# Lecture Notes in Computer Science     14697

Founding Editors

Gerhard Goos
Juris Hartmanis

The series Lecture Notes in Computer Science (LNCS), including its subseries Lecture Notes in Artificial Intelligence (LNAI) and Lecture Notes in Bioinformatics (LNBI), has established itself as a medium for the publication of new developments in computer science and information technology research, teaching, and education.

LNCS enjoys close cooperation with the computer science R & D community, the series counts many renowned academics among its volume editors and paper authors, and collaborates with prestigious societies. Its mission is to serve this international community by providing an invaluable service, mainly focused on the publication of conference and workshop proceedings and postproceedings. LNCS commenced publication in 1973.

Margherita Antona · Constantine Stephanidis
Editors

# Universal Access in Human-Computer Interaction

18th International Conference, UAHCI 2024
Held as Part of the 26th HCI International Conference, HCII 2024
Washington, DC, USA, June 29 – July 4, 2024
Proceedings, Part II

*Editors*
Margherita Antona
Foundation for Research and Technology -
Hellas (FORTH)
Heraklion, Crete, Greece

Constantine Stephanidis
University of Crete, and Foundation for
Research and Technology - Hellas (FORTH)
Heraklion, Crete, Greece

ISSN 0302-9743           ISSN 1611-3349 (electronic)
Lecture Notes in Computer Science
ISBN 978-3-031-60880-3      ISBN 978-3-031-60881-0 (eBook)
https://doi.org/10.1007/978-3-031-60881-0

# Foreword

This year we celebrate 40 years since the establishment of the HCI International (HCII) Conference, which has been a hub for presenting groundbreaking research and novel ideas and collaboration for people from all over the world.

The HCII conference was founded in 1984 by Prof. Gavriel Salvendy (Purdue University, USA, Tsinghua University, P.R. China, and University of Central Florida, USA) and the first event of the series, "1st USA-Japan Conference on Human-Computer Interaction", was held in Honolulu, Hawaii, USA, 18–20 August. Since then, HCI International is held jointly with several Thematic Areas and Affiliated Conferences, with each one under the auspices of a distinguished international Program Board and under one management and one registration. Twenty-six HCI International Conferences have been organized so far (every two years until 2013, and annually thereafter).

Over the years, this conference has served as a platform for scholars, researchers, industry experts and students to exchange ideas, connect, and address challenges in the ever-evolving HCI field. Throughout these 40 years, the conference has evolved itself, adapting to new technologies and emerging trends, while staying committed to its core mission of advancing knowledge and driving change.

As we celebrate this milestone anniversary, we reflect on the contributions of its founding members and appreciate the commitment of its current and past Affiliated Conference Program Board Chairs and members. We are also thankful to all past conference attendees who have shaped this community into what it is today.

The 26th International Conference on Human-Computer Interaction, HCI International 2024 (HCII 2024), was held as a 'hybrid' event at the Washington Hilton Hotel, Washington, DC, USA, during 29 June – 4 July 2024. It incorporated the 21 thematic areas and affiliated conferences listed below.

A total of 5108 individuals from academia, research institutes, industry, and government agencies from 85 countries submitted contributions, and 1271 papers and 309 posters were included in the volumes of the proceedings that were published just before the start of the conference, these are listed below. The contributions thoroughly cover the entire field of human-computer interaction, addressing major advances in knowledge and effective use of computers in a variety of application areas. These papers provide academics, researchers, engineers, scientists, practitioners and students with state-of-the-art information on the most recent advances in HCI.

The HCI International (HCII) conference also offers the option of presenting 'Late Breaking Work', and this applies both for papers and posters, with corresponding volumes of proceedings that will be published after the conference. Full papers will be included in the 'HCII 2024 - Late Breaking Papers' volumes of the proceedings to be published in the Springer LNCS series, while 'Poster Extended Abstracts' will be included as short research papers in the 'HCII 2024 - Late Breaking Posters' volumes to be published in the Springer CCIS series.

I would like to thank the Program Board Chairs and the members of the Program Boards of all thematic areas and affiliated conferences for their contribution towards the high scientific quality and overall success of the HCI International 2024 conference. Their manifold support in terms of paper reviewing (single-blind review process, with a minimum of two reviews per submission), session organization and their willingness to act as goodwill ambassadors for the conference is most highly appreciated.

This conference would not have been possible without the continuous and unwavering support and advice of Gavriel Salvendy, founder, General Chair Emeritus, and Scientific Advisor. For his outstanding efforts, I would like to express my sincere appreciation to Abbas Moallem, Communications Chair and Editor of HCI International News.

July 2024                                                          Constantine Stephanidis

# HCI International 2024 Thematic Areas
## and Affiliated Conferences

- HCI: Human-Computer Interaction Thematic Area
- HIMI: Human Interface and the Management of Information Thematic Area
- EPCE: 21st International Conference on Engineering Psychology and Cognitive Ergonomics
- AC: 18th International Conference on Augmented Cognition
- UAHCI: 18th International Conference on Universal Access in Human-Computer Interaction
- CCD: 16th International Conference on Cross-Cultural Design
- SCSM: 16th International Conference on Social Computing and Social Media
- VAMR: 16th International Conference on Virtual, Augmented and Mixed Reality
- DHM: 15th International Conference on Digital Human Modeling & Applications in Health, Safety, Ergonomics & Risk Management
- DUXU: 13th International Conference on Design, User Experience and Usability
- C&C: 12th International Conference on Culture and Computing
- DAPI: 12th International Conference on Distributed, Ambient and Pervasive Interactions
- HCIBGO: 11th International Conference on HCI in Business, Government and Organizations
- LCT: 11th International Conference on Learning and Collaboration Technologies
- ITAP: 10th International Conference on Human Aspects of IT for the Aged Population
- AIS: 6th International Conference on Adaptive Instructional Systems
- HCI-CPT: 6th International Conference on HCI for Cybersecurity, Privacy and Trust
- HCI-Games: 6th International Conference on HCI in Games
- MobiTAS: 6th International Conference on HCI in Mobility, Transport and Automotive Systems
- AI-HCI: 5th International Conference on Artificial Intelligence in HCI
- MOBILE: 5th International Conference on Human-Centered Design, Operation and Evaluation of Mobile Communications

# List of Conference Proceedings Volumes Appearing Before the Conference

1. LNCS 14684, Human-Computer Interaction: Part I, edited by Masaaki Kurosu and Ayako Hashizume
2. LNCS 14685, Human-Computer Interaction: Part II, edited by Masaaki Kurosu and Ayako Hashizume
3. LNCS 14686, Human-Computer Interaction: Part III, edited by Masaaki Kurosu and Ayako Hashizume
4. LNCS 14687, Human-Computer Interaction: Part IV, edited by Masaaki Kurosu and Ayako Hashizume
5. LNCS 14688, Human-Computer Interaction: Part V, edited by Masaaki Kurosu and Ayako Hashizume
6. LNCS 14689, Human Interface and the Management of Information: Part I, edited by Hirohiko Mori and Yumi Asahi
7. LNCS 14690, Human Interface and the Management of Information: Part II, edited by Hirohiko Mori and Yumi Asahi
8. LNCS 14691, Human Interface and the Management of Information: Part III, edited by Hirohiko Mori and Yumi Asahi
9. LNAI 14692, Engineering Psychology and Cognitive Ergonomics: Part I, edited by Don Harris and Wen-Chin Li
10. LNAI 14693, Engineering Psychology and Cognitive Ergonomics: Part II, edited by Don Harris and Wen-Chin Li
11. LNAI 14694, Augmented Cognition, Part I, edited by Dylan D. Schmorrow and Cali M. Fidopiastis
12. LNAI 14695, Augmented Cognition, Part II, edited by Dylan D. Schmorrow and Cali M. Fidopiastis
13. LNCS 14696, Universal Access in Human-Computer Interaction: Part I, edited by Margherita Antona and Constantine Stephanidis
14. LNCS 14697, Universal Access in Human-Computer Interaction: Part II, edited by Margherita Antona and Constantine Stephanidis
15. LNCS 14698, Universal Access in Human-Computer Interaction: Part III, edited by Margherita Antona and Constantine Stephanidis
16. LNCS 14699, Cross-Cultural Design: Part I, edited by Pei-Luen Patrick Rau
17. LNCS 14700, Cross-Cultural Design: Part II, edited by Pei-Luen Patrick Rau
18. LNCS 14701, Cross-Cultural Design: Part III, edited by Pei-Luen Patrick Rau
19. LNCS 14702, Cross-Cultural Design: Part IV, edited by Pei-Luen Patrick Rau
20. LNCS 14703, Social Computing and Social Media: Part I, edited by Adela Coman and Simona Vasilache
21. LNCS 14704, Social Computing and Social Media: Part II, edited by Adela Coman and Simona Vasilache
22. LNCS 14705, Social Computing and Social Media: Part III, edited by Adela Coman and Simona Vasilache

23. LNCS 14706, Virtual, Augmented and Mixed Reality: Part I, edited by Jessie Y. C. Chen and Gino Fragomeni
24. LNCS 14707, Virtual, Augmented and Mixed Reality: Part II, edited by Jessie Y. C. Chen and Gino Fragomeni
25. LNCS 14708, Virtual, Augmented and Mixed Reality: Part III, edited by Jessie Y. C. Chen and Gino Fragomeni
26. LNCS 14709, Digital Human Modeling and Applications in Health, Safety, Ergonomics and Risk Management: Part I, edited by Vincent G. Duffy
27. LNCS 14710, Digital Human Modeling and Applications in Health, Safety, Ergonomics and Risk Management: Part II, edited by Vincent G. Duffy
28. LNCS 14711, Digital Human Modeling and Applications in Health, Safety, Ergonomics and Risk Management: Part III, edited by Vincent G. Duffy
29. LNCS 14712, Design, User Experience, and Usability: Part I, edited by Aaron Marcus, Elizabeth Rosenzweig and Marcelo M. Soares
30. LNCS 14713, Design, User Experience, and Usability: Part II, edited by Aaron Marcus, Elizabeth Rosenzweig and Marcelo M. Soares
31. LNCS 14714, Design, User Experience, and Usability: Part III, edited by Aaron Marcus, Elizabeth Rosenzweig and Marcelo M. Soares
32. LNCS 14715, Design, User Experience, and Usability: Part IV, edited by Aaron Marcus, Elizabeth Rosenzweig and Marcelo M. Soares
33. LNCS 14716, Design, User Experience, and Usability: Part V, edited by Aaron Marcus, Elizabeth Rosenzweig and Marcelo M. Soares
34. LNCS 14717, Culture and Computing, edited by Matthias Rauterberg
35. LNCS 14718, Distributed, Ambient and Pervasive Interactions: Part I, edited by Norbert A. Streitz and Shin'ichi Konomi
36. LNCS 14719, Distributed, Ambient and Pervasive Interactions: Part II, edited by Norbert A. Streitz and Shin'ichi Konomi
37. LNCS 14720, HCI in Business, Government and Organizations: Part I, edited by Fiona Fui-Hoon Nah and Keng Leng Siau
38. LNCS 14721, HCI in Business, Government and Organizations: Part II, edited by Fiona Fui-Hoon Nah and Keng Leng Siau
39. LNCS 14722, Learning and Collaboration Technologies: Part I, edited by Panayiotis Zaphiris and Andri Ioannou
40. LNCS 14723, Learning and Collaboration Technologies: Part II, edited by Panayiotis Zaphiris and Andri Ioannou
41. LNCS 14724, Learning and Collaboration Technologies: Part III, edited by Panayiotis Zaphiris and Andri Ioannou
42. LNCS 14725, Human Aspects of IT for the Aged Population: Part I, edited by Qin Gao and Jia Zhou
43. LNCS 14726, Human Aspects of IT for the Aged Population: Part II, edited by Qin Gao and Jia Zhou
44. LNCS 14727, Adaptive Instructional System, edited by Robert A. Sottilare and Jessica Schwarz
45. LNCS 14728, HCI for Cybersecurity, Privacy and Trust: Part I, edited by Abbas Moallem
46. LNCS 14729, HCI for Cybersecurity, Privacy and Trust: Part II, edited by Abbas Moallem

47. LNCS 14730, HCI in Games: Part I, edited by Xiaowen Fang
48. LNCS 14731, HCI in Games: Part II, edited by Xiaowen Fang
49. LNCS 14732, HCI in Mobility, Transport and Automotive Systems: Part I, edited by Heidi Krömker
50. LNCS 14733, HCI in Mobility, Transport and Automotive Systems: Part II, edited by Heidi Krömker
51. LNAI 14734, Artificial Intelligence in HCI: Part I, edited by Helmut Degen and Stavroula Ntoa
52. LNAI 14735, Artificial Intelligence in HCI: Part II, edited by Helmut Degen and Stavroula Ntoa
53. LNAI 14736, Artificial Intelligence in HCI: Part III, edited by Helmut Degen and Stavroula Ntoa
54. LNCS 14737, Design, Operation and Evaluation of Mobile Communications: Part I, edited by June Wei and George Margetis
55. LNCS 14738, Design, Operation and Evaluation of Mobile Communications: Part II, edited by June Wei and George Margetis
56. CCIS 2114, HCI International 2024 Posters - Part I, edited by Constantine Stephanidis, Margherita Antona, Stavroula Ntoa and Gavriel Salvendy
57. CCIS 2115, HCI International 2024 Posters - Part II, edited by Constantine Stephanidis, Margherita Antona, Stavroula Ntoa and Gavriel Salvendy
58. CCIS 2116, HCI International 2024 Posters - Part III, edited by Constantine Stephanidis, Margherita Antona, Stavroula Ntoa and Gavriel Salvendy
59. CCIS 2117, HCI International 2024 Posters - Part IV, edited by Constantine Stephanidis, Margherita Antona, Stavroula Ntoa and Gavriel Salvendy
60. CCIS 2118, HCI International 2024 Posters - Part V, edited by Constantine Stephanidis, Margherita Antona, Stavroula Ntoa and Gavriel Salvendy
61. CCIS 2119, HCI International 2024 Posters - Part VI, edited by Constantine Stephanidis, Margherita Antona, Stavroula Ntoa and Gavriel Salvendy
62. CCIS 2120, HCI International 2024 Posters - Part VII, edited by Constantine Stephanidis, Margherita Antona, Stavroula Ntoa and Gavriel Salvendy

**https://2024.hci.international/proceedings**

# Preface

The 18th International Conference on Universal Access in Human-Computer Interaction (UAHCI 2024), an affiliated conference of the HCI International (HCII) conference, provided an established international forum for the exchange and dissemination of scientific information on theoretical, methodological, and empirical research that addresses all issues related to the attainment of universal access in the development of interactive software. It comprehensively addressed accessibility and quality of interaction in the user interface development life-cycle from a multidisciplinary perspective, taking into account dimensions of diversity, such as functional limitations, age, culture, background knowledge, etc., in the target user population, as well as various dimensions of diversity which affect the context of use and the technological platform and arise from the emergence of mobile, wearable, ubiquitous, and intelligent devices and technologies.

UAHCI 2024 aimed to help, promote, and encourage research by providing a forum for interaction and exchanges among researchers, academics, and practitioners in the field. The conference welcomed papers on the design, development, evaluation, use, and impact of user interfaces, as well as standardization, policy, and other non-technological issues that facilitate and promote universal access.

Universal access is not a new topic in the field of human-computer interaction and information technology. Yet, in the new interaction environment shaped by current technological advancements, it becomes of prominent importance to ensure that individuals have access to interactive products and services that span a wide variety of everyday life domains and are used in fundamental human activities. The papers accepted to this year's UAHCI conference present research, methods, and practices addressing universal access issues related to user experience and interaction, and approaches targeted to provide appropriate interaction means to individuals with specific disabilities, but also issues related to extended reality – a prominent technological medium presenting novel accessibility challenges, as well as advancements in learning and education.

Three volumes of the HCII 2024 proceedings are dedicated to this year's edition of the UAHCI conference. The first focuses on topics related to User Experience Design and Evaluation for Universal Access, and AI for Universal Access. The second focuses on topics related to Universal Access to Digital Services, Design for Cognitive Disabilities, and Universal Access to Virtual and Augmented Reality, while the third focuses on topics related to Universal Access to Learning and Education, Universal Access to Health and Wellbeing, and Universal Access to Information and Media.

Papers of these volumes were accepted for publication after a minimum of two single-blind reviews from the members of the UAHCI Program Board or, in some cases, from members of the Program Boards of other affiliated conferences. We would like to thank all of them for their invaluable contribution, support and efforts.

July 2024

Margherita Antona
Constantine Stephanidis

# 18th International Conference on Universal Access in Human-Computer Interaction (UAHCI 2024)

Program Board Chairs: **Margherita Antona**, *Foundation for Research and Technology - Hellas (FORTH), Greece*, and **Constantine Stephanidis**, *University of Crete and Foundation for Research and Technology - Hellas (FORTH), Greece*

- Basel Barakat, *University of Sunderland, UK*
- Joao Barroso, *INESC TEC and UTAD, Portugal*
- Ingo Bosse, *University of Teacher Education in Special Needs, Switzerland*
- Laura Burzagli, *National Research Council of Italy (CNR), Italy*
- Pedro J.S. Cardoso, *Universidade do Algarve, Portugal*
- Silvia Ceccacci, *University of Macerata, Italy*
- Nicole Darmawaskita, *Arizona State University, USA*
- Carlos Duarte, *Universidade de Lisboa, Portugal*
- Pier Luigi Emiliani, *National Research Council of Italy (CNR), Italy*
- Andrina Granic, *University of Split, Croatia*
- Gian Maria Greco, *Università di Macerata, Italy*
- Francesco Ermanno Guida, *Politecnico di Milano, Italy*
- Simeon Keates, *University of Chichester, UK*
- Georgios Kouroupetroglou, *National and Kapodistrian University of Athens, Greece*
- Monica Landoni, *Università della Svizzera Italiana, Switzerland*
- Barbara Leporini, *CNR-ISTI, Italy*
- John Magee, *Clark University, USA*
- Daniela Marghitu, *Auburn University, USA*
- Jorge Martin-Gutierrez, *Universidad de La Laguna, Spain*
- Maura Mengoni, *Università Politecnica delle Marche, Italy*
- Silvia Mirri, *University of Bologna, Italy*
- Federica Pallavicini, *Università degli Studi di Milano-Bicocca, Italy*
- João M. F. Rodrigues, *University of the Algarve, Portugal*
- Frode Eika Sandnes, *Oslo Metropolitan University, Norway*
- J. Andres Sandoval-Bringas, *Universidad Autónoma de Baja California Sur, Mexico*
- Muhammad Shoaib, *University College Cork, Ireland*
- Hiroki Takada, *University of Fukui, Japan*
- Philippe Truillet, *Université de Toulouse, France*
- Kevin C. Tseng, *National Taipei University of Technology, Taiwan*
- Gerhard Weber, *TU Dresden, Germany*

The full list with the Program Board Chairs and the members of the Program Boards of all thematic areas and affiliated conferences of HCII 2024 is available online at:

**http://www.hci.international/board-members-2024.php**

# HCI International 2025 Conference

The 27th International Conference on Human-Computer Interaction, HCI International 2025, will be held jointly with the affiliated conferences at the Swedish Exhibition & Congress Centre and Gothia Towers Hotel, Gothenburg, Sweden, June 22–27, 2025. It will cover a broad spectrum of themes related to Human-Computer Interaction, including theoretical issues, methods, tools, processes, and case studies in HCI design, as well as novel interaction techniques, interfaces, and applications. The proceedings will be published by Springer. More information will become available on the conference website: https://2025.hci.international/.

General Chair
Prof. Constantine Stephanidis
University of Crete and ICS-FORTH
Heraklion, Crete, Greece
Email: general_chair@2025.hci.international

**https://2025.hci.international/**

# Contents – Part II

**Universal Access to Digital Services**

Designing Cybersecurity Awareness Solutions for Young People in Rural
Developing Countries: Insights and Lessons Learned ...................... 3
   *Farzana Quayyum and Giske Naper Freberg*

Feedback as a Form of User Involvement in the Digital Realm .............. 19
   *Lukas Baumann and Susanne Dirks*

Co-creating Value with Cognitive Accessibility Features in Digital
Services: Enablers and Barriers ........................................ 32
   *Terhi Kärpänen*

Remote Secure Online Voting System Development ........................ 51
   *T. Matos and J. Guerreiro*

Designing for Inclusion and Diversity in Big Tech Reports: A Gray
Literature Analysis .................................................... 66
   *Ana Carolina Moises de Souza and Letizia Jaccheri*

How Order and Omission of Web Content Can Vary Unintentionally
Across User Cohorts: A Review ......................................... 80
   *Frode Eika Sandnes*

Mapable: Accessible Web-Based Indoor Maps for People with Diverse
Interaction and Information Needs ...................................... 100
   *Julian Striegl, Claudia Loitsch, Emma F. Etzold, and Gerhard Weber*

Exploring the Relationship Between Generation Z's Beauty Experience
and Brand Loyalty: A Comprehensive Study in the Experience Economy
Era ................................................................... 112
   *Shin-Yu Tsai and Hsien-Hui Tang*

Enhancing Customer Loyalty in Pure Internet Banking: An Analysis
of Experience and NPS Shifts Using S-O-R Theory ...................... 129
   *Qiu-Ze Wu, Yu-Ling Lien, Hsien-Hui Tang, and Michael T. Lai*

## Design for Cognitive Disabilities

Scaffolding for Inclusive Co-design: Supporting People with Cognitive
and Learning Disabilities .............................................. 151
    Leandro S. Guedes, Irene Zanardi, Marilina Mastrogiuseppe,
    Stefania Span, and Monica Landoni

Overcoming Challenges in Questioning People with Intellectual
Disabilities Regarding Their Digital Media Usage: Lessons Learned
from the EVE4all Project ............................................... 171
    Vanessa N. Heitplatz, Leevke Wilkens, Nele Maskut, Miriam Bursy,
    and Susanne Dirks

A Study on the Design of an Emotional Interaction Device for Children
with Autism Spectrum Disorder Based on Focused Attention Mindfulness ..... 186
    Yujia Jia, Jiaqi Wang, and Yujun Zhou

Experience-Oriented Intervention Strategy for Children with Autism
Spectrum Disorders and Their Families: A Framework of Design
and Evaluation ......................................................... 198
    Tsai-Ling Liao, Wei-Chi Chien, and Ling-Yi Lin

"Mum Helps Me When the Internet Messes Up...": Accessibility
of eHealth Services for People with Intellectual Disability .................. 213
    Claude L. Normand, Catharina Gustavsson,
    Kristin Alfredsson Ågren, Vanessa N. Heitplatz,
    Darren D. Chadwick, and Stefan Johansson

Interventions for Improving Road Surveillance for Teen Drivers
with Autism ............................................................ 231
    Erik Sand

DramaPlaya: A Multi-sensory Interactive Toolkit for the Home-Based
Drama Therapy of Children with Developmental Delays .................... 250
    Lingchuan Zhou, Han Zhang, and Yunqi Wang

## Universal Access to Virtual and Augmented Reality

Universally Designed Mobile Augmented Reality as a Digital Aid
for Banknote Recognition .............................................. 267
    Attila Bekkvik Szentirmai, Yavuz Inal, Anne Britt Torkildsby,
    and Ole Andreas Alsos

Enhancing Accessible Reading for All with Universally Designed
Augmented Reality – AReader: From Audio Narration to Talking AI
Avatars ............................................................ 282
    Attila Bekkvik Szentirmai

Attention and Sensory Processing in Augmented Reality: Empowering
ADHD Population .................................................. 301
    Shiva Ghasemi, Majid Behravan, Sunday D. Ubur,
    and Denis Gračanin

Virtual Reality Meets Low Vision: The Development and Analysis
of MagniVR as an Assistive Technology ............................. 321
    Cem Kaya, Baha Mert Ersoy, and Murat Karaca

Deaf and Hard of Hearing People's Perspectives on Augmented Reality
Interfaces for Improving the Accessibility of Smart Speakers ............... 334
    Roshan Mathew, Garreth W. Tigwell, and Roshan L. Peiris

Enhancing Electromobility Component Training Through Mixed Reality:
A Proposal Model .................................................. 358
    Ahmed Musule, Francisco J. Esparza, Leticia Neira-Tovar,
    and Christopher Diaz

Training Attention Skills in Individuals with Neurodevelopmental
Disorders Using Virtual Reality and Eye-Tracking Technology ............... 368
    Alberto Patti, Francesco Vona, Anna Barberio,
    Marco Domenico Buttiglione, Ivan Crusco, Marco Mores,
    and Franca Garzotto

EasyCaption: Investigating the Impact of Prolonged Exposure
to Captioning on VR HMD on General Population ....................... 382
    Sunday D. Ubur, Naome A. Etori, Shiva Ghasemi, Kenneth King,
    Denis Gračanin, and Maria Gini

Shared Boundary Interfaces: Can One Fit All? A Controlled
Study on Virtual Reality vs Touch-Screen Interfaces on Persons
with Neurodevelopmental Disorders ..................................... 404
    Francesco Vona, Eleonora Beccaluva, Marco Mores,
    and Franca Garzotto

Correction to: A Study on the Design of an Emotional Interaction Device
for Children with Autism Spectrum Disorder Based on Focused Attention
Mindfulness ........................................................... C1
  *Yujia Jia, Jiaqi Wang, and Yujun Zhou*

**Author Index** ........................................................ 419

# Universal Access to Digital Services

# Designing Cybersecurity Awareness Solutions for Young People in Rural Developing Countries: Insights and Lessons Learned

Farzana Quayyum[(✉)] [iD] and Giske Naper Freberg

Norwegian University of Science and Technology (NTNU), Trondheim, Norway
farzana.quayyum@ntnu.no

**Abstract.** Cybersecurity challenges and the need for awareness are well-recognized in developed countries, but this still needs attention in less-developed countries. This paper presents a design science research study exploring which factors we should consider when designing cybersecurity awareness solutions for young people in developing countries. We have developed prototypes of mini-cybersecurity awareness applications and conducted a pilot study with six participants (aged 16-30) from the Gambia. Our findings show that factors like the influence of culture and social constructs, literacy, language competence, and the way of introducing cybersecurity concepts are essential to consider when designing and developing cybersecurity awareness resources. The findings of this study will guide future researchers to create more inclusive cybersecurity awareness resources for users in developing countries and from diverse backgrounds.

**Keywords:** Cybersecurity awareness · Human factors of cybersecurity · Developing countries · Diversity and inclusion

## 1 Introduction

Understanding user needs is at the core of software engineering. Integrating human-centered methodologies into software engineering has recently been a hot topic. Although user-centric design and research are expanding, Baez and Casati [6] pointed out that very little has been done in the area of developing software for disadvantaged and vulnerable people. Some researchers have conducted studies where they designed software for vulnerable people, for example, software for physically disabled people [2,28]. According to Mary C. Ruof [26], along with physically and mentally challenged people, the vulnerable population also includes economically or educationally disadvantaged people. To ensure diversity and inclusion in the software engineering process, it is necessary that we include and consider a diverse group of users (including the disadvantaged population) and see how diversity influences the needs of each user group.

Education and training on cybersecurity have been a focus in Western and well-developed countries for many years. In cybersecurity awareness research,

M. Antona and C. Stephanidis (Eds.): HCII 2024, LNCS 14697, pp. 3–18, 2024.
https://doi.org/10.1007/978-3-031-60881-0_1

many research studies have been conducted to design and develop educational resources for children and adults (e.g., [9,14,32]). However, most of these studies are done in Western and developed countries, keeping the user groups from these specific parts of the world in mind. Developing cybersecurity awareness solutions for the economically or educationally disadvantaged population, such as the young generation in developing countries and least developed countries (LDCs), still lacks attention. Limited studies have explored cybersecurity issues in developing countries (e.g., [12,21]), but the amount of research is inadequate and lacking. The users' needs and facilitating learning factors can vary depending on the socio-economic diversity of the user groups, which are very different in developing countries compared to Western and developed nations.

Access to technologies, the internet, and digital resources are correlated with the economic status of an individual and a family [7]. Illiteracy, poverty, and a weak economy are common phenomenons in LDCs; thus, people's familiarity and competence with the digital world are also weak compared to those living in developed countries. However, the accessibility of the internet and digital devices is increasing globally, including the developing countries and LDCs. So, with this increased engagement with digital technologies, the need for cybersecurity awareness also emerged. However, considering that people in LDCs have limited knowledge about technologies and maybe even a limited level of education, designing and developing cybersecurity educational resources for them is a challenge. Thus, we address the following research question in this study: *What factors should we consider when developing cybersecurity awareness solutions for young users in developing countries?*

The outline of this paper is as follows: we discuss the background of this study and related works in Sect. 2, whereas in Sect. 3, we present our research methodologies. In Sect. 4, we present the results of this study, followed by a discussion of the findings in Sect. 5. In the end, we conclude our paper in Sect. 6, highlighting the future directions of our work.

## 2    Background and Related Work

"Developing countries" is a collective term that refers to countries that suffer from a weak economy and various socio-economic difficulties that constrain the population's prosperity in terms of development, living standard, and welfare. The recent COVID-19 pandemic has accelerated the use of technologies worldwide. During the pandemic, the need and importance of technological development in developing countries have again come to light, underlining the digital gaps and how much we need to bridge this gap. Although providing internet connectivity and digital technologies is a crucial part of the development, making the technologies available only is not enough [3]. Training, adapting, and learning the correct usage of the technologies are just as necessary as availability. According to Poushter et al., [22], the smartphone ownership gap between developed and developing nations is narrowing. The use of social media in developing countries is also on the rise. Even though there is rapid growth in the numbers of internet access and digital media usage, developing countries are still facing an immense challenge in providing digital literacy and security training for their populations. Various research studies have shown that measures should be taken to escalate the cyber awareness level amongst people in developing countries (e.g., [1,10]). Yet, cybersecurity awareness in developing countries is still an under-researched area and faces various challenges, including the lack of comprehensive initiatives, limited governmental support, inadequate cybersecurity curricula or extramural activities, limited budgets, and lack of resources [17,29].

Education and training on cybersecurity are not new and have been a focus in Western and well-developed countries for many years. Several tools, games, courses, training materials, and other learning activities are available to help people learn about cybersecurity and be aware of the issues internet usage can bring. Many of these available resources are targeted toward children and teenagers as they are one of the most vulnerable groups to targeted cyber attacks. Examples of such educational resources include games like Be Internet Awesome[1] by Google, CyberCIEGE [11], interactive books like Cyberheroes [30] and so on. There are various educational solutions for adults as well, including [5,25]. However, most of these studies are done, and resources are developed with an audience in mind, which is located in developed countries. Many children and young people born or living in developed countries are growing up in a digital world surrounded by many advanced technologies and devices. Young people in developing countries, on the other hand, may not have had the same environment and exposure to the digital world. Many get access to the internet and own personal devices like mobile phones, smartphones, and computers when they become young adults or even later. Thus, they might embrace the digital world for the first time without any prior knowledge.

Maoneke et al. [19] conducted a study in 2018 to identify cyberspace risks for adolescents in Namibia. The researcher found many risks, including exposure to inappropriate content (such as pornographic content, harmful content, and violent videos), cyberbullying, stranger dangers, privacy violations, etc., as the common risks the young generation faces online. Some other studies have also explored the cybersecurity risks and the need for awareness in the context of developing countries (example includes [18,20]). Bernadas and Soriano [7] investigate the diversity of internet connectivity in developing countries and the link of privacy behaviors of the youth with the diversity of connectivity in terms of information literacy. Von Solms and Von Solms [29] propose a cyber-safety curriculum for teachers in junior or primary schools using open educational resources. Nevertheless, many of the existing studies conducted in the African region contribute to the cybersecurity awareness needs from a strategic and policy-making perspective. As the majority of the resources are designed and developed with the users of developed nations in mind, there is a shortage of research into the habits and user needs when providing cybersecurity education for users in developing countries and rural areas.

---

[1] https://beinternetawesome.withgoogle.com/en_us/.

## 3  Methodology

In this study, we have used a design science research approach [15] and developed prototypes of mini-educational applications (apps) on cybersecurity. This paper presents the results of a pilot study where we tested the prototypes with six users. To develop the prototypes for this study, we have collaborated with a Norwegian company named Leap Learning[2] that develops educational solutions for children and adults with an aim to bridge the educational and digital divides around the world. This company is actively working with many developing countries in Sub-Saharan Africa. As they already have a connection and functional platform in that region, we collaborated with Leap Learning to construct initial prototypes of the educational apps and to conduct a pilot testing with participants from a Sub-Saharan African nation (i.e., the Gambia). Our main focus for this study is to identify the needs of our targeted user groups and understand the issues we must consider when designing cybersecurity educational solutions for our specific user domain. Therefore, we have focused on exploring the user needs using the existing design templates and development platform of Leap Learning. In the following section, we describe our methodology and the prototypes.

### 3.1  Design and Development

**Development Platform.** Our prototypes contain designs and functionalities that pre-exist in the development platform of Leap Learning. After implementing the templates in the development platform, we added content and relevant illustrations to each app. After the initial implementation, changes could be made to each app, such as updating the number of activities, levels, features and locations, and adding new material.

**Content Elicitation.** Based on the findings from relevant literature [24,27], we identified the common cybersecurity risks that young people face nowadays, such as privacy, password security, online strangers, cyberbullying, phishing, identity theft, and many others. For our pilot study, we chose not to focus on all cybersecurity issues in one iteration cycle following the design science research strategy's iterative cycle principles. Instead, we selected three common cybersecurity risks (namely, online contact, privacy, and password security) identified in the literature for the initial iteration and this pilot study. To formulate the questions for the apps, we mainly took inspiration from the cybersecurity awareness curriculum by Google[3]. In addition, findings from the literature [24,27,31] were used as inspiration. Since our target audience was from rural areas in developing countries and might not have great digital competence, we kept the prototypes basic and informative. We decided to make the apps available in English to reach a wider audience. In the Gambia, English is the official language, and most of the population speaks, writes, or understands English orally to a certain level.

---

[2] https://leaplearning.no/.
[3] https://beinternetawesome.withgoogle.com/en_us.

**Functionality Elicitation.** From the literature (e.g., [4,14,24,30]), we have seen that storytelling, quizzes, visualization, and the inclusion of gamification elements were among the common functionalities and practices applied to raise cybersecurity awareness. Our selected design template uses three different game approaches, including quizzes, storytelling (to provide information), and prioritizing. We have employed these three functionalities for the prototype applications as utilizing the same approach for all the apps could bore the participants and make them feel less driven to test out the apps. Another reason behind different approaches is that they may help us determine which approach works best for the targeted audience.

**Prototype Development.** For all three topics (online contact, privacy, and password security), we have developed one informative app and one quiz app each. For the topic of password security, we have developed one additional app using the prioritizing approach (to test the user's understanding of password strengths). Thus, we have developed and tested a total of seven mini-apps (using three approaches). The approaches are further described below.

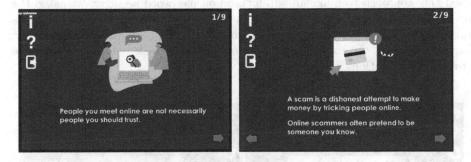

**Fig. 1.** Informative app, focused on online strangers

**The Informative App.** An informative app informs users about a topic by giving useful information in a textual format. This app format includes short sentences accompanied by an illustration and aims to explain a relevant aspect concisely and descriptively. Each sentence on the app tells users about security issues that may arise while using the internet and the possible consequences. Figure 1 displays two screenshots from the working prototype of the informative app on online strangers

**The Quiz App.** To challenge the user and test if they have understood and learned from the informative app, we included a quiz-inspired "Select Sentence" app. This app asks the user a question, and the user is given three alternative answers to choose from. This app features a drag-and-drop functionality where the user needs to drag the correct answer into the answer slot. When the user

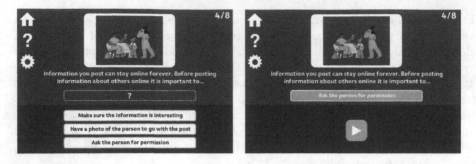

**Fig. 2.** Quiz app, focused on sharing personal information online

drags the correct answer to the answer slot, it will turn green and play a celebrating sound. Figure 2 displays an example of a quiz with the view of the interface before and after answering.

**Priority App.** The next approach is a priority app, where the user prioritizes the given alternatives from "best to worst" or "worst to best." We have used this approach to make an app focused on password security; we asked the users, for example, to arrange some given passwords according to their strengths in terms of security. This app also incorporates drag-and-drop functionality. Figure 3 displays an implemented view of a priority task before and after the correct prioritization.

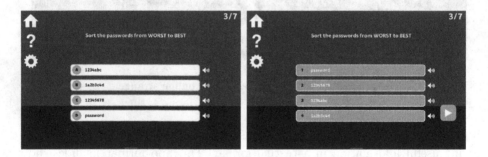

**Fig. 3.** Priority app, focused on password security

## 3.2   Participant Recruitment

Initially, we recruited eight participants for the pilot test, including six from the Gambia. In addition, we recruited two participants (one from Syria and one from Eritrea) living in Norway (who had recently arrived in Norway as refugees from their respective countries). However, to ensure better consistency of the analysis and the findings, we only present the results from the pilot test with the six participants from Gambia in this paper. The participants in the Gambia were primarily students from vocational schools. The representatives from Leap Learning contacted the students through their schools and recruited them. An overview of the participants can be seen in Table 1. The age range of the participants varied from 16 to 30 years. As this research project was carried out in a Norwegian institution, we complied with Norway's ethical regulations. We took approval from the Norwegian Agency for Shared Services in Education and Research[4] to collect personal data from the users. Before the user testing, we explained the purpose and objectives of the study to each participant. All the participants were required to sign an informed consent. The participants were also informed about their right to withdraw from the process.

## 3.3  Data Collection

During the pilot study with the prototypes, we observed the participants interacting with the apps, followed by a brief interview. The observation was used to discover whether the apps were simple for the participants and whether they had any issues while attempting them independently. Another goal of this testing and observation was understanding the users' needs for future development. Due to time limitations, we tested the apps on at least two cybersecurity topics with each participant. Afterward, we conducted semi-structured interviews [13] so the participants or the interviewer could ask follow-up questions if needed. The purpose of the semi-structured interviews was to know the demographic information about the participant and the participant's feedback and reflections on the tested applications. Demographic data included age, country of origin, and the user's previous experience with digital media. While obtaining the participants' feedback after interacting with the working prototype, we asked them if they had any difficulties understanding how to use any of the apps, if they learned anything new when using the apps, and what they enjoyed about the apps.

## 3.4  Data Analysis

The collected data consisted of notes and comments from the observation phase and recorded audio files from the interviews. We performed a qualitative analysis with the interview transcripts and observation data. For the data from the observations, we conducted a qualitative categorization analysis following Preece et al. [23]. This approach involves looking for incidents and patterns in the data. For example, a pattern could be any incident where multiple participants struggled with a task or similar comments made by participants during the test session. When analyzing the transcripts and observation notes, we looked for similar facts or themes that appeared multiple times and would be helpful for us to improve the apps in the future. We present the results from the pilot test in Sect. 4 and then further discuss the themes and related findings in Sect. 5.

---

[4] https://sikt.no/en/home.

## 4    Results

To give an overview of the participants' digital competence, we start by summarizing the results of participants' digital usage and whether or not they had access to digital devices and the internet in their daily lives. Most participants owned a smartphone and were familiar with social media, as shown in Table 1.

**Table 1.** Overview of the participants

| ID | Age | Digital device | Internet access | Social media | Email |
|----|-----|----------------|-----------------|--------------|-------|
| P1 | 16 | No | Only at school | No | No |
| P2 | 18 | Smartphone | Yes | Facebook, WhatsApp, Twitter | No |
| P3 | 17 | Phone, computer | Yes | Instagram, WhatsApp, Twitter, Google | Yes |
| P4 | 23 | Phone | Yes | No | Yes |
| P5 | 23 | Phone, computer | Yes | Facebook, WhatsApp, Instagram | No |
| P6 | 30 | Phone, computer | Yes | Instagram, Facebook, WhatsApp, Snapchat | Yes |

### 4.1    Participants' Interactions with the Apps

Overall, the participants interacted with the informative apps on the tablet seemingly well; they did not struggle with the app's navigation and could proceed to the next screen without difficulty. However, with the other two types of apps (quiz and priority apps) that had "drag-and-drop" functionality, some of the participants struggled and needed some time to understand how it works. The main issue observed during the user testing was understanding certain words and terms. There were many online security-related concepts or related words that some participants struggled to pronounce and understand the meaning or the concept. Malicious, extortion, digital footprint, and catfishing are some examples of such words the participants found difficult. The term "friend request" was also new to the participant who had no social media.

### 4.2    Participants' Reflections on the Apps

Participants' reflections on the apps were diverse. Some participants thoroughly reflected on their experiences, while some were comparatively reserved in their responses. When asked if they had previously received any cybersecurity training or education, all eight participants answered "No". As a result, their interactions with the apps were their first encounter with cybersecurity topics in an educational setting. Every participant gave positive feedback regarding learning from the applications. For example, participants P1, P2, and P5 acknowledged how the apps taught them about privacy and the risks of sharing personal information with strangers. Participants P2, P3, and P6 said that the applications assisted in learning secure password practices. Participant P5 also mentioned learning about scamming and how online strangers can scam people if they get private information about the individual.

Along with asking about what they learned from the apps, we also asked the participants if they were familiar with any information presented in the apps (prior to testing the apps). Even though the participants had not received formal training, some had a basic understanding of online security issues. For instance, participants P2 and P3 mentioned they knew they should not share passwords with others; participant P1 knew they should not share personal information like phone numbers or photos with strangers. Participant P6 also added that she had knowledge about scamming risks as she had experienced it in real life.

We further asked the participants which topic or app they enjoyed most. All the participants who tested the password app mentioned that password security was their favorite topic. The priority app on passwords (arranging the given passwords) seemed to be a favorite of multiple participants. As stated by participant P6, *"When it came to finding the rating from the least to the most important, I found that really interesting because it was testing me, and it was a little difficult"*.

### 4.3   Participants' Perception of the Apps' Language

When asked how they understood the language in the apps, the majority of participants replied, *"there were a few words I did not know"*. A spelling error was discovered in one of the apps by participant P6, which shows that the language was easy enough for this participant to identify any mistakes. Nevertheless, it also depended on the proficiency level of the participant himself. The general response was that the sentences were "not too long and difficult." Since Participant P4 was not proficient in reading English but was proficient in speaking and understanding the language, the participant had trouble reading the content from the apps. The participant, however, remarked that the language was "really easy" to understand after being assisted by the observer to try the apps and read the app's contents aloud.

## 5   Findings and Discussion

In this section, we discuss the findings of this study and the lessons we learned about what factors to consider when developing cybersecurity awareness solutions for users in developing countries, followed by the potential limitations.

### 5.1   Existing Cybersecurity Knowledge and Experience

In Sect. 4.2, we mentioned that some participants mentioned having an awareness of privacy, passwords, and scams, even though they said they did not get any formal education or training on cybersecurity before participating in our study. From the interviews and conversations with the participants, it is apparent that they became aware of these security issues from their real-life experiences. For example, three participants (P2, P5, and P6) mentioned experiencing scamming attempts on social media. The participants who have smartphones or computers reported knowing about passwords, which they seem to have achieved due to using these devices. However, even though the participants know they should not share their passwords, they still lack awareness about secure passwords, recommended password-strength practices, etc. Overall, the results of this study suggest that young people in rural developing countries are capable of comprehending cybersecurity challenges if given the right guidance and education. Even though some of the participants had trouble understanding certain terminology and words used in the apps, they were able to understand the concept after being explained.

## 5.2   Factors We Should Consider

From the results, we can say that despite living in rural areas in developing countries with limited digital access and opportunities, young people are exposed to online security threats, as highlighted by earlier studies as well (e.g., [19,29]). Thus, emphasis on cybersecurity training is needed to make them responsible and sensible users of the internet and digital tools and technologies. Nevertheless, depending on the available access to technologies and differences in the learning environment and culture of the users in different parts of the world, our proposed solutions should be relevant and inclusive for our targeted audience. From observing the participants and talking to them, we have identified some aspects that need to be considered when developing digital cybersecurity education platforms for an audience in underdeveloped areas of the world. In the following section, we present these identified factors.

**Influence of Culture and Social Constructs.** It is crucial to adjust cultural and local content when communicating new information, as we discovered from the pilot study in the Gambia. To reach a wider audience, we created our apps in English and used language that could be easier for the general public to understand. However, several terms were used in the apps to present the cybersecurity topics, which the participants struggled to understand or could not relate to. One participant, for instance, was confused about what a "pet" was (the term was used in the password app). Others could not have understood the phrases used to describe banking and financial services (to describe financial fraud or scam) because having a bank account is uncommon in rural areas. Preece et al. [23] emphasized the importance of formulations, language, or jargon when formulating the interview guide. This aspect became evident in our study when the participants were asked the following question: *"What gender do you identify as?"* . In developed countries, especially in Western culture, asking a gender question may seem correct or normal. However, cultural customs may be far more traditional in rural areas of least-developed nations like the Gambia; gender roles and identification in these nations have not been questioned. Therefore, the participants were quite unfamiliar with a question that had been phrased in this way. To ensure that each participant understood the question, we had to repeat it and rephrase it.

Social constructs and phenomena in rural areas differ from those in Western countries. Particularly in rural areas, society is more traditional than in urban areas. Thus, topics that deal with, for example, sexuality and gender identification are rarely or never a topic of conversation. Having a pet in a household is not a common phenomenon. These terms refer to phenomena and constructions common in societies in developed countries. So, culture and social context are essential to consider; each country is different regarding cybersecurity awareness, the extent of technological advancement, cyber crimes, and their ability to handle these matters at a societal or national level. Chang and Cobbel [10] also highlighted in their study how a country's context and social structure could create challenges and influence the effectiveness of a cybersecurity awareness program.

Moreover, it was evident from the observation that some participants found it challenging to use some of the apps' features (like the drag-and-drop functionality) or answer questions. However, when asked about their struggles during the interview, they did not reflect on these difficulties and expressed that there were no challenges in understanding the apps and that the process was "easy." This behavior might indicate that the participants were concerned with answering the questions in a manner they believed would be pleasing or expected by the interviewer rather than being straightforward with their opinions. Such social desirability tendencies can also be associated with cultural constructs, as suggested by existing research [8, 16].

**Literacy and Language Competence.** The language and literacy levels of people in rural areas or in many developing countries are not necessarily correlated to their age. It depends on how much schooling they have received throughout their lives. Though English is the official language of the Gambia, and people may have a certain level of proficiency in the English language, they still have issues comprehending the concepts in English. During our study, some participants needed help in reading and understanding the information provided in the apps because some participants could understand oral English but were not good at reading and understanding. To address this gap between oral understating and literacy levels, including sounds and audio of written contents could be part of the solution. The audio could accompany the textual visualization, giving illiterate people equal access as illiteracy is a common problem in underdeveloped countries and areas. Another interesting example was observed while interviewing Participant P1. When asked about the learning outcomes from the apps, participant P1 replied by reciting some text from the app word by word. However, she did not reflect upon what she had read and the context of the information. This can indicate that she was more concerned with remembering the words and sentences by heart rather than reflecting on what she was reading.

**Introducing Cybersecurity Terms and Concepts.** Cybersecurity is a field where many special terms and terminology are used. Introducing these special terms and terminologies to the target audience is challenging if the literacy level is low or absent. As stated in Sect. 4.1, "malicious," "catfishing," "blackmail," "extortion," and "digital footprint" are examples of cybersecurity terms the participants struggled to interpret. Nevertheless, these are some common cybersecurity risks and are important to include when educating about cybersecurity. Identifying ways to help people understand these cybersecurity topics is essential, even if they have no or low literacy level. One suggested approach could be to connect with real-life situations and examples to explain the terms and help them understand the consequences and the preventative measures.

While interviewing Participant P2 after testing the apps, she shared her experience about an episode when she almost got scammed by a stranger on Facebook. The scammer convinced her to pay money for some products that the scammer promised to send her from abroad. Participant P2 shared this with one of her relatives, and the relative then explained that it was a scam. She spontaneously recounted this occurrence with the interviewer because she could see the similarities between this incident and the information provided in one of the apps. This way, it was easier for this participant to understand the concept of a scam, how it works, and the consequences. Thus, relating the cybersecurity concepts with real-life scenarios will help increase awareness even if the target audience lacks formal education. Also, a gradual introduction of the terms will allow the user to process the information gradually by dividing the topics and relevant information into levels based on the complexity of the topic and related difficulties. When a user acquires a foundational understanding of cybersecurity topics, introducing difficult words can follow at a higher level.

**Reflection on the Actions.** One of the main takeaways from the study by Adelola et al. [1] was the importance of measuring and testing the users' knowledge and ability level. The purpose of providing comprehension tests is to encourage users to reflect and think critically about the data presented. In addition, it can give an indication to the educator whether or not the information fits the needs of the target audience. Our quiz-inspired prototype included a "Select Sentence" functionality and a prioritization functionality for the password security topic. These functionalities were implemented using a drag-and-drop feature. Both of these functionality types aimed to test whether or not the user comprehended the information provided in the informative apps. The participant had to finish the task by giving the right response in order to go on to the next one. The apps gave users feedback on their answers by becoming green when the right response or solution was supplied, as described in Sect. 3.1. However, it was found throughout the observations that this feature pushed some users to attempt several solutions until they found the right one rather than reflecting before choosing an answer. Therefore, it is necessary to keep in mind that when designing educational tools or resources, there should be opportunities for the users to reflect on their actions and learning. Giving the user one or two chances to submit the right response before moving on to the next task may help us avoid this problem in future iterations. The user can receive feedback or a score on the tasks they completed correctly and incorrectly once all the tasks have been completed. This strategy might also be more motivating and promote focus and reflection.

## 5.3   Limitations and Future Work

The primary limitation of this study is that our sample size was small. We acknowledge that studying a larger sample size would have given more versatile results and related findings. As we have mentioned earlier, this is a pilot study; thus, we plan to make further improvements to the existing prototypes and continue with more studies in multiple phases. Another limitation is that the apps are primarily written in English. The majority of young people in The Gambia can understand spoken English. Still, as we found during the study, they may need to develop their written English skills to fully comprehend the context and significance of the app's content. However, we chose to use English to reach a wider audience and make our study applicable to people from different countries.

This pilot study provided us with a number of suggestions for alterations and enhancements to the current prototypes. For example, the results from this study indicated what kind of functionality might seem easy (like the informative app) or complex (like the drag-and-drop) for the target group of users. Our findings about language proficiency and familiarity with the terminologies would guide us in designing better educational resources for these user groups. As part of our ongoing research and future work, we aim to improve the current apps and continue more studies to evaluate the prototypes further and explore the issues. Future research can also explore participatory design approaches to design cybersecurity resources with and for such diverse user groups.

## 6   Conclusion

This paper presents the findings of our study exploring how we can create inclusive and efficient cybersecurity awareness solutions for young users in rural developing countries. In Western and developing nations, the "cyber maturity" level varies. To better meet user needs worldwide, we need to be more inclusive in our overall cybersecurity awareness research. The positive findings of this study suggest that, when given the right tools and learning opportunities, young people from developing countries or LDCs are well capable of understanding and comprehending the concepts and etiquette of cybersecurity, even though they may not currently have access to institutional higher education and lack experience using digital tools. With this study, we aim to encourage more work in making our designs more inclusive and develop cybersecurity educational resources for people in developing countries that will better meet their needs.

**Acknowledgment.** We thank all the participants and Leap Learning for contributing to this project. We also note that the presented work of this paper is a research collaboration between Leap Learning and the researchers for this study; there was no financial involvement. We also acknowledge the support and guidance provided by Professor Letizia Jaccheri during the project.

# References

1. Adelola, T., Dawson, R., Batmaz, F.: The urgent need for an enforced awareness programme to create internet security awareness in Nigeria. In: Proceedings of the 17th International Conference on Information Integration and Web-based Applications & Services, pp. 1–7 (2015)
2. Alzahrani, M., Uitdenbogerd, A.L., Spichkova, M.: Impact of animated objects on autistic and non-autistic users. In: Proceedings of the 2022 ACM/IEEE 44th International Conference on Software Engineering: Software Engineering in Society, pp. 102–112 (2022)
3. Aruleba, K., Jere, N.: Exploring digital transforming challenges in rural areas of south Africa through a systematic review of empirical studies. Sci. Afr. **16**, e01190 (2022)
4. Baciu-Ureche, O.G., Sleeman, C., Moody, W.C., Matthews, S.J.: The adventures of scriptkitty: using the raspberry pi to teach adolescents about internet safety. In: Proceedings of the 20th Annual SIG Conference on Information Technology Education, pp. 118–123 (2019)
5. Bacud, M.L., Mäses, S.: Game-based learning for cybersecurity awareness training programmes in the public sector. In: ECEL 2021 20th European Conference on e-Learning, p. 50. Academic Conferences International limited (2021)
6. Baez, M., Casati, F.: Agile development for vulnerable populations: lessons learned and recommendations. In: Proceedings of the 40th International Conference on Software Engineering: Software Engineering in Society, pp. 33–36 (2018)
7. Bernadas, J.M.A.C., Soriano, C.R.: Online privacy behavior among youth in the global south: a closer look at diversity of connectivity and information literacy. J. Inf. Commun. Ethics Soc. **17**(1), 17–30 (2018)
8. Bernardi, R.A.: Associations between Hofstede's cultural constructs and social desirability response bias. J. Bus. Ethics **65**, 43–53 (2006)
9. Bioglio, L., Capecchi, S., Peiretti, F., Sayed, D., Torasso, A., Pensa, R.G.: A social network simulation game to raise awareness of privacy among school children. IEEE Trans. Learn. Technol. **12**(4), 456–469 (2018)
10. Chang, L.Y., Coppel, N.: Building cyber security awareness in a developing country: lessons from Myanmar. Comput. Secur. **97**, 101959 (2020)
11. Cone, B.D., Irvine, C.E., Thompson, M.F., Nguyen, T.D.: A video game for cyber security training and awareness. Comput. Secur. **26**(1), 63–72 (2007)
12. Da Veiga, A., Loock, M., Renaud, K.: Cyber4dev-q: calibrating cyber awareness in the developing country context. Electron. J. Inf. Syst. Dev. Ctries. **88**(1), e12198 (2022)
13. Galletta, A.: Mastering the Semi-structured Interview and Beyond: From Research Design to Analysis and Publication, vol. 18. NYU Press (2013)
14. Giannakas, F., Kambourakis, G., Gritzalis, S.: Cyberaware: a mobile game-based app for cybersecurity education and awareness. In: 2015 International Conference on Interactive Mobile Communication Technologies and Learning (IMCL), pp. 54–58. IEEE (2015)

15. Hevner, A.R., March, S.T., Park, J., Ram, S.: Design science in information systems research. Manag. Inf. Syst. Q. **28**(1), 6 (2008)
16. Kim, S.H., Kim, S.: Ethnic differences in social desirability bias: effects on the analysis of public service motivation. Rev. Publ. Pers. Adm. **37**(4), 472–491 (2017)
17. Kortjan, N., von Solms, R.: Cyber security education in developing countries: a South African perspective. In: Jonas, K., Rai, I.A., Tchuente, M. (eds.) AFRICOMM 2012. LNICST, vol. 119, pp. 289–297. Springer, Heidelberg (2013). https://doi.org/10.1007/978-3-642-41178-6_30
18. Kritzinger, E., Loock, M., Mwim, E.N.: Cyber safety awareness and culture planning in South Africa. In: Castiglione, A., Pop, F., Ficco, M., Palmieri, F. (eds.) CSS 2018. LNCS, vol. 11161, pp. 317–326. Springer, Cham (2018). https://doi.org/10.1007/978-3-030-01689-0_25
19. Maoneke, P.B., Shava, F.B., Gamundani, A.M., Bere-Chitauro, M., Nhamu, I.: ICTS use and cyberspace risks faced by adolescents in Namibia. In: Proceedings of the Second African Conference for Human Computer Interaction: Thriving Communities, pp. 1–9 (2018)
20. Naidoo, T., Kritzinger, E., Loock, M.: Cyber safety education: towards a cyber-safety awareness framework for primary schools. In: International Conference on e-Learning, p. 272. Academic Conferences International Limited (2013)
21. Owusu, A., Broni Jnr, F., Akakpo, P.: Preliminary insights into the concerns of online privacy and security among millennials in a developing economy. J. Theor. Appl. Inf. Technol. **15**(11), 3063–3076 (2019)
22. Poushter, J., Bishop, C., Chwe, H.: Social media use continues to rise in developing countries but plateaus across developed ones. Pew Res. Center **22**, 2–19 (2018)
23. Preece, J., Sharp, H., Rogers, Y.: Interaction Design: Beyond Human-Computer Interaction. John Wiley & Sons, London (2015)
24. Quayyum, F., Cruzes, D.S., Jaccheri, L.: Cybersecurity awareness for children: a systematic literature review. Int. J. Child Comput. Interact. **30**, 100343 (2021)
25. Raisi, S., Ghasemshirazi, S., Shirvani, G.: UltraLearn: next-generation cybersecurity learning platform. In: 2021 12th International Conference on Information and Knowledge Technology (IKT), pp. 83–88. IEEE (2021)
26. Ruof, M.C.: Vulnerability, vulnerable populations, and policy. Kennedy Inst. Ethics J. **14**(4), 411–425 (2004)
27. Švábenský, V., Vykopal, J., Čeleda, P.: What are cybersecurity education papers about? a systematic literature review of SIGCSE and ITICSE conferences. In: Proceedings of the 51st ACM Technical Symposium on Computer Science Education, pp. 2–8 (2020)
28. Torrado, J.C., et al.: Developing software for motivating individuals with intellectual disabilities to do outdoor physical activity. In: Proceedings of the ACM/IEEE 42nd International Conference on Software Engineering: Software Engineering in Society, pp. 81–84 (2020)
29. Von Solms, R., Von Solms, S.: Cyber safety education in developing countries. J. Syst. Cybern. Inform. **30**(2), 14–19 (2015)
30. Zhang-Kennedy, L., Abdelaziz, Y., Chiasson, S.: Cyberheroes: the design and evaluation of an interactive ebook to educate children about online privacy. Int. J. Child-Comput. Interact. **13**, 10–18 (2017)

31. Zhang-Kennedy, L., Chiasson, S.: A systematic review of multimedia tools for cybersecurity awareness and education. ACM Comput. Surv. (CSUR) **54**(1), 1–39 (2021)
32. Zhao, J., et al.: I make up a silly name' understanding children's perception of privacy risks online. In: Proceedings of the 2019 CHI Conference on Human Factors in Computing Systems, pp. 1–13 (2019)

# Feedback as a Form of User Involvement in the Digital Realm

Lukas Baumann[✉] [iD] and Susanne Dirks [iD]

TU Dortmund University, Dortmund, Germany
lukas.baumann@tu-dortmund.de

**Abstract.** Since the adoption of the Web Accessibility Directive (WAD, 2016) customer feedback and complaint management have also become relevant for public sector bodies in the European Union in terms of digital accessibility, because it requires the implementation of a feedback mechanism that allows people to report accessibility issues or request additional information about inaccessible content. Although some people are aware of their digital accessibility rights and the obligation for public sector bodies PSBs to appropriately handle their feedback on existing barriers granted by the WAD, a significant number of people with disabilities, stakeholders, and the general public still lack comprehensive knowledge about the WAD and its associated requirements. In the context of the results from the EU-funded UPowerWAD project, the term 'feedback' and its potential andlimitations for the inclusion of people with disabilities in a digital world are discussed. Based on the presented results, the involvement of users, especially in the context of accessibility, from the very beginning is emphasized.

**Keywords:** feedback mechanism · complaint system · user involvement · participation · disability · web accessibility directive

## 1 Introduction

In the digital realm, complaint management mechanisms can help to address the needs of different target groups. In companies, for example, adequate complaint management contributes to customer loyalty because it gives customers the feeling that they are being valued and that their feedback can make a difference [1]. Furthermore, commercial online stores can only be successful if the needs and expectations of customers are known, and the response is appropriate [2, 3]. Since the adoption of the Web Accessibility Directive (WAD, 2016), customer feedback and complaint management have also become relevant for public sector bodies (PSBs) in the European Union (EU) in terms of digital accessibility. The WAD requires the implementation of a feedback mechanism that allows people to report accessibility issues or request additional information about inaccessible content. The creation of appropriate conditions for digital participation is an increasingly important political and societal task due to the continuous shift of social processes into the digital space and the associated new forms of inequality [4–7]. Heitplatz and Bühler emphasize that "digital participation has become a new key factor for

M. Antona and C. Stephanidis (Eds.): HCII 2024, LNCS 14697, pp. 19–31, 2024.
https://doi.org/10.1007/978-3-031-60881-0_2

participation opportunities which complements the traditional ways of living" [8]. Even though the WAD applies to PSBs, the demand for fully accessible online services is also relevant for the private sector. In today's reality, where all matters of everyday life, including participating in public life become almost impossible without using online services, digital accessibility is essential for people with disabilities.

The term 'feedback' is linked to various aspects such as user involvement, participation, citizenship, and bottom-up social processes. Hence, in this paper, the term 'feedback' and its potential for the inclusion of people with disabilities in a digital world are discussed. This includes a classification of feedback and feedback mechanisms based on results obtained from various research projects. Furthermore, the impacts and potential of feedback for improving the accessibility of digital services as well as further aspects of improving participation and empowerment in the digital world are addressed.

The motivation for this contribution arose from the UPowerWAD project (2022–2024) and its results. This project was funded by the Erasmus + Programme of the European Union to raise awareness and empower people with disabilities to provide actionable feedback and improve the accessibility of PSBs' websites in the context of the feedback mechanism of the WAD [9].

## 2   Classifying Feedback

According to Najar et al. "User feedback can be considered as complaints and suggestions, which can be instrumented in the organization to improve its services and products" [10]. Important characteristics of feedback are summarized below:

– Feedback is personalized information.
– Feedback is descriptive and based on direct observation.
– Feedback can be described as an informal assessment process.
– Feedback has the purpose of helping to achieve the receiver's best potential [11].

### 2.1   Feedback Through Complaints

Feedback generally reflects the experience of using or applying information or services and can be neutral, positive, or negative. Complaints are a special feedback form and should be treated with particular care.

A complaint can be described as "a customer's expression of dissatisfaction with a product or a service" [12]. In general, feedback or complaints contain direct input from customers, which means receiving valuable information on a service or product [1]. If complaints are not handled properly further negative customer responses will appear. Customer complaints are therefore viewed as an indicator to determine whether a service-oriented business operates well [13]. Handling complaints is mostly realized within the organization or by ombudspersons or other services [14]. In business, complaint management systems are part of Customer Relationship Management (CRM) [12]. The management of customer complaints usually affects the level of customer satisfaction and is often an important tool in organizations to maximize customer satisfaction [10, 12]. Common problems in CRM typically refer to problems in the complaints process (e.g., the customer is not aware of the appropriate channel for complaints) and problems in the complaint management (e.g., missing channel for asking for further information) [12].

In technology development, feedback is often collected through usability tests, assessments, and evaluations. It is common practice to ask participants for their opinions on usability problems or design suggestions [15]. This type of feedback is closely related to participatory approaches where users, developers, and designers share knowledge, ideas, and suggestions on usability and design aspects [16]. Here, the feedback usually relates to experiences and considerations about the suitability of the technical system for its context of use [17]. A variety of methods are available to involve users in the development of technologies and technical systems. One form of feedback in usability evaluation is an approach in which users are asked to comment on designs asynchronously in online ad hoc groups ("social design feedback") [17]. The key features of this type of feedback are the engagement between users and developers and the ability for users to see and respond to other participants' comments. In general, user involvement in usability evaluation is seen as valuable [18, 19].

Feedback and reputation systems can also be found in every e-commerce marketplace [20]. Digital platforms use these mechanisms to evaluate the transactions between sellers and retailers. In this context, the feedback mechanism can be described as a specific type of formal control mechanism [21]. In their article on feedback mechanisms on digital platforms, Steur and Seiter [21] propose various design criteria for the provision of feedback. This helps to further categorize the feedback mechanism of the WAD. On the one hand, feedback mechanisms differ in terms of their reciprocity. For example, feedback according to the WAD can be described as "one-sided feedback", as only users can report barriers. On the other hand, feedback mechanisms differ in terms of the restriction of input options. According to the WAD, the feedback mechanism must be barrier-free, i.e. it must be made accessible to all and therefore various input options must be implemented. Feedback mechanisms can be used to collect either qualitative or quantitative data or both types of data. Experience has shown that feedback on the accessibility of a website or application tends to be qualitative. Users usually describe a specific accessibility problem. Furthermore, submission categories can also differ. The WADs feedback mechanism relates to digital accessibility and is usually implemented as an independent mechanism. For general complaints, PSBs often use a general feedback channel. For the collection of quantitative data, most feedback mechanisms use a specific scale level. For qualitative data, often no specific rating system is used.

## 2.2 Feedback and Digital Accessibility

The WAD aims to improve the accessibility of PSBs' websites and mobile applications and harmonize standards across the EU to reduce digital barriers and give people with disabilities better access to digital public services. The feedback mechanism of the WAD intends to provide people with disabilities the opportunity to actively participate in the improvement of digital accessibility.

The results of the first monitoring period of the WAD have shown that most websites and mobile applications of public institutions do not meet the respective accessibility requirements. At the same time, there is almost no feedback on still existing barriers [22]. This implies a need for action on both the website owners' and the users' side. To enable user feedback, the mechanisms implemented for providing feedback need to be accessible. On websites that are not accessible in general, these mechanisms are also not accessible. However, all digital services must be accessible, offering the widest possible choice to potential or actual recipients based on access to the best available information. There must be means to assess preferences when making service-related decisions and to communicate and resolve grievances [23].

Another problem is that vulnerable people or people with disabilities often tend not to complain [14]. One of the reasons is that they are often given the impression that the perceived problems are caused by their personal characteristics and that they are not entitled to special provisions. If people with disabilities do not complain, this can mean that they are not aware of their right or have limited opportunities to claim this right [24]. Thus, it cannot be assumed that people with disabilities do not give feedback because they have no interest in doing so, but rather because it is made difficult for them to do so. Therefore, it is important to investigate whether people want to participate or not and, if so, what conditions must be met [25].

In general, it is crucial to find ways to include people with disabilities in all processes that affect them [26]. To enable true self-advocacy, the focus must be on the people expressing their views and needs [27]. Involving the intended user groups from the beginning of the development process is necessary to know the users' needs and expectations and to be able to respond to them appropriately [2, 3]. Many experts emphasize that the application of inclusive approaches has positive effects not only for vulnerable people but for all people [14, 28]. Pilgrim et al. summarize, that "the views of people with disabilities are crucial for improving services" [27].

In the context of citizenship, Ashibly and Chiong emphasize that public institutions must implement and provide services that meet the wishes and requirements of all people to achieve a high level of acceptance and user-friendliness [29]. Involving users throughout the design and development process helps to better understand and ultimately meet users' needs and expectations [30]. Wirtz and Kurtz concluded in their work that a user-centered strategy in the design and implementation of e-government services is crucial for successful portal management, especially at the local level [31]. The opportunity to respond to and assess the services of public institutions can lead to greater trust, a positive attitude towards public transparency, and, if the feedback is meaningful and accepted, improved service quality [32–34]. Furthermore, effective complaints and redress procedures support the perceived integrity of PSBs [23]. This means that good governance is closely linked to the perceived fairness of the system. This in turn is crucial for the level of trust that citizens place in public institutions. In summary, the inclusion of the user perspective is a key aspect in the successful implementation and acceptance of digital services provided by PSBs [35].

## 3   Insights from the UPowerWAD Project

Although some people are aware of their digital accessibility rights and the obligation for PSBs to appropriately handle their feedback on existing barriers granted by the WAD, a significant number of people with disabilities, stakeholders, and the general public still lack comprehensive knowledge about the WAD and its associated requirements. The

EU-funded UPowerWAD project has tackled these issues. During the project, the use of accessibility feedback mechanisms was analyzed, measures to raise awareness of the WAD were developed, suggestions for improving feedback mechanisms were made and the basis for implementing training courses on accessibility and feedback mechanisms was laid.

## 3.1 Project Results

Within the UPowerWAD project, the four main results described below were developed.

The **Methodological Toolkit** helps to understand the technical and motivational barriers that prevent users from giving feedback [36]. It also includes a general introduction to feedback mechanisms and their relevance for the user as well as a description of ways to improve users' willingness to provide feedback and the quality of feedback content [37]. As part of qualitative field research, interviews were conducted with people with disabilities in three of the four partner countries, who were asked about their experiences with digital accessibility and feedback mechanisms [36]. The interviews revealed that feedback on existing barriers is usually not given for three different reasons:

- The feedback mechanisms cannot be used because of insufficient accessibility.
- The user is accustomed to circumventing the problem.
- Their feedback is not valued by the website owner and the existing problems are not resolved [37, 38].

The **Interactive Repository of Best Practices** includes a list of best practices for implementing feedback mechanisms that effectively support people with disabilities in providing feedback on web accessibility issues. It shows good practice examples of feedback mechanisms that facilitate structured and actionable feedback on accessibility issues as well as an overview of proven approaches to encourage and improve feedback [38]. The document can be used by different stakeholders and can help to understand what actions and provisions can be expected from PSBs. Understanding the best practices presented can help users assess the quality of the feedback mechanism and its impact on user feedback and understand its relevance. According to Baumann et al., the recommendations developed for the WAD feedback mechanisms can be used for any type of feedback [36]. Even if they were not developed primarily for this purpose, they can also help to raise awareness among PSBs and other website owners to prioritize accessibility and user feedback.

The **Model Curriculum** contains general information and a framework that can be used to develop specific courses for training people with disabilities. Such training should aim towards raising awareness of the right to digital accessibility and the existing feedback mechanisms and to develop general knowledge about accessibility on the Internet [39]. The modules included in the model curriculum aim to empower users with disabilities to improve the accessibility of PSBs' websites and mobile applications by providing structured and actionable feedback on existing digital barriers. The model curriculum targets organizations of persons with disabilities (OPDs) and Vocational educational training (VET) providers who wish to offer training to their members and the general public.

Within the curriculum, the following four main steps in providing structured and actionable feedback are outlined:

1. Identifying the accessibility issue(s).
2. Locating the accessibility statement for information about the feedback mechanism.
3. Identifying the most appropriate feedback channel.
4. Reporting the accessibility issue.

The model curriculum provides a rather abstract description of the content relevant for courses on the WAD feedback mechanism and digital accessibility in general. It can be used as a general framework in all countries of the EU. To be able to work with the curriculum in specific training situations, the teaching material needs to be adapted to national contexts and, if necessary, supplemented with specific examples. Due to its modular structure, the contents of the model curriculum can be easily adapted to the needs of learning groups with different levels of background experience.

In the final phase of the project, the Practical Guidelines were developed as a supplement to the model curriculum. The guidelines aim is to show VET providers and OPDs how they can empower people with disabilities to engage constructively with web accessibility, the feedback mechanism, and the operators of websites and mobile applications. Its main purpose is to provide information for the creation of training courses based on the model curriculum [40].

## 3.2 Prerequisites for Actionable Feedback

During the project, a comprehensive understanding of the methods, prerequisites, and procedures necessary to enable people with disabilities to provide actionable feedback was developed. The results of the project showed that, in general, the following improvements can be achieved when people with (and without) disabilities provide actionable feedback on existing digital barriers. First, actionable feedback can be used to identify specific barriers and challenges for people with disabilities while using digital services and websites. Also, feedback from users with disabilities ensures that the implementation of the WAD is tailored to the needs of end users, making accessibility improvements more comprehensive and effective. Different users may encounter different barriers and therefore provide feedback on different issues. Hence, it is important to gather feedback from people with a wide range of user needs. This way, public websites can get feedback from people with different types of disabilities and can improve the accessibility of their digital services in all regards. Thirdly, the improvement of the accessibility of digital content and services is an ongoing process. The use of actionable feedback supports this process by facilitating iterative updates and refinements to digital content and platforms. These ongoing adjustments are important to keep pace with the constant evolution of digital content and accessibility standards. Lastly, obtaining and implementing actionable feedback strengthens the participation and self-efficacy of people with disabilities. In this way, users are involved in improving the digital accessibility of digital content and services. This improved digital accessibility also benefits other people with and without disabilities. As revealed in the interviews, people with disabilities often do not see themselves as valued members of society. Ultimately, an appropriate approach to user feedback and an appreciative response to received feedback can greatly promote the willingness to provide it.

Beyond this, the research within the project has shown that feedback on accessibility is scarce because the users often do not find the right feedback channel or are not aware of the option to give feedback via a provided mechanism. Providing training for people with disabilities helps to equip them with the appropriate technical skills and know-how for providing actionable feedback on accessibility issues. However, it is important to emphasize that the ultimate responsibility for implementing accessible websites and mobile applications rests with the website owner. By raising awareness of the importance of feedback for improving digital accessibility, the quality and level of user feedback can be increased.

The project results also highlight the role of OPDs and PSBs, stakeholders, community groups, and government initiatives in disseminating knowledge about digital accessibility and encouraging persons with disabilities to learn more about their rights. OPDs play a crucial role in reaching out to the community of persons with disabilities at all levels. One necessity is adequate guidance and support for these organizations in this regard, e.g. through collaborations with VET providers, accessibility specialists, or research institutions.

Finally, web and application developers also play a crucial role in improving digital accessibility. Accessibility requirements, technical guidelines, and legal requirements must become a natural part of their training and profession. Current legislation to ensure the digital participation of people with disabilities, such as the WAD or the *European Accessibility Act* (EAA) [41], has significantly increased the demand from public bodies for developers who can create accessible websites and mobile applications. Especially for web developers who have little or no experience in the field of digital accessibility, user feedback provides valuable insights into potential barriers and how they can be improved.

## 4 Discussion

The research summarized in this paper, and particularly the results of the UPowerWAD project, show that the participation of people with disabilities in evaluating the usability and accessibility of digital services can help to increase the overall accessibility and improve the possibilities for participation. According to Følstad, user feedback in the context of design studies is primarily used to expand knowledge about users' expectations and habits [17]. Especially for target group-related issues that tend to go beyond general usability requirements, such as accessibility, users with disabilities should be considered experts, which makes their feedback even more useful. Evidence from usability evaluations shows that feedback can also be used to gain understanding that cannot be derived from other data sources, as it reflects 'real-world' use [17].

This highlights how important it is that feedback mechanisms meet the different needs of users with disabilities so that reporting a barrier is generally possible [14]. A complaint management system must be "conspicuous, easily accessible and simple to operate". It should take into account the needs of different social groups" [23]. In line with the outcomes of the UPowerWAD project, Kormpho et al. emphasize the importance of providing multiple channels for reporting [12].

Furthermore, Bosch has already shown in 2005 that companies need to introduce tools and concepts that enable a better understanding of customer needs instead of just finding a solution to the identified problem [1]. Such tools and concepts can transform traditional complaint management into an exciting process and learning experience for associates. To implement a successful process, an appropriate level of management commitment seems to be crucial. As already mentioned, it is essential to view feedback as a gift. This includes allowing both users and the responsible parties to give feedback, express gratitude, clarify the feedback, and reflect on the feedback received [11].

Pietilä et al. emphasize the connection between the willingness to participate in a study or provide feedback and a noticeable change because of prior participation [42]. This connection was also observed in the UPowerWAD project. People with disabilities are more willing to give feedback on digital barriers if they previously had positive experiences in handling their feedback. Appreciative feedback from the website owner and a resolution of the reported problem was described as very motivating. Conversely, the absence of any kind of reaction led to the interviewees generally no longer giving feedback.

Not only the actual handling of feedback but also the opportunity to see other people's comments can be a motivating aspect for giving feedback. Websites such as *FixMyStreet* [43] in the UK or *report-antisemitism* [44] in Germany provide an example of how to create a centralized overview for reporting on a particular topic. A solution to support the implementation of the WAD is the *Public Barrier Tracker* which would allow users to obtain information on the status of their complaint [45]. These approaches also help to balance the asymmetrical relationship between the user and service provider: "Any positive discrimination measure that favors the citizen contributes to a more balanced system" [23].

Feedback and complaint management of accessibility issues can also benefit from new technologies. For example, Alenezy and Akhlaq have developed *Fix-It*, a public complaint management system that is used via an Android app and connects directly to the service provider [46]. In addition, rule-based chatbots or AI chatbots can be used to engage in a dialog with the user, or machine learning approaches help to classify complaints to save time and effort [12]. According to Morgeson et al., these solutions are often preferred by users due to their inherent speed of response or balance of customization and attention [47]. Social media is also perceived as an effective tool for feedback and interaction, especially for citizen empowerment and direct interaction with authorities [48]. If accessible, social media platforms can have a positive influence on the digital participation of people with disabilities [49, 50].

In this context, it is also important to note that the resources available to an organization influence the extent to which it can provide these opportunities [14]. In addition to financial resources and technical capabilities, PSBs must have the "appropriate skills and competencies to respond appropriately to the wishes of disabled people" [28]. The results from the UPowerWAD project can not only help to empower people with disabilities but also inform and train PSBs about digital accessibility and appropriate methods for implementing the feedback mechanism. As mentioned in the practical guidelines, demonstrating the relevance of accessibility and user feedback, for example by inviting a person with a disability to give a guest lecture, can also help to motivate and raise awareness [41].

## 5  Conclusion

The research outcomes summarized in this paper help to understand that the implementation of "effective feedback requires that the giver, the receiver, and the environment are carefully considered" [11]. The lack of reported barriers on the websites of PSBs in the EU combined with a multitude of co-existing digital barriers is not only a technical but a multifactorial problem. The opportunity to provide feedback is a valuable resource for improving digital participation for people with and without disabilities. It is important to note that potential exclusion due to existing digital barriers can only be prevented if the transformation processes are designed together with people with disabilities.

In conclusion, the WAD and the provided feedback mechanism can be seen as a good example and forerunner for a systematic change in the valuation of digital accessibility. It needs to be emphasized that the improvement of the accessibility of PSBs websites will also depend on the number of complaints received [32].

To resolve the remaining problems, the design and development of public digital services must be rethought, and user involvement must be enabled from the very beginning. This is especially important because from 2025 onwards, the implementation of digital accessibility not only applies to the public sector but will also need to be adopted in the private sector due to the EAA.

**Acknowledgments.** The UPowerWAD project was realized by the Department of Rehabilitation Technology at the TU Dortmund University (Germany) in cooperation with the European Blind Union, Funka (Sweden), and the Synthesis Center for Research and Education (Cyprus). The project receives funding from the Erasmus+ Programme of the European Union (Project ID: 2021-1-DE02-KA220-VET-000033176).

**Disclosure of Interests.** The authors have no competing interests to declare that are relevant to the content of this article.

## References

1. Bosch, G.V., Enríquez, F.T.: TQM and QFD: exploiting a customer complaint management system. Int. J. Qual. Reliab. Manag. **22**(1), 30–37 (2005)
2. Adiyarta, K., Napitupulu, D., Nurdianto, H., Rahim, R., Ahmar, A.: User acceptance of E-government services based on TRAM model. IOP Conf. Ser.: Mater. Sci. Eng. **352** (2018)

3. Akkaya, C., Zepic, R., Krcmar, H.: E-Government und Open Government in Deutschland aus Bürgerperspektive: Gestern, heute und morgen. In: Kutscher, N., Ley, T., Seelmeyer, U., Siller, F., Tillmann, A., Zorn, I. (eds.) Handbuch Soziale Arbeit und Digitalisierung, pp. 402–413. Beltz Juventa, Weinheim (2020)
4. Altmeppen, K.D.: Teilhabe: Grundbegriffe der Kommunikations-und Medienethik (Teil 16). Communicatio Socialis **52**(2), 187–192 (2019)
5. Dobransky, K., Hargittai, E.: Unrealized potential: Exploring the digital disability divide. Poetics **58**, 18–28 (2016)
6. Dirks, S., Bühler, C.: Digital Empowerment - or how to overcome the second level digital divide for people with cognitive disabilities. INFORMATIK 2021, Lecture Notes in Informatics (LNI), vol. 15, Gesellschaft für Informatik, Bonn (2021)
7. Rawat, P., Morris, J.C.: The Effects of Technology and Institutions on E-Participation. Routledge, New York (2021)
8. Heitplatz, V.N., Bühler, C.: Digital participation of people with intellectual disabilities living in residential institutions – perspectives, barriers and implications. In: Antona, M., Stephanidis, C. (eds.) Universal Access in Human-Computer Interaction. Lecture Notes in Computer Science, pp. 353–370. Springer, Cham (2023)
9. UPowerWAD. https://www.funka.com/en/projekt/upower-wad/. Accessed 16 Feb 2024
10. Najar, A.S., Al-Sukhni, H.A., Aghakhani, N.: The application of service-oriented architecture in E-complaint system. In: Second International Conference on Communication Software and Networks, Singapore, pp. 280–283 (2010)
11. Jug, R., Jiang, X.S., Bean, S.M.: Giving and receiving effective feedback: a review article and how-to guide. Arch. Pathol. Lab. Med. **143**(2), 244–250 (2019)
12. Kormpho, P., Liawsomboon, P., Phongoen, N., Pongpaichet, S.: Smart complaint management system. In: Seventh ICT International Student Project Conference (ICT-ISPC), pp. 1–6 (2018)
13. Trappey, A.J.C., Lee, C.H., Chen, W.P., Trappey, C.V.: A framework of customer complaint handling system. In: 7th International Conference on Service Systems and Service Management, Proceedings of ICSSSM 2010, pp. 879–884 (2010)
14. Brennan, C., Sourdin, T., Williams, J., Burstyner, N., Gill, C.: Consumer vulnerability and complaint handling: challenges, opportunities and dispute system design. Int. J. Consum. Stud. **41**(6), 638–646 (2017)
15. Følstad, A., Law, E., Hornbæk, K.: Analysis in practical usability evaluation: a survey study. In: Chi, E., Höök, K. (eds.) Proceedings of the SIGCHI Conference on Human Factors in Computing Systems (CHI 2012), pp. 2127–2136. ACM, New York (2012)
16. Greenbaum, J., Kyng, M.: Design at work. Lawrence Erlbaum Associates, Hillsdale (1991)
17. Følstad, A.: Users' design feedback in usability evaluation: a literature review. Hum. Cent. Comput. Inf. Sci. **7**(1), 1–19 (2017)

18. Fischer, B., Peine, A., Östlund, B.: The importance of user involvement: a systematic review of involving older users in technology design. Gerontologist **60**(7), 513–523 (2020)
19. Kujula, S.: User involvement: a review of the benefits and challenges. Behav. Inf. Technol. **22**(1), 1–16 (2023)
20. Tadelis, S.: Reputation and feedback systems in online platform markets. Annu. Rev. Econ. **8**, 321–340 (2016)
21. Steur, A.J., Seiter, M.: Properties of feedback mechanisms on digital platforms: an exploratory study. J. Bus. Econ. **91**(4), 479–526 (2021)
22. Web Accessibility Directive - Monitoring Reports. https://digital-strategy.ec.europa.eu/en/lib rary/web-accessibility-directive-monitoring-reports. Accessed 14 Jan 2024
23. Brewer, B.: Citizen or customer? complaints handling in the public sector. Int. Rev. Adm. Sci. **73**(4), 549–556 (2007)
24. Klausner, M.: Postkategoriales Teilhaberecht und (trans-)kategoriale Selbstvertretung von Menschen mit Behinderung: Kollektivierungsprozesse durch die Mobilisierung von Recht. Zeitschrift für Kultur- und Kollektivwissenschaft **7**(1), 153–186 (2021)
25. Scheu, B., Autrata, O.: Partizipation und Soziale Arbeit: Einflussnahme auf das subjektiv Ganze. Springer Fachmedien, Wiesbaden (2013)
26. Charlton, J.I.: Nothing About Us Without Us. University of California Press (1998)
27. Pilgrim, D., Todhunter, C., Pearson, M.: Accounting for disability: customer feedback or citizen complaints? Disabil. Soc. **12**(1), 3–15 (1997)
28. Bühler, C.: Accessibility über Desktopanwendungen hinaus – Barrierefreiheit. Informatik-Spektrum **40**(6), 501–510 (2017)
29. Alshibly, H., Chiong, R.: Customer empowerment: does it influence electronic government success? A citizen-centric perspective. Electron. Commer. Res. Appl. **14**(6), 393–404 (2015)
30. Herendy, C.: How to learn about users and understand their needs? User experience, mental models and research at public administration websites. ST **41**(1), 5–17 (2018)
31. Wirtz, B.W., Kurtz, O.T.: Local e-government and user satisfaction with city portals – the citizens' service preference perspective. Int. Rev. Publ. Nonprofit Market. **13**(3), 265–287 (2016)
32. Allen, B., Tamindael, L.E., Bickerton, S.H., Cho, W.: Does citizen coproduction lead to better urban services in smart cities projects? An empirical study on e-participation in a mobile big data platform. Gov. Inf. Quart. **37**(1), 101412 (2020)
33. Kim, S.: Public trust in government in Japan and South Korea: does the rise of critical citizens matter? Publ. Adm. Rev. **70**(5), 801–810 (2010)
34. Kim, S., Lee, J.: E-participation, transparency, and trust in local government. Publ. Adm. Rev. **72**(6), 819–828 (2012)

35. Stember, J., Hesse, E.: Handlungsempfehlungen aus Deutscher Sicht. In: Stember, J., Eixels-berger, W., Spichiger, A. (eds.) Wirkungen von E-Government: Impulse für eine wirkungs-gesteuerte und technikinduzierte Verwaltungsreform, pp. 79–84. Springer Fachmedien, Wiesbaden (2018)
36. Baumann, L., Dirks, S., Kemeny, P., Laurin, S., Zapata, S.M-, Bosselmann, L., et al.: Involving, empowering, and training end users with disabilities to fully participate in the web accessibility directive objectives. In: First Results from the UPowerWAD Project. Stud Health Technol Inform 2023, vol. 306, pp. 364–370 (2023)
37. UPowerWAD Toolkit. https://www.funka.com/en/projekt/upower-wad/main-activities-and-results/toolkit. Accessed 16 Feb 2024
38. UPowerWAD Repository. https://www.funka.com/en/projekt/upower-wad/main-activities-and-results/repository. Accessed 16 Feb 2024
39. UPowerWAD Model Curriculum. https://www.funka.com/en/projekt/upower-wad/main-act ivities-and-results/curriculum. Accessed 16 Feb 2024
40. UPowerWAD Practical Guidelines. https://www.funka.com/en/projekt/upower-wad/main-act ivities-and-results/practical-guidelines. Accessed 16 Feb 2024
41. Directive (EU) 2019/882 of the European Parliament and of the Council of 17 April 2019 on the Accessibility Requirements for Products and Services. https://eur-lex.europa.eu/legal-content/EN/TXT/HTML/?uri=CELEX:32019L0882. Accessed 16 Feb 2024
42. Pietilä, I., Meriläinen, N., Varsaluoma, J., Väänänen, K.: Understanding youths' needs for digital societal participation: towards an inclusive virtual council. Behav. Inf. Technol. **40**(5), 483–496 (2021)
43. FixMyStreet. https://www.fixmystreet.com. Accessed 16 Feb 2024
44. RIAS. https://report-antisemitism.de. Accessed 16 Feb 2024
45. Alarcon, D., Andreasson, K., Mucha, J., Nietzio, A., Sawicka, A., Snaprud, M.: A public bar-rier tracker to support the web accessibility directive. In: Miesenberger, K., Kouroupetroglou, G. (eds.) Computers Helping People with Special Needs: 16th International Conference, ICCHP 2018. LNCS, vol. 10896, pp. 22–26. Springer, Heidelberg (2018)
46. Abdulrahman, A.F., Akhlaq, M.: Fix-it: design and implementation of a public complaint management system. In: 2023 International Conference on Computer Science, Information Technology and Engineering (ICCoSITE), pp. 858–862 (2023)
47. Morgeson, F.V., Hult, G.T.M., Mithas, S., Keiningham, T., Fornell, C.: Turning complain-ing customers into loyal customers: moderators of the complaint handling-customer loyalty relationship. J. Mark. **84**(5), 79–99 (2020)
48. Widodo, I.M., Sutarman: empowering public opinion through android applications for com-munity participation and complaint management. KLIK: Kajian Ilmiah Informatika dan Komputer **4**(3) (2023)

49. Anderson, S., Araten-Bergman, T., Steel, G.: Adults with intellectual disabilities as users of social media: a scoping review. Br. J. Learn. Disabil. **51**, 544–564 (2023)
50. Sweet, K.S., LeBlanc, J.K., Stough, L.M., Sweany, N.: Community building and knowledge sharing by individuals with disabilities using social media. J. Comput. Assist. Learn. **36**, 1–11 (2020)

# Co-creating Value with Cognitive Accessibility Features in Digital Services: Enablers and Barriers

Terhi Kärpänen[1,2]([⊠]) [iD]

[1] Laurea University of Applied Sciences, Ratatie 22, Vantaa, Finland
[2] University of Helsinki, Yliopistonkatu 4, 00100 Helsinki, Finland
`terhi.karpanen@helsinki.fi`

**Abstract.** Digital services should be accessible to all people regardless of their possible disabilities or limitations. Currently, many people are excluded from digital services due to disabilities or limitations in using digital services. Moreover, cognitive accessibility features, such as better usability and understandable content, usually create value for all users, even those without disabilities. This paper argues that failing to design cognitively accessible digital services challenges value co-creation – there is a danger of value co-destruction. To identify enablers for and barriers to designing cognitively accessible digital services, semi-structured in-depth interviews with accessibility experts and professionals were conducted.

**Keywords:** Web Accessibility · Cognitive Accessibility · Value Co-Creation · Value Co-Destruction · Digital Services

## 1 Introduction

*Strive not to be a success, but rather to be of value.* – Albert Einstein.

Currently, many people are excluded from digital services due to disabilities or limitations in using digital services. With the rapid growth of services provided through the Internet and mobile devices, a part of the population risks being excluded from basic services in both the private and public sectors [1]. The European Commission [2] has stated that five million persons with disabilities in the European Union (EU) do not use the Internet due to some form of disability. According to the World Wide Web Consortium (W3C) [3], digital services should be designed to be accessible to all because web accessibility benefits individuals, businesses, and society. Web accessibility encompasses all disabilities that affect access to the Internet and allows everyone to perceive, understand, navigate, and interact with the Internet [1, 3]. Cognitive accessibility features (e.g., understandable content and usability) can be seen as part of a web accessibility entity. Cognitive accessibility in digital services benefits people with cognitive and learning disabilities, people with different language skills and people with memory problems. People who have cognitive disabilities perceive the benefits of digital services and want to use them as a part of daily life [4, 5].

M. Antona and C. Stephanidis (Eds.): HCII 2024, LNCS 14697, pp. 32–50, 2024.
https://doi.org/10.1007/978-3-031-60881-0_3

Vargo and Lusch [6] first introduced the concept of service-dominant logic – services are valuable when customers use them to their benefit. If service users cannot use the services intended for them, value co-creation does not occur [6]. Therefore, proper service design is fundamentally important. The concept of value co-destruction has been defined "as an interactional process between service systems that results in a decline in at least one of the systems" well-being [7]. If digital services cannot be used due to their use of difficult language or content and their creators have not considered cognitive accessibility features, they do not bring value to their users and this leads to a misuse of resources. Organizations may misuse customers' resources by not responding to customer expectations and by not fulfilling the value proposition. For example, if service providers do not have enough resources to design digital services, value can be co-destructed [7–9].

Previous studies have focused on the user perspective in order to understand how accessible digital services create value for service users (e.g., by providing a better customer experience) [10–13]. Value co-destruction related to accessibility has been studied, for example, in the public sector [8] and in the elderly care network context [14], but the focus has not been on accessibility or purely digital services. Relatively little research has focused on the organization's enablers for or barriers to implementing cognitively accessible digital services. The related studies have addressed the factors for adaptation and the motivation to implement accessible services [15–17]. A study by Velleman et al. [15] revealed accessible digital service benefits and enablers. Regarding digital service barriers, studies by Leitner et al. [16] and Crabb et al. [18] have partially made references to the topic. Although previous research has focused on accessibility, it has not focused on investigating the enablers or barriers from the point of view of organizations or of considering cognitively accessible digital services. This cognitive accessibility viewpoint gives new information to value co-creation and value co-destruction research because value co-creation and value co-destruction concepts essentially involve the use and misuse of resources [7]. There is a research gap in relation to understanding the enablers and barriers in this context.

Responding to this gap, this study investigates web accessibility experts' and professionals' perceptions of organizational barriers and enablers when designing cognitively accessible digital services. This knowledge can be used to support organizations' design of digital services that generate value for all customers and prevent value co-destruction. Semi-structured in-depth interviews with web accessibility experts and professionals were conducted in Finland. The advantage of in-depth interviews is that the researcher gains a more accurate picture of the respondent's position or behavior [19]. The chosen data analysis technique is content analysis. The content analysis aims to organize and elicit meaning from data [20].

The remainder of this paper is organized as follows: first, the relevant literature is presented and the theoretical baseline for this study is set out by creating an understanding of cognitive accessibility and its enablers and barriers in digital services, as well as an understanding of the literature on value co-creation and value co-destruction. Second, the results of the empirical study are presented, based on in-depth interviews. Finally, the theoretical contribution of the research results is discussed.

## 2 Literature Review

### 2.1 Cognitive Accessibility in Digital Services

According to the Strategy for the Rights of Persons with Disabilities [21], one in six people in the EU has a disability that ranges from mild to severe and over a third of people aged over 75 have disabilities that restrict them to some extent in physical and digital environments. There are limited statistics regarding people affected by barriers to cognitive accessibility in a digital environment [22]. The national unions in EU countries have published some statistics, and, e.g., in Finland, there are up to 650 000–750 000 citizens who have difficulty reading or understanding the common language [23]. Considering these numbers, accessibility should be considered an important part of digital service implementation. According to a report by the European Commission [24], digital services can include a large range of online services, ranging from simple websites to Internet infrastructure services and online platforms. People with disabilities (e.g., long-term physical, mental, intellectual or sensory impairments) should have equal access to digital services, on an equal basis to others [22, 25]. People with cognitive limitations can encounter different kinds of cognitive challenges in digital services that affect the use of the digital services (e.g., loss of memory, problems with information processing or a lack of concentration) [26, 27].

Cognitive accessibility in digital services benefits people with cognitive and learning disabilities, and it also benefits people with memory problems (e.g., elderly people) or people with language challenges (e.g., people with immigrant backgrounds). According to the WHO [28], various factors can create barriers for people who have disabilities which can be seen to also be barriers for people who have cognitive disabilities or limitations (e.g., there can be a lack of consultation with and involvement of persons with disabilities or a lack of accessibility). Making websites and applications usable for people with cognitive and learning disabilities affects every part of design and development [27]. According to the W3C [27], technology provides opportunities for people to interact with content and to process information in ways that are simpler and more usable to them, such as navigating web content easily and accessing information in multiple formats. The main cognitive functions which challenge the use of digital services can be related to attention, reading, writing, concentration, operating tasks, memory, time and understanding [22, 26]. Based on the work of Leskelä [26], the cognitive challenges can be also related to orientation difficulties with speech ability and the production of spoken and written language.

The technical requirements of web accessibility are guided by commonly agreed standards and national legislation in EU countries [1]. However, the importance of the web accessibility field, cognitive accessibility (which offers individuals opportunities to engage with content and process information in ways that are more user-friendly for them), is not part of national legislation. The W3C [27] has developed Web Content Accessibility Guidelines (WCAG) and supplemental guidance (Cognitive Accessibility Guidance), which provide ways to improve cognitive accessibility. The guidelines may give guidance to organizations and their experts, and to content creators, in order for them to follow the web accessibility rules in the digital service design process, but despite the guidance, web accessibility often remains unsatisfactory [29]. The Cognitive

Accessibility Guidance has some similarities with the usability heuristics for user interface design created by Nielsen [30]. Regarding understandable content, Mäkipää and Isohella [31] have developed heuristics for accessible online text production, which can partly support the design of cognitively accessible digital content. Cognitive accessibility features (e.g., understandable content) are features that require manual checks (e.g., some automation tools related to accessibility testing do not reveal all the accessibility issues) [32].

## 2.2 Barriers to and Enablers for Designing Cognitively Accessible Digital Services

Despite the guidelines, many people face problems when using digital services. The possible actions that have been taken to remove accessibility obstacles (e.g., legal frameworks, web accessibility requirements and standardization, design considerations and education) have been noted by the European Commission [22]. A study related to cognitive accessibility [17] indicated that guidelines or recommendations could motivate web developers to consider people with disabilities in their projects.

The studies of Velleman et al. [15] and Leitner et al. [16] did not focus on actual enablers but more on factors for adaptation and the motivation to implement accessible services. The study by Velleman et al. [15] revealed factors related to the adoption and implementation of accessibility standards within municipalities. The factors with high influence were, for example, resources, quality assurance, knowledge, budget, managerial decisions, guidelines, and legislation [15]. The study by Leitner et al. [16] revealed different dimensions related to the motivation factors: economic, social and technical dimensions. The economic dimension revealed the fear of a negative image and the importance of website; the social dimension revealed social commitment and top management support; and the technical dimension was related to website quality [16].

Barriers to using cognitively accessible digital services have been studied by people who have cognitive disabilities or limitations, and the studies have revealed the problems they have in understanding language [33, 34]. There are a few studies [17, 18, 35] that have looked at the web-accessibility barriers from the perspective of service providers. The study by Crabb et al. [18] highlighted the developers' understanding of the accessibility practice and the methods that are used to implement it. The interviewees of the study discussed how the lack of understanding of how a person with a disability uses technology impacts how technology interactions are designed, and there should be more co-operation with different service users [18]. The study by Pichiliani and Pizzolato [17] revealed that the barriers related to web developers were a lack of knowledge, a lack of time to implement the needed features, the organizational culture, and a lack of user testing. The study by Leitner et al. [16] regarding web accessibility implementation in private-sector organizations and its motivations and business impact revealed barriers such as a lack of knowledge of the social, business, and technical benefits of web accessibility, a lack of awareness, a lack of top management support, misconceptions, corporate design requirements and differences in what is considered an accessible design.

## 2.3 Value Co-creation and Value Co-destruction in Digital Services

Vargo and Lusch [6], first introduced the concept of service-dominant logic and the concept of value co-creation. According to Vargo and Lusch [6], customers can be seen as the co-creators or co-producers of value, and the firm's role is to offer value propositions. Based on the findings of Payne et al. [36], value co-creation involves the supplier offering superior value propositions, which are relevant to its customers. Value is created in cooperation between the customer and the service provider. Based on the work of Rintamäki et al. [37], a value proposition is purpose-built when it is relevant from the customer's point of view, based on the competencies and resources of the service provider, and when it differentiates from competitors in a positive way. When the value is relevant to the customer, it may lead to benefits to the supplier through, for example, revenue or referrals [36]. According to the service-dominant logic, services should be seen as the fundamental unit of exchange – only when users can use the services that service providers offer, can value be created and appropriated [6]. To support value co-creation, a service provider should consider the subjectivity of value and how customers use a service.

There is the difficulty of defining value because of the subjectivity involved in attributing value. Value in use (use value) is based on subjective benefit [38]. Value can mean different things to different people in different contexts and in different ways [39]. Mitronen and Rintamäki [38] argued that, in understanding the concept of value, the role of benefits and sacrifices is central: how the service helps the customer achieve the customer's goals, the kind of feelings it arouses and the changes that result from the transaction. Customer value can have many dimensions: economical (equal to price), functional, emotional and symbolic dimensions [38]. Functional value focuses on satisfying customer needs, saving the customer time and effort. Emotional value is a matter of feelings, which produces positive feelings and experiences for the customer or, respectively, eliminates negative emotions and experiences. Symbolic value is based on the meanings the customer attaches to a service [38]. Smith and Colgate [40] recognized functional, hedonistic, and symbolic values. Hedonistic value refers to the experiential value created by the product via the feelings and senses it provokes [40]. Zhang et al. [41] discussed similar divisions but described the types of value in terms of functional, emotional, and social value.

Value co-creation can also lead to unwanted results. If users cannot use digital services due to a lack of cognitive accessibility features, e.g., language, the expectations of users have not been met and the value can be co-destructed [42]. Also if, for example, service providers do not have enough resources to design digital services, value can be co-destructed [7–9, 43]. There is interconnection between value co-creation and value co-destruction. Lumivalo et al. [44] argue that value co-creation and value co-destruction interact dynamically—either weakening or strengthening—during service encounters among service actors. According to Chowdhury et al. [45], the cooperation between producer and customer can create tensions if either ambiguity or role conflicts are used opportunistically or for power games, which can potentially weaken value co-creation. A lack of consonance between actors can cause value co-destruction [8]. Because value is subjective and users can experience it in different ways, value co-creation can lead to value co-destruction. In general, the existing value co-destruction studies can be divided into studies that focus on resource abuse [43, 46], actors' deviation from routine procedures, understandings and commitments [9] and studies that focus on both causes of resource misuse [41].

The term "cognitive accessibility" refers to people who have problems processing information. Cognitive disabilities include cognitive impairments and difficulties in performing activities and participation due to such impairments. People with cognitive disabilities may experience difficulties in communication due to reduced capacity in mental functions, such as orientation, attention, memory, abstraction, organization and planning, experience and management of time, problem-solving, language, and calculation [3, 47]. When digital services are not cognitively accessible e.g. the content is not understandable, individuals with cognitive impairments may feel excluded or disengaged.

Based on the work of Järvi et al. [48], value co-destruction is present if a customer experiences a service failure. Organizations may misuse customers' resources by not responding to customer expectations and by not fulfilling the value proposition [42]. Engen et al. [8] identified a lack of transparency, mistakes, a lack of bureaucratic competence and an inability to serve as the causes of value co-destruction. Plé and Chumpitaz Cáceres [7] defined the co-destruction of value in the interaction between the producer and the customer as happening when the resources (i.e., the producer and the customer) are intentionally misused to prevent the formation of value co-creation or to cause interference. The lack of knowledge of how to design cognitively accessible digital services may lead to value co-destruction. Kashif and Zarkada [49] stated that value co-creation may lead to accidental value co-destruction due to a lack of sufficient knowledge. Failing to address cognitive accessibility can harm a company's reputation and customer loyalty. In particular, the public sector can face value co-destruction when interactive parties fail to integrate resources in a mutually beneficial manner [8]. Understanding customer value and the process whereby value is co-created is a major concern for organizations, and is fundamental to competitiveness [42]. In many countries, some legal requirements and regulations mandate accessibility standards, including some features of cognitive accessibility for certain industries and services. It's important to understand the barriers and enablers when designing cognitively accessible services to prevent value co-destruction.

## 3   Method

To better understand the enablers and barriers related to implementing cognitive accessibility features in digital services, web accessibility experts and professionals were interviewed.

### 3.1   Interviewees

The interviewees were experts, lecturers, or professionals in accessibility and/or cognitive accessibility located in southern Finland. The interviewees were chosen based on their expertise on cognitive accessibility and accessibility field. In total, ten experts were interviewed. The experience in years varied by half a year to 23 years. The interviewees were informed of the interview topic beforehand and were asked for their consent to utilize their responses in the research. In cases where anonymity for the interviewees and their companies was promised, the anonymity of the individuals and/or groups involved in the research was a priority and respected in the research: personal information was kept confidential [50]. The interviewees were numbered. The interviewees' information is summarized in Table 1 and the interview guide is in Appendix.

**Table 1.** The interviewees

| Interviewee | Field of experience | Experience in years |
| --- | --- | --- |
| P1 | Accessibility Expert | 1 year |
| P2 | Accessibility Expert | ½ year |
| P3 | Accessibility Specialist | 20 |
| P4 | Accessibility and usability specialist | 18 |
| P5 | Development Manager | 23 |
| P6 | Accessibility Specialist | 5 |
| P7 | Accessibility Expert | 2 |
| P8 | Lecturer | 1 |
| P9 | Accessibility Expert | 20 |
| P10 | Lecturer | 3 |

### 3.2 Data Collection

In this research, semi-structured in-depth interviews were used to understand and explore the experts' perspectives on the research subject. In-depth interviews provide more detailed information than what is available through other data collection methods, and the researcher gains a more accurate picture of the respondent's position or behavior [19, 51]. The interviews were conducted between November 2021 and September 2023. The interviews lasted between 50 and 70 min.

### 3.3 Data Analysis

The chosen data analysis technique was content analysis, and the process of content analysis followed the guidelines provided by Bengtsson [20]. Content analysis can be used on all types of written texts and thus is suitable for semi-structured interviews. All the interviews were transcribed by following the transcription procedure [52]. The data was coded and then grouped into categories and subcategories. Next, a cross-case matrix was created to represent the interviewees in rows and the themes in columns. The following categories were found from the interviews:

1. Cognitive accessibility features
2. Barriers to implementing cognitively accessible digital services
3. Enablers when implementing cognitively accessible digital services

# 4  Results

This section presents the results by category and the characteristics of the research. Before any actual research questions related to the research were asked, the interviewees described the meaning of web accessibility and cognitive accessibility in their own words. All the interviewees understood the meanings of the terms web accessibility and cognitive accessibility.

## 4.1  Cognitive Accessibility Features

Cognitive accessibility was seen as part of web accessibility. All the interviewees mentioned that the term cognitive accessibility is related to either information handling or information processing. One interviewee mentioned that cognitive accessibility is related to more than just information processing – cognitively accessible design digital services should provide a feeling of security to service users:

> P4: There is more than just information processing. Cognitive accessibility can relate to feelings of security and knowledge.

Overall, the term cognitive accessibility was understood broadly. Although the interviewees understood the meaning of cognitive accessibility, they thought that the term can be hard to understand for other people (e.g., content creators or service providers). The interviewees specified that the main target group for people who particularly benefit from cognitively accessible digital services are people with different kinds of cognitive disabilities or limitations, but all people benefit from cognitively accessible digital services. According to the interviewees, organizations do not understand all existing benefits, and thus there is a need to better communicate about them. The understanding of the benefits of cognitively accessible digital services was gained from the perspective of users and organizations:

> P6: Organizations benefit from the functionality of the website. The customer contacts will decrease in number if digital services are working, and this also reduces costs.

## 4.2  The Barriers to Implementing Cognitively Accessible Digital Services

The interviewees were asked to think of possible barriers and why service providers have not provided cognitively accessible digital services. Some barriers were more relevant for smaller organizations, such as money. Otherwise, a diverse range of barriers was mentioned, and the barriers were seen as similar in organizations of different sizes. The most common barrier was the lack of knowledge.

> P4: Organizations do not have enough understanding about this subject and more training is needed.

Other barriers mentioned were a lack of money, a lack of positive attitudes, a lack of professional competence, complex terms, conservative organizational culture and a feeling of inadequacy.

*P5: The groups that benefit from cognitively accessible services are diverse and the question is: How do I serve everyone? The feeling of inadequacy. It is impossible to consider all the groups who need cognitively accessible services.*

Barriers mentioned in the interviews are listed in Table 2.

**Table 2.** The barriers to implementing cognitively accessible digital services

| Barriers' | Interviewee | Selected quotations |
| --- | --- | --- |
| Lack of knowledge | P2, P3, P4, P6, P7, P8, P9, P10 | *'There should be an understanding of how to implement and design accessible services.'* |
| Lack of money | P2, P6 | *'A lack of money can be one barrier.'* |
| Lack of positive attitudes | P1, P6 | *'It could be the attitude problem. No interest to search information.'* |
| Lack of professional competence | P9, P10 | *'More focus on professional skills. It does not mean that if you have ten fingers, you can play like a professional pianist.'* |
| Feeling of inadequacy | P5 | *'It is too much. How do I serve everyone?'* |
| Complex terms | P8 | *'Difficult to understand what accessibility or cognitive accessibility means.'* |
| Conservative organizational culture | P9 | *'Conservative way of thinking. No willingness to understand new ideas.'* |

All the interviewees mentioned that one option for removing possible barriers is to test the digital services either by using accessibility experts, experienced specialists or focus groups. One interviewee suggested an application with which service providers can check the requirements easily.

*P2: An easy application could be developed for service providers with which they could see the requirements or the correctness of the information.*

One interviewee mentioned the possibility of using students to test the services. Also, official usability tests were suggested to organizations.

*P8: Universities can offer testing help and students who can, e.g., do a thesis or projects surrounding cognitive accessibility.*

*P10: Organizations may use more usability tests or studies because accessibility is part of usability.*

## 4.3   The Enablers When Implementing Cognitively Accessible Digital Services

Furthermore, the interviewees' were asked their opinions in relation to the possible enablers that service providers may encounter. The enablers in this context were the factors, practices, policies, or resources within an organization that help make digital consumer services more accessible to individuals with cognitive disabilities. The answers were based on the interviewees' feelings and understanding of possible enablers. According to the interviewees, the most common enabler was checklists or guidelines. Other enablers were believed to be customer base expansion, legislation, money, and cost savings, hiring or involving people with cognitive disabilities, outsourcing services, organizational culture and other benefits, such as search engine optimization (SEO) or brand image. Especially in bigger organizations, money was seen as an enabler.

*P4: It should be understood that people with disabilities have money, and everyone has money, so the services should be designed to suit everyone.*

Also, social responsibility and organizational culture were mentioned.

*P6: From the social responsibility point of view, services should be made easy to use for all people. Attitude affects everything.*

Three of the interviewees (P5, P6, P9) mentioned that one option for ensuring the accessibility of digital services is involving people or hiring employees for organizations who have cognitive difficulties or asking their opinion via focus groups:

*P5: Organizations should take small steps to enter the world of accessibility. One could take into consideration one user group at a time, starting with immigrants and linguistic challenges, for example.*

Four of the interviewees (P1, P2, P6, P7) mentioned that the Internet is full of usable checklists regarding cognitive accessibility and how to design usable and understandable websites.

One interviewee mentioned that society has put effort to promote accessibility.

*P7: There are many accessibility trainings available, both paid and free, because society invests so much in it.*

The problem is how content creators or employees in organizations digital departments will find or search for this information.

*P8: Accessibility terminology may be difficult to understand. The question is how to find information about trainings.*

All the enablers have been listed in Table 3.

**Table 3.** The enablers for implementing cognitively accessible digital services

| Enablers | Interviewee | Selected quotations |
|---|---|---|
| Checklists and other material | P1, P2, P6, P7, P8, P10 | 'There should be easy checklists for companies.' |
| Legislation | P5, P6, P8, P10 | 'Legislation is the stick.' |
| Money and cost-saving | P6, P4, P8 | 'Big organizations can spend more money to design accessible services.' |
| Customer base extension | P3, P4, P10 | 'Designing for all brings more customers.' |
| Hiring or involving people with cognitive disabilities | P5, P6, P9 | 'Organizations should be involved to design process more people with cognitive disabilities.' |
| Other benefits e.g. improvements to SEO or brand | P9, P10 | 'Better brand image with accessible digital services.' |
| Outsourcing services | P9 | 'Bigger organizations can buy services from professionals.' |
| Social responsibility, organizational culture | P6 | 'Everyone should have a responsible mindset.' |

## 5  Discussion

This study aimed to identify the perceptions of experts and professionals in web accessibility in relation to organizational enablers and barriers when designing cognitively accessible digital services. The research question was as follows: What are the organizational enablers and barriers when designing and creating cognitively accessible digital services? To be able to respond to that question, in-depth interviews were conducted with accessibility experts and professionals in Finland.

According to the interviewees, there can be different kinds of barriers when organizations design cognitively accessible digital services. Some of the barriers may vary depending on the size of the organization, most importantly the lack of financial resources available for service design. Interviewees answered almost unanimously that the most common barrier was the lack of knowledge. Lack of knowledge has also been mentioned in earlier studies [16, 17]. According to the interviewees, information is available on the Internet, but the dilemma is how and which keywords to use to search for it. Also, complex terms in the accessibility field may contribute to the problem. This is something not mentioned in earlier research.

Other barriers were related to conservative organization culture, a lack of professional competence, a lack of positive attitudes and feelings of inadequacy. A lack of money and a lack of positive attitudes were mentioned in the studies of Pichiliani and Pizzolato [17] and Leitner et al. [16]. The feeling of inadequacy was a barrier that was not mentioned in the previous studies. The group of people who need cognitively accessible digital services is diverse, and being aware of the whole group's needs requires

time, money, knowledge, and other resources, which may lead to feelings of inadequacy. Organizational culture may be seen as a barrier but also an enabler. Pichiliani
and Pizzolato [17] also identified this barrier. Leitner et al. [16] pointed out the lack of
top management support, which can be considered part of organizational culture. If the
organizational culture is conservative and not permissive, there is no willingness to make
improvements to digital services unless it is required by legislation. One new barrier was
a lack of professional competence. This can lead to a situation where, for example, an
inexperienced person and not a professional, can be hired in the organization to create
online content. Content creation is one of the most important activities in the cognitive
accessibility field.

The most common enabler according to the interviewees was the web accessibility
checklists. Other enablers were customer base expansion, legislation, money and cost
savings, hiring or involving people with cognitive disabilities, outsourcing services,
organizational culture and other benefits, e.g., SEO or brand image. The interview results
revealed that some of the enablers were partly similar to those mentioned in previous
studies related to web accessibility motivations and adaptations [15–17]. Velleman et al.
[15] and a European Commission report [22] mentioned legislation and guidelines, which
were also mentioned in this study. The study by Leitner et al. [16] showed economic,
social and technical structures. However, the study by Leitner et al., [16] focused on
overall web accessibility motivation factors and adaptations. One interviewer mentioned
the other benefits that cognitively accessible digital services may bring to an organization,
such as better search engine optimization. Although the web accessibility benefits of
digital services have been reported in earlier studies [15–17], service providers may
not actually understand the benefits. A study by Pichiliani and Pizzolato [17] focused
on cognitively accessible digital service enablers, and they raised the importance of
guidelines. The importance of different guidelines was mentioned in the interview results,
but the problem according to the interviewees was that the Internet is full of good
checklists regarding cognitive accessibility, but service providers are not able to search
for that information. Hiring people with cognitive disabilities to work in companies or
outsourcing services were not mentioned in earlier studies. A European Commission
pilot study [22] suggested involving user participation in the design process, but not as
an employee.

## 5.1 Value Co-destruction

This paper argued that failing to design cognitively accessible digital services challenges
value co-creation – there is a danger of value co-destruction. Understanding enablers
and barriers may prevent service providers' and users value co-destruction. If organizations misuse customers' resources and do not fulfill their value proposition position, the
expectations are not met [42]. As Vargo and Lusch [6] point out, services are valuable
only if people can use them. If digital services cannot be used due to their use of difficult
language or content, they do not bring value to their users. This leads to resource misuse.

The interviewees mentioned the lack of resources and lack of knowledge as the most critical barriers that explain why service providers may not design cognitively accessible digital services. According to Plé and Chumpitaz Cáceres [7], if an actor lacks resources, such as the time or skills needed to engage in value co-creation, the process can fail. Kashif and Zarkada [49] mentioned the lack of knowledge as a reason for value co-destruction. Based on Plé and Chumpitaz Cáceres [7] and Kashif and Zarkada [49], statements about knowledge lacking a role in value co-destruction, this should be seen as one of the critical factors regarding misuse of one's resources. Cluley and Radnor [39] have stated that value can mean different things to different people in different contexts and in different ways. User expectations can be subjective. Stressful situations and obstacles can create barriers for service users [8]. When service providers provide usable and understandable digital services, the risk of bad customer experiences is lower. In the study by Engen et al. [8], one of the causes of value co-destruction was the inability to serve. There are situations in the digital environment when the services do not reach the customer. These problems can be related to a lack of usability or a lack of understandable content, which are the main features of cognitive accessibility. To mitigate value co-destruction related to cognitive accessibility, service providers should prioritize cognitive accessibility features in digital services.

## 5.2 Practical Implications

According to the interview results, there are many enablers for cognitively accessible digital services and there are many barriers as well. As the study results revealed, guidelines are one step that can be taken to enable organizations to consider cognitive accessibility features in digital services. More support and guidance are needed in order to be able to support organizations to design accessible services. As the interview results showed, there are some guidelines on the Internet, but the problem is establishing how to search for that information.

A good baseline for support is to use web accessibility standards (WCAG), which may provide a baseline for implementing accessible services. However, this standard does not provide all the cognitive accessibility requirements. Therefore, one option is to use the W3C's supplemental guidance (Cognitive Accessibility Guidance) [27]. However, these standards may be complex and difficult to understand due to the complex terminology of cognitive accessibility. The terms should be rephrased or improve the search engine optimization for information that is available on the Internet. More training for content creators and service providers regarding web accessibility will help service providers understand the broad field of accessibility and the features of cognitive accessibility.

Based on the interview results, one enabler was legislation. Currently, the Web Accessibility Directive of 2016 requires that all public sector websites and applications in the EU member states implement, enforce and maintain a uniform set of accessibility standards [53]. Each EU country has formed its own legislation based on the directive. The newer directive, the European Accessibility Act 2019 (EAA) requires that both public and private sector actors guarantee the accessibility of certain products and services. All EU countries need to cover this directive in their national legislation by 2025. However, only some of the cognitive accessibility features have been defined in the current legislation. When legislation requirements are not definite for organizations, the question of social responsibility arises [54]. When legislation does not exist, the importance of the topic is not seen as relevant in digital services' daily activities. In the future, cognitive accessibility features should be considered in national legislation.

## 5.3   Limitations and Further Research

The findings of this study are subject to certain limitations. The number of interviewees was small. The interviews were conducted in a geographically small area, the southern part of Finland. Also, the experience years of interviewees varied.

This study was based on cognitive accessibility in digital services. Concentrating on overall web accessibility and the technical requirements may lead to different kinds of barriers and enablers. In this study, the size of the organization was not specified for the interviewers. There can be different kinds of barriers and enablers depending on the size of an organization.

Future research is needed considering the enablers and barriers that cognitive accessibility in digital services may bring to organizations. Future studies need to collect a larger group of people who are working with digital services on a daily basis (e.g., those who are providing content for digital services). Understanding the content providers' knowledge of cognitive accessibility may give more insight into 'how to overcome the barriers and formulate support.' Further studies can investigate the barriers and enablers for a particular size of organization. The term cognitive accessibility is familiar to web accessibility experts and professionals but it is still an unclear term to other people. More research is required in the field where the term is understood and in order to foster an understanding of the enablers and barriers in this field.

## 6   Conclusions

In this paper, the interview results were presented regarding the enablers and barriers encountered when designing cognitively accessible digital services. The interviewees were accessibility experts and professionals in Finland. This paper argued that failing to design cognitively accessible digital services challenges value co-creation as it brings about a danger of value co-destruction.

Firstly, several steps can be taken to remove barriers and enhance enablers for cognitively accessible digital services within an organization. The results provide evidence that one of the biggest barriers was a lack of knowledge and the most common enabler was supporting organizations by providing guidelines and checklists and enhancing knowledge of cognitive accessibility. If service providers are not familiar with the term cognitive accessibility and the possible benefits of cognitive accessibility, they do not understand what to search for online. Digital services are changing rapidly. New digital channels and new requirements for providing accessible digital services that cater to the circumstances of all people arise. Once designed, a website or web store constantly needs updates. The features of cognitive accessibility should open more practical ways for web designers and content providers to design and provide content.

Secondly, there should be more information available for organizations about how cognitive accessibility in digital services can enhance their digital services. When the benefits have been understood, more support is needed in order to be able to implement the requirements for a digital service's content and platform. Organizations should educate employees on cognitive accessibility and its importance. This includes educating designers, developers, content creators and customer service staff. Organizations should foster a culture that values and champions accessibility as an integral part of the design and development process (e.g., they should foster a culture that involves users with cognitive disabilities in the digital service design process and tests digital services with users regularly). When the understanding of cognitively accessible importance and benefits arise, there is no danger of value co-destruction.

Thirdly, more research is needed on how digital services can co-create value or co-destruct value for people who have cognitive disabilities. Value co-creation and co-destruction should be viewed in the same research. According to Lumivalo et al. [44] value co-destruction should be studied in connection with value co-creation to understand its uniqueness and the dynamics between the two.

**Acknowledgments.** I would like to thank all the interviewees who gave their valuable insights to foster this research.

# Appendix

### In-depth Interview Guide
At the beginning of each interview, the participants were reminded about the topic of the interview and permission for the interview was requested.

1. Please describe your name and field of expertise.
2. How long you have been in your current position as a web accessibility or cognitive accessibility specialist or expert?
3. Please describe what web accessibility means.
4. Please describe what cognitive accessibility means.
5. Please describe what could be the benefits of using cognitively accessible features in digital services for the service user and the service provider.
6. Please describe what barriers there could be to implementing cognitive accessibility features in digital services.
7. What kind of support should be offered to service providers so that they can provide accessible and cognitively accessible digital services?
8. Please describe what could be enablers for implementing cognitive accessibility features in digital services.
9. How can service providers make sure that their digital services are cognitively accessible?

# References

1. European Commission. Web Accessibility. https://digital-strategy.ec.europa.eu/en/policies/web-accessibility. Accessed 15 Aug 2023
2. European Commission. Web Accessibility Directive: Websites of Public Sector Bodies Must be Accessible as of Now. https://digital-strategy.ec.europa.eu/en/news/web-accessibility-directive-websites-public-sector-bodies-must-be-accessible-now. Accessed 20 Sept 2023
3. W3C. Introduction to Web Accessibility. https://www.w3.org/WAI/fundamentals/accessibility-intro/. Accessed 30 Oct 2023
4. Chalghoumi, H., Cobigo, V., Jutai, J.: Ethical issues related to IT adoption by elderly persons with cognitive impairments. Stud. Health Technol. Informat. **242**, 59–63 (2017)
5. Holmes, K.M., O'Loughlin, N.: The experiences of people with learning disabilities on social networking sites. Br. J. Learn. Disabil. **42**, 1–5 (2014). https://doi.org/10.1111/bld.12001
6. Vargo, S.L., Lusch, R.F.: Evolving to a new dominant logic for marketing. J. Mark. **68**(1), 1–17 (2004). https://doi.org/10.1509/jmkg.68.1.1.24036
7. Plé, L., Chumpitaz Cáceres, R.: Not always co-creation: introducing interactional co-destruction of value in service-dominant logic. J. Serv. Mark. **24**(6), 430–437 (2010). https://doi.org/10.1108/08876041011072546
8. Engen, M., Fransson, M., Quist, J., Skålén, P.: Continuing the development of the public service logic: a study of value co-destruction in public services. Public Manag. Rev. **23**, 1–20 (2020). https://doi.org/10.1080/14719037.2020.1720354
9. Echeverri, P., Skålén, P.: Co-creation and co-destruction: a practice theory based study of interactive value formation. Mark. Theory **11**(3), 351–373 (2011). https://doi.org/10.1177/1470593111408181
10. Abad-Alcalá, L., Llorente-Barroso, C., Sánchez-Valle, M., Viñarás-Abad, M., Pretel-Jiménez, M.: Electronic government, and online tasks: towards the autonomy and empowerment of senior citizens. Profession. Inform. **26**(1), 34–42 (2017). https://doi.org/10.3145/epi.2017.ene.04
11. Calvo, R., Seyedarabi, F., Savva, A.: Beyond web content accessibility guidelines: expert accessibility reviews. In: Proceedings of the 7th International Conference on Software Development and Technologies for Enhancing Accessibility and Fighting Info-exclusion (DSAI 2016), pp. 77–84. Association for Computing Machinery, New York (2016). https://doi.org/10.1145/3019943.3019955
12. Gonçalves, R., Rocha, T., Martins, J., et al.: Evaluation of e-commerce websites accessibility and usability: an e-commerce platform analysis with the inclusion of blind users. Univ. Access Inf. Soc. **17**(3), 567–583 (2018). https://doi.org/10.1007/s10209-017-0557-5
13. Palani, S., Fourney, A., Williams, S., Larson, K., Spiridonova, I., Morris, M.R.: An eye tracking study of web search by people with and without dyslexia. In: Proceedings of the 43rd International ACM SIGIR Conference on Research and Development in Information Retrieval, pp. 729–738. Association for Computing Machinery, New York (2020). https://doi.org/10.1145/3397271.3401103
14. Čaić, M., Odekerken-Schröder, G., Mahr, D.: Service robots: value co-creation and co-destruction in elderly care networks. J. Serv. Manag. **29**(2), 178–205 (2018). https://doi.org/10.1108/JOSM-07-2017-0179
15. Velleman, E.M., Nahuis, I., van der Geest, T.: Factors explaining adoption and implementation processes for web accessibility standards within eGovernment systems and organizations. Univ. Access Inf. Soc. **16**(1), 173–190 (2015). https://doi.org/10.1007/s10209-015-0449-5
16. Leitner, M.-L., Strauss, C., Stummer, C.: Web accessibility implementation in private sector organizations: motivations and business impact. Univ. Access Inf. Soc. **15**(2), 249–260 (2014). https://doi.org/10.1007/s10209-014-0380-1

17. Pichiliani, T., Pizzolato, E.: A survey on the awareness of Brazilian web development community about cognitive accessibility. In Proceedings of the 18th Brazilian Symposium on Human Factors in Computing Systems (IHC 2019), pp. 8, 1–11. Association for Computing Machinery, New York (2019). https://doi.org/10.1145/3357155.3358448

18. Crabb, M., Heron, M., Jones, R., Armstrong, M., Reid, H. Y., Wilson, A.: Developing accessible services: understanding current knowledge and areas for future support. In: Proceedings of the 2019 CHI Conference on Human Factors in Computing Systems (CHI 2019), pp. 216, 1–12. Association for Computing Machinery, New York (2019). https://doi.org/10.1145/329 0605.3300446

19. Ghauri, P.N., Grønhaug, K., Strange, R.: Research Methods in Business Studies (Fifth). University Press, Cambridge (2020)

20. Bengtsson, M.: How to plan and perform a qualitative study using content analysis. Nursing Plus Open **2** 8–14 (2016). https://doi.org/10.1016/j.npls.2016.01.001

21. European Commission. European Disability Strategy 2010–2020: A renewed commitment to a barrier-free Europe. https://eur-lex.europa.eu/LexUriServ/LexUriServ.do?uri=COM%3A2 010%3A0636%3AFIN%3Aen%3APDF. Accessed 15 Aug 2023

22. European Commission. Pilot project study: Inclusive web-accessibility for persons with cognitive disabilities. https://digital-strategy.ec.europa.eu/en/library/commission-publishes-study-inclusive-web-accessibility-persons-cognitive-disabilities. Accessed 15 Aug 2023

23. The Finnish Centre for Easy Language/Selkokeskus. Selkokielen tarve. https://selkokeskus.fi/selkokieli/selkokielen-tarve/. Accessed 15 Oct 2023

24. European Commission. The Digital Services Act package. https://digital-strategy.ec.europa.eu/en/policies/digital-services-act-package. Accessed 30 Nov 2023

25. United Nations. Convention on the Rights of Persons with Disabilities – Article 9: Accessibility. https://www.un.org/development/desa/disabilities/convention-on-the-rights-of-persons-with-disabilities/article-9-accessibility.html. Accessed 30 Nov 2023

26. Leskelä, L.S.: Saavutettavan kielen opas. Kehitysvammaliitto ry. Oppimateriaalikeskus, Helsinki (2019)

27. W3C. Cognitive Accessibility Guidance. https://www.w3.org/WAI/WCAG2/supplemental/# cognitiveaccessibilityguidance/. Accessed 30 Nov 2023

28. World Health Organisation. Disability, World Health Organisation. https://www.who.int/news-room/fact-sheets/detail/disability-and-health/. Accessed 30 Nov 2023

29. Vollenwyder, B., Iten, G.H., Brühlmann, F., Opwis, K., Mekler, E.D.: Salient beliefs influencing the intention to consider web accessibility. Comput. Hum. Behav. **92**, 352–360 (2019). https://doi.org/10.1016/j.chb.2018.11.016

30. Nielsen, J.: Enhancing the explanatory power of usability heuristics. In: Proceedings of the SIGCHI Conference on Human Factors in Computing Systems (CHI 1994), pp. 152–158. Association for Computing Machinery, New York (1994). https://doi.org/10.1145/191666. 191729

31. Mäkipää, J.-P., Isohella, S.: Designing heuristics for accessible online text production. Scand. J. Inf. Syst. **34**(1), 5 (2022)

32. Laamanen, M., Ladonlahti, T., Puupponen, H., Kärkkäinen, T. Does the law matter? an empirical study on the accessibility of Finnish higher education institutions' web pages, pp. 1–17. Universal Access in the Information Society (2022). https://doi.org/10.1007/s10209-022-009 31-6

33. Johansson, S., Gulliksen, J., Lantz, A.: Cognitive accessibility for mentally disabled persons. In: Abascal, J., Barbosa, S., Fetter, M., Gross, T., Palanque, P., Winckler, M. (eds.) Human-Computer Interaction – INTERACT 2015: 15th IFIP TC 13 International Conference, Bamberg, Germany, September 14-18, 2015, Proceedings, Part I, pp. 418–435. Springer, Cham (2015). https://doi.org/10.1007/978-3-319-22701-6_31

34. Watfern, C., Heck, C., Rule, C., Baldwin, P., Boydell, K.M.: Feasibility and acceptability of a mental health website for adults with an intellectual disability. Qualit. Eval. JMIR Mental Health **6**(3), e12958 (2019). https://doi.org/10.2196/12958
35. Inal, Y., Guribye, F., Rajanen, D., Rajanen, M., Rost, M.: Perspectives and practices of digital accessibility: a survey of user experience professionals in Nordic countries. In: Proceedings of the 11th Nordic Conference on Human-Computer Interaction: Shaping Experiences, Shaping Society (NordiCHI 2020), Article 63, 1–11. Association for Computing Machinery, New York (2020). https://doi.org/10.1145/3419249.3420119
36. Payne, A.F., Storbacka, K., Frow, P.: Managing the co-creation of value. J. Acad. Mark. Sci. **36**, 83–96 (2008). https://doi.org/10.1007/s11747-007-0070-0
37. Rintamäki, T., Kuusela, H., Mitronen, L.: Identifying competitive customer value propositions in retailing. Manag. Serv. Qual. **17**(6), 621–634 (2007)
38. Mitronen, L., Rintamäki, T.: Arvopohjainen toimintalogiikka julkisen sektorin palvelujen ohjausjärjestelmissä. In: Anttonen, A., et al. (ed.) Julkisen ja yksityisen rajalla: julkisen palvelun muutos, pp. 174–216. Tampere University Press, Tampere (2012)
39. Cluley, R., Radnor, Z.: Rethinking co-creation: the fluid and relational process of value co-creation in public service organizations. Publ. Money Manag. **41**(7), 563–572 (2021). https://doi.org/10.1080/09540962.2020.1719672
40. Smith, B., Colgate, M.: Customer value creation: a practical framework. J. Market. Theory Pract. **15**(1), 7–23 (2007). https://doi.org/10.2753/MTP1069-6679150101
41. Zhang, T., Lu, C., Torres, E., Chen, P.-J.: Engaging customers in value co-creation or co-destruction online. J. Serv. Mark. **32**(1), 57–69 (2018). https://doi.org/10.1108/JSM-01-2017-0027
42. Smith, A.: The value co-destruction process: a customer resource perspective. Eur. J. Mark. **47**(11/12), 1889–1909 (2013). https://doi.org/10.1108/EJM-08-2011-0420
43. Vafeas, M., Hughes, T., Hilton, T.: Antecedents to value diminution: a dyadic perspective. Mark. Theory **16**(4), 469–491 (2016). https://doi.org/10.1177/1470593116652005
44. Lumivalo, J., Tuunanen, T., Salo, M.: Value co-destruction: a conceptual review and future research agenda. J. Serv. Res. **27**(2), 159–176 (2023). https://doi.org/10.1177/10946705231177504
45. Chowdhury, I., Gruber, T., Zolkiewski, J.: Every cloud has a silver lining—Exploring the dark side of value co-creation in B2B service networks. Indust. Market. Manag. **55**, 97–109 (2016). https://doi.org/10.1016/j.indmarman.2016.02.016
46. Robertson, N., Polonsky, M., McQuilken, L.: Are my symptoms serious Dr Google? a resource-based typology of value co-destruction in online self-diagnosis. Australas. Market. J. **22**(3), 246–256 (2014). https://doi.org/10.1016/j.ausmj.2014.08.009
47. Scherer, M.J., Federici, S., Tiberio, L., Pigliautile, M., Corradi, F., Meloni, F.: ICF core set for matching older adults with dementia and technology. Ageing Int. **37**, 414–440 (2012). https://doi.org/10.1007/s12126-010-9093-9
48. Järvi, H., Kähkönen, A.-K., Torvinen, H.: When value co-creation fails: reasons that lead to value co-destruction. Scand. J. Manag. **34**(1), 63–77 (2018). https://doi.org/10.1016/j.scaman.2018.01.002
49. Kashif, M., Zarkada, A.: Value co-destruction between customers and frontline employees: a social system perspective. Int. J. Bank Market. **33**(6), 627–691 (2015). https://doi.org/10.1108/IJBM-09-2014-0121
50. Eriksson, P., Kovalainen, A.: Case study research. In: Qualitative Methods in Business Research: Introducing Qualitative Methods, pp. 115–136. SAGE Publications Ltd., London (2008)

51. Boyce, C., Neale, P.: Conducting in-depth interviews: a guide for designing and conducting in-depth interviews for evaluation input. Pathfinder International Tool Series, Monitoring and Evaluation-2. https://nyhealthfoundation.org/wp-content/uploads/2019/02/m_e_tool_series_indepth_interviews-1.pdf. Accessed 30 Oct 2023
52. Bailey, J.: First steps in qualitative data analysis: transcribing. Fam. Pract. **25**(2), 127–131 (2008). https://doi.org/10.1093/fampra/cmn003
53. European Commission. Web Accessibility Directive: Websites of public sector bodies must be accessible as of now. https://digital-strategy.ec.europa.eu/en/news/web-accessibility-direct ive-websites-public-sector-bodies-must-be-accessible-now. Accessed 30 Oct 2023
54. Kärpänen, T.: Corporate digital responsibility and accessibility in digital services. In: Katherine Blashki (Ed.) Proceedings of the International Conferences on Interfaces and Human Computer Interaction 2022 and Game and Entertainment Technologies 2022. International Association for the Development of the Information Society, pp. 92–98 (2022). https://doi.org/10.33965/IHCI_GET2022_202205L012

# Remote Secure Online Voting System Development

T. Matos(✉) 🆔 and J. Guerreiro 🆔

NOVA LINCS and FCT and ISE, University of the Algarve, 8005-139 Faro, Portugal
`a52888@ualg.pt`, `jdguerreiro@ualg.pt`

**Abstract.** Remote online elections have been studied and applied throughout the years in several countries with different approaches and distinct secure mechanisms. Online elections collect sensitive information therefore, the system, must guarantee confidentiality, integrity, privacy, security and be auditable to ensure a successful and creditable election process.

A distinct web-based system approach, as far known, was developed using data processing, backend, storage and frontend components secured by cipher suites and an independent developed asymmetric cryptography key management system. Both, cipher suites and the key manage system, ensure authentication, authorization and vote encryption before storage, making it impossible to visualize election results primary to vote counting initiation and user's votes choices.

The developed system implements a mechanism to verify enabled users accesses in a specific election and ensure if they already voted, avoiding repeated votes. Encrypts, stores votes and users in distinct database tables to avoid, even with direct database access, the knowledge of who has voted so far and what was the vote direction, displaying statistics information of the already casted number of votes, being, the election committee, able to monitor effectiveness, before the voting period ends.

The developed and implemented databases follows ACID (Atomicity, Consistency, Isolation and Durability) properties, assuring each statement in a transaction is treated as a single unit preventing data loss and corruption, ensuring consistency, isolating user transactions, guaranteeing no transaction interferes with another and, on the event of a system failure, is assured that all executed transactions are saved and no data is lost.

**Keywords:** Security · Cibersecurity · Remote Online Voting · System Development

## 1 Introduction

Elections are a key point in any democracy allowing the people to individually choose their representatives. Nowadays, elections are, in every democratic country, used to select the ruling or regional governments for a mandate. Paper

© The Author(s), under exclusive license to Springer Nature Switzerland AG 2024
M. Antona and C. Stephanidis (Eds.): HCII 2024, LNCS 14697, pp. 51–65, 2024.
https://doi.org/10.1007/978-3-031-60881-0_4

elections are the most common ones where every voter selects a candidate from a ballot and places the vote paper into an urn. Votes are never associated with the voter and results are counted and shown to the population.

Recently, different forms of election have been addressed, elections via letter using post offices that deliver votes to the counting tables or the use of electronic elections for voters to submit their choices, by either using a predefined machine set and localization, similar to paper elections, or by using remote election software and internet technologies.

A remote elections software must be reliable, secure and ensure that user's identity and the privacy of their vote choices are not compromised, therefore cryptography and secured communications assume an relevant importance.

In this article, integrated on the Accessible security and privacy topic, a research study and a remote election software was developed that can be used in any type of elections, following the best security and privacy practices to ensure voters can cast their votes without being compromised and the election follows a predefined secure workflow until the results are made public.

The systems requirements to properly define the system architecture were [1,2]:

- **Ballot flexibility**: The system must be able to have different type of ballots, from yes or no to multiple parties ballots;
- **Voter flexibility**: Must be able to have different list of eligible voters for distinct elections;
- **Spontaneity**: Must require as little preparation as possible;
- **Remote participation**: Possibility to cast a vote from wherever the voter chooses;
- **Usability**: The system must be usable for everybody;
- **Strict Voting**: Cast votes only on the ballot candidates or by not selecting any candidate, resulting in a blank vote;
- **logging**: There must be registered log information without compromising individual privacy for the system to be auditable.

An election is a sensitive procedure that differs in candidates and eligible voters on each election, therefore several issues were considered for the system development:

- **Eligibility**: Only eligible voters are accepted;
- **Uniqueness**: Only a single vote can be accepted from each voter;
- **Equality**: Every eligible voter can access the election results after the results are public, regardless if the voter casted or not a vote;
- **Secrecy**: The system cannot link a voter to his vote, even with direct access to the database, nevertheless the voter must only vote once;
- **Integrity**: Impossibility to replace a casted vote with another vote;
- **Robustness**: The system must always perform its functions regardless of any eventual problem.

By following all these requirements, the system will successfully conduct a remote election.

The remainder of this article is organized as follows: In Sect. 2 Related work is presented. Section 3 describes the System Architecture. The developed Application Programmable Interface (API) Module is presented in Subsect. 3.1, the databases are presented in Subsect. 3.2 while Sect. 4 presents the System Security and Sect. 5 concludes the article.

## 2   Related Work

Throughout the years election systems have been used and are a reality in several countries. Switzerland [3], Estonia [4] and Norway [5] are perfect examples of such use.

Dyachkova et al. [6] developed a completely anonymous real time public network voting system. The authors system uses two different user's permissions, regular users and administrators. The first can cast a vote and visualize results after they became public, while the administrators cannot vote, but can create, delete elections, define users and groups, and publish results. Users authenticate using a single password and for the ballot creation and for signature the authors used an algorithm named "blind", based on RSA encryption. The ring signature protocol was used for data transmission to protect and anonymize eligible voters and prevent repeated votes. The system architecture is a node network connected to each other and a storage server that receives the nodes data, maintaining voter's anonymity.

Varshney et al. [7] proposed a system where the voter registers and authenticates identifying themselves with an random id and password generated by the system after a form fulfillment. On the election day, voters may cast their vote within a 10 s window to submit their choice. After a successful submission, a numeric code is automatically generated to identify the voter's voting location and choice which is encrypted by AES and stored on the database. Due to the AES complexity, even with a smaller key size of 128 bits, the generated numeric code maintains its confidentiality. The presented system does not allow, after the vote is casted, the same user to access the ballot again. To ensure integrity, any election system must be auditable, Alamleh et al. [8] mentioned. The authors also refereed that an election system must be stored in a safe environment to maintain confidentiality, integrity, availability and also logs must be made available for eventual audits.

The Sliusar et al. [9] proposed system is based on Blockchain technology. The system requires an identification confirmation, where the user presents a document and automatically the system generates a QR code, which is verified and registered by an authorized independent third party operator into the Blockchain, followed by the a token generation that will function as a ballot associated to the user, like a virtual wallet with a time limit. When the user casts his vote, a transaction between the user's wallet and the candidate's wallet is established, maintaining anonymity, because it cannot be traced back to the user's identity. The vote is stored and the user can visualize his vote at any time. The Blockchain technology guarantees transparency, anonymity, reliability, and security due to the fact that there is no need for electoral authorities, only the voter is able to see his vote and it is impossible to hack a chain block without affecting all others, avoiding, therefore, eventual vote tampering. Blockchain, with its a decentralized technology, assures fault tolerance, increases efficiency and faster processing, increasing civic engagement where the voter can participate in an election regardless of his location. The only problem of Sliusar et al. system is the need of guaranteeing the voter's identification assuring the voter is indeed the same person of the identification document.

Schmidt et al. [10] state that an election system should be outsourced to verified third parties called Voting Service Providers (VSP). A VSP should provide secure building, hardware, software and skilled personnel to ensure a secure electronic election. The authors refer that a VSP must be trustworthy, regulated and supervised by proper authorities. The hosting and operational processing are provided by the VSP therefore they must also secure communications via SSL/TLS. Some servers are connected to the external unprotected network (internet) to receive the votes and other are not, therefore it is required the implementation of all trusted and secured components like communication, storage and erasure, cryptography, logging and monitoring, installation, configuration and personnel for a proper electronic election to be held, maintaining system availability and protection.

An evaluation of remote internet voting as the next step in governance was performed by Ruth et al. [11]. The authors stated that the challenge was not technological but political, despite handling problems like data security, password protection, anonymity and server overload. The constituencies representation, discrimination and other political issues are concerns to be dealt by public officials. The authors also mentioned that remote voting elections were held in the United States and in Europe. In the last case, countries noticed that voters who normally describe themselves as abstainers choose internet voting. Different identification ways were described by the authors, in the USA, voters used their social security number, in Spain a smart card with a PIN code was used but it was counterproductive because only a small number of voters used the system. In Estonia a digital identification with two PINs was implemented where the first was used as a credential to access and cast the ballot, the second to encrypt and store it into the server. Voter anonymity was kept using "double envelope" security in which the digital ballot is not decrypted until the voter's identity was separated from it. Several Estonian parties expressed concerns over the system usage, especially regarding vote secrecy and, due to the unsupervised nature of the system, concerns of potentiate illegal pressure, coercion, or inducement of voters. Kate el al also mentioned that the Estonia System did not meet the expectations and only a small percentage of electors used the system and stated that these type of systems are convenient and can be secured in maintaining the voters anonymity but the assurance that votes are genuinely free of choice is a problem that does not occur in physical regular paper elections.

Kate et al. [12] used a message digest embedded in a random image file as an authentication system. The message digest used a SHA2 hashing algorithm with a generated 256 bit string and the vote was encrypted with AES protocol and then stored. When elections terminate, the votes are decrypted and results are announced. Yang et al. [13] implemented a complex three ballot model for end-to-end verifiability where every voter holds one of the ballots that can be used to verify the bulletin board results, calculate the final result and compare it with the published results. The system is resistant to coercion and does not require any cryptography while votes are being casted, they are encrypted and signed when stored. On tallying, the signature is verified and the vote is decrypted and counted.

The use of biometric fingerprint to authenticate voters was presented by Agarwal et al. [14] in their developed system. The reading of the biometrical is physical, so the voters address themselves to a voting station, and a comparison between the stored and the voter fingerprint is done by hashing. The votes are not encrypted and only the vote casting is stored to prevent vote duplication.

Annar Shankar et al. [15] proposed a system for migrants to cast votes, consisting in three modules: a mobile application, a backend server and a web application. The mobile application verifies the voter's ID requiring a One Time Password (OTP). Voters can temporarily change their voting location, the system requests a voter photo, a digital copy of its ID and the new location. Voters can also verify their activity by scanning an encrypted QR code present on the web application in the voting station. The backend server is responsible for storing the voter personal details in a database and respond to voter requests. Generating parties list and counting votes are also another responsibility of the backend server. On election day the voter scans a QR code on the website and sends their details to the server, triggering an event on the voting location. The web application on the polling station listens to the trigger and displays the constituency list allowing the voter to vote which is then stored anonymously by encrypting it to avoid tampering. The web application is placed at the polling station by the election commission. After displaying the list of parties, the application enables a 3 min timer camera and microphone to avoid malpractices. If the voter face is detected the vote buttons are enabled. After a vote has been casted it is encrypted and sent to a distributed server to avoid data tampering. Each voter must be present on election booth to cast the vote to avoid forgery.

All of these systems have pros and cons, the encryption before storing makes it harder to change data, using the decentralized Blockchain functionalities is a

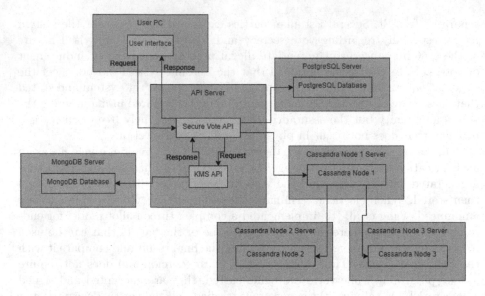

**Fig. 1.** System Architecture.

good option to guarantee security and and anonymity, using a VSP may also be a good solution, nevertheless some counter backs in the presented systems like the obligation to physically access the voting system, or to physically authenticate to vote, or even having a small windows to select the voter choice may be seen as an issue.

The developed Remote Secure Online Voting system presented in this article is a different approach contributing to remote election systems that can be applied to any kind of elections assuring security and anonymity. In the next Section the developed System Architecture is presented.

## 3　System Architecture

The system architecture is presented in Fig. 1, composed by an user interface, a Application Programming Interface (API) module with two API, Secure Vote and the Key Management System (KMS), a relational and two non-relational databases, one using Cassandra database system distributed nodes and mongoDB. Figure 1 diagram shows the APIs and servers usage for each used database system. Taking advantage of the decentralized nature of Cassandra the server usage of every node is optimal and if a crash or Denial of Service(DOS)/Distributed Denial of Service(DDoS) attacks occurs all will remain working. MongoDB and PostgreSQL separate servers mitigates possible data compromises, isolating such attempts to specific servers.

An election system requires a logical component to process data [16,17], so the development of a API module was essential to be used as an interface between users, databases storage and the Cassandra nodes in order to secure data. In Subsect. 3.1 the API module will be detailed while the databases will be presented in Subsect. 3.2.

## 3.1 Application Programming Interface Module

As stated before, an API is a interface to access distinct software modules, supplying end-points to invoke a specific method or class [18]. The most used API model is the Representational State Transfer, also known as REST, which was the logical choice for the developed remote election system in order to access the electoral module in a indirect, secured and encrypted way. Two distinct API were developed in this module, the first, Secure Vote API, that allows the creation of an election, vote casting, vote tallying and results presentation. All accesses and operations are stored in a log for eventual auditing. Each user has dedicated endpoints, forms and permissions. The system defines a set of permissions, Regular for voters, Manager to create elections, ballots, initiate and end election periods, tally and display results, Auditor to visualize all logs and audit the system and the last, Admin, accesses all system options.

The system also defines, for each election, a set of data entities, defined and properly mapped to their properties [16,17,19–25], each with a distinct role:

- **User**: The user class contains all operations regarding users like user registration, account verification, update and delete, login, password recovery, regenerate signature key, change permission, block and unblock user, blacklist, user verification. All of these options depend on the user permissions previously described;
- **Election**: This class has operations to create, update and delete elections, generate and regenerate the election keys that are responsible for vote casting encryption and decryption. The generation and regeneration of election key are only available before the start date/time of the election. Every user can visualize the results, after the election end date, just managers can access the voters list but not on which candidate or group of candidates they have voted on;
- **Vote**: The vote class has only one operation, the vote itself. The votes are directly associated to an election but never to a user, so no one can visualize, not even in the database, the users vote. Tallying is also the vote class responsibility, counting each candidate or group of candidates votes;
- **Log**: All interactions in the system are stored in two types of logs, internal and election logs. The first, auditors can visualize accesses, admins and system actions, while the second auditors can visualize all election actions performed by all users while the election period is available;
- **Blacklist**: This class supplies operations to add and remove emails to and from the blacklist. The blacklist blocks emails from registering an account in order to block eventual email spam.

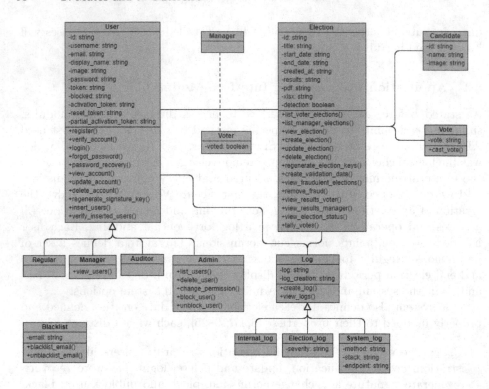

**Fig. 2.** Secure Vote module API Class Diagram.

The second API is KMS, developed to secure encryption keys since they are a major concern and cannot be compromised [1]. A key management system allows its users to manage their encryption keys. Users can create, retrieve, update and delete keys [26]. The Secure Vote module will have an external KMS, so if an attack occurs on the Secure Vote API it will not affect the KMS and vice-versa. In this case, the KMS will have its own API to allow the Secure Vote API to create, retrieve, update and delete keys regarding elections and user signatures. Due to the sensitive nature of the private keys, they are encrypted when stored while the public keys do not require such encryption.

In Fig. 3 it is possible to visualize the lack of relationships between entities because they are not required to properly execute their operations. The KMS API main functionality is to secure the public and private keys and operations, like key creation, retrieval, update or delete. This API also stores logs of all actions performed between the Secure Vote API, the non-relational database and the KMS API. The KMS API has its own entities and operations:

- **Key**: The Secure Vote API uses the KMS API to create, retrieve, update and delete keys. Voter signature keys are used while casting the vote and election keys are used to encrypt and decrypt votes;
- **Log**: This class stores all actions performed by the system to be audit and checked if any unauthorized access occurred;

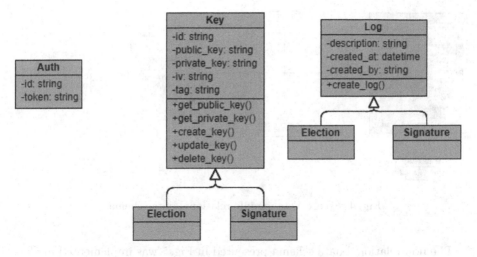

**Fig. 3.** KMS API Class Diagram.

- **Auth**: The auth class has a middle-ware in all endpoints checking if the token exists and if is a valid one. Each token is generated with a secret associated to each system. If one of these tokens is compromised, the keys cannot be retrieved because they are encrypted and also of because the API answer is encrypted before it is sent.

### 3.2 Databases

The databases architecture are a division in two of the diagram presented in Fig. 2, a relational and non-relational databases for data decentralization ans security.

The relational database was implemented to deal with data manipulation on multiples tables and consistency also because of the transactions amount needed to ensure candidates, voters, managers, election data storage. PostgreSQL was chosen because is ACID-complaint features and automatic updates to stored procedures preventing therefore SQL injection. Figure 4 describe the schema used for the Secure Vote user, candidate, manager, voters and elections data, while Fig. 5 describe the Secure Vote non-relational data schema where the votes and logs are stored.

Votes and log operations, performed by both API, cannot fail during vote casting, therefore the databases must be, always available To mitigate this problem, Cassandra database system was implemented because of its distributed NoSQL wide-column storage system developed by Apache for high availability, and its architecture that does not present a single point of failure, so far. Also because Cassandra prepared statements prevents NoSQL injection attacks, assigning extra security to the election system. However, Cassandra is not ACID-complaint, due to the lack of transactions, but the implemented operations do not require any transactions, they are single not sequenced queries.

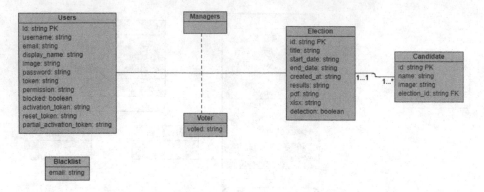

**Fig. 4.** Secure Vote module relational data schema.

The non-relational data schema presented in Fig. 5 was implemented in Cassandra distributed database system for the votes of the electors, internal operations log, election transactions log and system logs. The votes were implemented in the non-relational database without any identification of the voter, so it cannot be back traced which voter voted on what candidate, not even with database access, because there is no registration of the user, nevertheless the user cannot vote a second time, managed in the transaction database, assuring voter's anonymity and confidentiality.

Comparing the diagram presented in Fig. 3.1 with the schema in Fig. 4, some attributes are no present because permissions have to be stored with the users data. Several tokens are also stored, a reset token is used when a user recovers its password and a activation token is used to verify if the submitted email is actually a real user email, accomplished with a activation email sent to the registered user email.

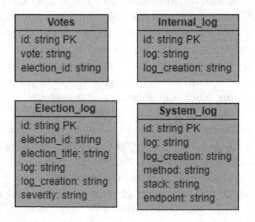

**Fig. 5.** Secure Vote module non-relational data schema.

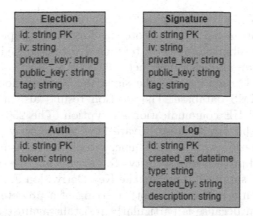

**Fig. 6.** KMS data schema.

The KMS database is stored in MongoDB because is schemeless, where data can change the schema without having to alter the database itself, allowing keys to be stored regardless of what encryption type is used.

Figure 6 represents the developed schema to store KMS operations where each table is a key type to improve data organization. All election, signatures, authentication keys and all transactions logs performed are stored in the schema.

All data must be secured, therefore in Sect. 4 all applied system security is detailed.

## 4  System Security

Nowadays there are several cipher suites that can be applied to secure applications, supplying algorithms for key exchange to protect shared keys, bulk encryption to encrypt client/server messages and message authentication to verify integrity, combined with TLS or SSL protocols [27]. Remote elections must be secured [28], therefore a
TLS_ECDHE_ECDSA_WITH_AES_256_GCM_RSA_4096_SHA256_K571
cipher suite was used for both Secure Vote and KMS APIs, where the algorithms ECDHE was applied for key exchange, ECDSA for signature verification, AES_256_GCM and RSA_4096 are the bulk encryption algorithms used, HMAC is for message authentication and K571 is the elliptic curve used. The cipher suite used was combined with TLS over TCP for secure transport connections.

### 4.1  Cipher Suite Implementation in the Remote Secure Online System

Secure Vote and KMS uses ECDHE together with AES_256_GCM to encrypt the data exchanged between themselves where every API communication has always a different encryption keys. For signing votes and integrity check, Secure

Vote API uses SHA-256 together with ECDSA to verify if a vote cast belong to the actual voter who casted it. If the vote was forged or tampered, is discarded, but the attempt to submit a forged or tempered vote is logged for auditors and authorities to confirm and eventually act.

AES-256-GCM is used encrypt the signature and election private keys to be stored in the KMS database. The election results also use this algorithm combined with ECDHE communication encryption. The 256 bit key was chosen instead of 128 bit key because private keys are sensitive information and GCM mode of operation was due to its encrypted data integrity capabilities for communication and private keys security. To encrypt and decrypt using AES, a 256 bit key must be supplied, therefore the Key Derivation Function (KDF) was applied to transform a string into another string of a predetermined size. The function was chosen because is particularly resistant against ASIC and brute-force attacks to decipher encrypted messages and passwords [29]. The KDF or scrypt was applied when creating signature or election keys, where the user must insert a 12-character key, transformed by the function in a 256 bit or 32 characters long string to be used with AES. RSA is used in Secure Vote to encrypt the vote casting, using on the client side, the public key, and on the server side a private key to decrypt the votes while HMAC is used to provide a way to verify if the submitted cast is the same that arrives in the API. ECDSA already provides a way to verify integrity, but HMAC reinforces these transactions because it is a sensitive process and must be handled with special care to avoid tampered votes.

### 4.2 Complementary Security Applied in the Remote Secure Online System

To identify and authenticate both users and services consumed by the Secure Vote API [30,31] a JSON Web Token (JWT), which is a token represented as a string, converted from a JSON object, to digitally sign using HMAC, was used. These tokens in the Secure Vote API are used to verify permissions in each endpoint checking on the database if a user or service has permissions to access. KMS API also uses JWT to authenticate requests while always requiring authentication in all its endpoints.

Stored procedures and parameterized statements, which are not mutually exclusive and can be both used at the same time [32], were also used in the system to mitigate possible SQL and NoSQL injection attacks.

DOS attacks are one of the biggest threats in the internet nowadays, API endpoints can be subjected to such attacks, and an attacker can send constantly requests [30,31] therefore a rate limiter that defines the maximum number of IP address requests is recommended. Both API, Secure Vote and KMS uses Express.js framework that integrates a rate limiter on the endpoints to mitigate this kind of attacks.

To deal with Cross Site Request Forgery (CSRF), exploitation of the existing trust between application and browser, when requests arrive on an API from dubious sources, an extension of the XML-HttpRequest, Cross Origin Resource

Sharing (CORS) is applied, providing permissions to access resources in cross origin requests through a set of HTTP headers enforced by the client. The validation of these headers is performed in the server site. Both API, Secure Vote and KMS uses these mechanisms to control access and prevent CSRF attacks.

### 4.3   Resilient and Security Tests

The Remote Secure Online Voting System is now being tested by security personal in the University of Algarve, where several tests have been applied. Tests like brute force, ASIC and dictionary attacks have been performed and as far, unsuccessful. Tools like DirBuster, Dirb, Webroot.pl and Burp Suite have been unsuccessfully used for brute force attacks. DOS and DDOS attacks have been performed with tools like LOIC, HOIC, Slowloris and RUDY. Despite of the attacks diminish communications, the system never stopped and still was able to continue working. Several other tests are being prepared to be enforced on the system to test the resiliency and integrity.

## 5   Conclusions and Future Work

All democratic democracies need elections for people free choice to select their rulers. So far, several attempts have been made to implement electronic, digital, and remote election systems, but not all of them were successful. One of the main issues is public trust, so the authors intended to contribute by providing a possible solution that can be applied in remote secure online elections. The design architecture, ciphers, redundancy, and complementary security applied on the system ensures that a possible solution can be used in remote elections, providing integrity, data segregation, confidentiality, privacy and secure transactions. The system is completely auditable, all transactions, internal, external, election and system logs are saved and accessible. Several security tests and cyberattacks have been made and yet unsuccessful, others will follow, as future work, to ensure that the product is secure to be on production.

**ACKNOWLEDGEMENTS.** This work was supported by NOVA LINCS (UIDB/04516/2020) with the financial support of FCT.IP.

## References

1. Kiayias, A., Korman, M., Walluck, D.: An internet voting system supporting user privacy. In: 2006 22nd Annual Computer Security Applications Conference (ACSAC 2006), IEEE, December 2006
2. Kulyk, O., Neumann, S., Volkamer, M., Feier, C., Koster, T.: Electronic voting with fully distributed trust and maximized flexibility regarding ballot design. In: 2014 6th International Conference on Electronic Voting: Verifying the Vote (EVOTE), IEEE, October 2014

3.  Serdult, U., Germann, M., Mendez, F., Portenier, A., Wellig, C.: Fifteen years of internet voting in Switzerland [history, governance and use]. In: 2015 Second International Conference on eDemocracy; eGovernment (ICEDEG), IEEE, April 2015
4.  Heiberg, S., Willemson, J.: Verifiable internet voting in Estonia. In: 2014 6th International Conference on Electronic Voting: Verifying the Vote (EVOTE), IEEE, October 2014
5.  Markussen, R., Ronquillo, L., Schürmann, C.: Trust in internet election observing the Norwegian decryption and counting ceremony. In: 2014 6th International Conference on Electronic Voting: Verifying the Vote (EVOTE), IEEE, October 2014
6.  Dyachkova, I., Rakitskiy, A.: Development of the remote anonimous voting system and the analysis of its vulnerabilities. In: 2021 Ural Symposium on Biomedical Engineering, Radioelectronics and Information Technology (USBEREIT), IEEE, May 2021
7.  Varshney, K., Johari, R., Ujjwal, R.L.: Remote online voting system using aneka platform. In: 2018 7th International Conference on Reliability, Infocom Technologies and Optimization (Trends and Future Directions) (ICRITO), IEEE, August 2018
8.  Alamleh, H., AlQahtani, A.A.S.: Analysis of the design requirements for remote internet-based e-voting systems. In: 2021 IEEE World AI IoT Congress (AIIoT), IEEE, May 2021
9.  Sliusar, V., Fyodorov, A., Volkov, A., Fyodorov, P., Pascari, V.: Blockchain technology application for electronic voting systems. In: 2021 IEEE Conference of Russian Young Researchers in Electrical and Electronic Engineering (ElConRus), IEEE, January 2021
10. Schmidt, A., Langer, L., Buchmann, J., Volkamer, M.: Specification of a voting service provider. In: 2009 First International Workshop on Requirements Engineering for e-Voting Systems, IEEE, August 2009
11. Ruth, S., Mercer, D.: Voting from the home or office? Don't hold your breath. IEEE Internet Comput. **11**, 68–71 (2007)
12. Kate, N., Katti, J.: Security of remote voting system based on visual cryptography and Sha. In: 2016 International Conference on Computing Communication Control and automation (ICCUBEA), IEEE, August 2016
13. Yang, J., Jing, S., Jia, L.: RVBT: a remote voting scheme based on three-ballot. In: 2020 16th International Conference on Computational Intelligence and Security (CIS), IEEE, November 2020
14. Agarwal, S., Haider, A., Jamwal, A., Dev, P., Chandel, R.: Biometric based secured remote electronic voting system. In: 2020 7th International Conference on Smart Structures and Systems (ICSSS), IEEE, July 2020
15. Harsshanth, S., et al.: Migrant voting system-solution to gain the lost votes. In: 2021 2nd International Conference on Smart Electronics and Communication (ICOSEC), IEEE, October 2021
16. Rosasooria, Y., Mahamad, A.K., Saon, S., Isa, M.A.M., Yamaguchi, S., Ahmadon, M.A.: E-voting on blockchain using solidity language. In: 2020 Third International Conference on Vocational Education and Electrical Engineering (ICVEE), IEEE, October 2020
17. Jangada, A., Dadlani, N., Raina, S., Sooraj, V., Buchade, A.: De-centralized voting system using blockchain. In: 2022 IEEE International Conference on Blockchain and Distributed Systems Security (ICBDS), IEEE, September 2022

18. Eilertsen, A.M., Bagge, A.H.: Exploring api/client co-evolution. In: 2018 IEEE/ACM 2nd International Workshop on API Usage and Evolution (WAPI), pp. 10–13 (2018)
19. Li, Y., et al.: A blockchain-based self-tallying voting protocol in decentralized IoT. IEEE Trans. Dependable Secure Comput. **19**, 119–130 (2022)
20. Salman, W., Yakovlev, V., Alani, S.: Analysis of the traditional voting system and transition to the online voting system in the republic of Iraq. In: 2021 3rd International Congress on Human-Computer Interaction, Optimization and Robotic Applications (HORA), IEEE, June 2021
21. Al-madani, A.M., Gaikwad, A.T., Mahale, V., Ahmed, Z.A.: Decentralized e-voting system based on smart contract by using blockchain technology. In: 2020 International Conference on Smart Innovations in Design, Environment, Management, Planning and Computing (ICSIDEMPC), IEEE, October 2020
22. Kumar, D., Kumar Dwivedi, R.: Blockchain and internet of things (IoT) enabled smart e-voting system. In: 2023 International Conference on Intelligent Data Communication Technologies and Internet of Things (IDCIoT), IEEE, January 2023
23. Peter, G., Stonier, A.A., Sherine, A.: Development of mobile application for e-voting system using 3-step security for preventing phishing attack. In: 2022 2nd International Conference on Advance Computing and Innovative Technologies in Engineering (ICACITE), IEEE, April 2022
24. Pranitha, G., Rukmini, T., Shankar, T.N., Sah, B., Kumar, N., Padhy, S.: Utilization of blockchain in e-voting system. In: 2022 2nd International Conference on Intelligent Technologies (CONIT), IEEE, June 2022
25. Govindaraj, R., et al.: Online voting system using cloud computing. In: International Research Journal of Modernization in Engineering (2022)
26. Roman, R., Alcaraz, C., Lopez, J., Sklavos, N.: Key management systems for sensor networks in the context of the internet of things. Comput. Elect. Eng. **37**, 147–159 (2011)
27. Microsoft: Cipher suites in tls/ssl (schannel ssp) (2023). https://learn.microsoft.com/en-au/windows/win32/secauthn/ciphersuites-in-schannel
28. Schryen, G.: Security aspects of internet voting. In: Proceedings of the 37th Annual Hawaii International Conference on System Sciences, IEEE (2004)
29. Le Duong, V.T., Tran, T.H., Pham, H.L., Lam, D.K., Nakashima, Y.: MRSA: a high-efficiency multi romix scrypt accelerator for cryptocurrency mining and data security. IEEE Access **9**, 168383–168396 (2021)
30. Lauer, T.W.: The risk of e-voting (2004)
31. Jefferson, D., Rubin, A.D., Simons, B., Wagner, D.: Analyzing internet voting security. Commun. ACM **47**, 59–64 (2004)
32. Chao-yang, Z.: Dos attack analysis and study of new measures to prevent. In: 2011 International Conference on Intelligence Science and Information Engineering, IEEE, August 2011

# Designing for Inclusion and Diversity in Big Tech Reports: A Gray Literature Analysis

Ana Carolina Moises de Souza(✉) and Letizia Jaccheri

Norwegian University of Science and Technology, Trondheim 7491, Norway
{ana.c.m.de.souza,letizia.jaccheri}@ntnu.no

**Abstract.** This study investigates whether big technology companies (Google, Amazon, Meta, Apple, Microsoft) comprehensively report inclusion and diversity actions in their software product and service design. Therefore, this research aims to address the gap in reporting on designing for inclusion actions carried out during product and service design. Using a gray literature review approach, we examined reports from a variety of sources, including Corporate Social Responsibility (CSR), Diversity, Equity and Inclusion (DEI), Environment, Social and Governance (ESG), and others. Thematic analysis was applied to synthesize the results and answer the main research question: How are inclusion and diversity actions reported by big tech companies during the design of software products? Our study shows that while diversity in the workplace is frequently reported, actions related to diversity and inclusion in software design are unreported. Google, Apple and Microsoft provide more detailed insights into inclusive design approaches in their reports, while Meta and Amazon focus predominantly on environmental initiatives and workplace diversity. The findings highlight the need for standardized reporting practices and greater transparency in the software design process. We offer recommendations on what to report regarding software development in inclusion and diversity reports.

**Keywords:** social sustainability · diversity · designing for inclusion · software development · corporate social responsibility

## 1 Introduction

Over the past two decades, the evolution of the technology industry has led big technology companies to expand their role beyond mere innovation and market dominance. These companies are now embracing broader and more impactful social responsibility. As stakeholders increasingly demand transparency and ethical practices, big techs find themselves at the crossroads of Corporate Social Responsibility (CSR), Diversity, Equity, and Inclusion (DEI), and Environmental, Social, and Governance (ESG).

The pioneering efforts of early advocates in reporting social responsibilities, such as Ben & Jerry's, offer an overview of how social justice is relevant to corporate reputation [8,17]. Contemporary reports from major technologies such as

M. Antona and C. Stephanidis (Eds.): HCII 2024, LNCS 14697, pp. 66–79, 2024.
https://doi.org/10.1007/978-3-031-60881-0_5

Google, Amazon, Meta (Facebook), Apple and Microsoft (GAMAM or GAFAM [30]) represent their commitment to building a better society.

But what do all these big techs have in common? The production, innovation, and design of new software products and services. When comparing these tech companies to traditional manufacturing sectors (using a car manufacturer as an example), a difference emerges. Car manufacturers are required to report on the social and environmental impacts of their products, the production process, and overall business practices. In contrast, software companies often lack clear reporting mechanisms that detail the social and environmental impacts of both their development processes and the resulting software products.

The hypothesis of this study is that big tech may not be reporting the diversity and inclusion of their software, especially when designing it. However, they are focusing the report on diversity and inclusion related to the workplace. Calero et al. investigated whether actions during software development and in the software product were reported in CSR, they identified actions at the organizational level but were not related to the software product or process [7]. Souza et al. identified that financial companies do not address sustainability systematically in their software development, but only sustainability initiatives implemented at an organizational level [26].

The aim of this study is to verify whether designing for diversity and inclusion is reported in the reports of the big tech companies concerning their products and services. Therefore, our main research question is: How are inclusion and diversity actions reported by big tech companies during the design of software products? To answer this, our study design is performed by conducting a gray literature review [1, 19] of the reports (CSR, DEI, ESG, and other sources) and thematic analysis to synthesize the findings [9].

During our review, we identified several challenges in finding specific reports that disclose approaches to designing for inclusion and diversity, particularly in the software they sell and provide. We ended up with five reports, which we read to identify actions related to Universal Design [18], Participatory Design [24], and User-Centered Design [13]. Google, Apple and Microsoft were the companies that covered inclusive design approaches in more detail in their report that would be related to the design of their software products. Meta and Amazon's reports were mostly concentrated on environmental initiatives and workplace diversity. Although we found a few instances, our study has shown a need for reporting the practices adopted in the design process of software, a more standardized way of presenting this information, and facilitating access to these reports.

This extended abstract is structured as follows: Sect. 2 provides background on diversity and inclusion. Section 3 details the methods employed in this study, and Sect. 4 presents the results. Section 5 discusses the implications for the practice and limitations. We conclude our study in Sect. 6.

## 2   Background

Designing for diversity and inclusion is the intentional and inclusive approach to creating products, services, or systems that meet the needs of a diverse group with different needs [21]. Himmelsbach et al., refer to diversity in different dimensions and argue that diversity has multifaceted and social implications [12]. The dimensions are: cultural, gender, age, ability, ethnic, racial, and cognitive diversity [12].

In the context of reporting initiatives related to social aspects, diversity and inclusion have been reported by the big techs at the organizational level [10]. The previous findings are also confirmed in the study of Rodriguez Perez et al., in which diversity was perceived by the increased participation of women in teams and inclusion was targeted at employees with different nationalities in the area of software development [20]. The question that still remains here is: how are inclusion and diversity actions reported by big tech companies during the design of software products?

Szlavi and Soares [27] venture into the field of inclusive design, challenging conventional gender norms in web interfaces and advocating inclusive design principles that take intersectional factors into account. Their study investigates the application of inclusive design on the websites of big tech companies such as Microsoft, Apple, Google and Meta. The findings highlight the need for further research to address the exclusion of transgender and non-binary individuals in software design. In the context of software engineering, an intersectional approach involves examining how various aspects of identity, such as gender, race and socioeconomic status, intersect to influence individuals' experiences in the field of technology. This perspective recognizes that people's experiences are shaped by several factors beyond gender [11].

The importance of acknowledging design assumptions in user interface and interaction design is highlighted by Bardzell [3]. The author argues that each design project creates an "ideal user," and the design's success relies on how closely real users align with this ideal. The concept of self-disclosure is explored, highlighting how software shapes user identities and the empowerment potential of transparent processes. The study provides insights into the feminist Human-Computer Interaction (HCI) agenda, proposing two contributions: critique-based and generative. Critique-based involves analyzing designs to reveal unintended consequences, while generative contributions use feminist approaches in decision-making to influence tangible design outcomes. The author advocates recognizing and developing feminism's generative role in HCI to move beyond merely identifying sexism and create concrete, positive impacts in design practices.

Burnet et al. study introduces GenderMag, a systematic evaluation method for identifying gender-inclusiveness issues in problem-solving software [6]. It is based on five facets drawn from gender differences in the use and usability of software, aiming to design for diverse problem-solving facets statistically clustered by gender. GenderMag has been iteratively evolved and tested across various settings and evaluators, demonstrating its applicability beyond problem-solving software [28]. The method is available for use, with ongoing beta-testing in HCI education and production software settings globally, aiming to help software teams create gender-inclusive products and address pervasive issues in problem-solving software.

In the context of social sustainability theory, inclusion and diversity serve as paths to realizing social justice [2]. Souza et al. conducted a systematic literature review, reporting on existing research that explores the social dimension of sustainability in the specific context of software development [25]. The studies in the review propose tools and strategies to address diversity and inclusion as components of social sustainability. Therefore, designing for inclusion and diversity is a practical way to achieve social sustainability in software engineering, helping to prevent social erosion and the accumulation of social debt in software development [4].

Together, these studies align with the goal of identifying actions in big tech's CSR, ESG, and DEI reports, emphasizing the importance of inclusive design practices at both organizational and product/service levels. We aim to contribute to uncovering whether the big tech reports the existing practices applied in designing product and services related to Universal Design, Participatory Design and User-Centered Design.

## 3   Methods

### 3.1   Gray Literature Review

Gray literature covers a variety of information produced outside regular publication channels, often not well covered in scientific databases. In academic terms, it refers to information from government, academia, business and industry, in electronic or printed formats, not controlled by commercial publishers [19]. Furthermore, scholars have adopted a definition of gray literature that does not require intellectual property rights protection [1]. This definition recognizes the wide availability of web publishing platforms such as blogs, repositories, reports, and preprint servers such as arxiv. In line with this understanding of gray literature, our analysis focuses on CSR, DEI and ESG reports available on big tech websites.

We developed a search string to capture relevant gray literature related to diversity, inclusion, corporate responsibility, and sustainability reports of the big techs. The search string used in the Google search contained the following terms:

> *diversity OR inclusion report OR "corporate responsibility report" OR sustainability and "apple OR meta OR google OR microsoft OR amazon"*

Documents were included if they were reports pertaining to diversity, inclusion, corporate responsibility, or sustainability from the specified companies (Google, Amazon, Meta, Apple, Microsoft). The search prioritized reports directly accessible online and in pdf format corresponding to the fiscal years 2022 and 2023. The documents were excluded if they did not relate to the specified themes or if they were duplicates. Reports published before 2022, corresponding to previous fiscal years, were not selected. Additionally, materials not directly associated with the selected companies were excluded. We also identified that some reports did not cover the entire fiscal year; instead, they were progress reports detailing initiatives up to the mid-year point. In such cases, these reports were excluded from the review process.

We prioritized the most recent results from the search. This means no specific date restrictions were applied to ensure a comprehensive retrieval of relevant gray literature.

Following the search, three PDF reports from Meta, Google, and Microsoft, published in both 2002 and 2023, were downloaded for further analysis. We navigated through Apple and Amazon webpages, specifically their sustainability and environment pages, to obtain their reports. These reports are an important part of the gray literature as they represent the data collected and examined in detail during the review process. In the end, we downloaded five pdf documents.

The pdf documents were added to MAXQDA[1] to start the analysis. We started by fully reading each report. During this process, we discover references to more detailed reports about diversity and inclusion. We started a snowballing process from the original document or seed to check for other relevant information in the sources provided in the seed. From there, we downloaded five additional reports and added them to be read as well. In Table 1, we detail a list of the five analyzed reports. The next section explains how we carried out the analysis of these reports.

**Table 1.** Big Techs reports analyzed in the study.

| Title | Company | Pages N# | Fiscal Year | Retrieval Date |
|---|---|---|---|---|
| Google Diversity Annual Report 2023 | Google | 115 | 2022 | 30th Dec 2023 |
| 2022 Amazon Sustainability Report | Amazon | 82 | 2022 | 30th Dec 2023 |
| 2023 Sustainability Report | Meta | 60 | 2022 | 28th Dec 2023 |
| Environmental Social Governance Report | Apple | 85 | 2022 | 18th Jan 2024 |
| Global Diversity & Inclusion Report 2023 | Microsoft | 37 | 2023 | 18th Jan 2024 |

## 3.2   Thematic Analysis

Thematic analysis was employed to consolidate findings pertaining to the diversity and inclusion related to the design addressed in the reports. This approach involves systematically reviewing the data, identifying recurring ideas, themes, and then organizing these themes into higher-order categories that encapsulate the overall essence of the data [9]. Within the MAXQDA tool, three steps were executed: open coding, theme synthesis, and cross-case analysis among the reports.

After thoroughly reading all the reports, we initiated the open-coding phase. Our investigation lens relied on finding evidence of designing for inclusion and

[1] https://www.maxqda.com/.

diversity in the process of developing software products and services. Basically, we sought answers to our initial hypothesis: *big tech companies might not be reporting on how they address inclusion and diversity in their software products and services.*

During the initial open-coding phase, we began identifying themes that could support some of the evidence found. The higher themes related to design disciplines were identified to group the open-ended: Universal Design (UD), Participatory Design (PD), and User-Centered Design (UCD). These design disciplines, when applied in the context of software development, contribute to creating products and services that are not only functional but also inclusive, user-friendly, and aligned with the diverse needs of the intended audience [29]. Those higher themes helped us to clearly understand which initiatives related to these disciplines were found in the companies' report.

To enhance our analysis, we also conducted keyword searches in the selected reports using terms such as "design," "inclusion," "inclusive," and "diversity." This additional step allowed us to further contextualize how these words were used in the text and grasp the underlying meanings. The results of this complementary analysis will be presented in the next section (Table 2).

**Table 2.** Summary of High themes, Themes and codes.

| High Theme | Theme | Codes |
| --- | --- | --- |
| Universal Design | Inclusive Design | education, guidelines for inclusive design, inclusive technology to eliminate biases, skin tone representation, inclusivity in interpersonal communication, gender identities |
|  | Accessiblity | deaf and hard of hearing technologies, mobility assistive technologies, accessible reading technologies, speech features |
| Participatory Design | Diverse Stakeholders | individuals with disabilities, underrepresented co-creation |
| User-Centered Design | Usability | unspoken |

# 4   Results

In this section, we present the results of our analysis based on the design disciplines we have identified as higher themes. In each subsection, we describe what we have found in the reports selected. After these subsection, we explore what has been discussed in the report for each company. Finally, we provide some recommendations to these companies to cover this subject in their reports.

## 4.1   Universal Design

Universal Design is an approach to design that aims to create products and environments that are accessible and usable by people of all abilities, ages, and backgrounds without the need for adaptation or specialized design. As explained by Iwarsson and Ståhl [14] "universal design is synonymous to 'design for all' and represents an approach to design that incorporates products as well as building features which, to the great-est extent possible, can be used by everyone."

In the context of software development, Universal Design involves creating software interfaces and interactions that are inclusive and user-friendly for a diverse range of users, including those with disabilities or varying levels of technological expertise [5].

**Inclusive Design.** Google openly shared its scale for broader use, aiming to improve inclusivity in product development by considering diverse needs, values, and skin tones.

Apple stands out with a comprehensive approach to inclusive design. The company launched videos during the Worldwide Developers Conference (WWDC) on inclusive design processes and practices. Apple offers guidelines, courses, and activities to support developers in building inclusive apps, considering factors like age, gender, race, language, and socio-economic context. Guidelines such as the Human Interface Guidelines[2], The Practice of Inclusive Design[3], and The Process of Inclusive Design[4] are available online for developers. The company emphasizes respectful communication and equitable person recognition in device cameras with different skin tones as well.

Microsoft introduced inclusive features in Microsoft 365, allowing users to specify pronouns in their profiles. This feature, identified through interviews with LGBTQIA+ communities, promotes a sense of belonging and inclusion by preserving their gender identities. Another feature in Micrsoft 365 profiles is the possibility of recording the correct pronunciation of your name, avoiding mispronunciation, and allowing inclusivity in interpersonal communication. Microsoft AI for Accessibility is a technology that provides recommendations to connect Neurodivergent job-seekers with potential employers.

Amazon focuses on inclusive technology to eliminate biases, leveraging artificial intelligence to eliminate biases in hiring. The company strives to address workplace biases that disproportionately affect women and other marginalized groups.

In Meta's sustainability report, there is a very general statement about designing new apps and services with diverse needs and values in mind. This may be because, from their perspective, this report is not intended to cover the social aspects of software. Nevertheless, we argue that when reporting on sustainability, it is crucial to address environmental, social, and other relevant dimensions of sustainability.

**Accessibility.** Google shows commitment through features that promote accessible reading technologies, such as Reading Mode, which allows customization

---

[2] https://developer.apple.com/design/human-interface-guidelines/inclusion.

[3] https://developer.apple.com/videos/play/wwdc2021/10275/.

[4] https://developer.apple.com/videos/play/wwdc2021/10304/.

and text-to-speech capabilities. Live Caption provides spoken-word captions and user-typed responses read aloud. Collaborates with the disability community to create adaptive smartphone features, enhancing online experiences for all users. Speech features created in a digitized voice help facilitate communication.

Apple demonstrates commitment to accessibility through privacy and inclusive design, as highlighted in the ESG report. Deaf and hard of hearing technologies introduced during COVID-19, consisting of iOS 14 Sound Recognition, sign language in FaceTime, and LiveCaptions positively impacted social sustainability. Mobility assistive technologies in society, such as Door Detection, People Detection, and Apple Watch mirroring, help to assist people with mobility constraints and blindness. Speech features to enable Siri to have diverse profiles of voices help address inclusion. Ongoing software development focuses on tools for navigation, health, and communication, catering to diverse user needs.

Microsoft advances accessibility with the Seeing AI app, allowing blind or low-vision users to read and distinguish currency symbols and menu options. According to Microsoft, this solution is "an app for visually impaired people that narrates the world around you[5]" and offers a range of solutions, including speech-to-text, captioning, narrator, and immersive reader, supporting individuals with disabilities.

Amazon extends accessibility features across devices and entertainment, concentrating on vision, hearing, mobility, learning, and speech. Key initiatives involve voiceview screen readers, enabling navigation through voice commands, and enhancing the user experience.

Although Meta's Sustainability report does not explicitly mention accessibility, a closer look at their webpages reveals blogs and reports focused on accessibility resources. This discovery implies a commitment to accessibility, and it could be beneficial to enhance the Sustainability report by including relevant links and sharing these online resources.

## 4.2   Participatory Design

Participatory Design is a collaborative approach that engages end-users in design and decision-making processes, ensuring continuous consideration of their perspectives and needs throughout the design lifecycle [24]. In software development, Participatory Design actively involves end-users, diverse stakeholders, and relevant parties in the design phase, facilitating the creation of solutions closely aligned with user expectations and requirements.

Google mentions efforts to address biases and create more representative artificial intelligence datasets, but it does not explicitly clarify whether individuals from underrepresented communities actively participated in the design and decision-making processes. For a more definitive determination of participatory design, specific details about the involvement of end-users in shaping the Automated Speech Recognition (ASR) technologies would be needed.

---

[5] https://www.microsoft.com/en-us/garage/wall-of-fame/seeing-ai/.

In the Microsoft report, there is no explicit mention of Participatory Design, but it does highlight an inclusive approach to innovation and development. The emphasis on investing in ideas developed by or in collaboration with individuals with disabilities suggests a commitment to incorporating diverse perspectives and needs. Also, Microsoft reported that employees with disabilities have been a driving force behind Microsoft Innovations. Their participation in the designing and development of software products has been raising the demand for more dedicated features for people with disabilities, showing the tangible outcomes of an inclusive approach to innovation.

During our analysis, we did not discover any additional information in the reports from Apple, Amazon, and Meta that would provide evidence of the application of participatory design principles in the development of their products.

### 4.3  User-Centered Design

User-Centered Design is an iterative design process that prioritizes the end-user's needs, preferences, and experiences. It involves understanding users' behaviors, expectations, and challenges to create products that are intuitive and enjoyable to use [16]. User-Centered Design in software development revolves around placing the user at the center of the design process. It includes techniques such as user research, usability testing, and feedback loops to continuously refine and improve the user experience [23].

None of the companies have explicitly reported user-centered or usability tests, metrics, or concerns related to User-Centered Design for their products. However, readers can infer that initiatives pertaining to User-Centered Design are implicitly addressed when the companies mention accessibility, inclusion, or inclusive design. For example, when Google mentions collaboration with the "disability community to create features that make smartphones more adaptable to the needs of all users, enhancing the online experience for everyone" it indicates a consideration for diverse user experiences.

## 5  Discussion and Limitations

### 5.1  Implications for the Practice

Reporting on corporate social responsibility (CSR), sustainability (environmental, social, governance) and diversity, equity and inclusion (DEI) efforts is often considered an additional task for many companies that feel obliged to report due to government, market and investor pressures, as well as society's expectations [15,22]. However, the benefits of such reporting can outweigh the challenges and pressures placed on companies. When large technology companies disclose their positive social impacts, they demonstrate transparency, reliability and credibility [22]. These positive impacts are reflected in the promotion of gender, cultural and racial equality in internal opportunities and can have long-term effects on the customers who buy and use their solutions.

Despite the existing pressures, much clarity is still needed in these reports. The results of this study indicate that only a few companies report high levels of design for inclusion and diversity, with Apple being a benchmark when it comes to launching and communicating such initiatives. It is essential to emphasize practical actions in these reports, which aim to inform consumers and investors about how big techs' values are achieved and perpetuated in society.

While Landrum and Ohsowski [15] argue that current standards lack specificity regarding what should be reported, there is still a need to report the social impacts of software. Reporting on inclusion and diversity initiatives in software design allows smaller companies to learn from large technology companies. In addition, these reports can act as mechanisms to build trust in solutions and encourage continued use. Designing for inclusion and diversity serves to bridge the gap between diverse groups, offering ordinary people the opportunity to understand how these concerns are being addressed.

## But What Can We Do in Practice?

- Report the software's Social Impacts: Big technology companies bear significant responsibility for the products and services they create. Technology has become a fundamental part of our society, altering the way people interact, shop, live, and consume. In this context, a practical step is to clearly articulate initiatives in the design of new technologies. This involves not only providing information about diversity and inclusion in the workplace but also assessing and reporting the social impacts of their software products. Disclosing the social impact of software presents an opportunity to prevent hate speech, data privacy violations, data leaks, digital divides, and discriminatory prejudices.
- Report the Social Features: Social features refer to the functionalities of the software that directly contribute to addressing social concerns. For instance, as artificial intelligence technology advances, the need for transparency becomes more evident. Information on how these technologies are designed with inclusion and diversity in mind, along with involving diverse groups in developing and testing products, can be part of these reports.
- Report Critical User Feedback Analysis: Another essential action is to listen to how people are affected by a new product or service from a human perspective. Reporting on these efforts can contribute to a more humanitarian use of technology.

The practical implications require a holistic and proactive approach to big technology. In fact, by reporting social impacts, incorporating design for inclusion, and critically analyzing user feedback, big tech companies might be able to meet society's expectations while building trust, preventing potential problems, and contributing to a more responsible and sustainable society.

## 5.2  Key Themes Beyond Inclusion and Diversity in Software Development

If not designing for inclusion and diversity in their software product, what else is being reported? Based on our cross-analysis of reports provided by Google, Amazon, Meta, Apple, and Microsoft, several commonalities emerged from the analysis:

- Sustainable building design, carbon footprint reduction, and circular supply chain systems.
- Diversity is recognized in workforce composition, supply chain, and organizational culture.
- Initiatives include increasing employees with diverse backgrounds, supplier diversity, and forming partnerships with diversity advocates.
- Inclusion is a latent theme discussed in roles, report content, supplier diversity, and shared language among leadership.
- The concept of creating inclusive work environments and fostering diverse representation is present.
- Companies discuss inclusivity in workplace practices, benefits, mental health support, and promotion of internal and external experiences.
- Recognition of diverse skin tones, initiatives for marginalized communities, and addressing systemic racism are highlighted.
- Global perspective in addressing societal issues on a worldwide scale, including education, accessibility, and online safety for diverse groups.
- Commitment to broader societal issues, such as privacy, human rights, sustainability, and alignment with Sustainable Development Goals.
- Organization's leadership commitment to principles of design, diversity, inclusion, and sustainability.

We recognize the efforts of big tech companies to provide such reports over the years. In this study, we intend to shed light on opportunities to report actions related to inclusion and diversity during software development and in the software product. For this, we offered three recommendations that invite companies to consider and incorporate into their reporting practices.

## 5.3  Threat to Validity

In this study, we researched documents available online in the form of a report. One possible bias addressed is the lack of information from different sources. To minimize this, we accessed the companies' websites to search for more information and other reports. We also carried out snowballing by opening links to reports that could be included in the research. In addition, we clearly defined the inclusion criteria for selecting reports while conducting the gray literature. However, it is important to note that there may be reports that were overlooked for two reasons: a) the names of the reports were not specific i.e. DEI, b) they were not easy to find on the company's website. These problems occurred at Amazon,

Apple and Meta. For example, Meta's sustainability reports do not have a link to what would be its DEI report and the name of this report is "Responsible Business". In the case of Apple, the DEI initiatives are reported in their ESG reports. In the case of Amazon, we did mot find an DEI report, but we did find a website on Diversity and Inclusion in the workplace.

Another threat we are addressing is the lack of robust methodologies that would require a standardized report among all companies. As the aim of this study is not to compare each report with another, we minimized this by checking whether the reports followed current reporting frameworks, such as the Sustainability Accounting Standards Board (SASB)[6], Task Force on Climate-related Financial Disclosures (TCFD)[7] Global Reporting Indicators (GRI)[8], and United Nations Guiding Principles (UNGP)[9].

A final limitation is the fact that these reports change over time; we selected reports from years 2022 and 2023. We did not check the reports for other years. We cannot generalize our conclusions based only on the selected reports. In-depth research is needed to check all the years. Nevertheless, we believe that even in older reports, there is limited emphasis on designing for inclusion and diversity in areas like software development, given the emerging nature of this concern.

# 6   Conclusion

With this study, our objective is to highlight the importance of disseminating diversity and inclusion actions used in the design of products and services, especially during software development. Despite the various ways of reporting diversity, the way in which designing for diversity and inclusion in software is addressed is still minimal relative to all other concerns reported. The results reveal significant disparities in the way information is presented. While one report integrates diversity and inclusion, another discloses related information on different websites not mentioned in the report. This raises questions about transparency, raising doubts about whether these companies evaluate the accessibility implementation of their products, whether they create products that truly promote inclusion, and whether these products are designed to address diversity broadly across different diversity groups. In this study, we identified opportunities to improve reporting, adding the social impacts of the software, analyzing user feedback from a humanistic perspective and listing the characteristics that positively impact society.

---

[6] https://sasb.org/.
[7] https://www.fsb-tcfd.org/.
[8] https://www.globalreporting.org/standards/.
[9] https://www.ungpreporting.org/resources/salicnt-human-rights-issues/.

# References

1. Adams, R., Smart, P., Huff, A.S.: Shades of grey: guidelines for working with the grey literature in systematic reviews for management and organizational studies. Other Change Management Strategy (Topic), POL (2017)
2. Ajmal, M.M., Khan, M., Hussain, M., Helo, P.: Conceptualizing and incorporating social sustainability in the business world. Int. J. Sustain. Dev. World Ecol. 25(4), 327–339 (2018)
3. Bardzell, S.: Feminist HCI: taking stock and outlining an agenda for design. In: Proceedings of the SIGCHI Conference on Human Factors in Computing Systems, pp. 1301–1310 (2010)
4. Betz, S., et al.: Sustainability debt: A metaphor to support sustainability design decisions (2015)
5. Burgstahler, S.: Universal design: Process, principles, and applications (2021). https://www.washington.edu/doit/universal-design-process-principles-and-applications. Accessed 28 Jan 2024
6. Burnett, M., et al.: GenderMag: a method for evaluating software's gender inclusiveness. Interact. Comput. 28(6), 760–787 (2016)
7. Calero, C., Guzmán, I.G.R.D., Moraga, M.A., García, F.: Is software sustainability considered in the CSR of software industry? J. Sustain. Dev. World Ecol. 26, 439–459 (2019)
8. Ciszek, E., Logan, N.: Challenging the dialogic promise: how Ben & Jerry's support for black lives matter fosters Dissensus on social media. J. Pub. Relat. Res. 30(3), 115–127 (2018)
9. Cruzes, D.S., Dyba, T.: Recommended steps for thematic synthesis in software engineering. In: 2011 International Symposium on Empirical Software Engineering and Measurement, pp. 275–284. IEEE (2011)
10. Fet, A.M., Knudson, H.: Implementing Corporate Social Responsibility (2017)
11. Gren, L.: On gender, ethnicity, and culture in empirical software engineering research. In: Proceedings of the 11th International Workshop on Cooperative and Human Aspects of Software Engineering, pp. 77–78 (2018)
12. Himmelsbach, J., Schwarz, S., Gerdenitsch, C., Wais-Zechmann, B., Bobeth, J., Tscheligi, M.: Do we care about diversity in human computer interaction: a comprehensive content analysis on diversity dimensions in research. In: Proceedings of the 2019 CHI Conference on Human Factors in Computing Systems, pp. 1–16. CHI 2019, Association for Computing Machinery, New York, NY, USA (2019)
13. ISO, E.: 9241–210: Human-centered design for interactive systems. Deutsches Institut für Normung (2010)
14. Iwarsson, S., Ståhl, A.: Accessibility, usability and universal design-positioning and definition of concepts describing person-environment relationships. Disabil. Rehabil. 25(2), 57–66 (2003)
15. Landrum, N.E., Ohsowski, B.M.: Identifying worldviews on corporate sustainability: a content analysis of corporate sustainability reports. Bus. Strateg. Environ. 27, 128–151 (2018)
16. Law, C.M., Jaeger, P.T., McKay, E.: User-centered design in universal design resources? Univ. Access Inf. Soc. 9, 327–335 (2010)
17. Lim, J.S., Young, C.: Effects of issue ownership, perceived fit, and authenticity in corporate social advocacy on corporate reputation. Pub. Relat. Rev. 47, 102071 (2021)

18. North Carolina State University, College of Design: Center for Universal Design (2024). https://design.ncsu.edu/research/center-for-universal-design/. Accessed 1 Feb 2024

19. Rainer, A., Williams, A.: using blog-like documents to investigate software practice: benefits, challenges, and research directions. J. Softw. Evol. Process **31**, e2197 (2019)

20. Rodríguez-Pérez, G., Nadri, R., Nagappan, M.: Perceived diversity in software engineering: a systematic literature review. Empir. Softw. Eng. **26**(5), 102 (2021)

21. Sears, A., Jacko, J.A. (eds.): Human-Computer Interaction. CRC Press, Boca Raton (2009)

22. Sethi, S., Martell, T.F., Demir, M.C.: Enhancing the role and effectiveness of corporate social responsibility (CSR) reports: the missing element of content verification and integrity assurance. J. Bus. Ethics **144**, 59–82 (2017)

23. Shamonsky, D.: The viability of user-centered and human-centered design practices with natural user interfaces (NUIs). In: Marcus, A., Rosenzweig, E., Soares, M.M. (eds.) Design, User Experience, and Usability. HCII 2023. LNCS, vol. 14030, pp. 297–307. Springer, Cham (2023). https://doi.org/10.1007/978-3-031-35699-5_22

24. Simonsen, J., Robertson, T.: Routledge International Handbook of Participatory Design. Routledge, London (2012)

25. de Souza, A.C.M., Cruzes, D.S., Jaccheri, L., Krogstie, J.: Social sustainability approaches for software development: a systematic literature review. In: Kadgien, R., Jedlitschka, A., Janes, A., Lenarduzzi, V., Li, X. (eds.) Product-Focused Software Process Improvement - 24th International Conference, PROFES 2023, Dornbirn, Austria, December 10-13, 2023, Proceedings, Part I. LNCS, vol. 14483, pp. 478–494. Springer, Cham (2023). https://doi.org/10.1007/978-3-031-49266-2_33

26. de Souza, A.C.M., Reinehr, S., Malucelli, A.: Sustainable software engineering: an empirical study of the Brazilian financial sector. In: Canciglieri Junior, O., Noël, F., Rivest, L., Bouras, A. (eds.) Product Lifecycle Management. Green and Blue Technologies to Support Smart and Sustainable Organizations, pp. 115–129 (2022)

27. Szlavi, A., S. Guedes, L.: Gender inclusive design in technology: case studies and guidelines. In: Marcus, A., Rosenzweig, E., Soares, M.M. (eds.) Design, User Experience, and Usability. HCII 2023. LNCS, vol. 14030, pp. 343–354. Springer, Cham (2023). https://doi.org/10.1007/978-3-031-35699-5_25

28. Vorvoreanu, M., Zhang, L., Huang, Y.H., Hilderbrand, C., Steine-Hanson, Z., Burnett, M.: From gender biases to gender-inclusive design: an empirical investigation. In: Proceedings of the 2019 CHI Conference on Human Factors in Computing Systems, pp. 1–14 (2019)

29. Waller, S.D., Bradley, M.D., Hosking, I.M., Clarkson, P.J.: Making the case for inclusive design. Appl. Ergon. **46**, 297–303 (2015)

30. Wichowski, A.: The Information Trade: How Big Tech Conquers Countries, Challenges Our Rights, and Transforms Our World. HarperCollins, New York (2020)

# How Order and Omission of Web Content Can Vary Unintentionally Across User Cohorts: A Review

Frode Eika Sandnes(✉) ⓘ

Oslo Metropolitan University, 0130 Oslo, Norway
frodes@oslomet.no

**Abstract.** Information has become more accessible than ever due to web technologies, standards, and assistive technologies. Still, here are unresolved issues that can hinder equal access to all. This study reports on work-in-progress that explores how various implementation choices can affect what information, and the order information is presented to different user groups. First, potential situations are reviewed where content is rendered differently for different users. Three user groups are considered, namely default browser users, low vision users that rely on browser magnification, and screen reader users. Potential consequences of different content and presentation orders are discussed. Implications of this study include raising awareness of the importance of presentation order and the potential risk of multiple presentation orders; stakeholders should be encouraged to strive for consistent and meaningful content for all users.

**Keywords:** accessibility · low vision · web · presentation order · html · screen reader · contrast · semantic coding · CSS · sticky elements · protrusion · collision · responsive layout · reflow

## 1   Introduction

One key goal of universal accessibility is to achieve equal access to information for all users. Attention is often directed towards providing access due to reduced functioning using alternative modalities. For example, screen reader users rely on alternative text representations as substitutes for images. Obviously, a text snippet is not equivalent to an image, although they may communicate quite similar messages. Still a visually oriented user will get a slightly different message from an image than the message a screen reader user will get from a text snippet. One may therefore argue that access to information can never be truly equal as the modalities are notably different. Yet, we should strive to make different representations as similar as possible.

This study is addressing a subtle, yet important aspect of accessibility, namely that of content presentation order and content omissions. If two user groups are presented with a list of items in different order one may argue that they have access to the same information and thereby have equal access. Yet, the presentation order of information can have a significant impact on how the information is perceived. Implicitly, we tend to find the first information more important than information presented later. We tend to rank tasks on to-do lists in order of urgency. Journalists tend to front-load the most important points in news stories with less important details further down the text. Ranking lists and leaderboards are commonly used to rank the performance of competitors, such as who ran the fastest, which academics have the most citations or publications [1].

So, if two different user groups receive the same information in a different order, it follows that there is a chance that the information will be perceived differently by the two groups. But is this a prominent issue? This study focuses on three user groups, namely default browser users, magnification users and screen reader users. Default browser users typically have uncorrected, or close to uncorrected, vision, and access content as presented. Magnification users typically have reduced vision yet prefer to access information visually yet often adjust the text size in the browser for improved comfort of reading. Screen reader users are typically technically blind, legally blind, or low-vision users who prefer non-visual information [2] and thus use a screen reader to access information via Braille (sense of touch) or text-to-speech (sense of hearing).

We can use an example from contemporary web design to illustrate how the presentation order can become different for these three user groups. Figure 1 shows a common web design pattern found on many responsive websites. The page is coded with three div boxes in the order $A$, $B$, and $C$ (see Fig. 2). Screen reader users will therefore be presented with the boxes in the order $A$, $B$, $C$ since it typically presents contents in coding order. For the other two groups (default browser users and magnification users) the order will be $A$, $C$, $B$ if we assume a typical $F$-style reading pattern where users read or scan the contents of a page from left to right, top to bottom [3]. This is because box $B$ is a child of box $A$ and therefore appears further down the page, while box $C$ is vertically aligned at the same level as box $A$. Next, Fig. 3 shows the result after a magnifier user increases the text size from 200% to 250%. Because of the magnification there is no longer space for box $A$ and $C$ to be horizontally side by side and box $C$ has been pushed down below box $B$, giving a presentation order of $A$, $B$, $C$. The two visually oriented user groups receive the content in a different order. However, box $C$ has disappeared from the view giving a presentation order of $A$, $B$. The sequence $A$, $B$ is different from $A$, $B$, $C$ since box $C$ is missing. This is a realistic scenario if the user is unaware of the box $C$ below which would have to be discovered through scrolling and exploration [4]. Such scenarios can become both a significant usability and accessibility problem if box $C$ contains important information needed immediately such as a navigation menu. This example results in different presentation orders for all the three user groups.

Many real-world cases exhibiting the problems illustrated in the previous example can be observed. These observations indicate that it may be hard to manually consider all possible cases and permutations in a complex development project, or that there is limited awareness regarding diverging content order challenges. This work thus directs the attention towards the challenges associated with diverging content order and consequences thereof. It is argued that a key accessibility goal is to ensure that all user groups are presented, to the extent possible, content in the same order. Also, an automatic tool intended for detecting divergent presentation order was designed and is described herein. The purpose of such a tool is for web developers to apply adjustments and corrections once potential problems are identified.

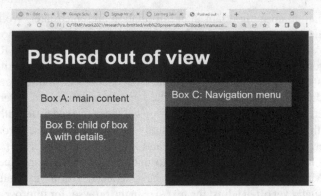

**Fig. 1.** All contents are visible on the page with 200% text size (box order *A*, *C*, and *B*).

```
17    <div style="width: 200px;height: 200px;background: ■greenyellow;float:left; color:□
18        <p id="p2" style="">Box A: main content</p>
19        <div style="width: 150px;height: 100px;background: □rgb(252, 13, 13);float:left;
20            <p id="p2" style="margin: 5%;">Box B: child of box A with details.</p>
21        </div>
22    </div>
23    <div style="width: 200px;background: □rgb(248, 11, 122);float:left;">
24        <p id="p2" style="margin: 5%;">Box C: Navigation menu</p>
25    </div>
```

**Fig. 2.** Html-source in VS-code for the webpage rendered in Figs. 2 and 3. The boxes are marked in the sequence Box *A* (line 18), Box *B* (line 20), Box *C* (line 24).

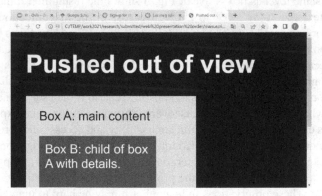

**Fig. 3.** Box *C* (navigation menu) is pushed out of view (below box *B*) with 250% text size (box order *A* and *B*).

This paper is organized as follows. The next section starts by reviewing related work on tools for automatic checking of rendering failures on the web. Next, situations that may result in different presentation orders are reviewed.

## 2 Related Works

The World Wide Web Consortium (W3C) Web Content Accessibility Guidelines (WCAG) provides relatively clear, concrete, and comprehensive advice on how to make content on the web more accessible to all computer users. These guidelines are referred to in the legislatures of several countries as well as other standards such as EN 301 549. These guidelines have also been revised several times to capture technological advancements and changes in technology use. There has also been a relatively intense interest in tools that can help web developers adhere to such guidelines [5–9]. Panchekha et al. [10] gave a representative summary of key visual accessibility issues including sufficiently large text (14 pixels), resizable text, no more than 80 characters per line, no horizontal scrolling, hierarchical headings, no overlapping texts, no overlapping texts and images, sufficient line spacing, sufficient color contrast, vertically aligned columns (Western languages), and sufficiently large buttons. Several of these recommendations address visual aspects of readability [11–13]. Web Accessibility Visual Evaluator (WAVE) is an example of a frequently mentioned tool that attempts to address a wide range of accessibility issues visually [14] while other tools focus on specific yet important issues such as color contrast [15, 16]. A recent review of accessibility research revealed that most of the accessibility research addressed reduced low vision [17].

Much of the focus is visually oriented although many of the issues described in WCAG are non-visual and apply to screen reader users that rely on Braille or text-to-speech. Although the content must be designed to be fully non-visually accessible one may argue that visual elements provide important visual cues for users that rely on visual stimuli, such as most low-visual acuity users. Jay et al. [18] demonstrated the importance of visual embellishments through an eye-tracking experiment where default web pages were compared to text-only pages stripped for visual embellishments. They concluded that visual embellishments should be reintroduced after accessibility transformations. A similar argument has been the rationale for reflowing archival scanned documents allowing low-vision users to visually inspect the original presentation, with its artifacts, without the burden of horizontal scrolling [19].

A study of what web developers ask about on technical discussions forums showed that browser issues were among the most common [20]. Walsh et al. [21] reported that more than a million questions connected to responsive web design had been posted on StackOverflow. Mazinanian [22] argued that CSS styling definitions are hard to maintain and often result in problems, and that this has triggered the emergence of CSS pre-processors that reduces the developers' need to maintain CSS across versions and browsers. The difficulty of debugging layout issues has also been pointed out as a key challenge [23]. However, browsers have increasingly incorporated development tools that make it easier to inspect the effects of markup on the visual layout. Another challenge that has been pointed out is that traditional testing methodologies do not capture visual mistakes [24] and that other methods such as image-processing based approaches may be more suitable. Walsh et al. pointed out that it is not always feasible with manual visual inspection as it depends on some form of "oracle" to declare correctness. They therefore argued for automatic tools [25]. Guérin [26] provided a thorough review of typical visual web application problems. In a related study the same research group proposed declaration of human readable assertions with a visual focus [27]. Similarly, Chang et al. [28] proposed visual test scripts based on similar principles.

Such testing is sometimes referred to as visual regression testing (VRT), defined as the testing of the emergence of old bugs with the introduction of new changes. It can be used to verify consistency across versions to prevent the visual layouts are broken with new releases and updates [29]. Also, this approach has been used for cross browser consistency check to ensure that web pages render identically across different browsers [30–32] or different mobile form factors [33]. A variation on this approach can also be used to check for internal visual consistency within the different views of the same application version [34]. Simply put, this image-based approach compares screenshots of the two versions to detect differences [35, 36] and sometimes well-known image processing libraries such as OpenCV are used [37]. It is argued that automatic tools can help quickly draw the testers attention towards differences that otherwise can be hard to spot manually. Walsh et al. [21] argued that spot-checking, that is, the checking of certain configurations such as mobile, tablet, and desktop is an unreliable means of detecting failures, and claimed that many code modifications that cause unintentional regressions make their way undetected to production websites.

Typical rendering failures include overlapping text, component occlusion, or missing images [38]. A drawback of such approaches is that small changes in the interface can lead to many detected differences. The tester may thus be overwhelmed with erroneous error reports, and it may be difficult to detect the actual cause of the problem. An example of such a situation is the insertion of an element, such as a page header shifting the remaining content downwards. Simple image-comparison methods are unable to effectively situations with responsive layouts that depend on the client configurations. To achieve this more sophisticated scale and translation invariant image registration methods would be needed. Moreover, visual approaches are not relevant for checking how web pages are rendered textually by screen readers.

Some approaches for detecting cross browser issues use structural information and rendered screenshots, most notably the Document Object Model (DOM) as used in the WebDiff tool [39] and X-PERT tool [40], but also crawling information [41]. One approach is to build an alignment graph that attempts to capture the relative alignment of the elements on a page. The html elements were found by querying the DOM and their respective relative positions and dimensions were determined using their XPaths.

A handful of authors proposed methods for automatically repairing issues [24, 31, 42]. Mahajan et al. [31, 32] argued that there may be a lack of expertise and time to resolve issues.

To sum up, testing for cross browser issues involves checking the similarity of the different page renderings. However, simply comparing screenshots is not sufficient to determine check rendering failures on responsive web pages that adapt to the client configuration. Responsiveness can in theory refer to any user configuration. Although these configurations usually are visual, they do not necessarily have to be so. Web pages that respond to smartphone viewing orientation is one example of responsiveness [43]. The width is narrower in portrait mode compared to landscape mode, while the height is longer in portrait mode compared to landscape mode. Typical rendering issues can be that content overflows on the sides of the viewport, or that some content occludes other contents. A truly responsive page will tailor the content to the dimensions of the viewport. Dark mode versus light mode can also be considered responsiveness as pages are rendered in dark mode if the user has set this as a preference in the browser [44]. Responsiveness could also include aspects such as font choices, line spacing, word spacing, letter spacing, etc., which attributes are easily configurable in some ePub readers.

However, responsiveness is probably most often associated with dynamic layout and reflowed pages where the content is adjusted to fit the width of the viewport, thereby avoiding horizontal scrolling [45–47]. The rationale is that content is viewed on a range of devices with different display configurations. WCAG success criterion 1.4.10 addresses the problems associated with scrolling in two dimensions. The viewport widths can be dramatically different for smartphones and desktops [48]. Failures can occur when pages are rendered for given widths and a substantial amount of research attention has been directed towards detecting rendering failures on responsive web pages. A commonly cited argument is that it is hard to manually detect rendering failures with many different viewport widths. ReDeCheck is one tool [49, 50] that analyzes the DOM tree. This tool is also the basis for other reflow checking tools [51].

Althomali et al. [52] described three types of rendering failures that can occur with different viewport widths, namely element collision failures where one element occludes another element, element protrusion failures where an element extend beyond the width of a parent element, and viewport protrusion where an element extends beyond the width of the viewport (Figs. 4, 5, 6, 7 and 8). In this study the term occlusion will be used to describe collision since a collision usually will make one element fully or partially occlude the other element. Overflow will be used to refer to protrusion since element protrusions means that the elements overflow their bounds. Althomali et al. also distinguished between observable and non-observable collisions. They argued that it is difficult to spot collisions between elements with borders if only the borders are colliding as the colliding elements still will appear to be uniformly spaced. They claimed that such issues cannot be detected by simply analyzing the DOM alone without visual information about the rendering. Their tool VISER (VISual VERifier) therefore used Selenium WebDriver to query the browser about the actual visual rendering.

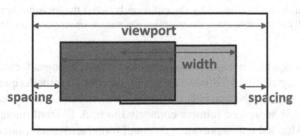

**Fig. 4.** Partial occlusion caused by collision of two boxes with fixed width positioned relative to the left and right margins, respectively with a narrow viewport (inspired by [52]).

In a more recent work on the repair tool layout Dr Althomali et al. [42] also addressed wrapping failures. Wrapping failures occur when content wraps when it should not, and

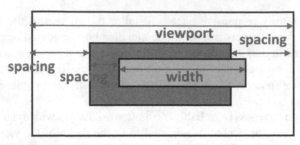

**Fig. 5.** Element overflow (obtrusion) with a narrow viewport. The green box has a fixed width and obtrudes its magenta parent box whose left and right margins are positioned relative to the viewport sides (inspired by [52]).

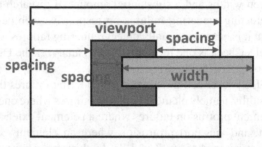

**Fig. 6.** Viewport overflow (obtrusion). The fixed width green box partially appears outside the narrow viewport (inspired by [52]).

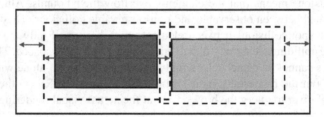

**Fig. 7.** The partial occlusion caused by the collision between the invisible borders of the two boxes is not visually observable since the visible areas remain intact (inspired by [52]).

small range failures which occur when a layout chaotically changes for small changes in viewport widths. Small range failures can occur with erroneous media query definitions. Their tool works by downloading pages with *wget* which then are analyzed by their tool. Ryou and Ryu [53] addressed failures connected to back to front rendering in html5. Wu et al. [54] addressed issues prevalent on small form factor smartphone devices such as readable font sizes, cluttered texts, and distorted layouts. The smartphone use case is important as it is the only means of accessing the web for many users [55].

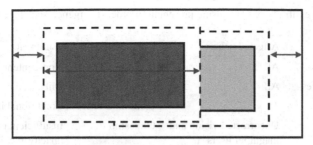

**Fig. 8.** The box occlusion due to the collision is visually observable since parts of the visible green area suggest that another part of the box is hidden behind the magenta box (inspired by [52].

Other issues that have been subjected to automatic checking includes failures caused by dynamically loaded web pages [56] and internationalization (i18n) pages where different languages consume different amount of real estate which can lead to overflow (protrusion) failures of the template does not scale accordingly [57].

It appears that the main objective of most automatic tools for checking responsive layout is handling a diversity of display types with different viewport widths and not accessibility per se. Reflow is also dependent on the text size and the viewport width. Responsive web pages that reflow correctly according to both width and text size are also contributing to accessibility, as low vision users typically increase and decrease the text size dynamically according to the reading situation [19].

An issue discussed among accessibility practitioners that has not seemingly received much research attention is that of diverging presentation order for different user groups. The order in which content is presented to display users and screen reader users can easily diverge. However, research conducted in a range of disciplines suggests that presentation order is important, for example a competitors' position on a leaderboard [58], the order of the results returned by search engines [59], the order products are presented according to price and perceived quality [60], and the order save, cancel, and next buttons are presented on web pages [61]. Typically, the content presentation order signal importance, where the first items are weighed as more important than later occurring items. Hence, it may be potentially problematic if different user groups are presented content in different orders.

This work complements and extends ongoing research into the responsive web such as the impact of sticky elements and cookie consent notices in small viewports [62] and how reflow can introduce hyphenation issues [63].

## 3   A Review of Potential Omission and Order Issues on the Web

Table 1 summarizes potential accessibility issues that can result in content absence or diverging presentation orders for different users. This review considers default browser users, i.e., users without vision correction that browse content with the default rendering, browser magnification users, i.e., low vision users that magnify the content in the browser to compensate for reduced visual acuity, and screen reader users, typically users that are technically or legally blind that access the content with a screen reader and text to speech

**Table 1.** Accessibility issues causing presentation order divergence and content absence.

| Issue | Affected cohort | Content issue | Comment |
|---|---|---|---|
| Html comments | All | Omission | Non-content |
| Console messages | All | Omission | Only seen by developers |
| Media queries | " | Omission, order | Conditional inclusion |
| Imperceivable | Uncorrected vision and magnifier users | Omission | Insufficient contrast, opacity, etc |
| Disabled content | " | " | Hidden from view |
| Occlusions | " | " | Hidden behind view |
| Out-of-view | " | " | Hidden behind borders |
| No semantic coding | Screen readers | " | Complicated navigation |
| No alternative text | " | " | Image content inaccessible |
| Dynamic content | " | " | Screen reader unaware of changes |
| Sticky content | Magnifier users | " | Hidden behind sticky elements |
| Position directives | " | " | Appear outside viewport |
| Position directives | All | Order | Implicit ordering |
| Order directives | Screen readers | " | Order directives ignored |
| Floating elements | Magnifier users | " | Flouting out of view |

or braille output devices. Note that screen readers are occasionally used by other user groups such as users diagnosed with dyslexia. Default browser users and magnification browser users rely on visual cues, while screen reader users rely on audio cues (text-to-speech) or tactile cues (Braille output devices). Note that if content is diverging for one group, it will also be diving for the other groups. For instance, if content is missing for one group, it is present for another. Whether the presence or absence of content is the intention is a matter of definition. In this text the divergence will refer to divergence from the norm defined as default browser users, as most web content is designed for and tested with default browser users. First, issues causing differences in content are reviewed. Second, issues causing diverging presentation orders are examined.

### 3.1 Omitting Content

Missing content is defined herein as content somewhat coded and contained within the webpage source but not rendered such that it is perceivable to the users.

An example of an explicit mechanism that can cause differentiated renderings is media queries based on client characteristics such as width, color capabilities, page orientation, etc. Media queries are CSS directives that define how content is presented to all or some of the user groups. Consequently, when used incorrectly media queries can contribute towards the discrimination against certain user groups by removing content given certain conditions. Websites that omit certain content in narrow viewports are examples of this.

**Blocking Screen Reader Users.** Missing semantic coding or missing alternative text may result in visually rendered content becoming inaccessible to screen reader users. Most common issues are missing alternative texts for images [64, 65], insufficient markup of tables [66] and semantic coding of layout [67]. A related issue is that of dynamic or live content where the content is updated after a web page has loaded, for instance search results. If the page is not coded with appropriate ARIA markup the updated content may not reach the screen reader users [68]. These issues are well documented but were included in the taxonomy for completeness.

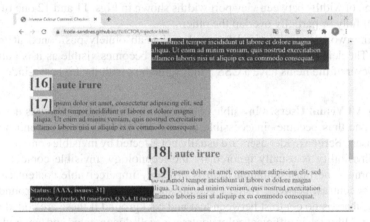

**Fig. 9.** Sticky element in the bottom left corner (150% text size).

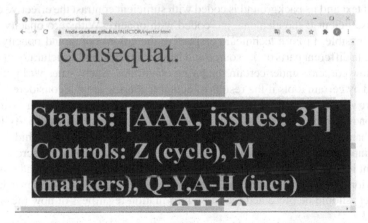

**Fig. 10.** Sticky elements obstructing the magnified view (500% text size).

**Blocking Magnifier Users (Visual).** Sticky and fixed elements can cause problems for magnified browser users [62]. These will be collectively referred to as sticky elements.

Simply explained, sticky elements are boxes that remain in view regardless of how the page is scrolled. Sticky mechanisms are typically optimized for default browser viewing giving users access to important page functionality such as search or navigation regardless of where one is on a long page, such as a news site. However, with magnification activated such sticky elements will also be magnified accordingly and consequently occlude larger parts of the display real estate (see Figs. 9 and 10). With high magnifications it is not uncommon for a sticky element to consume the entire real estate making the other content inaccessible. This is especially problematic if the designers have not provided mechanisms for hiding or dismissing the sticky elements.

Content may also be omitted for magnifier users if content is absolutely positioned horizontally outside the viewport. Also, content may be obstructed by other content. For example, imagine two boxes $A$ and $B$ anchored to the left and right margins (see Fig. 11). For a range of widths between viewport widths shown in Figs. 11 and 12 one of the two boxes will fully or partially overlap the other.

Imagine two identically sized boxes $A$ and $B$ absolutely positioned at the same position. The default outcome is that the last item becomes visible as it is painted the last. However, if the items have a CSS $z$-index, the box with the highest $z$-index will be visible.

**Blocking All Visual Users.** Invisible content is content that somehow is not visually rendered and thus becomes inaccessible to both default browser users and magnified browser users. Screen reader users are usually not affected by invisible content as coding causing invisibility is usually ignored by the technology. Invisible content can take several forms. The most common form is probably imperceivable content caused by insufficient contrast between visual elements such as text and the background. In the worst case there is no contrast between text and background if these are coded with the same color. Although insufficient color contrast is well-documented and covered by most accessibility audit regimes [69–71] it was included in the taxonomy for completeness.

Even if text and its background is coded with sufficient contrast the effective contrast may be insufficient if the elements are coded with opacity. With zero opacity content becomes invisible. From a technical perspective the color coding and opacity coding may reside in different parts of the source and be semantically and structurally unrelated, yet somehow coincide under certain rendering conditions. Such issues will perhaps go undetected by certain tools if the results of actual rendering are not considered.

The browser can also be instructed not to show a given element. Such instructions may be conducted by setting visibility property to hidden or display property to none. Such mechanisms are typically used in visual interfaces to temporarily hide or show certain components. However, such directives are typically ignored by screen readers and content intended to be missing thus becomes perceivable to screen reader users. In such situations the unintentional content may be perceived as noise. A premise herein is that all users should be presented the same information regardless of how the webpage is accessed.

The last two categories of invisible content are probably not common but could potentially occur by accident. The first of the two are occlusions in which elements are positioned such that one occludes the other element making it invisible to the users. The other is content positioned outside the view. If an element is coded with negative coordinates, it will not be visible in the viewport. What becomes occluded and what becomes visible usually depends on the coding order and as the most recently painted element appears on top. However, depth directives (z-index) will override coding order if specified. Occlusions and out-of-view problems can also potentially cause a reverse problem. Imagine a page is incorrectly coded with occlusions and/or out-of-view issues, and visually inspected with a verification that the content is as inspected. The invisible information may not be important and may be forgotten by the designers. However, when accessed with a screen reader this content is reported and may appear as noise and divert the users' attention away from important contents.

**Blocking All Users.** An html-comment is an example of content not rendered to any users. Comments are hidden in plain view but can be read by inspecting the webpage source. Comments are usually intended for developers and not the readers and is therefore not an accessibility issue as comments are omitted from all types of webpage renderings.

Another perhaps obscure example is console output. The console is usually used by developers for debugging web applications. Such output is not rendered in the browser and therefore not visible to regular users. Such content, which can be formatted using CSS styles, is only available via the console window that needs to be explicitly opened (see Fig. 11). Some web sites do communicate certain content via the console window such as job openings for web developers.

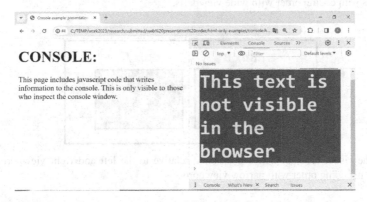

**Fig. 11.** Console output content not visible via the browser or screen reader.

### 3.2  Diverging Presentation Order

As with missing contents media queries can also be used to alter the presentation order for some of the user groups. This could be done in several ways, for instance by positioning elements differently for different viewport widths. Although theoretically possible, such issues are probably uncommon.

**Divergence for All Users.** Certain fixed and floating positioning specifications in CSS can cause the presentation order to become different for individuals that rely on magnified browser contents. For example, imagine two boxes $A$ and $B$ of width $w$ relatively positioned a certain distance slightly greater than their widths from the left and right borders, respectively at the same vertical level. In a wide view the first box A will appear on the left and the second box $B$ will appear on the right (see Fig. 12). It is here assumed that the width is larger than $4w$. However, in a narrow view, say a width of $2w$, the second box $B$ will appear on the left and the first box $A$ will appear on the right since their positioning are relative to the right and left borders respectively and will thus be "pushed" to the other side (see Fig. 13). If the width is $3w$ the first box $A$ will be occluded by the second box $B$ (missing content). A similar effect could also occur if the two boxes were positioned relatively to the top and bottom borders, respectively, along the same horizontal position. The same situation can also occur vertically with reference to the top and bottom viewport margins.

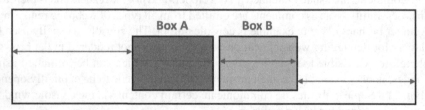

**Fig. 12.** The visual order of boxes positioned relative to the left and right viewport margins corresponds with coding order with wide viewports.

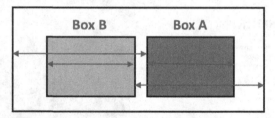

**Fig. 13.** The visual order of boxes positioned relative to the left and right viewport margins diverges from coding order with narrow viewports.

CSS media-queries can also be set up with unique element orderings for different cohorts. For instance, there could be one media query with settings for screen readers, and two different media queries that will trigger for magnifier users and uncorrected vision users, respectively, each with unique element orderings.

**Divergence for Screen Reader Users.** Usually, a web page is rendered in the order it is coded. However, CSS order properties allow the presentation order of elements to be specified explicitly. This means that the last element on a page can appear on top if it is ordered as the first element. Order properties are typically ignored by screen readers which will typically present the content in coding order. The result is that the screen reader users receive content in a different order than visual browser users.

The CSS wrap-reverse property can cause divergence between the order presented to the screen-readers and magnifier users. While the screen reader will present the floating elements in coding order (see Fig. 14), the reverse wrapped floating elements will appear in reverse order (last first) if the margin causes elements to wrap (see Fig. 15).

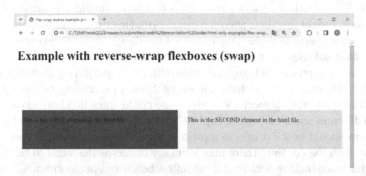

**Fig. 14.** Flexbox elements in coding order (browser magnification 125%).

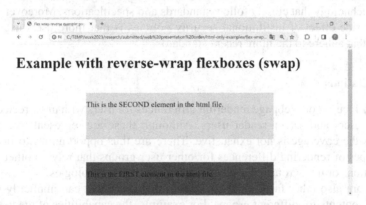

**Fig. 15.** Flexbox elements reverse wrapped when vertically stacked as their width exceed the viewport width when magnified to 150% in the browser. The last element is placed in before the first element.

**Divergence for Magnifier Users (Visual).** With certain contemporary web designs, the presentation order can become different at different browser magnification rates due to floating text boxes. An example of this was illustrated with the three boxes *A*, *B* and *C* in Figs. 1, 2 and 3 in the introduction. Such patterns can for instance represent a situation where box *A* represents a certain content with sub-content in box *B* where box *C* contained a navigation menu. In a wide view box, *A* and *B* will be side by side and the content of *B* will appear before the content of *C* with the order *A*, *B*, *C*. However, in a narrow view box *B* will reflow and be pushed to the bottom of the page and thus appear after *C*, with the order *A*, *C*, *B*. The presentation order depends on the width of the viewport or the text size. If box *B* contained a navigation menu it can be problematic if this important element is pushed out of view to the bottom of the page with a high magnification setting.

# 4  Discussion

One may question the goal of automatically repairing issues as attempted in several studies [24, 31, 32, 42]. An alternative view is that tools should not automatically fix issues; the tools should only draw attention to issues that need to be addressed manually to uncover potentially serious underlying reasons. One should assume and expect that web developers have sufficient competences to resolve issues once these have been pointed out by the tools. The process of being presented with issues and having to resolve this will potentially lead to useful and productive learning thereby preventing the same problems from reoccurring in future projects. Moreover, one could argue that how a layout should respond to different widths should be explicitly specified by the designer, and that these specifications should be the results of a process involving users and how they perceive and interact with the content. There may be many concerns that need to be taken into consideration when making decisions about reflow behavior. An algorithm will not know what the users need and how issues should be resolved. Perhaps cross browser issues are less of a threat currently than they were one or two decades ago due to improvements in browser technology that closely follow standards and specifications. Moreover, perhaps a positive side effect of institutional security policies is that more users use updated browsers that adhere to the more recent standards.

## 4.1  Limitations

This study focused on webpage rendering differences for users with uncorrected vision, magnifier users and screen-reader users. Although these are representative of many web users the coverage is not exhaustive. There are thus opportunities to investigate similar types of rendering differences for other user groups that rely on other browser configurations or user groups that rely on other assistive technologies.

There are also other factors not covered in this study that can implicitly result in diverging contents for different groups. For example, the capabilities of the users input devices can affect the degree of access to contents, for instance if the content depends on image input such as QR-codes [72], or text intense queries [73–75].

# 5  Conclusions

Situations that can cause differences in how web contents are presented differently to different groups were presented together with a review of the literature on automatic checking of web sites. This study focused on users with uncorrected vision, magnifier users and screen-reader users. An array of hypothetical situations was presented. Future work should explore to what degree these issues are prevalent in frequently used websites. The test cases discussed herein have been made available to the research community at https://github.com/frode-sandnes/PRESENTATION-ORDER. Live examples can be viewed at https://frode-sandnes.github.io/PRESENTATION-ORDER/.

# References

1. Sandnes, F.E.: A simple back-of-the-envelope test for self-citations using Google Scholar author profiles. Scientometrics **124**(2), 1685–1689 (2020)
2. Sandnes, F.E.: What do low-vision users really want from smart glasses? Faces, text and perhaps no glasses at all. In: Miesenberger, K., Bühler, C., Penaz, P. (eds.) ICCHP 2016. LNCS, vol. 9758, pp. 187–194. Springer, Cham (2016). https://doi.org/10.1007/978-3-319-41264-1_25
3. Pernice, K., Whitenton, K., Nielsen, J.: How People Read Online: The Eyetracking Evidence. Fremont, USA: Nielsen Norman Group (2014)
4. Hosking, I.M., Clarkson, P.J.: Now you see it, now you don't: understanding user interface visibility. In: Antona, M., Stephanidis, C. (eds.) UAHCI 2017. LNCS, vol. 10279, pp. 436–445. Springer, Cham (2017). https://doi.org/10.1007/978-3-319-58700-4_35
5. Abascal, J., Arrue, M., Fajardo, I., Garay, N., Tomás, J.: The use of guidelines to automatically verify Web accessibility. Univ. Access Inf. Soc. **3**(1), 71–79 (2004)
6. Brajnik, G.: Comparing accessibility evaluation tools: a method for tool effectiveness. Univ. Access Inf. Soc. **3**(3), 252–263 (2004)
7. Abduganiev, S.G.: Towards automated web accessibility evaluation: a comparative study. Int. J. Inf. Technol. Comput. Sci. **9**(9), 18–44 (2017)
8. Abascal, J., Arrue, M., Valencia, X.: Tools for web accessibility evaluation. In: Yesilada, Y., Harper, S. (eds.) Web accessibility. HIS, pp. 479–503. Springer, London (2019). https://doi.org/10.1007/978-1-4471-7440-0_26
9. Alsaeedi, A.: Comparing web accessibility evaluation tools and evaluating the accessibility of webpages: proposed frameworks. Information **11**(1), 40 (2020)
10. Panchekha, P., Geller, A.T., Ernst, M.D., Tatlock, Z., Kamil, S.: Verifying that web pages have accessible layout. ACM SIGPLAN Not. **53**(4), 1–14 (2018)
11. Eika, E.: Universally designed text on the web: towards readability criteria based on antipatterns. Stud. Health Technol. Inform. **229**, 461–470 (2016)
12. Eika, E., Sandnes, F.E.: Authoring WCAG2.0-compliant texts for the web through text readability visualization. In: Antona, M., Stephanidis, C. (eds.) Universal Access in Human-Computer Interaction. Methods, Techniques, and Best Practices: 10th International Conference, UAHCI 2016, Held as Part of HCI International 2016, Toronto, ON, Canada, July 17-22, 2016, Proceedings, Part I, pp. 49–58. Springer International Publishing, Cham (2016). https://doi.org/10.1007/978-3-319-40250-5_5
13. Eika, E., Sandnes, F.E.: Assessing the reading level of web texts for WCAG2.0 compliance—can it be done automatically? In: Di Bucchianico, G., Kercher, P. (eds.) Advances in Design for Inclusion, pp. 361–371. Springer International Publishing, Cham (2016). https://doi.org/10.1007/978-3-319-41962-6_32
14. Kasday, L.R.: A tool to evaluate universal Web accessibility. In: Proceedings on the 2000 Conference on Universal Usability, pp. 161–162 (2000)
15. Sandnes, F.E., Zhao, A.: An interactive color picker that ensures WCAG2.0 compliant color contrast levels. Procedia Comput. Sci. **67**, 87–94 (2015)
16. Sandnes, F.E.: Inverse color contrast checker: automatically suggesting color adjustments that meet contrast requirements on the web. In: The 23rd International ACM SIGACCESS Conference on Computers and Accessibility, ACM (2021)
17. Sandnes, F.E.: Is there an imbalance in the supply and demand for universal accessibility knowledge? Twenty years of UAIS papers viewed through the lens of WCAG. UAIS **21**(2), 333–349 (2022)
18. Jay, C., Stevens, R., Glencross, M., Chalmers, A., Yang, C.: How people use presentation to search for a link: expanding the understanding of accessibility on the web. UAIS **6**(3), 307–320 (2007)

19. Sandnes, F.E.: Lost in OCR-Translation: pixel-based text reflow to the rescue: magnification of archival raster image documents in the browser without horizontal scrolling. In: PETRAE 2022 (pp. 500–506), ACM (2022)
20. Bajaj, K., Pattabiraman, K., Mesbah, A.: Mining questions asked by web developers. In: Proceedings of 11th Working Conference on Mining Software Repositories (pp. 112–121), (2014)
21. Walsh, T.A., Kapfhammer, G.M., McMinn, P.: Automatically identifying potential regressions in the layout of responsive web pages. Softw. Testing, Verification Reliabil. **30**(6), e1748 (2020)
22. Mazinanian, D.: Refactoring and migration of cascading style sheets: towards optimization and improved maintainability. In: 2016 International Symposium on Foundations of Software Engineering (pp. 1057–1059), ACM (2016)
23. Burg, B., Ko, A.J., Ernst, M.D.: Explaining visual changes in web interfaces. In: Symposium on User Interface Software & Technology (pp. 259–268), ACM (2015)
24. Stocco, A., Yandrapally, R., Mesbah, A.: Visual web test repair. In: 26th Joint Meeting on European Software Engineering Conference and Symposium on the Foundations of Software Engineering (pp. 503–514), ACM (2018)
25. Walsh, T.A., Kapfhammer, G.M., McMinn, P.: Automated layout failure detection for responsive web pages without an explicit oracle. In: 26th International Symposium on Software Testing and Analysis (pp. 192–202), ACM (2017)
26. Guérin, F.: Testing web applications through layout constraints: tools and applications. Doctoral dissertation, Université du Québec à Chicoutimi (2017)
27. Hallé, S., Bergeron, N., Guérin, F., Le Breton, G., Beroual, O.: Declarative layout constraints for testing web applications. J. Logical Algebraic Methods Programm. **85**(5), 737–758 (2016)
28. Chang, T.H., Yeh, T., Miller, R.C.: GUI testing using computer vision. In: Conference on Human Factors in Computing Systems (pp. 1535–1544), ACM (2010)
29. Tanno, H., Adachi, Y., Yoshimura, Y., Natsukawa, K., Iwasaki, H.: Region-based detection of essential differences in image-based visual regression testing. J. Inf. Process. **28**, 268–278 (2020)
30. Saar, T., Dumas, M., Kaljuve, M., Semenenko, N.: Browserbite: cross-browser testing via image processing. Softw. Pract. Exper. **46**(11), 1459–1477 (2016)
31. Mahajan, S., Alameer, A., McMinn, P., Halfond, W.G.: Automated repair of layout cross browser issues using search-based techniques. In: International Symposium on Software Testing and Analysis, pp. 249–260. ACM (2017)
32. Mahajan, S., Alameer, A., McMinn, P., Halfond, W.G.: XFix: an automated tool for the repair of layout cross browser issues. In: International Symposium on Software Testing and Analysis, pp. 368–371. ACM (2017)
33. Moran, K., Li, B., Bernal-Cárdenas, C., Jelf, D., Poshyvanyk, D.: Automated reporting of GUI design violations for mobile apps. In: 40th International Conference Software Engineering, pp. 165–175 (2018)
34. Mahajan, S., Gadde, K.B., Pasala, A., Halfond, W.G.: Detecting and localizing visual inconsistencies in web applications. In: APSEC 2016, pp. 361–364. IEEE (2016)
35. Mahajan, S., Li, B., Behnamghader, P., Halfond, W.G.: Using visual symptoms for debugging presentation failures in web applications. In: ICST 2016, pp. 191–201. IEEE (2016)
36. Mahajan, S., Halfond, W. G.: WebSee: A tool for debugging HTML presentation failures. In: ICST 2015, pp. 1–8. IEEE (2015)
37. Mahajan, S., Halfond, W.G.: Finding HTML presentation failures using image comparison techniques. In: International Conference Automated Software Engineering, pp. 91–96. ACM/IEEE (2014)

38. Liu, Z., Chen, C., Wang, J., Huang, Y., Jun, H., Wang, Q.: Nighthawk: fully automated localizing UI display issues via visual understanding. IEEE Trans. Softw. Eng. **49**(1), 403–418 (2023). https://doi.org/10.1109/TSE.2022.3150876

39. Choudhary, S.R., Versee, H., Orso, A.: WEBDIFF: automated identification of cross-browser issues in web applications. In: International Conference Software Maintenance, pp. 1–10. IEEE (2010)

40. Choudhary, S.R., Prasad, M.R., Orso, A.: X-PERT: accurate identification of cross-browser issues in web applications. In: ICSE 2013, pp. 702–711. IEEE (2013)

41. Choudhary, S.R., Prasad, M.R., Orso, A.: CrossCheck: combining crawling and differencing to better detect cross-browser incompatibilities in web applications. ICST **12**, 171–180 (2012)

42. Althomali, I., Kapfhammer, G.M., McMinn, P.: Automated repair of responsive web page layouts. In: ICST 2022, pp. 140–150. IEEE (2022)

43. Amalfitano, D., Riccio, V., Paiva, A.C., Fasolino, A.R.: Why does the orientation change mess up my Android application? From GUI failures to code faults. Softw. Testing Verification Reliabil. **28**(1), e1654 (2018)

44. Pedersen, L.A., Einarsson, S.S., Rikheim, F.A., Sandnes, F.E.: User interfaces in dark mode during daytime – improved productivity or just cool-looking? In: Antona, M., Stephanidis, C. (eds.) HCII 2020. LNCS, vol. 12188, pp. 178–187. Springer, Cham (2020). https://doi.org/10.1007/978-3-030-49282-3_13

45. Dick, W.E.: Operational overhead caused by horizontal scrolling text. Technical note (2017). Accessed 19 Mar 2022. http://nosetothepage.org/Fitz/2dScroll.html

46. Hallett, E.C., et al.: The usability of magnification methods: a comparative study between screen magnifiers and responsive web design. In: Yamamoto, S. (ed.) Human Interface and the Management of Information. Information and Knowledge Design: 17th International Conference, HCI International 2015, Los Angeles, CA, USA, August 2-7, 2015, Proceedings, Part I, pp. 181–189. Springer International Publishing, Cham (2015). https://doi.org/10.1007/978-3-319-20612-7_18

47. Öquist, G., Lundin, K.: Eye movement study of reading text on a mobile phone using paging, scrolling, leading, and RSVP. In: MUM '07, pp. 176–183. ACM (2007). https://doi.org/10.1145/1329469.1329493

48. Mahajan, S., Abolhassani, N., McMinn, P., Halfond, W.G.: Automated repair of mobile friendly problems in web pages. In: International Conference Software Engineering, pp. 140–150 (2018)

49. Walsh, T.A., McMinn, P., Kapfhammer, G.M.: Automatic detection of potential layout faults following changes to responsive web pages. In: ASE 2015, pp. 709–714. IEEE (2015)

50. Walsh, T.A., Kapfhammer, G.M., McMinn, P.: ReDeCheck: an automatic layout failure checking tool for responsively designed web pages. In: International Symposium on Software Testing and Analysis, pp. 360–363. ACM (2017)

51. Althomali, I., Kapfhammer, G.M., McMinn, P.: Automated visual classification of DOM-based presentation failure reports for responsive web pages. Softw. Testing, Verification Reliabil. **31**(4), e1756 (2021)

52. Althomali, I., Kapfhammer, G.M., McMinn, P.: Automatic visual verification of layout failures in responsively designed web pages. In: ICST 2019, pp. 183–193. IEEE (2019)

53. Ryou, Y., Ryu, S.: Automatic detection of visibility faults by layout changes in HTML5 web pages. In: ICST 2018, pp. 182–192. IEEE (2018)

54. Wu, A., Tong, W., Dwyer, T., Lee, B., Isenberg, P., Qu, H.: MobileVisFixer: tailoring web visualizations for mobile phones leveraging an explainable reinforcement learning framework. IEEE Trans. Vis. Comput. Graph. **27**(2), 464–474 (2020)

55. Sankhi, P., Sandnes, F.E.: A glimpse into smartphone screen reader use among blind teenagers in rural Nepal. Disabil. Rehabil. Assist. Technol. **17**(8), 875–881 (2022)

56. Li, W., Harrold, M.J., Görg, C.: Detecting user-visible failures in AJAX web applications by analyzing users' interaction behaviors. In: International Conference Automated Software Engineering, pp. 155–158. IEEE (2010)

57. Mahajan, S., Alameer, A., McMinn, P., Halfond, W.G.: Effective automated repair of internationalization presentation failures in web applications using style similarity clustering and search-based techniques. Softw. Testing, Verification Reliabil. **31**(1–2), e1746 (2021)

58. Chernbumroong, S., Sureephong, P., Muangmoon, O.O.: The effect of leaderboard in different goal-setting levels. In: ICDAMT 2017, pp. 230–234. IEEE (2017)

59. Chen, H., Dumais, S.: Bringing order to the web: automatically categorizing search results. In: Proceedings of Human Factors in Computing Systems, pp. 145–152. ACM (2000)

60. Suk, K., Lee, J., Lichtenstein, D.R.: The influence of price presentation order on consumer choice. J. Mark. Res. **49**(5), 708–717 (2012)

61. Bangor, A.W., Miller, J.T.: The design and presentation order of web page buttons. In: Proceedings of Human Factors and Ergonomics Society Annual Meeting, vol. 49, no. 15, pp. 1449–1453. Sage, Los Angeles (2005)

62. Sandnes, F.E.: "Consent notices are obstructing my view": Viewing sticky elements on responsive websites under the magnifying glass. Displays 102579 (2023)

63. Sandnes, F.E.: To wrap or not to wrap? A study of how long words are split when reflowed on magnified web pages. Univ. Access in the Inf. Soc., 1–13 (2023)

64. McEwan, T., Weerts, B.: ALT text and basic accessibility. In: Proceedings of British HCI Group Annual Conference on People and Computers, vol. 2, pp. 71–74 (2007)

65. Sandnes, F.E.: Towards "Image Reflow" on the web: avoiding excessive panning of magnified images by multiplexing automatically cropped regions of interest. In: Nocera, J.A., Lárusdóttir, M.K., Petrie, H., Piccinno, A., Winckler, M. (eds.) Human-Computer Interaction – INTERACT 2023: 19th IFIP TC13 International Conference, York, UK, August 28 – September 1, 2023, Proceedings, Part IV, pp. 315–319. Springer Nature Switzerland, Cham (2023). https://doi.org/10.1007/978-3-031-42293-5_29

66. Amtmann, D., Johnson, K., Cook, D.: Making web-based tables accessible for users of screen readers. Library Hi Tech **20**(2), 221–231 (2002)

67. Harper, S., Bechhofer, S.: Semantic triage for increased web accessibility. IBM Syst. J. **44**(3), 637–648 (2005)

68. Thiessen, P., Hockema, S.: WAI-ARIA live regions: eBuddy IM as a case example. In: W4A, pp. 1–9. ACM (2010)

69. Hansen, F., Krivan, J.J., Sandnes, F.E.: Still not readable? An interactive tool for recommending color pairs with sufficient contrast based on existing visual designs. In: ASSETS 2019, pp. 636–638. ACM (2019)

70. Sandnes, F.E.: Understanding WCAG2.0 color contrast requirements through 3D color space visualization. Stud. Health Technol. Inform **229**, 366–375 (2016)

71. Sandnes, F.E.: An image-based visual strategy for working with color contrasts during design. In: Miesenberger, K., Kouroupetroglou, G. (eds.) Computers Helping People with Special Needs: 16th International Conference, ICCHP 2018, Linz, Austria, July 11-13, 2018, Proceedings, Part I, pp. 35–42. Springer International Publishing, Cham (2018). https://doi.org/10.1007/978-3-319-94277-3_7

72. Huang, Y.P., Chang, Y.T., Sandnes, F.E.: Ubiquitous information transfer across different platforms by QR codes. J. Mobile Multimedia **6**(1), 003–014 (2010)

73. Sandnes, F.E., Thorkildssen, H.W., Arvei, A., Buverad, J.O.: Techniques for fast and easy mobile text-entry with three-keys. In: Proceedings of the 37th Annual Hawaii International Conference on System Sciences, p. 10. IEEE (2004)

74. Sandnes, F.E.: Evaluating mobile text entry strategies with finite state automata. In: Proceedings of the 7th International Conference on Human Computer Interaction with Mobile Devices & Services, pp. 115–121. ACM (2005)

75. Sandnes, F.E., Jian, H.L.: Pair-wise variability index: evaluating the cognitive difficulty of using mobile text entry systems. In: International Conference on Mobile Human-Computer Interaction (pp. 347–350). Springer, Cham (2004).https://doi.org/10.1007/978-3-540-28637-0_35

# Mapable: Accessible Web-Based Indoor Maps for People with Diverse Interaction and Information Needs

Julian Striegl, Claudia Loitsch, Emma F. Etzold[✉], and Gerhard Weber

Chair of Human-Computer Interaction, Technische Universität Dresden,
Nöthnitzer Straße 46, 01187 Dresden, Germany
{julian.striegl,claudia.loitsch,emma_franziska.etzold
gerhard.weber}@tu-dresden.de

**Abstract.** Access to digital maps and geospatial information has become an integral part of modern applications to support mobility. However, for people with visual and mobility impairment, provided digital solutions are insufficient, target only one of the mentioned user groups, or are exclusively developed for outdoor environments. Research on accessible web-based indoor maps for people with impairments is still sparse. This paper presents the concept and prototype of an accessible web application that provides indoor map data and information on accessibility features of buildings to users with visual impairment, blindness, mobility impairment, and users without impairments. Results of a user study with 24 participants from all target groups show good to excellent usability (mean SUS score: 80), with room for improvement for users with severe visual impairment and blindness (mean SUS score: 66.7).

**Keywords:** Indoor Maps · Building Information · OpenStreetMap · Accessibility · Visual Impairments · Mobility Impairments

## 1 Introduction

For individuals with disabilities to independently plan and execute trips to unfamiliar buildings, detailed information regarding the accessibility of these destinations is essential. This necessity is underscored in studies by Mueller and Engel [9,25], highlighting the importance of comprehensive accessibility data. Orientation and navigation in indoor environments require tailored geospatial information beyond the perception of the immediate environment [14], which can be particularly challenging for people with visual or mobility impairments [19,21]. These user groups require granular information about landmarks, points of interest (POIs), barriers, and accessibility features to create a sufficient mental map of the environment and to navigate effectively [13,31]. Constantinescu et al. surveyed 820 relevant indoor accessibility features for people with disabilities [7]. However, there are hardly any freely available digital indoor maps of public buildings, nor do existing geographic information systems contain sufficient data about indoor accessibility [31]. While solutions for accessible outdoor

navigation have already been established[1,2,3], accessible systems for indoor orientation and navigation support are still sparse. In many cases, applications
supporting mobility follow map-based concepts. However, developing accessible
map applications is a challenging task that involves creating alternative interaction modalities and adaptable user interfaces to meet the needs and abilities of
people with disabilities [4, 12].

Unfortunately, as previous studies have shown [22], major map vendors have
been found to need to catch up in meeting the needs of this target group. Furthermore, existing solutions for improving accessibility of map-based mobility-
supporting apps focus only on some user groups with impairments [33] and do
not consider the diverse needs and preferences of individuals with and without
impairments regarding indoor information and digital interaction modalities [9].

This paper introduces an accessible web application designed to assist individuals, both with and without disabilities, in obtaining customized information essential for planning trips and navigating unfamiliar indoor environments.
Unlike applications targeting a single group, this solution caters to three distinct user categories: individuals with visual and mobility impairments, as well
as those without any impairments. The user interface and user experience design
adhere to technical accessibility standards while offering a customized information retrieval and interaction approach. This design is grounded in a comprehensive study by Mueller and Engel [25], which highlighted the significant and varied
informational needs of these groups. Such information is crucial for enabling people with impairments to orient themselves more effectively and independently
within unfamiliar buildings. The proposed concept primarily facilitates the pre-
visit or on-site search for essential accessibility-related information about buildings, allowing users to determine accessible routes to unfamiliar destinations.
This functionality aligns with common tasks found in map browsers for buildings. Furthermore, the application accommodates a broad spectrum of information queries, specifically tailored to meet the diverse needs of people with
disabilities.

Section 2 provides related research. Section 3 proposes the concept and design
of an accessible web application for indoor map data to meet the diverse interaction and information needs of people with disabilities. Section 4 presents the
methodology and results of a conducted user study and discusses implications
and limitations. A brief conclusion is drawn in Sect. 5.

## 2   Related Work

Maps and technical mobility aids are essential tools that help individuals with
visual impairment (VI) and mobility impairment (MI) to orient themselves and

---

[1] BlindSquare, http://www.blindsquare.com/, retrieved: April 15, 2023.

[2] Soundscape, https://www.microsoft.com/en-us/research/product/soundscape/, retrieved: April 15, 2023.

[3] Nav by ViaOpta: https://apps.apple.com/de/app/nav-by-viaopta/id908435532,
retrieved: April 15, 2023.

navigate their surroundings. These resources are utilized during both the planning and execution stages of a trip [25].

Tactile maps (e.g., in swell paper or thermoformed reliefs) are effective for people with VI to acquire spatial knowledge of an unfamiliar urban environment [3,11]. Tactile maps are suitable for orientation and mobility training [15] but have limitations, such as the inability to represent a large amount of information or specific details such as distances [3]. The creation of tactile maps is costly and time-consuming. Although automation approaches have been investigated [6,24,29], there are no mature and available solutions that limit their efficiency for personal use.

Augmenting paper-based tactile maps with acoustic or haptic information is a promising approach for increasing the information density displayed on tactile maps. For example, TPad is a mobile application for the iPad that allows users to interact with indoor map data through two-handed exploration, auditory icons, and audio commands [23]. Engel et al. investigated interaction techniques with audio-tactile indoor maps (printed on swell paper) that are usable with a digital pen and a smartphone app to support finding a target in a building through sonification [10]. Although audio-tactile approaches seem adequate for indoor map accessibility, their disadvantages remain in producing printed materials, which limits their use to service facilities.

People with visual impairments can also experience spatial relationships through haptic map exploration and feedback via vibration and sonification directly on a typical touchscreen, which is effective for both indoor [1,32] and outdoor environments [8,18,27].

Another approach to improve the accessibility of maps is the presentation of spatial data in virtual, auditory, or verbal form, as shown, e.g., by [17,30]. Auditory Maps, a 3D sound system developed by Heuten et al. [17], allows blind users to identify geographic objects in a city and navigate through a virtual walkthrough, an auditory flashlight walkthrough, and an auditory flashlight bird's eye view. Striegl et al. [30] presented an app-based orientation support system for blind users using landmark-based orientation descriptions, which resulted in good cognitive maps and good acceptance and usability.

Only a few studies investigated improving map accessibility through web-based technologies, i.e., providing compatibility with screen readers or text-to-speech technologies and following standard guidelines such as the Web Content Accessibility Guidelines (WCAG), e.g., [20,28]. Klaus et al. [20] developed a web application that allows users to customize map style, retrieve verbal information in text and speech, and perform classic map functions such as searching, zooming, and panning. The web application aims for WCAG compliance with automatically generated semantic descriptions and adjustable colors, contrasts, and labels. In a pilot study, Rottmann et al. [28] found that an additional list view created a viable alternative for making map content accessible in an accessible mobile map application. Feedback emphasized the need for meaningful classification and order of listed items for users with visual impairments or blindness.

In summary, maps can be accessible to people with visual impairments through graphical adaptations such as tactile maps and multiple modalities such as sound and vibration. However, current systems are often designed for specific target groups. Universal approaches for indoor maps that cater to diverse needs, such as profile-based tailoring, still require investigation. Research on web-based map accessibility is sparse despite the widespread use of web-based and indoor location-based services [16]. The importance of this issue has been discussed at events such as the *W3C-OGC Workshop on Maps for the Web*[4]. This paper proposes a concept, prototype, and study of accessible web-based indoor maps to fill these gaps.

## 3  Concept and Design

*Target Groups:* The target group for this web application encompasses a diverse and inclusive community, primarily consisting of individuals with varying degrees of visual and mobility impairments. This includes people who are blind, those with partial vision or visual impairments, individuals with mobility impairments, and people without such impairments.

*Requirements:* To fulfill the needs of the target groups, we first carried out a literature-based requirements analysis, through which we determined the required building information and the requirements for the web application itself. We researched the challenges, needs, and preferences of people with visual or mobility impairments who need assistance with orientation in buildings. We identified specific requirements for accessible digital indoor maps catering to the needs of people with low vision, blindness, and mobility impairments and those without such impairments.

Firstly, the map should provide users with crucial information regarding navigation and safety, including information about open spaces, the location of entrances, environmental features, stairs, elevators, ground changes, or obstacles [21,25].

Secondly, accessibility information should be tailored to the specific needs of users. For example, the map should provide information about tactile paving or speech-enabled elevators for visually impaired users and fine-gained information about stairs, ramps, elevators, and accessible restrooms for people with mobility impairments [7,9,31].

Thirdly, the application should be accessible according to WCAG and provide features to customize the map's appearance according to the user's needs, such as adjustable font size and support for assistive technologies such as screen readers [21]. To enhance the application's usability, features known from existing map applications are required, including searching for buildings and indoor rooms and classic interaction techniques such as panning, zooming, changing building layers, selecting indoor objects, and inserting a legend.

---

[4] W3C-OGC Workshop on Maps for the Web, https://www.w3.org/2020/maps/report, retrieved: April 15, 2023.

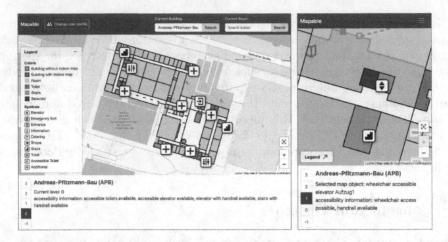

**Fig. 1.** Screenshots of the application with a selected building. Left: General building information with the selected profile for users with VI. Right: Zoom on a selected indoor element with information for users with MI on a mobile device.

*Architecture:* Our approach uses a web application to provide broad accessibility, which complies extensively with the WCAG – thereby implementing accessibility guidelines in the technical foundation of the system – and adapts to different screen sizes and devices. The web application was built using NodeJS. The Leaflet library was used to display the map. The data basis is OpenStreetMap (OSM) data with the advantage that anyone can add information to a building. However, it is a prerequisite that data and accessibility information on a building are available in OSM. Data reconciliation is performed by the server once a day to update the building data used in the application.

*User Interface:* The user interface is vertically divided into three sections: the header, containing settings and a search bar; the map, including zoom buttons and a collapsible legend; and the information area, displaying accessibility features of the building or selected indoor elements. In the settings, the map's appearance, such as line thickness, color strength, or font size, can be adjusted to fulfill the requirements. Users can, furthermore, choose a color blindness (none, red-green, blue-yellow, black-white) to switch the color pallet used.

On focusing the building search's input field, a dropdown list is opened, containing all building names with indoor map data inside the map's current viewport. Users can search for a building by its name without knowing its spatial position. On the map, buildings with indoor map data are highlighted by color, allowing sighted users to recognize which buildings provide an indoor map quickly. By zooming on a building, the indoor map becomes visible. Alternatively, users can click or touch on a building or use the building search to zoom in on it and center it on the map.

Figure 1 (left) shows that the indoor map comprises a building outline, color-highlighted rooms, stairs, and elevators. Restrooms, e.g., have a different fill color than rooms of other types or staircases. The map also includes the representation of tactile paving.

There are icons for special POIs, grouped in a plus icon according to a semantic zoom manner, depending on the zoom level: (wheelchair-accessible) restrooms, stairs, elevators, ramps, entries and exits, emergency exits, service points, stores, and catering locations.

Users can select rooms, staircases, or elevators by clicking on the element or icon or searching for it by room number or type. By selecting a building or indoor element, further information is displayed in the information area.

Screen reader users can search for buildings, get summarized accessibility information for each building level, and search for indoor objects to get information on specific POIs. Furthermore, menus and settings can also be accessed via a screen reader. Due to the complexity of indoor maps with numerous objects in multi-level buildings, it would have been difficult for screen reader users to switch between levels and select individual objects sequentially or through explore-by-touch. Therefore, the map object was designed to be ignored by screen readers. Nevertheless, as stated above, map data and accessibility information are made accessible via the search functionality for this user group.

*User Profiles:* In the app settings, users can choose between three profiles: profile for users with VI, with MI, and without impairments. The displayed information on the map and in the information area is tailored to the selected profile. In the VI profile, the location of tactile paving is added to the map (if available), and information on handrails, braille labels, and elevators with speech output is added to the information area. In the MI profile, information on the wheelchair accessibility of indoor elements (such as elevators and toilets), ramps, and the existence of handrails are given. Users can, furthermore, adjust in the settings which accessibility features should be included visually on the map and in the information section of the application. The design decision, which features are predefined in a profile, is based on preliminary investigations [7,25].

## 4    Evaluation

To investigate the usability of the developed application, a user study was conducted as a single-arm trial with participants from the target group, including people with VI, MI, and people without impairment.

### 4.1    Participants

24 people participated in the study (18 male, 5 female, 1 diverse). This included 8 people without impairment, 8 with mild visual impairment (MVI) such as limited visual acuity, color blindness, and mild gaze paresis, 6 with severe visual impairment (SVI), such as blindness, and 2 with MI. The average age of participants was 30 years, ranging from 20 to 60.

## 4.2   Methodology

Participants were introduced to the project and tested the application independently on a mobile device in a laboratory setting. They could use their smartphone or a provided device. Android smartphones and tablets were available for the latter, and the participants could choose which one they wanted to use.

Participants were not required to complete a specific set of tasks. Instead, they could explore the application with or without their assistive technologies and use the functions freely in an exploratory manner. With this approach, participants could use their usual interaction mechanisms and ascertain if their expectations of the application were met. The investigator was available for questions, and the interaction with the application was observed. For people with SVI who did not use their own smartphone for the experiment, the investigator activated the screen reader before handing over the provided device. Afterward, participants either filled out connected questionnaires or dictated their answers to the investigator.

General technology acceptance (TA) and competence beliefs (TCB) were measured using sub-scales of the technology commitment model [26], as those may affect the perceived usability. The system's usability was measured using the system usability scale (SUS) [5], and results were interpreted according to Bangor et al. [2]. Accordingly, a mean SUS score above 72.75 was interpreted as *good* and above 85.58 as *excellent* usability. In contrast, a mean SUS score between 52.01 and 72.75 is considered *okay* and corresponds to marginally acceptable usability [2].

Additionally, participants were asked open questions regarding additional functionalities and possible improvements as a formative evaluation of the application. All participants had to sign a privacy policy and consent form to comply with data protection provisions.

## 4.3   Results

Overall, the SUS results indicated good to excellent usability above all groups (mean (M): 80, standard deviation (STD): 14.47). As shown in Fig. 2, the usability was rated as good to excellent by participants without impairments (NI) (M: 85.31) and participants with MVI (M: 87.19). SUS results for participants with MI indicated good usability (M: 70, STD: 10.61). The SUS results for participants with SVI states a marginal acceptable usability, with a high STD (M: 66.7, STD: 19.34). When comparing SUS results for the SVI group to SUS results of NI, MVI, and MI combined, a significant difference could be seen (unpaired t-test, $p = 0.0060$). While the technology commitment model results generally indicated a good TA and TCB among participants (TA M: 15.54/20, TA STD: 2.67, TCB M: 14.5/20, TCB STD: 1.93), some differences between participating groups could be seen. Participants with no visual impairment (NI & MI) showed a slightly higher TA (M: 16.20, STD: 1.81) than participants with MVI and SVI (M: 15.07, STD: 3.12). However, differences were insignificant (unpaired t-test, $p = 0.3179$). Furthermore, participants with MI scored lower for technology competence beliefs than the other participants (M: 13, STD: 4.24).

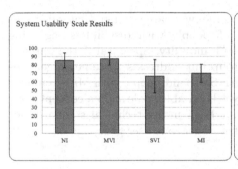
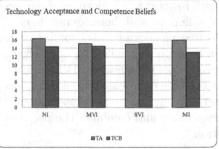

**Fig. 2.** SUS, TA, and TCB results for people without impairment (NI), mild visual impairment (MVI), severe visual impairment (SVI), and people with mobility impairment (MI).

## 4.4 Discussion

While, overall, the perceived usability of the system was good to excellent, there was a significant difference in the SUS results between the group of participants with SVI and the remaining participants (NI, MVI, and MI). Technology acceptance and technology competence beliefs showed no significant differences between groups, which indicates room for improvement regarding the usability for SVI users. These results follow the answers to open questions on additional functionalities and possible improvements, as participants with SVI had the most comments and requests for additional functionalities and improvements to the presented application. Participants mainly wanted more fine-grained information on rooms, POIs, landmarks, and accessibility features (e.g., by not only providing the information that the bathroom in a building is accessible, but by indicating which specific features make it accessible). Furthermore, people with SVI requested the possibility of using the digital map with the explore-by-touch functionality of the screen reader and comments to further improve the usability of the search function via screen readers. Participants positively mentioned that the digital map application is easily usable for people with MVI and enables the collaborative planning of trips between users with and without impairments.

*Limitations:* The presented user study focused on investigating the application's usability after one-time use. Usability and acceptance after a long time of use was not considered. Therefore, results could be influenced by a novelty effect. Furthermore, while the study included people with NI, MVI, SVI, and MI, group size was not uniform, with the MI group having only 2 participants. As this exploratory study mainly used the SUS to investigate usability for different user groups, there can be a bias related to the accessibility of the user interface in comparison to the amount of accessibility information obtained through the presented indoor maps. Furthermore, participants from the SVI group could not compare the indoor information provided through the app to ground truth. This should be taken into consideration in follow-up studies.

*Contribution:* We developed an accessible web application that addresses the different and heterogeneous needs of people with disabilities regarding information-seeking tasks for better indoor mobility. Specifically, the application is not only focused on one target group but addresses three heterogeneous user groups: people with MVI, people with SVI, and people with MI. No indoor map service or research application has yet been able to develop a concept, user interface, and user experience design that both meets technical standards for accessibility and combines the needs of heterogeneous user groups in one application.

## 5    Conclusion

Supporting autonomous orientation and navigation in unfamiliar environments plays a crucial role in including people with disabilities in everyday social and work life. Approaches to improve orientation and navigation in indoor environments tend to address the accessibility needs of a specific user group only. The presented application for accessible web-based indoor map data *Mapable* addresses the different needs and preferences of users with and without disabilities, specifically, by tailoring interaction concepts, presented information, and user interface experience. Mapable provides access to indoor data retrieved from OSM by a map view and in text form, with customizable map design and informational content. The study results showed good to excellent usability among the diverse group of people with mild and severe visual impairments, people with mobility impairments, and people without disabilities. Room for improvement was indicated for people with SVI and will be addressed in future work. Similar to related research, the study results showed the high need for more detailed accessibility information for public indoor spaces.

**Acknowledgements.** Application development was supported by Sebastian Rottmann, Fabian Lüders, Lisa-Marie Schäfer, Till Große, Tomasz Ludyga and Adrian Köhler. This work was partially funded by the Federal Ministry of Labour and Social Affairs (BMAS) under the grant number 01KM151112.

## References

1. Adams, R., Pawluk, D., Fields, M., Clingman, R.: Multiomodal application for the perception of spaces (maps). In: Proceedings of the 17th International ACM SIGACCESS Conference on Computers & Accessibility. ASSETS '15, pp. 393–394. Association for Computing Machinery, New York, NY, USA (2015). https://doi.org/10.1145/2700648.2811386
2. Bangor, A., Kortum, P.T., Miller, J.T.: An empirical evaluation of the system usability scale. Int. J. Hum.-Comput. Interact. **24**(6), 574–594 (2008). https://doi.org/10.1080/10447310802205776
3. Brock, A., Jouffrais, C.: Interactive audio-tactile maps for visually impaired people. SIGACCESS Access. Comput. (113), 3–12 (2015). https://doi.org/10.1145/2850440.2850441

4. Brock, A.M., et al.: SIG: making maps accessible and putting accessibility in maps. In: Extended Abstracts of the 2018 CHI Conference on Human Factors in Computing Systems. CHI EA '18, pp. 1–4. Association for Computing Machinery, New York, NY, USA (Apr 2018). https://doi.org/10.1145/3170427.3185373
5. Brooke, J.: SUS - a quick and dirty usability scale (1996)
6. Clark, J., Clark, D.: Creating tactile maps for the blind using a GIS (1994)
7. Constantinescu, A., Müller, K., Loitsch, C., Zappe, S., Stiefelhagen, R.: Traveling to unknown buildings: accessibility features for indoor maps. In: Miesenberger, K., Kouroupetroglou, G., Mavrou, K., Manduchi, R., Covarrubias Rodriguez, M., Penáz, P. (eds.) ICCHP-AAATE 2022, Part I. LNCS, vol. 13341, pp. 221–228. Springer, Cham (2022). https://doi.org/10.1007/978-3-031-08648-9_26
8. Darvishy, A., Hutter, H.-P., Grossenbacher, M., Merz, D.: Touch explorer: exploring digital maps for visually impaired people. In: Miesenberger, K., Manduchi, R., Covarrubias Rodriguez, M., Peñáz, P. (eds.) ICCHP 2020. LNCS, vol. 12376, pp. 427–434. Springer, Cham (2020). https://doi.org/10.1007/978-3-030-58796-3_50
9. Engel, C., et al.: Travelling more independently: a requirements analysis for accessible journeys to unknown buildings for people with visual impairments. In: ASSETS 2020 - 22nd International ACM SIGACCESS Conference on Computers and Accessibility. Association for Computing Machinery, Inc. (2020). https://doi.org/10.1145/3373625.3417022
10. Engel, C., Weber, G.: ATIM: automated generation of interactive, audio-tactile indoor maps by means of a digital pen. In: Miesenberger, K., Kouroupetroglou, G., Mavrou, K., Manduchi, R., Covarrubias Rodriguez, M., Penáz, P. (eds.) ICCHP-AAATE 2022. LNCS, vol. 13341, pp. 123–133. Springer, Cham (2022). https://doi.org/10.1007/978-3-031-08648-9_15
11. Espinosa, M.A., Ungar, S., Ochaíta, E., Blades, M., Spencer, C.: Comparing methods for introducing blind and visually impaired people to unfamiliar urban environments. J. Environ. Psychol. **18**(3), 277–287 (1998). https://doi.org/10.1006/jevp.1998.0097
12. Froehlich, J.E., et al.: Grand challenges in accessible maps. Interactions **26**(2), 78–81 (2019). https://doi.org/10.1145/3301657
13. Fryer, L., Freeman, J., Pring, L.: What verbal orientation information do blind and partially sighted people need to find their way around? A study of everyday navigation strategies in people with impaired vision. Br. J. Vis. Impair. **31**(2), 123–138 (2013). https://doi.org/10.1177/0264619613485079
14. Giudice, N.A., Guenther, B.A., Jensen, N.A., Haase, K.N.: Cognitive mapping without vision: Comparing wayfinding performance after learning from digital touchscreen-based multimodal maps vs. embossed tactile overlays. Front. Hum. Neurosci. **14**, 87 (2020). https://doi.org/10.3389/fnhum.2020.00087
15. Goldschmidt, M.: Orientation and mobility training to people with visual impairments. In: Mobility of Visually Impaired People: Fundamentals and ICT Assistive Technologies, pp. 237–261 (2018). https://doi.org/10.1007/978-3-319 54446-5_8
16. Grand View Research: Digital Map Data - Market Analysis From 2016 to 2027. Technical report, Grand View Research, Inc. (2019)
17. Heuten, W., Henze, N., Boll, S.: Interactive exploration of city maps with auditory torches. In: CHI '07 Extended Abstracts on Human Factors in Computing Systems. CHI EA '07, pp. 1959–1964. Association for Computing Machinery, New York, NY, USA (2007). https://doi.org/10.1145/1240866.1240932

18. Kaklanis, N., Votis, K., Tzovaras, D.: A mobile interactive maps application for a visually impaired audience. In: Proceedings of the 10th International Cross-Disciplinary Conference on Web Accessibility. W4A '13, pp. 1–2. Association for Computing Machinery, Rio de Janeiro, Brazil, May 2013. https://doi.org/10.1145/2461121.2461152

19. Kandalan, R.N., Namuduri, K.: Techniques for constructing indoor navigation systems for the visually impaired: a review. IEEE Trans. Hum.-Mach. Syst. **50**(6), 492–506 (2020). https://doi.org/10.1109/THMS.2020.3016051

20. Klaus, H., Marano, D., Neuschmid, J., Schrenk, M., Wasserburger, W.: AccessibleMap. In: Miesenberger, K., Karshmer, A., Penaz, P., Zagler, W. (eds.) ICCHP 2012. LNCS, vol. 7383, pp. 536–543. Springer, Heidelberg (2012). https://doi.org/10.1007/978-3-642-31534-3_79

21. Loitsch, C., Müller, K., Engel, C., Weber, G., Stiefelhagen, R.: AccessibleMaps: addressing gaps in maps for people with visual and mobility impairments. In: Miesenberger, K., Manduchi, R., Covarrubias Rodriguez, M., Peňáz, P. (eds.) ICCHP 2020. LNCS, vol. 12377, pp. 286–296. Springer, Cham (2020). https://doi.org/10.1007/978-3-030-58805-2_34

22. Medina, J.L., Cagnin, M.I., Paiva, D.M.B.: Investigating accessibility on web-based maps. ACM SIGAPP Appl. Comput. Rev. **15**(2), 17–26 (2015). https://doi.org/10.1145/2815169.2815171

23. Melfi, G., Baumgarten, J., Müller, K., Stiefelhagen, R.: An audio-tactile system for visually impaired people to explore indoor maps. In: Miesenberger, K., Kouroupetroglou, G., Mavrou, K., Manduchi, R., Covarrubias Rodriguez, M., Penáz, P. (eds.) ICCHP-AAATE 2022, Part I. LNCS, vol. 13341, pp. 134–142. Springer, Cham (2022). https://doi.org/10.1007/978-3-031-08648-9_16

24. Miele, J.A., Landau, S., Gilden, D.: Talking TMAP: automated generation of audio-tactile maps using Smith-Kettlewell's TMAP software. Br. J. Vis. Impair. **24**(2), 93–100 (2006). https://doi.org/10.1177/0264619606064436

25. Müller, K., Engel, C., Loitsch, C., Stiefelhagen, R., Weber, G.: Traveling more independently: a study on the diverse needs and challenges of people with visual or mobility impairments in unfamiliar indoor environments. ACM Trans. Access. Comput. **15**(2) (2022). https://doi.org/10.1145/3514255

26. Neyer, F.J., Felber, J., Gebhardt, C.: Entwicklung und validierung einer kurzskala zur erfassung von technikbereitschaft. Diagnostica **58**(2), 87 (2012). https://doi.org/10.1026/0012-1924/a000067

27. Poppinga, B., Magnusson, C., Pielot, M., Rassmus-Gröhn, K.: TouchOver map: audio-tactile exploration of interactive maps. In: Proceedings of the 13th International Conference on Human Computer Interaction with Mobile Devices and Services. MobileHCI '11, pp. 545–550. Association for Computing Machinery, New York, NY, USA, August 2011. https://doi.org/10.1145/2037373.2037458

28. Rottmann, S., Loitsch, C., Weber, G.: Accessible mobile map application and interaction for people with visual or mobility impairments. In: Proceedings of Mensch Und Computer 2022. MuC '22, pp. 119–127. Association for Computing Machinery, New York, NY, USA (2022). https://doi.org/10.1145/3543758.3543780

29. Štampach, R., Mulíčková, E.: Automated generation of tactile maps. J. Maps **12**(sup1), 532–540 (2016). https://doi.org/10.1080/17445647.2016.1196622

30. Striegl, J., Felchow, J., Loitsch, C., Weber, G.: Accessible indoor orientation support by landmark-based navigation. In: Antona, M., Stephanidis, C. (eds.) HCII 2023. LNCS, vol. 14020, pp. 510–524. Springer, Cham (2023). https://doi.org/10.1007/978-3-031-35681-0_34

31. Striegl, J., Lotisch, C., Schmalfuss-Schwarz, J., Weber, G.: Analysis of indoor maps accounting the needs of people with impairments. In: Miesenberger, K., Manduchi, R., Covarrubias Rodriguez, M., Peňáz, P. (eds.) ICCHP 2020. LNCS, vol. 12377, pp. 305–314. Springer, Cham (2020). https://doi.org/10.1007/978-3-030-58805-2_36

32. Su, J., Rosenzweig, A., Goel, A., de Lara, E., Truong, K.N.: Timbremap: enabling the visually-impaired to use maps on touch-enabled devices. In: Proceedings of the 12th International Conference on Human Computer Interaction with Mobile Devices and Services. MobileHCI '10, pp. 17–26. Association for Computing Machinery, New York, NY, USA (Sep 2010). https://doi.org/10.1145/1851600.1851606

33. Tannert, B., Kirkham, R., Schöning, J.: Analyzing accessibility barriers using cost-benefit analysis to design reliable navigation services for wheelchair users. In: Lamas, D., Loizides, F., Nacke, L., Petrie, H., Winckler, M., Zaphiris, P. (eds.) INTERACT 2019, Part I. LNCS, vol. 11746, pp. 202–223. Springer, Cham (2019). https://doi.org/10.1007/978-3-030-29381-9_13

# Exploring the Relationship Between Generation Z's Beauty Experience and Brand Loyalty: A Comprehensive Study in the Experience Economy Era

Shin-Yu Tsai(✉) ⓘ and Hsien-Hui Tang ⓘ

National Taiwan University of Science and Technology, Taipei City 106335, Taiwan (R.O.C.)
ariel880521@gmail.com

**Abstract.** In the era of the experience-driven economy, consumer demands are evolving towards highly personalized and unique service experiences. Concurrently, demographic shifts, particularly the rise of Generation Z, forecast a significant change in consumer behavior within the beauty industry. This generation, known for its emphasis on diverse beauty facets, significantly influences the cosmetics market. However, amidst fierce brand competition, Generation Z exhibits a declining sense of brand loyalty amid a multitude of options.

This study aims to investigate the relationship between Generation Z's preferences in beauty experiences and their loyalty towards specific brands. To accomplish this, a comprehensive "Demand-Experience-Loyalty" framework was developed, using theoretical perspectives. In-Dept interviews were conducted, unveiling the intricate details of Generation Z's consumption experiences of beauty products. The encoded findings provided invaluable insights that delineate the nuanced demands and unique attributes of this demographic segment, enabling brands to better understand their target audience.

The research underscores the pivotal role of products as the central driver of the consumer experience, with communication serving as a guiding force in purchase decisions. Simultaneously, service and environment support and fortify these experiences. Moreover, a distinctive pattern of loyalty behavior, tethered to specific product categories, was observed among Generation Z consumers. This sheds light on the dynamic interplay among loyalty, consumer needs, and experience domains, serving as a crucial guide for future strategies in both academic discourse and practical brand management.

**Keywords:** Brand Loyalty · Generation Z · Experience Framework

## 1 Introduction

In the era of the experience economy, consumer demands are increasingly fragmented and refined. The shift from a product-centric approach to service differentiation has become imperative, as companies strive to enhance value through customized services. With the saturation of the service economy, we have now entered the current era of experience.

M. Antona and C. Stephanidis (Eds.): HCII 2024, LNCS 14697, pp. 112–128, 2024.
https://doi.org/10.1007/978-3-031-60881-0_8

Additionally, emerging demographics are influencing market dynamics. Generation Z, as the new dominant consumer group, exhibits a willingness to express individuality and stands out from the crowd, not only demonstrating a pursuit of beauty but also impacting the traditional operations of the cosmetics industry.

Looking towards the future, cosmetics brands must meet the personalized and nuanced experiential demands of consumers while considering how to capture the attention of Generation Z. However, the decreasing brand loyalty among Generation Z poses a challenge to the loyalty strategies that companies have relied on in the past.

Against this backdrop, this paper poses the research question: "What is the relationship between Generation Z and beauty brand loyalty through experience analysis?" The aim is to explore the decision-making considerations and experiential perceptions of Generation Z beauty consumers, thereby assisting brands in utilizing experience design to enhance loyalty. The objectives are: (1) Conduct in-depth interviews to understand the value, experiential preferences, and differences in brand loyalty among beauty consumers of different loyalty types. (2) Code the interview results based on the research framework, clustering similar opinions and sentiments. (3) Connect demands, experiences, and loyalty performance to explore the dynamic relationships between them, and cross-examine the insights of different brand loyalists.

## 2 Literature Review

### 2.1 The New Mindset and Framework in the Experience Economy

In the context of the experience economy, the concept of Experience Thinking (X Thinking) elucidates that brands act as creators of experiences, while individuals serve as co-creators of the brand, with experience serving as the bridge for communication of needs and values between the two (Huang & Lai, 2020).

Additionally, the Holistic Experience Model (HXM) further defines four domains that influence experiences, namely product, environment, service, and communication (Lai & Tang, 2023) (see Fig. 1):

1. Product Experience: The core offering sold by the brand, which can be a product or service, catering to varying degrees of user experience needs.
2. Environment Experience: The experiential field where brands facilitate interactions between products and users, encompassing the establishment of physical and digital environments.
3. Service Experience: The assistance provided by brands to purchasers or users throughout the consumption process, which can be conveyed through employee training and the cultivation of corporate culture to transmit brand values.
4. Communication Experience: The experiences resulting from the interaction between brands and consumers, aiding consumers in memorizing key brand concepts and thereby promoting consumption (Wijaya, 2013).

### 2.2 Generation Z and Beauty Industry

The new generation of young consumers possesses a significant demand for cosmetics, viewing makeup as a major pathway to embracing the principle of "be yourself" (Clark,

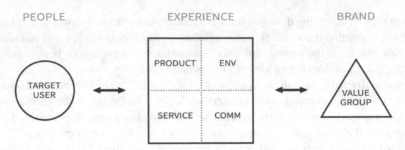

**Fig. 1.** The Holistic Experience Model

2019). 70% of Generation Z beauty shoppers identify themselves as "beauty enthusiasts," with their perception of beauty revolving around "authenticity and the freedom of diversity," challenging the traditional frameworks of the beauty industry (Biondi, 2021).

As digital natives, they are accustomed to showcasing themselves across various social platforms (Biondi, 2021), gradually becoming co-creators of brands. However, reports indicate that Generation Z exhibits the lowest brand loyalty among all generations (Droesch, 2019). Coupled with the highly prevalent "multi-brand preference" trend in the cosmetics industry (TMO Group, 2020), cosmetic companies face increasing challenges in maintaining brand loyalty.

The emergence of community marketing, the embrace of diverse and inclusive cultures, and Generation Z's expressive nature collectively exert significant influence and present challenges to the cosmetics industry.

### 2.3 Brand Loyalty

Brand loyalty is commonly used to measure the relationship between brands and customers, representing consumers' behavior, intention, and inclination to repeatedly purchase a particular brand (Brown, 1953; Zeithaml, 1988; Balding & Rubinson, 1996). Enhancing brand loyalty can increase brand revenue and generate positive word-of-mouth (Gounaris & Stathakopoulos, 2004).

In this study, various loyalty measurement methods were considered, and ultimately, the four groups of customer types suggest by marketing professor Philip Kotler were selected to encompass the breadth of consumer behavior. This method categorizes loyalty into four types from high to low (Kotler & Keller, 2016):

1. Hard-core Loyals: Customers who buy exclusively from a brand.
2. Split Loyals: Customers loyal to two or three brands in a particular category.
3. Shifting Loyals: Consumers who shift loyalty from one brand to another.
4. Switchers: Customers with no sense of loyalty to any brand.

## 3   Methodologies

The research process consists of two stages: contextual inquiry and in-depth interviews. The initial findings from contextual inquiry provide the basis for the subsequent interviews. In-depth interviews are the focal point of the study, employing thematic analysis to compile interview content and ultimately understand the analysis of experience and brand loyalty.

### 3.1 Contextual Exploration

To achieve the research objectives, contextual exploration was conducted initially. Six preliminary interviews with cosmetics consumers were conducted to grasp the makeup behavior and consumption patterns of Generation Z. Field observations were also utilized to compile domains of experience, serving as reference material for subsequent interviews, as shown in Table 1.

Table 1. The Items and Definitions of Experience Domains from Field observations

| Experince Domains | Items and Definition |
|---|---|
| Product | Product variety, price, functionality, color, fragrance, texture, packaging, compatibility with multi-functional combinations, ease of use, and composition |
| Environment | Physical environment elements include sample displays, mirrors, makeup removal areas, display arrangements, layout planning, lighting designs, color materials, etc. (Wu, 1995); while digital environment elements include online website designs, app designs, and interface interaction experiences |
| Service | The ability to solve problems, behavioral attitudes, service professionalism, and sales behavior (such as suggesting additional purchases at checkout, actively addressing customer needs, etc.) |
| Communication | The production and distribution of promotional materials (such as offline billboards and direct mail), in-store signage (product descriptions and tutorials, product pairing recommendations, discounts and promotions, customer reviews and ratings), in-store events, utilization of media promotion channels, and brand collaborations |

### 3.2 Framework Establishment:

Based on Lai and Tang's (2023) Holistic Experience Model, the research framework integrates findings from the preliminary contextual exploration and relevant literature. The framework incorporates theories such as Maslow's (1943) hierarchy of needs, Keller's perceived value (1993), the Holistic Experience Model (Lai & Tang, 2023), and Kotler and Keller's (2016) four loyalty classifications, establishing an "Demand-Experience-Loyalty" framework, as illustrated in Fig. 2.

### 3.3 Respondent Selection

Based on the research framework, a questionnaire for recruiting interviewees was designed. Interviewees were selected based on the following criteria: (1) selecting

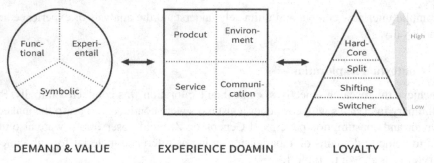

DEMAND & VALUE          EXPERIENCE DOAMIN          LOYALTY

**Fig. 2.** The "Demand-Experience-Loyalty" framework

respondents aged 18 to 27 to align with the age range of Generation Z, (2) ensuring interviewees have a certain level of makeup needs by excluding respondents who apply makeup only 1 to 2 times per week or purchasing makeup less than once a year, and (3) to ensure comprehensive use of makeup products, interviewees who selected three or more options out of five makeup categories (base makeup, facial contouring, eyebrow makeup, eye makeup, and lip makeup) were selected as interview subjects.

152 responses were collected from the questionnaire survey, from which 18 representative interviewees were selected. Finally, the interview content was coded into the corresponding research framework to present comprehensive insights into the experiences of new generation cosmetics brands.

## 4   Result

This paper explores Generation Z from an experiential perspective and proposes an innovative experience analysis framework applied to the cosmetics industry, yielding the following research findings.

### 4.1   Beauty Demand Value of Generation Z

Generation Z consumers purchase and apply cosmetics to fulfill their needs for self-esteem and self-actualization (Maslow, 1943), as well as to achieve symbolic value (Keller, 1993). This signifies their pursuit of showcasing a sense of accomplishment and belonging through makeup, aiming to actualize their personal image and align with symbolic elements such as the culture, identity, and values of a brand. Through coding and summarization, this study presents specific insights into the unique needs of Generation Z:

**Pursuit of Lifestyle Attitude.**   For the demand values of Generation Z, makeup not only assists in self-expression but also represents the expression of lifestyle attitude, as individuals who engage in makeup are seen as "being attentive and responsible for their lives (p137)." Furthermore, respondents perceive themselves as "gradually becoming more beautiful (p141)" during the makeup process, resulting in "increased self-preference (p150)" and positive motivation in life.

**Management of Virtual Identity.** People change their makeup according to different social occasions. In these situations, Generation Z cosmetics consumers place the highest emphasis on occasions requiring "photography (p020/p038/p137/p141)", with some extreme cases where individuals state they do not need makeup "if there will be no photographic record (p126)". This illustrates that the maintenance of the social facade has transcended from physical to digital realms, with the younger generation emphasizing the management of virtual identity as a key aspect of life.

**Personal Image Shaping.** Many Generation Z cosmetics consumers have personal preferences in makeup styles, using makeup not only to achieve their ideal appearance but also to choose brands that match their self-perception rather than blindly following brand styles. For example, a respondent with a "youthful teenage (p145)" persona prefers the Korean makeup brand ETUDE HOUSE, which exudes a "spring-like, pink (p126)" atmosphere.

## 4.2   The Different Emphasis of Experience Domains

This study identified product and communication as the primary domains influencing consumer decision-making in four experience domains. Products serve as the core of all experiences, while communication guides decision-making. Services and environments complement each other, enhancing the product's emphasis.

**Primary Domains in Beauty Experience – Product Domain.** The classification of cosmetics in the market is often inflexible and standardized, failing to meet consumers' real usage needs. Therefore, based on the respondents' definitions and classifications of cosmetics, this study organized three types of cosmetic products:

*Base Makeup Type.* Base makeup includes foundation and contouring products, representing the "most basic (p121)," "most frequently used (p137)," and "largest area (p147)" of the overall makeup. Base makeup products are highly related to individual skin types and conditions, with consumers having different product efficacy needs based on external factors, such as weather and time:

> "When it's cold or my face is dry, I use liquid foundation; when my face is oily or in the summer, I use pressed powder." (p141)

> "When pressed for time, I use pressed powder or something similar to BB cream because it's quick to apply." (p020)

*Color Cosmetics Type.* Color cosmetics include products with rich colors such as lipstick, blush, and eyeshadow, primarily "influencing personal style (p137)" and meeting the demands of image shaping.

Consumers seek freshness and richness in their purchases, often exhibiting "experimental (p121)" buying behavior, and consider factors such as skin tone and dressing style:

> "At first, everyone around me bought eye palettes of pink or orange tone...but later I found out they didn't really suit me, so I bought this palette of earth tone...it matches my skin tone and daily outfit." (p020)

*Eyebrow and Eyelash Enhancement Type.* Eyebrow and eyelash enhancement products include products for the eye area, such as eyebrow pencils, eyeliners, and mascaras, which rely on the user's "personal skills (p038)" and emphasize product usability.

These products also subtly affect personal style and are linked to the demands of image shaping. For example, using an angled eyebrow pencil to create a "neat (p051)" look or using mascara to create a "natural and clean (p121)" appearance instead of a bold one. Some people also enhance their brows and lashes for perfect imaging when taking photos, corresponding to Generation Z's emphasis on virtual identity:

> "Because the makeup may not be very noticeable in the photos, so you have to apply heavier… I usually use a softer eyeliner pencil, but when going out with friends, we'll take photos. So, I'll change to a more noticeable liquid eyeliner, and maybe apply the mascara a couple more times." (p141)

**Primary Domains in Beauty Experience – Communication Domain.** Generation Z is adept at using various channels to acquire information. This study identified the most commonly used information channels for Generation Z consumers in Taiwan, namely YouTube, Instagram, Dcard, and Xiaohongshu. These channels all have a social nature, demonstrating the integration of information acquisition with their daily entertainment.

*Discovering New Brands: YouTube and Instagram.* Generation Z beauty consumers rely on YouTube to acquire makeup knowledge, indicating that they "learn about brands mostly from YouTube (p027)." They filter complex online information through makeup YouTubers, following individuals with similar conditions:

> "I'm a vegetarian… I only watch vegan KOLs because it's like they've already filtered out brands that don't meet my needs." (p011)

Instagram serves as a complement to YouTube, with many of the influencers and makeup YouTubers followed on Instagram overlapping. The informational utility of Instagram is lower, as influencers mainly incorporate brand information inadvertently through daily sharing. Generation Z also learns makeup techniques from these makeup YouTubers or influencers to improve themselves and enhance positive emotions, corresponding to the demand value of pursuing attitudes towards life:

> "If the photos they shared are really pretty, I'll remember them particularly. I'm like, wow, she's so pretty! I really want to learn her makeup steps. And when I see pretty things, I'll have a good mood." (p141)

*In-depth Comparison of Products: Dcard and Xiaohongshu.* After initially familiarizing themselves with makeup brands, consumers then extensively compare and research product information in more depth. Dcard is Taiwan's largest anonymous community platform with dedicated beauty discussion boards. Respondents mainly use Dcard to search for "reviews or unboxing (p068)" of products and compare comments from ordinary netizens, considering them to be more authentic.

Xiaohongshu[1] is a well-known Chinese online shopping and social app. Generation Z finds it "more suitable for comparison (p007)" among many similar products because of its "fast update rate" and "four-grid layout (p007)" compared with other channels (see Fig. 3). Today, digital networks empower consumers, allowing them to generate topics for brands (Lin, 2021). Communication messages have surpassed the scope that companies can control (Saukko, 2016), and user-generated content (UGC) is flourishing. Generation Z resonates more with this authentic content.

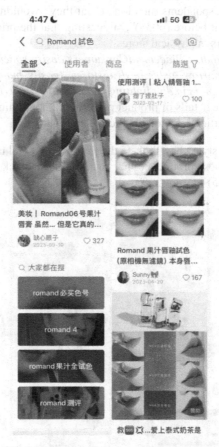

**Fig. 3.** The four-grid layout of Xiaohongshu

## Secondary Domains in Beauty Experience – Environment Domain

*Characteristics of Beauty Retail Channels in Taiwan.* In Taiwan, there is a wide variety of channels for selling cosmetics, with drugstores and e-commerce platforms being the

---

[1] Xiaohongshu is the official English name of the app, referred to as "RED" by Chinese data monitoring companies, and also commonly known as "Little Red Book" online.

most frequently visited by consumers, accounting for 91.9% and 65.4%, respectively. These channels are comprehensive shopping avenues that bring together multiple brands for sale, indicating that today's consumers prefer a "one-stop shopping" experience (Rhodes & Zhou, 2019).

Furthermore, the survey reveals that only 38 respondents prefer either purely online or offline shopping, indicating that Gen Z beauty consumers in Taiwan embrace a hybrid shopping model that spans both online and offline channels, highlighting the importance of brand omnichannel operations. Even though Gen Z is adept at online shopping (Google, 2016), some respondents mentioned that they "wouldn't buy a brand online if they've never bought it before (p038)", suggesting that the primary experience with beauty brands still occurs in physical stores.

*Store Design and Product Placement**Consumers desire spacious and well-lit environments, as they find narrow aisles in drugstores "easily bump into others (p126 / p137)", or that "trying colors in dim lighting makes it look ugly (p137)".* Some respondents pay attention to the details of product placement, mentioning that the visual style of "Knolling (p145)" particularly attracts them (see Fig. 4):

"… like the knolling style, they'll place the products flat and laid out. I'm particularly interested in those products rather than the usual stacked ones, which are less appealing." (p145)

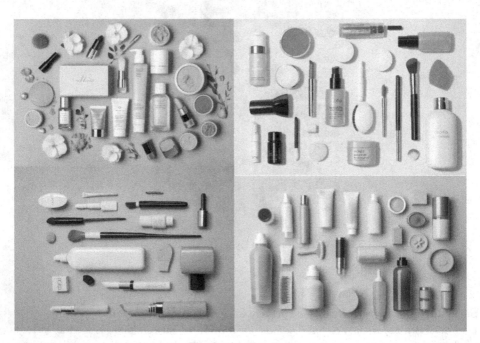

**Fig. 4.** Knolling Style

Moreover, placing special product packaging on the outer periphery of counters easily catches respondents' attention. Combined with themed environments inside the store, a consistent brand value can be conveyed:

"There was one season at M.A.C when they were all about pink and creamy pearl glow. The packages on display and even the LED boards in the store were in that color... Really caught my eyes. And then there was another time when they had this whole zodiac theme going on, which was pretty cool too." (p027)

However, the above environmental findings are the opinions of a minority of respondents. Most Gen Z beauty respondents described that "there isn't much difference in the design (p150)" and found it easy to blend the experiences of product, service, and other domains, indicating a relatively weak individual experience with the environment.

### Secondary Domains in Beauty Experience – Service Domain

*Language and Attitude.* Interviewees mentioned feeling ignored or encountering two-faced attitudes from the service staff at the counters. Despite expecting good service at higher-end counters, the actual experience often falls short, leading to negative perceptions of service and satisfaction (Baskaran, 2011):

"One time, I went with my mom and aunt to C brand, thinking it's supposed to be all fancy and upscale. But when we just asked about a few items, the staff acted like we were wasting their time or something. I mean, there were plenty of them around, and it's not like they were swamped with customers. They just brushed us off, and it was really disappointing." (p027)

Consumers also value the language used by service staff and their sincerity. While salespersons praise customers to boost sales, such practices can inadvertently foster perceptions of "insincere and unthoughtful" (p068) or a deficiency in providing objective explanations and comparisons, thereby eliciting consumer disfavor.

"That color clearly doesn't match my skin tone, yet she said it looks great and suits me well... It felt like she was just talking nonsense." (p141)

"One of my male friends wanted to buy makeup for his girlfriend at a counter, but he's unfamiliar with the prices. The salesperson told him it was only 1200TWD. I thought, what do you mean 'only'? She didn't help him compare the prices or explain if there were discounts or better deals. She just said 'it's only 1200TWD,' and it made me really uncomfortable, like, do you even know how to speak?" (Interviewee p150)

*Explorative Sample Trying Experience.* Generation Z Beauty consumers place emphasis on trying product. If the sample products are not well-maintained or the makeup removers are not provided, consumers may abandon their purchase altogether:

"The cleanliness of sample products affects whether I want to try them. If the environment is disgusting, I won't buy anything. The same goes for makeup removal because I want to leave the store feeling clean." (p020)

During the experiences of sample trying, Generation Z Beauty consumers dislike service staff influencing their shopping choices and prefer a playful and self-explorative shopping experience. Therefore, they often prefer the "relaxed (p027)" atmosphere of drugstores, where they can explore freely, compared to the "pressure (p141)" felt at department store counters due to the attentive staff and aggressive sales tactics:

"Some sales might kindly suggest that the product I'm looking at didn't suit my skin tone, but I just want to give it a try anyway. I don't like feeling restricted." (p147)

The service expectations of Generation Z manifest differently across various product categories. While counters now often provide full-face makeup services for fundamental items, consumers exhibit contentment with such provisions. However, concerning colorful cosmetics or eyebrow and eyelash products, which involve personal aesthetic preferences, consumers are less inclined to accept makeup application services, indicating the importance Generation Z places on shaping their personal image:

"I might not like how the salesperson applies eyeshadow on me. Because everyone's preferences are different, so I prefer not to try it on my face." (p150)

### 4.3   Generation Z's Beauty Brand Loyalty

**Low Loyalty and a Mix-and-Match of Multiple Brands.** In the survey, Generation Z makeup enthusiasts with high loyalty accounted for 35%, those with compound loyalty accounted for 34%, while those with low loyalty accounted for 57%, indicating that non-loyalists make up the majority. This widespread low loyalty attitude may be attributed to their digital native identity (Brooks, 2022; Dani, 2022; Rawat, 2023), continuously changing brand choices due to rapid information changes, indicating that makeup was like "fast fashion (p121)", and often paying attention to "what's trending lately (p145)."

The study found that Generation Z beauty consumers construct their personal makeup combinations through multi-brand mix-and-match. Respondents explained that "each brand buys different items (p141)", leading to "low repetition of brands (p121)" in personal possession, resulting in a "one category corresponds to one brand" purchasing pattern:

"For foundation, I currently use Estée Lauder; for eyeliner, I specifically use a certain brand, always KISSME; I like Maybelline mascara and would repurchase it; and then for eyeshadow, it's Colourpop, which is highly pigmented and blends well" (p150)

This is because consumers' recognition path of the brand starts with the popular product lines before moving on to the brand. They select products based on each brand's respective strengths and expertise, such as "When it comes to M.A.C, I always think of makeup, but for foundation, I would consider trying the famous counter brands like NARS, MAKE UP FOR EVER, or Lancôme (p027)". Therefore, Generation Z's beauty loyalty tends to lean towards "category" loyalty rather than "brand" loyalty.

**Details and Levels of Category Loyalty.** Applied to the classification of cosmetics in this study, hierarchical loyalty differences can be summarized. Consumers are most likely to develop high loyalty in the basic makeup type because the products "affect the skin's condition (p150)", and they would "rather spend more to get the perfect one (p027)". Respondents' choices of foundation brands are also concentrated on a few highly recognized and highly rated big brands, showing the highest attitudinal loyalty among all categories.

Next, the eyebrow and eyelash enhancement type tend to generate fixed usage habits and preferences due to the dual needs of usability and style shaping, gradually accumulating behavioral loyalty through experience (Dick & Basu, 1994), described as "using the same one for several years" or "not buying other brands anymore."

Lastly, loyalty to the color cosmetics type is the lowest, and consumers of all loyalty levels are easily influenced by new product releases or trend influences to purchase multiple brands, or even in cases where they "don't know the brand name and just buy it because the color is pretty (p141)", lacking both loyalty and brand awareness.

**Correspondence between Other Experience Domains and Loyalty**
*Communication Domain.* In addition to products, another significant domain of experience—communication, is mostly associated with low loyalty consumers having a habit of continuously receiving new information, resulting in an increase in the number of brands they come into contact with and replacement of them.

High loyalty consumers can be divided into two categories: those who frequently pay attention to information and those who do not. The former mainly needs to check periodically whether the brands they are loyal to have "new products released (p027)", while the latter mainly relies on word-of-mouth recommendations from friends and family as they have a stable shopping pattern.

*Service Domain.* In interviews, when asked about the most memorable Moments of Truth (MOT) from past experiences (Wang & Zhu, 2022), most responses focused on the service domain, indicating that service most influences consumers' experience outcomes and overall evaluations. This pursuit of service is particularly prominent among highly loyal individuals, as they already have fixed brand preferences and habits, so they value the purchase process experience more than information that assists in brand selection:

> "In addition to the makeup expertise, whether they will consider the customer's needs, such as telling me about recent promotions or advising me on how to mix and match more cost-effectively, is also very important." (p150)

However, the influence of service does not necessarily rise to brand value and may not directly affect brand loyalty. As mentioned above, interviewee p027 once had a terrible service experience at C brand but still has high loyalty to the brand, indicating that "I think bad attitude is a personal issue and does not affect the brand."

*Environment Domain.* Finally, the environment domain holds less significance concerning brand loyalty among Generation Z beauty consumers. They often overlook spatial design in beauty stores, given the product-oriented focus of the beauty retail industry.

Conversely, certain industries, such as the hotel and catering sectors, prioritize service provision, striving to deliver a comprehensive customer experience. Consequently, they invest more heavily in environmental design to enhance overall customer satisfaction and loyalty. For instance, the spatial design in the hotel industry is tailored to meet individuals' needs for privacy and socialization (Barbour, 2015), while environmental design in catering emphasizes seating layout, circulation planning, and acoustic considerations (Maffei & Dong, 2016).

Thus, while the environment domain is not negligible, its influence appears to be relatively diminished in shaping the beauty shopping experience for Generation Z.

## 5  Discussion

### 5.1  Insights of Experience Framework in Consumer Journey

In the 5A consumer journey model (Kotler et al., 2021), the communication domain dominates the initial stages of Aware and Appeal, initiating the subsequent progression of experiences. Besides obtaining virtual communication messages through various social media platforms, Generation Z highly values recommendations from friends and family, using them directly as decision-making criteria in the Awareness, Appeal, and Ask stages, bypassing the tedious process of research and comparison:

> "Even last time I bought mascara, I couldn't be bothered to check, I just asked my friends straight up… Basically, once I get their input, I'll probably just go with it." (p073)

Among them, family members play a pivotal role, influencing the initial brand awareness of Generation Z. Interviews revealed that mothers serve as significant beauty guidance figures, with participants predisposed to favor brands recommended by their mothers, gradually developing loyalty to specific brands:

> "Shu uemura got me hooked all because of my mom. She's been using their cleansing oil ever since I can remember… Whatever she buys, I just follow, and I ended up liking their foundation too." (p027)

Moving into the Ask and Act stages, product display and maintenance within the environment, as well as the impact of service on the sample trying experience, are more significant. Moreover, the efficacy of word-of-mouth extends beyond the virtual domain to the physical domain. Generation Z enjoys exchanging and trying out cosmetics at friends' gatherings, expanding the scope of product trying beyond brand stores:

> "My friends love sharing their makeup with me. Sometimes, when we hang out or stay over at each other's places, we start exchanging makeup products. It's like a mini makeup party." (p073)

In summary, communication initiates the experiential process, while the environment and service domains follow suit, with products threading through the entire journey to create a sustained experience. Within the customer journey, it is noteworthy that interpersonal interactions and word-of-mouth promotion are crucial in Generation Z's consumer behavior, leading to an expansion of the experience framework across multiple domains. This study suggests that brands should integrate virtual and physical experiences, attempting to expand personal networks and digital information into offline collective promotional platforms, representing an innovative direction for brands' future word-of-mouth experiences.

## 5.2  Comparison Between Experience Framework and Other Business Analysis Tools

In today's fierce business competition, enterprises employ comprehensive strategic analysis tools to enhance competitiveness. Among them, Customer Relationship Management (CRM) and Customer Experience Management (CXM) have emerged as important tools leading to enterprise success.

CRM systems utilize personalized interaction and data analysis to accurately predict customer needs (Peppers & Rogers, 1993; Payne & Frow, 2005), while CXM not only focuses on transactional behavior but also emphasizes building emotional resonance and coherent narratives (Holbrook & Hirschman, 1982). Both CRM and CXM emphasize the design of touchpoints in the customer journey, and research indicates that touchpoint interactions involve multidimensional operations (Brakus et al., 2009; Design Management Institute, 2023; Hwang & Seo, 2016; Schmitt & Zarantonello, 2013). However, there is limited research proposing a clear framework to define these dimensions.

In this regard, this study provides a comprehensive experience framework that includes all touchpoints' experience design, spanning both physical and virtual realms, assisting enterprises in systematically analyzing existing infrastructure and planning future strategies. Taking the beauty industry as an example, through the experience framework, it can be discovered that consumers are least concerned about environmental design, but physical environments remain important. Meanwhile, products and communication are the core focal points. Therefore, it is inferred that a possible strategy for beauty brands is to "highlight product display through environmental design and transform online communication."

For instance, a large-scale beauty store in Japan, @cosme TOKYO, converts digital platform information such as popularity rankings and user experiences into physical ranking boards (see Fig. 5). These boards are prominently displayed at the entrance, showcasing trial products of popular items one by one and adjusting displays weekly based on online information, successfully creating buzz and attracting customer engagement.

In summary, enterprises can utilize the experience framework to identify their strengths and allocate resources, and can concretely correlate the value of each domain to loyalty analysis, assisting enterprises in targeted improvements. Compared to commonly used business tools, the experience framework provides innovative and comprehensive analysis, contributing to the transformation of experiences in enterprises.

**Fig. 5.** @cosme TOKYO BEST COSME AWARD CORNER

# 6  Conclusion

This study examines Generation Z from the perspective of experience and applies the analytical framework of "Demand-Experience-Loyalty" to the beauty industry to establish a comprehensive view of experience. The following results were found:

First, in terms of demand, apart from correlating the overall beauty demands of Generation Z with existing demand value theories, this study further analyzes and summarizes three types of demand differences: pursuit of lifestyle attitude, management of virtual identity, and personal image shaping. The discovery of deep-seated demands provides brands with new perspectives to plan customer segmentation strategies that are more aligned with real situations.

Second, regarding the experience, this study identifies that among the four domains of experience, the primary domains influencing consumer decision-making for Generation Z are the product and communication domains. Products serve as the core of brand experience, while communication guides decision-making direction. Additionally, service and environment domain complement each other to enhance the presentation of products. Through an understanding of different experience domains, enterprises can identify their own advantages and assist in resource allocation to achieve comprehensive strategic planning.

Third, in terms of loyalty, this study validates the declining brand loyalty of Generation Z beauty consumers, as well as the specific loyalty behavior dominated by product categories in the makeup market. Corresponding to the classification of cosmetics in this study, hierarchical loyalty differences can be summarized, ranging from the base makeup type, the eyebrow and eyelash enhancement type, to the colorful cosmetics type, demonstrating loyalty hierarchies from high to low. Understanding the loyalty behavior of Generation Z can help position beauty brands and enhance brand loyalty in a rapidly changing market.

Fourth, through the coherent context of the 5A consumer path, this study finds that Generation Z primarily advances subsequent experiences through the communication domain in the early stages of shopping, and emphasizes word-of-mouth promotion in various stages of the journey and experience domains, finally explaining the trend of virtual and real integration experiences. Mapping experience domains to various stages of the consumer path can assist brands in executing more detailed touchpoint designs and driving the progression of customer journeys.

In conclusion, this study analyzes the relationship between Generation Z and beauty brand loyalty through the experience framework, not only acquiring an in-depth understanding of the personal experience connotations of Generation Z but also uncovering numerous details of experience design and the significance of brands in the minds of beauty consumers. Integrating the above findings and insights, the research results provide innovative operational suggestions and perspectives for beauty brands, assisting in the derivation and application of experience strategies for the new generation, and can also serve as a reference for other consumer and retail markets.

**Disclosure of Interests.**    The authors have no competing interests to declare that are relevant to the content of this article.

# References

1. Baldinger, A.L., Rubinson, J.: Brand loyalty: the link between attitude and behavior. J. Advert. Res. **36**(6), 22–34 (1996)
2. Barbour, F.: The role of psychology in hotel design. Int. J. Architect. Arts Appl. **1**(2), 45–51 (2015)
3. Baskaran, K.: Success of retail in India: The customer experience management scenario. Int. J. Electron. Market. Retail. **4**(2/3), 206 (2011). https://doi.org/10.1504/IJEMR.2011.043048
4. Biondi, A.: How Gen Z is changing beauty. Vogue Business (2021). https://www.voguebusiness.com/beauty/gen-z-changing-beauty
5. Brakus, J., Josko, J., Schmitt, B.H., Zarantonello, L.: Brand Experience: what is it? How Is It Measured? Does It Affect Loyalty? **73**(3), 52–68 (2009). https://doi.org/10.1509/jmkg.73.3.52
6. Brooks, R.: 3 Things You Need To Know About Gen Z And Brand Loyalty. Forbes (2022). https://www.forbes.com/sites/forbesagencycouncil/2022/08/10/3-things-you-need-to-know-about-gen-z-and-brand-loyalty/?sh=37d4367dc4f2
7. Brown, G.H.: Brand loyalty—fact or fiction. Trademark Reporter **43**, 251 (1953)
8. Clark, K.: How Gen Z is changing the face of modern beauty [Paramount]. How Gen Z is changing the face of modern beauty (2019). https://www.paramount.com/news/audience-insights/how-gen-z-is-changing-the-face-of-modern-beauty
9. Dani, J.: Gen Z didn't kill brand loyalty, but it looks different. Retail Dive (2022). https://www.retaildive.com/news/gen-z-brand-loyalty-retailers-individuality-pricing/636558/
10. Design Management Institute. What is Design Management?. https://www.dmi.org/page/what_is_design_manag (2023)
11. Dick, A.S., Basu, K.: Customer loyalty: toward an integrated conceptual framework. J. Acad. Mark. Sci. **22**(2), 99–113 (1994). https://doi.org/10.1177/0092070394222001
12. Droesch, B.: Millennials and Gen Zers are less inclined to participate in loyalty programs. Insider Intelligence (2019). https://www.insiderintelligence.com/content/millennials-gen-z-less-inclined-to-participate-in-loyalty-programs
13. Google. Generation Z, New insights into the mobile-first mindset of teens (2016)
14. Gounaris, S., Stathakopoulos, V.: Antecedents and consequences of brand loyalty: an empirical study. J. Brand Manag. **11**(4), 283–306 (2004). https://doi.org/10.1057/palgrave.bm.2540174
15. Holbrook, M.B., Hirschman, E.C.: The experiential aspects of consumption: consumer fantasies, feelings, and fun. J. Cons. Res. **9**(2), 132–140 (1982)

16. Huang, F., Lai, Z.-J.: Experience Thinking. Tianjin Science and Technology Press (2020)
17. Hwang, J., Seo, S.: A critical review of research on customer experience management: theoretical, methodological and cultural perspectives. Int. J. Contemp. Hosp. Manag. **28**(10), 2218–2246 (2016). https://doi.org/10.1108/IJCHM-04-2015-0192
18. Keller, K.L.: Conceptualizing, measuring, and managing customer-based brand equity. J. Mark. **57**, 1–22 (1993)
19. Kotler, P., Keller, L.K.: Marketing management (15th). Pearson (2016)
20. Kotler, P., Kartajaya, H., Setiawan, I.: Marketing 5.0: Technology for Humanity. (1st ed.). Wiley (2021)
21. Lai, M., Tang, H.-H.: Experience design's transformation towards experience-driven transformation: a practical perspective. IASDR 2023: Life-Changing Design (2023). https://doi.org/10.21606/iasdr.2023.366
22. Lin, K.W.: [Lin Ke Wei E-commerce Column] What is UGC? Let users create new topics for the brand. Inside (2021). https://www.inside.com.tw/article/22167-ugc-content-marketing
23. Maffei, L., Dong, H.: Acoustic design in restaurants: a case study. Appl. Acoust. **108**, 88–98 (2016)
24. Maslow, A.H.: A theory of human motivation. Psychol. Rev. **50**, 370–396 (1943)
25. Payne, A., Frow, P.: A strategic framework for customer relationship management. J. Mark. **69**(4), 167–176 (2005)
26. Peppers, D., Rogers, M.: The one to one future: building relationships one customer at a time. Doubleday (1993)
27. Rawat, J.: Cracking the code of Gen-Z loyalty programs. Forbes (2023). https://www.forbes.com/sites/forbesbusinesscouncil/2023/08/10/cracking-the-code-of-gen-z-loyalty-programs/?sh=2b431f291a78
28. Rhodes, A., Zhou, J.: Consumer search and retail market structure. Manage. Sci. **65**(6), 2607–2623 (2019). https://doi.org/10.1287/mnsc.2018.3058
29. Saukko, T.: Paths to purchase: the role of the online environment and the fluctuation of customer brand engagement (2016)
30. Schmitt, B., Zarantonello, L.: Consumer experience and experiential marketing: a critical review. Rev. Market. Res. **10**, 25–61 (2013). Emerald Group Publishing Limited. https://doi.org/10.1108/S1548-6435(2013)0000010006
31. TMO Group. China Cosmetics Industry Report (2020)
32. Wang, Z.-Q., Zhu, H.-B.: Peak Experience: Insights into Hidden and Unknown Needs, Mastering Key Moments to Influence Customer Decisions. Common Wealth Magazine Co., Ltd (2022)
33. Wijaya, B.S.: Dimensions of brand image: a conceptual review from the perspective of brand communication. Eur. J. Bus. Manage. 5(31) (2013)
34. Wu, J.-S.: Exhibition Design. New Image Publishing Co., Ltd., Chadstone (1995)
35. Zeithaml, V.A.: Consumer perceptions of price, quality, and value: a means-end model and synthesis of evidence. J. Mark. **52**(3), 2–22 (1988). https://doi.org/10.1177/002224298805200302

# Enhancing Customer Loyalty in Pure Internet Banking: An Analysis of Experience and NPS Shifts Using S-O-R Theory

Qiu-Ze Wu[1], Yu-Ling Lien[1], Hsien-Hui Tang[1(✉)], and Michael T. Lai[2,3,4]

[1] National Taiwan University of Science and Technology, Taipei, Taiwan
drhhtang@gapps.ntust.edu.tw
[2] X Thinking Institute, Shanghai, China
[3] TANG Consulting, Shanghai, China
[4] Tongji University, Shanghai, China

**Abstract.** In the evolving FinTech landscape, traditional financial institutions are embracing digital transformations, accelerated by the COVID epidemic. This study investigates the customer experience in pure Internet banking, utilizing a mixed-method approach that blends qualitative and quantitative research. It incorporates the Stimulus-Organism-Response (S-O-R) framework within the context of ser-vice design, probing the perceptual link between experience domains and custom-er loyalty. The research specifically analyzes the relationship between customer experience variances and loyalty shifts among different Net Promoter Score (NPS) subgroups, pinpointing the primary factors that facilitate loyalty enhance-ment from lower to higher NPS levels.

Findings reveal that functional and spiritual values predominantly influence the NPS transition from low to medium, with service elements and communication being pivotal in affecting these values, respectively. This insight is instrumental for businesses seeking to refine their experience domains, ensuring a comprehensive understanding of customer needs, and thereby elevating product quality and cus-tomer experience. By focusing on loyalty levels in service details, this study aims to spur innovation and enhance the customer experience in the digital banking sector, aligning closely with driving customer loyalty.

**Keywords:** Customer Experience · experience domains · Perceived Value · Customer Loyalty · Pure Internet Banking

## 1 Introduction

In the wake of technological advancement and digital integration, the global financial technology (FinTech) sector is witnessing significant activity. This includes a paradigm shift in the traditional financial industry towards digital transformation. A 2017 PwC survey highlighted a substantial increase in consumer reliance on online banking channels, rising from 27% in 2012 to 46% in 2017. Further emphasizing this trend, McKinsey & Company (Barquin, S., 2018) reported a 1.5 to 3-fold increase in online banking penetration in Asia between 2015 and 2018. The onset of the COVID-19 pandemic accelerated

M. Antona and C. Stephanidis (Eds.): HCII 2024, LNCS 14697, pp. 129–148, 2024.
https://doi.org/10.1007/978-3-031-60881-0_9

this shift; for instance, Deloitte (2022) noted a doubling in the number of first-time Internet banking users in Sweden from 2020 to 2021. The Asian market has been particularly receptive to this digital banking evolution. Japan led the way with the establishment of Japan Net Bank in 2000, followed by significant growth in entities like Rakuten Bank. Between 2020 and 2022, Taiwan issued a total of three pure Internet banking licens-es to establish financial brands and provide services in a completely online, non-physical way, declaring that the banking industry has officially entered the all-digital era. With the rapid development of information technology and Internet technology, the form of service provision has changed. This wave has also swept through the financial industry, resulting in the rapid growth of fintech in recent years. Pure Inter-net banking, with its branding and service delivery through an all-digital channel, is highly capable of integrating technology and quickly adapting and expanding its services. As of the third quarter of 2023, a stark contrast in market share between traditional and Internet-only banks is evident, with the former holding 88.40% and the latter only 11.60%. The overall number of accounts opened by the three Internet-only banks in Taiwan had accumulated to 2,177,908, with LINE Bank, which opened on April 22, 2021, having the largest number of accumulated accounts at 1,656,046 accounts. The market share of LINE bank business increased to 8.82% in two years. Compared to the other two pure Inter-net banks, LINE Bank controls 76% of the pure Internet banking market (FSC, 2023). Innovative forms of services seem to change people's expectations of digital banking, as well as their attitudes and behaviors towards traditional financial services (Saksonova & Kuzmina-Merlino, 2017).

The LINE company's business is not only banking, it also controls the social media business in Taiwan. LINE's business includes not only banking, but it also controls the social media business in Taiwan. According to DIGITAL 2023: TAIWAN (Kemp, 2023), in 2022, 90.7% of Taiwan's Internet users aged 16–64 (90.4% of all social media users) will be using LINE, and 50.7% of these users will report that their favorite social media platform is LINE. It can be seen that LINE Bank has great potential for development in the pure Internet banking business. Despite technological advancements in the sector, the prevalent strategy of price-oriented competition among banking services appears unsustainable. This approach is hampered by minimal differentiation in services, low switching costs for customers, and a general lack of brand loyalty. Furthermore, the emphasis on rapid market entry often leads to a technology-centric approach to ser-vice innovation, overlooking the crucial understanding of customers' actual needs and behavioral patterns. This misalignment between technological advancements and user experience complicates the technology's role in enhancing brand value and establish-ing a loyalty feedback loop. The Net Promoter Score (NPS), a metric developed by Frederick Reichheld (2003), serves as a pivotal tool for assessing customer loyalty and guiding business improvements, with implications for long-term growth. For Internet-only banks like LINE Bank, which operates with a significantly lower market share than traditional banks, prioritizing the transition of customers from low to medium NPS is crucial. Elevating NPS is not just about enhancing the brand image; it's about building a stable customer base and mitigating negative customer perceptions. Therefore, this study would like to investigate what are the factors affecting the movement of internet-only banking customers from low NPS to medium NPS in the framework of experience domains and perceived value.

1. The primary aim of this study is to explore the differential factors in customer experience and the transition of loyalty among customers within low to medium Net Promoter Score (NPS) subgroups in the context of the experience economy, with a specific focus on pure Internet banking. To accomplish this, the study is structured around several key objectives: Apply the Stimulus-Organism-Response (S-O-R) theory to enhance the understanding of customer internal needs from service reception to loyalty formation and pinpoint key brand experiences.
2. Employ NPS segmentation to assess the varying needs of customers across different loyalty levels, aiding companies in formulating specific loyalty conversion strategies and tailoring their offerings within the constraints of limited resources.
3. Integrates the S-O-R framework into the context of service design research, employing structural equation modeling to examine the interactions between service delivery (stimulus), perceived value (organism), and customer loyalty (response). We hypothesize that spiritual, emotional, and functional values positively influence customer loyalty and that the domains of experience, such as product, service, environment, and communication, significantly affect these values.

## 2  Literature Review

### 2.1  Pure Internet Banking

Pure Internet Banking is internationally recognized as a banking model that operates exclusively through digital channels, eschewing physical branches and face-to-face customer service. However, the specifics of this definition vary by country. The Taiwan Financial Supervisory Commission (2018) defines an Internet-only bank as an entity that primarily uses the Internet or other electronic transmission channels for delivering financial products and services. These banks perform functions like those of commercial banks, with the stipulation that their operations are limited to the head office and customer service centers, barring any other physical locations for sales activities. This operational model, distinct from traditional banking, significantly reduces the costs associated with physical service provisions (Fathima, 2020; Sha & Mohammed, 2017).

Globally, Internet-only banks can be differentiated based on their operational models. In Europe and the United States, where financial services penetration is high, the model predominantly focuses on distinguishing from traditional banking through technological innovation and enhanced customer experiences (Johnson, Christensen, & Kagermann, 2008). Conversely, in Asia, the approach is often based on a diversified shareholder structure, encompassing sectors like e-commerce, telecommunications, and retail. This approach aims to leverage extensive customer bases and integrate various business operations to create a comprehensive ecosystem (Peltoniemi & Vuori, 2004). Depending on the shareholder composition, pure Internet banks can be classified into four categories: "technology creation", "bank/financial holding company investment", "group enterprise investment," and "group-bank joint ventures". The majority of European and American pure Internet banks fall into the first two categories, whereas the latter two are more prevalent in Asia.

## 2.2  Customer Loyalty

Customer loyalty is a multifaceted concept influenced by various factors such as experience domains and pricing. It is characterized by a degree of attitudinal favoritism towards a company, leading to repeat purchases and providing a competitive edge (Dick & Basu, 1994; Bagram & Khan, 2012). In academic research, multiple indicators have been employed to measure customer loyalty, each with its unique focus and implications. Gronholdt et al. (2000) identified four key indicators: customers' willingness to repurchase, value tolerance, propensity to recommend a brand, and willingness to cross-purchase. Among these, the willingness to repurchase and the likelihood of recommending emerged as the most robust measures of loyalty.

The Net Promoter Score (NPS), introduced by Reichheld (2003) and further developed by Reichheld and Markey (2011), is a widely adopted industry metric. It categorizes customer relationships into three groups and offers both a broad, industry-wide perspective and an insightful, customer-centric view. The simplicity and comparability of the NPS make it particularly useful for companies with limited resources, enabling them to quickly assess customer relationships and prioritize strategic initiatives. This study adopts the NPS as a suitable measure, aligning with its aim to offer a comprehensive view of the brand's industry position and insights into customer perceptions and potential behaviors.

In summary, customer loyalty can be categorized into 'attitudinal loyalty' and 'behavioral loyalty'. Attitudinal loyalty emphasizes maintaining a relationship with the service provider (Zeithaml, 2000), while behavioral loyalty focuses on the frequency and nature of specific purchasing actions among available options (Neal, 1999). Therefore, this study will examine both behavioral and attitudinal dimensions of customer loyalty.

## 2.3  Perceived Value and Experience Domains

Perceived value is fundamentally the customer's cognitive evaluation of a product or service (Zeithaml, 1988), instrumental in determining whether customer needs and expectations are met (Ji, 2012). It forms the basis of attitude, which in turn predicts behavioral intentions (Fishbein & Ajzen, 1972). To predict customer loyalty, understanding these intentions is crucial. This study adopts the perceived value measure proposed by Sweeney & Soutar (2001), further refined using Maslow's Hierarchy of Needs Theory (Maslow, 1943). The components of perceived value are categorized as "spiritual value", "emotional value", and "functional value". Spiritual value relates to self-worth and belonging, emotional value to positive emotions and safety, and functional value to meeting basic usage needs.

Experience domains emerge from the interaction between service providers and receivers during the service delivery process. It represents the gap between customer expectations and their actual perceptions of the service received (Parasuraman et al., 1985). High-experience domains are a key strategy for fostering customer loyalty (Brun et al., 2014). Traditionally, experience domains evaluations focused on 'concrete' service providers. However, as services become more intangible and complex, existing measures need adaptation to this evolving economic landscape. The shift from a goods-dominant to a service-dominant logic in the market (Vargo & Lusch, 2008) underscores the transition towards more dynamic, intangible, and operational aspects of service delivery. In the contemporary experience economy (Pine & Gilmore, 1998), service providers increasingly offer complex, intangible, and permeable experiences (Huang & Lai, 2020). Customer experience, as defined by Tsai & Liu (2021), is the perception formed through interactions with firms. These experiences are multi-faceted, involving various dimensions of interaction (Grönroos, 2008; Rojas & Camarero, 2008).

According to Lai & Tang (2023), the customer experience can be structured into four dimensions: product, service, environment, and communication. Each plays a unique role in shaping the overall experience. 'Products' include both tangible and intangible elements offered by enterprises. 'Services' encompass the behaviors of service provision and receipt, facilitated through both personnel and digital channels. The 'environment' refers to the interactional field between enterprises and customers, including both physical and digital settings. Lastly, 'communication' involves the mediums through which enterprises engage and build relationships with customers, both directly and indirectly (Keller & Swaminathan, 2019). When these dimensions are effectively aligned, they contribute to positive perceived value (Farnham & Newbery, 2013), enhancing customers' overall perception of experience domains.

In summary, the evolution towards a service-dominant logic in the experience economy necessitates a broader understanding of experience domains. It extends beyond mere transactional interactions to encompass a holistic view where products, services, environment, and communication collectively define the customer experience. This comprehensive approach is essential for accurately capturing the nuances of modern experience domains in an increasingly digital and customer-centric world.

## 2.4 S-O-R Theory

The Stimulus-Organism-Response (S-O-R) theory, as proposed by environmental psychologists Mehrabian & Russell (1974), offers a framework to understand behavioral responses as a product of internal perceptions. This model augments the traditional Stimulus-Response (S-R) theory by incorporating affective cognition as a mediator between external stimuli and behavioral responses. It underscores the initiative and complexity of the organism in the process. "Stimulus" refers to external environmental inputs, "Organism" to the internal perception of these stimuli, and "Response" to the resultant behavioral performance. This theory, which emphasizes the interplay between external stimuli and internal perceptions leading to specific behaviors, is particularly useful in assessing customer experiences across various environmental contexts (Waqas et al., 2021).

In this study, the S-O-R model is employed to dissect how external environmental factors – specifically, services in brand interactions – act as stimuli that generate internal customer perceptions, influencing loyalty behavior. This approach is apt for exploring the factors that affect customer loyalty in the banking sector, a domain currently grappling with widespread issues of low customer loyalty. Customer loyalty is crucial for firms to establish a competitive advantage (Dick & Basu, 1994; Mehmood et al., 2012), and perceived value, formed post-interaction with products and services, constructs the initial stage of "perceived loyalty" (Wu et al., 2011).

The banking industry, as the focus of this study, confronts a pervasive challenge of low customer loyalty, a factor critical for building a competitive advantage (Dick & Basu, 1994; Mehmood et al., 2012). In this context, "perceived loyalty", which emanates from customers' valuation of received products and services, forms the initial phase of the loyalty hierarchy (Wu et al., 2011). Within the experience economy, the nature of experience domains is shifting towards increased intangibility and complexity, leading customers to seek deeper, more intrinsic experiences. The congruence of a company's products, services, and values plays a pivotal role in fostering positive perceived value (Farnham & Newbery, 2013). Experience domains gauged through the dynamics of service exchange, are instrumental in aligning what firms offer with customer expectations. This alignment is crucial for initiating a positive revenue cycle (Heskett et al., 2008). Moreover, experience domains are a key determinant in a cascade effect involving customer satisfaction, loyalty, and repurchase intention. Thus, maintaining high experience domains is essential for fostering customer loyalty, a vital component in the competitive positioning of banks (Brun et al., 2014).

In conclusion, this study establishes a comprehensive framework encompassing the following elements, as depicted in Fig. 1: The "Stimulus" is represented by the "experience domains" provided by the enterprise. The "Organism" is the internal "perceived value" experienced by the customer post-service. The "Response" is the resulting customer loyalty, which is a direct outcome of the internal perception. To analyze these components, the study employs the concept of NPS to segment customers. This approach enables an investigation into how different loyalty groups place varying emphases on service and perceived value. A primary objective is to explore strategies for positively transitioning customer loyalty from low to medium NPS levels. This is particularly relevant given the observed instability of customer loyalty within the financial industry. Based on this framework, the study proposes the following hypotheses to guide the empirical investigation:

H1. Spiritual Value has a positive influence on Customer Loyalty.

H2. Emotional Value has a positive influence on Customer Loyalty.

H3. Functional Value has a positive influence on Customer Loyalty.

H4. Product has a positive influence on Spiritual Value.

H5. Product has a positive influence on Emotional Value.

H6. Product has a positive influence on Functional Value.

H7. Service has a positive influence on Spiritual Value.

H8. Service has a positive influence on Emotional Value.

H9. Service has a positive influence on Functional Value.

H10. Environment has a positive influence on Spiritual Value.

H11. Environment has a positive influence on Emotional Value.

H12. Environment has a positive influence on Functional Value.

H13. Communication has a positive influence on Spiritual Value.

H14. Communication has a positive influence on Emotional Value.

H15. Communication has a positive influence on Functional Value.

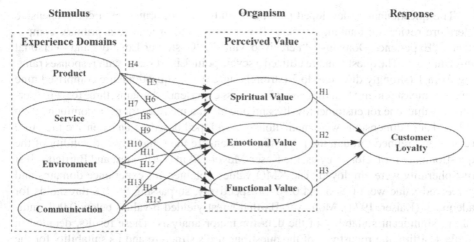

**Fig. 1.** Structural model

# 3  Methodology

In this study, a case-mixed analysis of a pure internet banking app "LINE Bank" is used to investigate how experience domains and perceived value affect changes in customer loyalty, and how this affects the shift in NPS from "low to medium". The research process includes: Stage 1 "Questionnaire Survey", Stage 2 "Model Construction and Hypothesis Measurement".

## 3.1  Data Collection and Sampling

The primary data for this study was collected through an online questionnaire survey, conducted from January 26, 2022, to February 14, 2022, in Taiwan. Focusing on LINE Bank as a case study, the target demographic comprised individuals who had previous experience using this service. To ensure the validity and relevance of the responses, screening questions were incorporated into the questionnaire. Before the development of the questionnaire, preliminary insights into the service's current state and customer behaviors and experiences were gathered. This was achieved through a series of semi-structured interviews. The interview guide focused on three key areas: user background, motivation, and context and experience with LINE Bank. These interviews, totaling six, were instrumental in uncovering core usage patterns and key motivational factors of the customers. Building upon the insights gained from these interviews, an online questionnaire was constructed. This questionnaire aimed to delve deeper into the findings, particularly focusing on the aspects highlighted in the interviews. A pilot test of this questionnaire was then conducted with a sample of 40 customers. The feedback received was critical in providing a comprehensive understanding of customer usage, service influence, and experience. This feedback also served as a guiding reference for the final design of the questionnaire.

The questionnaire, developed post-pilot study, was informed by a comprehensive literature review on banking services. It was structured around four primary components: "Experience Domains", "Perceived Value", "Customer Loyalty" and "Personal Information". The questionnaire utilized a seven-point Likert scale, with responses ranging from 1 (strongly disagree) to 7 (strongly agree). The questionnaire comprised nine levels of measurement: four dimensions to assess experience domains, three to gauge perceived value, one for customer loyalty, and one official measure for net recommendation value. These dimensions were meticulously developed based on an extensive literature review and refined through the pilot study. To ensure the reliability and validity of the questionnaire for factor analysis, the Kaser-Meyer-Olkin (KMO) test and Bartlett's Test of Sphericity were employed. The KMO values obtained for experience domains and perceived value were 0.886 and 0.904, respectively, surpassing the 0.8 thresholds for adequacy (Kaiser, 1974). Moreover, Bartlett's test yielded p-values below 0.001, indicating significant suitability of the data for factor analysis. These results, detailed in Table 1, affirm the robustness of the questionnaire's structure and its suitability for the intended analysis.

### 3.2 Measurement Model and Measurement Scales

For quantitative analysis, this study utilized Structural Equation Modeling (SEM), specifically employing Partial Least Squares (PLS) analysis via SmartPLS 4.0 software. SEM is a widely recognized method in social and behavioral sciences due to its effectiveness in exploring causal relationships among variables, validating research models, and facilitating multilevel analysis. The analytical process of SEM in this study included two stages: model construction and hypothesis testing. The measurement model concentrated on validating whether the chosen indicators accurately represented the latent variables. This involved examining the relationships between these indicators and their corresponding latent variables. The structural model, on the other hand, focused on the interrelations among the latent variables themselves, particularly investigating predictive and causal relationships between independent and dependent variables. To ensure the robustness of the models, the study first undertook covariance and reliability analyses during the measurement model evaluation phase. Subsequently, in the structural model evaluation phase, the efficacy of the structural model and its explanatory power were assessed using the R-Square Score. Finally, the significance and strength of the model paths were determined through bootstrap analysis, employing 5000 samples to test the assumptions.

Reliability is the reliability of the measurement results, which includes the consistency and stability of the measurement results. Consistency is required for the measures in the variables, and good stability is indicated by the fact that there are no large differences in the repeated measurements of the same group of questions. A high level of consistency and stability indicates a high level of reliability. In this study, Construct reliability (CR) and Cronbach's alpha were used. Composite reliability (CR) can be regarded as the internal consistency of a construct, and a value of CR greater than 0.6 indicates an acceptable level of construct consistency (Fornell & Larcker, 1981), while some scholars have adopted a more stringent criterion, which is a value greater than 0.7 (Hair, Black, Anderson, & Tatham, 2013); and Cronbach's α is a measure of reliability, and Cronbach's $\alpha$ is a measure of stability. Some scholars have adopted a more stringent criterion, suggesting that the composite reliability should be greater than 0.7 (Hair, Black, Anderson, & Tatham, 2013), while the Cronbach's alpha coefficient should be acceptable with a criterion of greater than 0.7, and greater than 0.8 is considered to be good (Nunnally, 1978). Validity refers to the validity of a measure, and a high validity indicates the truthfulness and accuracy of the measurement results. Validity can be categorized into Convergent zvalidity and Discriminate Validity. Convergent validity refers to the high degree of correlation between the measures of a variable when measured by the same or different methods. Factor loadings: The correlation between the variables and the factors should reach a standard value of 0.5 or more (Nunnally, 1978). Average Variance Extracted (AVE): the average explanatory power of the variables over the latent variables, which should reach a standard value of 0.5 or above (Fornell & Larcker, 1981), with higher coefficients indicating better convergent validity. The discriminant validity is the correlation between different variables, and if it has the discriminant validity, it means that several variables are different from each other and have differentiation. The test of discriminant validity is based on Fornell & Larcker's standard, which consists of (1) the correlation coefficients between the variables should be less than 0.85 (Klein et al., 2004). (2) The square root of the mean variable extraction of each variable should be larger than the correlation coefficient of each variable (Fornell & Larcker, 1981). (3) In a cross-loading matrix, the individual metric loadings of one variable need to be higher than the loadings of the other variables (Chin, 1998). In this study, the Coefficient of Determination ($R^2$) was used to assess the explanatory power of the structural model, and the value closer to 1 means higher explanatory power, and the $R^2$ value close to 0.50 can be regarded as medium explanatory power, and the $R^2$ value close to 0.75 can be regarded as high explanatory power (Hairet al., 2014).

# 4   Results

## 4.1   Descriptive Statistics

A total of 437 questionnaires were collected. After excluding invalid samples, a total of 370 valid samples were collected, representing 84.67% of the total sample. Among the valid samples, there were 263 females, accounting for 71.1% of the total sample, and 107 males, accounting for 28.9% of the total sample. The majority of the respondents were young and medium-aged, aged 21–30, with a total of 260 respondents, accounting for 70.3% of the total sample, followed by those aged 31–40, with a total of 56 respondents, accounting for 15.1% of the total sample. The occupation of most respondents was student, with a total of 122 respondents (32.7%). Disposable income was an open-ended question, with the highest percentage of respondents in the range of NT$10,001 - NT$30,000, with 113 respondents (30.5%), followed by NT$30,001 - NT$150,000, with 111 respondents (30%).

## 4.2   Measurement Model Assessment

Tables 2 and 3 summarize the evaluation of the model during the model measurement phase of the study. The results show that the questionnaire meets the criteria for each

**Table 1.** Summary of items.

| Variables | Code | Item content | References |
|---|---|---|---|
| **Experience Domains** | **Product** | | Kaabachi, S., Ben Mrad, S., & Barreto, T. (2022) Kotler & Armstrong (2015) |
| | PR1 | LINE Bank provides me suitable selection of products/services, e.g., Time Deposit, Quick Credit | |
| | PR2 | LINE Bank provides a wide range of products/service packages, e.g., transferring money, managing finances, borrowing, etc | |
| | PR3 | LINE Bank provides the products/services with the features I want, e.g., free transfer fee | |
| | PR4 | LINE Bank provides the product/service that fulfills what I need | |
| | **Service** | | Shankar & Jebarajakirthy (2019) Parasuraman, A., Zeithaml, V. A., & Malhotra, A. (2005) |
| | SE1 | I can open an account in LINE Bank easily | |
| | SE2 | I can deposit money in LINE Bank easily | |
| | SE3 | I can finish transactions in LINE Bank easily | |
| | SE4 | I can retrieve the accurate transaction details on my account | |
| | **Environment** | | Kaabachi et al. (2022) |
| | EN1 | LINE Bank has a great reward system | |

(*continued*)

**Table 1.** (*continued*)

| Variables | Code | Item content | References |
|---|---|---|---|
| | EN2 | The app design that includes the user interface and user experience between LINE Bank and Line Ecosystem are consistent | |
| | EN3 | I can seamlessly move between LINE Bank and Line Ecosystem, e.g., LINE Pay and LINE TV | |
| | EN4 | I can seamlessly move between LINE Bank and other platforms or channels, e.g., online stores, department stores | |
| | EN5 | LINE Bank provides various service scenarios that fulfill what I need | |
| | **Communication** | | Windasari et al. (2022) |
| | CO1 | Debit Card provided by LINE Bank is different from other banks | |
| | CO2 | Information and interface provided by LINE Bank about its services is simple and easy to understand | |
| | CO3 | Financial products provided by LINE Bank are different from other banks | |
| **Perceived Value** | **Spiritual Value** | | Windasari et al. (2022) Schuitema et al. (2013) |
| | SV1 | LINE Bank has a good reputation | |
| | SV2 | Brand Image of LINE Bank suits me better compared with the other digital-only banks in Taiwan | |
| | SV3 | Opinions and usage from people around me led me to use LINE Bank | |

(*continued*)

**Table 1.** (*continued*)

| Variables | Code | Item content | References |
|---|---|---|---|
| | **Emotional Value** | | Windasari et al. (2022) Yang et al. (2004) |
| | EV1 | Using LINE Bank is safe and secure | |
| | EV2 | LINE Bank is easy to use | |
| | EV3 | Using LINE Bank is interesting | |
| | **Functional Value** | | Windasari et al. (2022) Babin& Darden & Griffin(1994) |
| | FV1 | LINE Bank is convenient | |
| | FV2 | LINE Bank saves my time and cost | |
| | FV3 | LINE Bank provides what I need | |
| **Customer Loyalty** | LO1 | I intend to continue using LINE Bank | Gronholdt, Martensen& Kristensen (2000) |
| | LO2 | I would like to say positive things about LINE Bank to other people | |

Notes: The Cronbach-a coefficients for Product, Service, Environment, Communication, Spiritual Value, Emotional Value, Functional Value, and Customer Loyalty, segmented by low-to-medium NPS categories, are 0.868, 0.859, 0.877, 0.838, 0.826, 0.866, 0.911, 0.849, respectively, and the total reliability of the questionnaire is 0.968

of the tests, is free of covariance has good reliability, and meets the criteria for both convergent and discriminant validity.

### 4.3 Structural Model Assessment

In order to confirm the linkage of the hypotheses, this study conducted structural model evaluation after the measurement model evaluation. Figure 2 shows the modeling results of the structural equations including R-Square, path significance, and path coefficient for each variable. The result shows that the smallest $R^2$ of the variables is 0.604, which is greater than 0.5, so the structural model has moderate explanatory power. Table 4 shows the results of hypothesis checking in this study.

Except for H2, H10 and H11, all relationships are significant statistically, as seen in Table 4, as all p-values are < 0.05. More specifically, Customer Loyalty was favorably associated with Spiritual Value ($\rho < 0.001$, $\beta = 0.310$) and Functional Value($\rho < 0.001$, $\beta = 0.481$). Spiritual Value was favorably associated with Product($\rho < 0.05$, $\beta = 0.175$), Service($\rho < 0.05$, $\beta = 0.175$) and Communication($\rho < 0.001$, $\beta = 0.441$). Similarly, Functional Value was favorably associated with Product($\rho < 0.001$, $\beta = 0.249$), Service($\rho < 0.001$, $\beta = 0.311$), Environment($\rho < 0.001$, $\beta = 0.221$) and Communication($\rho < 0.001$, $\beta = 0.215$).

**Table 2.** The result of measurement model assessment.

| Construct scales | Code | VIF | Cronbach's α | CR | Outer loadings | AVE |
|---|---|---|---|---|---|---|
| Product | PR1 | 2.080 | 0.868 | 0.910 | 0.845 | 0.717 |
|  | PR2 | 1.683 |  |  | 0.768 |  |
|  | PR3 | 2.457 |  |  | 0.876 |  |
|  | PR4 | 2.584 |  |  | 0.893 |  |
| Service | SE1 | 2.042 | 0.859 | 0.904 | 0.841 | 0.703 |
|  | SE2 | 1.981 |  |  | 0.816 |  |
|  | SE3 | 2.588 |  |  | 0.890 |  |
|  | SE4 | 1.817 |  |  | 0.804 |  |
| Environment | EN1 | 1.706 | 0.877 | 0.910 | 0.760 | 0.671 |
|  | EN2 | 2.309 |  |  | 0.830 |  |
|  | EN3 | 2.401 |  |  | 0.820 |  |
|  | EN4 | 2.196 |  |  | 0.829 |  |
|  | EN5 | 2.156 |  |  | 0.852 |  |
| Communication | CO1 | 1.751 | 0.838 | 0.902 | 0.860 | 0.755 |
|  | CO2 | 2.399 |  |  | 0.896 |  |
|  | CO3 | 2.077 |  |  | 0.850 |  |
| Spiritual Value | SV1 | 1.987 | 0.826 | 0.896 | 0.883 | 0.741 |
|  | SV2 | 1.933 |  |  | 0.872 |  |
|  | SV3 | 1.745 |  |  | 0.827 |  |
| Emotional Value | EV1 | 2.188 | 0.866 | 0.918 | 0.869 | 0.788 |
|  | EV2 | 2.651 |  |  | 0.918 |  |
|  | EV3 | 2.109 |  |  | 0.876 |  |
| Functional Value | FV1 | 3.540 | 0.911 | 0.944 | 0.931 | 0.849 |
|  | FV2 | 2.547 |  |  | 0.895 |  |
|  | FV3 | 3.793 |  |  | 0.938 |  |
| Customer Loyalty | LO1 | 2.191 | 0.849 | 0.930 | 0.930 | 0.869 |
|  | LO2 | 2.191 |  |  | 0.934 |  |

Source: Authors' calculation

**Table 3.** Results of discriminant validity using Fornell-Larcker criterion.

|    | PR    | SE    | EN    | CO    | SV    | EV    | FV    | LO    |
|----|-------|-------|-------|-------|-------|-------|-------|-------|
| PR | 0.847 |       |       |       |       |       |       |       |
| SE | 0.674 | 0.838 |       |       |       |       |       |       |
| EN | 0.679 | 0.643 | 0.819 |       |       |       |       |       |
| CO | 0.628 | 0.623 | 0.717 | 0.869 |       |       |       |       |
| SV | 0.638 | 0.632 | 0.647 | 0.731 | 0.861 |       |       |       |
| EV | 0.678 | 0.708 | 0.643 | 0.688 | 0.767 | 0.888 |       |       |
| FV | 0.744 | 0.754 | 0.744 | 0.723 | 0.697 | 0.778 | 0.922 |       |
| LO | 0.685 | 0.620 | 0.634 | 0.580 | 0.686 | 0.666 | 0.739 | 0.932 |

Source: Authors' calculation

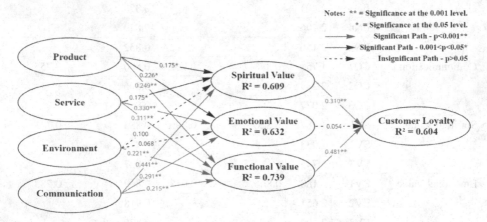

**Fig. 2.** Results of structural equation modeling.

**Table 4.** Hypothesis testing results

| Hypothesis/path | Standard deviation | T-statistics | P-values | Results |
|-----------------|--------------------|--------------|----------|---------|
| H1. SV → LO | 0.094 | 3.298 | 0.001** | Supported |
| H2. EV → LO | 0.094 | 0.578 | 0.564 | Not Supported |
| H3. FV → LO | 0.087 | 5.546 | 0.000** | Supported |
| H4. PR → SV | 0.063 | 2.769 | 0.006* | Supported |
| H5. PR → EV | 0.081 | 2.810 | 0.005* | Supported |

(*continued*)

**Table 4.** *(continued)*

| Hypothesis/path | Standard deviation | T-statistics | P-values | Results |
|---|---|---|---|---|
| H6. PR → FV | 0.062 | 4.030 | 0.000** | Supported |
| H7. SE → SV | 0.072 | 2.424 | 0.015* | Supported |
| H8. SE → EV | 0.075 | 4.429 | 0.000** | Supported |
| H9. SE → FV | 0.061 | 5.097 | 0.000** | Supported |
| H10. EN → SV | 0.082 | 1.218 | 0.223 | Not Supported |
| H11. EN → EV | 0.081 | 0.846 | 0.398 | Not Supported |
| H12. EN → FV | 0.062 | 3.541 | 0.000** | Supported |
| H13. CO → SV | 0.075 | 5.878 | 0.000** | Supported |
| H14. CO → EV | 0.074 | 3.948 | 0.000** | Supported |
| H15. CO → FV | 0.064 | 3.333 | 0.001** | Supported |

Source: Authors' calculation

## 5  Discussion

The results of this study show that the majority of LINE Bank users are students between the ages of 21 and 30, and it seems to imply the most of the respondents are students and from Generation Z. The results of this study show that LINE Bank's experience domains and perceived value affect the shift from low NPS to medium NPS. The S-O-R theoretical framework was used to investigate the effects of experience domains and perceived value on the transfer from low NPS to medium NPS, and it was found that functional value (H3) had the greatest effect on customer loyalty, followed by spiritual value (H1), and emotional value (H2) did not affect the transfer of loyalty. Reviewing the results of the questionnaire, it can be inferred that this may be because when using pure Internet banking services, users of low and medium NPS are more concerned about convenience and ease of use, as well as how much money they can save about their interests. Spiritual value also affects customer loyalty transfer this may be because low and medium NPS users are more concerned about whether LINE Bank has a good image, whether the style and image are suitable for them, and other people's opinions on the use of LINE Bank, etc. The spiritual value affects the loyalty transfer of low and medium NPS users. Emotional values do not affect loyalty transfer, probably because they believe that purely Internet banking products should be safe and enjoyable to use.

The study's findings suggest that optimizing brand reputation and minimizing customer dissatisfaction at LINE Bank could be effectively achieved by focusing on enhancing both Functional and Spiritual Values. Functional Value, having a more substantial impact, is significantly influenced by all four experience domains, particularly the 'Service' aspect. This highlights the importance of making financial services user-friendly and easily navigable, considering their inherent complexity. If LINE Bank wants to optimize its brand reputation and reduce the negative impact on customers, it can focus on enhancing customers' Functional Value and Spiritual Value. Functional Value, having a more substantial impact, is significantly influenced by all four experience domains, particularly the 'Service' aspect. This highlights the importance of making financial services user-friendly and easily navigable, considering their inherent complexity. On the other hand, Spiritual Value is primarily driven by effective 'Communication'. While the 'Product' and 'Service' dimensions exert weaker influences on Spiritual Value, they still play a role in reinforcing the brand's image. LINE Bank must maintain consistent and meaningful communication with its customers, which helps in building a positive brand image and reputation. Incorporating unique product features, such as simplified friend transfers, and increasing service usability can augment this effort.

For LINE Bank to focus on creating an 'exclusive value' that minimizes negative impacts on customers, starting with 'Functional Value' as communicated through the 'Service' experience is recommended. When the service experience meets customers' personal needs at various stages effectively, it not only satisfies but also elevates their perception of value to a spiritual level. This transformation from functional to spiritual value can lead to enhanced customer satisfaction and loyalty, further solidifying LINE Bank's competitive position in the market.

It is worth noting that while "functional value" is one of the main directions for optimizing the customer experience, improving the experience of low and medium-group customers also requires attention to their "spiritual value", which may mean that for this group, Generation Z, pure online banking services not only need to optimize customer experience from the four dimensions of experience domains but also pay more attention to the spiritual value of customers. Therefore, the functions provided by online banking services may no longer be limited to basic deposit and withdrawal and other related financial services, but they may be more concerned about whether the brand image and value concept of the enterprise is in line with their spiritual values and values. The "communication" experience has the most significant impact on "spiritual values", and it can be understood that "communication" is the best way to establish a "positive spiritual value" experience. Companies need to strengthen communication with customers to tap into their needs and convey a sense of reassurance and trustworthiness to attract customers to use their products. Users who perceive full value from the communication experience have a higher chance of establishing positive spiritual value. A review of the questionnaire revealed that the experience of "communication" varied among the low NPS. On the whole, novelty, simplicity, and modernity were the main feelings of customers in the communication experience, while "familiarity with LINE and good experiences in the past" led to a "trustworthy brand reputation" and "complete and consistent innovation" shaped a "truly innovative financial service", which made customers feel that LINE Bank was better than other banks and in line with the value recognition, and thus most likely to create positive effects in terms of competitor selection and willingness to do business. The card face design In addition to the visual image that creates a short-term, strong attraction, the "card face design" also creates an implicit communication effect that conveys a differentiated market positioning and serves as one of the ways to convey "newness", which in turn achieves the effect of increasing motivation to apply and value recognition. The simple communication style in marketing and product information not only allows customers to learn on their own in terms of functional value but also mentally enables some customers to "choose the most suitable financial service". In addition, the simple communication style of the marketing and product information not only allows customers to learn about the functionality and value of the product, but also gives some customers a sense of belonging to the financial product that best suits their needs, and the feeling of being able to confidently control their assets.

# 6 Conclusion

To explore the relationship between customer experience and loyalty and the strategy of loyalty transfer, this study is based on the current development of the industry and the existing literature, as well as the industry and academic aspects, to deepen the understanding of the brand experience of the Real Pure Internet Banking, and to examine in both directions the service perspectives that can be used to establish a loyal relationship. From a quantitative perspective, we analyze the hypotheses of the two parts of the research model, firstly, how experience domains as an external stimulus affect intrinsic perceptual values, and the extent to which the three perceptual values affect customer loyalty, and objectively analyze the validity of the hypotheses, their path relationships, and their strengths. The study's results proved that Functional Value, followed by Spiritual Value, is the most influential factor in the transfer of loyalty of pure Internet banking customers. All four service qualities highly influence the "Functional Value" of Internet-only customers, while the "Spiritual Value" is influenced by "Product, Service and Communication" and not by "Environmental" factors, with "Communication" being the most influential factor on the "Spiritual Value". The impact of the research topic will be extended to the related digitalized financial services other than pure Internet banking, breaking through the existing level of exploration of financial innovation service strategies.

To optimize the functional value for its users, LINE Bank could focus on streamlining customer interactions. Introducing AI-driven features that simplify repetitive tasks and enhance the user experience could significantly increase ease of use. AI-assisted financial services, offering intuitive and user-friendly interfaces, could play a pivotal role in enhancing customer satisfaction. In terms of elevating spiritual value, a more personalized communication strategy could be key. Utilizing AI technology to create personalized service assistants and delivering brand messages that resonate with customers' values could strengthen customer engagement. In-app push notifications tailored to individual preferences could foster a deeper connection between the bank and its users. Furthermore, aligning with the values of Generation Z, an emphasis on social responsibility and sustainability could be beneficial. By integrating socially responsible and SDG-aligned financial products, such as green investment options or features enabling charitable donations, LINE Bank can extend its experience domains beyond traditional banking. This not only meets the basic financial needs but also aligns with the brand's commitment to social responsibility, appealing to customers' desire to make a positive impact.

Further, to optimize the functional value of LINE Bank, it may be possible to simplify repetitive operations for customers by introducing more customer-friendly features, such as artificial intelligence to assist in financial services, making it easier for customers to use. Optimizing LINE Bank's spiritual value may be achieved by implementing a more personalized communication strategy, such as using artificial intelligence technology to allow customers to set up personalized service assistants or delivering brand messages in line with customer values through in-app push notifications. At the same time, it emphasizes its commitment to social responsibility and sustainability to strengthen its brand image and resonate with Gen Z values. To satisfy both functional and spiritual values, LINE Bank could also consider developing financial products that are socially responsible or in line with the SDGs, such as green investment or charitable donation features, which not only provide basic financial services but also demonstrate the brand's commitment to giving back to society. Through these concrete measures, LINE Bank can more effectively improve the quality of its services and increase customer loyalty, thereby contributing to NPS loyalty transfer. Overall, this study helps pure Internet banking firms to understand their customers across the four dimensions of experience domains, which in turn guides them to improve their products and optimize the customer experience, as well as to examine the details of experience domains in terms of loyalty levels, to conduct experience domains Management and minimize negative customer impact. By implementing these strategies, LINE Bank can enhance the quality of its experience domains and foster stronger customer loyalty, contributing to an effective NPS loyalty transfer.

This research offers invaluable insights for online-only banking firms, aiding them in comprehending customer perspectives across the four domains of experience. It propels them towards enhancing products, optimizing customer experiences, and examining service delivery nuances at different loyalty levels for effective Service Quality Management. Academically, it deepens the discourse on customer experience in pure online banking. Through the S-O-R theoretical framework, it establishes a link between digital service innovation and loyalty in the banking industry and provides a benchmark for reference, adding verifiable loyalty metrics to the total experience architecture of people-experience-brand, enriching the competitive landscape of the financial ecosystem.

# References

1. Ajzen, I., Fishbein, M.: Attitudes and normative beliefs as factors influencing behavioral intentions. J. Pers. Soc. Psychol. 21(1), 1 (1972)
2. Babin, B.J., Darden, W.R., Griffin, M.: Work and/or fun: measuring hedonic and utilitarian shopping value. J. Consum. Res. 20, 644–656 (1994). https://doi.org/10.1086/209376
3. Bagram, M.M.M., Khan, S.: Attaining customer loyalty! The role of consumer attitude and consumer behavior. Int. Rev. Manag. Bus. Res. 1(1), 1–8 (2012)
4. Barquin, S.: Asia's digital banking race: giving customers what they want. McKinsey & Company (2018). https://www.mckinsey.com/~/media/mckinsey/industries/financial%20s ervices/our%20insights/reaching%20asias%20digital%20banking%20customers/asias-dig ital-banking-race-web-final.pdf
5. Brun, I., Rajaobelina, L., Ricard, L.: Online relationship quality: scale development and initial testing. Int. J. Bank Mark. 32(1), 527 (2014). https://doi.org/10.1108/IJBM-02-2013-0022
6. Chin, W.W.: The partial least squares approach to structural equation modeling. Mod. Methods Bus. Res. 295(2), 295–336 (1998)
7. Dick, A.S., Basu, K.: Customer loyalty: toward an integrated conceptual framework. J. Acad. Mark. Sci. 22, 99–113 (1994)

8. Deloitte Switzerland: DIGITALISATION OF BANKING online during the COVID-19 pandemic (2022). https://www2.deloitte.com/ch/en/pages/financialservices/articles/digitalis ation-banking-online-covid-19-pandemic.html

9. Farnham, K., Newbery, P.: Experience Design: A Framework for Integrating Brand, Experience, and Value. John Wiley & Sons (2013)

10. Financial Supervisory Commission R.O.C.(Taiwan). Digital deposit account business statistics. Banking Bureau of the Financial Supervisory Authority Commission (2023). https://www.fsc.gov.tw/userfiles/file/%E6%95%B8%E4%BD%8D%E5%AD%98%E6% AC%BE%E5%B8%B3%E6%88%B6%E9%96%8B%E6%88%B6%E6%95%B8%E7% B5%B1%E8%A8%88112Q3.zip

11. Fornell, C., Larcker, D.F.: Evaluating structural equation models with unobservable variables and measurement error. J. Mark. Res. **18**, 39–50 (1981). https://doi.org/10.2307/3151312

12. Gronholdt, L., Martensen, A., Kristensen, K.: The relationship between customer satisfaction and loyalty: cross-industry differences. Total Qual. Manag. **11**(4–6), 509–514 (2000). https:// doi.org/10.1080/09544120050007823

13. Hair, J.F., Black, W.C., Babin, B.J., Anderson, R.E.: Multivariate Data Analysis. Pearson Education Limited (2013)

14. Hair, J.F., Gabriel, M., Patel, V.: AMOS covariance-based structural equation modeling (CB-SEM): guidelines on its application as a marketing research tool. Braz. J. Mark. **13**(2) (2014)

15. Heskett, J.L., Jones, T.O., Loveman, G.W., Earl Sasser, J.W., Schlesinger, L.A.: Putting the service-profit chain to work. Harv. Bus. Rev. (2008). https://hbr.org/2008/07/putting-the-ser vice-profit-chain-to-work

16. Huang, J., Lai, M.T.: X Thinking. Tianjin Science and Technology Press (2020). http://www. xthinking.cn/tysw/index_128.aspx

17. Johnson, M.W., Christensen, C.M., Kagermann, H.: Reinventing your business model. Harv. Bus. Rev. **86**(12), 50–59 (2008)

18. Kaabachi, S., Ben Mrad, S., Barreto, T.: Reshaping the bank experience for GEN Z in France. J. Mark. Anal. **10**, 1–13 (2022). https://doi.org/10.1057/s41270-022-00173-8

19. Kaiser, H.F.: An index of factorial simplicity. Psychometrika **39**(1), 31–36 (1974)

20. Keller, K.L., Swaminathan, V.: Strategic Brand Management: Building, Measuring, and Managing Brand Equity, Global Edition (2019)

21. Kemp, S.: Digital 2023: Taiwan (2023). https://datareportal.com/reports/digital-2023-taiwan

22. Klein, J., Dawar, N.: Corporate social responsibility and consumers' attributions and brand evaluations in a product–harm crisis. Int. J. Res. Mark. **21**(3), 203–217 (2004)

23. Kotler, P., Burton, S., Deans, K., Brown, L., Armstrong, G.: Marketing. Pearson Higher Education AU (2015)

24. Lai, M.T., Tang, H.-H.: Experience design's transformation towards experience-driven transformation: a practical perspective (2023)

25. Maslow, A.H.: Preface to motivation theory. Psychosom. Med. **5**(1), 85–92 (1943)

26. Mehmood, M.M., Bagram, Khan, S.: Attaining Customer Loyalty! The Role of Consumer Attitude and Consumer Behavior. Int. Rev. Manag. Bus. Res. (2012). https://www.scinapse. io/papers/2108811116

27. Mehrabian, A., Russell, J.A.: An Approach to Environmental Psychology. The MIT Press (pp. xii, 266) (1974)

28. Mohammed, S., Sha, N., Uddin, M.A.: Determinants of Islamic banks acceptance in Oman. Int. Rev. Manag. Mark. **7**(1), 398–402 (2017)

29. Neal, W.D.: Satisfaction is nice, but value drives loyalty. Mark. Res. **11**(1), 20–23 (1999)

30. Nunnally, J.C.: Psychometric theory (2d ed). McGraw-Hill (1978)

31. Parasuraman, A., Zeithaml, V.A., Berry, L.L.: A conceptual model of service quality and its implications for future research. J. Mark. **49**(4), 41–50 (1985)

32. Parasuraman, A., Zeithaml, V.A., Malhotra, A.: E-S-QUAL: a multiple-item scale for assessing electronic service quality. J. Serv. Res. **7**(3), 213–233 (2005). https://doi.org/10.1177/1094670504271156

33. Peltoniemi, M., Vuori, E.: Business ecosystem as the new approach to complex adaptive business environments. In: Proceedings of eBusiness Research Forum, vol. 2, no. 22, pp. 267–281 (2004)

34. Pine, B.J., Gilmore, J.H.: Welcome to the Experience Economy, vol. 76, no. 4, pp. 97–105. Harvard Business Review Press, Cambridge, MA, USA (1998)

35. PwC Survey: Digital Banking in Indonesia (2018). (n.d.)

36. Reichheld, F.F.: The One Number You Need to Grow. Harvard Business Review (2003). https://hbr.org/2003/12/the-one-number-you-need-to-grow

37. Reichheld, F.F., Markey, R.: The Ultimate Question 2.0: How Net Promoter Companies Thrive in a Customer-driven World. Harvard Business Press (2011)

38. Rojas, C., Camarero, C.: Visitors' experience, mood and satisfaction in a heritage context: evidence from an interpretation center. Tour. Manag. **29**, 525–537 (2008). https://doi.org/10.1016/j.tourman.2007.06.004

39. Saksonova, S., Kuzmina-Merlino, I.: Fintech as financial innovation—the possibilities and problems of implementation. Eur. Res. Stud. J. XX(Issue 3A), 961–973 (2017). https://doi.org/10.35808/ersj/757

40. Schuitema, G., Anable, J., Skippon, S., Kinnear, N.: The role of instrumental, hedonic and symbolic attributes in the intention to adopt electric vehicles. Transp. Res. Part A: Policy Pract. **48**, 39–49 (2013). https://doi.org/10.1016/j.tra.2012.10.004

41. Shankar, A., Jebarajakirthy, C.: The influence of e-banking service quality on customer loyalty: a moderated mediation approach. Int. J. Bank Mark. **37**(5), 1119–1142 (2019). https://doi.org/10.1108/IJBM-03-2018-0063

42. Sweeney, J.C., Soutar, G.N.: Consumer perceived value: the development of a multiple item scale. J. Retailing **77**(2), 203–220 (2001)

43. Tsai, M.-H., Liu, Y.-K.: Research on experience strategy design of new tea drink brands under scenario thinking——taking HEYTEA as an example. Art Sci. Technol. **34**(7), 178–180 (2021)

44. Vargo, S.L., Lusch, R.F.: Service-dominant logic: continuing the evolution. J. Acad. Mark. Sci. **36**, 1–10 (2008)

45. Waqas, M., Hamzah, Z.L.B., Salleh, N.A.M.: Customer experience: a systematic literature review and consumer culture theory-based conceptualisation. Manag. Rev. Q. **71**(1), 135–176 (2021)

46. Windasari, N.A., Kusumawati, N., Larasati, N., Amelia, R.P.: Digital-only banking experience: insights from gen Y and gen Z. J. Innov. Knowl. **7**(2), 100170 (2022). https://doi.org/10.1016/j.jik.2022.100170

47. Wu, L.-W., Chang, K.-H., Chung, P.-M.: The exploration of perceived value, relationship quality, and loyalty stage. Taiwan Acad. Manag. J. **11**(1), 1–28 (2011). https://doi.org/10.6295/TAMJ.2011.1101.01

48. Yang, Z., Jun, M., Peterson, R.T.: Measuring customer perceived online service quality. Int. J. Oper. Prod. Manag. **24**(11), 1149 (2004)

49. Zeithaml, V.A.: Consumer perceptions of price, quality, and value: a means-end model and synthesis of evidence. J. Mark. **52**(3), 2–22 (1988)

50. Zeithaml, V.A.: Service quality, profitability, and the economic worth of customers: what we know and what we need to learn. J. Acad. Mark. Sci. **28**, 67–85 (2000)

**Design for Cognitive Disabilities**

# Scaffolding for Inclusive Co-design: Supporting People with Cognitive and Learning Disabilities

Leandro S. Guedes[1(✉)], Irene Zanardi[1], Marilina Mastrogiuseppe[2],
Stefania Span[3], and Monica Landoni[1]

[1] Università della Svizzera Italiana (USI), Lugano, Switzerland
{leandro.soares.guedes,irene.zanardi,monica.landoni}@usi.ch
[2] University of Trieste, Trieste, Italy
marilina.mastrogiuseppe@units.it
[3] Cooperativa Sociale Trieste Integrazione a m. ANFFAS Onlus, Trieste, Italy
http://luxia.inf.usi.ch/

**Abstract.** This paper presents a framework for integrating scaffolding in co-design sessions with people with cognitive and learning disabilities. While scaffolding has been recognized for enhancing participant engagement in co-design, its application lacks standardization. Our study pursues three primary objectives: (1) Present two case studies involving an Augmented Reality application and the ACCESS+ museum application, highlighting specific user needs; (2) Adapt the concept of scaffolding to support the informal learning needed to interact with technology while having an active role in co-design (3) Discuss how to revisit collaborative design to become more accessible and inclusive as to empower people with cognitive and learning disabilities. Through a methodical approach of task subdivision, prompt initiation, assessment of understanding, support through prompting and fading, and repetition if needed, our framework demonstrates how tailored scaffolding can effectively engage participants, emphasizing the importance of integrating diverse perspectives in technology development.

**Keywords:** Co-design · Scaffolding · Method · Cognitive and Learning Disabilities · Intellectual Disabilities · Guidelines · Inclusion

## 1 Introduction

As computing and information technology are growing, so are diverse ways of providing accessible and inclusive interactions. The generation of new or dedicated approaches to co-design is essential for creating accessible experiences and providing inclusive interaction with technology. Including people with disabilities in designing new tools provides real accessible solutions for everyone. While this is well known nowadays, researchers and practitioners still lack guidelines and methods to work with participants with different abilities.

An important target group that proportionally lacks literature [20] is people with cognitive and learning disabilities. In this paper, we use the W3C COGA

© The Author(s), under exclusive license to Springer Nature Switzerland AG 2024
M. Antona and C. Stephanidis (Eds.): HCII 2024, LNCS 14697, pp. 151–170, 2024.
https://doi.org/10.1007/978-3-031-60881-0_10

definition of cognitive disabilities [31], which includes, but is not limited to: cognitive disabilities, learning disabilities, intellectual disabilities, and specific learning disabilities. For this reason, and considering our target participants, we decided to cluster our work under the name "cognitive and learning disabilities."

When running technological projects aimed at people with cognitive and learning disabilities, supporting procedures should be used to enable participants to solve a task, express their ideas and desires, or both [7]. Based on the homonymous metaphor [45], Scaffolding, an evidence-based educational practice (EBE), has a long history of application and success in facilitating the learning of people with learning disabilities. Typically it involves a structured interaction between a knowledgeable other (e.g., educator, researcher, caregiver, support worker) and a learning protagonist (child or adult), intending to help the latter to achieve a specific goal by providing tailored assistance [8]. This paper involves technology and tools as a way to assist people with cognitive disabilities (Fig. 1). The concept of scaffolding is conceived around introducing temporary support to help achieve an objective that would otherwise prove out of reach. The supportive elements are subsequently removed when they are no longer needed. Scaffolding enables transferring these symbolic elements into different contexts, such as the well-known learning one and the specific acquisition of technological skills.

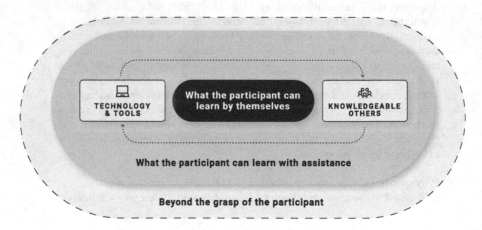

**Fig. 1.** Participants' knowledge and assistance with scaffolding, based on [41].

Scaffolding procedures seem particularly promising in supporting co-design activities in the various phases of ideation, prototyping, and evaluation as well as earlier on during user data collection leading to the extraction of user requirements. However, we could not find any paper introducing guidelines to date. This paper strives to comprehensively respond to the research question, "How can scaffolding effectively assist and empower individuals with cognitive and learning disabilities to participate in the co-design of innovative technologies?"

We will focus on how scaffolding can help engage and empower participants involved in co-design activities, taking care of all the different design steps. Starting from making sure the focus of the design is clearly and effectively communicated, supporting the roles participants can play, and facilitating any proposed activity while collecting and assessing new ideas as triggered by having task-oriented interaction with existing tools. All of this is accomplished by using as many communication channels as appropriate, checking the need for further explanations, and providing those when needed. In doing this we also acknowledge the different forms of prompts to be accessible to our co-designers. In this paper, we make three overall contributions to the HCI community:

1. We adapt and expand the concept of scaffolding first introduced by Wood et al. [45] as a metaphor to support learning, to be used in the collaborative design of technology with people with cognitive and learning disabilities;
2. Describe case studies to empirically expose how scaffolding support can empower people with cognitive and learning disabilities during co-design sessions;
3. Propose scaffolding steps as guidelines toward inclusive co-design.

This paper is organized as follows: we introduce the background and related works in Sect. 2. In Sect. 3, we outline the research methodology employed in our studies. In Sect. 4, we discuss two case studies that feature the key takeaways from co-design sessions and showcase the role played by scaffolding. We then introduce a framework for scaffolding in Sect. 5. Then, we engage in discussion, elaborate on limitations and future considerations in Sect. 6, and finally reflect and share lessons learned in Sect. 7.

## 2 Background and Related Work

### 2.1 People with Cognitive and Learning Disabilities

Cognitive and learning disabilities encompass a broad range of conditions that may affect abilities to: learn, communicate, read, write, perform math, or process sensory input; comprehend or process new or complex information and acquire new skills; and use memory and attention or visual, language, or numerical thinking. While some cognitive functions might be impaired, others can remain unaffected or even contribute to talents [23]. Cognitive and learning disabilities can also involve intellectual impairments affecting understanding and language skills.

Beyond cognitive abilities, social and practical domains play a crucial role. The social domain covers empathy, interpersonal skills, and the ability to form friendships, while the practical domain involves self-management in education, work, and leisure [36]. People with the same diagnosis can exhibit a high degree of variability in characteristics, influenced by differences in cognitive skills like language, memory, attention, and visual-perceptual abilities [40]. This variability affects personality and social-practical environmental adaptation.

Terminology and classifications for these disorders vary internationally [42]. Interventions in cognitive disabilities follow a bio-psycho-social approach, emphasizing person-environment interaction and the importance of individualized supports to enhance functioning [30]. Effective interventions, under the framework of evidence-based education (EBE), must be tailored to the individual's specific needs and environmental interactions, as outlined by the International Classification of Functioning, Disability and Health (ICF) [26]. Scaffolding methods within EBE have proven effective in supporting the learning processes of those with disabilities [22].

## 2.2 Scaffolding

Over the past two decades, the concept of scaffolding has become a key metaphor in psychology and education, initially representing how caregivers such as teachers assist in a child's learning and development. This idea, first elaborated by Wood, Bruner, and Ross [46], draws heavily from Vygotsky's concept of the zone of proximal development (ZPD) [41]. ZPD – as seen in Fig. 1 – represents the range where learners are capable only with support from someone with more knowledge or expertise. An enriched version of the metaphor has been created over the years, with applications to the study of parent-child and teacher-student interactions involving learners with learning disabilities (e.g. [35]).

In a comprehensive review of the field, van de Pol et al. [37] scrutinizes the most important areas of scaffolding:

1. **Contingency**: This involves the caregiver adjusting the level of assistance according to the learner's competence. Strategies the caregiver could use to personalize the learner's assistance include actions that can be executed simultaneously:
   - **Physical prompts**: Giving physical help, such as accompanying the learner's action with body movements.
   - **Gestural prompts**: Using gestures like pointing or nodding.
   - **Verbal prompts**: Providing verbal feedback, hints, or questions.
2. **Fading**: The gradual withdrawal of support as the learner gains more and more competence [9]. For example, reducing physical assistance from guiding a finger to less direct forms of help, like verbal prompts.
3. **Transfer of Responsibility**: As fading increases, the learner's responsibility to independently perform the task increases and evolves with the ultimate aim of achieving the action spontaneously, without the need for assistance.

Throughout the entire process, a pivotal role is played by evaluation strategies [38]. Effective support can be initiated and gradually ended based on the learner's responses to the received assistance. The explicit control of the analysis can help both parties to develop inter-subjectivity [28].

## 2.3   From Scaffolding to Co-design

Scaffolding has been increasingly used in recent years to explore social support in technology-mediated learning environments [3,50], as it improves learning and self-regulation while co-designing [50]. In this study, we refer to co-design as a verb to indicate the act of incorporating community members in the design process [49] to ensure the rights of individuals with cognitive disabilities [16].

Co-design developed from the long tradition of Participatory Design, and it incorporates a variety of methods and tools aimed at giving participants power over the design process. Because of the focus on user engagement, different approaches target different user groups, such as persons with disabilities [27]. When involving individuals with cognitive and learning disabilities, it is crucial to have multiple means of eliciting needs while also keeping attention and engagement [11]. As an example, Co-Design Beyond Words (CDBW) aims to facilitate various forms of expression that do not depend on verbal communication, which amounts to a reflection-in-action process [44]. To enhance user engagement and bridge the knowledge gap between researchers and participants, one approach is to involve users with concrete objects [11,44] or prototypes that can aid in increasing their involvement [6,13,34,47].

In this context, scaffolding has been used more or less implicitly to aid sessions. In HCI, Active Support (AS) investigates how varying degrees of engagement might be allowed through graded assistance, with fading serving as the key to reducing support [6]. This is particularly important when taking into account the different participation levels that might be attained throughout a session [34]. Regarding engagement with prototypes, [47] emphasizes the necessity of stimulating conversation to extract their viewpoints. To facilitate requirement elicitation, tools and materials themselves can act as a scaffold [15,25,44] and encourage engagement [10]. Their use also requires building or removing scaffolds *in situ* to accommodate the participant's experience [21]. Most broadly, scaffolding is used to structure not only the tasks but also the session itself [5], social relationships [44,48], collaboration between participants [39,43], and the environment [44].

While scaffolding has become common in co-design, there is no set of rules that standardize the approach for co-design tasks with people with cognitive and learning disabilities. As a result, our primary focus is on using scaffolding to encourage their active participation in co-design. We intend to formulate guidelines for scaffolding to aid designers in carrying out such studies effectively.

## 3   Methodology

This section presents a comprehensive overview of our data collection and analysis method, along with the ethical considerations we adhered to during the research process. It also provides detailed insights into the participants involved in our two case studies. These studies are practical applications of the scaffolding method in real-world co-design activities. Through them, we aim to deepen our understanding of scaffolding's role in enhancing collaborative design, thereby solidifying the foundations of our research findings.

## 3.1  Participants

Our research sessions included eight participants in total. In Case Study I, we had four participants (P1, P2, P3, and P4) attending in person and one participant (P5) attending virtually as she usually does. In Case Study II, we had seven participants (P1, P2, P3, P4, P6, P7, and P8). They are part of an association that supports people with cognitive and learning disabilities and actively involves them in studying several topics on display at the museum. The association recruited participants who were asked to interact with the application as part of their daily study routine. Nonetheless, participants could choose whether to be part of the study and be free to drop out at any point. Table 1 denotes the participant demographics for this case study.

**Table 1.** Participants described in all of the case studies presented in this paper.

| ID | Gender | Age | Country | Case Study | Disabilities |
|---|---|---|---|---|---|
| P1 | Woman | 20–25 | Italy | I and II | Moderate Cognitive Disabilities |
| P2 | Woman | 40–45 | Italy | I and II | Moderate Cognitive Disabilities |
| P3 | Man | 30–35 | Italy | I and II | Moderate Cognitive Disabilities and Epilepsy |
| P4 | Man | 60–65 | Italy | I and II | Mild Cognitive Disabilities and Tetraparesis |
| P5 | Woman | 30–35 | Italy | I | Mild Cognitive Disabilities |
| P6 | Woman | 50–55 | Italy | II | Moderate Cognitive Disabilities and Spastic Paraparesis |
| P7 | Woman | 50–55 | Italy | II | Moderate Cognitive Disabilities |
| P8 | Man | 25–30 | Italy | II | Moderate Cognitive Disabilities and Non-verbal |

## 3.2  Research Team and Collaboration

We worked with a multidisciplinary team during both case studies, including one educator and one assistant, a psychologist, and three computer science researchers. We collaborated with participants and professionals from the ANF-FAS support center and with the Trieste Natural History Museum, which also provided access to their content and physical space.

## 3.3  Data Collection and Analysis

We recorded audio and video in a local cloud service for future data analysis, and access was strictly limited to the researchers conducting the research. All procedures were conducted by the paper authors.

Each participant session included an Educator as participant assistant, providing support when needed; the collaborating psychologist took notes, while a researcher conducted the sessions. All potentially identifying information was redacted in the transcription process.

Qualitative analysis was conducted, and we coded the data to extract categories, highlights, and trends. We adapted Gibbs' Reflective Cycle [2] as a framework based on thematic analysis [1]. This reflective model, consisting of six stages – Description, Feelings, Evaluation, Analysis, Conclusion, and Action Plan – allowed us to deeply examine our interactions, identify points of success, and continuously improve our research approach. We gathered notes, photos, and videos collected from the aforementioned studies, and we identified common threads and patterns of experience, extracting insights useful for developing guidelines.

### 3.4 Ethical Considerations

We applied strict security protocols in handling participant data from our Case Studies. The partner association handled communicating consent, ensuring each participant and their legal guardians were aware of the study and informed them of the possibility of discontinuing participation at any time. Additionally, the research was reviewed and approved by the Ethics Committees of the institutions involved (USI – Decision CE-2023-11 – and ANFFAS).

## 4 Case Studies

The following case studies helped shape a co-design structure that focuses on increasing, and interpreting the participation of people with cognitive and learning disabilities. Each case study has its own goal, participant pool, assessment criteria, and findings.

### 4.1 Case Study I: AR Interaction

This Case Study revolves around scaffolding when designing an Augmented Reality (AR) application called AIMusem [14] and assessing the interaction and perception of AR by people with cognitive and learning disabilities before, during, or after a museum visit [12]. We designed and developed an application to test how AR can provide support and is perceived in this context. The project's primary objective was to create an inclusive AR experience that would assist participants in engaging with museum content. In this Case Study, we are focusing on the 3D dinosaur exhibits. Participants were instructed to complete three tasks using a smartphone camera (1) target the Quick Response (QR) codes of a brown dinosaur, (2) target the QR code of a white dinosaur, and (3) read the textual description or use a text-to-speech (TTS) feature to hear the text read aloud. Figure 2 illustrates participants engaging with the application.

(a) Participant P1      (b) Participant P2      (c) Participant P3      (d) Participant P4

**Fig. 2.** Participants interacting with dinosaur content using an AR application.

**Method:** We used a task-oriented approach to engage participants with the proposed technology. Therefore, participants were encouraged to hold a smartphone and interact with the content themselves. The first, third, and fourth authors conducted this research to assess user perceptions and the success rate in accomplishing the proposed tasks: *Find the dinosaur by pointing the smartphone camera to the QR code; Approach and describe more details of the dinosaur; Read the textual description available; Rotate around the QR code and check the face and tail of the dinosaur.* The second research goal was to assess the scaffolding level needed to execute each task successfully. We recorded and took notes of the participants' interactions for further analysis. The study consisted of two sections: a hands-on and a virtual session.

**Procedure:** We facilitated a hands-on session that took an hour to assess our participants' interaction with the application. We aimed to evaluate the application's intuitiveness, identify areas that required improvement, and gather insights for future iterations. First, we proposed engaging freely with the application, then we proposed exploring the content in greater depth by providing specific prompts, and last, we proposed manipulating and turning around the object while holding the device. Participant P5 was not present in person but wanted to contribute, so we made a video call to include her in this study.

**Findings:** The analysis revealed the following themes:

**Using Scaffolding to Assess Understanding:** During the session, we encouraged participants to interact with AR. We realized that instructions like *"Please, approach the object"* were ambiguous to P1, P2, and P3 since it was unclear whether the object referred to was the device or the QR code. They interpreted it to mean bringing the device closer to their face rather than bringing it closer to the QR code– the intended action. To address this, we employed a well-established method of providing instructions with a **time delay**. Initially, we assisted in guiding the motion using a **physical prompt**. Then we used fading to reduce the physical prompt and replace it with **verbal cues** after the autonomous use of the smartphone was successfully learned. We also provided **gestural prompts** to guide the interaction, pointing to where they should move the device. When participants were presented with the words *"enlarge"* or *"reduce,"* the same misunderstanding arose, as the object of the action was unclear.

**Prompting or Explaining:** P2 unintentionally covered the smartphone's camera with her fingers and questioned whether the power had run out. Once we informed her that her fingers were causing the obstruction, she modified her grip and repositioned the device to uncover the camera. Our **verbal prompt** prevented her from becoming frustrated and enabled her to complete the task successfully.

**Assisting a Participant:** P4 has a motor disability. The participant easily accomplished all of the tasks and only needed assistance holding the smartphone and focusing on the QR code. The **physical scaffolding** he required was related to his motor ability: knowledgeable others assisted him in achieving the proposed goal by helping him hold the device.

**Providing Peer Feedback:** Participant P5 needed a few minutes to understand how AR functioned and behaved as she interacted with it through her computer screen. Initially, she thought it was a video, and we demonstrated how both work (the camera and the QR code) so she could associate that the camera was pointing at the QR code and generating the image on the screen. We used text-to-speech to describe the 3D object, a dinosaur, with the following sentence: "Hi, I am a dinosaur". After carefully looking and listening, P5 was ready to express a critical perspective, she said: *"We have never met a dinosaur because it no longer exists, but it seems like a nice way of seeing it"*. She added: *"It is a good idea for someone who can't read [to hear the dinosaur introducing itself]. You could provide generic audio like "Hi, I'm a dinosaur, I was alive, and I am not living anymore. I was herbivorous"*. Scaffolding lowered obstacles to engaging with AR technology while creating an environment in which mistakes are the fault of the design, not of the user. Thanks to the feedback mechanism that it promoted, scaffolding framed the object of investigation as *in fieri*, encouraging a mindset of improvement and eventually making the participant act as an **expert**, a knowledgeable other (Fig. 1), providing concrete assistance for simplifying the content for her peers.

## 4.2   Case Study II: Accessible Application

This Case Study highlights scaffolding when co-designing a museum application called ACCESS+ [29,32]. We evaluated the usability of the museum website and a previous museum tablet application to gather feedback and requirements from participants and then we moved to iterate the design of the ACCESS+ app. To iterate and make ACCESS+ more accessible, the co-design process involved three research visits with stakeholders (museum professionals, educators, psychologists, and technology experts) and individuals with cognitive and learning disabilities to understand their needs and collect requirements. In this paper, we are providing examples and highlighting how we scaffolded the first research visit, composed of several days and research sessions.

**Method:** During our first session, we evaluated the usability of an existing museum website and tablet application. This session aimed to determine what participants liked and disliked about the current solutions. We used a task-based approach to engage them and, ultimately, asked about their preferences. Tasks included finding the museum page, the dinosaur page, the museum address, the museum opening time, and a specific room on the museum map. The qualitative research focused on their preferences between devices, solutions, and UI elements.

The following sessions focused primarily on enhancing the ACCESS+ application. The participants engaged in a two-step process where they initially visited the museum and later utilized the application to retrieve information related to their visits. Through a task-based usability testing approach, participants could customize various aspects such as icon and text sizes, backgrounds, labels, and voices to cater to individual preferences and requirements. Users also made sense of the museum content by looking at symbols using AAC and listening to full-text text-to-speech with personalized tone, pitch, and highlight settings. Some participants shared their thoughts, actively engaging with the re-design and improvement of the accessibility of each choice and prompting us toward the addition of new features based on what they deemed to be unclear or missing. Other participants provided non-verbal feedback that their educators interpreted.

**Procedure:** We engaged with a group of participants, of which seven attended the initial sessions (Table 1). Through a series of interactive sessions and discussions, we worked together to make the museum's digital content more accessible. We used a combination of activities to trigger co-design and gathered more participant feedback. This insight implicitly and explicitly enabled us to improve the app between visits. Our visits started with focus groups to get to know the participants and understand their prior knowledge about the content we planned to introduce – museum animals. The group discussed the content through written responses or drawings according to their abilities, and we reviewed the key details about each animal as described with easy-to-read (E2R) text produced by the participants together with their educators. Following each museum visit, participants engaged with the app, giving them a preview of the captivating encounters they had at the museum. We also asked questions during the study to assess their technology habits and preferences. These activities were carefully planned in collaboration with stakeholders to ensure alignment with the visit's educational objectives and participants' interests.

**Findings:** The following research disclosed several significant themes.

**Eliciting Previous Knowledge to Solve a Task:** In our first session, participants were asked to inform us about specific information provided by the website. For this task, participants were asked to identify when the museum was open. After carefully reading the page, participant P7 said, "*I don't recall by heart, but I went there in the morning last time; they presumably still open in the morning.*" Initially, the participant used her previous knowledge to answer the question, rather than information seeking the content of the website. We then specifically asked her to consider and focus on the content of the website and refer to the times listed there, helping her to get a better understanding of the task by also giving a hint on how to achieve it. After scaffolding, she provided specific times listed in the website's information, and she was able to derive the correct answer. In this example, the researchers provided a scaffold to support the participant's thinking process using **verbal prompts** and further scaffolding to help her retrieve the necessary information.

**Expressing and Acknowledging Self-efficacy:** We provided participants with **verbal and gestural scaffolding** as we tasked them with searching for the museum address and admission fee. We aimed to evaluate how comprehensible street names, numbers, references, and ticket prices were for them. Although all participants were able to complete the task, P1 stood out by completing it quickly and displaying a high level of self-efficacy: *"I told you I knew how to use the tablet"*. Acknowledging and celebrating users' accomplishments can foster a positive and encouraging environment, which is crucial for their engagement in research tasks.

**Scaffolding Aiding Navigation:** In the first session using the ACCESS+ app, the first objective involved finding a particular animal within the menu. Upon reaching the correct page, a picture and the initial portion of content were presented (Fig 3b). To access more information, participants had to scroll down. While the majority of participants managed to scroll autonomously, a few required **verbal or gestural** prompts as a scaffolded approach. Notably, during this task, P4 encountered distractions and moments of frustration, necessitating a supportive atmosphere to facilitate full participation.

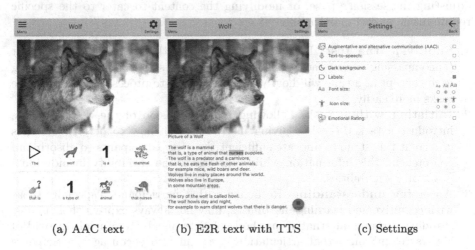

(a) AAC text          (b) E2R text with TTS          (c) Settings

**Fig. 3.** ACCESS+ app with different features.

**Scaffolding to Understand Audio and Visual Contents:** We conducted tests involving easy-to-read text paired with text-to-speech and word highlighting (refer to Fig. 3b). During these tests, P2 effectively utilized the TTS feature following **verbal** instructions. However, P7 encountered challenges in adjusting the voice speed to their preference. While some participants found the TTS feature to be beneficial, others required additional clarification or experienced difficulties in concentrating when simultaneously reading and listening to the text. Notably, P8, a non-verbal participant who relies on Augmentative and Alternative Communication (AAC) for communication, played a crucial role in the testing process. P8 communicated using their AAC notebook and **gestures**, offering valuable insights as a daily AAC user. Their input proved invaluable in identifying complex pictograms (see Fig. 3a). P8 expressed satisfaction with the ability to interact with the interface, listening to individual pictograms with the assistance of TTS. In P1's feedback, she described the experience as "*Very easy! I pressed an image, and the iPad spoke.*"

## 5    A Framework for Scaffolding

When co-designing with people with cognitive and learning disabilities, it is well understood that research sessions must be properly planned (e.g., [11,27, 44]). Once researchers have completed their planning for the research visit and associated activities, they can employ scaffolding during the session.

This approach is designed to assist and actively involve participants throughout the co-design session. Therefore, researchers can opt for an adaptable approach, recognizing that each participant may possess unique needs and capabilities. This customization may entail utilizing various communication methods, adjusting the session's pace, or modifying the content to cater to the specific requirements of each participant.

1. **Subdivide the test.** Initiate by subdividing the elements of your test (encompassing various activities and tasks) into small chunks. Introducing each concept at a time will help your participants to process and execute the tasks more easily.
2. **Initiating with a task.** Following the subdivision of the test elements, introduce a task [17] while giving instructions on how to perform it. It is crucial at this stage to allocate sufficient time for participants to absorb and comprehend this information while considering the variability in individual processing capabilities.
3. **Assessing understanding.** Recognizing that participants, especially those with cognitive and learning disabilities, may not always express their understanding verbally, alternative methods of assessment are crucial. Instead of always relying on verbal articulation, you can also encourage participants to demonstrate their comprehension through actions or any other form of expression (e.g. pointing to pictograms). For instance, rather than asking, "*What do you think this means?*", prompt them with action-oriented queries

like, *"Can you show me how you would do that?"* or *"What would you do next?"* These practical demonstrations offer insights into their grasp of the concept. While assessing understanding in this manner, you may discover areas where the concept was not fully comprehended. By creatively encouraging participants to **show** rather than **tell**, their ability to execute a task can effectively reveal their level of understanding. This step can be executed more than once if needed. You can also use different strategies – such as allowing a bigger time delay for any prompt – as a way to accommodate the participants' needs. Additionally, when suitable, facilitating peer interactions can further enhance the assessment and learning process.

4. **Support understanding through prompting.** In contrast to conventional methods, where researchers typically avoid providing prompts or explanations to minimize bias, our approach involves the strategic use of prompts to aid participants in understanding and interacting with the tasks. Prompting can take various forms, such as verbal cues, gestures, physical aids, or a combination thereof. These prompts are designed to offer additional contextual information, making it easier for participants to grasp complex concepts or navigate intricate tasks. Moreover, we may introduce a **time delay** between the prompt and the participant's response to allow them more time for thoughtful consideration, accommodating their individual pace and requirements, as recommended by Merrill (1992) [24]. For instance, in Case Study I, we utilized prompts to guide participants in understanding how to approach a 3D model effectively. In Case Study II, participants were encouraged to locate specific information on websites and applications with the assistance of prompts. When participants struggle to provide responses due to insufficient understanding, we adopt an incremental approach, breaking down the support into smaller and manageable steps. This technique allows facilitators to support the participants' understanding step by step, providing just enough assistance for them to accomplish a single task.

5. **Fading.** Fading, the gradual reduction of aid, is accomplished by adhering to specified rules: physical and gestural assistance is reduced, and verbal suggestions are limited. When utilizing an application, for example, the quantity and quality of physical prompts are gradually reduced. Case Study I – interacting with AR – illustrates a situation in which participants required physical instructions until they independently learned how to hold and point the smartphone at the QR code. The fading process was implemented by progressively minimizing physical assistance – for instance, transitioning from direct hand guidance to lighter touches on the elbow – and substituting them with verbal cues. Fading should be used only when necessary, skipping this stage if prompting must be repeated, or if the study is completed in a short session and fading is not utilized.

6. **Repeat if needed.** Repeat the process (items 3–4) of assessing understanding and supporting understanding through prompting by going one question or task at a time whenever needed. You can move to the next task if the participant already learned or you can proceed with your planned study.

164    L. S. Guedes et al.

The previous steps are essential to support people with cognitive and learning disabilities during co-design. One example of scaffolding applied to Case Study I is depicted in Fig. 4. It is critical to document both successes and failures throughout the process. On the one hand, using a structured approach for carrying out the activity can aid in participant engagement. Collecting information about the scaffolds, on the other hand, can provide vital information about the participant's understanding and, as a result, can aid in interpreting their input.

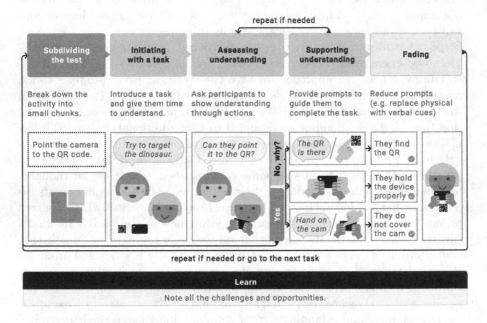

**Fig. 4.** Scaffolding layers applied to Case Study I: AR interaction.

## 6   Discussion

We have defined the role of scaffolding in co-designing with people with cognitive and learning disabilities and introduced case studies to demonstrate examples of scaffolding throughout the collaborative design cycle. We chose scaffolding for its research-backed effectiveness [4] and alignment with Applied Behavioral Analysis [19]. Unlike Cooperative learning [18], which emphasizes group activities, scaffolding offers tailored support. This method suits learners with cognitive disabilities, providing gradual learning through explicit instructions and support, ensuring individualized assistance for effective task performance. Since our goal was to ensure inclusivity and individualized support for participants with cognitive and learning disabilities during the co-design process, scaffolding was deemed more appropriate. It allowed us to provide tailored guidance to each participant according to their unique needs and abilities.

The first Case Study (Sect. 4.1), a hands-on experience, highlighted areas for advancement in AR technology and device sensors, surfacing the need for a sensor to detect when the camera is being obstructed and a tutorial on how to approach and downscale an object. It also helped us realize the importance of (1) establishing a good personal relationship with our participants and (2) how crucial it was to provide detailed instructions for conducting the proposed tasks, not only verbally but also physically – accompanying the verbal cues with physical gestures. Another important element that emerged was that each participant needed a different level of scaffolding related to their physical and cognitive needs, interest, and their level of engagement with the task. This amount of care paid out in the quality of the feedback we collected, enabling us to redesign the application.

In our second Case Study (Sect. 4.2), we co-designed a museum application that displayed complementary museum content. We used scaffolding to assist participants in eliciting prior information and completing the suggested activities, helping us to iterate the design of the application based on their invaluable feedback. We also gave them several forms of cues, drawing their attention vocally and pointing gestures to labels, numbers, letters, and icons as clues to help them on tasks. When eliciting prior information, we underscored the importance of understanding how participants approach tasks and access information, necessitating scaffolding techniques to redirect participants' focus toward the relevant content. The ability to use verbal and gestural scaffolding effectively not only supported participants in completing tasks but also empowered them. We recognized that encouragement and praise for accomplishments helped participants to complete their tasks with confidence. Finally, the study's findings highlighted the importance of scaffolding, self-efficacy acknowledgment, and effective communication channels in creating technology solutions that make museums more inclusive and enjoyable for all.

By scaffolding the session, participants were better equipped to engage with the technology and offer meaningful feedback. Fading the session gradually, allowed participants to gain confidence and independence in their interactions with the technology. By implementing these adjustments, we created an inclusive research environment where participants felt valued, heard, and empowered to provide valuable feedback. Moreover, when the same participants are involved over time, as in Case Study II, scaffolding can help to exchange and consequentially acquire new knowledge and skills. This contributed to the success of our research outcomes, as we were able to gather rich observations and insights that informed the development of more accessible and user-friendly technologies.

Additionally, the scaffolding approach emphasizes the provision of temporary, adjustable, and tailored support for learning and engagement in co-design activities [6,44]. This approach recognizes the unique requirements of individuals with cognitive and learning disabilities and the need to differentiate assistance based on their specific needs and abilities [27]. By collaborating with professionals who work closely with them, we gain valuable insights into the specific challenges and strengths of each participant. Scaffolding acknowledges these challenges and incorporates strategies to reduce cognitive load, such as breaking down information into smaller, manageable chunks and providing ample time for participants to respond.

It is important to point out that a balance and a trade-off exist between providing scaffolding by prompting, allowing users to understand independently, and figuring out how to complete tasks across the stated case studies. Following educators' advice, we provided detailed instructions that were often tailored on the fly [33] in a reflection-in-action process [44] to fit the participants' specific abilities and needs. This approach enabled us to adapt tasks, both in terms of presentation and overall complexity, to suit the different needs and abilities of the participants. Given it was their first exposure to the presented technology, we wanted to avoid them feeling lost and frustrated by the lack of guidance. Instead, we provided encouragement and support to maintain their engagement when performing the proposed tasks. However, it is important to notice that this happens during the co-design process, where it is essential to facilitate and guide the use of technology. The same approach would not be appropriate when running a formal summative evaluation session.

## 6.1  Limitations and Future Work

Further research is needed to validate and refine these guidelines with participants with a diverse range of disabilities and note their effectiveness for research on various technologies. Another limitation is that with scaffolding comes researcher discretion and variability around what the 'prompting' might be. An area for future work is systematizing the prompting to make it more consistent across conditions. Finally, a last limitation is that more work needs to be done to understand the repercussions of focus group scaffolding when more than one participant is present, and the abilities and scaffolding necessary to move to the next layer of information are not consistent across participants.

Areas for future work involve testing and refining the guidelines and related steps with a wider spectrum of cognitive and learning disabilities, with more than one participant present (as in a focus group), and with a varied and diverse range of technologies. Future work can further inquire into how to include and actively involve different players in our research, such as educators and clinicians, to promote their engagement while drawing from their areas of expertise, knowledge, and skills. Additionally, more research may also explore and consider ways to empower the role of participant caretakers, educators, and assistants in co-design as this research continues to inform how we might help scaffold understanding and co-create technologies that are more accessible.

## 7  Conclusions

The voices of people with cognitive and learning disabilities can be amplified in research by allowing them to participate actively and make contributions. Scaffolding co-design sessions is one of the means to improve their participant, however, it lacked a systematized structure for its use. We found that scaffolding in co-design serves as a means of empowering individuals, enabling them to become more independent over time. As participants gain new skills and confidence, they can better contribute to the design process. Moreover, by enhancing co-design with a scaffolding approach, we cultivate more active and engaged participants who can provide valuable input. This approach not only improves the immediate outcomes of the co-design process but could also offer long-lasting benefits as individuals develop their abilities and become more self-reliant contributors to technology design while acquiring essential digital skills.

**Acknowledgements.** We would like to thank SNSF for funding this research, ANF-FAS and The Civic Museum of Natural History of Trieste for collaborating with this research, and our amazing co-designers for making this work possible.

# References

1. Adams, A., Lunt, P., Cairns, P.: A qualititative approach to HCI research (2008)
2. Adeani, I.S., Febriani, R.B., Syafryadin, S.: Using Gibbs' reflective cycle in making reflections of literary analysis. Indones. EFL J. **6**(2), 139–148 (2020)
3. Alexander, E., Bresciani, S., Eppler, M.: Knowledge scaffolding visualizations: a guiding framework. Knowl. Manag. E-Learn. **7**, 179–198 (2015)
4. Bakken, R.K., Næss, K.A.B., Lemons, C.J., Hjetland, H.N.: A systematic review and meta-analysis of reading and writing interventions for students with disorders of intellectual development. Educ. Sci. **11**(10) (2021). https://doi.org/10.3390/educsci11100638, https://www.mdpi.com/2227-7102/11/10/638
5. Benton, L., Vasalou, A., Khaled, R., Johnson, H., Gooch, D.: Diversity for design: a framework for involving neurodiverse children in the technology design process. In: Proceedings of the SIGCHI Conference on Human Factors in Computing Systems, pp. 3747–3756 (2014)
6. Bircanin, F., Brereton, M., Sitbon, L., Ploderer, B., Azaabanye Bayor, A., Koplick, S.: Including adults with severe intellectual disabilities in co-design through active support. In: Proceedings of the 2021 CHI Conference on Human Factors in Computing Systems. CHI '21. Association for Computing Machinery, New York, NY, USA (2021). https://doi.org/10.1145/3411764.3445057
7. Catarci, T., De Giovanni, L., Gabrielli, S., Kimani, S., Mirabella, V.: Scaffolding the design of accessible eLearning content: a user-centered approach and cognitive perspective. Cogn. Process. **9**, 209–216 (2008)
8. Cengher, M., Budd, A.F., Farrell, N.C., Fienup, D.M.: A review of prompt-fading procedures: Implications for effective and efficient skill acquisition. J. Dev. Phys. Disabil. **30**, 155–173 (2018)
9. Collins, A.M.: Cognitive apprenticeship: teaching the craft of reading, writing, and mathematics. Technical report no. 403 (1987)
10. Frauenberger, C., Good, J., Alcorn, A., Pain, H.: Supporting the design contributions of children with autism spectrum conditions. In: Proceedings of the 11th International Conference on Interaction Design and Children, pp. 134–143 (2012)
11. Gibson, R.C., Dunlop, M.D., Bouamrane, M.M.: Lessons from expert focus groups on how to better support adults with mild intellectual disabilities to engage in co-design. In: Proceedings of the 22nd International ACM SIGACCESS Conference on Computers and Accessibility, pp. 1–12 (2020)

12. Guedes, L.S., Zanardi, I., Mastrogiuseppe, M., Span, S., Landoni, M.: "Is this real?": assessing the usability and accessibility of augmented reality with people with intellectual disabilities. In: Antona, M., Stephanidis, C. (eds.) Universal Access in Human-Computer Interaction - HCII 2023. Lecture Notes in Computer Science, vol. 14021, pp. 91–110. Springer, Cham (2023)
13. Guedes, L.S., Zanardi, I., Span, S., Landoni, M.: Multisensory Diorama: Enhancing Accessibility and Engagement in Museums. In: Abdelnour Nocera, J., Kristín Lárusdóttir, M., Petrie, H., Piccinno, A., Winckler, M. (eds.) INTERACT 2023. LNCS, vol. 14143, pp. 628–637. Springer, Cham (2023). https://doi.org/10.1007/978-3-031-42283-6_34
14. Guedes, L.S., Marques, L.A., Vitório, G.: Enhancing interaction and accessibility in museums and exhibitions with augmented reality and screen readers. In: Miesenberger, K., Manduchi, R., Covarrubias Rodriguez, M., Peňáz, P. (eds.) ICCHP 2020. LNCS, vol. 12376, pp. 157–163. Springer, Cham (2020). https://doi.org/10.1007/978-3-030-58796-3_20
15. Hiniker, A., Sobel, K., Lee, B.: Co-designing with preschoolers using fictional inquiry and comicboarding. In: Proceedings of the 2017 CHI Conference on Human Factors in Computing Systems, pp. 5767–5772 (2017)
16. The Office of the High Commissioner for Human Rights is the leading United Nations: Conventions on the rights of persons with disabilities (2006). https://www.ohchr.org/en/instruments-mechanisms/instruments/convention-rights-persons-disabilities
17. Johansson, S., Gulliksen, J., Lantz, A.: User participation when users have mental and cognitive disabilities. In: Proceedings of the 17th International ACM SIGACCESS Conference on Computers and Accessibility. ASSETS '15, pp. 69–76. Association for Computing Machinery, New York, NY, USA (2015). https://doi.org/10.1145/2700648.2809849
18. Johnson, D.W., Johnson, R., Anderson, D.: Social interdependence and classroom climate. J. Psychol. **114**(1), 135–142 (1983)
19. Lovaas, O.I.: Teaching individuals with developmental delays: basic intervention techniques. Pro-ed (2003)
20. Mack, K., McDonnell, E., Jain, D., Lu Wang, L., Froehlich, J.E., Findlater, L.: What do we mean by "accessibility research"? A literature survey of accessibility papers in chi and assets from 1994 to 2019. In: Proceedings of the 2021 CHI Conference on Human Factors in Computing Systems. CHI '21. Association for Computing Machinery, New York, NY, USA (2021). https://doi.org/10.1145/3411764.3445412
21. Malinverni, L., Mora-Guiard, J., Padillo, V., Mairena, M., Hervás, A., Pares, N.: Participatory design strategies to enhance the creative contribution of children with special needs. In: Proceedings of the 2014 Conference on Interaction Design and Children, pp. 85–94 (2014)
22. Mastrogiuseppe, M., Guedes, L.S., Stefania, S., Patrizia, C., Monica, L.: Reconceptualizing inclusion in museum spaces: a multidisciplinary framework. In: Gomez Chova, L., Lopez Martinez, A., Candel Torres, I. (eds.) 14th International Conference of Education, Research and Innovation, pp. 7225–7233 (2021)
23. Meilleur, A.A.S., Jelenic, P., Mottron, L.: Prevalence of clinically and empirically defined talents and strengths in autism. J. Autism Dev. Disord. **45**, 1354–1367 (2015)
24. Merrill, D.C., Reiser, B.J., Ranney, M., Trafton, J.G.: Effective tutoring techniques: a comparison of human tutors and intelligent tutoring systems. J. Learn. Sci. **2**(3), 277–305 (1992)

25. Moraveji, N., Li, J., Ding, J., O'Kelley, P., Woolf, S.: Comicboarding: using comics as proxies for participatory design with children. In: Proceedings of the SIGCHI Conference on Human Factors in Computing Systems, pp. 1371–1374 (2007)
26. Organization, W.H.: International classification of functioning, disability and health: Icf (2001)
27. Robb, N., Boyle, B., Politis, Y., Newbutt, N., Kuo, H.J., Sung, C.: Participatory technology design for autism and cognitive disabilities: a narrative overview of issues and techniques. In: Recent Advances in Technologies for Inclusive Well-Being: Virtual Patients, Gamification and Simulation, pp. 469–485 (2021)
28. Ruiz-Primo, M., Furtak, E.: Informal formative assessment and scientific inquiry: exploring teachers' practices and student learning. Educ. Assess. **11**, 205–235 (2006)
29. Guedes, S., Zanardi, L., Mastrogiuseppe, I., Span, M., Landoni, M.S.: Co-designing a museum application with people with intellectual disabilities: findings and accessible redesign. In: Proceedings of the European Conference on Cognitive Ergonomics 2023. ECCE '23. Association for Computing Machinery, Swansea, Wales (2023). https://doi.org/10.1145/3605655.3605687
30. Schalock, R.L., Luckasson, R.A., Shogren, K.A.: The Renaming of mental retardation: understanding the change to the term intellectual disability. Intellect. Dev. Disabil. **45**(2), 116–124 (2007). https://doi.org/10.1352/1934-9556(2007)45[116:TROMRU]2.0.CO;2
31. Seeman-Horwitz, L., Ran, R., Lee, S., Bradley Montgomery, R.: Making content usable for people with cognitive and learning disabilities, May 2021. https://www.w3.org/TR/coga-usable/
32. Soares Guedes, L., Ferrari, V., Mastrogiuseppe, M., Span, S., Landoni, M.: ACCESS+: designing a museum application for people with intellectual disabilities. In: Miesenberger, K., Kouroupetroglou, G., Mavrou, K., Manduchi, R., Covarrubias Rodriguez, M., Penáz, P. (eds.) ICCHP-AAATE 2022. LNCS, vol. 13341, pp. 425–431. Springer, Cham (2022). https://doi.org/10.1007/978-3-031-08648-9_49
33. Soares Guedes, L., Landoni, M.: Meeting participants with intellectual disabilities during COVID-19 pandemic: challenges and improvisation. In: The 23rd International ACM SIGACCESS Conference on Computers and Accessibility. ASSETS '21. Association for Computing Machinery, New York, NY, USA (2021). https://doi.org/10.1145/3441852.3476566
34. Spencer González, H., Vega Córdova, V., Exss Cid, K., Jarpa Azagra, M., Álvarez-Aguado, I.: Including intellectual disability in participatory design processes: methodological adaptations and supports. In: Proceedings of the 16th Participatory Design Conference 2020-Participation (s) Otherwise-Volume 1, pp. 55–63 (2020)
35. Stone, C.A.: The metaphor of scaffolding: its utility for the field of learning disabilities. J. Learn. Disabil. **31**(4), 344–364 (1998). https://doi.org/10.1177/002221949803100404, pMID: 9666611
36. Tassé, M.J.: Adaptive behavior and functional life skills across the lifespan: conceptual and measurement issues. In: Lang, R., Sturmey, P. (eds.) Adaptive Behavior Strategies for Individuals with Intellectual and Developmental Disabilities. ACPS, pp. 1–20. Springer, Cham (2021). https://doi.org/10.1007/978-3-030-66441-1_1
37. van de Pol, J., Volman, M., Beishuizen, J.: Scaffolding in teacher-student interaction: a decade of research. Educ. Psychol. Rev. **22**(3), 271–297 (2010). https://doi.org/10.1007/s10648-010-9127-6
38. van de Pol, J., Volman, M., Beishuizen, J.: Patterns of contingent teaching in teacher-student interaction. Learn. Instr. **21**(1), 46–57 (2011). https://doi.org/10.1016/j.learninstruc.2009.10.004

39. Van Mechelen, M., Laenen, A., Zaman, B., Willems, B., Abeele, V.V.: Collaborative design thinking (CoDet): a co-design approach for high child-to-adult ratios. Int. J. Hum Comput Stud. **130**, 179–195 (2019)

40. Vicari, S., Bellucci, S., Carlesimo, G.A.: Visual and spatial long-term memory: differential pattern of impairments in Williams and down syndromes. Dev. Med. Child Neurol. **47**(5), 305–311 (2005). https://doi.org/10.1111/j.1469-8749.2005.tb01-141.x

41. Vygotsky, L.S.: Mind and Society: The Development of Higher Mental Processes. Harvard University Press, Cambridge, MA (1978). http://www.learning-theories.com/vygotskys-social-learning-theory.html

42. W3C: Cognitive and learning, March 2022. https://deploy-preview-113--wai-people-use-web.netlify.app/people-use-web/abilities-barriers-cognitive/

43. Warren, J.L., Antle, A.N., Kitson, A., Davoodi, A.: Lessons learned and future considerations for designing remotely facilitated co-design studies with children focused on socio-emotional experiences. In: Interaction Design and Children, pp. 37–49 (2022)

44. Wilson, C., Brereton, M., Ploderer, B., Sitbon, L.: Co-design beyond words: 'moments of interaction' with minimally-verbal children on the autism spectrum. In: Proceedings of the 2019 CHI Conference on Human Factors in Computing Systems, pp. 1–15 (2019)

45. Wood, D., Bruner, J.S., Ross, G.: The role of tutoring in problem solving*. J. Child Psychol. Psychiatry **17**(2), 89–100 (1976). https://doi.org/10.1111/j.1469-7610.1976.tb00381.x, https://acamh.onlinelibrary.wiley.com/doi/abs/10.1111/j.1469-7610.1976.tb00381.x

46. Wood, D., Bruner, J.S., Ross, G.: The role of tutoring in problem solving. J. Child Psychol. Psychiatry **17**(2), 89–100 (1976). https://doi.org/10.1111/j.1469-7610.1976.tb00381.x

47. Woodward, K., Kanjo, E., Brown, D.J., McGinnity, T., Harold, G.: In the hands of users with intellectual disabilities: co-designing tangible user interfaces for mental wellbeing. Pers. Ubiquit. Comput. 1–21 (2023)

48. Yip, J.C., et al.: Examining adult-child interactions in intergenerational participatory design. In: Proceedings of the 2017 CHI Conference on Human Factors in Computing Systems, pp. 5742–5754 (2017)

49. Zamenopoulos, T., Alexiou, K.: Co-design as collaborative research (2018)

50. Zhang, M., Quintana, C.: Scaffolding strategies for supporting middle school students' online inquiry processes. Comput. Educ. **58**, 181–196 (01 2012). https://doi.org/10.1016/j.compedu.2011.07.016

# Overcoming Challenges in Questioning People with Intellectual Disabilities Regarding Their Digital Media Usage: Lessons Learned from the EVE4all Project

Vanessa N. Heitplatz(✉) ⓘ, Leevke Wilkens ⓘ, Nele Maskut ⓘ, Miriam Bursy ⓘ, and Susanne Dirks ⓘ

Department of Rehabilitation Technology, TU Dortmund University, Dortmund, Germany
{Vanessa.heitplatz,leevke.wilkens,nele.maskut,miriam.bursy,
susanne.dirks}@tu-dortmund.de

**Abstract.** People with Intellectual Disabilities (ID) are often excluded from research due to a number of obstacles in questioning them (e.g. cognitive and linguistic abilities. To find out about common methods of questioning people with ID, a rapid review was conducted for this paper in December 2023. The evaluation of the research methods used by the studies in our sample shows that questionnaires, followed by interviews, are the most frequently used methods of gathering data and surveying people with intellectual disabilities. Those "classic" methods often do not meet the requirements of people with ID and other persons who have communication or intellectual impairments. This paper presents challenges and difficulties in questioning people with ID in the context of media and internet usage. It also tries to explain reasons for often not including them in current research. In addition, experiences from the EVE4all project are illustrated, in which several methodological approaches were used to ask people with ID about their opinion of the Easy Reading Add-On. Finally, new survey methods suitable for interviewing people with ID will be presented as examples.

**Keywords:** Evaluation · Methods · Disability · Intellectual Disability · EVE4all

## 1 Introduction

People with Intellectual Disabilities (ID) are often excluded from research due to a number of obstacles in questioning them (e.g. cognitive and linguistic abilities (see Sect. 2) [1 3]. This also applies to research about media and internet usage, even though more and more solutions are being developed for these groups of people (e.g. smartphone apps, browser extensions, training offers). Particularly when it comes to current issues (e.g. Internet and digital media usage), they are not being asked about their opinions, interests, and feelings. This leads to various misunderstandings, which in turn severely affect the quality of life and opportunities for participation of people with ID. For example, Heitplatz (2021) found that developed offers (e.g. workshops) for people with ID in

M. Antona and C. Stephanidis (Eds.): HCII 2024, LNCS 14697, pp. 171–185, 2024.
https://doi.org/10.1007/978-3-031-60881-0_11

residential facilities, aiming to promote their media skills, were not taken up because they did not reflect the reality of the resident's lives. The caregivers assumed that the residents toneded to learn their media skills on laptops. The residents, in turn, almost exclusively use smartphones or tablets and, therefore, did not take advantage of these offers [4]. Also, Alfredsson Ågren (2020a) states that new offers and workshops to enhance media literacy for people with ID often focus on their deficits and miss the potential to support their self-determination and autonomy [5]. This frustrates and demotivates people to learn new (digital) skills. Additionally, various studies [4, 6, 7] have shown that people with ID are much more aware of their obligations and risks when using the Internet than is often perceived by their social environment (i.e. parents, teachers, formal caregivers). Heitplatz, Bühler & Hastall (2019), for example, showed that many people with ID are well aware of the risks on the Internet and actively visit workshops and materials to inform themselves [8]. These studies clearly show significant shortcomings in various contexts influencing participation opportunities for people with ID. These misunderstandings result from decisions made over people's heads without asking them about their needs. In addition, there are several research gaps in media usage by people with ID. These include, for example, the use of social networks [8], research into media use in leisure time [5, 6] or knowledge about how people with ID acquire new information and content [9].

Using the experiences of two participatory development projects, Dirks (2019) illustrated that the participatory involvement of end users in the development process is also of central importance in the research and development of new technological products. Even if co-working with end users might be challenging at some points, most emerging problems can be solved [10].

**This paper** presents challenges and difficulties in questioning people with ID in the context of media and internet usage and tries to explain reasons for often not including them in current research (Sect. 2). In addition, experiences from the EVE4all project are illustrated, in which several methodological approaches were used to ask people with ID about their opinion of the Easy Reading Add-On (see Sect. 3.1). Finally, new survey methods suitable for interviewing people with ID will be presented as examples.

## 2  Challenges in Questioning People with Intellectual Disabilities

To understand the challenges of interviewing people with ID, it is first necessary to describe the group of people in detail.

### 2.1  People with Intellectual Disabilities

The ICF classifies components of health, i.e., body functions, body structures, activities, participation, and environmental factors (see Fig. 1). With the help of the ICF, health problems can be viewed holistically, and implications and measures for improving the state of health can be derived. In the following, challenges and impairments that make up the ID are assigned to the ICF's various components to understand better the problems that can arise when interviewing this group of people.

The American Association of Intellectual and Developmental Disabilities (AAIDD) [12] defines ID as an impairment that:

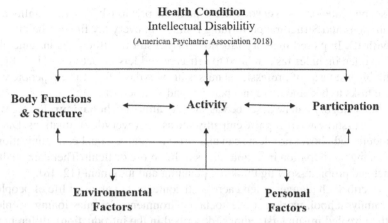

**Fig. 1.** Intellectual Disability along the ICF Classification

- Occurs before the age of eighteen.
- Affects mental and adaptive functions (Intellectual Functioning and Adaptive Behavior), and
- Interferes with the performance of activities in daily living contexts.

This definition clarifies that the diagnosis of ID is not tied to a predetermined age but that individual symptoms must be diagnosed during an individual's developmental phase. Thus, it is important that ID is an impairment that is not acquired as a result of an accident or illness in adulthood but rather in the phase of growing up, which distinguishes it from other diseases or syndromes (e.g. dementia, acquired brain damage). According to the DSM-5 [13], ID often occurs in combination with other disorders, such as Autism Spectrum Disorders, specific learning disorders or genetic disorders (e.g. fragile X-Syndrome, Rett-Syndrome). The following are categories in which challenges in everyday life for people with ID may occur depending on the severity of the impairment.

The first category is **communication and articulation**. As already described above, ID includes several disorders, such as Autism Spectrum Disorders, Rett-Syndrome or Down syndrome. Some of these diseases are particularly often associated with communication impairments (Body Functions and Structures of the ICF) and affect how these people interact with their environment [14, 15]. For example, people with Autism or Fragile X-Syndrome often show impairments in receptive and/or expressive structural language. This comprises the domains of semantics, including vocabulary, and word relations, and grammar [14]. People with Down Syndrome often suffer from hearing loss, craniofacial abnormities and hypertonia of speech muscles, leading to unintelligible speech output [15]. To generalize, the reasons for those and other communication difficulties are often muscle weaknesses, hearing problems, hypertonia, stroke, or respiratory tract infections leading to affections on speed and precision of speech movement [15]. As a result, the speech of affected people is often unintelligible or hardly understandable [15–17]. Early language difficulties are a risk for poor literacy skills, memory skills, and nonverbal abilities that impact everyday life, activities of daily living, and adaptive functions [16]. They affect their activity possibilities and participation opportunities.

The second category is **everyday life**. Due to the previously described influences on Body Functions and Structure, performing routines in everyday life can be difficult for people with ID. Impaired memory functions may result in difficulties in remembering tasks. This often includes tasks related to self-care and leisure activities [12, 18]. Thus, one of the biggest tasks of professional nurses in everyday life is to help people with ID with these tasks to become more independent and self-determinate.

The third category can be described as **socially adaptive behaviour**. People with ID may struggle to show and recognise empathy and assess (everyday) situations. Due to the factors mentioned above, problems can also arise in interpersonal communication with others, making participation in various areas of life more difficult. There are challenges in abstract and problem-solving thinking, planning and judgment [12, 18].

The described challenges extend across all contexts and areas of life of people with ID, e.g. family, school, work, and the social environment. For questioning people with ID and the revealed misunderstandings (described in the introduction), different points can be derived as a summary from the description of the group of people. On the one hand, impairments in communication and articulation play a central role in ID. This is difficult with surveys based on question-and-answer schemes. Depending on the severity of the communication impairment, it must be expected that verbal utterances may be only partially comprehensible, only with the help of technical aids (e.g. talkers) or even not comprehensible. Due to the problems described in the area of abstract thinking and problem-solving capabilities, conventional survey methods (see Sect. 2.2) can be a cognitive challenge for people with ID.

## 2.2 Common Methods for Questioning People with Intellectual Disabilities

To find out about common methods of questioning people with ID, a rapid review was conducted in December 2023. In ten databases, the following search terms were used: 'intellectual disability' or 'learning disability' or 'learning disabilities' or 'developmental disability' AND 'media use' OR 'smartphone'. After screening and exclusion of duplets, 38 studies were identified.

In 28 of the 38 identified studies, people with ID were asked their opinions (see Fig. 2). The graph shows that most of the studies are questionnaire studies (n = 16). Interviews are the second most popular method (n = 9). Less popular are focus group studies (n = 7) and using several methods of questioning (i.e. interviews and questionnaires) (n = 4). Additionally, observations were used in two studies [19, 20]. Interestingly, focus group studies can be differentiated between 'synchronous' and 'asynchronous' focus groups. Whereas the former refer to those focus groups that "typically take place in one setting, consist of six to 10 participants plus a moderator, and take several hours" [21], asynchronous focus groups are conducted over a longer period of time, for example via platforms such as secret Facebook groups. Bryan and Chung (2018) described their procedure as follows:

"The 10-week focus group was conducted using Secret Facebook Groups. This platform was chosen for three reasons. First, participants lived in several different states and travel to one spot was not possible, so an asynchronous online focus group made communication among them possible. Second, all 8 participants were already familiar with and had a presence on Facebook. Third, Facebook Secret Groups ensured privacy of any exchanges where asynchronous collaboration in sending and receiving ideas could occur anytime and from anyplace" [22].

The remaining 10 out of the 28 studies are so-called 'caregiver studies', which researched the opinion of caregivers (e.g. parents, family members, professionals) towards media usage.

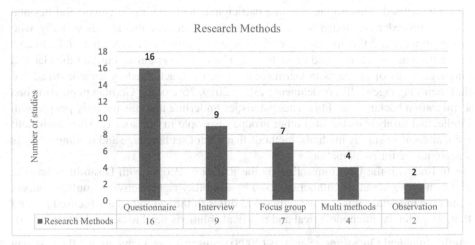

**Fig. 2.** Overview about identified studies from rapid review

The evaluation of the research methods used by the studies in our sample shows that questionnaires, followed by interviews, are the most frequently used methods of gathering data and surveying people with intellectual disabilities.

Of the 16 studies that used questionnaires, two were caregiver studies, and two others were studies in which people with intellectual disabilities and their caregivers were questioned. Altogether, 14 studies directly asked people with intellectual disabilities for their opinions. A closer look at the analysed data of fourteen studies shows that five questionnaire studies [5, 23–25] say that their questionnaires are adapted to the participants' needs (e.g. using easy language) without explaining this further. The authors of the remaining nine questionnaire studies [26–33] do not describe any adjustments or adaptations of the questionnaire to the participants' needs in their articles. The studies in our sample that used questionnaires are often part of large-scale studies that aim to achieve wide representation [34]. As can be seen in Fig. 2, some authors used multi-method approaches to investigate the media usage of people with ID; in particular, studies which surveyed people with intellectual disabilities and their caregivers on the same topic but with different methods seem to gain popularity [35–38].

### 2.3 Identified Challenges in Questioning People with ID

The results of the rapid review show that questionnaires and interviews are the most common methods of questioning people with ID in current research. This is a challenge for involving those people in research because those methods have different requirements, which are in contrast with described characteristics of ID (see Sect. 2.1).

**Linguistic and Cognitive Abilities as Requirements.** The results of the rapid review demonstrate that having the linguistic abilities to communicate, as well as having the cognitive abilities to understand the interview or questionnaire, are often described as essential preconditions for participation in a study: "To take part in the interview, they [participants] were required to communicate well enough verbally to be understood" [36]. In most of the major media usage studies [39–41], questionnaires or telephone interviews were used. This implies that the participants had specific linguistic abilities and that this procedure excluded people who could not articulate themselves verbally, who did not understand the questions, or who had a different native language. In Germany, 6.2 million adults cannot read or write [42]. Haug (2008) pointed out that the German language skills of migrants in Germany are often characterized by uncertainties, and that their language skills are deficient [43]. In 2019, 26% of the German population had a 'migration background' [44]. These statistics underline that it is not only people with intellectual disabilities but also other groups of people in our society who can benefit from alternative survey methods, methods that do not set language and reading skills as a prerequisite for participation.

In line with the UN Convention on the Rights of People with Disabilities and the claim 'nothing about us without us' used by disability rights activists, multiple papers state how important it is that not only the abilities of the individual are focused on, and that, accordingly, methodological and practical solutions need to be implemented [45].

**Methodological Questions.** Schäfers (2008) states that interviews are not the best way to survey every group of people due to the language requirements mentioned above [1]. Particular problems arise when surveying people with severe disabilities who cannot articulate themselves verbally or understand questions adequately. Previous experience reports on surveys of people with ID recommend an upper limit of 25 questions for questionnaire studies and a time limit of 30–40 min for interviews [46]. Some authors, however, say that their interviews with participants sometimes lasted longer than an hour [47]. A few studies chose other survey formats, such as focus groups. As Barr et al. (2003) noted:

> "it has been argued that focus groups have important advantages both in the dynamics present and the outcomes that can be achieved when attempting to gain insights into views of people for whom the usage of a questionnaire would be difficult if not impossible" [48].

However, the dynamics of focus groups have already been shown to help overcome existing barriers to including people with ID in research [49]. The characteristics of focus group studies allow wide-ranging adaptations to individual needs that are not isolated to those of people with ID. In addition, young children, older adults, and people who cannot read or write are more likely to participate in a focus group than to fill out a questionnaire. Heitplatz, Bühler & Hastall (2019) showed that focus groups, in combination with the Talking Mats method are an opportunity to allow even people with severe intellectual disabilities to express themselves during focus groups. The limitations of focus groups are revealed when it comes to discussing sensitive or very personal topics that should not be shared in a group (e.g. sexual abuse, violence, etc.) [50].

Additionally, three studies in the sample include several perspectives in multi-method studies on a specific research topic. For example, 38 [38] examined the media usage of adults with ID by interviewing both the parents of the people with ID and the people with ID themselves. The inclusion of different perspectives on a research topic is certainly helpful and is a first step towards including the opinions of people with disabilities. However, the studies found in the rapid review always used the same research method (i.e. questionnaires) for the different groups of people. Even if the participants with ID had help in filling out the questionnaires, it remains unclear whether the results of the questionnaires reflect their own opinion (and, if so, to what extent) or have been influenced by caregivers' opinions. In the literature, the call for participatory research methods is getting louder. 'Participatory research' is an umbrella term for collaborative approaches to the research of a specific topic. This approach "comprises a range of methodological approaches and techniques, all with the objective of handing power from the researcher to research participants [...]" [51]. A first step towards achieving this objective is considering people with ID as qualified and resourceful participants in research studies, as shown in the Easy Reading project (see Sect. 3) [10, 52]. It is the responsibility of researchers to design a research instrument that allows people with intellectual disabilities to participate and answer the questions [53].

However, such participative approaches require human, motivational, temporal, and financial resources. Large media usage studies (such as those mentioned in the introduction of this paper) are published annually, and so usually complete their recruitment, survey, and evaluation within one year. Obtaining such large and representative datasets means there is usually no time left for creative research methods, even though this should be part of the research process.

## 3 Lessons Learned from the EVE4all Project

In the "EVE4all – Easy Understanding for All" project, funded by the Federal Ministry of Education and Research (2022–2024), the 'Easy Reading' add-on developed in a previous project is being validated. The Easy Reading add-on was developed together with people with disabilities in the inclusive research and development project 'Easy Reading', a Horizon 2020 project (2018–2020) [10, 52]. Easy Reading is a free browser add-on that allows websites to be customized using various tools. Users can simplify the layout and content of websites (hiding graphics and images) or expand them (adding symbols or images) (Easy Reading, 2023). The primary target group for Easy Reading were people with ID. Even though the target group was expanded in the EVE4all project and specific usage contexts, such as formal and informal education was expanded, this primary target group is of great interest.

Thus, in the first steps of the EVE4all project, training courses for Easy Reading were developed and carried out in different institutions, such as sheltered workshops, residential facilities and vocational training centers. These trainings aimed to enable professionals, or end users, to use Easy Reading in various contexts. The overall aim was to ensure that, after the introductory training, the participants were able to use Easy Reading independently whenever the opportunity arose. Thus, the first challenge in the EVE4all project was to acquire institutions willing to participate and implement Easy

Reading. At this point, the project was faced with the so-called gatekeeper problem [54]. If the head of the institution, school or management level did not see the need or value of Easy Reading for their clients, it was nearly impossible to reach potential end-users. As the number of institutions participating in the implementation was not as high as hoped, Easy Reading was promoted at various (digital) events and exhibitions. This also included the distribution of handouts and other information material.

## 3.1  Validation Methods

Two approaches to validate Easy Reading were pursued. In the first approach, the project members collaborated closely with the institutions where trainings were carried out. In the second approach, information material and the project website were used to distribute an online questionnaire. This approach was chosen to reach as many Easy Reading users as possible.

In the institutions where training was provided, focus groups with end users were carried out. In these focus groups, questions regarding how they got to know Easy Reading, usage of Easy Reading in their everyday life and wishes and suggestions for improvement were asked. In order to react to the needs of the target group, the guidelines were handled in a flexible manner. This included reformulating the questions, changing the order in accordance with the given answers, providing additional explanations, giving examples and providing extra time to answer the questions. Furthermore, because some participants were anxious, it was emphasized that the focus group was not a test but that their opinions and experiences were of great value for the project. Additionally, some participants prepared notes upfront to the focus group. These notes are integrated into the analysis as an additional source of information.

In the second approach, a questionnaire was used and distributed online. The questionnaire consists of three parts (Usability, Getting to know and Usefulness, and General Feedback) and contains 45 items plus three questions about demographic information. Different well-known scales were used to create the questionnaire, such as System Usability Scale [55], Perceived Usefulness [56], Software Usability Measurement Inventory [57] as well as specific questions about Easy Reading. The answer scale was a five-point Likert scale. All items were adapted to Easy Reading. This questionnaire addresses primarily professionals and caregivers. Thus, to address the end users, such as people with ID directly, the questionnaire was translated into easy-to-read language and checked by a validation group for easy-to-read. This questionnaire was shorter and consisted of 24 items plus demographic information. The questionnaire has been available since September and is still online. In addition to the questionnaire, an invitation to provide feedback via voice message or instant messaging (WhatsApp, Signal, Threema) was sent out to lower the threshold for giving feedback.

## 3.2  Reflection of Used Validation Methods

Two focus groups with end users were carried out in the institutions with personal contact with the caregivers. These focus groups lasted about 30 min; four people participated in the first focus group and five in the second. Upfront to the focus groups, the participants had to sign a privacy statement. Even though the privacy statement was also translated into easy-to-read language, it was still rather complex due to the complexity of privacy statements itself. In Germany, privacy statements need to include the respective paragraph of the Data Protection Act. Therefore, before the focus groups were started, the interviewers explained the privacy statements. Afterwards, some end users decided against participation. Problematic as well was that due to the detailed explanation, the interest and attention for the focus group itself decreased. Furthermore, the participants were rather nervous, probably due to the unknown situation and because they antici-pated a test rather than conducting their opinions and experiences. Another problem was reaching the participants. The project members had to use the communication channel through caregivers and the management level. There was no communication channel directly to the end users. Thus, the gatekeeper problem [54] might have excluded addi-tional participants. Nevertheless, the focus groups provided valuable insights into the opinions and experiences of the end users with Easy Reading.

The first analysis of the questionnaire was carried out in October 2023. Even though various distribution channels were used, the response rate was rather low. So far, 29 people answered the questionnaire. Ten people answered the questionnaire in complex language, 19 in easy-to-read. However, the dropout rate was rather high, 60% did not complete the questionnaire. The risk for a high dropout rate and the difficulty to reach the intended target group with an online questionnaire [58] was known, nevertheless, this approach was chosen due to its broad distributions opportunities. Because in this digital distribution approach, support while answering the questionnaire could not be provided, an alternative to provide feedback was communicated. In addition to the links to the questionnaire, a mobile phone number was provided to allow for a simple and familiar communication channel. Everything from text or voice messages and calls would have been included in the analysis. However, by now, this communication channel was not used.

During the EVE4all project, the challenge was to reach as many people as possible without having any personal contact. Thus, 'traditional' methods, such as questionnaires were used in combination with an alternative communication channel. Although the questionnaire was provided in easy-to-read language, the drop-out rate shows that this approach is not appropriate. However, it remains unclear why communication via mobile phone was not used. One can only speculate that it is tedious to write to an unknown number, especially if the feedback is primarily for research purposes and the personal benefit remains unclear. Thus, alternative methods and approaches need to be developed and applied.

## 4   Be Creative! New Methods for Participatory Research

In order to design meaningful technology and training for the intended target group, for example, people with ID, another research approach is needed. Such an approach is participatory research. Participatory research is a generic term for research approaches that explore and influence social reality in partnership. The participatory research aims to understand and change social reality. One central aspect of participatory research is the involvement of co-researchers, who equally participate in every step of the research project [10, 52]. However, it can be differentiated into nine steps, who gradually describe the kind of participation [59]. While the overall goal should be the steps: Codetermination (6), partial decision-making power (7), decision-making power (8) and self-organization (9). Actions to enable participation at a lower level, for example, information (3), hearing-out (4) and involvement (5) are crucial groundwork. This is especially true for a target group, for which it is said that questioning or interviewing them holds challenges and difficulties (see Sect. 2.3). While the predecessor project Easy Reading, was a participatory research project per design [60], the EVE4all project is not a participatory research project, even though the aim is to involve the intended target group as much as possible, at least at the levels three-five. However, as illustrated in Sect. 3 the actions taken to involve people with ID in questionnaires and focus groups were not as successful as hoped for. Thus, in the following months a more creative approach will be taken. For this approach it will be necessary to work closely with institutions, so that people with ID can be reached with these methods and thus can participate in the research.

The first method is **photovoice**. In this method photos are taken by the participants with the aim to illustrate their thoughts and opinions and to use them in a follow-up conversation [61]. For the EVE4all project two approaches could be used. One is to identify potential challenges when using the internet. Second, taking pictures when using Easy Reading (add-on or mobile version). In the follow-up conversation, the photos can be used as stimulus or reminder for experienced barriers or the benefits. Additionally, this method can act as a motivation, because the participants have to first think actively about what to photograph. However, it has to be noted, that particularly the follow-up conversation requires a certain level of communication skills, even though the taken photos can be used as a source of data.

Another method is the **walking interview**. Together with the researcher the participants 'walk' around and talk about what they see, where they are and what they experience [62]. In the EVE4all project it is not really necessary to walk around, but researcher and participants can surf the internet together, while using Easy Reading. As well as the photovoice method, communication skills would be helpful and an additional source of information. However, observing what participants do in the internet and how they interact with Easy Reading will provide valuable information.

In addition to these more visual methods, additional communication aids can be developed and used in the follow-up conversation or during the interview. For example, symbols can be prepared to talk about barriers, experiences, wishes and so on. The selection of symbols needs to be prepared carefully and with consideration of the intended target group. Furthermore, Talking Mats [63] could be used to gain a more in depth insight of the usage of Easy Reading. The method **Talking Mats** has the additional benefit, that verbal communication skills are not required. Heitplatz (2021)was able to show in its study how well the combination of Talking Mats and focus groups works and what valuable insights can be drawn from it [4].

Coming from the empirical UX area (user experience design), **card sorting** may also be suitable for generating qualitative and quantitative statements about new technologies. Card sorting is mainly used in UX design in the analysis or conception phase. However, card sorting can also be helpful later on, for example if problems with the existing information architecture are suspected. Whether the method can be implemented well for people with ID is tested in the final project phase of the EVE4all project [64].

Finally, it would also be conceivable to carry out a **role-play** on a specific issue or topic. Depending on how the role-play is defined and implemented, communicative skills are not necessarily required. Particularly if several people are involved, the roles could be defined according to the needs and resources of the participants. Role-plays are primarily used as an empirical method in psychological research [65]. Role-plays have been considered less for collecting data from people with ID and might be an interesting way to get to know about their feeling regarding the Easy Reading Tool in our project.

Additionally, to these methods the direct interaction with the participants allows flexible adaptations in accordance to the participants' needs and the usage of Assistive Technology, e.g. speech-generating devices for communication. However, this flexibility by the researchers calls for a creative manner to conduct interviews. A strict guideline might be more hindering than beneficial. At the same time, it is important to follow basic interview rules, such as not asking leading questions or to put words in their mouths. This illustrates once again, that the importance of the researcher or interviewer cannot be stressed enough [53].

# 5 Conclusion

The results of the initial analysis of the methodological approaches of the EVE4all project illustrate the challenges researchers face when including a target group that may not be easy to reach and survey. 'Classical' methods such as questionnaires and interviews may reach their limits. However, these methods still need to be considered, especially when the goal is to reach as many participants as possible. Even though the outcome may not be as wished for. Thus, for (online) questionnaires, more individualized and creative approaches are needed. One approach could be to provide face-to-face support when filling out the questionnaire or introducing technical solutions (e.g. Avatars or virtual personas). This approach has different challenges as the participants still need to be reached in the first place, and the personnel costs must not be neglected.

The personal costs also need to be considered in the more personal and creative approaches presented in section four. In addition to the time needed for the methods itself, the recruitment process may also be cumbersome. The gatekeeper problem still applies, as heads of institutions and management still need to be convinced that their clients, students, residents are valuable participants in research. At the same time, the limited time and personnel resources in institutions should not be neglected by the researcher.

In summary, a research project to involve people with ID requires resources to overcome a variety of challenges. However, valuable and useful results can only be achieved if the target group is enabled to participate in such research projects. In an inclusive environment, everyone must have the means and opportunity to participate. It is the researcher's job to facilitate participation in his/her research and not the participants' job to match the description of a desired participant.

# References

1. Schäfers, M.: Lebensqualität aus Nutzersicht. Wie Menschen mit geistiger Behinderung ihre Lebenssituation beurteilen. VS Verlag für Sozialwissenschaften/GWV Fachverlage GmbH Wiesbaden, Wiesbaden (2008)
2. Schäfers, M., Schachler, V., Schneekloth, U., Wacker, E., Zeiler, E.: Forschungsbericht 471. Pretest Befragung in Einrichtungen der Behindertenhilfe. Abschlussbericht (2016). http://www.bmas.de/SharedDocs/Downloads/DE/PDF-Publikationen/Forschungsberichte/fb471-pretest-befragung-in-einrichtungen.pdf?__blob=publicationFile&v=1. Accessed 16 Jan 2018
3. Buchholz, M., Ferm, U., Holmgren, K.: Including persons with complex communication needs in research – a structured methodology based on Talking Mats (2016). https://www.isaac-online.org/conference/modules/request.php?module=oc_program&action=view.php&id=101&type=1&a=. Accessed 15 Jul 2020
4. Heitplatz, V.N.: Digitale Teilhabemöglichkeiten von Menschen mit intellektuellen Beeinträchtigungen im Wohnkontext. Perspektiven von Einrichtungsleitungen, Fachkräften und Bewohnenden. Eldorado - Repositorium der TU Dortmund (2021)
5. Ågren, K.A., Kjellberg, A., Hemmingsson, H.: Access to and use of the Internet among adolescents and young adults with intellectual disabilities in everyday settings. J. Intellect. Dev. Disabil. **45**, 89–98 (2020). https://doi.org/10.3109/13668250.2018.1518898
6. Ågren, K.A.: Internet use and digital participation in everyday life. Adolescents and young adults with intellectual disabilities. Linköpng University Medical Dissertations No. 1734. Department of Health, Medical and Caring Sciences Linköping University, Linköping (2020)
7. Chadwick, D., Quinn, S., Fullwood, C.: Perceptions of the risks and benefits of Internet access and use by people with intellectual disabilities. Br. J. Learn. Disabil. **45**, 21–31 (2017)
8. Shpigelman, C.-N.: Leveraging social capital of individuals with intellectual disabilities through participation on Facebook. J. Appl. Res. Intellect. Disabil. (JARID) **31**, e79–e91 (2018). https://doi.org/10.1111/jar.12321
9. Chadwick, D., Fullwood, C., Wesson, C.J.: Intellectual disability, identity, and the Internet. In: Luppicini, R. (ed.) Handbook of Research on Technoself, vol. 8, pp. 229–254. IGI Global, Pennsylvania (2013)
10. Dirks, S.: Empowering instead of hindering – challenges in participatory development of cognitively accessible software. In: Antona, M., Stephanidis, C. (eds.) HCII 2019. LNCS, vol. 11572, pp. 28–38. Springer, Cham (2019). https://doi.org/10.1007/978-3-030-23560-4_3
11. German Institute of Medical Documentation and Information: ICF (2019). https://www.dimdi.de/dynamic/en/classifications/icf/index.html. Accessed 30 Jan 2020
12. American Association of Intellectual and Developmental Disabilities: Definition of Intellectual Disability (2020). https://www.aaidd.org/intellectual-disability/definition. Accessed 29 Jul 2020
13. Falkai, P., Wittchen, H.-U. (eds.): Diagnostisches und statistisches Manual psychischer Störungen DSM-5®, 2nd edn. Hogrefe, Göttingen (2018)
14. Kjellmer, L., Fernell, E., Gillberg, C., Norrelgen, F.: Speech and language profiles in 4- to 6-year-old children with early diagnosis of autism spectrum disorder without intellectual disability. Neuropsychiatr. Dis. Treat. **14**, 2415–2427 (2018). https://doi.org/10.2147/NDT.S171971
15. Dodd, B., Thompson, L.: Speech disorder in children with Down's syndrome. J. Intellect. Disabil. Res. **45**, 308–316 (2001)
16. Marrus, N., Hall, L.: Intellectual disability and language disorder. Child Adolesc. Psychiatr. Clin. N. Am. **26**, 539–554 (2017). https://doi.org/10.1016/j.chc.2017.03.001

17. Norrelgen, F., et al.: Children with autism spectrum disorders who do not develop phrase speech in the preschool years. Autism **19**(8), 934–943 (2015). https://doi.org/10.1177/136 2361314556782
18. Lingg, A., Theunissen, G.: Psychische Störungen und geistige Behinderungen. Ein Lehrbuch und Kompendium für die Praxis, 7. aktualisierte Auflage. Lambertus-Verlag, Freiburg (2017)
19. Näslund, R., Gardelli, Å.: 'I know, I can, I will try': youths and adults with intellectual disabilities in Sweden using information and communication technology in their everyday life. Disabil. Soc. **28**, 1–13 (2013). https://doi.org/10.1080/09687599.2012.695528
20. Parsons, S., Daniels, H., Porter, J., Robertson, C.: Resources, staff beliefs and organizational culture: factors in the use of information and communication technology for adults with intellectual disabilities. J. Appl. Res. Intellect. Disabil. **21**, 19–33 (2008). https://doi.org/10.1111/j.1468-3148.2007.00361.x
21. Caron, J., Light, J.: "Social Media has opened a world of 'open communication:'" experiences of adults with cerebral palsy who use augmentative and alternative communication and social media. Augmentative Altern. Commun. **32**(1), 25–40 (2015). https://doi.org/10.3109/07434618.2015.1052887
22. Bryan, D.N., Chung, Y.: What adults who use AAC say about their use of mainstream mobile technologies. Assistive Technol. Outcomes Benefits (ATOB) **12**, 73–106 (2018)
23. Iglesias, O.B., Sánchez, L.E.G., Rodríguez, M.Á.A.: Do young people with Asperger syndrome or intellectual disability use social media and are they cyberbullied or cyberbullies in the same way as their peers? Psicothema **31**, 30–37 (2019). https://doi.org/10.7334/psicothema2018.243
24. Mendoza-González, A., et al.: An empiric study of the use of mobile technology by users with intellectual disability. In: Agredo-Delgado, V., Ruiz, P.H. (eds.) HCI-COLLAB 2018. CCIS, vol. 847, pp. 29–43. Springer, Cham (2019). https://doi.org/10.1007/978-3-030-05270-6_3
25. Shpigelman, C.-N., Gill, C.J.: Facebook use by persons with disabilities. J. Comput. Mediat. Commun. **19**, 610–624 (2014). https://doi.org/10.1111/jcc4.12059
26. Chiner, E., Gómez-Puerta, M.M., Cardona-Moltó, C.: Internet and people with intellectual disability: an approach to caregivers' concerns, prevention strategies and training needs. J. New Approaches Educ. Res. **6**(2), 153–158 (2017). https://doi.org/10.7821/naer.2017.7.243
27. Didden, R., et al.: Cyberbullying among students with intellectual and developmental disability in special education settings. Dev. Neurorehabil. **12**, 146–151 (2009). https://doi.org/10.1080/17518420902971356
28. Eghdam, A., Bartfai, A., Oldenburg, C., Koch, S.: How do persons with mild acquired cognitive impairment use information and communication technology and e-services? Results from a Swedish National Survey. PLoS ONE **11**, e0159362 (2016). https://doi.org/10.1371/journal.pone.0159362
29. Jenaro, C., Flores, N., Cruz, M., Pérez, M.C., Vega, V., Torres, V.A.: Internet and cell phone usage patterns among young adults with intellectual disabilities. J. Appl. Res. Intellect. Disabil. (JARID) **31**, 259–272 (2018). https://doi.org/10.1111/jar.12388
30. Lough, E., Fisher, M.H.: Internet use and online safety in adults with Williams syndrome. J. Intellect. Disabil. Res. (JIDR) **60**, 1020–1030 (2016). https://doi.org/10.1111/jir.12281
31. Patrick, P.A., Obermeyer, I., Xenakis, J., Crocitto, D., O'Hara, D.M.: Technology and social media use by adult patients with intellectual and/or developmental disabilities. Disabil. Health J. **13**, 100840 (2020). https://doi.org/10.1016/j.dhjo.2019.100840
32. Wehmeyer, M.L., Palmer, S.B., Smith, S.J., Davies, D.K., Stock, S.: The efficacy of technology use by people with intellectual disability: a single-subject design meta-analysis. J. Spec. Educ. Technol. **23**, 21–30 (2008). https://doi.org/10.1177/016264340802300303
33. White, P., Forrester-Jones, R.: Valuing e-inclusion: social media and the social networks of adolescents with intellectual disability. J. Intellect. Disabil. Online First **24**, 381–397 (2019). https://doi.org/10.1177/1744629518821240

34. Ågren, K.A., Kjellberg, A., Hemmingsson, H.: Digital participation? Internet use among adolescents with and without intellectual disabilities: a comparative study. New Media Soc. **22**, 146144481988839 (2020). https://doi.org/10.1177/1461444819888398

35. Haage, A., Bosse, I.K.: Media use of persons with disabilities. In: 11th International Conference, UAHCI 2017, held as part of HCI International 2017, vol. 10279, pp. 419–435 (2017)

36. Sallafranque-St-Louis, F., Normand, C.L.: From solitude to solicitation: how people with intellectual disability or autism spectrum disorder use the internet. Cyberpsychol. J. Psychosoc. Res. Cybersp. (2017). https://doi.org/10.5817/CP2017-1-7

37. Stiller, A., Weber, J., Strube, F., Mößle, T.: Caregiver reports of screen time use of children with autism spectrum disorder: a qualitative study. Behav. Sci. **9**, 56 (2019). https://doi.org/10.3390/bs9050056

38. Raspa, M., et al.: Mobile technology use and skills among individuals with fragile X syndrome: implications for healthcare decision making. J. Intellect. Disabil. Res. (JIDR) **62**, 821–832 (2018). https://doi.org/10.1111/jir.12537

39. ARD/ZDF-Forschungskommission: ARD/ZDF-Onlinestudie | ARD/ZDF-Forschungskommission (2020). http://www.ard-zdf-onlinestudie.de/. Accessed 15 Jul 2020

40. Medienpädagogischer Forschungsverbund Südwest: KIM-Studie 2018 - Kindheit, Internet, Medien. Basisuntersuchung zum Medienumgang 6- bis 13-Jähriger (2019). https://www.mpfs.de/fileadmin/files/Studien/KIM/2018/KIM-Studie_2018_web.pdf. Accessed 15 Jul 2020

41. Ofcom: Adults' Media Use & Attitudes. Report 2020 (2020). https://www.ofcom.org.uk/__data/assets/pdf_file/0031/196375/adults-media-use-and-attitudes-2020-report.pdf. Accessed 18 Aug 2020

42. Deutsche Welle: Zahl der Analphabeten in Deutschland geht zurück (2020). https://www.dw.com/de/zahl-der-analphabeten-in-deutschland-geht-zur%C3%BCck/a-48637432. Accessed 15 Jul 2020

43. Haug, S.: Sprachliche Integration von Migranten in Deutschland (2008). https://www.bamf.de/SharedDocs/Anlagen/DE/Forschung/WorkingPapers/wp14-sprachliche-integration.pdf?__blob=publicationFile&v=11. Accessed 23 Oct 2020

44. Statistisches Bundesamt: Bevölkerung mit Migrationshintergrund & Ausländer in Deutschland (2020). https://www.destatis.de/DE/Themen/Gesellschaft-Umwelt/Bevoelkerung/Migration-Integration/_inhalt.html. Accessed 18 Aug 2020

45. Niediek, I.: Wer nicht fragt, bekommt keine Antworten- Interviewtechniken unter besonderen Bedingungen. Zeitschrift für Inklusion (2016)

46. Gutiérrez, P., Martorell, A.: People with Intellectual Disability and ICTs. Comunicar Sci. J. Media Literacy **36**, 173–180 (2011). https://doi.org/10.3916/C36-2011-03-09

47. Shpigelman, C.-N.: Leveraging social capital of persons with intellectual disabilities through Facebook participation: the perspectives of family members and direct support staff. Intellect. Dev. Disabil. **55**, 407–418 (2017). https://doi.org/10.1352/1934-9556-55.6.407

48. Barr, O., McConkey, R., McConaghie, J.: Views of people with learning difficulties about current and future accommodation: the use of focus groups to promote discussion. Disabil. Soc. **18**, 577–597 (2003). https://doi.org/10.1080/0968759032000097834

49. Molin, M., Sorbring, E., Löfgren-Mårtenson, L.: Teachers' and parents' views on the Internet and social media usage by pupils with intellectual disabilities. J. Intellect. Disabil. **19**, 22–33 (2015). https://doi.org/10.1177/1744629514563558

50. Heitplatz, V.N., Bühler, C., Hastall, M.R.: Usage of digital media by people with intellectual disabilities: contrasting individuals' and formal caregivers' perspectives. J. Intellect. Disabil. (JOID) **26**, 420–441 (2021). https://doi.org/10.1177/1744629520971375

51. Participate: Participatory Research Methods – Participate (2020). https://participatesdgs.org/methods/. Accessed 23 Oct 2020
52. Miesenberger, K., Edler, C., Dirks, S., Bühler, C., Heumader, P.: User centered design and user participation in inclusive R&D. In: Miesenberger, K., Manduchi, R., Covarrubias Rodriguez, M., Peňáz, P. (eds.) ICCHP 2020. LNCS, vol. 12376, pp. 3–9. Springer, Cham (2020). https://doi.org/10.1007/978-3-030-58796-3_1
53. Wilkens, L.: "The Most Important Voices are Often the Hardest to Hear" - Einflüsse auf die standardisierte Interviewführung mit nicht oder wenig sprechenden Menschen, pp. 4–11. Uk & forschung (2019)
54. Buchner, T.: Das qualitative Interview mit Menschen mit sogenannter geistiger Behinderung- Ethische, methodologische und praktische Aspekte. In: Biewer, G. (ed.) Begegnung und Differenz: Menschen, Länder, Kulturen. Beiträge zur Heil- und Sonderpädagogik; [2. Tagung Internationale Sonderpädagogik, 28. - 30. 9. 2006 an der Universität Wien], pp. 516–528. Klinkhardt, Bad Heilbrunn (2008)
55. Brooke, J.: SUS: A 'Quick and Dirty' Usability Scale (1996). https://hell.meiert.org/core/pdf/sus.pdf. Accessed 2 Feb 2022
56. Davis, F.D., Bagozzi, R.P., Warshaw, P.R.: User acceptance of computer technology: a comparison of two theoretical models. Manage. Sci. **35**, 92–1003 (1989)
57. Kirakowski, J.: Software usability measurement inventory (2021). https://sumi.uxp.ie/about/whatis.html. Accessed 15 Jan 2024
58. Haage, A.: Informationsrepertoires von Menschen mit Beeinträchtigungen. Nomos Verlagsgesellschaft mbH & Co. KG (2021)
59. von Unger, H.: Partizipative Forschung. Springer Fachmedien Wiesbaden, Wiesbaden (2014). https://doi.org/10.1007/978-3-658-01290-8
60. Edler, C., Dirks, S.: D1.1 Methods and Tools for Recruitment (2018). https://www.easyreading.eu/wp-content/uploads/2019/04/D1.1.pdf
61. Wihofszky, P., et al.: Photovoice als partizipative methode: wirkungen auf individueller, gemeinschaftlicher und gesellschaftlicher Ebene. In: Hartung, S., Wihofszky, P., Wright, M.T. (eds.) Partizipative Forschung, pp. 85–141. Springer Fachmedien Wiesbaden, Wiesbaden (2020). https://doi.org/10.1007/978-3-658-30361-7_4
62. Kühl, J.: Walking Interviews als Methode zur Erhebung alltäglicher Raumproduktionen. Europa Regional **23**, 35–48 (2016)
63. Murphy, J., Cameron, L., Boa, S.: Talking Mats. A Resource to Enhance Communication, 3rd edn. Talking Mats, Shirling (2013)
64. Sinnig, C.: Informationsarchitektur meistern: 3 Card-Sorting-Methoden für eine bessere Navigation (2020). https://userlutions.com/blog/usability-analyse/card-sorting-informationsarchitektur/
65. Sader, M.: Rollenspiel als Forschungsmethode in unterschiedlichen Teilbereichen der Psychologie: Versuch einer Bestandsaufnahme. In: Sader, M. (ed.) Rollenspiel als Forschungsmethode, pp. 37–46. VS Verlag für Sozialwissenschaften, Wiesbaden (1986)

# A Study on the Design of an Emotional Interaction Device for Children with Autism Spectrum Disorder Based on Focused Attention Mindfulness

Yujia Jia$^{(\boxtimes)}$, Jiaqi Wang, and Yujun Zhou

Sichuan University Jinjiang College, Meishan 620860, Sichuan, China
Jiayujia163com@163.com

**Abstract.** In order to effectively alleviate the emotional stress of children with ASD in their daily lives, this study took the positive thinking exercise (FAM) and combined it with mandala coloring to create a recreational interactive device for children with ASD, as well as providing a new way of thinking about non-static FAM exercises. In this study, children's emotional changes were assessed during traditional mandala coloring exercises and interactive device intervention conditioning through group testing and interviews with healthcare professionals. The results indicated that the group moderated with the interactive device was more likely to stimulate children's interest and generate positive emotions.

**Keywords:** Children with ASD · MBCT · Mandala · Mindfulness-based design

## 1 Introduction

Autism is also known as Autism Spectrum Disorder (ASD). The problem of children with ASD is that they have poor performance in language and cognitive comprehension, and they are easily affected by the outside world and stress in terms of emotion, in order to regulate this negative emotion, some scholars have devoted themselves to research on how to enhance the socialization of children with ASD, for example, J Li and E Barakova et al. have developed a situational awareness tool (ApEn) to collect behavioral data related to stress expression and provide factual feedback on the stress level of children with ASD so as to regulate their negative emotions in time [1]. On this basis, mandala painting is gradually becoming an important modality of art therapy due to the function of mandala coloring training based on focused attention mindfulness (FAM) practice to regulate emotional disorders and enhance mental health and personality integrity. YC Liang et al. found that developing extended collaborative mandala coloring (CMC) can

---

The original version of the chapter has been revised. The first author's affiliation and e-mail address were corrected. A correction to this chapter can be found at
https://doi.org/10.1007/978-3-031-60881-0_26

M. Antona and C. Stephanidis (Eds.): HCII 2024, LNCS 14697, pp. 186–197, 2024.
https://doi.org/10.1007/978-3-031-60881-0_12

openly reveal the self in order to broaden the experience of interacting with others [2]. In addition, compared to traditional static mandala painting, many scholars have found that ASD children are guided by emotional expression products to gain insights into the laws of human emotions through multi-sensory pathways such as tactile, visual, and auditory senses. For example, Szatmari P et al. improved the social behavior of children with autism through the use of wearable devices for emotional recognition and mobile intervention in children with ASD [3]; Cochrane et al. enhanced the effect of positive cognitive processes through a nature soundscape responsive to their brainwave activity recorded with a Muse EEG headset [4]. Further, Claudia Daudén Roquet et al. designed a non-static mandala coloring exercise using the Anima working example prototype, which is an important attempt of non-static mindfulness practice in the field of human-computer interaction [5].

We believe that even though interaction technology has been gradually explored for monitoring users' emotions, more applications are still based on users' "sit-down" exercises. Considering the children with ASD (6–10 years old) should engage in more recreational social activities with their peers in order to improve their social and emotional expression skills, this study proposes an idea: transforming the Mandala Color Exercise in Positive Mindfulness Cognitive Therapy from a two-dimensional experience to a three-dimensional multimodal interaction, allowing children to receive both visual and behavioral stimuli on a physiological level, as well as psychologically regulated emotions and attention during the time they spend interacting with the product. The use of this entertaining interactive device allows children to get rid of the traditional sit-down "therapy" program, so that children in the interactive and entertainment process to relieve stress, increase interaction with peers, and enhance their socialization ability.

## 2   Research Method and Process

### 2.1   Participant Selection

This study was conducted in a special school (total 140 students, teachers and allied health workers 42 people), and the questionnaire was mainly distributed to the parents of the children, specialized teachers and related personnel in the special school, as it was considered that children with ASD do not have the ability to self-judge by completing the questionnaire.

This study required the cooperation of special school students, we obtained the review and approval of the school's Ethics Committee, in conjunction with the school's teacher and allied health workers, we selected 6 mildly symptomatic children aged 6–10 years with basic communication skills to be tested in accordance with the wishes of the children's parents and the children's personal wishes.

### 2.2   Participant Selection

**Materials.** Apple Watch (to provide HRV monitoring), laptop, interactive prototype (includes: Arduino, LED strip, thin-film pressure transducer, bi-directional rotary damper, acrylic blade, and metal stand).

**Installation Design.** Based on the study of different styles of mandala patterns, it is found that the flat style of the pattern of the use of color diversity, containing different cultural connotations of totems, design styles are numerous. Most of the mandala paintings are said to be round as the outer contour, the middle level superimposed irregular shapes, squares, polygons, etc., its symmetrical form of display graphics in the visual color tonal classification of the graphics do not use to give people a different visual experience. Accordingly, due to the research location in Guizhou minority areas, combined with the local cultural background, this program selects the characteristics of the local minority patterns and color schemes combined with the mandala design (Fig. 1).

**Fig. 1.** Classical ethnic style mandala design

## 2.3 Experimental Procedure

First, because children cannot accurately analyze their own emotional stress, a medical professional accompanied them throughout the experiment, and the stress detection software (real-time heart rate variability testing software) in the Apple Watch was used to provide factual feedback on the children's emotional changes. Secondly, the interactive device was able to feedback color changes according to the amount of force applied during rotation. Finally, mandala coloring was performed on the iPad (Figs. 2, 3 and 4).

In order to investigate the children's emotional changes after using the interactive device, this study divided six children into an experimental group and a control group; children in the control group, underwent a stress test and then completed the mandala coloring, followed by another stress test; children in the experimental group underwent a stress test and then engaged the children in a stress test after using the interactive device (the model), followed by another mandala coloring test.

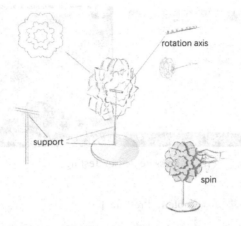

a.    Current prototype program design ideas

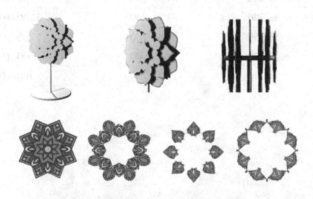

b. Mandala Pattern Layered Disassembly

c.  Appearance

**Fig. 2.**  Test prototype design

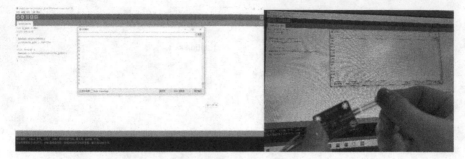

**Fig. 3.** Pressure Sensor Testing

**Table 1.** Pressure Test

|          | light intensity | medium strength | hard      |
|----------|-----------------|-----------------|-----------|
| Tester 1 | < = 400         | 400–750         | 750–1000  |
| Testers 2| < = 300         | 300–700         | 700–1000  |
| Testers 3| < = 350         | 300–700         | 700–900   |
| Testers 4| < = 240         | 240–600         | 600–1000  |
| Testers 5| < = 300         | 300–700         | 700–1000  |

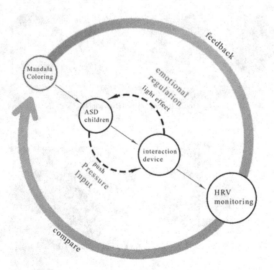

**Fig. 4.** Interaction Framework Schematic

**Experimental group test flow.**

1. The researchers introduced the experimental procedure and the use of the prototype to the accompanying medical staff and jointly explained it to the children.
2. Children were identified to clarify the experimental procedure and verbal consent was obtained from the children.
3. Wearing an Apple Watch and measuring HRV
4. Children were asked to turn the sub-interactive device at least 3 times to experience it, and were observed for mood and asked if they wanted to experience it again.
5. Children performed independent mandala coloring and measured HRV values.

**Control group test procedure.**

1. The researchers introduced the experimental procedure to the accompanying medical staff and jointly explained it to the children.
2. Children were identified to clarify the experimental procedure and verbal consent was obtained from the children.
3. Wearing an Apple Watch and measuring HRV
4. Allow children to train in mandala coloring under the guidance of medical personnel.
5. Children performed independent mandala coloring and measured HRV values.

# 3 Results

## 3.1 Research and Interview Results

The research population includes both online and offline, with a total of 320 valid questionnaires. Among the researchers, 49.35% were parents, 32.03% were rehabilitation teachers, and 18.61% were other groups; 61.04% of the researchers had difficulties in expressing their children's emotions; 56.26% of the researchers said that children with autism at home were treated in intervention centers and 21.65% were educated in special schools; 92.64% believed that the caring interactive products could help their children express their emotions correctly. Among them, 22.08% were treated in intervention institutions and 21.65% were sent to special education schools; 92.64% of the population believed that caring interactive products could help children express their emotions correctly (Fig. 5).

Based on the online questionnaire research, offline interviews were conducted, because the teachers of autistic children are the most familiar with the psychological and behavioral characteristics of autistic children as well as the process of Positive Thinking Therapy, taking into account the children's expressive barriers during face-to-face exchanges, and the teachers of autistic children are the most familiar with the process of Positive Thinking Therapy, therefore, a total of nine people, including teachers and medical staff, were chosen as the main targets of the interviews (Tables 1, 2 and 3).

According to the interview and research results, combined with ASD children's daily product needs, it shows that the product features that children mainly need are under the premise of considering the safety of product operation and interactive forms, combined with touch control and color and light interaction, it can attract and mobilize children's positive emotions and interactive positivity to the greatest extent possible (Figs. 6 and 7).

Which products help children express their emotions correctly?

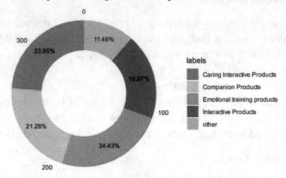

What features should an emotional interaction device have?

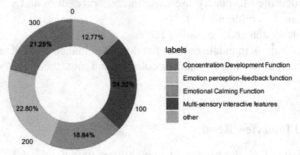

**Fig. 5.** Online research pie chart (example)

**Table 2.** Statistics on the basic information of teachers interviewed for children with ASD

| Number of interviews | sexes | dignity | Teaching experience (years) | Age of students taught (years) |
|---|---|---|---|---|
| 3 | women | language and literature teacher | 3–4 | 8–10 |
| 3 | daughter | resident teacher | 4–6 | 6–10 |
| 3 | women | medical personnel | 4–5 | 6–10 |

According to the user study, the tactile-emotional interaction mode design is carried out, firstly, the pressure tactile test is carried out on children aged 6–10 years old, when the subjects press the pressure module, there will be different colors of lights for feedback, and at the same time, the subjects are allowed to fill in the emotional rating scale. It was found that when the feedback color tends to be balanced between warm and cold, children's positive mood scores will be gradually stabilized; when the color appears to alternate, the interest of realistic children is enhanced.

**Fig. 6.** ASD Child Interaction Needs Analysis

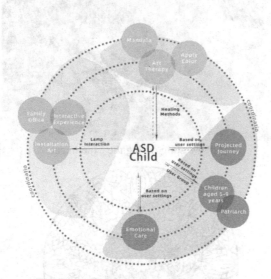

**Fig. 7.** ASD Child Interaction Positioning

## 3.2 Experimental Results

The results of the interviews and tests showed that the regulation of positive emotions was more pronounced in the children who added experiential interactions compared to experiencing traditional mandala coloring-only exercises.

During the experiment, it was found that children in the control group had more emotional ups and downs during the mandala coloring exercise and made more mistakes

**Table 3.** HRV changes in children during the experiment.

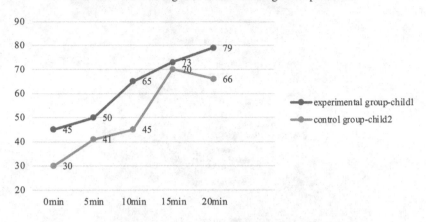

a. HRV testing during the experiment

b. Mandala coloring process

**Fig. 8.** Children during testing

during the coloring process. Children in the experimental group showed significant positive mood elevation, as well as better color selection and accuracy in the later stages of the mandala coloring process (Fig. 8).

## 4 Discussion

This study aims to make a recreational attempt to regulate the emotions of children with ASD, trying to change the mandala interaction from static painting to a dynamic recreational activity, so that children with ASD can enhance the interaction and emotional output with peers and release their nature during play. In our study, we found that compared with the static coloring process, the children showed good cooperation in using the interactive device, and showed higher interest in the interaction of the device's light effects, and the change of HRV showed that the children's emotional state could be improved more quickly, and they had a more reasonable choice of colors and were more accurate in the later process of filling in the mandala, while the control group's coloring practice under the traditional mode showed a higher interest in the traditional mode of coloring. Mandala coloring practice, on the other hand, was slower to improve children's moods and tended to show a decrease in concentration during later independent coloring practice. Since the current study found that positive mood production was more pronounced in children with the addition of experiential interactions than in children experiencing traditional mandala-only coloring practice, we intend to conduct a follow-up study to examine the effects of the addition of experiential interactions on children's mood. Therefore, we intend to conduct a follow-up in-depth study to validate the difference in the effects of the interactive form of dynamic healing versus the traditional static positive emotion practice.

However, some limitations appear in this study. Firstly, since the model and device sampling were generally effective, the accuracy of the model and the interaction experience will be improved in subsequent studies; furthermore, in the process of real-time emotion detection, the existing emotional stress software in the AppleStore and the Stress Watch and the SDNN detection in the Apple Watch were used to provide assistance to the healthcare workers even if the feedback is provided. Stress Watch and the SDNN detection that comes with the Apple Watch are currently used to provide the role of assisting healthcare workers to provide even though feedback, which can be combined with the interactive device in the future, and use professional HRV testing equipment, and increase the closeness of the interactive device to the children's emotions by adding a Wi-Fi transmission module to provide real-time feedback from the heart rate variability to the light changes.

## 5 Conclusion

This study attempts to supplement the existing cognitive practice methods with a "dynamic" and "interactive" mindfulness approach from the perspective of children with ASD. Since children with ASD are at the most critical stage of their lives in terms of value establishment and personality development, they need to innovate the traditional positive thinking exercises. In this study, the children's interaction with the interactive device stimulated their interest and enhanced their sense of participation, and we found that in this kind of recreational interaction, the children were more likely to communicate and play with each other, which could help them to cultivate their social behaviors. In addition, we found that in such entertaining interactions, children are more likely to actively communicate and play together, which helps children develop social behaviors, and thus our attempt also opens up new ideas for the future healing of children with ASD.

**Acknowledgments.** We thank all user study participants as well as the Guizhou Red Cross Society and local education bureau for their support and Sichuan University Jinjiang College for their joint efforts.

**Disclosure of Interests..**    The authors have no competing interests to declare that are relevant to the content of this article.

# References

1. Li, J., Barakova, E., Hu, J., et al.: ApEn: a stress-aware pen for children with autism spectrum disorder. In: International Work-Conference on the Interplay between Natural and Artificial Computation. Between Natural and Artificial Computation, pp. 281–290. Springer International Publishing, Cham (2022). https://doi.org/10.1007/978-3-031-06242-1_28
2. Liang, Y.C., Lin, M.L., Huang, D.H., Chiou, W.K.: Flow and interflow: the design principles of cooperative mandala coloring (CMC). In: Lecture Notes in Computer Science (Including Subseries Lecture Notes in Artificial Intelligence and Lecture Notes in Bioinformatics), 12192 LNCS, 337–355. Springer (2020). https://doi.org/10.1007/978-3-030-49788-0_25
3. Voss, C., Schwartz, J., Daniels, J., et al.: Effect of wearable digital intervention for improving socialization in children with autism spectrum disorder: a randomized clinical trial. JAMA Pediatr. **173**(5), 446–454 (2019). https://doi.org/10.1001/jamapediatrics.2019.0285
4. Cochrane, K.A., Loke, L., de Bérigny, C., Campbell, A.: Sounds in the moment: designing an interactive EEG nature soundscape for novice mindfulness meditators. In: Proceedings of the 30th Australian Conference on Computer-Human Interaction - OzCHI '18, 298–302, Melbourne, Australia. Association for Computing Machinery (2018).https://doi.org/10.1145/3292147.3292215
5. Roquet, C.D., Sas, C., Potts, D.: Exploring Anima: a brain-computer interface for peripheral materialization of mindfulness states during mandala coloring. Hum.-Comput. Interact. (2021). https://doi.org/10.1080/07370024.2021.1968864
6. Bin, Z., Xiaowei, M.: A review of educational rehabilitation research on children with autism. J. Teach. Educ. **2**(02), 104–110 (2015). https://doi.org/10.13718/j.cnki.jsjy.2015.02.015
7. Qian, X., Tang Hua, D.J., Xiao, S., et al.: Research on the status quo of autistic children in China--Taking Shanghai area as an example. Bus. Econ. **431**(19), 102–104 (2013)
8. Zhonghua, W., Dan, Y.: The current status and countermeasures of the current social cognition of autistic children. Talent (20), 236+238 (2016)
9. Mengqin, Z., Xing, L.: Current status of clinical application of mandala painting in psychological adjustment. General Pract. Nurs. **21**(06), 796–799 (2023)
10. Xiaoping, L.: An empirical study on the construction of "Doodle-Mandala painting intervention model" and its effect mechanism on autistic children. Shaanxi Normal University (2019). https://doi.org/10.27292/d.cnki.gsxfu.2019.001198

11. Jie, H.: Exploring the healing function of mandala painting. Central Acad. Fine Arts (2020). https://doi.org/10.27666/d.cnki.gzymc.2020.000055

12. Yuan, W.: Research on the application of color in improving communication ability of autistic children. Luxun Acad. Fine Arts (2022). https://doi.org/10.27217/d.cnki.glxmc.2022.000054

# Experience-Oriented Intervention Strategy for Children with Autism Spectrum Disorders and Their Families: A Framework of Design and Evaluation

Tsai-Ling Liao[1], Wei-Chi Chien[1(✉)], and Ling-Yi Lin[2]

[1] Department of Industrial Design, National Cheng Kung University, Tainan, Taiwan (R.O.C.)
chien@xtdesign.org
[2] Department of Occupational Therapy, National Cheng Kung University, Tainan, Taiwan (R.O.C.)

**Abstract.** This article provides a roadmap for interdisciplinary design teams, outlining how to craft experience-oriented intervention strategies that enhance family's collaboration. It explores methods for pinpointing design challenges within special needs populations and fosters an approach geared towards creating practical, real-world solutions that align with the perspectives of both designers and therapists. Highlighting the collaborative nature of the family, the article seeks to boost synergy across various fields of expertise, aiming to support the creation of effective and meaningful interventions for individuals with special needs.

**Keywords:** Autism Spectrum Disorders · Experience Design · Intervention Strategy · Parent-Child Interaction

## 1 Introduction

In 2023, Taiwan's Ministry of Health and Welfare reported an estimated 19,436 diagnoses of Autism Spectrum Disorders (ASD), highlighting a critical public health concern. The prevalence of ASD in the United States has dramatically increased from 1 in 150 in 1992 to 1 in 36 in 2023, accentuating the growing imperative for dedicated care and support for affected individuals. The *Diagnostic and Statistical Manual of Mental Disorders* (DSM-5), as outlined by the *Centers for Disease Control and Prevention* (2023), defines ASD as a pervasive neurodevelopmental condition characterized by challenges in social communication and interaction, alongside restricted behaviors and interests and significant hyper- or hypo-reactivity to sensory stimuli, including atypical exploration of sensory environments (*National Institute of Mental Health*, 2023).

Individuals with ASD exhibit a wide range of abilities; some excel in certain areas, while others struggle with daily living skills [1]. Challenges in performing everyday tasks can cause distress, with some individuals showing strong preferences for specific routines without meaningful purposes [2] or exhibiting avoidance behaviors [3]. Almost half of those with ASD have difficulties with activities of daily living (ADL) [4], impacting

M. Antona and C. Stephanidis (Eds.): HCII 2024, LNCS 14697, pp. 198–212, 2024.
https://doi.org/10.1007/978-3-031-60881-0_13

caregiver burden and future outlooks [5]. Current interventions often focus on social deficits, overlooking the importance of ADL in comprehensive development.

This study advocates for a holistic intervention approach that encompasses emotional well-being, family dynamics, and evidence-based practices to improve the lives of individuals with ASD. Echoing Fraunberger [6], it calls for a broad view in technology design for ASD, emphasizing philosophical, ethical, and moral considerations to enhance life quality. This research aims to extend beyond functional improvement, using ADL as a platform for communication, relationship building, and skill enhancement for autistic children.

To this end, we have convened an interdisciplinary team, including a design researcher (second author), an occupational therapist pursuing a master's in design (first author), and a professional therapist specializing in ASD and developmental psychology (third author). This team aims to identify significant design challenges and utilize technology to support ASD individuals in an experience-oriented rather than a technocratic manner [7]. We have developed a comprehensive framework to understand the dynamics of parent-child interactions within the daily routines of families affected by ASD, focusing on toothbrushing as a primary activity. This case study offers insights into enhancing parent-child engagement during toothbrushing routines in ASD families by applying theoretical principles and empathetic understanding to develop practical strategies. The interdisciplinary approach ensures the proposed design solutions meaningfully improve the lives of children with ASD and their families.

The subsequent sections will review background theories related to ASD, focusing on toothbrushing and ADL challenges, and discuss the concept of experience design within our framework. Moreover, we outline an evaluation strategy to inform future research, ultimately discussing the interdisciplinary nature of our study and suggesting avenues for future work.

## 2 Literature Review

### 2.1 Toothbrushing Challenges in ASD Children

Over half (53.6%) of children diagnosed with ASD exhibit atypical sensory processing [8], which can lead to either heightened or diminished responses to sensory stimuli compared to their neurotypical peers [9]. This divergence in sensory processing often complicates daily routines, particularly in personal hygiene and self-care [10], where tactile and visual sensitivities are pronounced. Toothbrushing presents significant challenges for this demographic. Research indicates that approximately 42% of children with ASD aged 5–12 exhibit aversion to toothbrushing, and nearly 58% require assistance with grooming tasks [11]. Hypersensitivity issues can result in resistance or non-cooperation during oral hygiene practices at home and in dental settings, as reported by parents. Responses to this resistance include frustration or inappropriate behaviors like swallowing toothpaste, leading to increased time and effort required from caregivers to ensure twice-daily toothbrushing compared to peers without ASD [12].

Parental feedback reveals that only half of the households with ASD-diagnosed children manage to maintain the recommended twice-daily toothbrushing routine. This shortfall is linked to a staggering 77% prevalence of tooth decay within this group. Factors contributing to less frequent brushing include time constraints (42%), the child's lack of cooperation (24%), fatigue, and the absence of adequate support [13]. Notably, children's reluctance and uncooperative behaviors pose significant obstacles for caregivers, potentially exacerbating the frequency of toothbrushing inadequacies. This situation contributes to a high incidence of dental decay among children with ASD [14], underscoring the need for improved oral health strategies. Furthermore, these challenges can strain the parent-child dynamic as recurring conflicts over toothbrushing accumulate, highlighting the critical need for targeted interventions to address these unique challenges.

## 2.2 Oral Health Care Intervention Strategies for Children with ASD

Interventions to improve oral health for individuals with ASD fall into three main categories: reducing hypersensitivity, providing education on toothbrushing techniques, and enhancing acceptance of oral health care.

One effective approach involves systematic desensitization, which gradually exposes children to stimuli that provoke anxiety, thereby reducing sensitivity and enhancing acceptance of dental care [15]. This method has demonstrated long-term effectiveness, with a significant portion of children (87.55%) becoming comfortable with using dental mirrors over a two-year follow-up period [16, 17]. Additionally, interventions like stimulus fading, which breaks down the toothbrushing process into incremental steps, have shown promise in improving compliance and extending the duration of toothbrushing among children with ASD [18].

An alternative intervention category adopts educational strategies, leveraging their visual learning preference [19] and interests in interactive artifacts [20]. Methods include video visualization [21–23], pictorial guides [24], augmented reality (VR) coaching systems like *Cheerbrush* [25], and learning methods such as social stories [26]. These principles involve converting steps into visual cues, task clarity, task-oriented specificity, and the "tell-show-do" approach [27–29].

The last category aims to enhance children's compliance by modifying the oral healthcare environment. Strategies include pre-surveying sensory needs, implementing reinforcement before dentist visits, adjusting schedules, and allowing ample time for children to proceed at their own pace.

Almost all interventions are designed for implementation by professionals, with less focus on empowering parents to apply these strategies at home. Consequently, caregivers often rely on trial and error to make toothbrushing a more enjoyable and effective routine for their children [30]. A significant number of parents (80%) report a lack of knowledge on how to brush the teeth of children with ASD effectively, seeking guidance through online resources (58%) or visual aids (50%) [12, 30]. This gap highlights the need for more accessible, parent-focused resources and training to avoid the frustration and conflicts that can arise from unsuccessful attempts.

Considering an experience-oriented perspective, designing interactive parent-child interventions has been shown to enhance the effectiveness of ADL interventions and improve the quality of life for families with developmentally delayed children, such as those with cerebral palsy or Down syndrome. However, for children with ASD, who often have unique social and psychological needs, it remains a question whether the same strategies that benefit children without social deficits can be equally effective, underscoring the need for tailored approaches that address the specific challenges faced by the ASD population.

## 2.3 Social Deficits and Relationship Development of ASD

Children with ASD exhibit marked differences in social engagement from infancy. Typically developing infants show a natural progression from dyadic (one-on-one) to triadic social interactions, demonstrating a preference for human faces, sustained eye contact, and reciprocal vocalizations. In contrast, children with ASD may show noticeable social interaction deficits as early as 6–8 months post-birth, including limited eye contact and diminished interest in social engagement [31, 32]. Interventions targeting these foundational social skills, such as enhancing eye contact and joint attention, effectively fostered emotional expression and social engagement in children with significant autistic symptoms [32].

Social skill development interventions are often conducted in clinical settings by specialists and may require intensive commitment, such as Applied Behavior Analysis (ABA) therapy for up to 40 h per week [33]. This intensive regimen can be stressful for the child and financially taxing for families. Adopting a family-centered care approach, which involves empowering families in decision-making and promoting collaborative efforts between parents and professionals, can mitigate family stress and improve parent-child interactions [34]. Models such as The SCERTS Model [35] and The Early Start Denver Model [36] enable parents to integrate social communication strategies into daily routines at home with specialist guidance. This method conserves medical resources and fosters skill generalization in natural settings.

Interestingly, the severity of ASD appears to have a correlation with the quality of parent-child relationships, suggesting an intervention challenge to think about forming meaningful connections between children with ASD and their caregivers [37]. Despite social interaction challenges, individuals with ASD possess the inherent need and ability to establish relationships, highlighting the necessity to support diverse strategies for social engagement. This perspective advocates for expanding intervention methods beyond clinical settings to home-based practices led by parents, emphasizing a directed approach to incorporating these strategies into everyday routines.

## 2.4 Experience Design and Its Role in ASD Interventions

Experience design emphasizes the psychological need for intrinsic motivation, driving individuals to seek meaningful engagements that provide closeness, such as interactions with loved ones [7, 38]. Self-determination theory highlights autonomy, competence, and relatedness as fundamental motivators that inspire individuals towards self-improvement, mastery, and meaningful relationships [39]. Activities that cater to these intrinsic needs tend to be more engaging and fulfilling, supporting the notion that enhancing family interactions can amplify the effectiveness of ADL training and lead to more positive familial experiences.

Sheldon categorizes ten experiences that generate positive affect [40], while Hassenzahl identifies six facets of positive interactions with interactive products, focusing on autonomy, competence, relatedness, meaningfulness, stimulation, and security [41]. The concept of relatedness is particularly significant in driving intrinsic motivation and fostering positive experiences, thus influencing the principles of interactive product design. In experience design, prioritizing the user's underlying desires over mere functionality is crucial. Hassenzahl proposes a three-tiered approach to experience design, emphasizing the importance of understanding users' true desires and crafting designs that facilitate meaningful experiences to meet these needs—ranging from the motivations behind actions, through the ways goals are achieved, to the operational aspects of the task [7].

In interventions targeting children with ASD, there is often a lack of focus on promoting positive family interactions. Daily activities like toothbrushing can become sources of friction within the parent-child dynamic if consistently approached negatively. By reimagining such routines to emphasize shared experiences rather than mere outcomes, we can foster a more meaningful connection between parents and children. Drawing from the principles of experience design, we posit that children with ASD might engage more actively in toothbrushing if it is transformed into an enjoyable bonding activity with their parents [42]. Interactive products have been shown to bolster relatedness through mechanisms like awareness, expressivity, physical closeness, gift-giving, joint activities, and reminiscing [43]. Our objective is to reinvent routine tasks such as toothbrushing into engaging rituals that strengthen the parent-child bond through the application of interactive elements [43, 44].

Ibañez's research [45] underlines the importance of joint activities in enhancing relatedness, suggesting that parents and children with ASD can improve their interactions during daily routines through effective guidance and engagement. Regular practice of daily routines in a familial context not only contributes to the child's social communication skills but also presents valuable opportunities for fostering communication and shared experiences, thereby enhancing relatedness within families affected by ASD.

## 3    Toward an Experience-Oriented Design Paradigm for ASD Interventions

### 3.1   Design Framework

This section outlines our interdisciplinary approach and illustrates how the concept of experience is integrated into formulating intervention strategies for ASD. Our development process, depicted in Fig. 1, begins with the initial problem recognition encountered by the first author in her efforts to devise toothbrushing training tools for children with ASD. This initial step sparked a comprehensive inquiry, encompassing a theoretical review, observations from the first author's practice, consultations with experts on toothbrushing techniques and ASD intervention theories, and an analysis of existing products. Incorporating an experience-oriented design perspective by the second author introduced innovative concepts into our strategy.

Drawing from these diverse sources, we could pinpoint the specific needs of children with ASD and their families, leading to the establishment of a design framework outlined in the subsequent sections of this paper. This framework guides our design process and lays out a strategy for future evaluation of our interventions. Also, the identified requirements were interpreted and transformed into our design proposal. As indicated in Fig. 1, the following steps for this project involve testing the design in practice and engaging in an iterative refinement process based on feedback and outcomes.

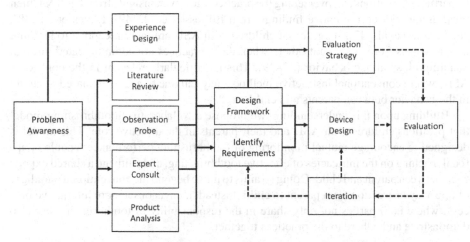

**Fig. 1.** Design research procedure

*Transitioning from Problems to Experience.* Our approach commenced with interviews with specialists to grasp the most pressing concerns in interventions for Autism Spectrum Disorders (ASD), integrating family feedback on the challenges and concerns they face in their child's daily life. Following this, our team conducted direct observations of children with ASD and their families to fully understand the real-world context and to develop insights that differ from those provided by experts alone.

We identified several core issues:

(i)  *Children with ASD often resist toothbrushing due to oral hypersensitivity, exhibiting uncooperative behaviors during the process.*

(ii)  *Parents face a stressful and time-consuming daily routine in brushing their ASD children's teeth, which diminishes both motivation and the frequency of toothbrushing sessions.*

(iii)  *There is a noticeable lack of confidence among parents in effecting positive changes in their children's living conditions.*

Addressing the toothbrushing difficulties faced by children with ASD is crucial. While therapists' interventions are valuable, we recognize from an experience design viewpoint the critical need to create motivational opportunities for both children with ASD and their parents during toothbrushing practices. Motivation in joint toothbrushing practices is a crucial facilitator for enhancing related skills.

Thus, moving from a problem-focused to a motivation-focused framework has critically shaped our strategy to alter the dynamics of parent-child toothbrushing interactions. Rather than solely focusing on enhancing therapists' ability to modify the behavior of children with ASD, our objective shifts towards introducing a new, shared experience for ASD families.

*Transitioning Requirements into Intervention Strategy.* Traditionally, the approach to teaching toothbrushing to children has seen parents in a predominantly directive role, imparting instructions and overseeing the practice. However, insights from Chiu & Chien [46], along with corroborative findings from Börjesson et al. [49], Hayes et al. [48], and Hussain et al. [47], suggest that children with ASD are more receptive to learning new practices from significant others when these practices are communicated through meaningful, symbolic behavior [47–49]. This is particularly relevant in the context of ASD, where conventional instructive methods may fail due to a lack of shared meaning in the behavior between parents and children.

Building upon this understanding, we propose a collaborative toothbrushing model that positions children with ASD and their parents in the directive role. This model is designed to encourage mutual monitoring of toothbrushing performance, enable reciprocal teaching on the intricacies of effective toothbrushing, and cultivate a shared experience between parent and child. Doing so aims to move beyond the conventional paradigm of one-way instruction from parent to child. Instead, it envisions a more interactive process, where both parties not only share in the responsibility of toothbrushing but also demonstrate and adhere to the practices together.

*Transitioning from Practices to Design Criteria.* In our journey to enhance toothbrushing practices within ASD families, the subsequent design challenge involves creating an appropriate design artifact. This artifact aims to dissect and transform the behavioral dynamics into structured rituals. Drawing on the P-E-O model proposed by Strong et al. [50], which delineates the complex interplay between personal (P), environmental (E), and occupational (O) factors affecting a child's performance. These dimensions guide our strategy for constructing an intervention device.

Occupational Enhancement through Device Design: Our device is tailored to provide detailed toothbrushing instructions, embracing the principles of repetition found in ABA interventions. This design ensures that children with ASD can acquire toothbrushing skills with their parents' support. Furthermore, the device encourages parents to follow the instructions, fostering a joint toothbrushing occupation and a new and shared activity between parent and child.

Environmental Integration: To augment the environmental context, the device is envisioned as a symbolic representation of the toothbrushing activity strategically placed in the bathroom. This placement helps ASD children more readily connect their experiences with their behavioral objectives, such as brushing their teeth alongside their parents and mutually monitoring the process. The device incorporates a clock that activates music around toothbrushing times each day, transforming toothbrushing into a ritualistic family activity enhancing the environmental cues that signal and support this shared practice.

Personal Guidance: From a personal perspective, the device includes instructional support for parents beforehand. With guidance from professional therapists, parents are equipped to utilize the device effectively, fostering a collaborative daily toothbrushing routine with their ASD children. This instructional component is crucial for empowering parents, ensuring they are well-informed and confident in creating a positive and engaging experience for themselves and their children.

In summary, by addressing the occupational, environmental, and personal dimensions through a carefully designed device, we aim to establish a more structured, enjoyable, and ritualistic approach to toothbrushing for ASD families. This holistic approach not only seeks to improve oral hygiene practices but also to strengthen family bonds and provide a framework for other daily activities.

## 3.2  BrushBond: A Device for Joint Toothbrushing

BrushBond (Fig. 2) represents our innovative approach to enhancing the toothbrushing experience for families with ASD children. This device is designed to transform toothbrushing from a mundane task into an engaging and collaborative activity. BrushBond is not just a toothbrushing aid; it's a tool for building routines, enhancing communication, and fostering connections between children with ASD and their parents. By incorporating elements of play, mutual engagement, and reward, toothbrushing becomes an eagerly anticipated activity, paving the way for more positive experiences in daily life. The initial prototype, illustrated in Fig. 3, outlines a four-step usage process:

1. Reminding Music: The device plays a familiar melody to signal that it's time for toothbrushing, serving as an auditory cue to begin the routine.
2. Toothbrushing Instruction: It provides visual guidance by illuminating specific teeth to indicate where to brush, simplifying the process and adding a game-like element.
3. Mutual Tooth Check: After brushing, a pushbutton on the device is pressed following a mutual inspection of each other's teeth, promoting interaction and cooperation.
4. Rewards: The device celebrates the completion of brushing all teeth with blinking lights, providing positive reinforcement and marking the end of the activity.

A Story-like Scenario Using BrushBond (see also Fig. 4):

*At 9 p.m., Tim, a child with ASD, is playing in the living room. Suddenly, a familiar melody starts playing from the bathroom. His mother approaches, telling Tim it's time for their toothbrushing game. Initially reluctant, Tim is drawn by the melody, associating it with a playful activity with his mother. This change in perception is partly due to the mother's recent learning session with a therapist, equipping her with strategies to guide Tim effectively.*

*Together, they head to the bathroom and activate the BrushBond device, initiating their toothbrushing ritual. The device lights up, indicating the specific teeth to start brushing. Mimicking his mother, Tim begins to brush his teeth accordingly. After declaring he's done, they check each other's teeth. With mutual confirmation that their molars are clean, they press the device's button together, moving on to the next set of teeth indicated by the device. This process of brushing, checking, and pressing the pushbutton is repeated until all teeth have been attended to. Upon completion, the device celebrates its achievement with blinking lights, marking a successful end to the ritual. This process, though time-consuming, strengthens their bond and smoothly transitions Tim to bedtime.*

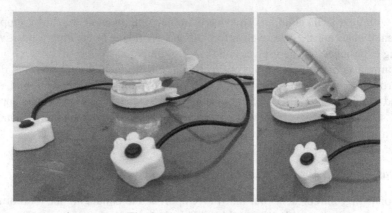

**Fig. 2.** Brushbond prototype

**Fig. 3.** Procedure of new ritual of tooth brushing

## 3.3 Evaluation Strategies of an Experience-Oriented Intervention Design

Evaluating the effectiveness of interventions aimed at improving toothbrushing practices in children with ASD requires a multi-dimensional approach. This evaluation encompasses assessing toothbrushing performance, the child's personal factors, the experience of using interactive products, rituals during toothbrushing, and the quality of parent-child interaction. Each domain plays a crucial role in understanding the intervention's impact and identifying areas for further improvement.

*Child's Personal Factors*

**Objective.** In every professional intervention practice, it is essential to understand cases' individual character. As mentioned before, ASD includes a wide range of disabilities. Understanding and evaluating their sensory processing, fine motor skills, social and communication abilities, and motivation are required, especially for ADL like toothbrushing.

**Tools:** Movement Assessment Battery for Children (MABC-2), Peabody Developmental Motor Scales - Second Edition (PDMS-2) [55] for motor skills, Sensory Profile (SP) [56], and Sensory Processing Measure (SPM) [57] for sensory processing. Additionally, tools like the Autism Behavior Checklist (ABC), Childhood Autism Rating Scale

(CARS) [58], and Social Responsiveness Scale (SRS) [59] assess ASD traits, social skills, and communication capabilities.

*Toothbrushing Performance*

**Objective.** Evaluation of this level inherits traditional intervention practices that focus on the performance quality based on the ASD's engaged problems. In our case, the evaluation includes the measure the frequency of toothbrushing, the accuracy of brushing techniques, and the level of parental assistance required.

For specific behaviors not covered by existing tools, the Custom Evaluations with the Goal Assessment Scale (GAS) [60] provides a flexible framework for setting personalized goals and measuring progress on a five-point scale, from −2 (current situation) to +2 (aspired improved situation), facilitating targeted assessments and interventions.

**Tools.** Observational data, Pediatric Evaluation of Disability Inventory (PEDI), and Vineland Adaptive Behavior Scales (VABS) to evaluate the child's abilities in ADL [51]. Higher scores are indicative of better ADL abilities and greater independence.

The design of GAS requires professional experience. An example in our case is shown in Table 1.

**Table 1.** Goal Assessment Scale: Rejection of toothbrushing as an example

| Score | Performance Description |
|---|---|
| 2 | After being reminded (by device or parent), the individual can actively indicate a desire to brush their teeth and proceed to the designated location |
| 1 | After being reminded (by device or parent), there is no resistance expressed through actions or words. However, it requires the adult to verbally remind 2–3 times before the individual proceeds to the toothbrushing location on their own |
| 0 | After being reminded (by device or parent), the individual can express their intention calmly, such as saying "I don't want to" or shaking their head. However, they can cooperate when given a direct command or request |
| −1 | After being reminded (by device or parent), slight physical assistance is needed, such as holding hands or gently supporting the head, to cooperate in moving to the toothbrushing location or engaging in toothbrushing. However, there is resistance during the process, such as crying, screaming, struggling, and attempting to escape |
| −2 | After being reminded (by device or parent), significant physical assistance is required, such as being held firmly or using straps and a safety seat, to cooperate in moving to the toothbrushing location or engaging in toothbrushing. Moreover, there is extreme resistance during the process, including crying, screaming, struggling, and attempting to escape |

*Experience Assessment*

**Objective.** This level of evaluation is necessary for understanding the social quality and product experience that the ASD children and their parents have, assessing the acceptance of the interactive device, the feelings of shared experience, and overall product impressions.

**Tools.** Experience Scales [52], AttrakDiff 2 [53], and the Technology Acceptance Model (TAM) + INTUI [54] to evaluate user toothbrushing experience, impressions, and acceptance of the interactive product. These evaluations, gathered through observation, interviews, and objective measures, will provide insights for design refinement.

This comprehensive evaluation framework allows for a detailed analysis of the intervention's effectiveness across multiple dimensions, guiding ongoing improvements and tailoring the intervention to better meet the needs of children with ASD and their families. Through structured assessments and feedback mechanisms, the intervention aims to enhance toothbrushing practices, promote independence, and foster positive parent-child interactions.

## 4   Conclusion

This study introduces an interactive design aimed at enhancing daily routines for autistic children and their families, using toothbrushing as a key example. While traditional therapies like PCIT [36, 61] and RDI [62] focus on improving parents' ability to teach social interaction and communication skills, they often fall short in real-world application for parents with ASD traits, due to a lack of flexibility and creativity.

This study outlines a multidisciplinary approach to designing interventions, emphasizing collaboration between designers and specialists to deeply understand and effectively address the needs of individuals with complex conditions, such as ASD. As can be seen in Fig. 4. It starts with employing an experience-oriented perspective to consider the fundamental motivation (relatedness) of the target behavior (toothbrushing ritual) and its dynamic interactions (joint toothbrushing guidance), advocating for a holistic perspective that goes beyond diagnosis-related traits. By recognizing the child and family as active participants in the design process, this approach aims to develop solutions that are both effective and tailored to the unique dynamics of each family.

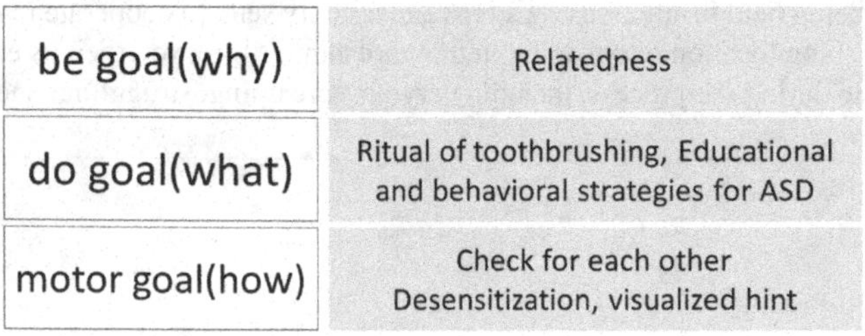

| be goal(why) | Relatedness |
| --- | --- |
| do goal(what) | Ritual of toothbrushing, Educational and behavioral strategies for ASD |
| motor goal(how) | Check for each other Desensitization, visualized hint |

**Fig. 4.** Experience-oriented design goals (based on [7], p.12)

This paper also recommends a feedback-driven process for iterative design adjustments, highlighting the importance of user experience evaluation and the integration of feedback from users with special needs to refine and assess the impact of the design on the main problem. This comprehensive approach ensures that interventions are adaptable and resonate with the specific needs and situations of families. Our future work is to continue the design research iteration and evaluate the potential of experience-oriented intervention design.

**Acknowledgement.** This project is funded by National Science and Technology Council, R.O.C. Taiwan (NSTC112-2410-H-006-075-).

# References

1. Lord, C., Elsabbagh, M., Baird, G., Veenstra-Vanderweele, J.: Autism spectrum disorder. Lancet **392**, 508–520 (2018)
2. Hsu, W.S., Ho, M.H.: Ritual behaviours of children with autism spectrum disorders in Taiwan. J. Intellect. Dev. Disabil. **34**, 290–295 (2009)
3. Astuti, E.Y., Sumarna, S.D., Ruswandy, D.: Toilet training programs for students with autism spectrum disorder (ASD) at special education school. Baltic J. Law Polit. **16**(3), 60–64 (2023)
4. Jasmin, E., Couture, M., McKinley, P., Reid, G., Fombonne, E., Gisel, E.: Sensori-motor and daily living skills of preschool children with autism spectrum disorders. J. Autism Dev. Disord. **39**, 231–241 (2009)
5. Lin, L.Y.: Factors associated with caregiving burden and maternal pessimism in mothers of adolescents with an autism spectrum disorder in Taiwan. Occup. Ther. Int. **18**, 96–105 (2011)
6. Fraunberger, C., Good, J., Parés, N.: Autism and technology beyond assistance & intervention. In: Proceedings of the Conference on Human Factors in Computing Systems, 07–12 May, pp. 3373–3378 (2016)
7. Hassenzahl, M.: Experience Design: Technology for All the Right Reasons. Morgan & Claypool Publishers (2010)
8. Jussila, K., et al.: Sensory abnormality and quantitative autism traits in children with and without autism spectrum disorder in an epidemiological population. J. Autism Dev. Disord. **50**, 180–188 (2020)
9. Mayer, J.L.: The relationship between autistic traits and atypical sensory functioning in neurotypical and ASD adults: a spectrum approach. J. Autism Dev. Disord. **47**, 316–327 (2017)
10. Lee, S.: Sensory processing abilities and activity of daily living skills in preschoolers with autism spectrum disorder. Am. J. Occup. Ther. **72**(4_Supplement_1), 7211505116p1 (2018). https://doi.org/10.5014/ajot.2018.72S1-PO5011
11. Ahmed, S., Waseem, H., Sadaf, A., Ashiq, R., Basit, H., Rose, S.: Daily living tasks affected by sensory and motor problems in children with autism aged 5–12 years. J. Heal. Med. Nurs. **92**, 7–12 (2021)
12. Naik, S.J., Vajaratkar, P.V.: Understanding parents' difficulties in executing activities of daily living of children with autism spectrum disorder: a qualitative descriptive study. Indian J. Occup. Ther. **51**, 107–112 (2019)
13. Campanaro, M., Huebner, C.E., Davis, B.E.: Facilitators and barriers to twice daily tooth brushing among children with special health care needs. Spec. Care Dent. **34**, 185–192 (2014)
14. Jaber, M.A.: Dental caries experience, oral health status and treatment needs of dental patients with autism. J. Appl. Oral Sci. **19**, 212–217 (2011)

15. Rachman, S.: Systematic desensitization. Psychol. Bull. **67**, 93–103 (1967)
16. Nelson, T.M., Chim, A., Sheller, B.L., McKinney, C.M., Scott, J.A.M.: Predicting successful dental examinations for children with autism spectrum disorder in the context of a dental desensitization program. J. Am. Dent. Assoc. **148**, 485–492 (2017)
17. Yost, Q., Nelson, T., Sheller, B., McKinney, C.M., Tressel, W., Chim, A.N.: Children with autism spectrum disorder are able to maintain dental skills: a two-year case review of desensitization treatment. Pediatr. Dent. **41**, 397–403 (2019)
18. Bishop, M.R., Kenzer, A.L., Coffman, C.M., Tarbox, C.M., Tarbox, J., Lanagan, T.M.: Using stimulus fading without escape extinction to increase compliance with toothbrushing in children with autism. Res. Autism Spectr. Disord. **7**, 680–686 (2013)
19. LeBlanc, L.A., et al.: Using Video modeling and reinforcement to teach perspective-taking skills to children with autism. J. Appl. Behav. Anal. **36**, 253–257 (2003)
20. Mesa-Gresa, P., Gil-Gómez, H., Lozano-Quilis, J.-A., Gil-Gómez, J.-A.: Effectiveness of virtual reality for children and adolescents with autism spectrum disorder: an evidence-based systematic review. Sensors **18**(8), 2486 (2018). https://doi.org/10.3390/s18082486
21. Aldi, C., et al.: Examining the Effects of video modeling and prompts to teach activities of daily living skills. Behav. Anal. Pract. **9**, 384–388 (2016)
22. Sallam, A.M., Badr, S.B.Y., Rashed, M.A.: Effectiveness of audiovisual modeling on the behavioral change toward oral and dental care in children with autism. Indian J. Dent. **4**, 184–190 (2013)
23. Shipley-Benamou, R., Lutzker, J.R., Taubman, M.: Teaching daily living skills to children with autism through instructional video modeling. J. Posit. Behav. Interv. **4**, 166–177 (2002)
24. Smutkeeree, A., Khrautieo, T., Thamseupsilp, S., Srimaneekarn, N., Rirattanapong, P., Wanpen, W.: The effectiveness of visual pedagogy for toothbrushing in children with autism spectrum disorder. J. Int. Soc. Prev. Commun. Dent. **10**, 415 (2020)
25. Zheng, Z.K., Sarkar, N., Swanson, A., Weitlauf, A., Warren, Z., Sarkar, N.: CheerBrush: a novel interactive augmented reality coaching system for toothbrushing skills in children with autism spectrum disorder. ACM Trans. Access. Comput. **14**, 1–20 (2021)
26. Marion, I.W., Nelson, T.M., Sheller, B., McKinney, C.M., Scott, J.A.M.: Dental stories for children with autism. Spec. Care Dent. **36**, 181–186 (2016)
27. Ikkanda, P.H., Ikkanda, Z.: Applied behavior analysis: behavior management of children with autism spectrum disorders in dental environments. J. Am. Dent. Assoc. **142**, 281–287 (2011)
28. Lyons, A.M., Leon, S.C., Phelps, C.E.R., Dunleavy, A.M.: The impact of child symptom severity on stress among parents of children with ASD: the moderating role of coping styles. J. Child Fam. Stud. **19**, 516–524 (2010)
29. Stigler, K.A., McDonald, B.C., Anand, A., Saykin, A.J., McDougle, C.J.: Structural and functional magnetic resonance imaging of autism spectrum disorders. Brain Res. **1380**, 146–161 (2011)
30. Teste, M., Broutin, A., Marty, M., Valéra, M.C., Cunha, F.S., Noirrit-Esclassan, E.: Toothbrushing in children with autism spectrum disorders: qualitative analysis of parental difficulties and solutions in France. Eur. Arch. Paediatr. Dent. **22**(6), 1049–1056 (2021)
31. Celani, G.: Human beings, animals and inanimate objects: what do people with autism like? Autism **6**, 93–102 (2002)
32. Alvarez, A., Lee, A.: Early forms of relatedness in autism: a longitudinal clinical and quantitative single-case study. Clin. Child Psychol. Psychiatry **9**, 499–518 (2004)
33. Vietze, P., Lax, L.E.: Early intervention aba for toddlers with ASD: effect of age and amount. Curr. Psychol. **39**, 1234–1244 (2020)
34. Gabovitch, E.M., Curtin, C.: Family-centered care for children with autism spectrum disorders: a review. Marriage Fam. Rev. **45**, 469–498 (2009)
35. Prizant, B.M., Wetherby, A.M., Rubin, E., Laurent, A.C.: The SCERTS model. Infants Young Child. **16**, 296–316 (2003)

36. Vismara, L.A., Rogers, S.J.: The early start Denver model: a case study of an innovative practice. J. Early Interv. **31**, 91–108 (2008)
37. Beurkens, N.M., Hobson, J.A., Hobson, R.P.: Autism severity and qualities of parent-child relations. J. Autism Dev. Disord. **43**, 168–178 (2013)
38. Sheldon, K.M., Bettencourt, B.A.: Psychological need-satisfaction and subjective well-being within social groups. Br. J. Soc. Psychol. **41**, 25–38 (2002)
39. Ryan, R.M., Deci, E.L.: Self-determination theory. In: Maggino, F. (ed.) Encyclopedia of Quality of Life and Well-Being Research. Springer, Cham (2000). https://doi.org/10.1007/978-3-319-69909-7_2630-2
40. Sheldon, K.M., Elliot, A.J., Kim, Y., Kasser, T.: What is satisfying about satisfying events? Testing 10 candidate psychological needs. J. Pers. Soc. Psychol. **80**, 325–339 (2001)
41. Hassenzahl, M., Diefenbach, S., Göritz, A.: Needs, affect, and interactive products – facets of user experience. Interact. Comput. **22**, 353–362 (2010)
42. Chien, W.C., Hassenzahl, M.: Technology-mediated relationship maintenance in romantic long-distance relationships: an autoethnographical research through design. Hum. Comput. Interact. **35**, 240–287 (2020)
43. Hassenzahl, M., Heidecker, S., Eckoldt, K., Diefenbach, S., Hillmann, U.: All you need is love: current strategies of mediating intimate relationships through technology. ACM Trans. Comput. Interact. **19**, 1–19 (2012)
44. Ozenc, F.K., Hagan, M.: Ritual design: crafting team rituals for meaningful organizational change. Adv. Intell. Syst. Comput. **585**, 146–157 (2018)
45. Ibañez, L.V., Kobak, K., Swanson, A., Wallace, L., Warren, Z., Stone, W.L.: Enhancing interactions during daily routines: a randomized controlled trial of a web-based tutorial for parents of young children with ASD. Autism Res. **11**, 667–678 (2018)
46. Chiu, Y.-C., Chien, W.-C.: Coping with autism spectrum disorder adolescents' emotional suppression with a "One-Bit" interactive device. In: Antona, M., Stephanidis, C. (eds.) Universal Access in Human-Computer Interaction. User and Context Diversity: 16th International Conference, UAHCI 2022, Held as Part of the 24th HCI International Conference, HCII 2022, Virtual Event, June 26 – July 1, 2022, Proceedings, Part II, pp. 332–342. Springer, Cham (2022). https://doi.org/10.1007/978-3-031-05039-8_24
47. Hussain, A., Abdullah, A., Husni, H., Mkpojiogu, E.O.C.: Interaction design principles for edutainment systems: enhancing the communication skills of children with autism spectrum disorders. Rev. Tec. La Fac. Ing. Univ. Del Zulia **39**, 45–50 (2016)
48. Hayes, G.R., Hirano, S., Marcu, G., Monibi, M., Nguyen, D.H., Yeganyan, M.: Interactive visual supports for children with autism. Pers. Ubiquit. Comput. **14**, 663–680 (2010)
49. Börjesson, P., Barendregt, W., Eriksson, E., Torgersson, O.: Designing technology for and with developmentally diverse children – a systematic literature review. In: Proceedings of the IDC 2015 14th International Conference on Interaction Design and Children, pp. 79–88 (2015)
50. Strong, S., Rigby, P., Stewart, D., Law, M., Letts, L., Cooper, B.: Application of the person-environment-occupation model: a practical tool. Can. J. Occup. Ther. **66**, 122–133 (1999)
51. Milne, S., Campbell, L., Cottier, C.: Accurate assessment of functional abilities in preschoolers for diagnostic and funding purposes: a comparison of the Vineland-3 and the PEDI-CAT. Aust. Occup. Ther. J. **67**, 31–38 (2020)
52. Laugwitz, B., Held, T., Schrepp, M.: Construction and evaluation of a user experience questionnaire. In: Holzinger, A. (ed.) USAB 2008. LNCS, vol. 5298, pp. 63–76. Springer, Heidelberg (2008). https://doi.org/10.1007/978-3-540-89350-9_6
53. Hassenzahl, M., Burmester, M., Koller, F.: AttrakDiff: Ein Fragebogen zur Messung wahrgenommener hedonischer und pragmatischer Qualität. In: Szwillus, G., Ziegler, J. (eds) Mensch & Computer 2003. Berichte des German Chapter of the ACM, vol. 57. Vieweg+Teubner Verlag. (2003)

54. Ameri Shahrabi, M., Ahaninjan, A., Nourbakhsh, H., Amani Ashlubolagh, M., Abdolmaleki, J., Mohamadi, M.: Assessing psychometric reliability and validity of technology acceptance model (TAM) among faculty members at Shahid Beheshti University. Manag. Sci. Lett. **3**, 2295–2300 (2013)
55. Piek, J.P., Hands, B., Licari, M.K.: Assessment of motor functioning in the preschool period. Neuropsychol. Rev. **22**, 402–413 (2012)
56. Tomchek, S.D., Dunn, W.: Sensory processing in children with and without autism: a comparative study using the short sensory profile. Am. J. Occup. Ther. **61**, 190–200 (2007)
57. Jorquera-Cabrera, S., Romero-Ayuso, D., Rodriguez-Gil, G., Triviño-Juárez, J.-M.: Assessment of sensory processing characteristics in children between 3 and 11 years old: a systematic review. Front. Pediatr. **5**, 57 (2017). https://doi.org/10.3389/fped.2017.00057
58. Rellini, E., Tortolani, D., Trillo, S., Carbone, S., Montecchi, F.: Childhood autism rating scale (CARS) and autism behavior checklist (ABC) correspondence and conflicts with DSM-IV criteria in diagnosis of autism. J. Autism Dev. Disord. **34**, 703–708 (2004)
59. Rotheram-Fuller, E., Kim, M., Seiple, D., Locke, J., Greenwell, R., Levin, D.: Social skills assessments for children with autism spectrum disorders. Autism **3**, 122 (2013)
60. James, K., Cuisck, A.: Goal attainment scaling as a method of clinical service evaluation. Am. J. Occup. Ther. **32**, 64–65 (1989)
61. Matson, M.L., Mahan, S., Matson, J.L.: Parent training: a review of methods for children with autism spectrum disorders. Res. Autism Spectr. Disord. **3**, 868–875 (2009)
62. Larkin, F., Guerin, S., Hobson, J.A., Gutstein, S.E.: The relationship development assessment - research version: preliminary validation of a clinical tool and coding schemes to measure parent-child interaction in autism. Clin. Child Psychol. Psychiatry **20**, 239–260 (2015)

# "Mum Helps Me When the Internet Messes Up…"

## Accessibility of eHealth Services for People with Intellectual Disability

Claude L. Normand[1] , Catharina Gustavsson[2,3,4] , Kristin Alfredsson Ågren[5] ,
Vanessa N. Heitplatz[6(✉)] , Darren D. Chadwick[7] , and Stefan Johansson[8,9]

[1] Department of Psychoeducation and Psychology, Université du Québec en Outaouais,
Gatineau, Qc, Canada
claude.normand@uqo.ca
[2] Center for Clinical Research Dalarna, Uppsala University, Falun, Sweden
[3] Department of Public Health and Caring Sciences, Uppsala University, Uppsala, Sweden
[4] School of Health and Welfare, Dalarna University, Falun, Sweden
[5] Department of Health, Medicine and Caring Sciences, Linköping University, Linköping,
Sweden
[6] Social Research Center and Rehabilitation Technology, TU Dortmund University,
Dortmund, Germany
vanessa.heitplatz@tu-dortmund.de
[7] School of Psychology, Liverpool John Moores University, Liverpool, UK
[8] Department of Media Technology and Interaction Design, School of Electrical Engineering
and Computer Science, KTH, Royal Institute of Technology, Stockholm, Sweden
stefan.johansson@begripsam.com
[9] Faculty of Engineering, Certec, Department of Design Studies, LTH, Lund University,
Lund, Sweden

**Abstract.** Many services have become digitized in society, including health services. Although there are many advantages to eHealth services, some segments of the population cannot reap those benefits. **Objectives**: This study aimed to: 1-describe how people with intellectual disability use the internet in Sweden; and 2-understand the nature of the contextual and personal barriers these users face when trying to access eHealth services in particular. **Methods**: Data from the nationwide survey "Swedes with Impairment and the Internet 2021" (SMFOI-21) were extracted for a subsample of 154 people with self-declared intellectual disability. **Results**: Findings reveal that people with intellectual disability used the internet predominantly for entertainment purposes. Challenges arose in more complex online activities, like internet searches, logging into eHealth services, booking medical appointments, and financial transactions. Participants relied on support from family, guardians or staff to read, write, create and memorise passwords, understand content, or solve technical problems encountered. They expressed a desire to engage more independently in the digital society but faced barriers due to the cognitive requirements of using apps and the internet as designed by computer scientists, difficulties in navigating complex online processes, such as eHealth services, and a lack of accessible infrastructure. Conclusion: This research

M. Antona and C. Stephanidis (Eds.): HCII 2024, LNCS 14697, pp. 213–230, 2024.
https://doi.org/10.1007/978-3-031-60881-0_14

214    C. L. Normand et al.

underscores the importance of improved accessibility, simplified interfaces, clearer instructions, and a supportive ecosystem to enhance their digital inclusion. It is a matter of people with intellectual disability being afforded equal rights to access health services.

**Keywords:** eHealth · Intellectual Disabilities · Digital Inclusion · Health Literacy · Impairments

# 1 Background

Many services have become digitized in society, including health services that used to be available only in person. The World Health Organization (WHO) defines eHealth as "The cost-effective and secure use of information and communications technologies in support of health and health-related fields, including health care services, health surveillance, health literature, and health education, knowledge and research" [1]. In recent years, the use of eHealth services has increased dramatically and eHealth offers a wide range of promising opportunities in the general population [2]. Therefore, offering digital health services should be an integral part of health priorities in communities worldwide [1].

However, research findings indicate that those who benefit the most from eHealth services are the populations with higher education, higher income, and younger age, with only one health issue [3]. This means that large parts of the population do not reap the benefits of eHealth. Furthermore, people not using eHealth have been found to be the ones that potentially need it the most [4]. People with lifelong impairments experience a disability digital divide in the use of eHealth services according to a Swedish nationwide survey study as they report greater difficulties in using eHealth than the population in general [5].

The digital divide is especially evident among people with intellectual impairments [5]. People with intellectual disability have difficulties in both intellectual functioning, with an IQ below 70, and difficulties in adaptive functioning, covering conceptual, social, and practical domains [6]. There is a large variation among individuals, but intellectual disability often necessitates lifelong support in many significant activities in daily life [7]. The overall prevalence is about 1–3% [8, 9]. In addition to those with a diagnosis of intellectual disability there exist a much larger number of people with intellectual impairments (including those with learning disabilities and those with borderline intellectual disability) who do not identify with this label and are often unknown to specialist disability services [8].

Significant healthcare inequalities have been identified for people with intellectual disability [8]. Barriers to effective healthcare that they experience can cause premature mortality from potentially avoidable causes [10, 11]. This group is also reportedly less involved in health decision making, often overlooked, and viewed as more vulnerable when considering their health literacy [12, 13]. Levels of health literacy are unknown for people with intellectual disabilities, with a surface functional and a deficit focus as observed in the extant literature [14]. People with low health literacy are more likely to delay seeking care and experience adverse outcomes. Indeed, low health literacy should be considered a significant public health issue [15]. A systematic review of online/eHealth interventions aimed at improving health equity among adult d/Deaf people has found a positive effect of electronic media when translated into sign language [16]. However, the authors warn that one needs to take into account the lower health literacy of the target audience, for example by providing interactive websites, graphics, animation, easy to understand video content, as well as usability testing, and feedback during the design process (p.553).

A scoping review [17] showed that people with impairments need digital health solutions that are designed to meet their specific needs in relation to the challenges they encounter in their living and working environments. Therefore, the health related disability digital divide could be referred to as the lack of accessible digital design of the eHealth services for all potential users. This seems to be the case especially for people with intellectual disability, as they were the subgroup in this study least likely to book medical or dental appointments online [5]. This is an alarming situation given that the prevalence of comorbid health conditions including diabetes, epilepsy, asthma, hearing loss, visual impairment, osteoporosis and Parkinson's disease is significantly higher in people with intellectual disabilities compared with the general population [18].

The lack of accessible design indicates a deficiency in following the human rights principles on health services, and digital accessibility [19]. This is further highlighted in a recent scoping review regarding accessibility of eHealth services, showing that only 6 out of 15 included studies specified the use of accessibility guidelines or standards in the development and evaluation of eHealth services [20]. Inclusion in digital health has never been more important due to the digitization of society exacerbated by the COVID-19 pandemic [21, 22]. Inclusion that should also hold for people with intellectual disability. Research shows that information and communication technology is used by people with intellectual disability [21, 23–27] and is perceived to be positive and essential in their everyday lives [28]. Although, as within the non-disabled population, there are some who do not wish to use technology [29].

In striving to achieve digital health equity, it is necessary to identify and address the barriers that may prevent people with intellectual disability from benefiting from digital health. There have been a number of reviews, which have highlighted and modelled the factors influencing the digital exclusion of people with intellectual disabilities. Chadwick et al. [30, 31] identified in their reviews barriers relating to: financial and economic disadvantage; negative societal attitudes and exclusion; lack of policy and governmental disdain; absent and inadequate support, education and training; and individual impairment related challenges in concert with poor ICT design. Lussier-Desrochers et al. [32] inspired by the Quebec Disability Creation Process [33] integrated a hub of personal and environmental resources that interact with digital devices and usage to account for digital inclusion or exclusion. They highlight that access to digital devices, sensorimotor, cognitive and technical requirements, as well as social codes and conventions (i.e. netiquette) all interact with personal abilities and support from the social or computer design environment to make digital participation possible. Johansson [34] identified the following prerequisites for participation in the digital society: access to the web, access to devices, access to applications, access to support, amenability to changes in practice, enabling and protective policy, law and regulation, lifelong education and learning, personal expectations and experiences regarding digital citizenship, competence and skill development, self-efficacy, personal and societal attitudes, affordability and accessible design.

These reviews demonstrate the complexity and multifactorial nature of digital participation and inclusion. Nonetheless, personal, environmental and societal factors affect upon digital exclusion, and when taking a social or interactionist perspective, underpinned by a belief in human rights, appropriate design of technology and societal and individual level supports provided to people with intellectual disability must be considered central.

In a recent review [35] of digital support of daily living for people with mild intellectual disability, the majority of the 46 included studies were small-scale, with the main finding that few studies did an inventory of the personal needs and preferences of people with intellectual disability in regard to what would be the most appropriate application in their personal physical and social context. Only three reported on eHealth services specifically, for example technology as facilitator for remote professional support.

Similar barriers and facilitators across studies were noted in the review, including the need for training and contextual difficulties due to failing technology. They also raised the absence of the voices of people with intellectual disability themselves in existing studies, as many relied on caretakers as respondents for them. This highlights the need for more in-depth qualitative studies giving voice to people with intellectual disability who access or use eHealth services.

## 1.1 Objectives

This study aimed to question people with intellectual disability regarding how they use the internet in general, and eHealth services specifically, in Sweden. Our objectives were to: 1 - describe their internet use, and 2 - understand the nature of the contextual and personal barriers users with intellectual disability face when navigating the internet in general, and eHealth services in particular.

## 2  Method

### 2.1 Study Design

The nationwide survey 'Swedes with Impairment and the Internet 2021' (SMFOI-21) uses a cross-sectional study design [27]. Every two years, this survey gathers data about Internet use from people with diverse types of impairments. The current study focuses on the qualitative survey data on internet use and eHealth services.

### 2.2 Participants

Data are taken from people with self-reported intellectual disability who had responded to the survey SMFOI-21. This sample comprised 154 respondents with intellectual disability. Participants completed the survey independently or with their proxy supporting them. However, answering the open-text questions was optional and gathered few responses.

## 2.3 Context of the Study

Sweden has a national eHealth portal called 1177.se. The same number is also a national telephone number for talking to a nurse who can provide health information. The portal has two parts: one part with health information pages, and one part where you log in to access personal interactive eHealth services. 1177.se is widely used. About 85% of the general Swedish population without impairments use 1177.se to find health information and log in to use services such as book healthcare appointments, read their healthcare records, renew prescriptions of medicines, etc. Among participants in SMFOI-21 who reported having intellectual disability, 56% had used 1177.se for accessing health information and 45% had used the logged in eHealth services [36].

## 2.4 Procedure of Data Collection

The SMFOI-21 survey was distributed from May 2021 to August 2021 via social media, disability rights organisations, local government municipalities and direct contacts. Respondents were also encouraged to pass the information on to other people they knew in the target population. Hence, non-probability purposive opportunity sampling was employed along with snowball sampling. Multiple sampling strategies are common and useful when trying to access often under-represented populations [37].

The survey was available either online, in paper format, by telephone or during an onsite interview. The survey contained questions about aspects of internet use. There were both questions with fixed response options and free text response options. The survey questions analysed in this study were the qualitative comments provided in response to the following questions:

1. Do you think the internet is difficult? Please describe in more detail why the internet is difficult.
2. If yes, what do you usually ask for help with?
3. Please tell us more about your attitude to doing different things on the internet.
4. How do you think the 1177.se healthcare information pages work? Feel free to describe in your own words.
5. How do you think the 1177.se logged in eHealth services work? Feel free to describe in your own words.
6. Please tell us more about your attitude to healthcare meetings via the internet.
7. Please describe your thoughts on your participation in the digital society.
8. Is there anything else you want to tell us?

## 2.5 Data Analysis

Both inductive and deductive content analysis were utilised to examine the comments provided in the open-ended questions. A combination of two conceptual frameworks of digital participation were applied deductively to the data corpus. Thus the difficulties described or strategies to overcome those difficulties when using internet in general, and eHealth services in particular, were coded as stemming from: (1) accessibility of digital devices per se (e.g. cost, negative attitudes) and applications (e.g. WiFi, design); (2) the cognitive, sensorimotor, or technical requirements of ICT devices or applications to navigate in cyberspace; (3) as well as the social codes and conventions needed to interact or communicate online, in accordance to Lussier-Desrochers et al.'s (2017) conceptualization of barriers and facilitators to online social participation. To account for data not covered by these categories, two broad prerequisites to digital inclusion from Johansson's thesis [34] were added: (4) policy, laws and regulation; and 5- praxis and practice. The latter covers education, social and technical support, expectations, competence, self-efficacy, and experiences.

## 3   Results

Before presenting results specific to eHealth information and services, we will give an overview of internet use by the participants. Numbers in parentheses refer to participants' identification numbers in the SMFOI-21 database.

### 3.1   Internet Use

Asked how they felt about their participation in digital society, survey respondents described what they could or liked to do. They also reported specific difficulties they encountered, and whom they usually turned to for support.

**This Is What I Do.**   Based on their accounts, people with intellectual disability use the internet primarily for entertainment purposes to watch movies, listen to music or find recipes. Different sites were used (e.g. YouTube, Spotify). "I think it's good to watch movies on your computer" (157). "I usually watch series and listen to music and such" (177). "On YouTube, you can find recipes" (1830). "I can choose videos on YouTube or songs on Spotify" (1348). "I think its fun, fun, to find new music" (1780)." I have a link already to YouTube" (315). They "like to play games on computer" (157), "watch sports" (261) or "read about history and news" (203). "While I like to use the internet for video services, music services, and to search for information and participate in forums, I avoid social media and some booking systems for care" (801).

Even though hesitation towards social media was expressed, the internet was also popular for communicating. "It feels good to be involved as you can contact family and friends" (133). "I use Facebook and Instagram when I want to share something exciting or fun that happened" (174). Another one "uses Google very much and image googling to communicate with pictures - shows parents, friends and teachers" (261). "I use Messenger to connect with friends" (587) or "meet classmates via Teams" (261).

Shopping and purchasing were also mentioned, like most people from the general population, "every now and then I buy things online" (174). As an example, "I just ordered a perfume on the internet" (1430). One participant listed advantages of making purchases online. "You do not have to go to different agents to buy tickets… You do not have to stand in line… and also avoid having too much cash on you" (1523). On the other hand, it can be "too easy to make a purchase…" Can be tricky not to go on advertising and so-called influencer sales, with the result that I buy more than I would online." (210)

**This is What I Need Help with.** After being asked if they found internet use difficult, respondents described why they thought it was difficult, what they needed help with, and what their general attitude was towards "doing different things on the internet". One participant summed it up as follows: "I can use the internet for fun things but have a hard time understanding difficult things that you need to know when you are an adult" (484). "Society assumes that at a certain age you have certain skills. But … I will never be able to do anything on [the] internet without help" (820).

*Everything.* The word "Everything" featured repeatedly in the accounts: "Everything is too fast for me" (281). "My guardian helps me with everything" (710). "Need help with everything from guardian or staff" (472). "With the help of assistants/parents, everything becomes easy to do via the internet, without their help, it would be impossible for me" (363). "I feel a little left out even though I get practical help using the internet" (363). "Without the help of another person, I am completely left out" (485). However, it's "hard to have to ask for help" (465). "I need help to handle matters like this [survey] on the internet. My mom is helping me write this" (484).

*Searching.* A closer look at the specific difficulties listed shows that the main obstacles had to do with the literacy level required for navigating the web, "because [all searches] require the ability to read and write" (485). Some people "cannot read and write" (1572) and therefore need someone to spell what they are looking for. "Mom usually helps me search for new stuff on YouTube" (128). "I can choose videos on YouTube or songs on Spotify if I get help searching first" (1348). Even with a basic level of literacy, "it is still too complicated to understand even though I can read. It needs to be further simplified" (468) since one can run into "difficult words that you don't understand what they mean" (1484). For Swedish users, "Zoom is difficult when it is written in English" (1830).

*Logging In.* Other challenges include creating a password that adhered to specific rules. "I don't understand passwords but know my own. I can't change my password because I don't understand what it means. If I am going to use any equipment other than my own, the password on that device must be changed to mine because that is what I will use" (1884). Once a password has been created, it is expected of users to memorise it. "I find it difficult to remember all the passwords you have to have" (267). "Mom helps me with passwords" (1706).

*Managing Money.* Online banking and shopping require many different steps that appear overwhelming. "I need help if I'm going to … pay invoices and book tickets. I'm afraid of being scammed, that's why I've never bought anything on the internet. My staff at the accommodation say that they are not allowed to help me … book tickets or order goods online… I don't want to order goods on the internet together with mom or dad. Then they see what they get as a birthday present" (699). "It is easy to shop on the internet, but it can be difficult to understand and compare what things cost in reality with different supplements, shipping, invoice fees, handling fees" (490). "I dare not shop on the internet. [I'm] afraid of being deceived. The staff at the property are not allowed to help me. That's why I buy everything in the shops" (699).

*Dealing with Technical Issues.* "I ask staff, friends or parents to show me or to guide me" (690) "when boxes come up" (660) "with incomprehensible error messages, logins, updates" (650), "something goes wrong" (670), I "pressed the wrong button" (1348) or "when things get messed up" (466). People can "also ask for help when [they] download something so [they] know it's nice or doesn't cost anything" (135). "To reboot, check connection, type in keywords" (1091). "When updating the iPad and various apps, icons often change and functions change. The iPad also wants to constantly add passwords. There should be an easier way to update...It's hard to relearn" (1348).

**This is What I Want.** When asked about their attitude toward internet use and digital participation, many comments implied that they would enjoy it better if they did not need to constantly ask for "help with everything" (654). "There are few things I can do myself on the internet. At the same time, it is necessary to use the internet" (485). Some say they "want to learn" (690), they "would love to take more courses, watch videos on how to do step by step" (261).

*Overcoming Exclusion.* In certain circumstances, law or systemic constraints restrain digital inclusion. "There is no access to broadband in the group homes in my municipality" (650) or "no internet at home" (818). House rules can interfere with digital participation also, if "the staff at the property are not allowed to help me" (699). "What is hard is that you get an iPod from [the rehabilitation service] but are not allowed to use it on YouTube" (1830). It's "difficult to shop online when you do not have a mobile ID or have a bank card" (1830). "It is mobile BankID that is the biggest problem. I can't have mobile BankID and then I'm limited in society" (627). "When you are not allowed to have mobile id... you cannot go by bus because you pay with mobile id; cannot go on coffee with a friend [because] they use Swish [a payment service] and I cannot." (818). "Luckily, my trustee has arranged for mobile BankID and Swish [a payment service], otherwise I would have been completely outside" (1348), but not everyone has the same good fortune, as the following quotation shows:

> "Unfortunately, [my guardian] has great difficulty in carrying out many of these matters, particularly banking, as there are an awful lot of regulations and prohibitions on the guardianship and performance of these tasks. This causes great difficulties for my guardian" (466).

Sometimes, the obstacles come from the negative attitudes or limited competence of people around them. One did not like having "big limitations, as I have a trustee. And trustee can't do much either" (2006):

> "Would make it easier if my trustee could have a BankID for me... so I could take part in health services... Have to go through forms sent by regular mail. I haven't even received my corona [COVID-19] passport yet, submitted the form 3 weeks ago. Those with BankID get theirs directly on their mobile" (1572).

"I want to be more involved, but my friends are unaccustomed" (1780). "It can be difficult to reach out to people who are not as involved in the digital society" (1523). Others claim they "have never been allowed to try and therefore cannot know how [they] would manage it" (1903). "My dad won't help me," (690) and "some assistants themselves find it difficult to navigate the net" (1348). Moreover, it appears they've been told that internet use "takes time out of the day" (705) "so it becomes a stress factor" (745).

"I feel very involved in the digital society, and rarely have difficulties in using the digital services that exist. It facilitates and simplifies a lot in my everyday life. But unfortunately, it can also lead to you becoming antisocial and sitting too much with the mobile phone instead of socializing." (1523).

Yet another declared they "can't use the internet as [they] don't have a computer or phone" (644).

## 3.2 Online Health Information and eHealth Services in Sweden

Following this overview of internet use by people with intellectual impairment, we now turn to how they access, or not, online health information, and eHealth services.

**The Health Information Pages in 1177.se.** Many people with intellectual disability do not seem to use online health information. When asked to reflect on the information on the 1177.se web site, some survey participants posted positive comments, but the majority reported it was difficult to access or to use.

*Good Content and Easy to Use.* Positive comments focused on how easy it was to use 1177.se. They found "It works very well" (801). It was rated "a good site with very good information" (267) and "a good navigation menu" (174). Some commented on the extensive information on the site: "There is a lot of good information about both diseases and treatments, as well as good advice in the event of outbreaks of major diseases, such as now during the COVID-19 pandemic" (1523). "However, it can be a lot of information, but it is still manageable. In addition, it is so easy with the search function to find specific information about, for example, diseases" (801).

*Cognitive Challenge Requires Social Support.* The majority of participants with intellectual disability who had tried using the eHealth website posted negative comments. Content being hard to understand was the most quoted difficulty. Some "can't read" (465) and "there is no read aloud button" (1081). Others said there is too "much information and do not really know where to look" (1081). Many acknowledged that even as adults, they needed their parents or a guardian to find and "to help [them] understand" (1096) the information. One suggested a "more personal approach" (943) to overcome such barriers.

**The eHealth Services in 1177.se.** Measures of eHealth services in SMFO1-21 include the use of digital identification to login as well as booking healthcare appointments online (to see a medical doctor or dentist) through 1177.se. Only a minority of people with intellectual disability book appointments online, although they are able to login with Mobile BankID or any other username and password. They tend to rely on others to borrow their ID to access 1177.se.

*Mixed Feelings and Experiences.* Only two participants posted exclusively positive comments. One wrote "good", the other elaborated by saying that "[logging] in via

BankID works well and easily. Then the headings for what you can do, book appointments, choose a reception, etc. are clear" (174). Descriptions of difficulties counterbalanced any other positive comments. "It sometimes works well and sometimes it's hard to get into it" (1484). "It works for the most part very well, however, they should simplify this with which health centres and other healthcare institutions you can see booked appointments with. Instead of having to add the health center in question, all booked appointments should be shown regardless of the healthcare provider" (1523). "It's easy to log in. It's messy when you're going to find doctor's appointment everyone's not active there when you get a call home and go into 1177 and want to see the time it's not there where it confuses" (1830). "It works pretty well. I like to see messages and read my journal, but I prefer to book doctor's appointments over the phone. I like to use various e-services, but for appointments, I prefer to consult with healthcare professionals before booking, or book doctor's appointments by phone. Once we wrote a question there, then the doctor called up, great!" (801).

Nevertheless, it is possible for persons with intellectual disability to overcome these difficulties. As explicitly stated, "it has become easier to log in" (267) and "I finally learned how they work" (606).

*Help Needed.*   As was the case when asked about the internet in general, the most common problem cited is that many people with intellectual disability rely on caretakers to use eHealth services. "It's possible if my parents help me" (471). However, even helpers can run into difficulties. "It's unnecessarily complicated to log in to, my assistants think" (383)."Their instructions need to be clearer and easy to read" (626). One particular problem in Sweden is that laws and regulations restrict who can have access to personal accounts. Thus, there is no legally correct method to share an account between a person with intellectual disability and designated tutors or trustees. Neither to share with relatives or staff. Therefore, if this still happens, the legal situation is unclear and the person with intellectual disability is then forced to give up control over their own identification and their own bank accounts. For example, staff in-group homes "say that they are not allowed to help me with my BankID.... They tell my guardian to do it, but I don't have a guardian. Don't think I need it. My mom or dad helps me with my BankID". (699).

On the other hand, Swedish parents have restricted access to their child's health file when the child is over 13 years old. "My mother is not allowed to order medicines for me, not to see my prescriptions and medical records even though I have many illnesses and medicines" (827). Meanwhile, this child complains, "I can't get a BankID, so I can't book appointments in healthcare" (827). One participant felt that the services were not designed to fit their personal needs: "It is not possible to book or cancel so much with the care because you always have to call. Their system doesn't suit me or the times of doctors who are in another county, or the rehabilitation that only has one reception to call" (490).

**Online Video Meetings for Healthcare.** Participants shared their attitude toward having healthcare appointments by video rather than in person.

*A Good Solution, Not a Panacea.* Many expressed positive attitudes towards online video meetings, such as "It has worked very well with speech therapist" (261), even though some might need to "get help to connect to meetings" (38). The possibility to have the meetings from home was deemed "great to avoid the hospital and possible infection" (748).

Although our data do not allow us to know whether online medical appointments were ever offered to them, survey participants without any experience with video meetings perceived the potential benefit of avoiding transport to attend medical appointments. "[I] think it would work" (135); "It seems simple and good then you do not have to go to the health centre" (236). It "would make it easier to avoid having to go away every time as I often have to visit the health care" (1572).

In addition, after having had some experience with video meetings for medical care, an overall positive attitude was tempered by the glitches that occurred during these online appointments. "During the pandemic, healthcare meetings via the internet have been a good solution, instead of the meetings having to be cancelled. It works reasonably well, but I still don't feel completely safe due to the fact that there may be disturbances that cause misunderstandings to arise" (801).

Care meetings via the internet are a good solution when there is no need for physical intervention and are a good way to avoid the spread of serious diseases. However, I find it difficult because I easily miss body language, and sometimes I miss what is said due to sometimes quality deficiencies during the video call (1523).

Nevertheless, participants clearly stated that they were "happy to meet them in real life instead" (1484) especially if they "have [their] family doctor that [they] like and want to go to" (587). They considered that "personal meetings are essential" (626), and "better in physical form" (705). Others expressed neutral attitudes towards online video meetings. Some admitted that they had not tried such meetings. "My disability is too great. My mother is usually the one who handles all contact with the healthcare system, either by phone or via meetings" (1348). Or "I can't connect one like that and I can't talk" (827). Its "difficult to have explanatory meetings when you need an interpreter, when you cannot describe for yourself what it is like" (356).

One participant said this technology was not relevant, another that it was "unsafe to use" and one noted that if you have a protected identity; it is not possible to have online video meetings. Despite a positive attitude towards the technology, one participant recognized that he would need some training before use. "If I was going to use them, I would have liked to ask certain things. I'm not sure how to do it" (723).

## 4   Discussion

As illustrated by conceptual frameworks of the prerequisites to digital inclusion of people with intellectual impairment [30, 32, 34, 38], accessibility of eHealth services depends on many factors. These include accessibility to the ICT devices and internet services, cognitively accessible design of applications and websites, expectations, education, and experience, as well as social support for overcoming technical challenges. All participants had access and experience of using a computer, tablet or smartphone, or had the expectation that they should as they volunteered to participate in the SMFOI-21 survey. They had the ability to answer the survey questions or were supported by proxies to do so.

One participant highlighted that, "fun things" are easier to do online, as demonstrated by the fact that the Internet is used primarily for entertainment and communication [22–27]. But the "difficult things" that adults are required to do can be out of reach for people with intellectual disability. Yet, they clearly expressed a desire to learn more and become more independent in their internet use. This is in line with recent studies which also found that people with intellectual disability often use digital media for leisure activities and often miss media competencies which go beyond scrolling and clicking "play" [39, 40]. Moreover, Heitplatz and collaborators [39] categorised different Internet User Types and stated that the "Help-Seeking-Realist" (the majority of people with intellectual disabilities) know about Internet risks and want to learn more about safer Internet usage. This idea that people with intellectual disabilities want to know more about how to stay safe online and to manage digital risks, including the risk of digital exclusion, has been replicated more widely [21, 41]. Clearly, we need to enhance the digital media competencies of people with intellectual disability. To do so will require education formats that fit the context and personal conditions of this group of people, education formats that can meet their heterogeneous developmental and individual support needs.

At present, reading and writing are prerequisites to logging in and navigating the web nearly everywhere. This barrier is serious enough to require help for "everything". This absolutist appraisal of their support needs provided by participants mirror societal notions that people with intellectual disabilities are unable to function independently. This accords with a narrative of dependency and such attributions may elicit negative emotions and beliefs about themselves [42]. These, in turn, may reduce individual beliefs regarding self-efficacy in relation to technology. For now, eHealth services in Sweden have not circumvented these systemic design issues. The SMFOI-21 2019 data analyses revealed that only 51% are able to use digital identification to log into 1177.se [5]. Further, only 22% book medical or dental appointments online [5]. Since the use of digital solutions surged during the Covid-19 pandemic, these numbers are likely to have increased slightly, though there is the suggestion that technology use may not persist [22, 43].

The most often cited solution to surmount problems encountered while using a computer or navigating online is to rely on someone for help (e.g. caregivers, parents). Utilising this support effectively in this context for online identification is problematic. Many eHealth services require the use of the third party identification technology called BankID which was found to be inaccessible by many of the participants. Since BankID is personal and confidential, asking for outside help to access eHealth services became problematic. The solution for many was to give away the control of the identification process to someone else. This is a breach of the rules issued by the bank and posed a risk, with people potentially losing the right to have a bank account. It also created a privacy problem especially in the context of high staff turnover, which is common for people with intellectual disabilities. The person having access to the other person's BankID is then given access to all that person's personal health information but also bank accounts, and many other very personal data. Even when a person has a legal guardian or trustee this problem remains since they cannot log in to their client's accounts without taking control over the client's personal BankID. This leaves persons with intellectual disability the difficult choice of either trying to log in to eHealth services without asking for help or exposing themselves to risks when they ask for help. As a result, many abstain from using the service at all. This mirrors the self-exclusion for the digital world identified in previous studies exploring the lived experiences of people with intellectual disabilities [44, 45].

These results show once again the dependencies of staff, relatives and other caregivers. Numerous studies [40, 46–48] have now shown that caregivers can have a positive (if they have a positive attitude towards digital participation) or negative (if they have a negative attitude towards digital participation) influence on participation opportunities. In the present study, however, they tended to have a negative influence, as the risks, fears and uncertainties of caregivers reduce participation opportunities. By relying on a caretaker or other supportive person to fix technical difficulties, adults with intellectual disability are deprived of autonomy and self-determination opportunities of making decisions regarding their online activities [31, 49]. On a daily basis, under most circumstances, adults with intellectual disability can rely on parents or staff to help when looking for a specific artist, video or logging into a Zoom meeting, for example. Unfortunately, not all helpers have the confidence or expertise to help [21, 35]. This barrier, however, should decline with coming generations. Nevertheless, caretakers can also exercise great control in giving access (or not) to ICT or to the internet, limiting the time spent online by refusing to help, and censoring access to social networking sites, pornography or dating sites to protect or reduce risks of cyber victimization, despite the fact that it has been demonstrated in past studies that youth and adults with intellectual disabilities can manage online risk [39, 50–52].

Like older adults, their health conditions require frequent encounters with healthcare providers that could potentially be facilitated by eHealth technologies [53]. The advantages of using video conference consultations to avoid possible contact with viruses as well as save time and money related to transportation issues were clearly recognized in our study and others as well [21]. As mandated by ethical codes for health professionals, medical appointments should be confidential to preserve one's dignity, privacy and autonomy (e.g. Swedish Medical Association, Swedish Association of physiotherapists, Canadian Medical Association, General Medical Council). When these appointments are done by video conference, needing and asking for help in order to use the application successfully could cross that line, thus invading one's privacy.

## 4.1 What Can Be Done?

Many solutions are available to overcome these limitations [12, 54–56]. In the specific case of the 1177.se website, requiring the use of a third party identity identification technology adds an extra layer of complexity. Some people with intellectual disabilities are prevented from using such technology since they do not conform to the requirements from the banks issuing the Bank ID. There is one other issuer of electronic ID in Sweden. Both providers have implemented design features such as face recognition or fingerprinting to log in, that could potentially overcome some of the problems. But there are few initiatives to provide knowledge on how to install and use this technology targeting people with intellectual disabilities. Identification and logging in on any website has been shown again and again to be a challenge for people with intellectual disability [21, 22, 27, 57].

Once logged in, reading simplified text supported by clear icons over a calm background can greatly facilitate comprehension. Nevertheless, a participative research study evaluating the use of a mental health website adapted for and by adults with an intellectual disability found that despite an Easy Read English feature, most participants accessed the audio function for some, if not all, of the textual content [57]. A function to convert text to audio to create the ability to listen to information rather than read it would be beneficial. Also, when having to type something, a function converting speech to text would be practical to find the right wording. And, when searching for something, word prediction or suggestions would be helpful. This technology does exist and is easy to implement. Complementing large chunks of text with video would benefit many users as suggested by the World Health Organization's global standards [1]. And, when people with cognitive impairments in Sweden collaborated on creating requirements for understandable texts, they formulated 19 recommendations [58]. A live chatbox to ask for help is yet another element that could facilitate the use of eHealth services by people with intellectual disability.

Finally, many of the barriers uncovered in this study could have been avoided or better addressed if the designers of eHealth information and eHealth services had collaborated in co-design activities with people with cognitive impairments [36] and tried harder to conform to standards for cognitive accessibility [59]. If eHealth applications were to apply these recommendations, one could expect an increase in the use of such applications by people who are often the ones who need it the most due to their greater heath needs, i.e. people with intellectual disability or other chronic conditions, leading to better quality of life, health and health equity [35].

As digital platforms become increasingly widespread for health communication and clinical treatment, it is critical to consider health equity in all phases of planning, development, evaluation, and implementation stages of eHealth services. This can be achieved by involving people with intellectual disability in these phases co-designing eHealth services [60]. Improving their accessibility is one important step for the Swedish population to reap the health benefits of these services.

## 5  Conclusion

Digital health technologies could have the potential to improve health outcomes for everyone, but they can also exacerbate health disparities if they are not designed and implemented with a focus on accessibility. Web accessibility standards are available, but they are not sufficient to make eHealth services accessible to all. Cognitive accessibility standards are lacking, impeding the rights of people with intellectual disability to equal access to health care. This is a serious issue for a population with higher rates of co-occurring impairments and health issues beyond their intellectual abilities.

In addition, this paper shows that even with specific topics such as eHealth, general problems and barriers limit people with intellectual disability in important opportunities for participation in our digitalized society. Despite advancing technological possibilities and solutions, these barriers still exist and must be addressed in future research and everyday applications.

# References

1. World Health Organization: Global strategy on digital health 2020–2025. https://www.who. int/publications/i/item/9789240020924 (2021)
2. Wynn, R., Gabarron, E., Johnsen, J.-A., Traver, V.: Special issue on e-health services. Int. J. Environ. Res. Public Health **17**(8), 2885 (2020). https://doi.org/10.3390/ijerph17082885
3. Wynn, R., Oyeyemi, S.O., Budrionis, A., Marco-Ruiz, L., Yigzaw, K.Y., Bellika, J.G.: Electronic health use in a representative sample of 18,497 respondents in norway (the seventh tromsø study - part 1): population-based questionnaire study. JMIR Med. Inform. (2020). https://doi.org/10.2196/13106
4. Reiners, F., Sturm, J., Bouw, L.J.W., Wouters, E.J.M.: Sociodemographic factors influencing the use of ehealth in people with chronic diseases. Int. J. Environ. Res. Public Health (2019). https://doi.org/10.3390/ijerph16040645
5. Pettersson, L., Johansson, S., Demmelmaier, I., Gustavsson, C.: Disability digital divide: survey of accessibility of eHealth services as perceived by people with and without impairment. BMC Public Health (2023). https://doi.org/10.1186/s12889-023-15094-z
6. American Psychiatric Association: Diagnostic and Statistical Manual of Mental Disorders, 5th edn. American Psychiatric Association Publishing (2022)
7. Schalock, R.L., Luckasson, R., Tassé, M.J.: Intellectual disability. Definition, diagnosis, classification, and systems of supports, 12th edn. aaidd, Silver Spring, MD (2021)
8. Emerson, E., et al.: People with learning disabilities in England 2011 (2012). https://www. glh.org.uk/pdfs/PWLDAR2011.pdf
9. Maulik, P.K., Mascarenhas, M.N., Mathers, C.D., Dua, T., Saxena, S.: Prevalence of intellectual disability: a meta-analysis of population-based studies. Res. Dev. Disabil. (2011). https://doi.org/10.1016/j.ridd.2010.12.018
10. O'Leary, L., Cooper, S.-A., Hughes-McCormack, L.: Early death and causes of death of people with intellectual disabilities: a systematic review. Res. Intell. Disabil (2018). https://doi.org/10.1111/jar.12417
11. Trollor, J., Srasuebkul, P., Xu, H., Howlett, S.: Cause of death and potentially avoidable deaths in Australian adults with intellectual disability using retrospective linked data. BMJ Open (2017). https://doi.org/10.1136/bmjopen-2016-013489
12. Chinn, D., Homeyard, C.: Easy read and accessible information for people with intellectual disabilities: Is it worth it? A meta-narrative literature review. Health Expectations : an Int. J. Public Participation Health Care Health Policy (2017). https://doi.org/10.1111/hex.12520
13. Geukes, C., Bruland, D., Latteck, Ä.-D.: Health literacy in people with intellectual disabilities: a mixed-method literature review. Kontakt (2018). https://doi.org/10.1016/j.kontakt. 2018.10.008
14. Latteck, Ä.-D., Bruland, D.: Inclusion of people with intellectual disabilities in health literacy: lessons learned from three participative projects for future initiatives. Int. J. Environ. Res. Public Health (2020). https://doi.org/10.3390/ijerph17072455
15. Henrard, G., Ketterer, F., Giet, D., Vanmeerbeek, M., Belche, J.-I., Buret, L.: La littératie en santé, un levier pour des systèmes de soins plus équitables ? Des outils pour armer les professionnels et impliquer les institutions: Santé Publique **S1**(HS1), 139–143 (2018). https://doi.org/10.3917/spub.184.0139
16. Morisod, K., Malebranche, M., Marti, J., Spycher, J., Grazioli, V.S., Bodenmann, P.: Interventions aimed at improving healthcare and health education equity for adult d/Deaf patients: a systematic review. Eur. J. Pub. Health (2022). https://doi.org/10.1093/eurpub/ckac056

17. Henni, S.H., Maurud, S., Fuglerud, K.S., Moen, A.: The experiences, needs and barriers of people with impairments related to usability and accessibility of digital health solutions, levels of involvement in the design process and strategies for participatory and universal design: a scoping review. BMC Public Health (2022). https://doi.org/10.1186/s12889-021-12393-1
18. Liao, P., Vajdic, C., Trollor, J., Reppermund, S.: Prevalence and incidence of physical health conditions in people with intellectual disability - a systematic review. PLoS ONE (2021). https://doi.org/10.1371/journal.pone.0256294
19. United Nations Enable: Convention on the Rights of Persons with Disabilities (2006). http://www.un.org/disabilities/default.asp?navid=12&pid=150
20. Jonsson, M., Johansson, S., Hussain, D., Gulliksen, J., Gustavsson, C.: Development and evaluation of ehealth services regarding accessibility: scoping literature review. J. Med. Internet Res. (2023). https://doi.org/10.2196/45118
21. Chadwick, D., et al.: Digital inclusion and participation of people with intellectual disabilities during COVID -19: A rapid review and international bricolage. Policy Practice Intel Disabi (2022). https://doi.org/10.1111/jppi.12410
22. Chadwick, D.D., Buell, S., Burgess, E., Peters, V.: "I would be lost without it but it's not the same" experiences of adults with intellectual disabilities of using information & communication technology during the COVID-19 global pandemic. Brit J Learn Disabil (2023). https://doi.org/10.1111/bld.12522
23. Alfredsson Ågren, K., Kjellberg, A., Hemmingsson, H.: Access to and use of the Internet among adolescents and young adults with intellectual disabilities in everyday settings. J. Intellect. Dev. Disabil. (2020). https://doi.org/10.3109/13668250.2018.1518898
24. Caton, S., Chapman, M.: The use of social media and people with intellectual disability: a systematic review and thematic analysis. J. Intellect. Dev. Disabil. (2016). https://doi.org/10.3109/13668250.2016.1153052
25. Chiner, E., Marcos Gómez-Puerta, M., Cardona-Moltó, C.: Internet and people with intellectual disability: an approach to caregivers' concerns, prevention strategies and training needs. J. New Approach. Educ. Res. 6(2), 153–158 (2017). https://doi.org/10.7821/naer.2017.7.243
26. Heitplatz, V.N., Bühler, C., Hastall, M.R.: Usage of digital media by people with intellectual disabilities: contrasting individuals' and formal caregivers' perspectives. J. Intell. Disabilities : JOID (2021). https://doi.org/10.1177/1744629520971375
27. Johansson, S., Gulliksen, J., Gustavsson, C.: Disability digital divide: the use of the internet, smartphones, computers and tablets among people with disabilities in Sweden. Univ. Access Inf. Soc. (2021). https://doi.org/10.1007/s10209-020-00714-x
28. Ågren, K.A., Hemmingsson, H., Kjellberg, A.: Internet activities and social and community participation among young people with learning disabilities. Brit J Learn Disabil (2023). https://doi.org/10.1111/bld.12519
29. Seale, J.: Wilderness and resistance: illuminating the digital inequalities experienced by adults with learning disabilities between 1970 and 1999. Disability Society (2019). https://doi.org/10.1080/09687599.2019.1576504
30. Chadwick, D., Wesson, C., Fullwood, C.: Internet access by people with intellectual disabilities: inequalities and opportunities. Future Internet (2013). https://doi.org/10.3390/fi5030376
31. Chadwick, D.D., Chapman, M., Caton, S.: Digital inclusion for people with an intellectual disability. In: Attrill-Smith, A., et al.: (eds.) The Oxford Handbook of Cyberpsychology, pp. 260–284. Oxford University Press (2019)
32. Lussier-Desrochers, D., et al.: Bridging the digital divide for people with intellectual disability. Cyberpsychol.: J. Psychosocial Res. Cybersp. 11(1), (2017). https://doi.org/10.5817/CP2017-1-1

33. Fougeyrollas, P.: Documenting environmental factors for preventing the handicap creation process: Quebec contributions relating to ICIDH and social participation of people with functional differences. Disabil. Rehabil. (1995). https://doi.org/10.3109/096382895091 66709

34. Johansson, S.: Design for Participation and Inclusion will Follow. Disabled People and the Digital Society. http://www.diva-portal.org/smash/get/diva2:1362526/FULLTEXT01.pdf (2019)

35. Oudshoorn, C.E.M., Frielink, N., Nijs, S.L.P., Embregts, P.J.C.M.: EHealth in the support of people with mild intellectual disability in daily life: a systematic review. J. Appl. Res. Intellect. Disabilities : JARID (2020). https://doi.org/10.1111/jar.12758

36. Johansson, S., Hedvall, P.-O., Larsdotter, M., Larsson, T.P., Gustavsson, C.: Co-Designing with extreme users: a framework for user participation in design processes. Scandinavian J. Disability Res. 25(1), 418–430 (2023). https://doi.org/10.16993/sjdr.952

37. Valerio, M.A., et al.: Comparing two sampling methods to engage hard-to-reach communities in research priority setting. BMC Med. Res. Methodol. (2016). https://doi.org/10.1186/s12 874-016-0242-z

38. Heitplatz, V.N.: Digitale Teilhabemöglichkeiten von Menschen mit intellektuellen Beeinträchtigungen im Wohnkontext. Perspektiven von Einrichtungsleitungen, Fachkräften und Bewohnenden. Eldorado - Repositorium der TU Dortmund (2021)

39. Heitplatz, V.N., Bühler, C., Hastall, M.R.: I Can't Do It, They Say! – Perceived Stigmatization Experiences of People with Intellectual Disabilities When Using and Accessing the Internet. In: Antona, M., Stephanidis, C. (eds.) HCII 2020. LNCS, vol. 12189, pp. 390–408. Springer, Cham (2020). https://doi.org/10.1007/978-3-030-49108-6_28

40. Ramsten, C., Blomberg, H.: Staff as advocates, moral guardians and enablers – using ICT for independence and participation in disability services. Scandinavian J. Disabil. Res. 21(1), 271–281 (2019). https://doi.org/10.16993/sjdr.608

41. Clements, F.A., Chadwick, D.D., Orchard, L.J.: 'I'm not the same person now': the psychological implications of online contact risk experiences for adults with intellectual disabilities. New Media Soc. (2023). https://doi.org/10.1177/14614448231217994

42. Scherer, K.R., Schorr, A., Johnstone, T. (eds.): Appraisal Processes in Emotion: Theory, Methods, Research. Oxford University PressNew York, NY (2001). https://doi.org/10.1093/oso/9780195130072.001.0001

43. Caton, S., et al.: Digital participation of people with profound and multiple learning disabilities during the Covid-19 pandemic in the UK. Brit J Learn Disabil (2023). https://doi.org/10.1111/bld.12501

44. Chadwick, D.D., Fullwood, C.: An online life like any other: identity, self-determination, and social networking among adults with intellectual disabilities. Cyberpsychol., Behav. Social Network. 21(1), 56–64 (2018). https://doi.org/10.1089/cyber.2016.0689

45. Darren David Chadwick: "You want to know that you're safe": experiences of risk, restriction and resilience online among people with an intellectual disability. Cyberpsychol.: J. Psychosocial Res. Cyberspace 16(3), (2022). https://doi.org/10.5817/CP2022-3-8

46. Alfredsson Ågren, K., Kjellberg, A., Hemmingsson, H.: Digital participation? Internet use among adolescents with and without intellectual disabilities: a comparative study. New Media Soc. (2020). https://doi.org/10.1177/1461444819888398

47. Chiner, E., Gómez-Puerta, M., Mengual-Andrés, S.: Opportunities and hazards of the internet for students with intellectual disabilities: the views of pre-service and in-service teachers. Int. J. Disabil. Develop. Educ. 68(4), 538–553 (2019). https://doi.org/10.1080/1034912X.2019.1696950

48. Heitplatz, V.N., Bühler, C., Hastall, M.R.: Caregivers' Influence on Smartphone Usage of People with Cognitive Disabilities: An Explorative Case Study in Germany. In: Antona, M., Stephanidis, C. (eds.) Universal Access in Human-Computer Interaction. 13th International Conference, UAHCI 2019, Held as Part of the 21st HCI International Conference, HCII 2019, Orlando, FL, USA, July 26–31, 2019, Proceedings, vol. 11573. LNCS Sublibrary: SL3 - Information Systems and Applications, incl. Internet/Web, and HCI, 11572–11573, pp. 98–115. SPRINGER, Cham, Switzerland (2019). https://doi.org/10.1007/978-3-030-235 63-5_9

49. Heitplatz, V., Wilkens, L., Bühler, C.: Gestaltungskonzepte und Beispiele zu digitalen Bildungsangeboten für heterogene Zielgruppen. In: Luthe, EW., Müller, S.V., Schiering, I. (ed.) Assistive Technologien im Sozial- und Gesundheitssektor. Gesundheit. Politik - Gesellschaft - Wirtschaft, pp. 311–335. SPRINGER, Wiesbaden (2022)

50. Molin, M., Sorbring, E., Löfgren-Mårtenson, L.: New Em@ncipatory landscapes? young people with intellectual disabilities, internet use, and identification processes. Adv. Social Work **18**(2), 645–662 (2017). https://doi.org/10.18060/21428

51. Seale, J.: The role of supporters in facilitating the use of technologies by adolescents and adults with learning disabilities: a place for positive risktaking? Eurp. J. Special Needs Educ. **29**, 220–236 (2014)

52. Seale, J., Chadwick, D.: How does risk mediate the ability of adolescents and adults with intellectual and developmental disabilities to live a normal life by using the Internet? Cyberpsychol.: J. Psycho. Res. Cyberspace **11**(1), (2017). https://doi.org/10.5817/CP2 017-1-2

53. Ware, P., et al.: Using eHealth technologies: interests, preferences, and concerns of older adults. Interact. J. Med. Res. (2017). https://doi.org/10.2196/ijmr.4447

54. Friedman, M.G., Bryen, D.N.: Web accessibility design recommendations for people with cognitive disabilities. TAD (2008). https://doi.org/10.3233/TAD-2007-19406

55. Karreman, J., van der Geest, T., Buursink, E.: Accessible website content guidelines for users with intellectual disabilities. Res. Intell. Disabil (2007). https://doi.org/10.1111/j.1468-3148. 2006.00353.x

56. Kennedy, H., Evans, S., Thomas, S.: Can the web be made accessible for people with intellectual disabilities? Inf. Soc. (2011). https://doi.org/10.1080/01972243.2011.534365

57. Watfern, C., Heck, C., Rule, C., Baldwin, P., Boydell, K.M.: Feasibility and acceptability of a mental health website for adults with an intellectual disability: qualitative evaluation. JMIR Mental Health (2019). https://doi.org/10.2196/12958

58. Begriplig Text: 19 råd för att skriva begripligt (2019). https://begripligtext.se/19-raden/

59. International Organization for Standardization: ISO 21801–1 Cognitive Accessibility - Part 1 General Guidelines (2020). https://www.iso.org/standard/71711.html

60. Müssener, U., et al.: Promoting healthy behaviors among adolescents and young adults with intellectual disability: protocol for developing a digital intervention with co-design workshops. JMIR Res. Protocols (2023). https://doi.org/10.2196/47877

# Interventions for Improving Road Surveillance for Teen Drivers with Autism

Erik Sand(✉) (iD)

University of Central Florida, Orlando, FL, USA
erik.sand@ucf.edu

**Abstract.** Learning to drive for any teen is a challenging process, especially for those who are on the autism spectrum. Challenges with executive function place extra demands for those teens and young adults. To better understand these difficulties, Nathaniel Wilson et al. consolidated all the literature from January 2000 to August 2017 that was guiding "the design of training interventions" for those on the spectrum. Wilson's work captured the objectives, findings, and limitations of 27 studies published during that period. This paper extends Wilson's review by summarizing the research done using Wilson's search criteria to May 2022 to better understand what interventions have been developed or studied, what elements of driving behavior are these interventions focused on improving, and what technologies and intervention techniques are being used to improve those behaviors. The final objective of this paper is to discuss design strategies that utilize game-based training with multi-modal monitoring to develop low-cost and scalable interventions to improve road surveillance and other driving behaviors. These design strategies include a full-function comprehensive training simulator, hybrid virtual reality for desktops, and very targeted solutions aimed at improving a particular skill. Low-cost and scalable interventions that can improve the driving behavior of this population, especially focusing on road surveillance, looks to be a promising area of research.

**Keywords:** autism spectrum disorder · driver training · teenage driving

## 1 Introduction

There are many important reasons for teens to learn how to drive, especially for teens on the autism spectrum. They range from driver safety to access to school and employment, to social inclusion, and to the overall ability for those with autism to live a life on par with their neurotypical counterparts. All of these are valid and important for the coming of age of teens. However, as any parent who's lived through their child's process of learning to drive can attest, having their child finally get a driver's license, and then driving on their own can create significant feelings of angst in those first few years of driving. Unfortunately, that feeling is well-founded. According to the CDC, motor vehicle accidents are the leading cause of death for teens in the United States with the accident rate among 16- 19-year-olds higher than any other group. Nearly 2,800 teens lost their lives in auto accidents in 2020 [1]. In addition, approximately 227,000 were

M. Antona and C. Stephanidis (Eds.): HCII 2024, LNCS 14697, pp. 231–249, 2024.
https://doi.org/10.1007/978-3-031-60881-0_15

treated in emergency rooms for auto accident-related injuries. The CDC estimates that the 13- to 19-year-old age group incurred about $40.7 billion in medical bills and work loss, resulting from these accidents that same year.

These first few years can be more troubling for parents of teens and young adults with ASD who do choose to learn to drive. Deficits in executive function (EF) may create additional challenges in the learning process for ASD teens. Compared to their TD counterparts, ASD teens show inefficiencies in some areas of EF that are inhibitors to safe driving [2]. A critical component of EF is working memory. Cox *et al.* (2016) [3] showed in simulated driving that teens with ASD exhibited reduced driving performance over their TD controls when increased working memory demands were placed on them. Walshe *et al.* (2017) [2] concluded from their literature review that deficient working memory contributes to reduced hazard detection and less attentive driving. As important as driving is for teens, the rate of licensure among teens on the spectrum is not equal to their traditionally developed (TD) counterparts. Several studies have surveyed the licensure rates of ASDs. Chee *et al.* (2015) [4] examined 100 young adults to determine attitudes towards driving in ASD and TD populations. The finding here was that only 34% of ASD had a license compared to 68% of TDs. A survey by Huang *et al.* (2012) [5] of driving eligible teens with ASD showed only 29% had driver's licenses or permits. Yet another survey of ASD adults by Deka *et al.* (2016) [6] on transportation mobility shows only 9.3% of those surveyed had driver's licenses. The takeaway from these studies is that ASDs appear not to be obtaining driver's licenses in numbers comparable to their TD peers. Further, for those ASDs that do obtain a license, studies show that it is taking them longer. Almberg *et al.* (2017) [7] revealed that ASDs need twice the amount of driving lessons of TDs. A survey by Daly *et al.* (2014) [8] had ASD respondents on average taking nearly two years longer than TDs in obtaining a driver's license.

A key piece of literature that sparked the author's interest in this topic (a parent of two teen drivers at the time) was a short article by McKnight and McKnight from 2003 entitled "Young Novice Drivers: Careless or clueless?" [9] This study reviewed over 2,000 accident reports involving teenage drivers ages 16 to 19 in Maryland and California. In the study, the authors read, coded, and analyzed each report for accident causes. These causes were categorized into broad categories that included Driving Preparation, Visual Search, Emergencies, Basic Control, Attention Level, as well as several others. There were many striking results to this study but the one that stood out is that nearly 44% of accidents in this study were attributed to poor visual search. Search, as defined by the authors included such fundamental driving constructs as searching ahead before turning, checking the mirrors and behind the vehicle before changing lanes, and fully scanning an intersection before entering. A more recent study by Curry *et al.* (2011) [10] corroborates the McKnight findings. This study collected crash data from the National Highway Traffic Safety Administration from July 2005 to December 2007 for 795 serious crashes involving 822 teen drivers. Twenty-one percent of these crashes were attributed to what Curry *et al.* defined as "inadequate surveillance" of current road conditions.

Though these studies on road surveillance did not focus on teens with autism, achieving adequate road surveillance is likely much more difficult for those teens on the spectrum. Two studies contained in a scoping review by Nathaniel Wilson *et al.* (2018) [11] review found issues in driving gaze and scan patterns of ASD teens compared to their TD peers. Sheppard *et al.* (2010) [12] found that the ASD group identified fewer hazards and in particular fewer hazards that involved a human figure. Reimer *et al.* (2013) [13] found that, when cognitive demands were increased with the ASD group, they tended to look away from the forward roadway presumably to reduce the cognitive load. Additionally, this study found that the ASD group tended to gaze much higher on the horizon than the TD controls group.

So, what does this mean for teens with autism who may be driving, learning to drive, or have an ambition to do so? Simply put, they will likely need extra time and assistance in learning to drive, given their potential differences in EF. Unfortunately, there seems little widely available to assist this population in this endeavor beyond one-on-one driving instruction done by parents or caregivers or by professional driving instructors. Entitled "Scoping Review of the Driving Behavior of and Driver Training Programs for People on the Autism Spectrum," Wilson *et al.* (2018) [11] sought to help better understand the current literature that was guiding the "design of training interventions" for those people with autism. This work looked at all publications done between January 2000 and August 2017 researching driver training for those on the autism spectrum. Twenty-seven articles in all were deemed to meet the author's inclusion criteria. The review summarized each publication's research team location, type of study, the study's objectives, participant population, key findings, and the study's limitations. Wilson went on to group these findings into four scoping classifications: participant performance in a driving simulator, participant performance in virtual reality driving, on-road driving and transport statistics, and barriers to obtaining a license.

The body of work contained in Wilson[1] is a significant step in understanding the differences in driving behavior and the issues ASDs face when learning to drive. However, given the pace of technology, significant environmental changes have taken place in the six years since the last study in the Wilson review was published. Recent advancements in virtual reality and artificial intelligence are now available not only to aid researchers in better understanding the differences between ASDs and TDs in their driving behavior, but aid in their driver training and even on-road performance. Therefore, this paper has three objectives. First, given the pace of technology, what work has been done since the Wilson study was first published? Utilizing Wilson's search methodology, this paper will summarize the work done since by borrowing the classification schemes presented in Wilson. The second objective is given both the Wilson corpus and beyond, summarize what interventions have been develop or studied, what elements of driving behavior these interventions are focused on improving and what are the technologies and intervention techniques used to do so. Though much of the work in Wilson and beyond studies the differences in driving characteristics and behaviors between drivers on the spectrum and neurotypical drivers, there has been work that focuses on driving interventions for those with autism and it needs to be summarized and understood. Finally, armed with this information, the final objective of this paper is to discuss design strategies that might utilize virtual reality, game-based training, and multi-modal monitoring to develop low-cost and scalable interventions to improve driving behaviors. Several of the studies found in Wilson used multi-modal strategies to monitor physiological factors

---

[1] Wilson and Wilson *et al.* (2018) will be used interchangeably through the remainder of this paper.

to determine and interpret a participant's affective state. The kinds of equipment used in these studies were likely state of the art at the time but were designed for use in a lab environment. Low-cost wearables are now available that can provide the same and better data. Additionally, recent projects undertaken by the author have utilized video games to help improve road surveillance of police officers. This game-based training was well received by the training organization and the officers that used it. Both the popularity of video games among teens (the most at-risk age group) and advances in inexpensive wearables and vision-based techniques that monitor physiological signals such as heart rate and respiration support the potential of developing effective interventions that leverage these technologies. Low-cost and scalable interventions improving the driving behavior of this population would be positively received.

## 2  Methods

The review methodology employed here borrowed extensively from Wilson. While Wilson searched peer-reviewed research articles written in English between January 2000 and August 2017, this review extended that work to peer reviewed articles in English published between August 2017 and March 2022. The keywords[2] from the search employed in Wilson were used across the University of Central Florida (UCF) Primo database with the aid of a UCF librarian. As the librarian produced search results, the abstracts were reviewed by the author. Like Wilson, articles were eliminated if they did not involve those with autism and did not include any research on driver training or driver skill development. Research was also excluded if it was not peer-reviewed, the full text was unavailable, it focused on disabilities other than ASD, or focused on transportation rather than independent driving.

Further classification of the studies included here was then performed following procedures outlined in Wilson. The studies were read by the author and grouped into five different scoping classifications depending on the focus of the article. These classifications included (1) on-road driving behaviors and transport statistics reports on drivers on the spectrum, (2) performance in driving simulators, (3) performance in virtual reality driving, (4) barriers to obtaining a license and training on drivers on the spectrum, and (5) literature reviews. The differentiation between simulator driving and driving in virtual reality outlined in Wilson was that the virtual reality classification used desktop computers (with monitors and interface equipment such as game controllers) as opposed to a full-functioning driving simulator. Other descriptive information was captured for analysis from each of the studies and included author and year of publication, location (country and university affiliation of listed author), number of citations (as determined

---

[2] The following search terms were used as appropriate: "Child development disorders, pervasive" OR "child developmental disorder*" OR "pervasive developmental disorder*" OR autism OR Asperger OR "autism spectrum disorder*" OR "autistic disorder*" OR "Develop- mental disabil*" AND "Automobile Driving" OR driving or "driv* training" OR "driver behaviour" OR "driver performance" OR "driver characteristic" OR "driv* education" OR "driv* testing" OR "driv* procedures" OR "driving hazard*" OR "car driv*"OR "automobile driv*" OR "driv* packages".

by Google Scholar at time of analysis), study objective, population, key findings, limitations, and gaze research. The Wilson review contained 27 studies. The criteria employed in this search yielded 23 papers.

## 3   Comparison of Key Categories

### 3.1   On-Road Driving Behaviors and Transport Statistics on Drivers on the Spectrum

Three additional studies were done in this category since the original Wilson article. Curry *et al.* (2018) [14] reviewed the licensure rates among adolescents and young adults with ASD, Curry *et al.* (2021) [15] compared motor vehicle crashes and traffic violations, while Vindin *et al.* (2021) [16] reviewed on-road driver training intervention. Regarding the licensure rates, Curry *et al.* (2018) [14] was consistent with the results of Daly *et al.* (2014) [8] reported in Wilson. Curry reviewed more than 52 thousand New Jersey residents born between 1987 and 1995 who were patients of the Children's Hospital of Philadelphia (CHOP) healthcare network. 609 of these patients had a confirmed spectrum diagnosis. Where Daley's sample of 172 drivers found that ASD drivers licensed nearly two years later than non-ASD drivers, Curry's database of New Jersey showed ASD drivers were licensing less than a year later than non-ASD's. The results of this larger sample size are encouraging for young ASD drivers. Using the same New Jersey data, an additional study was published by Curry *et al.* (2021) [15] comparing motor vehicle crashes, traffic violations, and license suspension. This study stands in some contrast to the Daly *et al.* (2014) [8] and D. J. Cox *et al.* (2017) [17] results contained in Wilson as it shows favorable crash and citation rates for ASD drivers. This later Curry *et al.* (2021) [15] report expanded the pool of drivers to include those born between 1987 and 2000 whose age of first visit to CHOP was between 12 and 15 (n = 71,476). These data revealed that adolescent and young adult drivers with ASD have "similar to lower crash rates compared with non-ASD drivers." Further, when the "rates of other adverse driving outcomes" were examined (i.e., moving violations and license suspensions), ASD drivers performed multiples better than non-ASD drivers in this sample. However, consistent with other studies, Curry *et al.* (2021) [15] reported that ASD drivers in the sample were more likely to crash while making left turns or U-turns for failure to yield the right of way. Finally, Vindin *et al.* (2021) [16] examined the results of a driving training program intended for those with ASD. This program was designed to help ASD's deal with many of the complex issues surrounding driving that were reported in Wilson such as multi-tasking and even simpler ones such as speed maintenance. The study reviewed the pre- and post- test results of both the driving training program and routine driving instruction. The on-road performance of the ASDs was reported as encouraging for both groups, but there was no significant difference between the two training regimes.

### 3.2   Performance in Driving Simulators

Seven new studies have been performed in this scoping classification since the Wilson review. Like Wilson, nearly all the studies compared ASD to neurotypical controls.

Six of these studies involved direct comparisons between teen and young adult drivers with ASD and matched neurotypical drivers. The seventh by Ross, Cox, *et al.* (2018) [18] involved comparing the attitude measures of novice ASD drivers and their parents before and after a driving simulator training intervention. One hundred eighty-six parents of novice neurotypical drivers were used in the study as a baseline. The Ross study reported that ASDs learning to drive have fewer positive and more negative feelings about driving than neurotypical controls. It also found that using a simulator as part of driving instruction improved these results for ASDs. This is consistent with the lone study reported in Wilson that used a simulator as a training intervention [17].

The remaining six studies in this group compared some elements of driving performance in the simulator between neurotypical and ASD drivers [19–24]. Bednarz, Kana, *et al.* (2021) [19], the most recent study of the group, was the first to look at how measures of Theory of Mind and executive function would predict how drivers might react to various road hazards. A study format similar to Sheppard E *et al.* (2010) [12] was employed where participants were shown both social and non-social hazards in the simulator. Sheppard defines a social hazard as one where a person is clearly visible such as a cyclist or a pedestrian and a non-social hazard as one where the person or driver of the vehicle is not. This study showed that lower performing scores in measures of theory of mind and executive function strongly correlate to a slower response to non-social hazards. The five remaining studies all measured some element of ability to maintain lane position and speed, the number of collisions, observance of traffic lights, and overall driving errors. In general, ASDs performed worse or on-par with their TD controls. Three studies reported on overall driving errors in the simulator [20–22]. Of these, two reported group differences with ASDs performing more poorly. Only D.Y.T. Chee *et al.* (2019) [21] reported no group differences. No Wilson study reported overall driving errors. Five studies reported lane position performance [20–24]. In contrast to Wilson, the Cox [22] and Dodwell [23] studies both found ASDs having a more difficult time maintaining lane position than TD controls while the remaining three studies did not. Though the sample sizes of the studies are relatively comparable, perhaps the difference can be explained by experience. Both the Ross and Cox studies use drivers that were slightly more experienced than the others. The same five studies compared ASD and TDs on collision with other vehicles. Only D.Y.T. Chee *et al.* (2019) [21] found group differences where ASDs performed more poorly. No study reported on the number of collisions in Wilson. Similarly, only one of the five studies reported group differences on elements of speed control. Cox [22] reported group difference in reckless driving where ASD participants drove greater than 20 miles per hour greater than the posted speed limit in the simulator. The remaining four studies did not report any group differences. This differing results might be explained in the statistical power of the study in that Cox [22] was comparing only seven new ASD drivers and ten new TD drivers.

Perhaps the biggest difference in the studies done in the Performance in Simulator Driving category since Wilson is the inclusion of physiological, cognitive, and attitude measures as predictors of tactical performance in the simulator, including one study correlating measures of Theory of Mind to tactical driving performance [19]. Only two studies in this Wilson scoping classification tested cognitive measures using clinical tests [3, 25], but neither tried to correlate any measure of the tactical performance in the simulator to these clinical scores. D.J. Cox *et al.* (2017) [17] tested the effects of cognitive demands on working memory and how that would affect simulated driving performance, but no clinical tests of executive function were used as predictor variables. Since Wilson, all but Ross *et al.* (2018) [18] correlated some aspects of physiological, cognitive, or attitude measures to group driving performance with all reporting at least one interaction between simulator performance and one of these measures. Measured within these studies were such cognitive measures as executive function, working memory, risk taking, impulsivity, inhibition, autism rating, and adult intelligence. Attitude measures included driving attitude, self-reported driving behavior, and perception of workload as well as three different tests for Theory of Mind. Physiological measures included heart rate, galvanic skin response, micro movements of the wrist, and elements of eye tracking.

Six of the seven studies report an interaction between a measure of executive function and a measure of driving performance with all six reporting that the interaction between a measure of executive function and one or more performance elements of simulated driving. Three studies [20–22] reported a strong interaction between BRIEF scores[3] and the number of overall driving mistakes. D.Y.T. Chee *et al.* (2019a) [20] found a strong interaction between DKEF-S scores[4] with the number of red-light tickets, and Autism Quotient (AQ) scores with the number of driving mistakes. Ross *et al.* (2019) [24] showed poor UFOV[5] scores presented higher lane position variance. Bednarz, Kana, *et al.* (2021) [19], which focused on measures of executive function and theory of mind, found that the measures of executive function employed in their study (UFOV Processing Speed and Selective Attention, and DKEF-S Trail Making) all had interactions with poorer responses to the presentation of social hazards. Important to reiterate here is that those who present with poorer executive function generally presented poorer driving performance in simulated driving.

Two studies tracked physiological measures in the simulator. D.Y.T. Chee *et al.* (2019) [21] tracked eye movement while D.J. Cox *et al.* (2020) [22] tracked heart rate, galvanic skin response, and micro-wrist movement in addition to eye movement. Regarding eye tracking, the Chee study found that ASDs had more overall fixations, particularly on the road ahead. This is consistent with the findings of Reimer *et al.* (2013) [13] reported in Wilson. Reimer reported that ASDs tended to fixate on distant objects and position their gaze high and to the right. D.Y.T. Chee *et al.* (2019) [21] also reported that ASDs fixate less on traffic lights, dwell less on potential hazards, and have a significant interaction between fixating on the road ahead and the number of simulator mistakes. The eye tracking in D.J. Cox *et al.* (2020) [22] found no significant difference in critical targets viewed and viewing the speedometer and dash of the simulator between the ASDs and TDs. However, when a trained driving instructor, blind to the two groups, reviewed replays of simulated driving performance, the instructor felt less comfortable with the ASD group than the TD. The Cox study also found that the ASD group showed

---

[3] Behavior Rating Inventory of Executive Function - designed to assess executive function behaviors in school age children. [26]

[4] Delis-Kaplan Executive Function System - first nationally standardized set of tests to evaluate higher level cognitive functions in both children and adults. [27]

[5] Useful Field of View - a cognitive assessment that reliably predicts crash risk in drivers. [28]

a more elevated heart rate in the more challenging segments of simulated driving than TD controls. No other physiological differences between groups were found in the Cox study.

## 3.3 Performance in Virtual Reality (VR)

Five studies [19, 29–32] were evaluated and placed in this category[6] because, like Wilson, they used a desktop computer to create a driving experience. Of the five, four studies directly compared performance of ASD to TD controls. Only Baker-Ericzén *et al.* (2021) [29] used a sample of only ASD to compare pre- and post-test success of a driver training intervention leveraging elements of both cognitive behavioral therapy and virtual reality training. Though Baker-Ericzén found the results of this study promising, the study was lacking controls that would have compared their intervention to one that didn't use cognitive behavioral therapy or virtual reality. Wade *et al.* (2017) [32] included here is a follow-on study to several others[7] referenced in Wilson. Important to note here is that this study is the only one in this scoping classification that's measuring gaze of the participants with the objective of using real time gaze feedback to improve the driving performance in the participants. The first part of Wade's study showed no difference between ASD and TD controls in gaze behavior while the second part of this study showed that real-time gaze feedback made no significant difference in participant performance. Similarly, a study by Bednarz, Kana, *et al.* (2021) [19] measured brain wave activity of its participants while responding to social and non-social hazards displayed in virtual reality. No group differences were found in accuracy of response, response time, and brain wave activity between groups when shown these hazards. The number of years driving, and the participant's age were better predictors of brain activity. The two studies by Patrick *et al.* [30, 31] sought to compare driving performance between ASDs and well-matched TD controls. Patrick *et al.* (2018) [30] hypothesized that driving performance parameters such as speed and lane maintenance of ASDs would not be performed as well as by TD controls, especially under cognitive load such as holding a conversation or tuning a radio. The results supported this hypothesis in all driving conditions tested. The second study, Patrick *et al.* (2020) [31], used the same VR driving environment and procedures. However, the participants in this study were given a series of clinical tests to determine levels of executive function, cognitive inhibition and impairment, and visual scanning and divided attention to develop correlations between these functions and driving performance. This study found the participant's speed of information processing mediated differences between ASD and non-ASD groups on speed and lane management. However, it also determined that there was no relationship between autism quotient scores (AQ) and driving performance.

## 3.4 Barriers to Obtaining a License and Training of Drivers on the Spectrum

There clearly has been a bigger focus on this topic in the literature since Wilson was first published. Where there were only three papers listed in the 17 years the Wilson

---

[6] Though one of the studies [32] was comprised of two significant sub-studies.

[7] Wade and several others from Vanderbilt University chronicled the development and leveraged the use of the Virtual Reality Adaptive Driving Intervention Architecture referenced in [32].

study covered. There are nine covered in the new time period. Eight of the nine studies derived information from at least one of three main constituent groups; those with ASD learning to drive, the parents or caregivers of those ASDs learning to drive, and the professional driving instructors - very often occupational therapists - that teach them. The ninth study was a literature review. Of the eight studies, six used questionnaires or interviews of some form. A seventh study, Silvi & Scott-Parker (2018) [33], chose to analyze posts from various on-line forums concerning driving behavior of those with ASD. The eighth study, Monahan *et al.* (2020) [34], was a published usability study on an author developed driver training application to ensure the application met "usability guidelines as well as the learning preferences" of ASDs. Though the Monahan study was helpful in improving the app, it didn't generalize further into the ASD community beyond noting that involving those familiar with ASDs early in the design process produces applications that are friendly to an ASD audience. The six studies employing some form of questionnaire or survey [18, 35–39] examined, in total, 422 responses. The groups comprising this total were young drivers with ASD (n = 28), parents and caregivers of young drivers with ASD (n = 109), parents of young TD drivers (n = 186) and driving instructors with experience in serving ASDs (n = 99). Two of the studies focused exclusively on the driving instructors [36, 37] while two of the studies focused exclusively on the parents and caregivers [18, 35].

Many consistent themes emerge in this new collection. All constituencies in these studies acknowledge that there are challenges to licensure intrinsic to ASDs that include the physical and social challenges ASDs face in executive function, motor skills, and social communication. However, the two studies that focused specifically on the experiences of the driving instructors [36, 37] noted that parents and caregivers of ASDs can be an impediment as well. The instructors interviewed in Vindin *et al.* (2021) [39] commented that "difficult parents" are a barrier to the process. Similarly, those identified as "relatives" in Silvi & Scott-Parker (2018) [33] held the view that the diagnosis of ASD and those personal characteristics associated with that diagnosis were significant barriers. However, the ASDs in the same study did not. They viewed the logistics of driving and the process of licensure to be a larger obstacle. In contrast, Myers *et al.* (2019) [36] noted several instructors who pointed to their most successful students were those whose parents were engaged in the process but promoted independence of their ASD children early. Parents interviewed in Kersten *et al.* (2020) [35] noted to be successful, they had to "gently push" even if the experience was out of the ASD's comfort zone. Parents had to eventually "let go" and allow the ASD the freedom to explore.

Another key theme that emerged in this classification was that instructional strategies unique to the individual ASD were likely the most successful. A notable quote from one of the driving instructors shared in Meyers *et al.* (2019) [36] was "if you've taught one student with ASD, then you've taught one student with ASD." Overall, it was observed that lessons should be shorter and more frequent to better handle social and concentration deficits exhibited by many ASDs [37]. The use of commentary driving was mentioned as a successful approach as well [36, 37]. However, there are cost and time challenges to utilizing professional driving instructors that result in lack of instruction or lower quality instruction provided by the parent or caregiver. All constituencies believe that success could be achieved and that ASD exhibit driving strengths as well that include excellent memorization skills and strict rule obeyance [37, 40].

## 4 Other Comparisons

### 4.1 Gaze and Scan

Three studies involving gaze and scan behavior[8] have been performed since Wilson [21, 22, 32]. All three of these studies involved direct measurement of the participant's eye location and focused on regions of interest while driving in a simulator (or in one instance on the road). Both Wade *et al.* (2017) [32] and D.Y.T. Chee *et al.* (2019) [21] measured the number of fixations and fixation duration on various predetermined targets such as road signs, rear view mirrors, and the simulated instrument clusters of the vehicle. Wade again confirmed the Reimer *et al.* (2013) [13] study showing that the median gaze of ASDs is slightly higher and to the right of TDs. The Wade study also used gaze location as a feedback mechanism to improve driving skills. This will be discussed in the section on driving interventions. D.J. Cox *et al.* (2020) [22] recorded a participant's eye position on the screen during a simulated drive such that the simulation could be replayed with the participant's gaze location superimposed on the replay. Like one of his previous studies [17], the gaze location was overlaid on the playback of the simulation and a reviewer measured the number of critical driving targets viewed by the participant. This study found no differences in the number of critical driving targets viewed by ASDs and TDs. Further, this study also had the participant perform an actual drive. Cameras recorded the participant's eye movements during the drive and a subsequent frame-by-frame analysis determined the participant's gaze behavior. A frame-by-frame analysis was made of film of the participant's driving an on-road course. No significant group differences were noted in glance behavior of on-road driving.

The Wilson review includes two of the most cited on gaze and scan behavior - Sheppard E *et al.* (2010) [12] and Reimer *et al.* (2013) [13] with 137 and 100 citations respectively[9]. Sheppard was the first to observe that those with autism perceive social hazards - those hazards involving people - more slowly than healthy controls. Reimer was the first to note that the average vertical and horizontal gaze positions of those drivers with autism is higher and to the right of those drivers traditionally developed. Two more studies in the Wilson review [41, 42] go on to perform direct measurement of gaze position to confirm Reimer's results. Sheppard *et al.* (2017) [43] goes on to extend their 2010 study by including direct measurement of gaze position and duration during the identification of driving hazards. Instead of merely having the participant identify different hazards, the Sheppard team measured where the participant was looking prior to acquiring sight of the hazard and where they looked during the identification of the

---

[8] For the purposes of this discussion, elements of gaze and scan behavior include (1) direct eye tracking or measurement of the participant while performing in VR or a simulator, (2) indirect measurement through clinical tests such as Uniform Field of View (UFOV) or Delis-Kaplan Executive Function System (D-KEFS), or (3) direct observation of gaze and scan behavior by a certified driving rehabilitation specialist.

[9] Source: Google Scholar at time of manuscript creation.

hazard. This study found that there were no pre-hazard group differences between ASD and TD in the number of fixations, the fixation duration, or the horizontal speed of the search. Additionally, this study found that once the hazard was seen, there was no difference between ASD and TD in time to respond. However, this study did show that ASDs were slower to fixate on the hazard than TDs.

Other studies on gaze and scan behavior were included in the Wilson review. Lian Zhang *et al.* (2015) [44] directly measured gaze position, pupil diameter, and blink rate, but no comparisons were made between ASDs and health controls in this study. The results of these measurements were used with other physiological measurements such as heart rate and galvanic skin response to develop AI models of a participant's affective state while driving. The aim of these models is to use the physiological conditions monitored to identify the affective state of a participant such that the difficulty of the simulator routine could be adjusted real-time to match the participant's affective state. D.J. Cox *et al.* (2017) [17] directly measured gaze during simulated driving. However, this gaze information was layered into a replay of the simulation such that a driving instructor could discuss the participants gaze and scan behaviors while reviewing a recording of the simulated exercise. A red cone was superimposed on the playback of a recording of the simulation that represented the driver's gaze direction and location during the simulated drive. Also in this study, a driving instructor, who was blind to the participants, reviewed the simulated drives and rated the ASD participant's visual scanning habits "uncomfortable." The remaining four studies examined in Wilson – D.Y. Chee *et al.* (2017) [40], Classen & Monahan (2013) [45], Monahan *et al.* (2012, 2013) [46, 47] - all used clinical tests to determine visual attention and motor response. In all four studies ASDs showed poorer visual attention and motor response than TDs.

### 4.2 Use of Physiological Monitoring

Three studies involving the use of physiological monitoring[10] have been performed since Wilson. Wade *et al.* (2017) [32] is included in this number as VR system employed in the study had the capability to monitor physiological signals but did not collect them in this particular study. Cox *et al.* (2020) [22] monitors the heart rate, galvanic skin response (GSR), and micro-movement as well as the driver's gaze position while in a driving simulator to determine differences between inexperienced (some with ASD) and experience drivers. In both on-road and simulated driving, inexperienced ASD drivers exhibited elevated heart rate and GSR over experienced drivers. A study by Bednarz, Stavrinos, *et al.* (2021) [48] places the participants in a magnetic resonance imaging device (MRI) to detect the participants brain activity to determine what areas of the brain were engaged when shown various types of driving hazards. In short, it was found that age was a better predictor of brainwave activity than group (ASD, ADHD, TD). The six studies published in Wilson [41, 42, 44, 49–51] were published by a collection of researchers associated with Vanderbilt University using their Virtual Reality Adaptive Driving Intervention Architecture (VADIA) – a VR driving simulator with an architecture that supports the monitoring and collection of various sensory inputs from the

---

[10] For the purposes of this discussion, physiological monitoring includes any monitoring of signals emanating from a participant's body. These would include such signals as heart rate, body temperature, brain wave activity, skin conductance, and others.

participant as well as gaze and scan information. These studies centered on developing a driver training intervention that can determine the affective state of the student driver and adjust the difficulty of the training exercise given the affective state of the trainee. In the six studies published, VADIA has collectively monitored participants' gaze, volumetric changes in blood (PPG), skin conductance (GSR), respiration, body temperature, electrical activity in the brain (EEG), heart activity (ECG), and the electrical activity in various muscles (EMG). The studies found each of these signals could be used as a feedback mechanism to adjust the difficulty of the driving routines. The next section goes into more detail.

## 4.3 Training Interventions

The collection of studies associated with VADIA mentioned above are all focused on developing a driver training intervention that use a combination of physiological signals to monitor a participant's affective state and adjust the level of difficulty of the driver training accordingly. Joshua Wade et al. (2014) [41] is the start of this collection of studies. Though no intervention was directly tested per say, this study used a small sample size to determine the feasibility of using VADIA to see if differences in the participant's gaze location could be determined real-time. The study did reveal differences between the ASD group and the TD group, but with a sample size of eight, nothing could be significantly concluded. Zhang et al. (2014) [51] and Lian Zhang et al. (2015) [44] investigated whether multi-modal fusion of driving performance data with physiological would be a better predictor of a participant's affective state than either performance or physiological data alone. Using a trained therapist to collect information on the participant's affective state at various points of the simulation, machine learning was used to map the data collected to the participant's affective state. It was concluded that feature fusion was an overall better predictor. Wade et al. (2015) [42] and Wade et al. (2017) [32] both extend the gaze paradigm further. Participants were required to progress through the training regimen in the simulator. The participants not only have to successfully complete the driving exercise but were also required to view various "regions of interest". Should the simulator not detect the participant's gaze on the required region of interest, the participant would fail that exercise. Participants showed a significant decrease in driving failures over controls. Bian et al. (2016) [49] adjusted the difficulty of various driving parameters given the detected engagement levels of the participant. Here, signals such as respiration and skin conductivity were used. Because of an extremely small sample size, it couldn't be determined if the training was more effective than controls, but participants noticed the difficulty level of the training changing and all stated that they were engaged with and enjoyed the training. Finally, Fan et al. (2018) [50] used participant EEG data captured while driving in a simulator. This study determined it was possible to use EEG data as another variable to determine a participant's cognitive workload and affective state.

Four other studies center around developing and testing interventions for driver training. In the Wilson collection, Brooks et al. (2016) [52] investigated using steering and pedal exercises in a driving simulator to improve the motor skills and coordination of pre-driving teens. A sample of ten ASDs were compared to 31 neurotypical control subjects. Though it took the ASD group longer, all participants in the study successfully completed the exercises. D. J. Cox *et al.* (2017) [17] set out to show that a virtual reality driving simulator training (VRDST) would improve overall driving performance and in particular, "driving-relevant" executive function. Though VRDST did not show improvement in driving related executive function, it did show significant skill improvement over routine driver training. Two other studies were performed on specific interventions since Wilson. Baker-Ericzen *et al.* (2021) [29] looked to improve driving related executive function and emotional regulation using a "manualized curriculum" they developed called Cognitive Behavioral Intervention for Driving (CBID). Participants met 1.5 h each week for 10 weeks in facilitated sessions that explored various aspects of their driving behavior. Pre- and post-assessment showed improved attitudes towards driving and improved performance in a driving simulator. Vindin *et al.* (2021) [16] developed an on-line driver training program (DTP) specifically for those learning drivers on the spectrum. Though the DTP showed significant improvement in driving performance, the improvement was not significant compared to routine driver training as a control.

## 5 Discussion

Three things can be concluded from the Wilson review and the subsequent one performed here. First, nearly all the research in both reviews supports the notion that there are differences in driving skills and rates of learning for those on the spectrum, especially for very new drivers. Additionally, these differences can be exacerbated by the apprehension and anxiety that many of those with ASD show in learning to drive [13, 18, 22]. Second, the literature supports that experience and training mitigate these differences and often the apprehension that comes with it [18, 29]. Those with ASD can become safe drivers [15, 18, 24, 39]. Third, though this combined review yielded over 50 studies, fewer than a dozen focused on only five unique training interventions. These interventions ranged from a full driving experience intelligent virtual reality simulator [32, 41, 42] to training steering and pedal motions [52] to training regimen leveraging cognitive behavioral theory to lessen the anxiety of new drivers [29].

What also stands from the review is that as important as training is, it is often not accessible to the learner with ASD [35–37, 39]. Professional driving instruction has been shown to be effective but can be prohibitively expensive. Though often with drawbacks, one-on-one driving instruction by a parent or caregiver can be effective as well but can be prohibitively time consuming for the parent or caregiver of the ASD learner. Time in a simulator (virtual reality or otherwise) has been shown to be effective as well in both training driving performance skills and lessening the anxiety of the learner [17, 18, 29]. However, their availability is often constrained and expensive. A third standout item is related to demographic. Several studies pointed out that previous driving experience lessened differences between ASDs and TDs therefore it is the youngest drivers with little to no experience who demonstrated the largest skill difference between comparable controls [22, 30]. In the general population, this is the demographic that has the most traffic accidents as well [1, 9].

Given this, there are three approaches to driver training platforms - all of which need to be steeped in pedagogy to serve this audience. First, there's the "all encompassing" approach as worked on by the Vanderbilt team. This approach would include a full-figured simulator and include the monitoring of gaze and physiological signals. A full simulator would allow the trainee the opportunity to "feel" the vehicle while the monitoring equipment allows for feedback during the training exercises. Much like other simulators and VR setups mentioned in this review, feedback can include things like noting the trainee is not looking at "regions of interest" and adjusting the difficulty of the training exercise per physiological signals. Other features might include a library of driving locations that are unique to the locale, thus creating familiarity when performing real-world driving. The advantage of this approach is that the training experience can be uniquely configured to the needs of the trainee thus helping the trainee learn to drive on their terms. The two key disadvantages are accessibility and cost. A system such as this could only be supported at a university or driving training center as it would be relatively expensive to build and maintain and would require use by many trainees to justify the cost. Further, there would be technical challenges as well in making a simulator such as this available to the public, the most notable of which is calibrating the thresholds of physiological signals to match many trainees. This approach might provide the most lifelike training experience but would have its challenges in setup and ongoing maintenance costs.

Second, there's the "one-off" approach as highlighted by the steering/pedal exercise. This approach targets specific areas of need such as steering and pedal coordination or road surveillance. The difference between the one-off approach and incorporating training exercises in the comprehensive simulator above is in the platform delivering the training. In the one-off approach, the training delivery platform is tailored and scoped only to the needs of the specific training mission. For example, like the steering and pedal coordination training, the training road surveillance techniques could be delivered using only a desktop computer coupled with an eye tracking device. There are clear advantages to this approach. The platforms can be low cost and very targeted to high need areas. Road surveillance is a great example of this. Given 44% of accidents in young teens can be attributed to poor road surveillance [9], low cost, targeted training could have a significant impact in this area. Several years ago, this author led a team of graduate students that built a road surveillance training game for a federal training agency. It was PC-based with an infinite runner game mechanic designed to teach law enforcement officers to look higher on the horizon while driving pursuit vehicles. It utilized a desk top PC coupled with a Tobi eye tracker and a Logitech G-25 game controller. Though no efficacy studies were ever done, it was well received by the agency. It proved to the agency that a targeted training platform could be developed quickly at low relative cost. Platforms such as this can be developed, hardened, and distributed to a wide range of users, thus making them accessible not just to driver training centers, but even for home use. However, these targeted applications are just that and shouldn't be mistaken for a comprehensive training experience.

There's a hybrid approach leveraging low-cost virtual reality, game-based learning, and inexpensive wearables. Like the one-off approach mentioned above, a desk top computer coupled with relatively inexpensive eye tracking and wearables can deliver training applications to a wide range of users. However, the hybrid solution considers a more complete training experience that could be delivered through a curriculum tailored for those young drivers with ASD. Like the full feature simulator described above, the availability of inexpensive wearables or effective computer vision-based approaches could potentially detect physiological signals thus creating a more intelligent driver training platform that provides feedback and adjusts difficulty during training. Training programs could potentially be delivered to home computers configured with the necessary equipment. Training applications could be game-based appealing to a younger audience that enjoys video games. With online training, there is more opportunity for creating a training experience tailored for and unique to the trainee. For example, training applications could potentially include driving scenarios of routes and locales important to the trainee. However, there are still potential issues. Calibrating physiological profiles and thresholds within training applications for a wide range of users still presents challenges as does calibrating any peripheral device for specific users. A Tobii eye tracker was used in the driving game this author helped create for the law enforcement community. Each new player session of the game required the user to perform Tobii's calibration routine. As this was a proof-of-concept application, the programming required to create and store unique user profiles was not performed, but this highlighted the work needed to scale and harden an application such as this.

In conclusion, ASDs, especially teens, are underserved in driver training. Novice ASD teen drivers show the greatest differences in driving performance when compared to their traditionally developed counterparts. Yet, for those teens who wish to learn to drive, their choices of how to learn are few. The availability of effective and inexpensive training solutions would help this community have the same opportunities as those teens not on the spectrum.

# 6 Limitations

The primary limitation of this review is the scope of the literature analyzed. Though the keywords from Wilson were used by a professional librarian, the results of the Wilson review were not able to be replicated with the databases available to the University of Central Florida library. Therefore, it's uncertain whether the search performed on the dates since Wilson provided an exhaustive list of studies that would match the criteria set forth by that study. Another limitation of this review is that it has been performed by only one author. As there were multiple authors involved in the Wilson review, a review by a single author introduces two different biases potentially not included in Wilson. First, the use of one author biases the interpretation of what should be included in the review. There were at least two instances where the author was unsure of whether these studies met the Wilson criteria for inclusion. Second, and perhaps more importantly, the interpretation of the findings of the studies included in this review was left up to only one reviewer – the author. A second or third reviewer would have left room for healthy debate that would have mitigated these biases.

**Acknowledgments.** The author would like to thank his Committee Chair, Dr. Charles Hughes of the University of Central Florida for all his help and guidance in the creation of this manuscript.

**Disclosure of Interests.** The author has no competing interests to declare that are relevant to the content of this article.

# References

1. Teen Drivers and Passengers: Get the Facts | Transportation Safety | Injury Center | CDC. https://www.cdc.gov/transportationsafety/teen_drivers/teendrivers_factsheet.html. Accessed 13 Jun 2023
2. Walshe, E.A., McIntosh, C.W., Romer, D., Winston, F.K.: Executive function capacities, negative driving behavior and crashes in young drivers. Int. J. Environ. Res. Public Health **14**, 1314 (2017). https://doi.org/10.3390/ijerph14111314
3. Cox, S.M., et al.: Driving simulator performance in novice drivers with autism spectrum disorder: the role of executive functions and basic motor skills. J. Autism Dev. Disord. **46**, 1379–1391 (2016)
4. Chee, D.Y.-T., et al.: Viewpoints on driving of individuals with and without autism spectrum disorder. Dev. Neurorehabil. **18**, 26–36 (2015). https://doi.org/10.3109/17518423.2014.964377
5. Huang, P., Kao, T., Curry, A.E., Durbin, D.R.: Factors associated with driving in teens with autism spectrum disorders. J. Dev. Behav. Pediatr. **33**, 70–74 (2012). https://doi.org/10.1097/DBP.0b013e31823a43b7
6. Deka, D., Feeley, C., Lubin, A.: Travel patterns, needs, and barriers of adults with autism spectrum disorder report from a survey. Transp. Res. Record., 9–16 (2016). https://doi.org/10.3141/2542-02
7. Almberg, M., Selander, H., Falkmer, M., Vaz, S., Ciccarelli, M., Falkmer, T.: Experiences of facilitators or barriers in driving education from learner and novice drivers with ADHD or ASD and their driving instructors. Dev. Neurorehabil. **20**, 59–67 (2017). https://doi.org/10.3109/17518423.2015.1058299
8. Daly, B., Nicholls, E., Patrick, K., Bosenbark, D., Schultheis, M.: Driving behaviors in adults with autism spectrum disorders. J. Autism Dev. Disorders **44** (2014). https://doi.org/10.1007/s10803-014-2166-y
9. McKnight, A.J., McKnight, A.S.: Young novice drivers: careless or clueless? Accid. Anal. Prev. **35**, 921–925 (2003)
10. Curry, A.E., Hafetz, J., Kallan, M.J., Winston, F.K., Durbin, D.R.: Prevalence of teen driver errors leading to serious motor vehicle crashes. Accid. Anal. Prev. **43**, 1285–1290 (2011). https://doi.org/10.1016/j.aap.2010.10.019
11. Wilson, N.J., Lee, H.C., Vaz, S., Vindin, P., Cordier, R.: Scoping review of the driving behaviour of and driver training programs for people on the autism spectrum. Behav. Neurol. **2018**, 6842306 (2018). https://doi.org/10.1155/2018/6842306
12. Sheppard, E., Ropar, D., Underwood, G., van Loon, E.: Brief report: driving hazard perception in autism. J. Autism Dev. Disord. **40**, 504–508 (2010). https://doi.org/10.1007/s10803-009-0890-5
13. Reimer, B., et al.: Brief report: examining driving behavior in young adults with high functioning autism spectrum disorders: a pilot study using a driving simulation paradigm. J. Autism Dev. Disord. **43**, 2211 (2013). https://doi.org/10.1007/s10803-013-1764-4
14. Curry, A.E., Yerys, B.E., Huang, P., Metzger, K.B.: Longitudinal study of driver licensing rates among adolescents and young adults with autism spectrum disorder. Autism: Int. J. Res. Pract. **22**, 479–488 (2018). https://doi.org/10.1177/1362361317699586

15. Curry, A.E., Metzger, K.B., Carey, M.E., Sartin, E.B., Huang, P., Yerys, B.E.: Comparison of motor vehicle crashes, traffic violations, and license suspensions between autistic and non-autistic adolescent and young adult drivers. J. Am. Acad. Child Adolesc. Psychiatry **60**, 913–923 (2021). https://doi.org/10.1016/j.jaac.2021.01.001

16. Vindin, P., Cordier, R., Wilson, N.J., Lee, H.: A driver training program intervention for student drivers with autism spectrum disorder: a multi-site randomised controlled trial. J. Autism Dev. Disord. **51**, 3707–3721 (2021). https://doi.org/10.1007/s10803-020-04825-5

17. Cox, D.J., et al.: Can youth with autism spectrum disorder use virtual reality driving simulation training to evaluate and improve driving performance? An exploratory study. J. Autism Dev. Disord. **47**, 2544–2555 (2017). https://doi.org/10.1007/s10803-017-3164-7

18. Ross, V., et al: Measuring the attitudes of novice drivers with autism spectrum disorder as an indication of apprehensive driving: going beyond basic abilities. Autism: Int. J. Res. Pract. **22**, 62–69 (2018). https://doi.org/10.1177/1362361317735959

19. Bednarz, H.M., Kana, R.K., Svancara, A.M., Sherrod, G.M., Stavrinos, D.: Neuropsychological predictors of driving hazard detection in autism spectrum disorder and ADHD. Child Neuropsychol. **27**, 857–887 (2021). https://doi.org/10.1080/09297049.2021.1908531

20. Chee, D.Y.T., Lee, H.C.Y., Patomella, A.-H., Falkmer, T.: Investigating the driving performance of drivers with and without autism spectrum disorders under complex driving conditions. Disabil. Rehabil. **41**, 1–8 (2019). https://doi.org/10.1080/09638288.2017.1370498

21. Chee, D.Y.T., Lee, H.Y., Patomella, A.-H., Falkmer, T.: The visual search patterns of drivers with autism spectrum disorders in complex driving scenarios. J. Transport Health **14** (2019). https://doi.org/10.1016/j.jth.2019.100597

22. Cox, D.J., et al.: A pilot study comparing newly licensed drivers with and without autism and experienced drivers in simulated and on-road driving. J. Autism Dev. Disord. **50**, 1258–1268 (2020). https://doi.org/10.1007/s10803-019-04341-1

23. Dodwell, A., Trick, L.M.: The effects of secondary tasks that involve listening and speaking on young adult drivers with traits associated with autism spectrum disorders: a pilot study with driving simulation. Transp. Res. Part F-Traffic Psychol. Behav. **69**, 120–134 (2020). https://doi.org/10.1016/j.trf.2019.12.011

24. Ross, V., et al.: The relation between driving errors and executive functioning in intellectually able young novice drivers with autism. Transp. Res. Part F, Traffic Psychol. Behav. **63F**, 38 (2019). https://doi.org/10.1016/j.trf.2019.03.003

25. Classen, S., Monahan, M., Wang, Y.: Driving characteristics of teens with attention deficit hyperactivity and autism spectrum disorder. Am. J. Occup. Ther. **67**, 644–673 (2013)

26. Behavior Rating Inventory of Executive Function I BRIEF. https://www.parinc.com/Products/Pkey/23. Accessed 18 May 2023

27. Delis-Kaplan Executive Function System. https://www.pearsonassessments.com/store/usassessments/en/Store/Professional-Assessments/Cognition-%26-Neuro/Delis-Kaplan-Executive-Function-System/p/100000618.html. Accessed 18 May 2023

28. UFOV Assessment. https://www.brainhq.com/partners/brainhq-for-clinicians/ufov/. Accessed 18 May 2023

29. Baker-Erlezén, M.J., Smith, L., Tran, A., Scarvie, K.: A cognitive behavioral intervention for driving for autistic teens and adults: a pilot study. Autism in Adulthood. **3**, 168–178 (2021). https://doi.org/10.1089/aut.2020.0009

30. Patrick, K.E., et al.: Driving comparisons between young adults with autism spectrum disorder and typical development. J. Dev. Behav. Pediatr. **39**, 451–460 (2018). https://doi.org/10.1097/DBP.0000000000000581

31. Patrick, K.E., et al.: Executive function "drives" differences in simulated driving performance between young adults with and without autism spectrum disorder. Child Neuropsychol. **26**, 649–665 (2020). https://doi.org/10.1080/09297049.2020.1713311

32. Wade, J., et al.: A pilot study assessing performance and visual attention of teenagers with ASD in a novel adaptive driving simulator. J. Autism Dev. Disord. **47**, 3405–3417 (2017). https://doi.org/10.1007/s10803-017-3261-7
33. Silvi, C., Scott-Parker, B.: Understanding the driving and licensing experiences of youth with autism. Transp. Res. Part F: Psychol. Behav. **58**, 769–781 (2018)
34. Monahan, M., OTD OTR/L CDRS, Brooks, J., Seeanner, J., Jenkins, C., Monahan, J.: Driver training application for individuals with autism. Assist. Technol. Outcomes Benefits **14**, 77–93 (2020)
35. Kersten, M., Coxon, K., Lee, H., Wilson, N.J.: In Their Own Time: parents gently push their autistic youth towards independent community mobility and participation. J. Autism Dev. Disord. **50**, 2806–2818 (2020). https://doi.org/10.1007/s10803-020-04384-9
36. Myers, R.K., Bonsu, J.M., Carey, M.E., Yerys, B.E., Mollen, C.J., Curry, A.E.: Teaching autistic adolescents and young adults to drive: perspectives of specialized driving instructors. Autism Adulthood: Challenges Manage. **1**, 202–209 (2019). https://doi.org/10.1089/aut.2018. 0054
37. Myers, R.K., Carey, M.E., Bonsu, J.M., Yerys, B.E., Mollen, C.J., Curry, A.E.: Behind the Wheel: specialized driving instructors' experiences and strategies for teaching autistic adolescents to drive. Am. J. Occup. Ther. **75**, 1–11 (2021). https://doi.org/10.5014/ajot.2021. 043406
38. Ross, V., et al.: Process of learning to drive by young persons with autism: experiences of the young persons themselves, parents, and driving instructors. Trans. Transp. Sci. **9**, 42–56 (2018)
39. Vindin, P., Wilson, N.J., Lee, H., Cordier, R.: The experience of learning to drive for people with autism spectrum disorder. Focus Autism Other Dev. Disabil. **36**, 225–236 (2021). https:// doi.org/10.1177/10883576211023312
40. Chee, D.Y., Lee, H.C., Patomella, A.-H., Falkmer, T.: Driving behaviour profile of drivers with autism spectrum disorder (ASD). J. Autism Dev. Disord. **47**, 2658–2670 (2017). https:// doi.org/10.1007/s10803-017-3178-1
41. Wade, J., et al.: Design of a virtual reality driving environment to assess performance of teenagers with ASD (2014). http://research.vuse.vanderbilt.edu/rasl/wp-content/uploads/ 2014/01/pdf/driving_HCI_2014.pdf
42. Wade, J., et al.: A virtual reality driving environment for training safe gaze patterns: application in individuals with ASD. In: Antona, M., Stephanidis, C. (eds.) Universal Access in Human-Computer Interaction. Access to Learning, Health and Well-Being: 9th International Conference, UAHCI 2015, Held as Part of HCI International 2015, Los Angeles, CA, USA, August 2-7, 2015, Proceedings, Part III, pp. 689–697. Springer International Publishing, Cham (2015). https://doi.org/10.1007/978-3-319-20684-4_66
43. Sheppard, E., van Loon, E., Underwood, G., Ropar, D.: Attentional differences in a driving hazard perception task in adults with autism spectrum disorders. J. Autism Dev. Disorders **47**, 405–414 (2017). https://doi.org/10.1007/s10803-016-2965-4
44. Zhang, L., et al.: Multimodal fusion for cognitive load measurement in an adaptive virtual reality driving task for autism intervention (2015). http://research.vuse.vanderbilt.edu/rasl/ wp-content/uploads/2015/01/Fusion_HCI_2015.pdf
45. Classen, S., Monahan, M.: Evidence-based review on interventions and determinants of driving performance in teens with attention deficit hyperactivity disorder or autism spectrum disorder. Null. **14**, 188–193 (2013). https://doi.org/10.1080/15389588.2012.700747
46. Monahan, M., Classen, S., Helsel, P.V.: Pre-driving evaluation of a teen with attention deficit hyperactivity disorder and autism spectrum disorder. Can. J. Occup. Ther. **80**, 35–41 (2013)
47. Monahan, M., Classen, S., Helsel, P.: Pre-driving skills of a teen with attention deficit hyperactivity and autism spectrum disorder. Dev. Disabil. Spec. Interest Sect. Q. **35**, 1–4 (2012)

48. Bednarz, H.M., Stavrinos, D., Svancara, A.M., Sherrod, G.M., Deshpande, H.D., Kana, R.K.: Behind the wheels with autism and ADHD: brain networks involved in driving hazard detection. Transp. Res. Part F-Traffic Psychol. Behav. **77**, 274–292 (2021). https://doi.org/10.1016/j.trf.2021.01.007

49. Bian, D., Wade, J., Warren, Z., Sarkar, N.: Online engagement detection and task adaptation in a virtual reality based driving simulator for autism intervention. In: Antona, M., Stephanidis, C. (eds.) Universal Access in Human-Computer Interaction. Users and Context Diversity: 10th International Conference, UAHCI 2016, Held as Part of HCI International 2016, Toronto, ON, Canada, July 17-22, 2016, Proceedings, Part III, pp. 538–547. Springer International Publishing, Cham (2016). https://doi.org/10.1007/978-3-319-40238-3_51

50. Fan, J., Wade, J.W., Key, A.P., Warren, Z.E., Sarkar, N.: EEG-based affect and workload recognition in a virtual driving environment for ASD intervention. IEEE Trans. Biomed. Eng. **65**, 43–51 (2018). https://doi.org/10.1109/TBME.2017.2693157

51. Zhang, L., Wade, J.W., Bian, D., Swanson, A., Warren, Z., Sarkar, N.: Data fusion for difficulty adjustment in an adaptive virtual reality game system for autism intervention. In: Stephanidis, C. (ed.) HCI International 2014 - Posters' Extended Abstracts, pp. 648–652. Springer, Cham (2014). https://doi.org/10.1007/978-3-319-07854-0

52. Brooks, J., et al.: Training the motor aspects of pre-driving skills of young adults with and without autism spectrum disorder. J. Autism Dev. Disord.Disord. **46**, 2408–2426 (2016). https://doi.org/10.1007/s10803-016-2775-8

# DramaPlaya: A Multi-sensory Interactive Toolkit for the Home-Based Drama Therapy of Children with Developmental Delays

Lingchuan Zhou[1]([✉]) [iD], Han Zhang[2,3] [iD], and Yunqi Wang[4]

[1] Indiana University Bloomington, Bloomington, IN 47408, USA
lz47@iu.edu
[2] University of Nottingham Ningbo, China, 199 Taikang East Road, Ningbo 315100, China
hvxhz2@nottingham.edu.cn
[3] Ningbo Research Institute, Zhejiang University, 1 Qianhu South Road, Ningbo 315100, China
[4] HD Ningbo School, Ningbo 315000, China
1801226@stu.hdschools.org

**Abstract.** Psychosocial problems are the most common and persistent mental health issues among children with developmental delays (CDD). Notably, drama therapy has shown immense potential in alleviating psychological and behavioral symptoms in CDD, ultimately fostering positive behavioral transformations. This study proposes a novel, AI-enhanced drama therapy framework, aptly named "DramaPlaya", which can be implemented within the comforts of one's home. By addressing the prevalent obstacles surrounding accessibility and engagement in traditional drama therapeutic approaches, this research aims to redefine the landscape of CDD therapy.

"DramaPlaya" integrates a multi-sensory interactive toolkit with an online visualization system, aimed at enhancing engagement during therapy sessions and overcoming the lack of highly specialized therapists that impedes consistent therapeutic progress. Through qualitative methods involving in-depth interviews with therapists and caregivers, the study reveals critical insights into the engagement dynamics of CDD within home-based drama therapy sessions. The proposed toolkit employs a human-centered design, validated in specialized educational and theatrical environments, to deliver a personalized and engaging therapeutic experience. The findings of this study underscore the potential of "DramaPlaya" to establish a more dynamic and tailored avenue of interaction for children with developmental delays, thus potentially revolutionizing the accessibility and quality of home-based therapy for this demographic.

**Keywords:** Drama therapy · Tele-therapy · Children with Developmental Delays · Mental Health

## 1 Introduction

A large majority of children with developmental delays (CDD) exhibit behavioral and psychological symptoms such as aggression, destruction, or emotional distress, often stemming from deficits in social-emotional development [1, 2]. These delays or atypical

M. Antona and C. Stephanidis (Eds.): HCII 2024, LNCS 14697, pp. 250–263, 2024.
https://doi.org/10.1007/978-3-031-60881-0_16

patterns can appear across various developmental domains such as autism spectrum disorder (ASD), attention deficit hyperactivity disorder (ADHD), Down syndrome (DS), etc. Disturbances in social-emotional development, for example, attachment issues and difficulties in emotion regulation, pose challenges for CDD in forming relationships, appropriately responding to others, and adjusting themselves to diverse social scenarios [3, 4]. Persistent deficits in social-emotional health cause regression in their abilities of facial expression, visual communication, and verbal integration [5, 6]. Unfortunately, the large majority of CDD face a life-long disorder that poses significant challenges to themselves, their families, and the social welfare organizations [7, 8].

A variety of therapeutic strategies, including cognitive behavior therapy, music therapy, and parent-child interaction therapy, have been crafted to bolster the social-emotional development of CDD. In particular, activating intervention, for example, drama therapy, stands out as a pivotal approach, crucial for not only modeling behaviors and revealing fears but also for cultivating social synchronization and coping capabilities in young individuals facing psychosocial challenges [7, 8]. Under the guidance of a drama therapist, the child actively participates in structured activities like storytelling, role-playing, puppetry, and improvisational games, fostering a creative and therapeutic environment [9]. Additionally, it encourages verbal and non-verbal expression, making it an appealing alternative for children who find traditional cognitive behavior therapy challenging or boring. Access to long-term and consistent therapy sessions remains challenging for CDD and their caregivers, with the scarcity of trained therapists and transportation issues [10]. As the COVID-19 pandemic exacerbated resource barriers, some art therapists and psychotherapists sought the opportunity to shift their practice trajectory to the online mode. Hence, tele-therapy delivery has been applied in mental health care as an alternative solution to enhance the accessibility and intervention diversity [11]. However, few studies explored tele-therapy platforms to facilitate drama practices, especially to solve psychosocial issues for individuals with special needs. One recent study investigated the feasibility of conducting remote drama practices among adult participants with serious mental illness. This pilot attempt validated the positive effects and convenience of the virtual format of drama therapy sessions, which were preferred by the majority of participants [10]. Consequently, it is essential to pinpoint the barriers and requirements of designing a tele-therapy platform specific for children with special needs and examine how existing assistive technologies can augment such tele-therapy practices.

To bridge this gap, the study conducted observations and semi-structured interviews with a cohort of 5 therapists and 12 caregivers. Its primary objective was to explore the underlying factors that impede the accessibility and level of engagement in drama therapy for individuals diagnosed with CDD. The accessibility of drama therapy is restricted owing to (1) a scarcity of adequately trained professionals in the field [12]; (2) poor engagement level during traditional therapy sessions [13]; (3) varying levels of acceptance exhibited by different children [14] and (4) the lack of quantitative evaluation of developmental progress. Concurrently, our research adopted a co-design methodology, collaborating with caregivers and therapists, to identify opportunities facilitated by technological mediation that can effectively support the tele-therapy sessions within their customary practices.

**Fig. 1.** DramaPlaya design prototype

This paper presents a case study that explores the efficacy of a personalised drama practice toolkit designed for home use. This comprehensive toolkit comprises an interactive multi-sensory stimulation device and an online drama therapy platform (refer to Fig. 1). Together, these innovative tools offer children with CDD a range of interactive stimuli, personalized content, and skill reinforcement [15]. The study's findings affirm that this tailored approach addresses the specific needs of individuals with CDD in the following areas:

1. Fulfilling the requirements of dynamic, individualized, and deeply engaging interactions for individuals with CDD.
2. Facilitating the development of social-emotional behaviors.
3. Supporting evidence-based interventions for caregivers while fostering effective communication between parents and therapists.

## 2 Related Works

### 2.1 Drama Therapy for CDD

Drama therapy is a dynamic form of psychotherapy that combines drama and theater techniques with various psychological theories, creating a safe, imaginative space for individuals to explore and address emotional and psychological issues through role-play, storytelling, and other interactive activities. This particular therapy, leveraging the dynamics of drama and theater, has been demonstrated as an effective intervention for CDD, especially for verbal and non-verbal expression development, social cognition, and sensory integration [7]. Wu et al. have documented that drama therapy plays a significant role in augmenting and sustaining levels of communication and cooperation both during and subsequent to intervention periods [16]. There is substantial evidence to suggest that drama therapy is particularly efficacious for children diagnosed with autism, manifesting in enhanced behavioral, expressive, and social competencies, alongside improved emotional well-being [3, 17]. Furthermore, drama-based methodologies have been recognized for their capacity to engage and stimulate interest in CDD, including those with Down Syndrome (DS) [18, 19], intellectual disabilities (ID) [20], and attention deficit hyperactivity disorder (ADHD) [21].

## 2.2  Multi-sensory Learning Environment in Special Education

Multi-sensory environments (MSEs) are educational mediums capable of catering to various learning styles by optimizing different senses, including visual, auditory, haptic, and kinesthetic [22]. It usually contains equipment that can create sound, light, and touch experiences in a specific room [23]. A remarkable example of interactive multi-sensory environments is MEDIATE, featuring a large display with dynamic digital elements, a multi-material tube offering various tactile effects, and a sound floor generating different sounds based on the child's position [24]. The system creates an adaptive stimulus depending on the behavioral patterns of autistic children, which aims to offer them a sense of agency and enhance their well-being. Game-based activities of MSEs for CDD combine language and physical movement tasks to improve engagement. For instance, The Magic Room, designed by Garzotto et al., provides mixed groups of children with interactive multi-sensory games that encourage positive behavior [13]. AEDLE exploits Augmented Reality (AR) to initiate digital drama therapy for pragmatic language skills training and the generalization process from the virtual environment to the real world [12].

In addition, the use of MSEs not only benefits children in a more playable way but also acts as a simple but powerful tool to include therapists or teachers in the content creation and personalization [13]. Children with different developmental delays exhibit diverse sensitivity to stimulation. According to Wuang and Su [25], children with down syndrome are reported to be under-responsive to sensory stimuli and lack efficient registration, while autistic children are more likely to be hypersensitive to environmental stimuli. By empowering therapists as creators and controllers, they can tailor the resources for CDD to align with the educational objectives.

## 2.3  Technical-Mediated Assessment in Interactive Therapy

Children with physical and mental disabilities have already been studied extensively regarding their physical functions in the context of HCI and their behavioral changes in the context of daily life, constituting a significant body of literature under the heading of assistive technology [26]. Given the nature of assistive technology, existing research, and applications range from low-tech/low-cost readily available devices to high-tech/specialized computer-aided tools [27]. Previous research demonstrated that assistive technology adopted in interactive play therapy not only boosted caregivers' confidence in child behavior management but also helped to reduce impulsive, aggressive, and defiant behavioral patterns among children [28].

In-home settings, a variety of devices and sensors have been deployed for automatic behavior assessment, ranging from accelerometers to sensing systems that identify stereotypical motor movements, enhancing the accuracy of behavior analysis while alleviating caregiver burden [29, 30]. However, the challenge remains to balance the technological stimuli with the natural interaction flow to avoid unwanted distractions [31]. Thus, the design of intuitive technology-mediated interventions that complement rather than intrude upon parent-child activities remains paramount [32].

## 3 Design Study Process

### 3.1 Observation and Interview

The primary challenge of this research lies in understanding the drama therapy process and our design inquiry. The first step involved first-hand observation of how drama therapy activities unfold, specifically focusing on the behavior of children with different developmental delays within the context of drama sessions. From February to April 2023, we observed 4 drama plays involving a total of 18 children with ASD or DS at Shanghai Children's Art Theater (SHCAT) [33] and therapy sessions for DS children at Ningbo LemonTree Special Education Institution (LemonTree).

At the SHCAT venue, two traditional drama productions were scheduled, "Storm" for those with ASD and "Down to Earth" for children with DS and ID, involving professional teams skilled in drama, music, and special education. These productions involved highly skilled professional teams proficient in drama, music, and special education. Each session, tailored for a small group of children aged 3 to 8, aimed to provide a personalized and immersive experience without any interference from caregivers. While caregivers were present as observers, they were strictly prohibited from intervening or guiding the children during the session.

These sessions featured interactive and multi-sensory elements, such as ambient lighting and textured decorations, tailored to the sensory sensitivities of each group. For instance, the environment for ASD-focused dramas was crafted to be more subtle, while the setting for DS and ID children included more vibrant stimuli. The performances incorporated personalized songs and activities, encouraging participation and socio-communicative behaviors.

Behavioral observations and ratings revealed varied engagement, with ASD children often participating quietly and DS/ID attendees showing more active involvement. The teams employed manual behavior ratings to encourage participation, though maintaining attention was occasionally challenging. Strategies to manage disruptive behaviors and foster engagement included positive reinforcement, adjusting sensory elements, and personalized interaction, demonstrating the adaptability and sensitivity of the therapeutic approach.

Following each session, we engaged in insightful discussions with caregivers, (See Fig. 2), to gather their perspectives on drama therapy and their observations of their children's behavior during the immersive drama plays. Caregivers expressed their appreciation for the positive impact of the drama plays on their children and expressed a desire to be more actively involved in such activities. For instance, C5 shared his enthusiasm, stating, *"The form of drama is interesting and attractive to my boy but hold monthly. I hope we can have a chance to attend more. If the content is not fixed but aligns to daily life to teach social skills, that would be great."* During the interactive segments, caregivers expressed concerns about the suitability of the activities for their children. As C3 explained, *"he needs much time to get familiar with the new environment. Our therapist spent nearly half a year to build rapport with him. It's better to prepare something that caters to his condition."* We also collected a few opinions on technology supporting online therapy. C7 reminded us of the importance of designing user-friendly household products, considering that grandparents or babysitters would be the primary users during daytime sessions.

**Summary of Interviews with Caregivers (C1~C12)**

| | | |
|---|---|---|
| C1 | 7yr ASD | The child is quiet in most of time and tends to not respond or actively engage in group activities. |
| C2 | 5yr ASD | She is quite energetic, often expressing herself without much regard for responses from others. |
| C3 | 5yr ASD | He does not like new environment, so we need times to let him feel comfortable in this environment (drama). However, such experiences are not common to see, only participated twice. |
| C4 | 12yr ASD | This drama content may not be well-suited for his age... too childish for him. |
| C5 | 6yr ASD | Such activity can be held more times, preferably with theatrical content that closely aligns with everyday life. |
| C6 | 9yr ASD | Hardly can we capture his attention... even show something he likes. |
| C7 | 6yr ASD | While I am aware of the existence of assistive learning robots and other products in the market, with elderly family members assisting in childcare, we prefer to take care of him by ourselves at home. |
| C8 | 3yr DS | Learning at home could result in significant savings on commuting and caregiving expenses. |
| C9 | 4yr DS | Both my husband and I work, and despite being exhausted upon returning home each day, we still invest a considerable amount of time attempting to communicate with our child. |
| C10 | 5yr DS | Teachers said the child's engagement was good, but I have no clear idea... this is a long-term effort. |
| C11 | 3yr DS | He needs time to go over what he learnt, and we parents should pay more attention to him. |
| C12 | 7yr DS | Actually he exhibits a strong affinity for novel experiences, as evidenced by his evident enjoyment of this recent drama activity. |

**Fig. 2.** Summary of interviews with caregivers (C1 to C12).

Moreover, we conducted interviews with five professionals in related fields, referring to T1 to T5 (See Fig. 3). The interview questions focused on the challenges encountered when children participated in drama sessions, their experiences with remote therapy, and their perspectives on technology-mediated home-based drama therapy. From a professional standpoint, it is crucial to ensure that the tools provided are adaptable enough to nurture the creativity of therapists. T3 emphasized the need to individualize every aspect for children, including the script, toys and props, session duration, and even the framework. Regarding the multisensory environment, T1 demonstrated how he adapted to the pandemic by conducting sessions through Zoom. *"We need to consider and personalize everything for children, such as the script, the toys and props, the time, and even the frame of the session."* When it came to the multi-sensory environment, T1 showed us how he worked during the pandemic through Zoom. *"We instructed parents and invited them to participate in the game with children. We may ask them to find all the reachable things at home, like a steel bowl, plastic paper, an apple, etc., using them as stimuli channels. Because children need more attractiveness to be engaged."* More than having drama therapy at home, T2 also mentioned the essence of taking daily practice. *"Rehabilitation is important... it helps generalize the skills in daily life."*

Summary of Interviews with Professionals (T1~T5)

| | | |
|---|---|---|
| Mr. Davies (T1) | Bamboozle Theatre, Co-Founder & Artistic Director | 1. Online, children require more engaging environments and stimuli.<br>2. Different children have varying interests, demanding long-term observation and practical experiences for effective understanding. |
| Mr. Travis Young (T2) | Art therapist | 1. Achieving complete rehabilitation to a certain extent in autism is challenging, necessitating persistent, long-term commitment to intervention and education, utilizing scientifically sound educational methods.<br>2. Digital tool can be seen as supportive for rehabilitation. It is useful during remote therapies.<br>3. Child patients exhibit sensitivity to sound and struggle with associating language with real-world objects. |
| Dr. Ma (T3) | Professional with ASD | 1. Response of every child to stimuli varies significantly. Therefore, whether we use sound, light, we use red color or green color requires therapists to carefully calibrate and comprehend these individualized reactions. But current digital tool cannot achieve this.<br>2. In most instances, digital products are used at home or in classroom, necessitating parental supervision. |
| Dr. Zhang (T4) | Professional with Down Syndrome | 1. We typically employ instructional methods designed for typically developing children when educating children with Down Syndrome. However, their learning pace tends to be slower, so we need to repeat again and again, especially confronting with abstract concepts. Notably, when instruction is situated within familiar and meaningful contexts, they are more likely to understand. |
| Dr. Lee (T5) | Professional with Down Syndrome | 1. It is very challenging to attract their attention during the class, neither to say online classes. We usually use attractive tools, languages and sound to help their engagement... they like to see some new things<br>2. It would be great if software solutions can help address emotional-behavioral challenges in daily life, enhance communication, and contribute to overall functional improvement. |

**Fig. 3.** Summary of interviews with professionals (T1 to T5).

## 3.2 Needs for and Barriers to Develop Technical-Mediated Drama Therapy Toolkit

Based on the evidence from the observation, the interview results with professionals and caregivers, and the literature review, we identified the main barriers to the accessibility of drama therapy for CDD, and the user needs of both stakeholders, CDD and therapists.

From the observation, we noticed that children with different developmental delays require different levels of environmental stimuli. Moreover, the preference, acceptance level and motion ability varied from child to child, which needed the therapist to build rapport with them. Compared with traditional therapy sessions, CDD had higher engagement levels and were more likely to acquire social-emotional skills.

The Interviews with caregivers highlighted the importance of access to trained therapists. The limited number of professionals would be the main impediment for CDD to get long-term and steady participation. Meanwhile, the professionals also agreed that technology can help them know the child better in the online condition.

Then, our research went to the conclusion of the four main factors that would impede the accessibility of drama therapy:

1. Insufficient availability of proficient practitioners;
2. Poor engagement level during conventional therapy sessions;

3. Variations in the individual levels of acceptance among children;
4. Absence of quantitative assessment methodologies for measuring developmental progress.

Based on our findings, we conducted a subsequent survey which helped us to understand the design features and desirable functionality of the home-based drama therapy toolkit (see Fig. 4).

Proposed design features rated on a 5-point scale from usefulness consideration (caregiver: n = 12, therapist: n = 5)

| Potential feature of the solution (from therapist perspective) | M | SD |
|---|---|---|
| 1  Support from real-time physiological data | 4.20 | 0.56 |
| 2  Tool for drama content creation and personalization | 3.60 | 0.64 |
| 3  Conduct drama therapy online | 3.40 | 1.04 |
| 4  Using digital tool for incentives to engage children in the therapy session | 3.00 | 0.40 |
| Potential feature of the solution (from caregiver perspective) | M | SD |
| 1  Daily drama practice for learning review and skill consolidation | 4.25 | 0.52 |
| 2  Feedback from therapist with physiological data support | 4.17 | 0.46 |
| 3  Taking drama therapy at home and meeting the therapist online | 3.91 | 0.91 |
| 4  Monitor for the therapy session | 3.50 | 0.91 |

**Fig. 4.** Proposed design features rated on a 5-point scale from usefulness consideration (caregiver: n = 12; professionals: n = 5).

Consequently, we conceptualized DramaPlaya, an innovative home-based drama practice toolkit that encompasses an interactive and multi-sensory stimulation device, complemented by an online therapy management system. These two components work together to provide children with developmental delays with interactive content, captivating experiences, and skill reinforcement. Moreover, therapists are empowered to craft and personalize content, tailoring stimuli to cater to specific needs. Not only does this toolkit aim to enhance the accessibility of drama therapy for children with CDD, but it also equips therapists with quantitative assessment capabilities. By seamlessly integrating visual and auditory data, the system can assess fluctuations in the child's emotions and mental state, offering real-time insights to the therapist.

## 4  DramaPlaya System

The development of the DramaPlaya system was grounded in the pedagogical framework of a multi-sensory learning environment [23]. This system is bifurcated into two primary functional modules, each tailored to distinct perspectives within the therapeutic session.

For the child, the system offers an interactive module, where the user engages with a digitally rendered panorama on both wall and floor projections. This interface maintains a visual connection with the therapist through a diminutive, unobtrusive window on the screen, preserving the child's immersion while ensuring therapeutic oversight.

From the therapist's standpoint, the system is equipped with a preparatory and control module. This allows for the pre-session arrangement of therapeutic content, real-time management during sessions, and the post-session development of practice schedules accessible via an online platform. The system's design is cognizant of the child's developmental stage, enabling skill reinforcement and consolidation to occur within the domicile, under the aegis of parental guidance.

### 4.1 Interaction Design

The main product consists of a two-way projector, a depth camera, a speaker, basic control buttons ("ON/OFF", Volume, Start) and contains one voice changer widget (with a microphone), two-foot widgets (with a 3D gyroscope, and a 3D accelerometer). The projector can simultaneously throw two 100-inch displays on the wall and the ground so that children can stand "in" the scene to interact with both displays. Accompanying sounds would be delivered via the speaker to create the drama environment. As shown in Fig. 5(c), the depth camera set at the end of a telescope enables video and detects body movements by capturing the skeleton joints of children, which supports the interaction with displays and the data analysis. The widgets could be taken out from the main product and worn on children's collars and shoes (see Fig. 5(f), (g)). The voice widget is used as a voice-changing toy for audio incentives and the foot widgets collect stomping data and provide adjustable vibrations for tactile feedback.

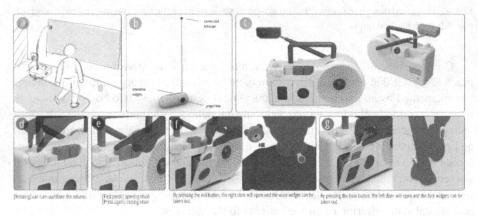

**Fig. 5.** DramaPlaya interaction design details.

### 4.2 Service System

The DramaPlaya system offers an array of functionalities, including content management and data records, specifically designed to cater to the unique needs and responses of children with developmental delays. This innovative platform allows therapists to personalize and adapt solutions to accommodate individual preferences, encompassing a wide range of aspects such as content, stimuli, and rewards. To ensure optimal engagement and monitoring of the child's behavioral states, the system provides real-time detection and contextual information, enabling therapists to closely monitor the dynamics of their participation. This valuable insight allows therapists to gauge the child's level of engagement and assess whether it falls within positive or negative parameters. (see Fig. 6.). In terms of data management, the system employs privacy-preserving features to securely store visual data (see Fig. 6. (d)), utilizing a 2D skeleton representation to capture and analyze body movements. Additionally, audio data collected from the voice widget's microphone undergoes thorough processing and evaluation to assess language proficiency and vocal expression. One notable advantage of the DramaPlaya system lies in its ability to tailor both content and interactions to suit the unique conditions of each child. This flexibility allows for the customization of plot difficulty, providing children with appropriate feedback and enabling therapists to seamlessly modify the timing of language and sensory integration training as needed. (see Fig. 6. (a)) (see Fig. 6. (c)). Furthermore, the system allows for personalized stimuli, granting therapists the freedom to adapt the drama environment settings to align with each child's preferences. This includes customizable features such as color schemes, background animations, sounds, avatar images, and rewards. By tailoring the environment to suit the child's individual needs, the DramaPlaya system ensures an immersive and engaging experience for optimal therapeutic outcomes.

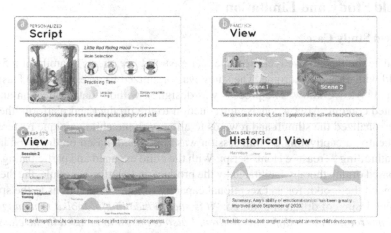

**Fig. 6.** DramaPlaya service system interface.

### 4.3 The Using Scenario

The DramaPlaya toolkit, designed to create a multi-sensory environment, monitors children's emotional responses, and assesses their mental states in real-time (refer to Fig. 1). For instance, in the "Treasure Hunt" script used at LemonTree, the session begins with a caregiver assisting the child with sensor widgets and activating the projector. The therapist initiates warm-up activities, such as "Mirror" from the toolkit or other familiar games, followed by the introduction of the day's script after a 10 to 15-min warm-up period.

*"...Today, the king of the Land of Equality gathers the children on the streets, hoping that they can unite and overcome challenges together. They must find three key items— lemons."* An icon denoting "Lemon" appears on the wall display, serving as a cue

throughout the drama. The child is represented on the wall with an avatar mask and virtual costume.

"...*Hao takes the torch and says, 'Thank you.' A joyful smile appears on his face.*" An NPC presenting the torch to the child emerges in the scenery. If the camera captures the child's movement, his figure on the display will hold a torch. The child pretends to raise the torch to illuminate the cave, and the environment will respond accordingly. The therapist will encourage him to integrate the language and facial expression, guiding the child in practicing how to show gratitude to others.

"...*With determination, Hao walks towards the rocky path.*" As the environment transitions to a rocky path, the floor displays updates accordingly. If the child walks on the rocky road, the foot widgets vibrate subtly to mimic the sensation of stepping on real rocks. The therapist monitors the emotional state of the kid, adjusting promptly if any discomfort to the stimuli is observed.

By the end of the session, the therapist will choose an ending ritual representing back to reality. She can either choose a game from the system or create one by herself.

## 5  Field Study and Limitation

### 5.1  Field Study Case

To evaluate the design, we recruited one therapist and her client, a family of a 5-year-old child with Down Syndrome. The study was organized to investigate the feasibility of DramaPlaya workflow. The process was designed without data collection and AI-augmented content. After a concise introduction to the product and platform, the therapist personalized the stimuli and rewards to align with the child's unique preferences. Subsequently, a captivating 20-min session was conducted, based on the second scene of the enthralling "Treasure Hunt" script. With the child engaged and participating in the home-based drama therapy facilitated by the product and platform module, the therapist commended the toolkit for its exceptional capacity to tailor interactions to the specific needs and desires of different children: "*it is such a meaningful toolkit to manage customized interactions with different children. I also expect it to be used in the classroom for more children participation...*" On the other hand, the therapist expressed her concerns regarding the engagement once children become familiar with the product and the long-term outcomes. "*If it could include more tools or props, digital materials as well, it will be more adaptable for therapists from different backgrounds, ... and it's better to control them in an easier but separate way for each incentive...*" she stated, "*The daily practice function sounds beneficial for children who have higher cognition level.*" Feedback from caregivers primarily revolved around the device cost and effectiveness of daily practice. "*We are worried about the cost of this device. If it is not frequently used nor versatile, it would be a burden for us.*"

### 5.2  Limitation

As described above, this field study was conducted using prototype devices. While acquainting the therapist with the toolkit, she invested considerable time in questioning and repeatedly testing to achieve a proficient grasp the prototype. This learning cost necessitates effort to seamlessly integrate the toolkit products and online platform, enabling therapists to navigate them fluidly during therapy sessions. Moreover, this study has a limitation of the small sample size because it was evaluated with only one therapist and one child with DS. Future design studies ought to seek extensive feedback from a larger cohort of therapists and children with diverse developmental delays, including those with ASD children.

## 6   Conclusion

The present study introduces DramaPlaya, an innovative framework for drama therapy enriched with AI, intended for home use. This concept combines a multi-sensory interactive device with an online service platform, aiming to enhance engagement and bridge the accessibility gap in drama therapy. For children with developmental delays, DramaPlaya offers an immersive and captivating experience, fostering improvement in their social-emotional behavior. Simultaneously, therapists benefit from the system's capabilities for personalized content and assessment, enabling them to cater to the diverse needs of CDD. Through observations and interviews, this research has identified key barriers and opportunities for leveraging technology-mediated approaches to support drama therapy for CDD. The toolkit addresses the need for dynamic, individualized, and engaging interactions while supporting social-emotional behavior development within the frame of drama therapy. In future work, we aim to involve users with varying developmental delays to refine and achieve a more inclusive design. Furthermore, our commitment to enhancing long-term engagement will be continued, as we explore the potential of daily practice.

## References

1. Bellman, M., Byrne, O., Sege, R.: Developmental assessment of children. BMJ **346**, e8687–e8687 (2013). https://doi.org/10.1136/bmj.e8687
2. Algozzine, B.: The emotionally disturbed child: disturbed or disturbing. J. Abnorm. Child Psychol. **5**, 205–211 (1977). https://doi.org/10.1007/BF00913096
3. Department of Human Sciences, Faculty of Psychology, Shahre Kord Branch, Islamic Azad University, Shahrekord, Iran., Rahimi Pordanjani, S.: Effectiveness of Drama Therapy on Social Skills of Autistic Children. Pract. Clin. Psychol. **9**, 9–18 (2021). https://doi.org/10.32598/jpcp.9.1.344.2
4. Bauminger, N.: The facilitation of social-emotional understanding and social interaction in high-functioning children with autism: intervention outcomes. J. Autism Dev. Disord. **32**, 283–298 (2002). https://doi.org/10.1023/A:1016378718278
5. Carter, A.S., Briggs-Gowan, M.J., Davis, N.O.: Assessment of young children's social-emotional development and psychopathology: recent advances and recommendations for practice. J. Child Psychol. Psychiatry **45**, 109–134 (2004). https://doi.org/10.1046/j.0021-9630.2003.00316.x
6. Karal, M.A., Wolfe, P.S.: Social story effectiveness on social interaction for students with autism (2024)
7. Berghs, M., Prick, A.-E.J.C., Vissers, C., van Hooren, S.: Drama therapy for children and adolescents with psychosocial problems: a systemic review on effects, means, therapeutic attitude, and supposed mechanisms of change. Children **9**, 1358 (2022). https://doi.org/10.3390/children9091358

8. Geiger, A., Shpigelman, C.-N., Feniger-Schaal, R.: The socio-emotional world of adolescents with intellectual disability: a drama therapy-based participatory action research. Arts Psychother. **70**, 101679 (2020). https://doi.org/10.1016/j.aip.2020.101679
9. Rashikj Canevska, O., Ramo Akgün, N.: Implementation and Benefits of Drama Therapy for Children with Special Educational Needs. Presented at the October 24 (2022)
10. Cheung, A., Agwu, V., Stojcevski, M., Wood, L., Fan, X.: A pilot remote drama therapy program using the co-active therapeutic theater model in people with serious mental illness. Community Ment. Health J. (2022). https://doi.org/10.1007/s10597-022-00977-z
11. Robledo Yamamoto, F., Voida, A., Voida, S.: From therapy to teletherapy: relocating mental health services online. Proc. ACM Hum.-Comput. Interact. **5**, 1–30 (2021). https://doi.org/10.1145/3479508
12. Park, J., Bae, G., Park, J., Park, S.K., Kim, Y.S., Lee, S.: AEDLE: designing drama therapy interface for improving pragmatic language skills of children with autism spectrum disorder using AR. In: Extended Abstracts of the 2023 CHI Conference on Human Factors in Computing Systems, pp. 1–7. ACM, Hamburg Germany (2023). https://doi.org/10.1145/3544549.3585809
13. Garzotto, F., Beccaluva, E., Gianotti, M., Riccardi, F.: Interactive Multisensory environments for primary school children. In: Proceedings of the 2020 CHI Conference on Human Factors in Computing Systems, pp. 1–12. ACM, Honolulu HI USA (2020). https://doi.org/10.1145/3313831.3376343
14. Zhang, H., Sun, X., Yao, C., Zhang, Y., Wang, Q., Lei, N.: design with caregivers: enhancing social interaction for children with down syndrome. In: Antona, M. and Stephanidis, C. (eds.) Universal Access in Human-Computer Interaction. User and Context Diversity. pp. 442–452. Springer International Publishing, Cham (2022). https://doi.org/10.1007/978-3-031-05039-8_32
15. Lobo, J., Matsuda, S., Futamata, I., Sakuta, R., Suzuki, K.: CHIMELIGHT: augmenting instruments in interactive music therapy for children with neurodevelopmental disorders. In: The 21st International ACM SIGACCESS Conference on Computers and Accessibility, pp. 124–135. ACM, Pittsburgh PA USA (2019). https://doi.org/10.1145/3308561.3353784
16. Wu, J., Chen, K., Ma, Y., Vomočilová, J.: Early intervention for children with intellectual and developmental disability using drama therapy techniques. Child Youth Serv. Rev. **109**, 104689 (2020). https://doi.org/10.1016/j.childyouth.2019.104689
17. Bololia, L., Williams, J., Macmahon, K., Goodall, K.: Dramatherapy for children and adolescents with autism spectrum disorder: a systematic integrative review. Arts Psychother. **80**, 101918 (2022). https://doi.org/10.1016/j.aip.2022.101918
18. Huria Kristen Batak Protestant Nommensen University, Batubara, J., Maniam, S., Universiti Pendidikan Sultan Idris: Enhancing Creativity through Musical Drama for Children with Special Needs (Down Syndrome) in Education of Disabled Children. Music Scholarsh. Probl. Muzykalnoj Nauki., 166–177 (2019). https://doi.org/10.17674/1997-0854.2019.2.166-177
19. Mottan, K.: Using drama to enhance communication and social skills among children with down syndrome
20. Barton-Hulsey, A., Sevcik, R.A., Romski, M.: Narrative language and reading comprehension in students with mild intellectual disabilities. Am. J. Intellect. Dev. Disabil. **122**, 392–408 (2017). https://doi.org/10.1352/1944-7558-122.5.392
21. Kejani, M., Raeisi, Z.: The effect of drama therapy on working memory and its components in primary school children with ADHD. Curr. Psychol. **41**, 417–426 (2022). https://doi.org/10.1007/s12144-019-00564-8
22. Komalasari, M.D., Pamungkas, B., Wihaskoro, A.M., Jana, P., Bahrum, A., Khairunnisa, N.Z.: Interactive multimedia based on multisensory as a model of inclusive education for student with learning difficulties. J. Phys. Conf. Ser. **1254**, 012057 (2019). https://doi.org/10.1088/1742-6596/1254/1/012057

23. Unwin, K.L., Powell, G., Jones, C.R.: The use of multi-sensory environments with autistic children: exploring the effect of having control of sensory changes. Autism **26**, 1379–1394 (2022). https://doi.org/10.1177/13623613211050176

24. Parés, N., et al.: Promotion of creative activity in children with severe autism through visuals in an interactive multisensory environment. In: Proceedings of the 2005 Conference on Interaction Design and Children, pp. 110–116. Association for Computing Machinery, New York, NY, USA (2005). https://doi.org/10.1145/1109540.1109555

25. Wuang, Y.-P., Su, C.-Y.: Correlations of sensory processing and visual organization ability with participation in school-aged children with down syndrome. Res. Dev. Disabil. **32**, 2398–2407 (2011). https://doi.org/10.1016/j.ridd.2011.07.020

26. Al-Moghyrah, D.H.: assistive technology use for students with down syndrome at mainstream schools in Riyadh, Saudi Arabia: Teachers' Perspectives. J. Educ. Pract. (2017)

27. Shahid, N.M.I., Law, E.L.-C., Verdezoto, N.: Technology-enhanced support for children with down syndrome: a systematic literature review. Int. J. Child-Comput. Interact. **31**, 100340 (2022). https://doi.org/10.1016/j.ijcci.2021.100340

28. Hatamzadeh, A., Pouretemad, H., Hassanabadi, H.: The effectiveness of parent – child interaction therapy for children with high functioning autism. Procedia - Soc. Behav. Sci. **5**, 994–997 (2010). https://doi.org/10.1016/j.sbspro.2010.07.224

29. Chikhaoui, M.T., Rabenorosoa, K., Andreff, N.: Kinematics and performance analysis of a novel concentric tube robotic structure with embedded soft micro-actuation. Mech. Mach. Theory **104**, 234–254 (2016). https://doi.org/10.1016/j.mechmachtheory.2016.06.005

30. Albinali, F., Goodwin, M.S., Intille, S.S.: Recognizing stereotypical motor movements in the laboratory and classroom: a case study with children on the autism spectrum. In: Proceedings of the 11th international conference on Ubiquitous computing, pp. 71–80. ACM, Orlando Florida USA (2009). https://doi.org/10.1145/1620545.1620555

31. Chen, Y.-Y., Li, Z., Rosner, D., Hiniker, A.: Understanding parents' perspectives on mealtime technology. Proc. ACM Interact. Mob. Wearable Ubiquitous Technol. **3**, 1–19 (2019). https://doi.org/10.1145/3314392

32. Jo, E., Bang, H., Ryu, M., Sung, E.J., Leem, S., Hong, H.: MAMAS: supporting parent-child mealtime interactions using automated tracking and speech recognition. Proc. ACM Hum. -Comput. Interact. **4**, 1–32 (2020). https://doi.org/10.1145/3392876

33. https://www.shcat.com.cn/en/

# Universal Access to Virtual and Augmented Reality

# Universally Designed Mobile Augmented Reality as a Digital Aid for Banknote Recognition

Attila Bekkvik Szentirmai[1]([✉]), Yavuz Inal[1], Anne Britt Torkildsby[1],
and Ole Andreas Alsos[2]

[1] Department of Design, Norwegian University of Science and Technology, Gjøvik, Norway
attila.b.szentirmai@ntnu.no

[2] Department of Design, Norwegian University of Science and Technology, Trondheim, Norway

**Abstract.** Fast and reliable banknote recognition for visually impaired individuals is often an unresolvable obstacle and requires personal assistance. Current assistive technologies, despite addressing blind users and users with low vision directly, commonly lack both portability and user-friendliness, thereby excluding a broader user demographic that could benefit from such solutions. This study introduces a digital aid strategy aimed at simplifying the identification of national and international banknotes across a diverse user spectrum, thus including individuals with varying visual, cognitive, and motor capabilities. Achieved through a mobile augmented reality application, this approach also advocates for incorporating Universal Design principles in crafting more encompassing mobile augmented reality applications. Additionally, the paper emphasizes the technology's potential to advance accessibility and mobile app development. The resulting prototype adheres to Universal Design standards, ensuring accessibility and usability for a wide array of users, regardless of their skills and abilities.

**Keywords:** Universal Design · Mobile Augmented Reality · Banknote Recognition · Assistive Technology · Accessibility · Usability

## 1 Introduction

Banknotes are designed for fast and efficient identification; however, individuals with diverse abilities, such as sensory or cognitive impairments, are often more vulnerable and dependent on assistance in banknote recognition scenarios. For instance, a blind person, due to sensory impairment, cannot identify a banknote by sight and may struggle further with distinguishing foreign banknotes that do not have tactile features. Similarly, for persons with cognitive impairments, e.g., dyslexia and dyscalculia, distinguishing between the notes and calculating values could be extra challenging [19]. Banknotes are often printed in different colors so people can identify and recognize them at a glance [39]. Color-driven recognition can be problematic for the unfamiliar, e.g., foreign people – with no reference to the banknote in question – and for people with color vision deficiency. Most banknotes carry a uniform shape and size to fit in pockets, but this uniformity can pose challenges for blind people in distinguishing between them. To mitigate this issue, several countries incorporated additional braille tactile textures into their banknotes [20]. This approach has proven to be ineffective because of a few major obstacles: (a) only a small number of blind people can read braille, (b) the tactile texture height is significantly compromised, and (c) the tactile information would not be useful for the people who do not understand the language [15].

In the past decade, multiple assistive technologies and approaches were marketed to aid, support, and guide users in banknote identification; however, these efforts primarily focused on assisting visually impaired individuals. The most widespread digital aids are standalone portable banknote scanners, using light sensors to read the color pattern of the notes and communicate their value audibly to the users [16, 26]. The major drawbacks of these solutions include cost, inflexibility, and practicality concerns.

A futuristic approach was introduced by Dunai et al. [9] in the form of a wearable assistive technology device. The solution has three main components: (1) an energy-efficient portable computer (Raspberry Pi), (2) sunglasses with an inbuilt infrared (IR) camera, and (3) a wirelessly connected smartphone. The recognition process is similar to the portable scanner's working mechanism. The IR camera scans and identifies the banknote, with the connected smartphone conveying the information audibly to users. Similarly, a Raspberry Pi-based banknote recognition system was developed by Lee et al. [21], but like other approaches solely designed for blind users, both solutions overlook the needs of most potential users.

Plenty of free and paid smartphone applications that promise banknote recognition have been developed mainly to help blind users with banknote recognition [e.g., 2, 14]. These solutions enhance mobility and flexibility and do not require additional hardware purchases, yet they still have certain limitations. Many of these applications are constructed based on Optical Character Recognition (OCR), leveraging the smartphone's CMOS camera sensor for image recognition [36]. However, the notes must be held steady, positioned on a flat surface, and illuminated optimally for precise banknote identification.

The evaluated technological approaches showed advantages and drawbacks concerning real-life usability, accessibility, and practicality. Among the methods assessed, smartphone applications stood out as particularly promising. That said, their design, which neither encompasses a broader user base and their associated needs nor the applied computer vision algorithms, exhibits potential for enhancement. Nonetheless, for applications to provide all-encompassing functionalities for a diverse audience, irrespective of their competencies, capacities, or limitations, it's essential to adhere to Universal Design (UD) principles [32]. UD pertains to designing products, systems, and environments that can be utilized and encountered by everyone to the greatest extent feasible, without requiring special equipment or adaptations [6, 8, 29], and "shall not exclude assistive devices for particular groups of persons with disabilities where this is needed" [25].

The limitations of OCR and CMOS technologies are making banknote recognition challenging on the go or in dynamically changing, e.g., indoor, outdoor, bright, and dark environments. This is where Augmented Reality (AR) image targets and advanced algorithms like Vuforia's [35] shine and are developed by prioritizing comprehensive image and feature recognition over limited text or pattern analysis. With this in mind, we decided to base our prototype on AR technology and utilized the seven principles of Universal Design of ICT [32] as our guiding framework. These are (1) Equitable Use, (2) Flexibility in Use, (3) Simple and Intuitive use, (4) Perceptible Information, (5) Tolerance for Error, (6) Low Physical Effort, and (7) Size and Space for Approach and Use. This approach aims to render the application accessible and usable for the broadest audience possible, regardless of their skills, abilities, or limitations [6, 29]. AR is an immersive, multisensory technology that seamlessly integrates digital information into the user's real-world surroundings in real-time. This digital content can encompass visual, auditory, tactile, or a combination thereof [4, 12]. Users can engage with and consume this digital content through wearable head-mounted solutions (HMD) or handheld AR-compatible smartphones, known as Mobile Augmented Reality (MAR) [3, 5].

AR historically presents significant accessibility and usability barriers [5, 11, 13, 30], while UD aims for barrier-free solutions [6, 29]. With this context in focus, the present study is committed to investigating the possibilities of universally designed mobile augmented reality applications. Limited literature focuses on human factors in AR research, with a few studies touching on HCI principles and usability heuristics, but rarely considers accessibility and diverse user abilities [2, 10, 11, 13, 14, 17, 18]. Therefore, a more encompassing approach is needed, leading this study to introduce a novel design methodology that integrates UD throughout the development of a MAR application.

## 2   Research Design

This research addresses the question: How can UD enhance the accessibility and usability of MAR applications? This inquiry delves into the applicability of UD principles in the design of AR. As previously mentioned, AR has historically lacked accessibility and usability. At the same time, the primary promise of UD lies in eliminating ICT barriers and enhancing accessibility and usability for a diverse user base. Additionally, we seek to answer the question: Can AR be a suitable platform for inclusive utility applications?

The research design consists of a series of phases to gain a comprehensive understanding and successful execution. An extensive study delves into various users' skills, abilities, goals, and preferences in the initial phase, establishing a foundation for subsequent stages. Building upon these insights, the second phase devises design objectives and requirement specifications customized to meet user needs. Subsequently, the third phase employs an iterative approach to guide the design and prototype development process, culminating in creating a fully functional minimum viable product. Lastly, the final phase involves testing with end-users and heuristic evaluations to validate findings and ensure alignment with user expectations.

## 3   Design Process

The design process followed and consisted of the following four phases: (1) mapping users' diverse skills, abilities, and situations, (2) formulating design objectives and requirement specifications, (3) iterative prototype development to implement the design ideas, and (4) design validation through users and experts.

### 3.1 Mapping Users' Diverse Skills, Abilities, and Situations (Phase 1)

Our objective is to tailor the design while considering the following issues:

**Digital-Literacy Barriers.** It is the ability to consume digital content. According to OECD's [24] worldwide survey, 26% of the population cannot use a computer, and a typical AR user belongs to the top 5% as a tech-savvy early adopter user. The survey indicates that to reach most users effectively, the strategy should involve targeting those with digital skill levels and designing a solution with minimal navigation, operational demands, and multitasking while emphasizing a highly simplified interface [24].

**Visual Barriers.** Most users are visual types and consume and interact with digital content primarily through graphical user interfaces. Most AR applications are highly dependent and built around visual elements, encompassing 2D, 3D, textural, and image-based information. Consequently, tackling prevalent obstacles such as myopia, color vision deficiency, and low color contrast sensitivity is imperative.

**Auditory Barriers.** Primarily impacting the elderly population aged 65 and above, this condition affects around 50% of this demographic, with a 5% prevalence observed globally [23, 38]. Despite being frequently disregarded, the potential of these AR features lies in their ability to provide mono, stereo, or spatial audio, thereby enhancing users' capabilities.

**Cognitive Barriers.** This can significantly influence users' decision-making, concentration, focus, memory retention, and perception of information. Cognitive impairments may arise from aging [37], innate conditions like dyslexia and dyscalculia [19], or temporary situations like fatigue or multitasking. Given this, it becomes essential to leverage the capabilities of AR, including computer vision and real-time object tracking. These capabilities can facilitate a user-friendly and intuitive design, automate user interactions, and simplify banknote recognition, all of which contribute to reducing the cognitive load on users.

**Motor Barriers.** This aspect can affect individuals to varying degrees, stemming from natural aging, Rheumatoid arthritis, accidents, inherent abilities, or situational factors like wearing gloves or handling items [31]. AR has various interaction styles and input mechanisms, integrating traditional keyboard, mouse, and touch gestures and emerging motion controllers, gaze controls, or air gestures. Thus, it is crucial to prioritize the provision of the most convenient and effortless interaction mechanisms for users.

**Cultural Barriers.** A diverse user base might use languages, data formats, and measurements, such as imperial or metric systems, reading order, and digital character sets. Accordingly, the core design should support the variety of these requirements and adapt a culturally sensitive design and language.

**Compatibility with Assistive Technologies.** Some users might use assistive technologies (AT) to operate their smartphones, regardless of our application's design. As a result, it is essential to guarantee compatibility with in-built ATs, such as screen readers and voice commands.

### 3.2 Formulating Design Objectives and Requirement Specifications (Phase 2)

To develop design objectives, we mapped the critical human factors, correlated them with UD principles, and set concrete design objectives based on UD guidelines. Regarding digital literacy, the principle of "Simple and intuitive use" (P3) aims to eliminate unnecessary elements and interaction tasks. For individuals with sensory disadvantages, "Equitable use" (P1) and "Perceptible Information" (P4) address concerns by incorporating high-contrast elements and multi-modal information presentation and also providing sensory feedback such as visual, auditory, and tactile cues.

Regarding motoric disadvantages, "Flexibility in use" (P2) and "Simple, intuitive use" (P3) accommodate various modes like portrait and landscape, handheld, and desktop while also simplifying interactions. "Tolerance for error" (P5) and "Low physical effort" (P6) ensure a forgiving interaction scheme and easy physical engagement. Cognitive disadvantages are targeted through the principle of "Simple, intuitive use" (P3), aiming to minimize on-screen elements and enhance predictability. Lastly, considering cultural and background diversity, the application should avoid culturally sensitive colours, visual elements, symbols and language and support various reading directions and non-Latin typography. In this way, the design addresses a spectrum of human factors, aiming to ensure inclusivity and accessibility for a wide array of users.

### 3.3 Iterative Prototype Development to Implement the Design Ideas (Phase 3)

We engaged in iterative prototype development to bring our design concepts to life and assess their effectiveness [7]. This process involved two primary phases: (1) Lo-fi prototyping (paper-based) and (2) Hi-fi prototyping (digital), aimed at crafting a user-testable minimum viable product that closely aligns with our final design.

**Lo-fi Prototyping.** Using quick and disposable paper prototypes to prevent bias towards initial ideas, the lo-fi prototyping phase explored various design concepts quickly. Early design stages involved sketching interface designs, layouts, and functionalities, linking them to the previous phase's findings and user personas to visualize application requirements. Each concept was followed by interactive testing of various ideas, scenarios, and situations, aiming to scrutinize, discuss, validate, and address design challenges. Initially, we generated sketches of 2D interface elements, identified optimal button placement, and explored potential difficulties related to screen orientation and user obstacles (see Fig. 1).

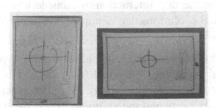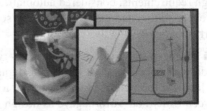

**Fig. 1.** Early sketches of the interface layout (on the left) and simulating accidental touches by holding the device (on the right)

Given the application's use context, it was necessary to simulate flexibility across varied use scenarios such as crowded places, single-handed operation, and multiple-screen orientations. This involved modeling on smartphones and tablets, considering the device's weight, dimensions, and user posture. Subsequently, we modeled use-case scenarios to identify the physical effort and dexterity requirements and to gather data concerning posture, size, and space for approach. Then, we simulated scenarios of visual distractions, encompassing factors such as color vision deficiencies, color contrast sensitivity, and blindness. This enabled us to strategically align our intended interaction approach with the seamless conveyance of multimodal information. It's important to clarify that simulation glasses aimed to enhance our comprehension of challenges rather than serving as a substitute for users with severe visual impairments.

**Fig. 2.** Modeling use of posture and psychical effort using different-sized devices (on the left) and simulating visual distractions with simulation glasses and eyepatches (on the right)

We observed that paper prototyping could have been more suitable for immersive technologies, seeing that simulating computer vision – e.g., live camera stream, its technical limitations, and the impact of the users' diverse environment – could be challenging. Modeling interaction styles by using physical objects, however, we found accurate, cost-effective, and relevant. In a handheld use-case scenario, we discovered that most users used their non-dominant hand to hold the phone and the dominant hand to hold the objects. This phenomenon must be considered in designing user interactions because concentrating the device's weight and accuracy demand on the users' nondominant hands can lead to potential difficulties in interface interaction. Also, we discovered that the natural interaction with MAR applications required both hands: One to hold the device and one to align the object (banknote) with them. The necessary physical effort using a big smartphone or tablet can be not just challenging but impossible for many. Furthermore, our initial design and button placement applying Fit's law [22] led to accidental touches in both portrait and landscape orientations. Therefore, we concluded and refined our design requirements, considered automatizing the user interaction by considering banknote recognition and magnification, and sought solutions that require significantly less effort (see Fig. 2).

**Hi-fi Prototyping.** To translate our observations from the lo-fi phase, we developed our design concepts into a functional digital prototype. We opted for Unity [33] as a development tool, coupled with Vuforia, a cutting-edge AR library [35]. The synergy between Unity and Vuforia gave us design flexibility and the ability to export the final project to major mobile platforms, such as Android and IOS.

We started the digital prototyping by making the recognition of banknotes possible through the smartphone's camera and initiated the process by creating image targets for

Vuforia. First, we scanned authentic banknotes, converted them into.jpg format, and then utilized Vuforia's Image-target generator for training their model to recognize our image targets (banknotes) in real-time (see Fig. 3). We scanned multiple images of various parts of each banknote to enhance accuracy and generate image targets. This ensured the system could recognize banknotes even when blended, wrinkled, or damaged.

Following this, we integrated functionalities to act upon recognition. Augmented text labels were added over the identified banknotes, offering a visual indication of both the banknote's name and its value. The app displayed the current exchange rate alongside the banknote's details for foreign currency. Concerning nonvisual users and multimodality, we introduced synthetic audio that simultaneously announces the label information on object recognition, providing an auditory interpretation of the label information. We integrated an automated application flow control to enhance interaction with the application, minimize the need for fine dexterity, and simplify complex gesture interactions (see Fig. 4).

Moreover, we incorporated a distance-based zoom function to eliminate the need for on-screen zoom buttons, which demand fine motor skills and accuracy. This alteration essentially made the smartphone function like a magnifying glass: When the user brings an object close to the camera, the digital information naturally enlarges (zooms in) - while moving the banknote farther from the camera reduces the scale of the digital content.

Fig. 3. Trained Image Target - Vuforia's feature recognition of 100 USD

We conducted a formative user evaluation on the hi-fi prototype to assess how it aligns with user requirements. The assessment included three participants, two males and one female, aged 25 to 54, providing diverse perspectives on the evaluation. Among the participants, two males primarily used smartphones as their primary ICT device and rated their technological proficiency above average. The female participant favored a desktop PC for daily use and described her technical proficiency as average. Additionally, two of the participants wore glasses and reported minor visual impairments. Notably, all participants had yet to gain experience with immersive technologies such as AR.

During the evaluation, participants engaged with the application, and any identified issues were incorporated into subsequent iterations, reflecting the continuous development process of the app. The think-aloud method was employed during the testing phase to comprehend users' perceptions and expectations thoroughly. This technique enabled participants to openly articulate their thoughts and emotions when they interacted with the app, offering invaluable insights into the design and uncovering potential challenges.

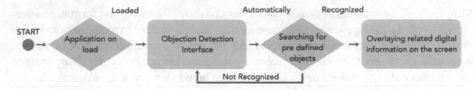

**Fig. 4.** Overview of the automatic object recognition function

Before the evaluation, participants were introduced to the app without training, mirroring a real-world discovery process. They were instructed to think aloud while navigating the app for the first time, openly sharing their thoughts, emotions, and points of confusion. Subsequently, participants were provided with various national and international banknotes and instructed to identify them. This identification process was observed across different settings, including indoor and outdoor environments and well-lit and dim conditions. One participant interacted with the application outdoors and in daylight. The other two participants tested the application indoors, where, on some testing rounds, the light was adjusted between off (dark), dim, and well-lit (bright) environments. An informal discussion was conducted following the test to gather more in-depth insights, opinions, and improvement suggestions. After the evaluation, our findings were discussed, design flaws were identified, and these issues were addressed in the subsequent iterations of the prototype.

**Design Implementation.** The initial digital iteration, represented by the hi-fi prototype, revealed a challenge concerning the changing backgrounds, adversely affecting digital text labels' legibility. To enhance readability, we refined these labels by incorporating symbols, sans-serif face type, and utilizing transparent high-contrast backgrounds that adhere to the physical banknotes' color scheme (see Fig. 5). Through the formative evaluation process, it became evident that users could need clarification, mistakenly assuming they were interacting with a camera application due to the live camera stream. This effect was also pronounced when users were multitasking or reopening the app. We implemented an "eye-shaped" silhouette design to address this issue and prevent misinterpretations. This design symbolizes the app's function, visually distinguishing the application from regular camera apps and assisting users with where to position their banknotes for recognition.

It became clear that beyond the visual adjustments, more auditory and tactile cues were necessary to communicate the application's nature and what users could anticipate from it. We refined the app so that non-visioned users can start using a screen reader, enabling all users to navigate the different stages of the application effectively. Also, we implemented an auditory welcome screen that instructs the user about the initial state and provides haptic feedback on banknote recognition - in companion with the auditory narration of the name, value, and exaggeration we implemented previously.

In scenarios with low lighting conditions, CMOS camera sensors can struggle to capture enough data for computer vision algorithms to identify banknotes accurately. To

**Fig. 5.** Recognition of banknote (hi-fi) before (on the left) and after (on the middle) and hand-free mode (on the right)

counteract this challenge, we incorporated a feature to utilize the smartphone's flashlight to light the banknote and enhance the recognition and tracking process. Additionally, coordinating the positioning of the phone and the banknote can pose difficulties, particularly for some users. To accommodate this, we introduced a third-person view "hand-free" mode by utilizing the front-facing camera. By activating this mode, users can place their devices (smartphone, tablet) on flat surfaces, e.g., table, lap, and position their banknotes towards the front-facing camera (see Fig. 5).

**Minimum Viable Product.** In the final iteration of the application, the graphical user interface is presented in two distinct layouts. The first layout, the splash/loading screen (Layout 1), incorporates branding elements that immediately communicate the application's identity to the user upon opening. The second layout (Layout 2) is the banknote recognition screen, serving as the primary interaction area for users. This interface welcomes users and provides clear audio-visual guidance for placing the banknote near the camera.

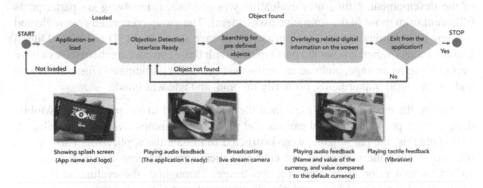

**Fig. 6.** Application flow diagram, visualizing the different states of the application

The application employs tactile feedback mechanisms during object recognition and generates a simplified visual representation of the banknote based on its color palette. This representation effectively conveys its value and exchange rate to the users. With non-sighted users in mind, the application has been designed to be fully functional through a screen reader or voice commands, both of which are supported by major mobile platforms. The process involves tapping the mobile screen to locate and select the application icon for users relying on screen readers. Once activated, the application provides a welcoming auditory prompt and guidance throughout the interaction. Tactile feedback is provided upon successful object recognition utilizing the device's haptic engine, and the identified banknote, along with its exchange rate, if applicable, is announced audibly.

Additionally, an alternative approach is provided for users who may not be able to interact with the screen, i.e., physically, they can place the mobile or tablet device on a stable surface and then activate the application using voice commands. This method utilizes the device's front-facing camera to offer a third-person perspective, allowing users to use the live camera stream as a mirror and interact effectively with the application. Figure 6 illustrates an application flow diagram visualizing the different states of the application.

### 3.4 Design Validation Through Users and Experts (Phase 4)

Our design process was firmly guided by the seven principles of UD throughout all stages of interaction, from design to development. To ensure the adherence of the developed prototype to UD principles, we conducted user and heuristic evaluations on the final prototype.

**Summative User Evaluation.** To validate our design choices, we tested each iteration of our digital prototypes to understand how the application aligns with user requirements and expectations. Our test devices incorporated smartphone and tablet devices, providing different screen sizes between 4.3 and 10 inches. Regarding the quality of the equipment, the prices vary between low-end and high-end. Toward the completion of the development, a final user evaluation was conducted, involving six participants (different from those in the formative assessment). The group comprised four male and two female individuals, ages 23 to 56, and an average age of 34.3 (SD = 12.03). Digital literacy ratings varied among the participants, with three considering themselves above average, two as average, and one as below average. Most participants (four out of six) had minor visual impairments, primarily myopia, and one was blind.

Before the evaluation, we explained the tasks at hand to the participants. Mobile devices with pre-installed applications and physical banknotes were then distributed. Following this, the participants were instructed to initiate the application. Participants tried to identify the banknotes and calculate their corresponding currency exchange values without prior instructions on app usage. Throughout the evaluation process, we recorded the proceedings and closely observed participants' interactions as they attempted to complete the assigned tasks.

The test results revealed that all participants successfully utilized the application to identify the provided banknotes, irrespective of their digital proficiency or capabilities. The auditory and visual clues made the app predictable, and no users had issues understanding, predicting, and executing the recognition function during ideal circumstances. Most users searched the application hamburger menu for additional features, e.g., flashlight activation or changing to a front-facing camera. Two activated the flashlight by minimizing the application and using options in the Android menu.

Most of the participants inquired whether the application could identify coins or counterfeit banknotes and proposed the inclusion of such functionalities. Notably, the blind participant appreciated the research on this subject, highlighting her intention to use the finished product. She emotionally mentioned how she has always depended on her husband in cash situations. She said with a touch of humor, "Now I won't need my husband anymore!".

**Heuristic Evaluation – Cognitive Walkthrough.** We also performed a cognitive walkthrough [28] on the final prototype with the involvement of three expert evaluators from the field of Universal Design of ICT. This walkthrough was instrumental in emulating the users' interactions with the prototype, enabling us to pinpoint potential sources of confusion or elements that could detrimentally affect the overall user experience. Before the start of the evaluation process, we set the seven UD-AR principles [30] as heuristics and the evaluation scope of application functions, which were banknote recognition on given local currencies (i.e., Norwegian Krone (NOK)) and banknote recognition and currency rate calculation on a given foreign currency (i.e., USD). Subsequently, three expert evaluators specializing in UD conducted a cognitive walkthrough, examining the application's functionalities and features. Each evaluator undertook this process individually, documenting their observations, critiques, and insights. Following their assessments, the evaluators convened to collectively review their findings, engaging in a thorough discussion to ensure a comprehensive evaluation and identify potential oversights. This collaborative review aimed to encompass a holistic perspective and ensure that all aspects of the application's usability and accessibility were thoroughly considered.

The application underwent an evaluation based on the UD heuristics for Mobile Augmented Reality [30], with experts reporting its adherence to critical factors. The experts highlighted its commitment to equitable access and information equivalence for a diverse user base (P1: Equitable use). The application's adaptability was noted, accommodating diverse user needs and orientations while ensuring accessibility for screen reader and voice command users (P2: Flexibility in use). Moreover, the experts acknowledged its user-friendly design, which caters even to those unfamiliar with AR technologies through automated interactions and multi-sensory cues (P3: Simple and intuitive use). For conveying information, the experts emphasized the application's effectiveness in using visual, auditory, and tactile cues to ensure perceivability (P4: Perceptible information). They appreciated how the application minimized errors with real-time updates (P5: Tolerance for error). Automation of banknote recognition and hands-free mode demonstrated its commitment to reducing physical effort and enhancing usability across user abilities (P6: Low physical effort). The application's adaptability extended to different user positions and environments, accommodating walking, standing, sitting, and lying down without compromising functionality (P7: Size and space for approach), as the experts' feedback highlighted. Finally, the experts concluded that the proposed banknote recognition prototype complied with the seven principles of UD.

## 4  Discussion and Conclusion

Our research has provided valuable insights into the Universal Design (UD) application in Mobile Augmented Reality (MAR) for facilitating banknote recognition and currency rate calculation. The adaptation of UD in MAR has the potential to reduce the barriers faced by those with, for example, visual or cognitive impairments or when language barriers occur. Currency recognition becomes particularly indispensable for visually impaired individuals, ensuring they can engage in exchange situations more independently and confidently, without apprehensions of being deceived or reliant on stigmatizing assistive technologies [27]. While most banknote recognition research focuses exclusively on visually impaired individuals [1, 2], there is potentially great value for more people regardless of their skills, abilities, or lack thereof. Being "disabled" or not is also strongly linked to the context or situation, e.g., trying to recognize foreign banknotes, foreign character sets, and labels during international travel - or swiftly verifying exchange rates without a calculator offers everyone convenience, speed, and accuracy. Thus, our research implies that emphasizing the UD of AR technologies can lead to a more expansive user base and cater to a broader market segment. While UD is necessary for some, it can benefit everyone, leading toward more accessible, usable, and sustainable products and services.

Through our validation process, we encountered design challenges highlighting AR-specific design flaws and offering broader lessons in developing mobile AR applications. One of the critical issues was the physical effort and considerable dexterity of using the application, requiring both hands to align the mobile device and the banknotes. This experience drove us to automate user interaction and consider hands-free modes, unitizing the front-facing cameras of the mobile device. This feature also eases the physical effort for a broader spectrum of MAR applications.

The problem of label readability with dynamic backgrounds highlighted the importance of context-aware design. With regular applications, the designers control the color palette and contrast ratios between the foreground and background. Yet, colors can change dynamically in MAR applications, where the background is the real world. Therefore, designers must consider techniques for context awareness to ensure information remains accessible across diverse background conditions.

MAR applications rely highly on camera streams; therefore, without visual or auditory tools, users could call wrong mental models, thinking they are using a camera application or cannot even predict app functions. Thus, designers and developers must adopt appropriate affordances that clarify the application's purpose. Finally, the design should consider adaptation to unlit conditions because dark environments could hinder object tracking and recognition. By offering adaptive lighting solutions, like activating a device's flashlight, we set a standard for ensuring functionality across various lighting conditions.

These challenges, solutions, and workarounds have implications beyond our specific application. They provide a framework for enhancing a broad range of AR applications by focusing on user diversity, context awareness, and UD principles. Our experience addressing these challenges forms a foundation for more accessible and efficient MAR experiences. The application of UD in our design resolved specific challenges within our banknote recognition prototype and brought to light novel features that could enhance the majority of other AR and MAR applications. By focusing on user diversity, physical accessibility, and environmental adaptation, we have demonstrated that AR can provide an ideal platform for highly inclusive applications.

Our research, therefore, makes a strong argument for the potential of using AR to develop inclusive utility tools. It highlights the importance of considering various user needs and the surrounding context during design and development, contributing to a more inclusive and engaging digital landscape. While the potential of AR in developing inclusive utility tools has yet to be widely recognized, our research underlines the possibilities it holds, provided that optimizing for user diversity, equity, and inclusion is in focus. With an increasing number of AR utility applications embracing UD principles, there exists a potential to set industry-wide practices for implementation, making a significant step toward social inclusion and hence tick off some of UN's sustainability goals at the same time, i.e., "Leave [ing] No One Behind" [34].

# References

1. Abilash, C.S., Dinakaran, M., Hari Vignesh, R., Anju, A.: Currency recognition for the visually impaired people. In: Proceedings of the 2022 IEEE Delhi Section Conference (DELCON), pp. 1–3. IEEE (2022). https://doi.org/10.1109/DELCON54057.2022.9753373
2. Angsupanich, S., Matayong, S.: A prototype real-time mobile application for Thai banknote recognition to support visually impaired persons. Universal Access in the Information Society, 1–16 (2023). https://doi.org/10.1007/s10209-023-01016-8
3. Aukstakalnis, S.: Practical Augmented Reality: A guide to the technologies, applications, and human factors for AR and VR. Addison-Wesley Professional (2016)
4. Azuma, R.T.: A survey of augmented reality. Presence: Teleoperators Virt. Environm. 6(4), 355–385 (1997)
5. Billinghurst, M., Clark, A., Lee, G.: A survey of augmented reality. Foundat. Trends® Hum.-Comput. Interact. 8(2–3), 73–272 (2015). https://doi.org/10.1561/1100000049
6. Björk, E.: Many become losers when the Universal Design perspective is neglected: Exploring the true cost of ignoring Universal Design principles. Technol. Disabil. 21(4), 117–125 (2009). https://doi.org/10.3233/TAD-2009-0286
7. Carr, M., Verner, J.: Prototyping and software development approaches. Department of Information Systems, pp. 319–338. City University of Hong Kong, Hong Kong (1997)
8. Darzentas, J., Miesenberger, K.: Design for all in information technology: a universal concern. In: Proceedings of the International Conference on Database and Expert Systems Applications, pp. 406–420. Springer, Berlin (2005). https://doi.org/10.1007/11546924_40
9. Dunai Dunai, L., Chillarón Pérez, M., Peris-Fajarnés, G., Lengua Lengua, I.: Euro banknote recognition system for blind people. Sensors 17(1), 184 (2017). https://doi.org/10.3390/s17010184
10. D'unsei, A., Grasset, R., Seichter, H., Billinghurst, M.: Applying HCI principles to AR systems design. In: Mixed Reality User Interfaces: Specification, Authoring, Adaptation (MRUI 2007) Workshop Proceedings, pp. 37–42 (2007). http://hdl.handle.net/10092/2340
11. Endsley, T.C., Sprehn, K., Brill, R.M., Ryan, K.J., Vincent, E.C., Martin, J.M.: Augmented reality design heuristics: Designing for dynamic interactions. In: Proceedings of the Human Factors and Ergonomics Society Annual Meeting, vol. 61(1), 2100–2104 (2017). https://doi.org/10.1177/1541931213602007
12. Furht, B.: Handbook of augmented reality. Springer Science & Business Media (2011)

13. Gabbard, J.L., Swan, J.E., II.: Usability engineering for augmented reality: employing user-based studies to inform design. IEEE Trans. Visual Comput. Graph. **14**(3), 513–525 (2008). https://doi.org/10.1109/TVCG.2008.24
14. Grijalva, F., Rodriguez, J.C., Larco, J., Orozco., L.: Smartphone recognition of the US banknotes' denomination, for visually impaired people. In: Proceedings of the 2010 IEEE ANDESCON, pp. 1–6. IEEE (2010). https://doi.org/10.1109/ANDESCON.2010.5631773
15. de Heij, H.: Banknote design for the visually impaired. DNB Occasional Stud. **130** (2009)
16. Hinwood, A., Preston, P., Suaning, G., Lovell, N.H.: Bank note recognition for the vision impaired. Australas. Phys. Eng. Sci. Med. **29**, 229–233 (2006). https://doi.org/10.1007/BF0 3178897
17. Ko, S.M., Chang, W.S., Ji, Y.G.: Usability principles for augmented reality applications in a smartphone environment. Inter. J. Hum.-Comput. Interact. **29**(8), 501–515 (2013). https://doi.org/10.1080/10447318.2012.722466
18. Kourouthanassis, P.E., Boletsis, C., Lekakos, G.: Demystifying the design of mobile augmented reality applications. Multimedia Tools Appli. **74**(3), 1045–1066 (2015). https://doi.org/10.1007/s11042-013-1710-7
19. Landerl, K., Bevan, A., Butterworth, B.: Developmental dyscalculia and basic numerical capacities: a study of 8–9-year-old students. Cognition **93**(2), 99–125 (2004). https://doi.org/10.1016/j.cognition.2003.11.004
20. Lederman, S.J., Hamilton, C.: Using tactile features to help functionally blind individuals denominate banknotes. Hum. Factors **44**(3), 413–428 (2002). https://doi.org/10.1518/001872 0024497646
21. Lee, J., Ahn, J., Lee, K.Y.: Development of a raspberry Pi-based banknote recognition system for the visually impaired. J. Soc. for e-Bus. Stud. **23**(2), 21–31 (2018)
22. MacKenzie, S.: Fitts' law as a research and design tool in human-computer interaction. Hum.-Comput. Interact. **7**(1), 91–139 (1992). https://doi.org/10.1207/s15327051hci0701_3
23. NIH - Age-Related Hearing Loss. https://www.nidcd.nih.gov/health/age-related-hearing-loss (Accessed 30 Jan 2024)
24. OECD - Skills Matter: Further Results from the Survey of Adult Skills, OECD Skills Studies, OECD Publishing, Paris. https://doi.org/10.1787/9789264258051-en (Accessed 30 Jan 2024)
25. OHCHR - Convention on the Rights of Persons with Disabilities, Article 2 – Definitions. https://www.ohchr.org/en/instruments-mechanisms/instruments/convention-rights-per sons-disabilities (Accessed 30 Jan 2024)
26. Papastavrou, S., Hadjiachilleos, D., Stylianou, G.: Blind-folded recognition of bank notes on the mobile phone. In: ACM SIGGRAPH 2010 Posters. ACM, Los Angeles, California (2010). https://doi.org/10.1145/1836845.1836919
27. Parette, P., Scherer, M.: Assistive technology use and stigma. Educ. Train. Dev. Disabil. **39**(3), 217–226 (2004)
28. Polson, P.G., Lewis, C., Rieman, J., Wharton, C.: Cognitive walkthroughs: a method for theory-based evaluation of user interfaces. Int. J. Man Mach. Stud. **36**(5), 741–773 (1992). https://doi.org/10.1016/0020-7373(92)90039-N
29. Story, M.F.: Maximizing usability: The principles of universal design. Assist. Technol. **10**(1), 4–12 (1998). https://doi.org/10.1080/10400435.1998.10131955
30. Szentirmai, A.B., Murano, P.: New universal design heuristics for mobile augmented reality applications. In: Proceedings of the International Conference on Human-Computer Interaction – Late Breaking Papers, pp. 404–418. Springer Nature Switzerland, Cham (2023). https://doi.org/10.1007/978-3-031-48041-6_27
31. Tutuncu, Z., Kavanaugh, A.: Rheumatic disease in the elderly: Rheumatoid arthritis. Clin. Geriatr. Med. **21**(3), 513–525 (2005). https://doi.org/10.1016/j.cger.2005.02.009
32. Universal Design Institute - Universal Design Principles. https://www.udinstitute.org/princi ples (Accessed 30 Jan 2024)

33. Unity Real Time Development Platform. https://unity.com/ (Accessed 30 Jan 2024)
34. UN Sustainable Development Group - Universal values principle two: Leave no one behind. https://unsdg.un.org/2030-agenda/universal-values/leave-no-one-behind (Accessed 30 Jan 2024)
35. Vuforia - Getting started with Vuforia engine in Unity. https://library.vuforia.com/articles/Training/getting-started-with-vuforia-in-unity.html#about (Accessed 30 Jan 2024)
36. Waghade, A.G., Zopate, A.V., Titare, A.G., Shelke, S.A.: Text extraction from text based image using Android. Inter. Res. J. Eng. Technol. (IRJET) **05**(3), 3304–3307 (2018)
37. WHO – Dementia. http://www.who.int/news-room/fact-sheets/detail/dementia (Accessed 30 Jan 2024)
38. WHO - Deafness and hearing loss. http://www.who.int/en/news-room/fact-sheets/detail/deafness-and-hearing-loss (Accessed 30 Jan 2024)
39. Williams, M.M., Anderson, R.G.: Currency design in the United States and abroad: counterfeit deterrence and visual accessibility. Federal Reserve Bank of St. Louis, pp. 371–414 (2007)

# Enhancing Accessible Reading for All with Universally Designed Augmented Reality – AReader: From Audio Narration to Talking AI Avatars

Attila Bekkvik Szentirmai[✉]

Faculty of Architecture and Design, Department of Design Mustad, Norwegian University of Science and Technology, Bygg 118, 315 Gjovik, Norway
attila.b.szentirmai@ntnu.com

**Abstract.** This paper introduces AReader, an innovative approach that combines Universal Design (UD) and Augmented Reality (AR) to enhance the universal accessibility of paper-based textual content. It targets a broad audience, including individuals with print and situational disabilities, emphasizing that reading challenges can affect anyone. The paper details the practical implementation of UD in AR, focusing on AR's context-aware, multimodal capabilities, and highlights a novel Visual Screen Reader feature. This feature is presented in two concepts: Text-to-Audio Narration with Visual Reading Guide and Text-to-AI-Video Narration. The paper also outlines a set of features and hands-on UD practices adaptable to a wide variety of AR applications. User testing has demonstrated that the prototype effectively enhances reading accessibility and usability across various user groups. The findings suggest that integrating UD principles with AR technologies can foster inclusive solutions, benefiting not only individuals with special needs but also contributing to broader societal inclusion.

**Keywords:** Universal Design · Augmented Reality · Assistive Technology · Text-to-Speech · Inclusive Technology · Digital Accessibility

## 1 Introduction

Reading unlocks a world of endless possibilities to access information. However, this access can become limited, burdensome, or inconvenient, particularly for an estimated 1.1 billion individuals with varying degrees of vision loss ("IAPB," 2020) or between the 395 million and 790 million people who struggle with dyslexia (Shaywitz, 1998). Beyond these groups, billions are also affected by emotional, physiological, or situational issues, as well as those who prefer alternative methods of accessing information other than reading. In our rapidly evolving information society, ensuring equal access to information is not merely necessary but a fundamental human right. This right is mandated by various international and national laws, standards, and regulations, including but not limited to the Convention on the Rights of Persons with Disabilities (Kanter 2006),

M. Antona and C. Stephanidis (Eds.): HCII 2024, LNCS 14697, pp. 282–300, 2024.
https://doi.org/10.1007/978-3-031-60881-0_18

the Americans with Disabilities Act (Lerblance 1992), or the Web Content Accessibility Guidelines (Wessel et al. 2021; Power et al. 2012 These standards are designed to ensure accessibility for individuals with various disabilities, including those unable to access or read printed materials referred to as print disabilities (Harpur 2017). The standards establish guidelines for creating content and environments that are more accessible, such as the use of alternative text for images for the blind, readable fonts, and clear language, which are particularly beneficial for people with dyslexia and other reading difficulties. Despite these mandates, the need for equal access to information continues to encounter barriers, even in critical domains such as reading (Harpur 2017).

Recognizing these challenges, this paper introduces AReader, a novel and innovative approach that integrates Universal Design (UD) with Augmented Reality (AR), making textual content accessible to broad audiences, regardless of their skills, abilities or circumstances. To understand the full significance of this approach, it is crucial to first consider the current state of assistive technologies. While these technologies are undoubtedly beneficial, they often fall short in terms of inclusivity, potentially leading to exclusivity, stigmatization, and inefficiency in addressing the broader needs of all users.

## 1.1 Assistive Technologies for Individuals with Print Disabilities

Assistive technologies (ATs) are specialized tools and devices designed to help individuals with tasks that otherwise might be difficult or impossible. These proprietary technologies, including both hardware and software, are crucial for addressing print disabilities. They assist in recognizing, capturing, processing, and communicating textual information in alternative formats for users with special needs (Virgili et al. 2018).

Magnification aids are crucial for visually impaired individuals, helping to enlarge content or specific areas of a display for easier viewing (Evans & Blenkhorn, 2008). Alongside these, Text-to-Speech (TTS) systems play a significant role by converting text into synthesized spoken language, benefiting not only those with visual impairments but also individuals with dyslexia (O'Malley 1995). In a similar vein, Screen Readers (SR) provide an auditory interpretation of visual content, including images, videos, and text, and offer contextual information like navigation and system status, primarily for digital displays (Oh et al., 2021). Furthermore, Optical Character Recognition (OCR) technology is essential in making non-predefined information accessible to both humans and machines, interpreting them through other assistive technologies like SRs (Islam et al. 2017; Guo et al. 2016; Eikvil 1993). This interconnected suite of technologies enhances accessibility, offering various solutions to overcome challenges faced by individuals with print disabilities.

While most ATs are integral parts of the major operating systems, such as macOS, Windows, iOS, and Android, their foundational functions and offerings have remained unchanged. The translation of innovative research into practical applications has been relatively slow and incremental, failing to keep pace with emerging technological trends and opportunities in the past decade. This outlook suggests that despite the substantial demand from billions of users and existing legal mandates, the ability to access and utilize services is not a central concern for industry stakeholders. This perspective may stem from the belief that the majority of the user base is unaffected by disabilities, leading to the assumption that prioritizing accessibility is not commercially viable. Generally,

ATs are viewed as specialized, "niche" tools intended solely for persons with disabilities. However, this perception could impede progressive development and overlook a broader population that could benefit from technologies designed to ease the burden of text reading. While ATs indeed facilitate accessibility, they also inadvertently create distinctions among users based on their specific needs. This approach can be more exclusive and stigmatizing than inclusive, thus neglecting a broader demographic in need.

The inability to access textual information could affect us all. Thus, segregating users based on deficits in skills and abilities is flawed. There are individuals with permanent, congenital disabilities and others who acquire disabilities temporarily through accidents or situational impacts. Situational disabilities can arise from specific contexts and environments, such as vision reduction in bright sunlight, hearing challenges in noisy areas, limited mobility in crowded spaces, or cognitive diminishment under stress (Gjøsæter et al. 2019; Wobbrock 2019). These situation dependent factors can reduce our skills and abilities, creating symptoms and barriers akin to those experienced by individuals with slight to severe disabilities. Therefore, a paradigm shift and a more universal approach are imperative, considering that loss of ability and its consequent hindrances can affect us all daily.

## 1.2   From Specialized Assistive Technologies to Universal Design

Universal Design (UD) is the design of products, systems, and environments for everyone, to the greatest extent possible, without the need for adoption or specialized equipment (Björk 2009; Darzentas & Miesenberger 2005; Story 1998). This approach extends beyond mere accessibility and disability concerns to encompass usability and user diversity. However, UD is often seen merely as an aspirational goal, stagnating within an initial focus on accessibility. Misconceptions such as UD being solely for the disabled, equating UD with accessibility, or viewing UD as a one-size-fits-all solution are prevalent. Contrary to these beliefs, UD aims to meet the diverse needs of all users. Yet, this ambitious approach is often deemed "impossible" or is limited by factors such as the laws of physics, material constraints, and technological limitations, which result in a narrow focus on accessibility. While accessibility is a prerequisite, since usability without accessibility is unattainable, overlooking usability and user diversity does not fully align with UD principles. Achieving UD goals, especially in the context of print disabilities, necessitates an integration with technologies capable of recognizing, capturing, converting, and communicating textual information in multimodal ways that enhance user senses. These capabilities align closely with the features of Augmented Reality (AR).

## 1.3   Augmented Reality: A New Frontier in Universal Accessibility

Augmented Reality (AR) is a multisensory, context-aware, immersive technology. It simultaneously overlays digital information with the users' physical environment (Billinghurst et al. 2015; Azuma 1997). Augmenting paper-based textual materials is a common practice in AR, such as AR books. However, these applications often overlook accessibility, neglecting user-centered design principles (Szentirmai & Murano 2023; Naranjo-Puentes et al. 2022; Herskovitz et al. 2020). Despite a few exceptions, AR is predominantly perceived and used as a visualization or entertainment tool, appealing mainly to early adopter tech-savvy users (Naranjo-Puentese et al. 2022; Herskovitz et al. 2020). This "stigma" significantly limits the exploration of AR's potential in enhancing accessibility and usability.

As a context-aware technology, AR has the capability to "see" for its users through camera vision, identify objects, and communicate information in a multimodal manner. It can convey audio information through speakers, using stereo, mono, or spatial sound, and present visual information in 2D or 3D, including static and dynamic imagery, through displays. Additionally, AR can "poke" users through tactile stimuli using haptic feedback. Accordingly, AR is not "just" a visualization tool. By manipulating visual stimuli, for instance, through enlarging, sharpening can be tailored to the specific needs of users, thereby compensating for their deficits in abilities. However, there's a common misconception that AR is more of a barrier to accessibility than a facilitator.

Only a limited number of research papers explore innovative AR approaches to enhance accessibility. Stearns et al. (2018) explore AR magnification using Microsoft HoloLens, highlighting its benefits for visually impaired users. Herskovitz et al. (2020) delves into AR's potential for blind users, creating accessible prototype alternatives for inaccessible AR applications, providing a roadmap for developers towards accessibility. Mambu et al. (2019) utilized a mobile AR platform, using computer vision to detect and announce objects auditory for enhancing daily activities for visually impaired individuals. Lastly, Gupta et al. (2019) developed an AR system to assist people with dyslexia, showing a significant decrease in reading time due to customizable text features. While these studies underscore the importance of accessibility in AR and inspired this paper, they also inadvertently highlight a critical oversight: providing value to the broader population in the form of universal solutions.

Within AR and its intersection with UD, the research landscape is relatively nascent. The pioneering study by Coughlan & Miele (2017) serves as a notable exception, asserting the significant potential of AR in reducing accessibility barriers and advocating AR as a UD tool. While their work stands as a foundational contribution in UD, other domains such as Universal Design for Learning (UDL) have also begun to recognize AR's beneficial impact on learning, as evidenced by studies like those of Stylianidou et al. (2020) and Walker et al. (2017). This gradual recognition in diverse areas underscores the versatility and far-reaching implications of AR in fostering inclusive environments.

However, UDL and UD are distinct concepts. UDL is a framework designed to address individual learning differences and optimize teaching and learning experiences in educational environments (Walker et al. 2017). In contrast, UD focuses on making products and environments accessible to all users. Both concepts aim for inclusivity and accessibility, but they target different domains. In other words, UDL might employ AR as a visualization tool for sighted students to enhance their learning comprehension, while providing alternative solutions, such as audiobooks, for visually impaired students (Walker et al. 2017) in the classroom. In contrast, applying UD principles in app design would render such differentiation unnecessary, as the application would be usable by all students, regardless of their skills and abilities.

Addressing this research gap, this paper presents the design and development of AReader, an AR prototype rooted in UD principles. Its aim is to provide a universally accessible, inclusive solution that eases the reading burden for all users, including those affected by print disabilities.

The paper is structured to first outline the required UD-AR features that can be implemented later in a variety of AR applications, followed by design validation through user testing. Subsequent sections delve into the broader implications of these findings within the UD-enhanced AR context, culminating with a reflection on future research directions in this field. Through this exploration, the paper seeks to reframe the perception of AR from a primarily visual-centric gaming tool to a technology fostering greater integration and participation in the digital society.

## 2    Research Design

The practice of UD in developing AR applications aligns with inclusive design philosophy and technological requirements. Addressing a novel intersection, this research pioneers the application of UD in AR, a domain yet to be fully explored by investigating: How Universally Designed Augmented Reality can enhance accessible and usable reading experiences, regardless of the users' skills and abilities? The research methodology is meticulously structured across several stages to guarantee comprehensive understanding and efficient execution. The initial stage lays the groundwork, identifying the preferences and needs of users with reading disabilities and examining the technological framework. Based on these preliminary insights, the research defines UD design objectives and AR requirement specifications. Following this, the project enters an iterative development phase, focusing on creating a user-testable prototype. Each iteration and design concept undergoes small-scale user testing with a diverse group of 3–5 participants, as suggested by Nielsen & Landauer (1993). This method provides immediate insights, guiding the development process. The final stage involves a more formal user testing with a diverse group of 12 participants, varying in age, skills, and abilities. This summative evaluation aims to ensure that the design aligns with the initial specifications and the broader goal of enhancing reading accessibility through the integration of UD in AR.

## 3    Design Process

This paper cannot encompass the entire detail of the design process due to scope limitations. However, the subsequent section offers a comprehensive overview of the pivotal considerations and discoveries encountered during the design phase. This overview aims to highlight critical elements of the design strategy, methodologies employed, and key insights gained, which collectively underpin the development of AReader.

### 3.1    User Needs Analysis and Feature Identification

Individuals with print disabilities exhibit distinct requirements for accessing and processing textual information. Users with print disabilities primarily need to interact with text in ways that mitigate their disability, making reading more manageable and comfortable. Based on research in Assistive Technology (AT), particularly focusing on Magnification (Stearns et al. 2018; Evans & Blenkhorn 2008), Text-to-Speech (TTS) (Craig &

Schroeder 2019; O'Malley 1995), Screen reader (SR) (Oh et al. 2021; Guo et al. 2016), and the utilization of AR (Mambu et al. 2019) the following priority list and feature set have been developed:

1. **Priority-Accessibility Features:** These are critical needs; without them, the application would not be usable for individuals with print disabilities.

   - Capture and Digital Conversion: Transforming printed text into a digital format for multimodal interpretation.
   - Auditory Access to Text: Text-to-speech tools are vital as they convert written text into spoken language, enabling users to absorb information through listening, thus circumventing visual reading challenges.
   - Enhanced Visibility: Magnification or other visual features aids are essential for enhancing the user's natural skills and abilities.

2. **Priority-Usability Features:** These features, while impacting accessibility, enhance the application's quality and convenience.

   - Consistent Reading Environment: A simplified, and consistent display is crucial. Uniform font size, style, and background color across digital content reduce visual strain and improve focus.
   - Guided Reading Assistance: Tools such as line guides or trackers are beneficial in following text, helping maintain the reading line and preventing users from losing their place.
   - Readability-Focused Fonts: Fonts designed for improved readability can significantly ease the reading process. These fonts feature characteristics that reduce visual confusion and enhance character recognition.

### 3.2 Technological Framework

In response to these user needs and priorities, the AR application must provide the following core functions:

- Identify and Capture Textual Content: To recognize the context and provide audio-visual assistance and interpretation to users.
- Multimodal Information Representation: Creating perceptible information by stimulating visual, auditory, and tactile senses. This includes providing Auditory Access to Text.
- Information Visualization: Employing visual enhancements such as a Consistent Reading Environment, Guided Reading Assistance, and Readability-Focused Fonts, along with visual guidance to enhance readability.
- Low Cost and High Availability: The technology should be accessible to a broader audience. The prototype must be built on widely available hardware, eliminating the need for proprietary or external devices.
- Development environment: The project will be built using Unity (v.2017.4), a universal engine capable for exporting prototypes to multiple systems (iOS, Android), and devices including phones, tablets, and head-mounted displays. AR development integrates the industry leading Vuforia engine v7 ("Vuforia," n.d.).

### 3.3 Requirement Specification for Universally Designed Augmented Reality

In our previous study (Szentirmai & Murano 2023), we developed UD heuristics for AR, reflecting the functions and needs identified in Sect. 3.1. The following requirements from Sect. 3.2 have been developed for implementation with UD:

1. Equitable Use (Accessibility)

   - AR pattern recognition: to detect text and convert it to speech, incorporating features such as Capture and Digital Conversion.
   - Visual Screen Reader: to visualize text and speech for comprehension while reading aloud, incorporating features such as Enhanced Visibility; Auditory Access to Text; Guided Reading Assistance.
   - Caption support on non-textual AR media.

2. Flexibility of Use (Accessibility & Usability)

   - Mobile AR support for portrait and landscape modes.
   - Head mounted AR support for natural first-person interaction.
   - Enhancing text visibility and sharpness through a digital render, regardless of environmental effects, incorporating Readability-Focused Fonts.
   - Provide natural magnification options for ease of zooming in and out of content.

3. Simple and Intuitive Use (Usability)

   - Intuitive UI with automatized functions for a minimal learning curve, facilitating a Consistent Reading Environment.
   - Hybrid natural interaction with physical and digital UI.
   - Avoiding the need for controllers or extra input devices.

4. Perceptible Information (Accessibility & Usability)

   - Multimodal information presentation (auditory, visual, tactile).
   - Visual enhancements for humans in different lighting conditions, incorporating Enhanced Visibility and Readability-Focused Fonts.
   - Visual enhancements for computer vision algorithms for detection and tracking the paper-based material.

5. *Tolerance for Error (Usability)*

   - Error prevention mechanisms that can break the application or the user experience.

6. Low Physical Effort (Accessibility & Usability)

   - Requiring minimal physical interaction, requiring no more than one hand, one finger usage.
   - Suitable for users with hard skin, wearing gloves or relying on physical ATs.
   - Suitable for users with varying degrees of motor skills.

7. Size and Space for Approach (Accessibility and Usability)

   - Interface design adaptable to various device sizes.
   - Comfortable usability in diverse physical postures.

- Functions available within reach to minimize motion sickness in head-mounted mode.

## 3.4  Implementation and Concept Development

Having established a requirement specification in Sect. 3.3, grounded in the principles of UD and tailored to meet the specific needs of users with reading disabilities in Sect. 3.1 and technological requirements in Sect. 3.2 this section focuses on the concrete concept development and design implementation. Each requirement outlined previously serves as a blueprint, characterized by iterative design and development, where concepts are built, tested, and refined. This user-centered design approach ensures that the technology developed is not only innovative but also empathetic and inclusive. The following section provides an overview about the concept development implementation and reasoning behind the choices.

**Hybrid Interface and Interaction styles.**  The seamless integration of physical "real" objects and reality is critical and requires a hybrid interface approach in AR. The hybrid nature possesses a physical paper-based textual information and a digital overlay rendered on the user's AR display. The development of the physical interface involved selecting text that introduces the Raspberry Pi, complementing our other research projects within the same topic. The A4 paper base, with the textual information served as a trackable image marker for the computer vision algorithm and provided the bases of the overlayed Visual Screen Reader (VSR) as shown in Fig. 1.

**Fig. 1.**  A) Physical Interface and Computer Vision Pattern; B) AReader Hybrid Interface Elements including Visual Screen Reader, AReader button and 3D augmentation of the Raspberry Pi.

The design process involved evaluating various concepts to address the limitations such as angle, distance, and graphic complexity of AR image targets. The chosen solution was a graphical design that balances visual appeal for human users with the efficiency, by providing enough complexity required for computer vision algorithms for identification and tracking (see Fig. 1A). This approach ensures the textual information availability without the AR component, visual appeal, and a more coherent design with the AR component, rather than the use of abstract markers. To accommodate both Head-Mounted and Handheld modes, a unique hybrid AReader button, integrating printed and digital elements, was designed as shown in Fig. 1 and Fig. 2. This button serves as the primary interaction input for the app, activating the main functions of the Visual Screen Reader (VSR). Further details are provided in the Visual Screen Reader section.

**Head Mounted Interaction.** In head-mounted display (HMD) mode, users experience the world from a first-person perspective by looking at a stereoscopic live video stream of the physical environment, mimicking the natural perception of the real world rendered on the smartphone's display (Ballestin et al. 2018). Interaction styles are therefore adapted for this perspective. HMD users engage with the paper-based text as they would in real life, enabling natural interaction. The AReader button, distinguishable in both design and function, is visually prominent on the paper, facilitating recognition by both human and computer vision (see Fig. 1A and Fig. 2A). Its design incorporates a recognizable image pattern, part of the identified image marker. When this specific button pattern is detected, a digital overlay highlights the button, making it visually stand out. User interaction prompts the button to change color; the app then sends haptic feedback, and AR reading commences. While the haptic feedback is crucial for non-visioned users, the additional visual and auditory clues confirm the interaction for all users. Direct interaction with the paper-based text means users can initiate the VSR function by tapping the print with a hand, finger, or any physical pointer, enhancing "freedom" and flexibility in usage. This interaction style, optimized for HMD view, emphasizes natural engagement with content. It incorporates visual affordances, a printed layout that is visually distinct, and audiovisual and tactile feedback, all contributing to an intuitive user experience.

A) Activation of the Virtual Button in Head-Mounted Display (HMD) Mode

B) Activation of the Virtual Button in Handheld Mode

**Fig. 2.** A) Activation of the Virtual Button in Head-Mounted Mode by touching the paper base; B) Activation of the Virtual Button through the mobile screen in Handheld Mode.

**Handheld Interaction.** Utilizing a mobile phone, with which most users are already familiar with. However, implementing AR can introduce unique challenges. The standard interaction involves placing the paper-based text on a table and hovering over it to activate the VSR options. Since holding the phone occupies one hand, using both hands —one to hold the phone and the other to interact with the paper-based AReader button—can be difficult, as observed during testing sessions. To address this, a novel hybrid approach has been developed. This approach allows users to interact with the paper-based material directly by touching it, but they can also activate the AReader by tapping the same button through the mobile screen as shown in Fig. 2B. The button remains the same in appearance and location, following the paper-based format, and can be activated via the smartphone screen with a simple touch. This offers users flexibility and leverages intuitive smartphone interactions.

The design adapts to different screen sizes, with both portrait and landscape modes; determined by reading the device's gyroscope, ensuring better ergonomics and a comfortable grip. For users interested in audio narration, the phone screen can be turned off, and the paper base set aside to listen to the audio. However, the visual reader guidance and talking avatars provide a visual element to follow.

Testing sessions revealed that holding the phone over the paper-base can be tiresome, especially with longer text to interpret. Consequently, a Mobile view of the VSR was implemented to reduce this physical effort. This feature allows the content played by the VSR to be displayed as a regular full screen 2D video on the user's screen with a touch gesture as shown in Fig. 3C. This transformation enables users to convert paper-based text into an "audiobook" or a visual reader guide or an AI lecture seamlessly within a second. Further details are provided in the following and in the Text-to-AI-Video Narration section.

**Visual Screen Reader.** *Text-to-Audio Narration with Reading Guidance.* The Visual Screen Reader (VSR) is the foundational feature of the application, transforming paper-based text into an audiobook or a visual reading guide, similar to a karaoke machine, by highlighting the text following the synthetic speech as shown in Fig. 3A. This feature incorporates functions such as Enhanced Visibility, Auditory Access to Text, and Guided Reading Assistance (see Sect. 3.1). Accordingly, the design must be both accessible and usable, addressing the specific needs of print-disabled users. It is equipped with functionalities for text detection, user notification, control provision, and visual tracking enhancements. When users view paper-based text, either in HMD or handheld mode, they first receive a haptic notification indicating that the application has recognized the text. The textual part of the physical paper is overlaid with a sharp text render, using a sans-serif font type for better readability. The digital render provides consistent visibility regardless of lighting conditions. Upon user interaction, the VSR starts "playing" the text by interpreting it with synthetic speech, while simultaneously highlighting the sections being read, thus providing visual guidance to its users. After triggering the screen reader, the paper base is no longer needed, and the phone can also be taken away while the user consumes the content audibly.

**Fig. 3.** A) Text-to-Audio Narration with Visual Reading Guidance; B) Text-to-AI-Video Narration; C) Transition from AR to Traditional Full-Screen 2D Video

*Text-to-AI-Video Narration.* During the testing of the first versions of the VSR, it was observed that visioned users, while finding the feature useful, also perceived it as somewhat dull and unengaging. In response to this, enhancements were explored to improve the user experience for these individuals. Inspired by the work of Tang et al. (2008) and the feedback of younger generations who keenly follow celebrities and influencers as interest. Accordingly, an AI-based concept has been devised: the Text-to-AI-Video Narration feature. This approach differs from the original Text-to-Audio Narration, this feature turns paper-based text into a celebrity video lecture. It displays an AI avatar that mimics both the natural voice and appearance of a celebrity, interpreting auditory and visually with captions the printed textual content. Multiple concepts for the design and placement of these AI tutors were tested, targeting ideal positioning for both HMD and handheld users. A range of AR effects, including hologram visuals and chroma-key technology, were evaluated to enhance the user experience. These concepts were eventually narrowed down to the final concept presented here shown in Fig. 3.B and C. To increase accessibility for visioned users, captions were added to the video narration. The creation of the AI video content involved online tools such as ParrotAI ("Parrot Ai," 2024) and Kapwing ("Kapwing," 2024).

**Magnification.** Various methods have been explored to implement magnification. Drawing inspiration from previous work of Stearns et al. (2018), a more intuitive and effortless approach was developed to minimize the need for complex interactions. The visibility of the paper-based text is enhanced by overlaying it with a digital AR render that remains sharp and visible. Leveraging the AR render of the text, a natural zoom interaction has been adapted. In HMD mode, when users lean closer to the target, the text remains sharp, clear, and becomes magnified (Fig. 4A). A similar effect is achieved in handheld mode, where users can magnify the text on the smartphone screen by simply bringing the phone closer to the printed material. This approach allows for an effortless and intuitive zooming experience, enhancing the readability of the text.

**Fig. 4.** A) Natural Magnification (Zoom) function; B) Digital mode, using image file on a pc screen in Handheld mode.

**Digital Mode.** AReader's functionality is not dependent on the specific nature of the target material (paper-base), but rather on the computer vision's ability to recognize and track the target. Consequently, all functionalities of the app remain accessible when the image target is displayed in a digital format, such as an image file or PDF on a digital screen. In other words, users can use AReader by opening the paper base in digital format on their laptops, tablets, or other devices without the need for the paper base as shown in Fig. 4B, promoting further flexibility in use.

**Situational and Environmental Adaptations.** Recognizing that users may operate the app in various settings, the prototype supports Bluetooth connection for headphones with active noise canceling and hearing aids. Additionally, for users in dimly lit areas, where computer vision's accuracy could be compromised, a flashlight function has been implemented. This feature assists users in navigating dark spaces, illuminating the image marker, and ensuring it remains trackable even in low-light conditions as shown in Fig. 5.

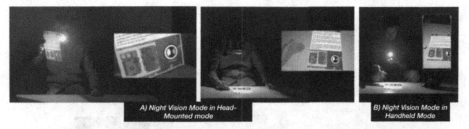

**Fig. 5.** A) Night Vision Mode in Head-Mounted mode; B) Night Vision Mode in Handheld mode

**Compatibility with Other Assistive Technologies.** The prototype is designed to integrate seamlessly with Android screen readers and voice command ATs, ensuring that visually impaired individuals can easily find and start the application using their ATs.

### 3.5 Overview of Prototype Workflow

AReader starts in handheld mode with a live camera feed that searches for text. Once it identifies the text, users receive haptic feedback and VSR is overlayed. Options include either Text-to-Audio Narration with Visual Guidance or Text-to-AI-Video. Users can manage this content (Play, Pause, Reset) using the AReader button, available both as a physical print and a digital touchscreen option. Additionally, a hamburger menu offers options to switch to Head-Mounted mode or activate the flashlight to enhance visibility as shown in Fig. 6.

### 3.6 Summative Design Validation with Users

**Participant Profile and Evaluation Procedure.** The evaluation involved 12 participants: 7 females (58.33%) and 5 males (41.67%), with ages ranging from 18 to over 65 years. The group reported diverse cognitive and visual impairments, including Dyslexia (25%), Dyscalculia (8.33%), and various levels of visual impairments such as 2 individuals with blindness (16.67%), one with color vision deficiency (8.33%), and four mild cases (33.33%) of myopia or hyperopia. All participation was voluntary, and the data was anonymized to ensure the protection of participants' identities, adhering to ethical research standards.

Participants were initially oriented with the equipment and briefed on the research objectives and app functionalities. The interaction began in handheld mode to facilitate

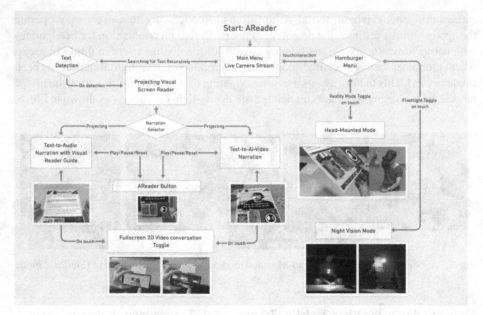

**Fig. 6.** Workflow of the AReader Prototype

exploration of interactions and controls. This was followed by mounting the smartphone in the headset for the HMD experience, with participants typically taking 3–6 min to become familiarized. Subsequently, participants task was to be engaged with the content through their preferred modalities – including text-to-audio narration, text-to-AI-video narration, head mounted, or handheld mode until they felt they learned the content about the Raspberry Pi. This learning phase typically lasted 6–10 min. After the task, participants completed an online survey, assessing user experience, and reading comprehension. In three instances, personal assistance was provided due to the inaccessibility of the online form.

**User Experience.**    All users were able to operate and receive information through the prototype, suggesting that the accessibility goals were met. Interaction preferences, however, were equally divided, with 50% of participants favoring handheld mode and the remaining 50% preferring a combination of both modes, none preferring HMD mode alone, indicating the need for adaptable AR solutions. The prototype received overly high satisfaction (8.25/10) and intuitiveness ratings (9.33/10), with low standard deviations (0.83 and 0.85, respectively), which suggests a consensus on its effectiveness and ease of use. Some participants expressed a particular fondness for specific features. One participant noted, "AI celebrities were funny as [...]. I want this on my laptop ", while another mentioned, "[...] converting text to video is awesome" as a highlight. Users with severe visual impairments rated the prototype high, however, one expressed concern about navigating through longer texts "How will this work if I want to use it on my bible? Do I need to use the phone on every page?", others mentioned the need for a currently missing feature for speech speed adjustment. On one occasion, a blind user presented the blank side of a paper to the camera. As a result, the app did not interact with the user, leading to a few second of uncertainty. This hiccup was not mentioned in the users' positive survey response. One person reported increased sweating while using the prototype, but no cyber-sickness symptoms were noted otherwise. Most participants who were wearing glasses reported comfort issues wearing the headset. Suggestions for improvement included better accommodation for glasses and enhanced VSR controls navigating through the text back and forth.

**Comprehension Assessment.** Measuring information comprehension, a six-question multiple-choice questionnaire was developed addressing various aspects of the Raspberry Pi, such as its primary purpose, development origin, size, used operating system, potential uses, and target group. Most responses were correct; however, four participants (33.33%) gave incorrect answers about the Raspberry Pi's origin and two (16.67%) made an error listing its use-cases. The positive results indicating AReader can enhance achieving information comprehension of paper-based textual content.

Overall, the prototype received positive feedback regarding user experience and intuitiveness. All participants could interact with the app and achieve learning objectives. Ergonomic and comfort issues were identified with the HMD mode. While these findings are outside our control, they highlight important considerations for the broader adoption of AR technologies.

## 4 Discussion and Conclusion

This research provided valuable insights integrating UD with AR to enhance accessible textual content consumption. Answering the primary research question, "How can Universally Designed Augmented Reality enhance accessible and usable reading experiences for users of varying skills and abilities?" The findings suggest that AReader significantly advances accessibility by incorporating assistive features and strengths of text-to-speech (Craig & Schroeder 2019; O'Malley 1995) and screen reader technologies (Oh et al. 2021; Guo et al. 2016) in one universal AR solution. All test participants, regardless of their skills, abilities were able to use the prototype and consume the paper-based textual content. Thus, the integration of AR and UD showcases AR's capability to enhance accessibility and inclusion, offering benefits to a wider array of users, not limited to those with special needs by fostering equitable use. Supporting the perspective put forth by Coughlan and Miele (2017).

### 4.1 Diverse User Preferences in Multimodal Content Accessibility

User testing with a diverse participant group yielded valuable feedback, highlighting distinct values and preferences. The Text-to-Audio Narration function, turning paper-based media into digital, was particularly appreciated by older users (50 and above) and those with severe visual impairments. This group, already dependent on assistive technologies for consuming textual content, found the feature's simple and intuitive use advantageous. In contrast, the Text-to-AI-Video Narration appealed more to younger users and those with dyslexia, finding the natural-sounding, human-like interpretations highly engaging. Notably, users with dyslexia expressed a preference for the human sounding (Craig & Schroeder 2019) and human-like AI (Tang et. al. 2008) narration over visual text guidance. This preference underscores the significance of enhancing user experience, not just accessibility, for individuals with special needs. These diverse preferences underline the critical importance of flexibility in use incorporating multiple content modalities within a single application to effectively cater to a wide range of users ensuring perceptible information.

In examining the preferences for HMD and Handheld modes, a significant divergence emerged. Concerning low physical effort 50% of users favored the handheld mode for its convenience, and 50% appreciated the flexibility of both modes. Notably, none exclusively preferred the HMD option. This trend underscores the practical and comfort challenges associated with HMDs. The process of starting the application on a mobile phone, switching to HMD mode within the app, and adjusting the headset was seen as overly complex. Additionally, users reported discomfort related to the headset's weight and the difficulty of wearing it with glasses. Some users innovatively adopted a "head mounted handheld" approach, holding the headset to their eyes without using the straps. Concerning physical comfort, one user noted increased sweating, but there were no reports of cybersickness (Martirosov et al. 2022; LaViola 2000). Indicating the reduction of the size and space for approach and use and the stationary HMD design (Szentirmai & Murano 2023), did not trigger cybersickness symptoms. Notably, all participants, including the oldest at 76, found the application to be intuitive and user-friendly. This finding reinforces the concept that AR technology, when designed with UD principles, can be accessible and easy to use for a broad spectrum of users (Björk 2009; Story 1998), regardless of their technical expertise.

## 4.2 Accessibility Beyond Special Needs

This paper asserts that the context and situation of use can render anyone susceptible to challenges in accessing textual information, a perspective on situational disabilities supported by Gjøsæter et al. (2019). Consequently, AT features, traditionally designed for individuals with special needs, can offer significant benefits to a wider population affected by the symptoms of disabilities. It is imperative to recognize that UD is not a replacement for accessibility research, design, or development. Rather, it is a complementary approach that builds upon that knowledge. For instance, AReader exemplifies this integration. Unlike conventional ATs for print disabilities such as TTS, SR, OCR scanners, AReader integrates these functionalities into a single application. This multimodal approach, encompassing audio, visual, and tactile elements, extends its utility beyond the demographic with print disabilities. Such approach not only mitigates the need for specialized hardware and software for users with special needs but also plays a crucial role in diminishing segregation and stigma among users. However, this broadened approach does not diminish the importance of focusing on users with special needs. The wealth of knowledge and techniques derived from accessibility research and traditional ATs are the cornerstones for UD. In essence, UD should be viewed as an extension, not a replacement, of the existing practice concerning users with special needs. For instance, the development of AReader drew inspiration from Mambu et al. (2019), and Stearns et al. (2018) who utilized AR for aiding blind and the visually impaired, significantly motivating this research. These innovative accessibility studies have been instrumental in the design and development of AReader.

### 4.3 Implications for Inclusive Accessibility

This study implies that AR, when integrated with UD, emerges as a potent tool for accessibility while fostering broad inclusivity. This approach encourages a reevaluation of accessibility features, shifting them from being marginalized and niche to widely recognized and mainstream, thus expanding their impact. A paradigm shift is needed in the perception of accessibility: from a feature exclusive to users with special needs to a holistic view where applications are inclusively designed for all users, eliminating segregation and stigma.

Furthermore, this research challenges the prevailing view of AR as merely a visualization or entertainment tool, highlighting its practical potential. The practical implementation of AReader can be generalized and benefit augmenting paper-based materials, as commonly used in AR books, making these resources accessible, including those with visual impairments or dyslexia. This approach is crucial for AR in educational settings, which is integral to lifelong learning and should cater to individuals with diverse abilities. By ensuring universal accessibility for AR applications, there's no need to distinguish users based on their abilities. The intuitive nature of AR has the potential to attract a wider user base, which could lead to a more diverse array of practical applications. This research serves as a blueprint for making paper-based educational AR applications more accessible, paving the way for more inclusive AR experiences in the future.

It is important to note that AReader is not a groundbreaking technological marvel. The prototype is built on a game engine and AR libraries that are nearly a decade old, thus ensuring broad device compatibility with legacy smartphones. AReader does not depend on expensive proprietary hardware. In handheld mode, it requires only a smartphone, while in head-mounted mode, it is compatible with any simple cardboard system with a camera hole. The prototype deliberately avoids the need for advanced depth sensing, Lidar sensors, or controllers, relying instead on paper, ink, and a smartphone application. This approach highlights a critical change in the barriers to mainstream AR adoption. Historically, the requirement for expensive and exotic hardware was a significant obstacle. However, the current bottleneck lies not in hardware limitations but in the scarcity of meaningful content ("PerkinsCoie," 2019), a lack of awareness about the technology's capabilities beyond the visuals, and a deficit in user-centered design in development.

Given this landscape, there is an urgent need for further research into the integration of UD with AR. Future studies should providing developers and designers with the necessary hands-on guidance and inspiration to create accessible and inclusive AR solutions. This research direction is crucial for shifting the current technological focus from hardware to designs that cater to a wider and more diverse user base.

### 4.4 Limitations

One of the primary limitations of this study is the relatively small scale of user testing, validating the final design with only 12 participants. However, the recruited user base was notably diverse, reflecting a wide spectrum of needs and preferences. The prototype and the task in converting textual information into audio and video is relatively simple, thereby enhancing the relevance and applicability and generalization of the results.

Regarding the prototype, it was tested using one paper-based concept focused on teaching about Raspberry Pi during the summative evaluation. While the design and layout of the prototype are easily adaptable for various topics and is in alignment with the architecture of typical AR-book design, this limitation must be acknowledged. Additionally, the feature for converting text to alternative media was rendered in advance, rather than in real time. This decision was made for the convenience of user testing, avoiding dependency on APIs or internet connectivity. However, for future iterations, real-time content generation should be incorporated to assess and address potential issues, such as errors in conversion. Although the current focus was on UD and conceptual development, subsequent versions of the application should explore these areas further to enhance functionality and user experience.

## 4.5 Conclusion

In conclusion, this research contributes to the fields of AR and accessibility, offering new insights and directions for the development of Universally Designed AR technologies. AReader received a highly positive reception from its users and set the groundwork for further innovations in human-computer interaction, potentially benefiting a wider spectrum of users and AR applications. As AR continues to evolve, achieving mainstream adoption, Universal Design will be crucial in ensuring that these technological advancements benefit all members of society, fostering a more inclusive and accessible digital world.

# References

Azuma, R.T.: A survey of augmented reality. Presence: Teleoperators Virt. Environ. 6(4), 355–385 (1997)

Ballestin, G., Solari, F., Chessa, M.: Perception and action in peripersonal space: A comparison between video and optical see-through augmented reality devices. In: 2018 IEEE International Symposium on Mixed and Augmented Reality Adjunct (ISMAR-Adjunct), pp. 184–189. IEEE (2018)

Billinghurst, M., Clark, A., Lee, G.: A survey of augmented reality. Foundat. Trends® Hum.–Comput. Interact. 8(2–3), 73–272 (2015)

Björk, E.: Many become losers when the Universal Design perspective is neglected: exploring the true cost of ignoring Universal Design principles. Technol. Disabil. 21(4), 117–125 (2009)

Coughlan, J. M., Miele, J.: AR4VI: AR as an accessibility tool for people with visual impairments. In: 2017 IEEE International Symposium on Mixed and Augmented Reality (ISMAR-Adjunct), pp. 288–292. IEEE (2017)

Craig, S.D., Schroeder, N.L.: Text-to-speech software and learning: investigating the relevancy of the voice effect. J. Educ. Comput. Res. 57(6), 1534–1548 (2019)

Darzentas, J., Miesenberger, K.: Design for all in information technology: a universal concern. In: International Conference on Database and Expert Systems Applications, pp. 406–420. Springer , Berlin Heidelberg (2005). https://doi.org/10.1007/11546924_40

Evans, G., Blenkhorn, P.: Screen readers and screen magnifiers. In: Assistive Technology for Visually Impaired and Blind People, pp. 449–495 (2008)

Eikvil, L.: Optical Character Recognition. J. Vis. Impairment Blindness **84**, 507–509 (1990)

Gupta, T., Sisodia, M., Fazulbhoy, S., Raju, M., Agrawal, S.: Improving accessibility for dyslexic impairments using augmented reality. In: 2019 International Conference on Computer Communication and Informatics (ICCCI), pp. 1–4. IEEE (2019)

Guo, A., Chen, X. A., Qi, H., White, S., Ghosh, S., Asakawa, C., Bigham, J.P.: VizLens: a robust and interactive screen reader for interfaces in the real world. In: Proceedings of the 29th Annual Symposium on User Interface Software and Technology, pp. 651–664 (2016)

Gjøsæter, T., Radianti, J., Chen, W.: Understanding situational disabilities and situational awareness in disasters. In: International Conference on Information Systems for Crisis Response and Management (2019)

Harpur, P.: Discrimination, Copyright, and Equality: Opening the e-Book for the Print-Disabled. Cambridge University Press (2017)

Herskovitz, J., Wu, J., White, S., Pavel, A., Reyes, G., Guo, A., Bigham, J. P.: Making mobile augmented reality applications accessible. In: Proceedings of the 22nd International ACM SIGACCESS Conference on Computers and Accessibility, pp. 1–14 (2020)

Islam, N., Islam, Z., Noor, N.: A survey on optical character recognition system. arXiv preprint arXiv:1710.05703 (2017)

Kanter, A.S.: The promise and challenge of the United Nations Convention on the Rights of Persons with Disabilities. Syracuse J. Int'l L. & Com. **34**, 287 (2006)

Kapwing AI Video Editor, https://www.kapwing.com/ai, (Accessed 31 Jan 2024)

LaViola, J.J., Jr.: A discussion of cybersickness in virtual environments. ACM Sigchi Bull. **32**(1), 47–56 (2000)

Lerblance, P.: Introducing the Americans with Disabilities Act: Promises and Challenges. USFL Rev. **27**, 149 (1992)

Mambu, J. Y., Anderson, E., Wahyudi, A., Keyeh, G., Dajoh, B.: Blind reader: an object identification mobile-based application for the blind using augmented reality detection. In: 2019 1st International Conference on Cybernetics and Intelligent System (ICORIS), vol. 1, pp. 138–141. IEEE (2019)

Martirosov, S., Bureš, M., Zítka, T.: Cyber sickness in low-immersive, semi-immersive, and fully immersive virtual reality. Virt. Real. **26**(1), 15–32 (2022)

Naranjo-Puentes, S., Escobar-Velásquez, C., Vendome, C., Linares-Vásquez, M.: A preliminary study on accessibility of augmented reality features in mobile apps. In: 2022 IEEE International Conference on Software Analysis, Evolution and Reengineering (SANER), pp. 454–458. IEEE (2022)

Nielsen, J., Landauer, T.K.: A mathematical model of the finding of usability problems. In: Proceedings of the INTERACT 1993 and CHI 1993 Conference on Human factors in Computing Systems, pp. 206–213 (1993)

O'Malley, M. H.: Text-to-speech conversion technology. In: Readings in Human–Computer Interaction, pp. 539–545. Morgan Kaufmann (1995)

Oh, U., Joh, H., Lee, Y.: Image accessibility for screen reader users: a systematic review and a road map. Electronics **10**(8), 953 (2021)

Parrot Ai Celebrity Voice Generator. https://www.tryparrotai.com/, (Accessed 31 Jan 2024)

PerkinsCoie 2019 VR/AR Survey Report. https://www.perkinscoie.com/images/content/2/1/v2/218679/2019-VR-AR-Survey-Digital-v1.pdf, (Accessed 31 Jan 2024)

Power, C., Freire, A., Petrie, H., Swallow, D.: Guidelines are only half of the story: accessibility problems encountered by blind users on the web. In: Proceedings of the SIGCHI Conference on Human Factors in Computing Systems, pp. 433–442 (2012)

Shaywitz, S.E.: Dyslexia. N. Engl. J. Med. **338**(5), 307–312 (1998)

Stearns, L., Findlater, L., Froehlich, J. E.: Design of an augmented reality magnification aid for low vision users. In: Proceedings of the 20th International ACM SIGACCESS Conference on Computers and Accessibility, pp. 28–39 (2018)

Story, M.F.: Maximizing usability: the principles of universal design. Assist. Technol. **10**(1), 4–12 (1998)

Stylianidou, N., Sofianidis, A., Manoli, E., Meletiou-Mavrotheris, M.: "Helping Nemo!"—Using augmented reality and alternate reality games in the context of universal design for learning. Educ. Sci. **10**(4), 95 (2020)

Szentirmai, A. B., Murano, P.: New universal design heuristics for mobile augmented reality applications. In: International Conference on Human-Computer Interaction, pp. 404–418. Springer Nature Switzerland (2023). https://doi.org/10.1007/978-3-031-48041-6_27

Tang, H., Fu, Y., Tu, J., Hasegawa-Johnson, M., Huang, T.S.: Humanoid audio–visual avatar with emotive text-to-speech synthesis. IEEE Trans. Multimedia **10**(6), 969–981 (2008)

IAPB Vision Atlas. https://www.iapb.org/learn/vision-atlas, (Accessed 31 Jan 2024)

Unity 2017.4.40. https://unity.com/releases/editor/whats-new/2017.4.40, (Accessed 31 Jan 2024)

Vuforia Library - Getting Started with Vuforia Engine in Unity. https://library.vuforia.com/articles/Training/getting-started-with-vuforia-in-unity.html#about, (Accessed 31 Jan 2024)

Virgili, G., Acosta, R., Bentley, S. A., Giacomelli, G., Allcock, C., Evans, J.R.: Reading aids for adults with low vision. Cochrane Database System. Rev. (4) (2018)

Walker, Z., McMahon, D.D., Rosenblatt, K., Arner, T.: Beyond Pokémon: Augmented reality is a universal design for learning tool. SAGE Open **7**(4), 2158244017737815 (2017)

Wessel, D., Kennecke, A. K., Heine, M.: WCAG and dyslexia—Improving the search function of websites for users with dyslexia (without making it worse for everyone else). In: Proceedings of Mensch und Computer 2021, pp. 168–179 (2021)

Wobbrock, J.O.: Situationally-induced impairments and disabilities. In: Web Accessibility: A Foundation for Research, pp. 59–92 (2019)

# Attention and Sensory Processing in Augmented Reality: Empowering ADHD Population

Shiva Ghasemi$^{(\boxtimes)}$ ⓘ, Majid Behravan ⓘ, Sunday D. Ubur ⓘ,
and Denis Gračanin ⓘ

Virginia Tech, Blacksburg, VA 24060, USA
{shivagh,behravan,uburs,gracanin}@vt.edu

**Abstract.** The brain's attention system is a complex and adaptive network of brain regions that enables individuals to interact effectively with their surroundings and perform complex tasks. This system involves the coordination of various brain regions, including the prefrontal cortex and the parietal lobes, to process and prioritize sensory information, manage tasks, and maintain focus. In this study, we investigate the intricate mechanisms underpinning the brain's attention system, followed by an exploration within the context of augmented reality (AR) settings. AR emerges as a viable technological intervention to address the multifaceted challenges faced by individuals with Attention Deficit Hyperactivity Disorder (ADHD). Given that the primary characteristics of ADHD include difficulties related to inattention, hyperactivity, and impulsivity, AR offers tailor-made solutions specifically designed to mitigate these challenges and enhance cognitive functioning. On the other hand, if these ADHD-related issues are not adequately addressed, it could lead to a worsening of their condition in AR. This underscores the importance of employing effective interventions such as AR to support individuals with ADHD in managing their symptoms. We examine the attentional mechanisms within AR environments and the sensory processing dynamics prevalent among the ADHD population. Our objective is to comprehensively address the attentional needs of this population in AR settings and offer a framework for designing cognitively accessible AR applications.

**Keywords:** Accessibility · ADHD · Attention · Augmented reality · Neurodiversity

## 1 Introduction

The definition of attention describes it as a limited resource for information processing [55]. Consider an attentionally demanding activity such as driving, a complex task that demands high levels of attention for safety and efficiency. Driving necessitates the adept handling of multiple cognitive processes: selecting what to focus on, maintaining concentration on critical tasks, managing distractions, and dividing attention among various inputs like traffic conditions, navigation, and vehicle control. Additionally, the ability to sustain vigilance, especially during prolonged periods of monotonous driving, is crucial [56].

Attention acts as a selective filter, enabling us to focus on relevant information while ignoring distractions, thus facilitating cognitive functions such as memory, learning, and decision-making. However, for individuals ADHD, this filtering process is impaired, leading to difficulties in maintaining focus, managing impulses, and organizing tasks. ADHD is a prevalent neurobehavioral condition affecting both children and adults worldwide. It is estimated that up to 5% of adults and between 6 to 9% of children and adolescents suffer from ADHD [1], making it a significant concern for public health and individual well-being. This disorder is characterized by a trio of symptoms: inattention, hyperactivity, and impulsivity, with inattention being a core feature [47] that disrupts social, academic, and occupational functions [22]. Individuals with ADHD have difficulty staying focused [53], following detailed instructions, and organizing tasks. They may also be easily distracted by irrelevant thoughts or stimuli, and often forget to complete tasks or responsibilities.

AR can intervene and provide support for attention in several innovative ways, including enhancing focus, engagement, and learning through the strategic use of digital augmentations [26]. By leveraging visual and auditory cues that blend seamlessly with the real-world environment, AR has the potential to direct the attention of individuals with ADHD towards specific tasks or information, aiding in sustained and selective attention. Little is known about sustained attention performance of adults with ADHD in AR settings. This targeted approach is particularly beneficial in mitigating the challenges associated with attention deficit by helping users prioritize sensory and cognitive processing without becoming overwhelmed. The four principles of attention-select, focus, divide, and sustain-are integral to the effective design and use of AR technologies. In practice, AR applications balance the presentation of digital augmentations, such as pop-up notifications or virtual objects, with the user's awareness of the real-world environment. This balance is critical to ensuring safe and effective interaction, as a lapse in attention could result in missed information or failure to notice real-world obstacles.

However, as AR applications becomes widespread, they raises concerns regarding sensory overload, a condition that occurs when an individual's sensory systems are bombarded with more information than they can process, leading to cognitive overload and an overwhelming sensation. The engagement of multiple sensory modalities in AR-visual, auditory, and sometimes haptic feedback-intensifies the risk of increasing the cognitive load on users. This potential for sensory overload underscores the importance of careful design in AR technologies, aiming to enrich the user experience without overwhelming their sensory processing capabilities. Therefore, we tackle ADHD challenges with a design approach to improve attention and daily function, offering key insights for developing inclusive AR solutions for this demographic.

The structure of this paper is organized as follows: Sect. 2 reviews related literature, summarizing interventions within the AR domain, including eye-tracking, brain-computer interface (BCIs) technology, and prevalent machine learning algorithms. Section 3 presents our conceptual framework, detailing the mechanisms of cognition and perception. In Sect. 4, the challenges faced by individuals with ADHD are discussed, along with corresponding AR interventions and solutions. Section 5 introduces our design proposal, and Sect. 6 provides the concluding remarks of the paper.

## 2    Related Works

The adoption of AR technology within ADHD research is garnering significant interest [6,10,24,45,49,52]. AR interventions present a promising strategy for ADHD, utilizing immersive experiences to enhance engagement and motivation. Offering real-time, personalized feedback and adaptable simulations, they facilitate skill training and behavior modification. This method suits ADHD individuals, potentially improving attention and learning outcomes. Yet, efficacy varies with symptom severity, personal preferences, and technological flexibility. Challenges remain in assessing long-term impacts, preventing over-reliance, and overcoming cost and access barriers to ensure equitable use.

### 2.1    AR Interventions for ADHD

AR's potential to improve social interaction, communication skills, and attention in children and adolescents with ADHD has been particularly promising [49]. This is further supported by Kaimara's exploration, which underscores AR's emerging role as an effective treatment approach, especially when coupled with cutting-edge technologies [25]. Additionally, AR introduces a novel dimension of flexibility and practicality by incorporating therapeutic light settings into users' daily routines, offering an innovative avenue for continuous light-based interventions [41]. Importantly, AR's capacity to enrich the real world with essential information addresses sensory impairments effectively [6,10,24,54]. While its application as an educational tool for children with special needs, including those with ADHD, highlights its interactive and immersive capabilities in facilitating ADHD management in pediatric settings [52].

Extending the scope of AR's impact, innovative approaches have combined AR with ADHD interventions to enhance social interactions [45]. AR's association with positive outcomes in ADHD contexts includes enhancements in behavior, cognitive function, and dual-tasking abilities in children [46]. Additionally, AR has been proposed as a valuable tool for enhancing specific cognitive skills, such as reading and spelling, through dedicated literacy programs for children with ADHD [51]. The development of AR serious games (ARGS) aims to train focused and selective attention in children with ADHD [3]. Research has also explored inattentional blindness [56] and attentional tunneling [50], examining cross-modality attention in AR, highlighting its comprehensive benefits in addressing ADHD-related challenges and showcasing its potential as a versatile intervention tool.

Research demonstrates AR's potential in enhancing literacy, specifically improving reading and spelling in children with ADHD [51], by offering tailored educational interventions. Further, AR's role extends to boosting memory recall in educational contexts, suggesting significant benefits for ADHD-related cognitive processes and information retention [58]. Game-based AR interventions have also shown to engage children with ADHD effectively, increasing satisfaction and potentially improving quality of life, while also strengthening crucial cognitive aspects [29]. These studies collectively underscore AR's versatility in addressing diverse challenges associated with ADHD, from literacy gaps to enhancing memory and cognitive engagement.

## 2.2 Visual Attention in Eye-Tracking

Eye tracking is a pivotal method for gauging where overt attention is directed, marking observable shifts in focus like gaze changes, in contrast to covert attention's internal shifts without eye movement [18]. This distinction aids in comprehending attention's role across various scenarios, including visual perception and spatial cognition. Leveraging eye-tracking technology, recent studies have probed the dynamics of how attention is oriented and maintained on particular stimuli, such as faces [36]. Eye movements, driven by visual-spatial attention, offer a direct measure of the direction and speed of attention in response to stimuli [59].

In practical terms, eye tracking is invaluable for analyzing attention-related behaviors in ADHD, revealing unique eye movement patterns like diminished fixation on faces and irregular scan paths [40]. Computerized eye-tracking training has been effective in improving saccadic movements and inhibitory control in ADHD, showcasing its potential for intervention [35]. Moreover, in the realm of e-learning, eye tracking supports customized educational strategies for ADHD, enhancing learning outcomes [27]. This technology's application underscores its significance in both understanding and addressing attention-related challenges, particularly within ADHD populations.

## 2.3 Attention in Brain-Computer Interfaces

Attention plays a pivotal role in Brain-Computer Interfaces (BCIs) research, influencing both the performance and applicability of BCIs across different domains. Electroencephalography (EEG), a non-invasive technique for monitoring brain activity, is instrumental in evaluating attention, particularly within AR environments. Studies have explored the use of EEG and eye tracking to distinguish between focused and divided attention in individuals wearing AR headsets, showing the capability of these technologies to monitor attention levels [33]. Moreover, EEG has revealed increased engagement and attention during AR tasks, marked by enhanced brain activity [37]. In the context of ADHD, multimedia interventions have been assessed through EEG, demonstrating improved attentional focus, as indicated by decreased theta wave activity [34]. Additionally, ethical considerations in BCI research are gaining attention, highlighting the importance of thorough evaluation and refinement of BCIs to enhance performance while addressing ethical implications.

## 2.4   Attention in Machine Learning

Machine learning (ML) algorithms are gaining traction for their role in AR interventions for ADHD, showcasing their capability in identifying and classifying the disorder through advanced neuroimaging techniques like MRI [15,17]. Research employing ML on extensive ADHD datasets has proven its effectiveness in the accurate identification and classification of ADHD, further supported by the achievement of detection accuracies up to 85.45% [11,15]. This highlights ML's significant potential in refining ADHD diagnosis and treatment strategies.

ML algorithms have been crafted for distinguishing ADHD from non-ADHD children using EEG signals, showcasing ML's broad applicability in ADHD diagnosis [39]. Further, ML aids in differentiating ADHD subtypes, assisting clinicians in timely patient identification [38]. Its application extends to accurately distinguishing between autism and ADHD, demonstrating ML's versatility in identifying neurodevelopmental disorders [13]. Moreover, ML's role in ADHD classification has evolved towards creating diagnostic tools incorporating VR and deep learning, highlighting innovative approaches in ADHD diagnostics [51,57]. Additionally, a Gaussian SVM-based ML model focusing on linear EEG features has proven effective in ADHD detection in clinical settings, demonstrating high accuracy and underscoring ML's role in early diagnosis and treatment. This approach emphasizes ML's capacity to improve diagnostic precision while minimizing computational demands through extensive data sets and stringent validation processes [2].

A cutting-edge EEG signal analysis method enhances ADHD detection by integrating Variational Mode Decomposition (VMD) with Hilbert Transform (HT). This approach refines the extraction and analysis of EEG rhythms-delta, theta, alpha, beta, and gamma-improving accuracy. By calculating entropy-based features from these rhythms, the technique assesses its efficiency in differentiating ADHD from non-ADHD subjects. Notably, the Extreme Learning Machine (ELM) classifier exhibits exceptional sensitivity, accuracy, and specificity in this context. The innovative VHERS model, as a result, stands out for its automatic ADHD detection capabilities, marking a substantial progress over previous methods and underscoring its applicability in real-time scenarios [28].

## 3   Conceptual Framework

Designing a context-aware AR system for ADHD necessitates a comprehensive integration of sensor technology, machine learning, and multimodal engagement strategies to dynamically adapt to an individual's environment and activity patterns. This approach ensures the system can effectively direct the user's attention towards relevant physical and virtual objects, enhancing engagement and seamlessly incorporating technology into daily life as suggested by Biocca et al. [7].

By leveraging advanced sensors and machine learning algorithms, the system gains a deep understanding of the user's context, including movement and environmental conditions, to select the most suitable modality-whether visual, auditory, or tactile-for engaging the user. This adaptive mechanism, underscored by a multidisciplinary approach that combines user experience design with robust data security, aims to tailor AR experiences to the unique needs of individuals with ADHD, minimizing sensory overload and enhancing cognitive functions.

Sensor integration, including accelerometers, gyroscopes, and GPS, provides valuable data on user orientation, motion patterns, and precise location tracking. Additionally, computer vision techniques through camera feeds offer insights into user movements, particularly in indoor settings where GPS may be less effective. Understanding the user's environment extends to deploying environmental sensors to assess ambient conditions such as light, temperature, and noise levels. This data, combined with location-based services and advanced mapping technologies, offers a comprehensive understanding of the user's context. Machine learning models trained on this diverse data can discern intricate patterns, enhancing the system's contextual awareness.

The importance of selecting the most appropriate modality for engaging user attention through a nuanced analysis of preferences, contextual relevance, and effectiveness of past interactions, facilitated by adaptive algorithms. These algorithms adjust to user feedback and changing conditions, prioritizing auditory notifications in visually demanding situations and haptic feedback in noisy environments, ensuring responsiveness to the dynamic nature of human activity. The integration of machine learning and artificial intelligence within a robust architectural framework is crucial for processing real-time data, adapting to shifts, and learning from user behavior, while maintaining stringent data security measures to protect privacy. Additionally, the text highlights the impact of ADHD on AR cognitive and neuroergonomic aspects, advocating for adaptive AR designs that minimize sensory overload risks and enhance cognitive functions, emphasizing the need for research into sensory overload, optimal exposure durations, and tailored AR experiences for learning and problem-solving.

The development of context-aware AR systems necessitates an in-depth understanding of human information processing, particularly how attention and cognition interact within these environments. Recognizing how individuals process, interact with, and respond to information can significantly refine AR technology design, making these systems more intuitive, effective, and cognitively compatible. This exploration into the nuances of attention-its influence on memory, multi-tasking, and decision-making-provides essential insights into optimizing AR experiences. By dissecting the complex dynamics of attentional mechanisms and their impact on cognitive functions, we aim to enhance AR technologies in ways that seamlessly align with human cognitive processes, thereby enriching user interaction and overall experience.

### 3.1   Human Information Processing

According to Wicken's human information processing model [56] as depicted in Fig. 1, sensory information is initially gathered through the Short-Term Sensory Store (STSS), where an abundance of environmental stimuli is received through our senses. The selection process then filters this information, guided by attention resources, to determine which stimuli will proceed to the next stage of

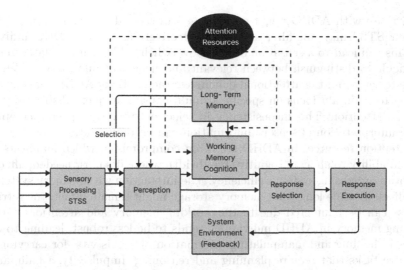

**Fig. 1.** A model of human-information processing stages [56].

processing. Once selected, this sensory input is channeled into perception, where it is interpreted, organized, and transformed into a coherent representation of the environment. Attention resources play a pivotal role throughout this process, as they allocate the cognitive bandwidth necessary to manage the flow and processing intensity of the information. Simultaneously, the model illustrates a bidirectional interaction with memory. Long-term memory provides a repository of past experiences and knowledge that can influence perception and decision-making processes. Conversely, new information can be consolidated into long-term memory for future use. Working memory serves as an active workspace where information is temporarily held and manipulated, facilitating cognitive functions such as reasoning, comprehension, and learning. Decision-making culminates in the response selection stage, where, based on the interplay of perception, memory, and cognitive evaluation, a suitable response to the stimuli is chosen. Following this, response execution occurs, wherein the selected action is carried out, whether it be a physical movement, verbal output, or another form of observable behavior. The model closes the loop with a system environment feedback component, which implies that the consequences of the executed response are observed and assessed, influencing subsequent sensory processing. This feedback mechanism ensures that cognitive processing is adaptive, allowing for the refinement of responses based on the success or failure of previous interactions with the environment. Thus, the model encapsulates a cyclical and interactive framework, demonstrating the complexity and dynamism of human information processing.

Compared to typical individuals, those with ADHD may show unique differences in their cognitive processing due to the disorder's fundamental issues related to attention, hyperactivity, and impulsivity. At the sensory processing stage, those with ADHD might experience an overload of sensory information, as their STSS may not filter stimuli as effectively as in non-ADHD individuals. This can lead to a sensation of being overwhelmed by sensory data, making it difficult to distinguish between relevant and irrelevant information. When it comes to selection, the attentional deficits characteristic of ADHD make it challenging to maintain focus on specific stimuli, causing frequent distractions and shifts in attention. This inconsistency in selection directly impacts perception, as the interpretation of sensory information can become erratic.

Attention resources in ADHD are often compromised, which manifests in a reduced ability to allocate cognitive bandwidth where it's most needed, affecting the entire processing system's efficiency. The interaction with memory systems is also affected; while long-term memory storage might remain intact, the retrieval process can be hampered due to the working memory and attentional issues. Working memory in ADHD individuals tends to be less robust, leading to difficulties in holding and manipulating information, which is vital for carrying out cognitive tasks that require planning and reasoning. Impulsivity, a hallmark of ADHD, can significantly influence response selection, leading to rapid decision-making often without full consideration of the consequences. This impulsiveness, coupled with potential hyperactivity, results in response execution that may be hasty or poorly coordinated. The actions taken might be less consistent and more variable than those of individuals without ADHD.

Ultimately, the system environment feedback, which closes the loop in cognitive processing, may not be as effective in those with ADHD. Due to the difficulties in sustaining attention and working with memory, learning from past experiences and adjusting subsequent behaviors can be challenging. Feedback may not lead to the same degree of behavioral adjustment as it might in individuals without ADHD, leading to a cycle that may not self-correct as efficiently. Interventions for ADHD typically focus on enhancing the efficiency of these cognitive processes, aiming to bolster attentional control, decrease impulsivity, and improve working memory capabilities.

## 3.2   Attention and Working Memory

Working memory (WM) and attention are crucial cognitive functions that are often affected in individuals with ADHD. Understanding how these processes occur in ADHD involves recognizing the challenges posed by the disorder and their impact on cognitive performance. WM is fundamentally about the top-down, active manipulation of data stored in short-term memory, a process central to cognitive functioning [23,30]. This cognitive system, responsible for the temporary storage and manipulation of information, is tightly interwoven with attention. The consensus in the scientific community is strong regarding the intimate linkage between WM and attention, highlighting their mutual dependence for efficient cognitive processing [4,42]. Attention not only plays a pivotal role in the entry and maintenance of information within working memory but also in the manipulation of this data, underscoring the symbiotic relationship between these two processes [14].

This interdependence is further elucidated through the dynamics of bottom-up and top-down processes; attention facilitates the initial transfer of information into working memory while also being subject to control by the contents of working memory itself, showcasing a bidirectional interaction [5,21]. Moreover, the capacity of multiple WM representations to concurrently direct attention emphasizes the complex, simultaneous control of attention by various elements within working memory [48].

Traditionally viewed as a one-way process where attention filters and allows only relevant information into short-term processing stores, the relationship between WM and selective attention is now recognized to be more nuanced [44]. The debate over the extent to which working memory influences attentional processes points to a more intricate and reciprocal interaction than previously thought, highlighting the sophistication of cognitive mechanisms at play [19]. WM deficits have been associated with the primary behavioral symptoms of ADHD, including inattention, hyperactivity, impulsivity, and the overall severity of the disorder [31].

### 3.3   Attention and Decision Making

Attention and decision-making are complex cognitive processes that are closely intertwined. Research has shown that attention plays a crucial role in guiding decision-making processes. For instance, studies have demonstrated a triple dissociation of attention and decision computations across the prefrontal cortex (PFC) [20]. This suggests that different subregions of the PFC are involved in attention-guided decision-making tasks. Furthermore, covert attention has been found to lead to faster and more accurate decision-making, highlighting the importance of attention in decision processes [43]. Additionally, the visual environment has been identified as a fundamental aspect of everyday decisions, with attention being a key factor in this process [8]. However, impulsive and risky decision-making are associated with ADHD [12]. Research has shown that individuals with ADHD exhibit suboptimal and inconsistent temporal decision-making, as well as risky decision-making, indicating a link between ADHD symptoms and decision-making inconsistencies [16]. The inclination towards risky decision-making in the ADHD population include difficulties with executive functioning, such as planning, inhibition control, and working memory, all of which are crucial for thoughtful decision-making. The exploration of risky decision-making within the ADHD demographic has yet to be thoroughly investigated. This gap in research presents an opportunity for scholars to delve deeper into the safety aspects of AR and its implications for individuals with ADHD.

### 3.4   Multi Task Attention

Attention and multitasking are critical cognitive functions that influence academic outcomes, particularly in individuals with ADHD, who often face challenges in managing multiple tasks simultaneously due to difficulties in sustaining attention and handling competing cognitive demands [31]. Digital interventions targeting ADHD have demonstrated improvements in attention, inhibition, and working memory, suggesting that such approaches can mitigate multitasking deficits in affected individuals [32]. Despite these advancements, the impact of technologies like VR on cognitive overload and attention spans in ADHD remains unclear, with research including that by Kaimara et al., indicating the need for further investigation into the relationship between ADHD and immersive technologies like AR and VR [25]. This highlights the potential of targeted interventions while also acknowledging the complexities of technology's effects on cognitive functions in ADHD.

## 4   Attention Guiding Mechanisms

Researchers have not yet agreed on how to best guide attention in immersive environments, though AR serious games and neurofeedback stand out as effective techniques. This opens a door to investigate enhancing attention via innovative methods like 3D UIs and adaptive context-aware technologies. This gap presents an opportunity to explore how attention can be enhanced through innovative approaches such as 3D user interfaces (UIs) and context-aware technologies. based on our literature review, several key features and considerations are paramount to ensure its effectiveness and accessibility, as depicted in Table 1. It is important to mention that, after conducting our research on a large scale and validating our proof of concept, this table will be updated to become more comprehensive.

**Table 1.** Challenges associated with ADHD and corresponding AR interventions.

| ADHD Challenges | AR Interventions and Solutions |
| --- | --- |
| Difficulty with Sustained Attention | Attention-Enhancing Tasks or Spatial Cues: Interactive tasks that progressively increase in complexity, along with spatial cues, to cultivate longer attention spans |
| Impaired Working Memory | Enhanced Cues and Interactive Feedback: Utilize visual and auditory cues, concise and digestible interface design, real-time feedback, and strategic repetition to aid memory retention and processing |
| Increased Distractibility | Customizable Sensory Environments: Offer control over sensory inputs to minimize distractions, ensuring focus remains on relevant tasks and stimuli |
| Executive Function Challenges | Gamified Learning Experiences: Incorporate gamification to enhance cognitive flexibility, planning, and decision-making through engaging and educational content |
| Difficulty with Spatial Orientation | Adaptive Navigation Aids: Utilize individual performance metrics to tailor navigation aids in 3D spaces, enhancing spatial orientation and reducing cognitive load |

(*continued*)

**Table 1.** (*continued*)

| ADHD Challenges | AR Interventions and Solutions |
| --- | --- |
| Overreliance on Multitasking | Real-Time Feedback Systems: Provide immediate feedback to manage multitasking effectively, reinforcing task completion and smooth transitions |
| Challenges with UI and Interaction Design | Intuitive Gamified Interfaces: Develop accessible, intuitive UIs using gamification to simplify navigation and interaction, reducing cognitive strain for ADHD users |
| Motivational Fluctuations | Personalized Engagement Strategies: Employ data analytics to customize tasks and rewards according to user motivation levels, fostering sustained engagement and interest |
| Processing Speed Variabilities | Pace-Adjustable Sensory Inputs: Allow users to adjust the pace of sensory inputs, accommodating different processing speeds and reducing the risk of overwhelm |

Several challenges inherent to ADHD can impact the experience within AR. Sustained attention is often a hurdle, as AR environments demand extended focus, which can be taxing for ADHD users, leading to faster cognitive fatigue. WM impairments, common in ADHD, can make it challenging to retain and manipulate information in real-time, thereby increasing cognitive load and complicating task performance. In the context of AR, addressing working memory deficits in individuals with ADHD is crucial for optimizing their AR experience. AR applications can be designed to accommodate working memory impairments by providing visual and auditory cues to aid in memory retention and retrieval. Additionally, the design of AR interfaces should consider the limited working memory capacity of individuals with ADHD, ensuring that the information presented is concise and easily digestible. Furthermore, incorporating interactive elements and real-time feedback in AR experiences can help individuals with ADHD engage their working memory more effectively.

The rich sensory nature of AR can also introduce numerous distractions; irrelevant stimuli can divert attention from the task at hand, impeding progress. Moreover, executive function challenges in planning, decision-making, and cognitive flexibility are significant obstacles when AR simulations present complex scenarios. Spatial orientation in three-dimensional spaces is another area of difficulty, especially when environments are intricate or navigation aids are lacking. An overreliance on multitasking within AR can heighten cognitive overload and impair task efficiency due to the frequent need to shift attention. User interface and interaction design pose additional challenges; non-intuitive or complicated interfaces can be especially burdensome for individuals with ADHD who may find it difficult to learn and recall navigational procedures.

Customizable sensory inputs allow users to tailor their sensory experience to avoid overstimulation or understimulation, which is critical for those prone to sensory processing challenges. The environment incorporates attention-enhancing tasks that become progressively more complex, helping users to expand their attention spans and cognitive processing abilities gradually.

An immediate feedback system is a cornerstone of this AR environment, offering users real-time responses that are essential for reinforcing learning outcomes and encouraging positive behavior, thus fostering motivation and a sense of achievement. The content within the AR is both educational and engaging; it leverages gamification techniques to maintain user interest and facilitate skill development and learning. Moreover, the use of data analytics is instrumental in personalizing the experience; by analyzing individual performance metrics, the environment adjusts task difficulty and types, thereby delivering a tailored and effective learning journey. These integrated features collectively aim to present an innovative educational tool designed specifically for the ADHD community, with the potential to markedly improve attentional control and learning outcomes.

Motivational fluctuations, often associated with ADHD, can affect user engagement with AR tasks, particularly if the environment lacks immediate feedback or rewards, potentially leading to reduced involvement and higher cognitive strain. Lastly, variabilities in processing speed may influence the ability of ADHD users to swiftly comprehend and respond to stimuli within AR simulations, which can result in feelings of overwhelm or frustration. These challenges necessitate careful design and consideration to ensure AR environments are accessible and supportive for users with ADHD (Fig. 2).

## 5   Design

Our study introduces a novel design concept that applies the SEEV model within an AR setting, specifically tailored to meet the varied requirements of individuals with ADHD. The SEEV model, recognized for its predictive capabilities in visual

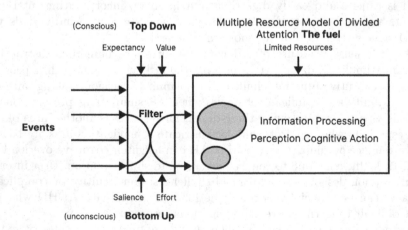

**Fig. 2.** SEEV model in design [56].

attention [56], incorporates four key factors-Salience, Effort, Expectancy, and Value-that are instrumental in the design of effective 3D UIs. By assessing the visual prominence of UI elements (Salience), the physical or cognitive exertion required to interact with them (Effort), the likelihood of encountering important information (Expectancy), and the perceived benefit of the interaction (Value), the model provides a comprehensive framework for managing and directing user attention. In Fig. 3, a pipeline of our work depicted our design system that begins with the application of the SEEV model to enhance situational awareness within an AR domain. Following the SEEV model, we implement our prototype in Apple Vision Pro headset, equipped with built-in eye-tracking technology used to collect eye tracking data to analyze complex patterns of fixations and saccades in relation to the visual stimuli and tasks can help distinguish between top-down and bottom-up attention influences.

AR prototype needs to accommodate a spectrum of ADHD types -categorized as low, medium, and high. This differentiation is essential to tailor the AR experience to the unique attentional capacities of each group. To this end, the prototype encompasses a triad of dual-task scenarios, each crafted to evaluate multitasking proficiency through the deployment of varied sensory modalities. The first scenario focuses on information retrieval, wherein participants are engaged in auditory information processing-such as listening to a lecture-while concurrently utilizing AR technology to search for specific information. The second scenario encompasses dynamic navigation, challenging participants to traverse a physical milieu whilst managing digital interactions, exemplified by holding a conversation or responding to virtual notifications through the AR interface. The third scenario is a collaborative endeavor, wherein participants engage in a live group discussion while processing textual information, such as reading an email, via the AR display.

Following task identification, eye-tracking technology is employed to collect data from participants engaged in these tasks. A particular emphasis is placed on including a substantial cohort of individuals diagnosed with ADHD, alongside a control group, to facilitate a comparative analysis. The setup for data collection is standardized, ensuring consistency across various tasks and participant experiences. This phase is critical for capturing the nuanced eye movement patterns that signify attentional engagement or distraction.

Prior to analysis, the collected eye-tracking data undergo a rigorous preprocessing phase. This includes the removal of noise, correction of data drifts, and addressing missing data points, ensuring the integrity of the dataset for feature extraction. Relevant features, such as fixation duration, saccade movements, and blink rate, are identified and extracted. These features are posited to be indicative of focused attention and are thus critical for the subsequent classification phase.

The core of our methodology involves employing Support Vector Machines (SVM) for the classification of preprocessed eye-tracking data. This process begins with a careful selection of features that robustly indicate attention patterns. The SVM model is then trained with a subset of this data, with model

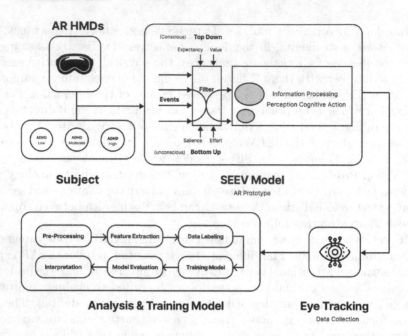

**Fig. 3.** Conceptual framework.

optimization undertaken to enhance accuracy and reliability through hyperparameter tuning. Validation of the model is conducted using a separate dataset, with performance evaluated through standard metrics such as accuracy, precision, recall, and F1 score.

The SVM algorithm is used from the scikit-learn library, a widely utilized machine learning toolkit in Python, to develop a classification model for our eye tracking data. The initial phase of our approach involved preparing the dataset, which was followed by the training of an SVM model to categorize each coordinate pair (x, y) into one of three categories: Area 1, Area 2, or neither. The feature set comprised the (x, y) coordinates, utilized to ascertain the focal area of the user. To effectively accomplish this, it was imperative to delineate the boundaries for Areas 1 and 2. For the sake of simplicity, we postulated that these areas could be approximated by rectangles, although more complex shapes could be considered depending on specific requirements. Additionally, certain data points, referred to as "pert area" points, were identified as either outliers or points of specific interest, necessitating further clarification regarding their role in the analysis of eye tracking.

During the data preparation phase, we assigned labels to the data contingent upon their designated areas: points within the confines of Area 1 received a label of 1, those within Area 2 were labeled 2, and points outside both areas were labeled 0. In terms of feature selection, we considered the x and y coordinates as primary features. The duration of gaze, represented by the 'time' attribute, was also evaluated as a potential feature, given its possible influence on classification outcomes. For model training, we utilized scikit-learn's Support Vector Classification (SVC), opting for the Radial Basis Function (RBF) kernel. The RBF kernel was selected due to its proven efficacy in managing non-linear data separations and intricate patterns, a common characteristic in eye tracking data where the subjects of interest, such as text and faces, do not manifest as linearly separable clusters in the feature space. Parameter selection was guided by existing literature, setting the regularization parameter C to a range of {26.5, 26.75, 27, 27.25, 27.5, 27.75, 28}. This decision was based on a study that identified optimal ranges for this parameter [9]. Similarly, the gamma parameter for the 'rbf' kernel was set to $\gamma = \{2^{-14.5}, 2^{-14.75}, 2^{-15}, 2^{-15.25}, 2^{-15.5}, 2^{-15.75}, 2^{-16}\}$, with the highest classification accuracy achieved at $C = 27$ and $\gamma = 2^{-15}$, indicating that such methodological approaches could be beneficial for optimizing parameters in eye tracking data classification.

In the final stage of model prediction and analysis, we leveraged the trained model to determine the focal area for each time point, allowing us to quantify the total duration spent focusing on each area, thus facilitating a comprehensive understanding of user engagement with the designated areas. Analysis of the SVM classification results enables the identification of distinct patterns of visual fixation and attention distribution, particularly among individuals with ADHD. These patterns offer unprecedented insights into the attentional dynamics facilitated by AR technology, highlighting differences and similarities in attention engagement compared to the control group. The findings of this research not only contribute to the academic understanding of ADHD in the context of emerging technologies but also offer practical implications for the design of AR experiences. Recommendations are provided for creating AR environments that are cognizant of the attentional needs of individuals with ADHD, potentially enhancing their engagement and learning outcomes. Furthermore, this study opens avenues for future research, suggesting the exploration of alternative machine learning models and the investigation of different cognitive tasks within AR settings.

Our pilot study has yielded promising initial findings regarding the use of AR technologies to aid individuals with ADHD in managing their attention. The study engaged a select group of individuals from the ADHD community, employing a prototype to demonstrate the potential of AR in facilitating attention management. Acknowledging the constraints imposed by the small sample size, we plan to expand our research to include a more diverse group of participants. The subsequent phase of the study will incorporate statistical analysis methods such as the t-Test and ANOVA, in conjunction with NASA Task Load Index (NASA-TLX), System Usability Scale (SUS), and User Experience Questionnaire (EUQ) questionnaires, aiming to compile a comprehensive dataset. This enriched dataset is expected to yield more precise and generalizable insights, deepening our understanding of how different ADHD groups allocate visual attention in AR environments. The findings from this research are projected to be instrumental in shaping the development of AR experiences that are finely tuned to meet the varied cognitive needs of users.

Additionally, the investigation aims to unearth patterns in eye movement and fixation data, which are instrumental in the creation of AR applications that are finely tuned to the attentional requirements of the ADHD population. By doing so, we strive to amplify their proficiency in managing attentional resources amidst multifaceted scenarios. The research identifies a conspicuous void in the current landscape-the absence of a design model adept at pinpointing the most conducive layout within immersive environments. Addressing this need is imperative, given that cognitive processes exhibit substantial variability across individuals. The quantity of information presented and its strategic placement are pivotal considerations that directly impact user satisfaction and efficacy.

## 6  Conclusion

We introduced a novel approach to enhance situational awareness in AR applications, particularly for individuals with ADHD. We identified a few gaps in current research when SEEV model have not been explored yet in AR domain for ADHD population. We proposed a comprehensive data-driven strategy, employing advanced eye-tracking technology and machine learning techniques, to scrutinize visual attention mechanisms. By conducting this research with a larger and diverse ADHD population, the study anticipates a robust foundation for further development in AR technologies. This research not only addresses a significant gap by exploring the nuances of attention management among individuals with ADHD in AR settings but also sets the stage for future developments in AR technology applications for educational, therapeutic, and recreational purposes for individuals with diverse cognitive profiles.

## References

1. Adams, R., Finn, P., Moes, E., Flannery, K., Rizzo, A.S.: Distractibility in attention/deficit/hyperactivity disorder (ADHD): the virtual reality classroom. Child Neuropsychol. **15**(2), 120–135 (2009)
2. Alim, A., Imtiaz, M.: Automatic identification of children with ADHD from EEG brain waves. Signals **4**(1), 193–205 (2023). https://doi.org/10.3390/signals4010010
3. Avila-Pesantez, D., Rivera, L.A., Vaca-Cardenas, L., Aguayo, S., Zuñiga, L.: Towards the improvement of ADHD children through augmented reality serious games: preliminary results. In: 2018 IEEE Global Engineering Education Conference (EDUCON), pp. 843–848. IEEE (2018)
4. Awh, E., Jonides, J., Reuter-Lorenz, P.A.: Rehearsal in spatial working memory. J. Exp. Psychol. Hum. Percept. Perform. **24**(3), 780 (1998)
5. Beck, V., Hollingworth, A., Luck, S.J.: Simultaneous control of attention by multiple working memory representations. Psychol. Sci. (2012). https://doi.org/10.1177/0956797612439068
6. Bimber, O., Raskar, R.: Spatial Augmented Reality: Merging Real and Virtual Worlds. CRC Press, Boca Raton (2005)

7. Biocca, F., Tang, A., Owen, C., Xiao, F.: Attention funnel: omnidirectional 3D cursor for mobile augmented reality platforms. In: Proceedings of the SIGCHI Conference on Human Factors in Computing Systems. CHI '06, pp. 1115–1122. Association for Computing Machinery, New York, NY, USA (2006). https://doi.org/10.1145/1124772.1124939, https://doi-org.ezproxy.lib.vt.edu/10.1145/1124772.1124939

8. Braver, T.S.: The variable nature of cognitive control: a dual mechanisms framework. Trends Cogn. Sci. **16**(2), 106–113 (2012)

9. Budiman, F.: SVM-RBF parameters testing optimization using cross validation and grid search to improve multiclass classification. Sci. Visual. **11**(1), 80–90 (2019)

10. Carmigniani, J., Furht, B.: Augmented reality: an overview. In: Handbook of Augmented Reality, pp. 3–46 (2011)

11. Chen, C.C., Wu, E.H.K., Chen, Y.Q., Tsai, H.J., Chung, C.R., Yeh, S.C.: Neuronal correlates of task irrelevant distractions enhance the detection of attention deficit/hyperactivity disorder. IEEE Trans. Neural Syst. Rehabil. Eng. **31**, 1302–1310 (2023). https://doi.org/10.1109/TNSRE.2023.3241649

12. Dekkers, T.J., de Water, E., Scheres, A.: Impulsive and risky decision-making in adolescents with attention-deficit/hyperactivity disorder (ADHD): the need for a developmental perspective. Curr. Opin. Psychol. **44**, 330–336 (2022)

13. Duda, M., Ma, R., Haber, N., Wall, D.: Use of machine learning for behavioral distinction of autism and ADHD. Transl. Psychiatry **6**(2), e732–e732 (2016)

14. Eriksson, J., Vogel, E.K., Lansner, A., Bergström, F., Nyberg, L.: Neurocognitive architecture of working memory. Neuron **88**(1), 33–46 (2015)

15. Eslami, T., Almuqhim, F., Raiker, J.S., Saeed, F.: Machine learning methods for diagnosing autism spectrum disorder and attention-deficit/hyperactivity disorder using functional and structural MRI: a survey. Front. Neuroinform. 62 (2021)

16. Gabrieli-Seri, O., Ert, E., Pollak, Y.: Symptoms of attention deficit/hyperactivity disorder are associated with sub-optimal and inconsistent temporal decision making. Brain Sci. **12**(10), 1312 (2022)

17. Ghiassian, S., Greiner, R., Jin, P., Brown, M.R.: Using functional or structural magnetic resonance images and personal characteristic data to identify ADHD and autism. PLoS ONE **11**(12), e0166934 (2016)

18. Hafed, Z.M., Chen, C.Y., Tian, X.: Vision, perception, and attention through the lens of microsaccades: mechanisms and implications. Front. Syst. Neurosci. **9**, 167 (2015)

19. Han, S.W., Kim, M.S.: Do the contents of working memory capture attention? Yes, but cognitive control matters. J. Exp. Psychol. Hum. Percept. Perform. (2009). https://doi.org/10.1037/a0016452

20. Hunt, L.T., et al.: Triple dissociation of attention and decision computations across prefrontal cortex. Nat. Neurosci. **21**(10), 1471–1481 (2018)

21. Hutchinson, J.B., Turk-Browne, N.B.: Memory-guided attention: control from multiple memory systems. Trends Cogn. Sci. (2012). https://doi.org/10.1016/j.tics.2012.10.003

22. Johnson, S., Kochhar, P., Hennessy, E., Marlow, N., Wolke, D., Hollis, C.: Antecedents of attention-deficit/hyperactivity disorder symptoms in children born extremely preterm. J. Dev. Behav. Pediatrics: JDBP **37**(4), 285 (2016)

23. Jones, D., Ghasemi, S., Gračanin, D., Azab, M.: Privacy, safety, and security in extended reality: user experience challenges for neurodiverse users. In: Moallem, A. (ed.) HCII 2023. LNCS, vol. 14045, pp. 511–528. Springer, Cham (2023). https://doi.org/10.1007/978-3-031-35822-7_33

24. Joseph, J., Vinay, M., Warrier, S.: Exploring the potential of augmented reality games for managing autism and ADHD: a promising alternative approach. Research Square preprint (2023)
25. Kaimara, P., Oikonomou, A., Deliyannis, I.: Could virtual reality applications pose real risks to children and adolescents? A systematic review of ethical issues and concerns. Virtual Reality 26(2), 697–735 (2022)
26. Keshav, N.U., Vogt-Lowell, K., Vahabzadeh, A., Sahin, N.T.: Digital attention-related augmented-reality game: significant correlation between student game performance and validated clinical measures of attention-deficit/hyperactivity disorder (ADHD). Children 6(6), 72 (2019)
27. Khan, A.R., Khosravi, S., Hussain, S., Ghannam, R., Zoha, A., Imran, M.A.: Execute: exploring eye tracking to support e-learning. In: Proceedings of the 2022 IEEE Global Engineering Education Conference (EDUCON), pp. 670–676. IEEE (2022)
28. Khare, S.K., Gaikwad, N.B., Bajaj, V.: VHERS: a novel variational mode decomposition and Hilbert transform-based EEG rhythm separation for automatic ADHD detection. IEEE Trans. Instrum. Meas. 71, 1–10 (2022)
29. Kim, S.C., Lee, H., Lee, H.S., Kim, G., Song, J.H.: Adjuvant therapy for attention in children with ADHD using game-type digital therapy. Int. J. Environ. Res. Publ. Health 19(22), 14982 (2022)
30. Kofler, M.J., Soto, E.F., Fosco, W.D., Irwin, L.N., Wells, E.L., Sarver, D.E.: Working memory and information processing in ADHD: evidence for directionality of effects. Neuropsychology 34(2), 127 (2020)
31. Kofler, M.J., Spiegel, J.A., Austin, K.E., Irwin, L.N., Soto, E.F., Sarver, D.E.: Are episodic buffer processes intact in ADHD? Experimental evidence and linkage with hyperactive behavior. J. Abnorm. Child Psychol. 46, 1171–1185 (2018)
32. Kollins, S.H., et al.: A novel digital intervention for actively reducing severity of paediatric ADHD (STARS-ADHD): a randomised controlled trial. Lancet Digit. Health 2(4), e168–e178. PLoS ONE 10(9), e0137173 (2015)
33. Kosmyna, N., Wu, Q., Hu, C.Y., Wang, Y., Scheirer, C., Maes, P.: Assessing internal and external attention in AR using brain computer interfaces: A pilot study. In: 2021 IEEE 17th International Conference on Wearable and Implantable Body Sensor Networks (BSN), pp. 1–6. IEEE (2021)
34. Lee, S.H., An, J.: Quantitative EEG evaluation of multimedia intervention program for ADHD children. In: Proceedings of the 4th International Symposium on Applied Sciences in Biomedical and Communication Technologies. ISABEL '11. ACM, New York (2011). https://doi.org/10.1145/2093698.2093714
35. Lee, T.L., Yeung, M.K., Sze, S.L., Chan, A.S.: Computerized eye-tracking training improves the saccadic eye movements of children with attention-deficit/hyperactivity disorder. Brain Sci. 10(12), 1016 (2020)
36. Leppänen, J.M.: Using eye tracking to understand infants' attentional bias for faces. Child Dev. Perspect. 10(3), 161–165 (2016)
37. Lim, Z.Y., Toa, C.K., Rao, E., Sim, K.S.: Development of augmented reality based applications for brain memory training. Int. J. Robot. Autom. Sci. 5(1), 13–20 (2023)
38. Lin, I.C., Chang, S.C., Huang, Y.J., Kuo, T.B., Chiu, H.W.: Distinguishing different types of attention deficit hyperactivity disorder in children using artificial neural network with clinical intelligent test. Front. Psychol. 13, 1067771 (2023)
39. Maniruzzaman, M., Shin, J., Hasan, M.A.M., Yasumura, A.: Efficient feature selection and machine learning based ADHD detection using EEG signal. Comput. Mater. Continua 72(3) (2022)

40. Mohammadhasani, N., Caprì, T., Nucita, A., Iannizzotto, G., Fabio, R.A.: Atypical visual scan path affects remembering in ADHD. J. Int. Neuropsychol. Soc. **26**(6), 557–566 (2020)

41. Mohammadrezaei, E., Ghasemi, S., Dongre, P., Gračanin, D., Zhang, H.: Systematic review of extended reality for smart built environments lighting design simulations. IEEE Access, 1 (2024). https://doi.org/10.1109/ACCESS.2024.3359167

42. Oberauer, K.: Working memory and attention—a conceptual analysis and review. J. Cogn. **2**(1) (2019)

43. Perkovic, S., Schoemann, M., Lagerkvist, C.J., Orquin, J.L.: Covert attention leads to fast and accurate decision-making. J. Exp. Psychol. Appl. **29**(1), 78 (2023)

44. Rajsic, J., Woodman, G.F.: Do we remember templates better so that we can reject distractors better? Attent. Percept. Psychophys. (2019). https://doi.org/10.3758/s13414-019-01721-8

45. Romero-Ayuso, D., et al.: Self-regulation in children with neurodevelopmental disorders "SR-MRehab: un colegio emocionante": a protocol study. Int. J. Environ. Res. Publ. Health **17**(12), 4198 (2020)

46. Shema-Shiratzky, S., et al.: Virtual reality training to enhance behavior and cognitive function among children with attention-deficit/hyperactivity disorder: brief report. Dev. Neurorehabil. **22**(6), 431–436 (2019)

47. Sonne, T., Marshall, P., Obel, C., Thomsen, P.H., Grønbæk, K.: An assistive technology design framework for ADHD. In: Proceedings of the 28th Australian Conference on Computer-Human Interaction. OzCHI '16, pp. 60–70. ACM, New York (2016). https://doi.org/10.1145/3010915.3010925

48. Summerfield, J.J., Lepsien, J., Gitelman, D.R., Mesulam, M., Nobre, A.C.: Orienting attention based on long-term memory experience. Neuron (2006). https://doi.org/10.1016/j.neuron.2006.01.021

49. Sweileh, W.: Analysis and mapping of scientific literature on virtual and augmented reality technologies used in the context of mental health disorders (1980–2021). J. Mental Health Train. Educ. Pract. (2023)

50. Syiem, B.V., Kelly, R.M., Goncalves, J., Velloso, E., Dingler, T.: Impact of task on attentional tunneling in handheld augmented reality. In: Proceedings of the 2021 CHI Conference on Human Factors in Computing Systems, pp. 1–14. ACM, Yokohama Japan, May 2021. https://doi.org/10.1145/3411764.3445580

51. Tosto, C., et al.: Exploring the effect of an augmented reality literacy programme for reading and spelling difficulties for children diagnosed with ADHD. Virtual Reality **25**, 879–894 (2021)

52. Vahabzadeh, A., Keshav, N.U., Abdus-Sabur, R., Huey, K., Liu, R., Sahin, N.T.: Improved socio-emotional and behavioral functioning in students with autism following school-based smartglasses intervention: multi-stage feasibility and controlled efficacy study. Behav. Sci. **8**(10), 85 (2018)

53. Volkow, N.D., Swanson, J.M.: Adult attention deficit-hyperactivity disorder. N. Engl. J. Med. **369**(20), 1935–1944 (2013)

54. Wagner, D., Schmalstieg, D.: Handheld augmented reality displays. In: IEEE Virtual Reality Conference (VR 2006), pp. 321–321 (2006). https://doi.org/10.1109/VR.2006.67

55. Wickens, C.D.: The structure of attentional resources. In: Attention and Performance VIII, pp. 239–257. Psychology Press (2014)

56. Wickens, C.D., Helton, W.S., Hollands, J.G., Banbury, S.: Engineering Psychology and Human Performance, 5th edn. Routledge, New York (2021). https://doi.org/10.4324/9781003177616

57. Wiguna, T., et al.: A four-step method for the development of an ADHD-VR digital game diagnostic tool prototype for children using a DL model. Front. Psych. **11**, 829 (2020)

58. Zhang, L., Luczak, T., Smith, E., Burch, R.F., et al.: Using Microsoft Hololens to improve memory recall in anatomy and physiology: a pilot study to examine the efficacy of using augmented reality in education. J. Educ. Technol. Dev. Exchange (JETDE) **12**(1), 2 (2019)

59. Zhang, Y.B., et al.: Using eye movements in the dot-probe paradigm to investigate attention bias in illness anxiety disorder. World J. Psychiatry **11**(3), 73 (2021)

# Virtual Reality Meets Low Vision: The Development and Analysis of MagniVR as an Assistive Technology

Cem Kaya$^{(\boxtimes)}$ ⓘ, Baha Mert Ersoy$^{(\boxtimes)}$ ⓘ, and Murat Karaca$^{(\boxtimes)}$ ⓘ

Sabancı University, İstanbul 34956, Turkey
{cemkaya,bersoy,muratkaraca}@sabanciuniv.edu

**Abstract.** This study presents MagniVR, an accessibility tool designed to enhance Virtual Reality experiences for individuals with low vision. The primary objective of this study was to develop and evaluate the effectiveness of MagniVR and provide a user-friendly tool for developers. MagniVR distinguishes itself by offering a customizable digital magnification tool that assists users in navigating and interacting within 3D virtual spaces. It can be integrated seamlessly with existing VR projects through the OpenXR framework during the development and offers flexibility in terms of camera and display positions on the user's avatar. The tool's design includes a user interface for customization and a magnifier display and camera.

**Keywords:** Spatial Computing · Metaverse · Virtual Reality · Unity · 3D · HCI · UX · DX · Accessibility · Low Vision · Assistive Technology

## 1 Introduction

Virtual Reality (VR) has transformed user interactions and experiences, but as a new platform, it still lacks critical accessibility standards and tools. This shortfall excludes a substantial population from engaging with VR. The World Health Organization reports that about 3.5% of the global population (284 million) are visually impaired, and 0.5% (39 million) are legally blind, with varying degrees of residual vision (Koyuncular, 2021). Similar to established platforms like web, desk-top, and mobile, VR also requires accessibility tools. However, due to VR's 3D nature, existing tools from other platforms don't seamlessly transfer. There may be more effective methods to enhance accessibility in VR, taking advantage of its 3D aspects.[1] The absence of such features in VR has been a focus for numerous research, one notably by SeeingVR. Their study explored the impact of various accessibility tools for low vision users (Zhao et al., 2019). Among these was a head-tracked magnification lens, which improved the ease of navigating menus and reading text for users. Building on this, this project aims to develop a more customizable and user-friendly magnification tool. There were two primary objectives: first, to evaluate the effectiveness of MagniVR in a VR environment, and second, to provide other

---

[1] An extended abstract along with preliminary data was presented at the IECHCI 2023 conference.

M. Antona and C. Stephanidis (Eds.): HCII 2024, LNCS 14697, pp. 321–333, 2024.
https://doi.org/10.1007/978-3-031-60881-0_20

developers with an easy-to-integrate accessibility tool. This project involved a two-phase user study with 18 participants.

## 2 Related Work

**SeeingVR.** SeeingVR is essentially a set of tools designed to improve the accessibility of virtual reality applications for users with low vision. They conducted a study to identify the challenges faced by users with low vision in VR. SeeingVR includes 14 tools which were simulated using a Wizard of Oz technique to augment a VR application with both visual and audio feedback. They conducted a study with 11 participants with low vision to evaluate the effectiveness of SeeingVR in improving the VR experience for users with low vision. The study involved a tutorial, a virtual task session, and an app experience session. The virtual task session included three tasks: menu navigation, visual search, and target shooting. Authors also tested the robustness of SeeingVR plugin with 10 popular VR apps, and evaluated the usability of the Unity toolkit with six developers. Authors concluded that their 14 accessibility tools helped people with low vision complete tasks in VR more quickly and accurately. Furthermore, they have concluded that these accessibility tools made VR more enjoyable for people with low vision. They have also discussed that even though accessibility guidelines for 2D media are matured, currently the are no VR-specific guidelines for accessibility and the space of accessibility is underexplored, and that their work has the potential to inspire the development of general accessibility standards for VR (Zhao et al. 2019).

**CLEVR.** This study investigates the usefulness and adaptability of a virtual reality application the research team has developed, called CLEVR, for people with low vision. The researchers designed and implemented an interaction interface based on user and expert feedback, evaluated it in a user study with 18 unpaid participants with low vision. The participants completed four tasks using CLEVR and then on a desktop computer for comparison. The tasks were intended to be representative of tasks that people would have to do regularly. The results of the study showed that 13 out of 18 participants were able to complete all tasks efficiently using CLEVR, demonstrating that VR accessibility tools have the potential to aid people with low vision. The participants also reported that the revised interaction system was more suitable and provided reliable control over regular aids and screens. However, 17 out of 18 participants indicated that using CLEVR was more demanding than using a desktop computer in terms of physical and mental strain. The results of this study suggest that VR can be a suitable aid to support the individual needs of people with low vision (Hoppe et al. 2020).

**Accessible News Reading.** This research aims to explore the potential of virtual reality as a platform for accessible news reading for individuals with low vision. The authors review the current state of low-vision reading aids, including print, digital devices, and audio, and highlight the limitations of these solutions for news reading regarding individuals with low vision. They then argue that VR has unique advantages as a reading platform for low vision, including comfort, mobility, wide visual field of view, multifunctionality, multimedia capabilities, and interactivity. Based on this, the authors propose a set of different design principles and a demo for VR reading applications, such as adjustable print and text layouts, smart text contrasting, an accessibility menu, image enhancement… In conclusion, the authors argue that VR has the potential to be an effective platform for accessible news reading for low vision and argue that further research should be conducted to better utilize what this medium has to offer (Wu et al., 2021).

**VRiAssist.** In this project an eye-tracking-based visual assistance tool for individuals with visual impairments in virtual reality environments was developed. The toolkit follows the user's eyes, allowing for precise corrections with respect to their specific visual impairments. VRiAssist offers features like distortion correction, color-brightness enhancement, and adjustable magnification, which address a range of vision related challenges. User studies have demonstrated that the toolkit is effective in improving users' vision in virtual environments, further highlighting the potential for accessibility tools like VRiAssist to enhance the overall accessibility in virtual reality environments.

The study aimed to assess the impact of harnessing the 3D Nature of the Metaverse, incorporating user hand movements, and distinguishing between camera and display on the efficacy, efficiency, and user satisfaction of magnification tools in Virtual Reality. Previous magnification solutions failed to fully exploit VR's 3D potential. For instance, SeeingVR's magnifier only enlarges the field of view's center, remaining fixed to the user's head. In contrast, VRiAssist only magnifies the specific area the user is looking at. MagniVR offers a unique approach, with the magnifier attached to the user's hand, allowing for manipulation in 3D space without affecting the overall field of view. We hypothesize that this design could optimize the use of a 3D medium like VR.

## 3   MagniVR

MagniVR aims to create a more accessible virtual reality experience for individuals with low vision by assisting them in navigating through 3D space, interacting with the virtual world through a customizable digital magnification tool. MagniVR has also been designed with DX, simplicity and ease of integration in mind. Developers need to import the prefab into their own project and set up the required OpenXR references using the GUI. The implementation involves acquiring references to the subcomponents of the XR rig, which typically takes a few minutes. As such, it is designed to be an accessible and efficient solution for any VR project that utilizes the OpenXR framework. MagniVR is also open source and enables further customization if required.

MagniVR consists of two main components: the user interface for customization and control, and the magnifier, which itself includes the display of the magnified content and the camera used for magnification. The display and the camera can separately be positioned in three different locations on the body: in front of the head, on the right hand, or on the left hand, providing flexibility and customization options for users. This design approach draws inspiration from the various magnification tool form factors from pre-existing designs tailored to meet the unique needs of individuals with low vision (Fig. 1).

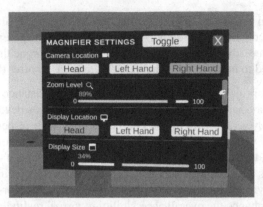

**Fig. 1.** MagniVR Control Interface

- Toggle MagniVR Button: A toggle button is available, allowing users to turn the magnifier on or off through the menu.
- Camera Location Buttons: This feature determines the location that the magnifier focuses on, enabling users to select a specific area to magnify.
- Zoom Level Slider: The user can manipulate the zoom level using the depicted slider, allowing for easy zooming in and out.
- Display Location Buttons: This feature enables users to specify the location of the display.
- Display Size Slider: The user can manipulate the display size by using the depicted slider.
- Menu Grab Bar: The gray cylinder, positioned on the right side of the menu, serves as a hold bar. Users can grasp this bar to freely move the menu around the VR environment, ensuring easy access at all times.
- Close Button: Closes the menu.

Beside these menu interactions we have added shortcuts for fast control over the tool. These shortcuts are magnifier toggle zoom in/out and menu summon. The shortcuts are determined by analyzing top VR applications and finding combinations with least button conflicts (Table 1).

**Table 1.** MagniVR Shortcuts

| Shortcuts | Left Hand | Right Hand |
|---|---|---|
| Toggle MagniVR | Press Primary and Secondary Buttons | Touch Primary and Secondary Buttons |
| Zoom in/out | Press the Joystick in while tilting it up/down | Touch Primary and Secondary Buttons |
| Summon Menu | Touch Primary and Secondary Buttons | Touch Primary and Secondary Buttons |

Moreover, the interface menu follows the user at a fixed distance while toggled on, ensuring it remains reachable even as the user moves within the VR environment, however is stationary when the user approaches the menu for closer inspection, allowing for more convenient interactions for users with low vision. The published Unity prefab accomplishes these goals. While inactive, the prefab has minimal impact on performance. Once activated, its resource usage is equivalent to a single camera and a render texture.

# 4 Evaluation

This study aims to evaluate how VR accessibility magnifiers affect the user experience for people with low vision in virtual reality environments. It also assesses the efficacy of MagniVR, especially relative to other existing tools like SeeingVR's magnification lens. From a technical standpoint, the project seeks to make the tool implementation easily accessible for developers using Unity's OpenXR toolkit. The goal of this study is to identify methods to enhance accessibility in Virtual Reality environments in an easy to integrate way.

## 4.1 Methodology

The project is divided into two phases. In the initial phase of the project, a basic prototype version of this tool was created and tested. The test consisted of 3 task groups, each group having 3 challenges. Each participant had to complete all of the challenges using 3 main configurations of the MagniVR: One featuring the magnifier display and camera on the right hand, another with the magnifier display on the right and the camera on the left hand, and the third with both positioned at the front of the head. The setup where both the camera and screen are placed in front of the head is a superset of the SeeingVR's magnification lens tool. Users tested the tool in all possible arrangements.

The tests were timed and afterwards participants were interviewed through a questionnaire. However, because completion times varied significantly due to participants' individual experiences, they were considered less informative and were consequently excluded from Phase 2. In the first phase of the study, there were six participants, of whom only three had low vision. These individuals formed the test group, while the other three participants, who had prescriptions, served as a baseline comparison group. The small size of the low vision group made it difficult to derive statistically significant results. Moreover, the tool used in this phase did not have a control menu, which restricted users to using controller shortcuts for operations. Finally, its design did not facilitate easy integration into other virtual reality projects (Fig. 2).

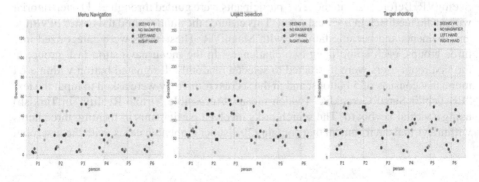

**Fig. 2.** The completion time of test rooms in Phase 1

The completion times for each test have been organized into separate plots based on the associated tasks. There are three plots, each corresponding to a task group, which consists of three associated tests. Within each task, there are 12 to 16 data points representing the completion times for the various tests participants were required to undertake. It's important to note that participants with prescriptions did not attempt to complete the test without using MagniVR (Fig. 3).

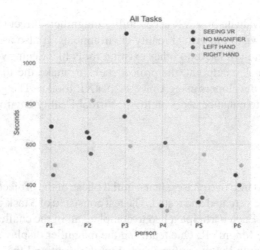

**Fig. 3.** The completion time of all tests in Phase 1

The figure above illustrates the total time spent by each participant on each task, with data points representing the sum of the completion times for the three sub-tests associated with their respective tasks. For two out of three participants with low vision, the time of completion for each task was the longest for tests without the use of MagniVR. It was rather surprising that this pattern did not hold true for one of the low vision participants. This unexpected discrepancy is thought to be a result of possible errors in measuring completion times and aspects of the experimental setup. During the interview, this particular participant expressed encountering substantial difficulties when trying to complete tasks without relying on any accessibility tools.

Regarding the accessibility tools, data suggests that there is no universally superior tool for this specific test setup (Table 2).

In Phase 2, to assess MagniVR, participants completed tasks analogous to those in SeeingVR. Before starting the tests, participants were guided through an 11-step tutorial with audio feedback in a virtual room. This ensured they understood the basics of virtual environments and became familiar with MagniVR. These tasks were categorized into three groups, each comprising two challenges. In the menu navigation task group, in the first room users were instructed to select a randomly designated button within a UI menu that consists of 5 buttons, and in the second room they were asked to input the text "Erişilebilir Sanal Gerçeklik" (which means "Accessible Virtual Reality" in Turkish) using a virtual keyboard. The search tasks involved participants in locating three items within a virtual environment that contains 29 distinct grabbable items, with the first room

**Table 2.** Demographics data for phase 2 participants

| ID | Sex | Age | Graduation Level | Legally Blind | Visual Acuity | Electronic device usage (hour) | VR use |
|---|---|---|---|---|---|---|---|
| P1 | F | 20–29 | High school | Yes | 20/100 | 5 + | No |
| P2 | M | 30 and above | University | Yes | 20/400 | 2–3 | No |
| P3 | F | 13–19 | Middle school | Yes | 20/400 | 5 + | Yes |
| P4 | M | Under 13 | Middle school | Yes | 20/400 | 2–3 | No |
| P5 | M | 20–29 | High school | Yes | 20/200 | 5 + | Yes |
| P6 | M | 30 and above | PhD | Yes | 20/400 | 5 + | No |
| P7 | M | Under 13 | Elementary school | Yes | 20/800 | 0–1 | No |
| P8 | F | Under 13 | Elementary school | Yes | 20/400 | 0–1 | No |
| P9 | M | Under 13 | Elementary school | Yes | Left: 20/800 Right: No vision | 2–3 | No |
| P10 | M | 13–19 | Middle school | Yes | 20/800 | 2–3 | No |
| P11 | F | 13–19 | High school | Yes | Left: 20/400 Right: No vision | 1–2 | Yes |
| P12 | M | 20–29 | High school | Yes | 20/400 | 5 + | No |

arranged in an organized manner and the second intentionally disorganized. Lastly, the shooting task required participants to pop red balloons using a dart gun. In the first room, the balloons followed a predictable pattern, whereas in the second room balloons' moving patterns varied. MagniVR allows the user to control the magnifier without any external help, and the flexibility of the magnification tool sets it apart from previously developed tools, such as SeeingVR (Fig. 4).

There were a total of 12 participants. Each participant filled out both a pre-test questionnaire and a post-test questionnaire. The MagniVR's effectiveness is evaluated through real-time test observations, the participants' performance in the tests they took part in, and their responses in the questionnaires they completed.

## 4.2  Effectiveness of MagniVR

Among the 12 participants, 10 found MagniVR to be beneficial for their tasks. Within this group of 10 participants, 9 expressed that MagniVR significantly aided them in exploring the virtual world. Participants were requested to assess the tool's effectiveness

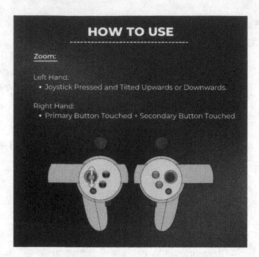

**Fig. 4.** English tutorial example

on a scale from 0 to 5, which yielded an average rating of 3.59. Among the three task categories, MagniVR received the highest praise for menu navigation, with five participants highlighting its helpfulness in this regard. Following closely was the search task, where 2 participants specifically noted the tool's assistance. No participants mentioned that MagniVR was particularly helpful for the shooting task due to the size of the targets and their distance from the user.

Out of 12 participants experimenting with different configurations of the MagniVR, a split in preference emerged. Five participants found it more comfortable to hold both the camera and the display in their dominant hand, thinking it allowed for better aiming. An equal number, another five participants, chose to keep both in their non-dominant hand. As one participant put it "I can interact with the VR environment using my dominant hand, can look around and read with the left and hide the display when not using the tool for better visibility (higher FOV) (directly translated from Turkish)". A smaller group, consisting of two participants, placed the camera and the display in front of their head. A few participants experimented with the configuration of separating the camera and display between their hands. As one participant explained, "I can take the camera in my right hand and the display in my left to search around the room or read lengthy text. However, in this specific environment, it was more convenient to simply teleport around(translated from Turkish)".

It should be noted that the majority of participants chose to teleport in front of objects they intended to interact with rather than utilizing MagniVR. Nevertheless, the tests were intentionally designed to prevent them from getting too close physically, encouraging them to rely on the tool instead. This simulation aimed to emulate VR scenarios where physical movement towards objects or teleportation options may not be feasible, thereby assessing the tool's effectiveness in such less accessible circumstances.

The most common complaint about MagniVR is about the control menu's interaction design. Most participants faced difficulty interacting with the control menu, with 5 out of the 12 participants specifically expressing their frustration regarding their experiences with control menu interactions (Fig. 5).

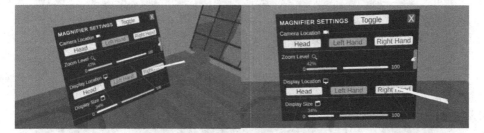

**Fig. 5.** Expected menu action examples.

When a user directs their pointer (represented as a ray in the virtual environment) toward a button on the menu, the button and the ray turn white, signaling that it is clickable. This aspect is functioning as intended.

The problem arises from a mismatch between the user's visual perception, where they believe they are engaging with the menu, and the actual interaction where the ray bypasses the menu and ends on an object behind it, leading to confusion and frustration. This visual inconsistency is especially problematic for individuals with low vision, as they already grapple with depth perception challenges (Fig. 6).

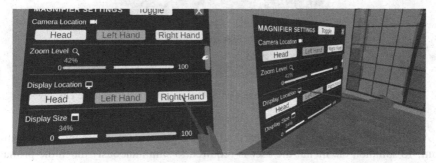

**Fig. 6.** Examples of Inaccurate Selection of UI Elements in Menus

A significant issue arises when participants use the MagniVR camera and display attached to their heads. They often attempt to interact with elements using hand rays, but mistakenly target the re-projection on the MagniVR display instead of the actual interaction element. This misalignment leads to missed interactions. One way to circumvent this issue is stretching one's arms approximately 30 cm forward or aiming beneath the display so that their reach extends in front of the screen, however, it should be noted that some participants had shorter arms, making this solution impossible. For this mode, the magnifier display can be placed closer to the head of the user to fix the problem (Figs. 7 and 8).

330 C. Kaya et al.

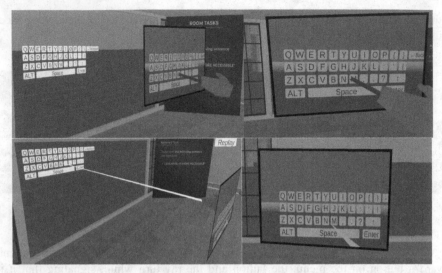

**Fig. 7.** Comparison of participants with varying arm lengths in research involving head-mounted magnifiers

**Fig. 8.** Image Demonstrating Successful Targeting from Beneath the Display

Another issue is about shortcuts, particularly the shortcut for summoning the control menu. To summon the menu, the user is required to simultaneously touch the primary and secondary buttons on both controllers. For toggling on the magnifier, a similar action is necessary: the user must touch the primary and secondary buttons on the right hand controller while simultaneously pressing the primary and secondary buttons on the left hand controller.

These shortcuts were designed with the intention of not conflicting with shortcuts used in other applications. This design choice aimed to ensure that the tool could be easily integrated into various projects without causing conflicts.

However, a significant problem emerged during testing. 9 out of 12 of the participants had no prior experience with virtual reality, so they were not familiar with the buttons. Consequently, they encountered difficulties when attempting to use these shortcuts. Specifically, participants frequently unintentionally summoned the control menu on when they were trying to activate the magnifier. This occurred because the menu summon shortcut did not require any active pressing interaction. Some of the new users found it preferable to rest their thumbs on the buttons, which resulted in them accidentally touching them and the continuous summoning of the menu. In addition to this the two shortcut sequences are quite similar, making them challenging for inexperienced users to execute accurately. Moreover, the absence of a menu despawn shortcut exacerbated the aforementioned issues.

Another major drawback of MagniVR is the lack of contrast and color control. The participants with lower acuity of color perception had difficulty reading some text elements depending on the background colors. During the tool's design phase, these features were considered but not implemented, as the primary focus of the test was solely on evaluating the magnification feature.

Additional feedback was gathered from participants, revealing various preferences. One individual suggested enlarging the buttons and spacing them further apart on the interface. Another preferred voice notifications upon button presses and voice commands for controlling the tool to improve the user experience. A third participant wished for a display with higher resolution. Additionally, a participant with vision in just one eye asked for the option to center the display in her line of sight.

## 5  Discussion

The results underscore the significant help of MagniVR for individuals with low vision, as evidenced by the feedback from 10 out of 12 participants who expressed clear satisfaction with its benefits. Notably, 9 of them reported being extremely satisfied with the tool. There were two exceptions: one participant, due to lack of color processing features, couldn't use the tool due to contrast-related issues, while another participant struggled with the controls but suggested that simplifying them would make the tool beneficial for her as well.

The initial concept for a low vision accessibility tool originated from a personal experience of one of the project's developers, who himself has low vision. While setting up his Meta Quest 2 VR device, he encountered difficulties interacting with the menu. The menu's small size, along with its behavior of shifting away and turning white when he approached and the lack of accessibility features, made it inaccessible for him. This anecdotal experience led to this study.

In designing the MagniVR menu during Phase 2, the initial approach was to allow participants the freedom to independently choose both their camera and display locations. However, this led to confusion among some participants. For example, if a participant switched the camera location to their right hand, the display would still remain on the left, making it challenging for them to then select the right hand for the display. To address this, MagniVR should consider a more straightforward design, like an interaction element that simultaneously adjusts both the camera and display locations. On the other hand, some participants did appreciate the ability to customize each location separately, enjoying the diverse combinations it offered. Instead of eliminating this option, it could be moved to an "advanced settings" section, preserving the flexibility for those who desire it.

In both the results of SeeingVR and this study, the magnification lens proved to be effective for menu navigation and text-related tasks. This research aimed to expand on the concept of a magnification lens by incorporating additional features. Unlike SeeingVR, which limited users to a single configuration, MagniVR offered various configurations. Furthermore, the inclusion of a control panel and shortcuts in MagniVR allowed for more precise control over the magnification tool, a feature which distinguishes MagniVR from SeeingVR. In this study, while menu navigation and text-related tasks were identified as the most suitable for MagniVR, participants also found it useful for search tasks as well.

### 5.1 Recommendations and Future Work

In the questionnaires, participants were also inquired about their interest in using MagniVR in augmented reality, enabling them to zoom in on objects to a similar extent as they can on a phone, but through a specialized device. The responses from all 12 participants expressed excitement, with explanations indicating that such a feature would greatly enhance their daily lives, highlighting the accessibility potential of augmented reality. It's worth mentioning that even before they were asked this, participants also brought up the idea of a device that would enable them to zoom in on real-world objects like they could in the virtual environments, emphasizing its potential convenience.

In addition to controller-based control and shortcut functionalities, the integration of advanced interaction modalities like hand gestures and eye-tracking-based controls, along with the introduction of specialized features such as ones in [VRiassist], would significantly enhance the capabilities of MagniVR.

Participants displayed different preferences in how they held the camera and display, highlighting the tool's flexibility in catering to individual needs. While the inclusion of advanced customization settings is crucial to accommodate power users, it is equally important to ensure that novice or casual users do not feel overwhelmed by advanced options. This demonstrated the challenges of addressing not only low vision issues but also the learning curve for inexperienced users, as novices faced particular difficulties when adapting to both VR and MagniVR simultaneously.

Considering that the application handles the final rendering process, incorporating such features into application development tools like game engines such as Unity could be a potential path forward for more accessible VR. The current implementation uses the OpenXR framework and does not require a significant developer input to implement.

Another way to increase the accessibility of VR technologies is by adding such tools at the OS and compositor level.

## 6   Conclusion

MagniVR has shown promising results as an assistive tool for people with low vision. In phase 2 of this study, out of 12 participants, 10 of them gave favorable feedback. This tool stands out due to its customizable configurations and control settings, providing a more personalized magnification experience compared to existing solutions. This project also provided important insights for the development of VR tools specifically designed for individuals with low vision. There is still potential for enhancements, particularly in color processing and making controls more user-friendly. As the popularity of VR continues to rise, tools like MagniVR will play a crucial role in making VR experiences inclusive and accessible to everyone.

**Acknowledgments.** As the MagniVR team, we want to thank Professor Kürşat Çağıltay for his guidance. Thanks to Mustafa Yardımcı for testing assistance, to our participants for their involvement, and to Sabancı University and the PURE program for their support.

**Disclosure of Interests.** The authors have no competing interests to declare that are relevant to the content of this article.

# References

Koyuncular, B.: The Population of Blind People in the World! In: Blindlook (2021) . https://www.blindlook.com/blog/detail/the-population-of-blind-people-in-the-world. (Accessed 19 Jan 2023)

Zhao, Y., Cutrell, E., Holz, C., et al.: SEEINGVR. In: Proceedings of the 2019 CHI Conference on Human Factors in Computing Systems (2019). https://doi.org/10.1145/3290605.3300341

Masnadi, S., Williamson, B., Gonzalez, A.N., LaViola, J.J.: VRIASSIST: An eye-tracked Virtual Reality Low Vision Assistance Tool. In: 2020 IEEE Conference on Virtual Reality and 3D User Interfaces Abstracts and Workshops (VRW), pp. 808–809 (2020). https://doi.org/10.1109/vrw50115.2020.00255

Wu, H.-Y., Calabrèse, A., Kornprobst, P.: Towards accessible news reading design in virtual reality for low vision. Multimedia Tools Appli. 80, 27259–27278 (2021). https://doi.org/10.1007/s11042-021-10899-9

Hoppe, A.H., Anken J., Schwarz T, et al.: CLEVR: A customizable interactive learning environment for users with low vision in virtual reality. In: The 22nd International ACM SIGACCESS Conference on Computers and Accessibility (2020). https://doi.org/10.1145/3373625.3418009

# Deaf and Hard of Hearing People's Perspectives on Augmented Reality Interfaces for Improving the Accessibility of Smart Speakers

Roshan Mathew(✉)⬤, Garreth W. Tigwell⬤, and Roshan L. Peiris⬤

Rochester Institute of Technology, Rochester, NY, USA
rm1299@rit.edu

**Abstract.** The continued evolution of voice recognition technology has led to its integration into many smart devices as the primary mode of user interaction. Smart speakers are among the most popular smart devices that utilize voice recognition to offer interactive functions and features to serve as a personal assistant and a control hub for smart homes. However, smart speakers rely primarily on voice recognition technology and are often inaccessible to Deaf and hard of hearing (DHH) individuals. While smart speakers such as the Amazon Echo Show have a built-in screen to provide visual interaction for DHH users through features such as "Tap to Alexa," these devices still require users to be positioned next to them. Though features such as "Tap to Alexa" improve the accessibility of smart speakers for DHH users, they are not functionally comparable solutions as they restrict DHH users from benefiting the same user freedom hearing users have in interacting with them from across the room or while performing another hands-on activity. To bridge this gap, we explore alternative approaches such as augmented reality (AR) wearables and various projection systems. We conducted a mixed-method study involving surveys and Wizard of Oz evaluations to investigate the proposed research objectives. The study's findings provide a deeper insight into the potential of AR projection interfaces as novel interaction methods to improve the accessibility of smart speakers for DHH people.

**Keywords:** Accessibility · Deaf and hard of hearing · Assistive Technologies · Smart speakers · Augmented Reality

## 1 Introduction and Motivation

The recent advancements in ubiquitous computing and speech recognition technologies have driven the widespread adoption of smart devices employing speech interfaces, enabling hands-free user interaction, and eliminating the need for display screens [4]. A smart speaker is one such voice-controlled smart device that is equipped with an intelligent virtual assistant, providing users with a natural

M. Antona and C. Stephanidis (Eds.): HCII 2024, LNCS 14697, pp. 334–357, 2024.
https://doi.org/10.1007/978-3-031-60881-0_21

language interface to ask questions, perform various tasks such as web browsing and music streaming, and control other smart devices within a home or office setting [2]. Smart speakers have become increasingly popular in the last decade, and factors such as language localization, the development of 5G infrastructure, advancements in Internet of Things (IoT) technology, and improvements in natural language processing have contributed to the steady growth of the smart speaker market [2]. Projections indicate that the global smart speaker market is expected to reach USD 15.6 billion by 2025, with a compound annual growth rate of 17.1% from 2020 to 2025 [2].

Voice-based interactions are more naturalistic and convenient to a wide range of users [37], including people with disabilities such as those with limited dexterity, limited mobility, visual impairments, and intellectual disabilities [19,25,28,33,38]. However, speech-controlled devices often pose accessibility challenges for people with hearing loss, especially those who do not use their voice or those who prefer to use sign language for communication [4,9]. Even Deaf and Hard of hearing (DHH) users who voice for themselves often find that smart speakers do not recognize their voice commands because speech recognition technologies are not yet capable enough to understand deaf speech [4,9]. Deaf speech signifies the accented speech of DHH individuals due to a partial or complete lack of acoustic feedback from their own vocal sounds [4]. Consequently, researchers have investigated alternative interaction methods beyond speech-based interactions for DHH individuals to engage with smart speakers. These alternative interaction methods included text-based interactions, text-to-speech (TTS) and automatic speech recognition (ASR), crowdsourced human captioning, gesture-based interactions, and sign-language input [4,8,10,11,24,34].

Studies have revealed that DHH individuals use personal assistant devices significantly less frequently compared to the general population, but DHH individuals have expressed a keen interest in utilizing these devices if they were equipped with alternative interaction methods, such as American Sign Language (ASL) interaction support [10,24]. However, current systems are incapable of accurately supporting sign-language-based interactions with smart speakers due to the lack of sign-language datasets needed to support modern deep-learning methods for sign recognition [11]. Perhaps due to the increased focus on the accessibility of smart speaker systems, some companies, such as Amazon and Google, have developed smart speakers (e.g., the Amazon Echo Show and Google Nest Hub), which include built-in screens that offer visual or text-based feedback for user interaction. However, these solutions require DHH users to be near the devices to interact using the smart speaker, either using a display screen or microphones or using computer vision or other sensing technologies to capture sign-language or gesture-based interactions.

Requiring DHH users to interact with smart speakers in its vicinity limits their freedom compared to hearing users who can interact from a distance or while engaged in other activities. Prior studies have shown that alternative interaction methods such as using text-based, ASR, or display screens are not functionally equivalent solutions for DHH users when compared to other user groups [9]. Therefore, further research is needed to explore potential interaction modalities that afford a functionally equivalent experience for DHH users as they engage with smart speakers in hands-free, mobile contexts.

Although not specifically focused on smart speakers, researchers have investigated alternative interaction modalities for on-body displays, body-worn projections, and other wearable displays, such as Augmented Reality (AR) smart glasses for displaying visual user interfaces (UIs) in mobile contexts. Wearable computing devices help bring technology closer to the users [36] and therefore, wearable devices utilizing AR and Spatial Augmented Reality (SAR) offer the potential advantage of leveraging the user's body and environment to be used as visual extensions of UIs of smart systems. However, to the best of our knowledge, there is no existing literature available that has explored the attitudes and preferences of DHH people in using AR interfaces as alternative approaches for smart speaker interactions.

Researchers who have conducted early studies on the accessibility of Conversational User Interfaces (CUIs) for DHH users have called for continued exploration of novel interaction methods before CUIs become ubiquitous in the world [9,34]. Therefore, the purpose of this study is to explore the potential of AR as an interaction modality with smart speakers that would facilitate a functionally equivalent experience for DHH users to that of hearing users, particularly for hands-free, mobile contexts. To this end, we conducted a mixed-method study involving an online survey with 247 DHH participants, followed by Wizard of Oz evaluations with 13 participants. The study findings offered valuable insights into various aspects of smart speaker usage among DHH participants, such as adoption rate, how frequently participants used smart speakers, their typical interaction patterns, where they preferred to place these devices in their homes or workplaces, their experiences managing accessibility challenges and their overall satisfaction with their current smart speakers. Participants also discussed their perspectives on using novel interaction methods using AR interfaces, such as smart glasses, and projected interfaces, such as tabletop, body-worn, and wrist-worn AR displays, to address the accessibility challenges of smart speakers.

The contributions of this research are twofold. Firstly, the study offers empirical knowledge of the current usage trends and the benefits and barriers of existing smart speakers from the perspective of DHH individuals. Secondly, the study provides a deeper understanding of whether AR and projected interfaces can serve as novel interaction methods for people with hearing loss to improve the accessibility of smart speakers and their broader applicability to a more extensive user base for such systems and devices.

## 2   Background and Related Work

### 2.1   DHH People and Speech-Controlled Devices

A study by Blair and Abdullah [5] investigating the challenges experienced by DHH users while using Smart Assistants (SAs), such as Siri, Google Assistant, and Alexa, found that even DHH individuals with profound deafness regularly engage with smart assistants, despite several barriers. These barriers include the lack of visual feedback or the need to be close to screen-based devices, SAs not understanding DHH users' spoken commands, inability to interact hands-free, and high-pitched voice responses from devices. All these lead to interruptions in the natural flow of functions and often limit DHH users on where and how the smart assistants can be used [5]. Researchers have been exploring alternative approaches to help overcome some of these challenges, such as sign language interaction, human computation to recognize deaf speech, and specialized mobile interfaces with text-to-speech capabilities to interact with speech-controlled devices [8–11]. Even though these studies proposed solutions that helped tackle some of the challenges DHH users face while interacting with voice-based smart devices, they still do not offer them the freedom to interact with speech-controlled devices in hands-free mobile contexts.

## 2.2   Alternative Interaction Modalities

**On-Body Projection Interfaces.** Researchers have been exploring the use of on-body displays for extending the UIs of wearable devices as this approach capitalizes on the constant proximity and immediate accessibility of our bodies, providing an "always-available" interface where users do not have to carry or retrieve another device for interaction [14,36,40,41]. PALMbit [41] employs a projector and camera mounted on the shoulder to project interfaces onto the user's palm, which is dynamically tracked in real-time, eliminating the requirement for markers. The system allowed user input through finger-to-finger touches. OmniTouch [13] utilizes a depth-sensing projection system worn on the shoulder to facilitate interactive multitouch applications on everyday surfaces, including the user's body and the surrounding environment. Skinput [15], involving a projection system enhanced by a sensing armband worn on the upper arm, relied on bioacoustic signals generated by skin touches on pre-learned locations on the arm and hand to track interactive interfaces. SixthSense [27], a wearable gestural interface that incorporates a pico-projector worn around the neck, projects interfaces onto the body or surroundings, allowing users to interact with them using natural hand gestures tracked through color markers worn on the fingers. LumiWatch [40], a self-contained smartwatch equipped with an integrated projector and touch sensing, turns the user's arm into a touchscreen, thus facilitating continuous 2D finger tracking with interactive, rectified graphics for a seamless experience. All these approaches primarily employed the forearm to display interfaces, and prior research has affirmed that forearms are the most preferred and universally accepted region of the body for projected touch interfaces [14,36]. This preference is attributed to the forearm's visual and physical accessibility, along with its affordances for control. Several conceptual projection-based smartwatches and smart bracelets have also been commercially publicized in recent years, such as Cicret [1], Ritot [3], and Haier Asu [26], indicating that such technology could become commercially available in the future.

**Body-Worn Projections.** One of the earliest instances of body-worn projectors involved a projector positioned on the user's shoulder to project images onto surfaces equipped with infrared (IR) reflected markers [20]. Utilizing an IR-emitting spotlight and a camera, this system allowed users to interact with the projected content by employing touch input through infrared reflective markers attached to the user's fingers. Blaskó et al. [6] investigated a simulated wrist-worn projection system, integrated with orientation and position-tracking technologies, to explore interaction techniques that facilitate ad-hoc data retrieval, content manipulation and presentation to minimize the need for users to look away from the projected image. Sakata et al. [35] conducted Wizard of Oz studies to evaluate the effectiveness of body-worn projection systems by comparing two scenarios: one involving the display of content on the user's palms using shoulder-mounted projectors and the other entailing the projection of both explicit and implicit information on the floor in front of the user through a lumbar-mounted projector. They concluded that palmtop displays provide easier viewing of information in mobile contexts as lumbar-mounted projectors would need stabilization methods to project content steadily. BOWL ProCam [22], a projector-camera system comprising a laser projector, a high-definition fish-eye camera, and attitude sensors worn on the upper chest area of the user evaluated interaction techniques that utilize nearby projection surfaces like the user's hands, as well as distant projection surfaces such as tabletops and walls. Attjector [21], a wearable and steerable camera-projector system equipped with Kinect and positioned above the user's shoulder, tracks the user's hand and dominant fingers to determine their current locus of attention to project content on that specific area. The researchers suggest that this projection system has potential applications in displaying large interactive user interfaces for mobile applications, with the projection dynamically following the user's focus of attention. OmniTouch [13] and SixthSense [27] (mentioned in the previous section) are also other notable lightweight body-worn projection systems that allow users to interact with projected content in their environment using gestures or touch input.

**Head-Mounted Displays.** Visual feedback on head-mounted displays (HMD) has been previously explored by many researchers as a solution to improve accessibility for DHH individuals in mobile contexts [12,16–18,29,30]. Most of these studies focused on providing captions, sound detection, and sound localization by leveraging the benefits offered by Mixed Reality (MR) technology devices such as Microsoft HoloLens and custom-built AR eyeglasses. The researchers found that using AR-based HMDs offered improved glanceability and better freedom for users to control the shape and placement of AR user interfaces (UIs) and captions in their environment using hand gestures [16]. In addition, the study by Olwal et al. [29] showed how DHH individuals could use HMDs to access captions and gain situational awareness and speaker recognition while engaged in other tasks. Their prototype, named Wearable Subtitles, is a lightweight, wearable head-worn display similar to eyeglasses and uses cloud-based speech-recognition technology to provide captions and sound awareness for DHH users

[29]. Prior research [7] has also demonstrated DHH individuals' preference for visual information on HMDs compared to smartphones and smartwatches in mobile contexts, mainly because it allows them to focus on the interaction or task at hand without the need to split their visual attention or break eye contact. The overall findings and usability evaluations of prototypes developed by Jain et al. [16–18] and Olwal et al. [29] showed that AR and HMD-based solutions are promising for improving the accessibility of DHH users in hands-free, mobile contexts.

### 2.3 Pairing AR Projection Systems and Speech-Controlled Devices for DHH Accessibility

Researchers have previously explored novel alternatives such as smartwatches, smartphones, and AR/MR HMDs to substitute traditional static text and screen-based methods to make information accessible for DHH users [7,16,29]. Of these new approaches, the findings regarding improved glanceability and user control while using AR/MR-based HMDs are undoubtedly encouraging. These studies demonstrated that AR-based displays to access speech and other visual feedback are a viable alternative.

AR projection systems interfaced with smart speakers could be a potential solution to enable DHH users to interact with the functions and features of voice-based smart devices in hands-free, mobile contexts. Projecting a speech-controlled device's UI in the DHH users' environment would offer them the freedom to engage from a distance (mobile contexts) and improved visual feedback for UI navigation and accessing captions. However, there is a lack of knowledge regarding the perspectives of DHH individuals about adopting AR projection technologies to interact with smart speakers. Therefore, our study explores the attitudes of DHH people toward using AR projection interfaces for improving the accessibility of smart speakers toward initial recommendations for the design and development of such systems.

## 3   Study 1

Our mixed-method research was approved by the Institutional Review Board (IRB). It consisted of two studies: a survey study and a follow-up Wizard of Oz evaluation of proof-of-concept prototypes of four alternative interaction methods. This section details the methodology employed for the survey study and presents the survey findings. Participants in the surveys had to meet two eligibility criteria: they needed to be 18 years of age or older and self-identify as DHH. Prior experience with a smart speaker was not a prerequisite for survey participation.

### 3.1   Methods

We recruited participants through ads on popular DHH forums, social media groups, and crowdsourcing apps. The survey included the following sections:

informed consent, screening questions based on the survey inclusion criteria described earlier, a concise overview of smart speakers featuring optional videos showcasing popular models (Amazon Echo, Google Nest), questions tailored for individuals with smart speaker experience, questions for those without such experience, an overview of the proposed AR interaction methods (head-mounted projections, on-body projections, body-worn projections, and tabletop projections) accompanied by image or video demonstrations, questions collecting participant feedback on these interaction methods, and finally, demographic questions.

For participants with prior smart speaker experience, the survey asked about their past interactions, contexts of use, interaction methods, frequency of use, and common barriers faced. For participants lacking previous smart speaker experience, we asked about their reasons for not considering these devices and the issues that needed addressing for them to consider using such technology. The demonstrations illustrating potential alternative interaction methods drew insights from existing research detailed in Sect. 2.2. On average, the survey took about 15 min to complete.

We used descriptive statistics to summarize participant demographics. Subsequently, we performed thematic analysis using an inductive, semantic approach to analyze open-text responses. We then generated codes to capture participant feedback and compared these codes across the samples. Following this comparison, we organized significant themes derived from the frequency of codes into higher-level categories. These categories described benefits, challenges, and participants' preferences regarding using AR interfaces as alternative interaction methods for smart speakers.

## 3.2   Participant Demographics

We received a total of 301 responses to the survey. After accounting for partial and duplicate surveys and those that did not meet the inclusion criteria, there were 247 valid responses. Out of the 247 valid participants, 16 identified as D/deaf, 216 as Hard of hearing (HoH), and 15 as "Other," primarily indicating hearing loss in one ear. Among these, 58 reported mild hearing loss (21 dB–40 dB), 110 had moderate hearing loss (41 dB–60 dB), 40 had severe hearing loss (61 dB–90 dB), nine had profound hearing loss (>90 dB), while 30 were uncertain about their degree of hearing loss. Among the 16 respondents identifying as D/deaf, five reported profound hearing loss, six indicated severe hearing loss, two each disclosed moderate and mild hearing loss, and one participant was unsure about their current level of hearing loss. Regarding assistive hearing devices, 105 participants did not use any, 61 wore hearing aids (HAs) in both ears, 50 in one ear, four had cochlear implants (CIs) in both ears, five in one ear, and four used a combination of cochlear implants and hearing aids (one on each side). Additionally, 18 participants mentioned having hearing aids or cochlear implants but not using them regularly. In terms of language proficiency, 202 participants were most fluent in English, 13 in ASL, 28 were fluent in both English and ASL, and four were most proficient in Spanish.

## 3.3  Findings

**Current Usage Trends for Smart Speakers.** Among the survey respondents, 193 had experience using a smart speaker, while 54 had not used one before. Among individuals lacking prior experience, only three participants self-identified as Deaf, while the remaining individuals identified either as HoH (N = 49) or under the category of "other" (N = 2, attributed to hearing loss due to tinnitus). Among those familiar with smart speakers, the most popular brands were Amazon Echo (N = 119), Google Nest Home (N = 48), Apple Home Pod (N = 8), and other brands (N = 18). Regarding usage frequency, 106 participants reported using their smart speakers many times daily, 23 used them about once a day, 20 used them four to six times a week, 12 used them two to three times a week, 10 used them once a week, and 22 used them every few weeks. Participants commonly placed their smart speakers in the living room (N = 67), bedrooms (N = 51), and kitchen (N = 48). Some also mentioned using them in their office (N = 9) or bathrooms (N = 3), while 15 participants had set up smart speakers in multiple rooms. The typical applications for smart speakers include entertainment (17.21%, such as games, trivia, and jokes), controlling other smart home devices (17%, such as lights and temperature), setting up lists (13.71%, such as groceries and to-do items), checking the weather (12.71%), scheduling (11.18%), information searches (9.43%), communication (9.21%), news updates (5.48%), online shopping (2.74%), and "other" (1.86%) miscellaneous features.

**Current Interaction Methods with Smart Speakers.** We asked the participants how they typically interact with their smart speakers. A total of 84 participants indicated using voice commands; 49 used a combination of voice and their smartphone's companion app (typing); 32 used a combination of voice, companion app, and the smart speaker's screen; 10 used a combination of voice and the screen interface on their smart speakers, five used a combination of the companion app and the smart speaker's screen interface, seven exclusively relied on the screen interface on their smart speakers, four solely used the companion app on their smartphones, and two sought assistance from their family members rather than directly interacting with the smart speakers.

Furthermore, we asked participants if they felt limited in any way when interacting with their smart speakers without using voice commands or receiving voice feedback. 153 participants thought they did not feel limited, while 40 believed they were limited in their interactions without voice commands. Of these 40 participants, 20 used only ASL or a combination of sign language and spoken English for communication. The other 20 participants used spoken English, but 12 reported having moderate or severe hearing loss. It is also worth noting that among those who did not feel limited, 70 participants reported they interacted with their smart speaker solely using voice commands, whereas 83 interacted using a combination of voice, the smart speaker screen, or the companion app. Of the 70 participants who interacted with their smart speaker solely using voice commands, 56 reported only mild or moderate hearing loss, and 14 had severe or profound hearing loss. Among the 83 participants who interacted using a combination of voice, the smart speaker screen, or the companion app, 59 reported mild or moderate hearing loss, and 24 reported severe or profound hearing loss.

Participants who did not prefer to use their voice were comfortable typing commands using the companion app or the smart speaker's screen interface. They did not think this type of interaction restricted their use of smart speakers. A participant noted, *"I have found that by using the smartphone app, I can eliminate having to interact with the speaker to complete non-voice functions."* On the other hand, some participants who felt limited because they could not use voice interaction noted that even using the companion app was not optimal, *"Sometimes it's inconvenient to run over to my smart speaker. Also, the actions I can do on the phone app are quite limiting as well."* They often had challenges with the device not understanding their speech or not hearing the voice response unless they turned up the volume very high. A participant said, *"I can't just tell the speaker what I want like most people because it doesn't understand me a lot of the time."* Other participants added that even if they could use their voice, they needed to be very close to the device, *"I have to stay near the speaker so I can talk clearly and hear the speaker better."* However, often they had to default to using the smart speaker screen, *"I have to go over to my desk and sit down to use the screen, rather than talking to it directly from anywhere in the room."*

**Satisfaction with Current Smart Speakers.** We asked participants to rate their experiences with the smart speakers they owned, and 62 participants noted that they were extremely satisfied, 101 participants stated that they were somewhat satisfied, 13 were neither satisfied nor dissatisfied, another 13 were somewhat dissatisfied, and four were extremely dissatisfied. Again, it is noteworthy that, out of the 62 participants who were extremely satisfied with their smart speakers, 26 used voice interactions, and another 30 participants could use their voice with the companion app or the smart speakers' screen interface. Of these 62 participants, 44 owned the Amazon Echo, 11 had the Google Nest Home, three used the Apple Home Pod, and four used other smart speakers. Regarding some of the most helpful features of their smart speakers, participants said the ability to view captioned content (for devices with a screen), hands-free activation and usage for several tasks, and different colored flashing lights for different features were the most beneficial. A participant added, *"I like being able to ask about the weather, without stopping what I'm doing. It is a challenge to hear the speaker if it's not positioned correctly, but if I keep it [...] fairly close, it's very convenient."*

Participants identified challenges related to the devices' understanding of deaf speech and the users' comprehension of voice responses as significant reasons for their dissatisfaction with smart speakers. A participant wrote, *"It doesn't always understand me and it gets incredibly frustrating trying to repeat the command over and over."* Other participants observed that while smart speakers with in-built screens are an improvement, they are still lacking in many ways. A participant, while expressing their frustration having to go near the device frequently, said, *"I want a hands-free experience. I want to be able to have a more intuitive experience. I want to be able to tell Alexa to do things, and not have to respond to many clarifying questions that are hard for me to hear."*

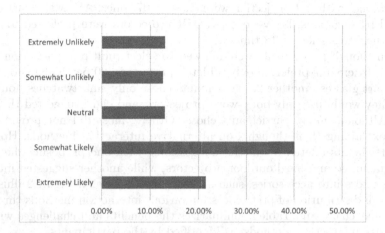

**Fig. 1.** Percentage distribution representing participants' likelihood to adopt the suggested alternative interaction modalities with smart speakers

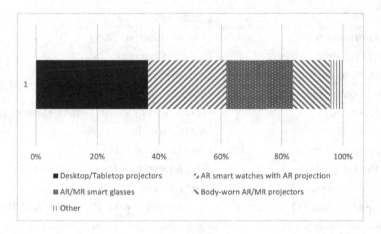

**Fig. 2.** Participants' preference for the type of interaction modalities with smart speakers

**Perceptions About Alternative Interaction Modalities.** We asked survey participants about their likelihood of using proposed alternative methods to interact with their smart speakers. Participants could also suggest their own novel interaction methods. Among the respondents, 53 expressed being extremely likely to use the proposed methods, 99 were somewhat likely, 31 were somewhat

344     R. Mathew et al.

unlikely, 32 were extremely unlikely, and 32 were unsure. Figure 1 shows participants' participants' likelihood of adopting the suggested alternative interaction modalities with smart speakers. Regarding the type of interaction methods they were most likely to use, desktop/tabletop projectors received 154 selections, smartwatches with AR projection were chosen 107 times, AR/MR smart glasses received 94 selections, body-worn AR/MR projectors were preferred 51 times, and "Other" was selected 18 times.

Even though participants were allowed to select multiple interaction methods, 49 participants preferred only tabletop projectors, 20 participants opted for only smart glasses, another 20 participants chose only smartwatches, four indicated they would use only body-worn projectors, and eight suggested their own ideas. Although many participants chose "Other," most did not provide comments explaining their thoughts on alternative interaction methods. However, two participants offered distinctive suggestions, with one proposing the use of ceiling-mounted and fixed outdoor projectors, while another suggested integrating projectors into accessories, such as necklaces or jewelry. Figure 2 illustrates the overall distribution of preferences for various interaction methods through a stacked bar chart, and Table 1 summarizes the benefits and challenges with the alternative interaction methods, as identified by the participants.

**Table 1.** Benefits and challenges with the proposed alternative interaction methods

| Benefits | Challenges |
| --- | --- |
| Visual Information (77) | Cost prohibitive (29) |
| Mobility/Portability (54) | Privacy Concerns (26) |
| Hands-free use for multitasking (37) | Device form factor (16) |
| Improved accessibility (29) | Physical discomfort (15) |
| Convenience (16) | Blocks field of vision (smart glasses) (14) |
| Ease of use (15) | Distractive (14) |
| Better accuracy and efficiency (12) | Learning curve (14) |
| Out-of-Pocket (11) | Finding surfaces for projection (13) |
| Inclusive Technology (11) | Safety concerns (13) |
| Larger display sizes (7) | Compatibility with Rx glasses and HAs (10) |
| Futuristic technology (6) | Usage in bright environments (8) |
| Other (5) | Other (39) |

## 4   Study 2

### 4.1   Methods

To gain a deeper understanding of the perspectives of DHH users regarding the proposed alternative interaction methods, we conducted a follow-up study, involving a Wizard of Oz evaluation of prototypes representing the proposed interaction methods. All participants had to be 18 years or older and were recruited based on how they identified in terms of their hearing loss, prior experience with smart speakers, and communication preferences.

At the beginning of the session, we explained the study's purpose and procedures to the participants. They were then asked to review and sign an Informed Consent form. To familiarize participants unfamiliar with the latest smart speaker models, we showed them common tasks performed by deaf users (checking the weather, browsing a recipe, setting timers/reminders, and managing a to-do list) using an Amazon Echo Show 10. Subsequently, we presented participants with four proof-of-concept prototypes simulating the proposed interaction methods: AR smart glasses, AR smart bands, body-worn projectors, and tabletop projectors.

We used Xreal Light AR smart glasses connected to a compatible smartphone for the head-mounted projection prototype. The on-body projection prototype involved participants wearing a smartwatch while projecting screen mock-ups onto their forearms using a Kodak Lumia 350 smart projector on a tripod. In the third prototype, body-worn projection, participants wore a neck holder mount with the mounted smart projector, allowing projection onto surfaces such as walls and tabletops. The fourth prototype, tabletop projection, featured the smart projector mounted on a tripod, projecting screen mock-ups onto a table surface. Figure 3 shows the Wizard of Oz configuration demonstrating the proof-of-concept prototypes for the four alternative AR projection interaction methods. We provided participants with a set of gestures, selected from prior studies on gesture interactions with wearable devices [31,32,42], to complete tasks like checking the weather, setting timers/reminders, and managing a to-do list.

Following the evaluation of each prototype, participants completed a short post-task questionnaire regarding their perspectives on the interaction method. Subsequently, we administered post-evaluation questions to gather overall preferences and feedback across themes such as interaction type, interaction space, interaction contexts, and privacy. Interaction types pertain to the mode of interaction and included head-mounted displays, on-body projections, body-worn projections, and tabletop projections. Interaction space referred to participant preferences regarding where they would like to view the visuals (three-dimensional space, nearby surfaces, on-body). Interaction contexts referred to participants' preferences for hands-free and mobile interactions. Privacy considerations involved participant preferences regarding device form factor (how large or discreet they would want the devices to be for use in personal and public spaces), and negotiating social expectations. Finally, participants were invited to share their overall thoughts and recommendations for implementing these interaction modalities.

## 4.2 Participant Demographics

We recruited thirteen participants for this study. Seven participants self-identified as Man (53.85%), five as Woman (38.46%), and one as Non-binary

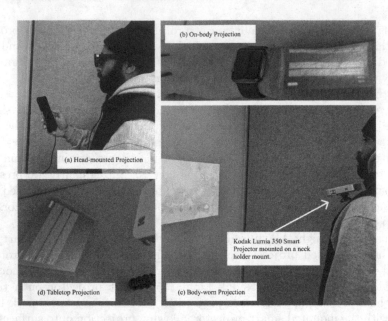

**Fig. 3.** The Wizard of Oz setup for: (a) Head-mounted projection, (b) On-body projections, (c) Body-worn projections, and (d) Tabletop projections

(7.69%). The participants ranged from 19 to 69 years old, with an average age of 44.69. Nine participants possessed prior experience with smart speakers (SS Exp), while four did not. Regarding the level of hearing loss (HL Level), two participants self-reported mild hearing loss (21 dB to 40 dB), eight reported moderate hearing loss (41 dB to 60 dB), one reported severe hearing loss (61 dB to 90 dB), and two reported profound hearing loss (>90 dB). Among the participants, five reported wearing hearing aids in both ears (HA 2E), one reported wearing a hearing aid in one ear (HA 1E), one reported using cochlear implants in both ears (CI 2E), and six reported not using any assistive hearing devices. In terms of communication methods, eight participants stated they used spoken English, four used both American Sign Language (ASL) and spoken English, and one participant exclusively used ASL. Table 2 shows the participant demographics for this study.

## 4.3    Findings

**Head-Mounted Displays.** Eight participants expressed that they were likely (Extremely likely (N = 3), Somewhat likely (N = 5)) to use head-mounted displays, such as AR smart glasses, to interact with a smart speaker, while five participants were unlikely to use them (Extremely unlikely (N = 2), Somewhat unlikely (N = 3)). Participants noted that visual information is much more accessible for people with hearing loss and emphasized that smart glasses would allow them to access information without the need to approach a smart hub.

**Table 2.** Participant Demographics

| ID | Gender | Age | SS Exp | HL Level | Devices | Languages |
|----|--------|-----|--------|----------|---------|-----------|
| IP1 | Man | 29 | Yes | Moderate | None | English |
| IP2 | Man | 63 | No | Moderate | None | English |
| IP3 | Man | 22 | Yes | Moderate | HA 2E | ASL, English |
| IP4 | Man | 19 | Yes | Moderate | HA 2E | ASL, English |
| IP5 | Man | 31 | Yes | Moderate | None | ASL, English |
| IP6 | Woman | 54 | No | Severe | HA 2E | English |
| IP7 | Woman | 60 | No | Profound | HA 2E | English |
| IP8 | Woman | 43 | Yes | Mild | None | English |
| IP9 | Woman | 41 | Yes | Mild | None | English |
| IP10 | Man | 49 | Yes | Profound | CI 2E | ASL |
| IP11 | Man | 69 | Yes | Moderate | HA 2E | ASL, English |
| IP12 | Woman | 68 | No | Moderate | None | English |
| IP13 | Non-binary | 33 | Yes | Moderate | HA 1E | English |

Participant IP12 underscored this point, stating, *"You would be able to see it and follow it. You wouldn't have to depend on hearing it and having it repeat and repeat until you get it. I learn better by vision anyway."* From an accessibility perspective, IP5, added, *"It would essentially or completely eliminate the need for voice-activation with the smart speaker home devices, providing an accessibility option for those who are DHH but also for those who are unable to speak clearly, loudly, or at all for various reasons."* Other participants also highlighted the benefits of the relatively hands-free use afforded by smart glasses as it helps with getting tasks done around the home while interacting with smart speakers.

Nevertheless, participants were also apprehensive that the information projected through the smart glasses would block their field of view and thus become a safety hazard. Concerns were also raised about compatibility with prescription glasses, as well as the desire for a sleek and fashionable design suitable for public settings. Participants expressed reluctance to wear clunky devices that would make it challenging to wear along with their hearing aids, cochlear implants, or other assistive hearing devices.

**On-Body Projections.** Eight participants stated that they were likely (Extremely likely (N = 3), Somewhat likely (N = 5)) to use on-body projection displays, such as AR smartwatches or smart bands, to interact with a smart speaker. Projecting screens onto the forearm instead of a smartphone or a comparatively smaller smartwatch screen allows users to benefit from a larger display area, which may enhance readability and usability. IP8 said, *"I guess always having the device on your person is a benefit. No need to look for a phone (companion app) or glasses or be in the same room as a device."* This discrete on-body projection not only facilitates mobility but also allows multitasking, even within public spaces. IP13 added, *"You can get the information that you want displayed on your arm. You can also hear it through the smart speakers. It would not make you stand out and it is rather cool."*

However, participants also voiced concerns regarding the potential visibility and readability of the projected content on the skin. Factors such as ambient light, especially in outdoor settings, and variations in skin tone were identified as potential challenges. Moreover, apprehensions were raised about the physical strain associated with holding one's arms up for extended periods during certain tasks and the interference of clothing with on-body projections, particularly on the forearms. IP11 recommended, *"Ensure that the projected display is bright, clear, and easily readable, even in various lighting conditions, to accommodate users with different visual abilities."*

**Body-Worn Projections.** Seven participants specified that they were likely (Extremely likely (N = 1), Somewhat likely (N = 6)) to use body-worn projection displays to interact with a smart speaker, whereas six participants were unlikely to use them ((Extremely unlikely (N = 3), Neutral (N = 2), Somewhat unlikely (N = 2)). The biggest advantages of body-worn projection displays are that users have better control over the size of the projection display, and it could potentially allow hands-free interaction using gestures or trackable touch input. IP11 emphasized this benefit, *"Users can interact with the projected display using touch input or gestures, keeping their hands free for other tasks and activities, which can be particularly beneficial for individuals with mobility impairments or those multitasking."*

Despite these advantages, participants identified several challenges associated with the use of body-worn projections. Although body-worn projectors allow users to be mobile, they still have to remain stationary and accurately orient the projector in order to project the content clearly onto a nearby surface. Finding a surface suitable for projection could be challenging in public spaces, and the clarity of projections might be affected by the lighting conditions and characteristics of the surface, such as color, material, and texture. Privacy also emerged as a significant concern, as the projected content is visible to nearby individuals, potentially compromising the confidentiality of sensitive or personal information. IP3 expressed this concern, noting, *"I think that the clip to project it would draw too much attention. like anybody who has lenses tacked onto their body draws a crowd, and it could end up being a bad situation in public, especially if the user is mostly or fully deaf."*

**Tabletop Projections.** Nine participants indicated that they were likely (Extremely likely (N = 3), Somewhat likely (N = 6)) to use tabletop projection displays to interact with a smart speaker. Four participants were either neutral (N = 1) or unlikely to use this type of projection (Extremely unlikely (N = 1), Somewhat unlikely (N = 2)). Participants perceived that tabletop projection displays shared both advantages and challenges with body-worn projection displays. However, due to the standalone nature of tabletop projectors, they were deemed more discreet and applicable in a broader range of mobile contexts. IP11, highlighted this, stating, *"The portable nature of standalone portable projectors allows for flexibility in the placement of tabletop projection displays, enabling users to create interactive environments in various settings or locations."* It was also observed that the portability of tabletop projectors might be compromised if the device is bulky. Additionally, since tabletop projectors are not wearable, they were considered more suitable for use in home or office settings. Participants also highlighted that many DHH people already wear assistive hearing devices, so they were hesitant to use additional wearable devices. IP6 stated, *"As someone who wears both glasses and hearing aids, I don't want too much else on my body. So the tabletop is my preference. But on-body projection sounds interesting as well."*

## Overall Preferences

*Interaction Type.* Participants were asked about their preference for the type of projection they were most likely to use. Tabletop projection displays (N = 6) were the most preferred, followed by on-body projection displays (N = 4), such as using smart watches or smart bands, then head-mounted displays (N = 3), such as AR smart glasses. Notably, none of the participants chose body-worn projection displays. These results are comparable to participant preferences from the survey study.

*Interaction Space.* Participants were queried regarding the interaction space they were most comfortable with. Six participants noted that they were most comfortable with projecting content onto surfaces around them, such as walls, tables, and countertops. While both tabletop and body-worn projection displays could achieve this, none of the participants selected body-worn projection displays when asked about their preferred type of interaction. This suggests that participants favor using tabletop projectors for projecting content onto the surfaces around them. Additionally, four participants indicated that they were most comfortable with using the three-dimensional space around them, which can be accomplished using AR smart glasses. Meanwhile, three participants were most comfortable with on-body projections, such as projections on forearms, wrists, or palms.

*Interaction Contexts.* To understand participants' perspectives on the most suitable types of projections for mobile, hands-free contexts, they were prompted to consider the types of interaction they would utilize when they were mobile or while multitasking. Six participants identified tabletop projection displays as the most fitting for such situations, while five participants thought head-mounted displays to be best suited to use in mobile, hands-free contexts. Notably, five out of the six participants favoring tabletop projection displays had previously chosen tabletop projection displays as their preferred interaction type. However, one participant, who had initially selected on-body projections as their preferred interaction type, believed that tabletop projection display was better suited for hands-free, mobile contexts. Similarly, two out of the five participants who opted for head-mounted displays for hands-free, mobile contexts had an overall preference for on-body projection displays. Furthermore, two participants expressed a preference for body-worn projection displays for use in mobile, hands-free scenarios, even though they had previously indicated that they had an overall preference for the tabletop and on-body projection interactions.

*Privacy.* Participants were probed to share their opinions on the privacy implications associated with the proposed interaction modalities. An overwhelming majority of the participants, comprising ten participants, asserted that head-mounted displays afford the highest level of privacy. Two participants believed that tabletop projection displays offer the most privacy, while one participant thought that body-worn projectors provide the most privacy. Participants were further queried about their choice of interaction modalities in different settings, such as public spaces and private spaces like their homes. Eight participants expressed a preference for using a head-mounted display in public spaces, whereas five participants indicated a preference for on-body projection displays. Notably, none of the participants selected tabletop or body-worn projection displays for use in public spaces. On the other hand, eight participants stated a likelihood of using tabletop projection displays at home or in private spaces, another four participants preferred body-worn projection displays in private spaces, and one participant favored head-mounted displays even at home. No participant chose on-body projection displays for use at home. Overall, only five participants exhibited similar preferences for interaction types in public and private spaces.

## Recommendations for Designing Alternative Interaction Methods for Smart Speakers

*Customization.* Participants suggested that alternative interaction methods should be adaptable to a diverse range of user needs. DHH users use various communication methods, including spoken language, written communication, and sign language. Therefore, both the projection devices and the gestures used for interaction should not hinder a user's preferred communication method. This was a concern for some participants about using on-body projections, particularly those on the forearm, using smart watches or smart bands on the forearm. IP2 expressed apprehension, stating, *"It's on the wrist, and ASL uses a lot of your arms, not just your hands. Making sure that it doesn't get in the way of communicating would be my biggest thing."* In addition, participants also emphasized the importance of customizable settings, including language preferences, font size, color contrast, and caption style, to address individual accessibility needs and preferences.

*Compatibility with Other Assistive Technology.* Another critical recommendation from participants was the necessity for projection devices to be compatible with other assistive technologies, such as HAs, CIs, and other hearing assistive technology devices. Participants highlighted the challenges with wearing devices such as smart glasses, which often need to go over behind-the-ear HAs or CIs or assistive hearing devices that are attached to the head. Additionally, some participants also suggested that it would be helpful for the projection devices to interface with HAs or CIs for direct audio streaming. Another significant concern participants had with smart glasses was regarding their compatibility with prescription glasses, with participants expressing a preference for the ability to use their own prescription lenses with smart glasses. Besides, participants also stressed the importance of designing intuitive and user-friendly interfaces, considering various alternative input methods for individuals with disabilities, including those with mobility impairments. Ensuring compatibility with the assistive devices used by diverse populations could enhance the usability of alternative interaction methods for smart speakers and smart hubs.

*Quality, Affordability, and Privacy.* Participants emphasized the necessity for high-quality projection devices to mitigate the risk of hardware or software malfunctions. Portable devices are also expected to possess extended battery life and durability to withstand occasional bumps or drops. At the same time, participants also underscored that such devices should be affordable. Participants also stressed that the projections should have clarity and visibility under varying ambient light conditions.

Moreover, participants pointed out the necessity for projection devices to maintain a discreet profile suitable for public use. They expressed reservations about devices that are bulky or not fashionable, as such attributes could attract unwanted attention. Additionally, participants were also not enthusiastic about interaction methods that are not discrete enough such that the display content is visible to those around them in public spaces. IP3 articulated this concern by stating, *"I believe it would attract too much attention. Individuals with lenses visibly attached to their bodies tend to gather a crowd, and this could potentially lead to unfavorable situations in public, particularly if the user is predominantly or completely deaf."*

## 5    Discussion

### 5.1    Current Usage Trends of Smart Speakers Among DHH Users

The findings from Study 1 highlighted a high adoption rate of smart speakers within the DHH community despite these devices primarily relying on voice-based interaction. 78.14% of the survey respondents in Study 1 and 69.23% of participants in Study 2 had previously used a smart speaker. This contrasts findings from prior research, which showed that most of their participants did not have experience with personal assistant devices (80.2%) or interactive personal assistants (58%) [10,34]. However, it is essential to note that most participants in the two prior studies used ASL for communication, whereas our study had more participants who self-identified as HoH. Among respondents with smart speaker experience, 54.92% reported using them multiple times daily. The top three uses included entertainment, such as playing games, trivia, and jokes; controlling other smart home devices, like lights and room temperatures; and creating shopping or to-do lists. This aligns with findings from prior research, indicating that the most common tasks users performed with Alexa were checking the weather, listening to music, and controlling other devices [10,23]. Amazon Echo devices were the most popular among users (61.66%), followed by the Google Nest Hub (24.87%). Participants chose to use smart speakers in living rooms (31.6%), bedrooms (26.42%), and kitchens (24.87%), which corroborates the findings from prior studies, which showed that living room, kitchen, and bedroom were the top choices [10].

The majority of users interacted with smart speakers using a combination of voice, a companion app, and the smart speaker's screen. Despite this, most participants did not perceive limitations regarding how they interact with smart speakers. It is worth noting that most of those who did not feel limited could use voice commands, at least to some extent, and participants who felt limitations predominantly used sign language for communication or reported moderate to severe hearing loss. While 84.46% of participants expressed satisfaction with their smart speakers, 63.21% indicated a likelihood of adopting proposed alternative interaction methods for smart speakers. This underscores the potential for improving the accessibility of this technology for the DHH community and that it is worth exploring alternatives that enhance smart speaker accessibility.

### 5.2  Perspectives of DHH People on Using AR Projection Interfaces as Alternative Interaction Methods for Smart Speakers

Across Study 1 and Study 2, most participants expressed that they would likely use AR projection interfaces to interact with smart speakers. In total, 152 participants (61.54%) out of 247 survey respondents in Study 1 reported a likelihood of adopting the proposed interaction methods. Findings from Study 2 revealed that tabletop projections were the most favored, with 9 out of thirteen participants (69.23%) stating a likelihood of adopting this interaction method. Conversely, body-worn projectors were the least preferred, with only 7 out of thirteen participants (53.85%) indicating a likelihood of using them. These participant preferences in Study 2 aligned with the outcomes of Study 1, where respondents indicated a higher preference for desktop/tabletop projectors (36.32%) and a lower preference for body-worn projectors (12.03%).

Although the majority of participants chose tabletop projections as their overall preference for an alternative interaction method, head-mounted displays emerged as the most preferred interaction method in public spaces and the second-most preferred interaction method in hands-free, mobile contexts. While participants acknowledged the benefits of head-mounted and on-body displays regarding mobility and privacy, the inclination towards tabletop projections is consistent with the findings that most participants prefer projecting content onto surrounding surfaces, including walls, tables, and countertops. Notably, tabletop projections also have the highest preference for mobile, hands-free contexts.

This preference is shaped by their current usage patterns of smart speakers, especially in private spaces like homes and offices. However, prior research has uncovered that the intrinsic properties of surfaces themselves can affect both the projected content and the feasibility of interactions [39]. Hence, it is crucial to carefully address considerations based on surface characteristics when implementing tabletop projections to alleviate perceptual issues caused by contextual and environmental interference.

In contrast, body-worn projection displays ranked the least preferred in terms of overall preference, interaction space, interaction contexts, and privacy. Despite offering mobility and convenience for use in hands-free contexts, such as during multitasking, body-worn projection displays still require users to remain relatively still. Designing a projection system capable of identifying the user's current locus of attention and projecting content onto that specific area [21] while incorporating image stabilization techniques could mitigate these concerns. Furthermore, participants perceived that these displays did not provide as much privacy as tabletop projection displays, both of which utilize nearby surfaces for projecting content. In addition, many DHH users already use hearing assistive devices and are reluctant to adopt additional wearable devices such as body-worn projectors, smart glasses or smart bands.

## 6   Limitations and Future Work

Our study is an early exploration aiming to gauge their attitudes regarding the use of AR projection interfaces to improve the accessibility of smart speakers. Limited existing research exists on this topic, making it a relatively uncharted area. Ideally, our study would have greatly benefited from an iterative participatory design approach for planning and developing proof-of-concept hardware prototypes. However, developing multiple hardware prototypes for each of the proposed interaction modalities was deemed out of scope due to time and resource constraints. While the simulations used in the Wizard of Oz study effectively demonstrated the concepts and potential use cases, they may not have provided participants with the same experience as with actual hardware prototypes. Additionally, this study would have benefited more from the participation of more individuals who are part of the Deaf community and use ASL as their primary language. However, it was challenging to conduct such targeted recruitment because people with hearing loss are a minority subsection of the population.

## 7   Conclusion

Our mixed-method study explored how people with hearing loss engage with smart speakers, delving into their usage contexts, interaction methods, frequency of use, and common challenges. To enhance smart speaker accessibility for deaf users, we introduced innovative interaction approaches using AR projection interfaces and assessed proof-of-concept prototypes for specific scenarios. The study's results provide a more profound understanding of how AR and projected interfaces can serve as innovative interaction methods, enhancing the accessibility of smart speakers for people with hearing loss.

**Acknowledgments.** The authors have no competing interests to declare that are relevant to the content of this article.

# References

1. Cicret projects emails, videos and games onto skin—daily mail online. https://www.dailymail.co.uk/sciencetech/article-2871401/The-bracelet-turns-ARM-touchscreen-Cicret-projects-emails-videos-games-skin.html
2. Smart speaker market size global forecast to 2021–2030. https://www.marketsandmarkets.com/Market-Reports/smart-speaker-market-44984088.html
3. This faceless watch has raised $400,000 on Indiegogo. https://www.nbcnews.com/id/wbna55692278
4. Bigham, J.P., Kushalnagar, R., Huang, T.H.K., Flores, J.P., Savage, S.: On how deaf people might use speech to control devices. In: Proceedings of the 19th International ACM SIGACCESS Conference on Computers and Accessibility. ASSETS '17, pp. 383–384. Association for Computing Machinery (2017). https://doi.org/10.1145/3132525.3134821
5. Blair, J., Abdullah, S.: It didn't sound good with my cochlear implants: understanding the challenges of using smart assistants for deaf and hard of hearing users, 4(4), 118:1–118:27 (2020). https://doi.org/10.1145/3432194
6. Blasko, G., Coriand, F., Feiner, S.: Exploring interaction with a simulated wrist-worn projection display. In: Ninth IEEE International Symposium on Wearable Computers (ISWC'05), pp. 2–9 (2005). https://doi.org/10.1109/ISWC.2005.21, ISSN: 2376-8541
7. Findlater, L., Chinh, B., Jain, D., Froehlich, J., Kushalnagar, R., Lin, A.C.: Deaf and hard-of-hearing individuals' preferences for wearable and mobile sound awareness technologies. In: Proceedings of the 2019 CHI Conference on Human Factors in Computing Systems. CHI '19, pp. 1–13. Association for Computing Machinery (2019). https://doi.org/10.1145/3290605.3300276
8. Fok, R., Kaur, H., Palani, S., Mott, M.E., Lasecki, W.S.: Towards more robust speech interactions for deaf and hard of hearing users. In: Proceedings of the 20th International ACM SIGACCESS Conference on Computers and Accessibility. ASSETS '18, pp. 57–67. Association for Computing Machinery (2018). https://doi.org/10.1145/3234695.3236343
9. Glasser, A., Mande, V., Huenerfauth, M.: Accessibility for deaf and hard of hearing users: sign language conversational user interfaces. In: Proceedings of the 2nd Conference on Conversational User Interfaces. CUI '20, pp. 1–3. Association for Computing Machinery (2020). https://doi.org/10.1145/3405755.3406158
10. Glasser, A., Mande, V., Huenerfauth, M.: Understanding deaf and hard-of-hearing users' interest in sign-language interaction with personal-assistant devices. In: Proceedings of the 18th International Web for All Conference. W4A '21, pp. 1–11. Association for Computing Machinery (2021). https://doi.org/10.1145/3430263.3452428

11. Glasser, A., Watkins, M., Hart, K., Lee, S., Huenerfauth, M.: Analyzing deaf and hard-of-hearing users' behavior, usage, and interaction with a personal assistant device that understands sign-language input. In: Proceedings of the 2022 CHI Conference on Human Factors in Computing Systems. CHI '22, pp. 1–12. Association for Computing Machinery (2022). https://doi.org/10.1145/3491102.3501987

12. Guo, R., et al.: HoloSound: combining speech and sound identification for deaf or hard of hearing users on a head-mounted display. In: Proceedings of the 22nd International ACM SIGACCESS Conference on Computers and Accessibility. ASSETS '20, pp. 1–4. Association for Computing Machinery (2020). https://doi.org/10.1145/3373625.3418031

13. Harrison, C., Benko, H., Wilson, A.D.: OmniTouch: wearable multitouch interaction everywhere. In: Proceedings of the 24th annual ACM Symposium on User Interface Software and Technology. UIST '11, pp. 441–450. Association for Computing Machinery. https://doi.org/10.1145/2047196.2047255

14. Harrison, C., Faste, H.: Implications of location and touch for on-body projected interfaces. In: Proceedings of the 2014 Conference on Designing Interactive Systems. DIS '14, pp. 543–552. Association for Computing Machinery (2014). https://doi.org/10.1145/2598510.2598587

15. Harrison, C., Tan, D., Morris, D.: Skinput: appropriating the body as an input surface. In: Proceedings of the SIGCHI Conference on Human Factors in Computing Systems. CHI '10, pp. 453–462. Association for Computing Machinery (2010). https://doi.org/10.1145/1753326.1753394

16. Jain, D., Chinh, B., Findlater, L., Kushalnagar, R., Froehlich, J.: Exploring augmented reality approaches to real-time captioning: A preliminary autoethnographic study. In: Proceedings of the 2018 ACM Conference Companion Publication on Designing Interactive Systems. DIS '18 Companion, pp. 7–11. Association for Computing Machinery (2018). https://doi.org/10.1145/3197391.3205404

17. Jain, D., et al.: Head-mounted display visualizations to support sound awareness for the deaf and hard of hearing. In: Proceedings of the 33rd Annual ACM Conference on Human Factors in Computing Systems. CHI '15, pp. 241–250. Association for Computing Machinery (2015). https://doi.org/10.1145/2702123.2702393

18. Jain, D., Franz, R., Findlater, L., Cannon, J., Kushalnagar, R., Froehlich, J.: Towards accessible conversations in a mobile context for people who are deaf and hard of hearing. In: Proceedings of the 20th International ACM SIGACCESS Conference on Computers and Accessibility. ASSETS '18, pp. 81–92. Association for Computing Machinery (2018). https://doi.org/10.1145/3234695.3236362

19. Kadylak, T., Blocker, K.A., Kovac, C.E., Rogers, W.A.: Understanding the potential of digital home assistant devices for older adults through their initial perceptions and attitudes, **21**(1), 1–10 (2022). https://doi.org/10.4017/gt.2022.21.1.486.06

20. Karitsuka, T., Sato, K.: A wearable mixed reality with an on-board projector. In: The Second IEEE and ACM International Symposium on Mixed and Augmented Reality, Proceedings, pp. 321–322 (2003). https://doi.org/10.1109/ISMAR.2003.1240740

21. Kratz, S., Rohs, M., Reitberger, F., Moldenhauer, J.: Attjector: an attention-following wearable projector. In: Kinect Workshop at Pervasive 2012, June 2012. https://www2.hci.uni-hannover.de/papers/kratz2012attjector.pdf

22. Kurata, T., Sakata, N., Kourogi, M., Okuma, T., Ohta, Y.: Interaction using nearby-and-far projection surfaces with a body-worn ProCam system, **6804** (2008). https://doi.org/10.1117/12.759311

23. Lopatovska, I., et al.: Talk to me: exploring user interactions with the Amazon Alexa. J. Librariansh. Inf. Sci. **51**(4), 984–997 (2019). https://doi.org/10.1177/0961000618759414, publisher: SAGE Publications Ltd

24. Mande, V., Glasser, A., Dingman, B., Huenerfauth, M.: Deaf users' preferences among wake-up approaches during sign-language interaction with personal assistant devices. In: Extended Abstracts of the 2021 CHI Conference on Human Factors in Computing Systems. CHI EA '21, pp. 1–6. Association for Computing Machinery (2021). https://doi.org/10.1145/3411763.3451592

25. Masina, F., et al.: Investigating the accessibility of voice assistants with impaired users: mixed methods study, **22**(9), e18431 (2020). https://doi.org/10.2196/18431

26. Miller, P.: ASU cast one smartwatch with built-in projector is now a real thing you can buy. https://www.theverge.com/circuitbreaker/2016/5/18/11700894/asu-cast-one-smartwatch-projector-released-china

27. Mistry, P., Maes, P., Chang, L.: WUW - wear UR world: a wearable gestural interface. In: CHI '09 Extended Abstracts on Human Factors in Computing Systems. CHI EA '09, pp. 4111–4116. Association for Computing Machinery (2009). https://doi.org/10.1145/1520340.1520626

28. Morris, J.T., Thompson, N.A.: User personas: smart speakers, home automation and people with disabilities (2020). http://hdl.handle.net/10211.3/215991, Publisher: California State University, Northridge

29. Olwal, A., et al.: Wearable subtitles: augmenting spoken communication with lightweight eyewear for all-day captioning. In: Proceedings of the 33rd Annual ACM Symposium on User Interface Software and Technology. UIST '20, pp. 1108–1120. Association for Computing Machinery (2020). https://doi.org/10.1145/3379337.3415817

30. Peng, Y.H., et al.: SpeechBubbles: enhancing captioning experiences for deaf and hard-of-hearing people in group conversations. In: Proceedings of the 2018 CHI Conference on Human Factors in Computing Systems. CHI '18, pp. 1–10. Association for Computing Machinery (2018). https://doi.org/10.1145/3173574.3173867

31. Piumsomboon, T., Clark, A., Billinghurst, M., Cockburn, A.: User-defined gestures for augmented reality. In: CHI '13 Extended Abstracts on Human Factors in Computing Systems. CHI EA '13, pp. 955–960. Association for Computing Machinery, New York, NY, USA, April 2013. https://doi.org/10.1145/2468356.2468527

32. Pomykalski, P., Woźniak, M.P., Woźniak, P.W., Grudzień, K., Zhao, S., Romanowski, A.: Considering wake gestures for smart assistant use. In: Extended Abstracts of the 2020 CHI Conference on Human Factors in Computing Systems. CHI EA '20, pp. 1–8. Association for Computing Machinery, New York, NY, USA, April 2020. https://doi.org/10.1145/3334480.3383089

33. Pradhan, A., Lazar, A., Findlater, L.: Use of intelligent voice assistants by older adults with low technology use, **27**(4), 31:1–31:27. https://doi.org/10.1145/3373759

34. Rodolitz, J., Gambill, E., Willis, B., Vogler, C., Kushalnagar, R.S.: Accessibility of voice-activated agents for people who are deaf or hard of hearing. http://hdl.handle.net/10211.3/210397, Publisher: California State University, Northridge

35. Sakata, N., Konishi, T., Nishida, S.: Mobile interfaces using body worn projector and camera. In: Shumaker, R. (ed.) VMR 2009. LNCS, vol. 5622, pp. 106–113. Springer, Heidelberg (2009). https://doi.org/10.1007/978-3-642-02771-0_12

36. Schneegass, S., Ogando, S., Alt, F.: Using on-body displays for extending the output of wearable devices. In: Proceedings of the 5th ACM International Symposium on Pervasive Displays. PerDis '16, pp. 67–74. Association for Computing Machinery (2016). https://doi.org/10.1145/2914920.2915021

37. Sciarretta, E., Alimenti, L.: Smart speakers for inclusion: how can intelligent virtual assistants really assist everybody? In: Kurosu, M. (ed.) HCII 2021. LNCS, vol. 12762, pp. 77–93. Springer, Cham (2021). https://doi.org/10.1007/978-3-030-78462-1_6
38. Smith, E., Sumner, P., Hedge, C., Powell, G.: Smart-speaker technology and intellectual disabilities: agency and wellbeing, **18**(4), 432–442 (2023). https://doi.org/10.1080/17483107.2020.1864670
39. Tigwell, G.W., Crabb, M.: Household surface interactions: understanding user input preferences and perceived home experiences. In: Proceedings of the 2020 CHI Conference on Human Factors in Computing Systems. CHI '20, pp. 1–14. Association for Computing Machinery, New York, NY, USA, April 2020. https://doi.org/10.1145/3313831.3376856
40. Xiao, R., Cao, T., Guo, N., Zhuo, J., Zhang, Y., Harrison, C.: LumiWatch: on-arm projected graphics and touch input. In: Proceedings of the 2018 CHI Conference on Human Factors in Computing Systems. CHI '18, pp. 1–11. Association for Computing Machinery (2018). https://doi.org/10.1145/3173574.3173669
41. Yamamoto, G., Sato, K.: PALMbit: a body interface utilizing light projection onto palms, **61**, 797–804 (2007). https://doi.org/10.3169/itej.61.797
42. Zhou, X., Williams, A.S., Ortega, F.R.: Eliciting multimodal gesture+speech interactions in a multi-object augmented reality environment. In: Proceedings of the 28th ACM Symposium on Virtual Reality Software and Technology. VRST '22, pp. 1–10. Association for Computing Machinery, New York, NY, USA, November 2022. https://doi.org/10.1145/3562939.3565637

# Enhancing Electromobility Component Training Through Mixed Reality: A Proposal Model

Ahmed Musule , Francisco J. Esparza , Leticia Neira-Tovar$^{(\boxtimes)}$ ,
and Christopher Diaz

University Autonomous of Nuevo León, San Nicolás de los Garza, NL, Mexico
{ahmed.musulelf,Javier.esparzamndz}@uanl.edu.mx,
Leticia.neira@gmail.com

**Abstract.** Mixed Reality (MR) has become a transformative tool, from a physical to a digital world, to create immersive educational experiences. This technology, leveraging the strengths of both virtual and augmented realities, provides an interactive platform where complex concepts can be visualized and understood in a more intuitive and engaging manner. This article presents an innovative MR application specifically designed to enhance training and familiarization with electric vehicle (EV) components and their operations. Targeting both students and professionals in the field of electromobility, the proposed MR model aims to support the theoretical knowledge and practical understanding of EV technologies. Through immersive and interactive learning experiences, users are introduced to the complexities of electric vehicles, including battery systems, electric motors, and charging mechanisms, among others. The application seeks to promote a deeper comprehension of social and environmental benefits of electric vehicles, thereby contributing to a more sustainable future in transportation. By leveraging the capabilities of MR within a Metaverse environment, the model offers a flexible and engaging educational tool that transcends geographical boundaries, making it accessible to learners and professionals worldwide. This initiative not only facilitates the acquisition of specialized knowledge in electromobility but also prepares individuals to actively participate in and contribute to the evolving landscape of electric vehicles. Through this advanced training tool, the project attempts to enhance the skills and competencies of future generations of engineers, technicians, and electromobility enthusiasts, ensuring they are well-equipped to drive the transition towards greener, more efficient transportation solutions.

**Keywords:** Electromobility · Metaverse simulators · Mixed Reality · Electromobility Components

## 1 Introduction

The integration of mixed reality (MR) in engineering education, particularly in electromobility, is important for interactive learning and training methodologies [1]. This approach is instrumental in demystifying the complexities of electric and hybrid vehicles, offering students and professionals alike a hands-on experience with the design

M. Antona and C. Stephanidis (Eds.): HCII 2024, LNCS 14697, pp. 358–367, 2024.
https://doi.org/10.1007/978-3-031-60881-0_22

fundamentals and operational intricacies of these advanced systems. Mixed reality environments facilitate a deeper understanding of vehicle components, fostering a more intuitive grasp of their functionalities and interconnections [2].

The adoption of MR technologies in educational settings aligns with the broader trend towards immersive learning experiences, where the theoretical and practical aspects of electromobility are seamlessly integrated. This is particularly relevant given the rapid advancements in vehicle technologies and the pressing need for a workforce well-versed in the principles of electric vehicles (EVs) and their contribution to sustainability [3].

It is possible to develop spatial science and develop synthetic data which can later be used for creating realistic, immersive environments [4]. These technologies play a pivotal role in simulating real-world scenarios, allowing for a more engaging and impactful learning experience. The use of synthetic data in MR applications, for instance, is revolutionizing the way we perceive and interact with digital twins of electric and autonomous vehicles, highlighting the importance of visual data in the industrial sector [5].

The integration of a metaverse with mixed reality (MR) technologies is identified as a critical element in eliminating geographical limitations for educational and professional training purposes. This integration facilitates a virtual environment where individuals from various global locations can participate in immersive learning and skill development sessions without the necessity for physical travel [6]. Consequently, the metaverse emerges as a vital tool in providing equitable access to education and training across different regions, thereby promoting a more inclusive and interconnected global community. This advancement underscores the significance of the metaverse in revolutionizing remote education and workforce training by offering a practical solution to the challenges of geographical and financial constraints.

A relevant factor in the design of virtual components is the identification of the methods and tools that the electro-automotive industry uses to model specialized parts and be able to digitize them with optimized techniques to reduce capacity problems and they can be visualized as if they were real, which is why the model includes the analysis of updated visualization methods. [7].

### 1.1 Objectives of the Study

The primary objective is to develop a versatile tool designed to facilitate a comprehensive understanding of automotive components and their proper application. By integrating user feedback, the system evolves in synchrony with its users, gathering insights that enable instructors to enhance the educational experience. This includes the teaching of microelectronic elements and the dynamics of robotic movements in automotive applications [8].

## 2 Related Work

A user-centered approach that involves user activities and interactions in the MX for design, development, and refinement [9]. This strategy gives priority to the training needs of operators, directly linking these needs to the educational outcomes and goals.

The inclusion of user feedback is crucial, creating an interactive experience that not only meets but also continually enhances the application. Our research involves a thorough analysis of current smart technology trends and their impact on the electric vehicle industry. Table 1 presents a selection of studies, illustrating the comprehensive scope of our research. This includes the technical aspects of electric and hybrid vehicle technologies to the innovative use of mixed reality and the metaverse in industrial training.

**Table 1.** Related studies on electric vehicles, mixed reality, and industrial training.

| Ref | Authors | Year | Focus Area | Methodology | Key Findings | Relevance to Current Study |
|---|---|---|---|---|---|---|
| [1] | Kucera et al. | 2018 | VR/AR in Mechatronics Education | Conference | Develops educational tools in Unity | Educational implications of MR |
| [2] | Almeida et al. | 2023 | VR in Industrial Training | Methodological | Innovates cross-platform VR training environments | Directly relates to VR's role in training |
| [3] | Un-Noor et al. | 2017 | Key EV Components and Technologies | Review | Comprehensive EV components study | Background on EV technologies for training |
| [4] | Çöltekin et al. | 2020 | Extended Reality in Spatial Sciences | Review | Highlights XR's potential in spatial sciences | Lays foundation for metaverse applications |
| [5] | Nassif et al. | 2024 | Synthetic Data in the Industrial Metaverse | Book | Discusses synthetic data's impact | Contextualizes data's role in the metaverse |
| [6] | Mystakidis | 2022 | Metaverse Overview | Encyclopedia | Defines Metaverse and potential impacts | Fundamental metaverse insights |
| [7] | Nassif et al. | 2024 | Visual Data in Industry | Book Chapter | Explores visual data's revolutionary role | Supports visual data's importance |
| [8] | Husain | 2021 | Electric and Hybrid Vehicles | Textbook | Overview of design fundamentals | Provides background on electromobility |
| [9] | Josan et al. | 2015 | 3D Visualization in Variable Gravity Models | Case Study | Developed VISR for enhanced human-machine interface | Demonstrates immersive training tools' potential |
| [10] | Kaluza et al. | 2019 | Mixed Reality in Automotive Engineering | Case Study | Uses MR for automotive lifecycle management | Shows MR application in engineering |

*(continued)*

**Table 1.** (*continued*)

| Ref | Authors | Year | Focus Area | Methodology | Key Findings | Relevance to Current Study |
|---|---|---|---|---|---|---|
| [11] | Šímová et al. | 2023 | Metaverse in Remote Working | Bibliometric Study | Analyzes remote working trends in the metaverse | Insights into metaverse for remote collaboration |
| [12] | Suryodiningrat et al. | 2023 | MR Systems in Education | Literature Review | Reviews MR in education systematically | Supports MR's educational utility |
| [13] | Chinoracký et al. | 2022 | Electromobility Market Trends | Literature Review | Reviews market trends and services | Market insight for electromobility training |
| [14] | Ali et al. | 2023 | Digital Twin Technology for EVs and AVs | Review | Reviews digital twin tech applications | Technical background for simulation models |
| [15] | Rohini et al. | 2022 | Electric Vehicle Components Review | Book Chapter | Discusses EV components in depth | Technical detail on EVs for simulator development |

## 3   Methodology

The process involved in the proposed model is structured by four distinct steps. These steps were conceptualized within the framework of the software life cycle methodology and were systematically executed according to the sequence illustrated in Fig. 1, to explore the proposed model for the development of a mixed reality trainer in a metaverse environment. The application seeks to increase efficiency in the way electromobility principles are understood, learned, and applied. It examines the fundamentals of the proposal and its relevance within the current landscape and the possibilities it offers to drive the growth and adoption of electromobility worldwide by having the possibility to receive training regarding the main components within the electromobility branch despite not being face-to-face with the expert.

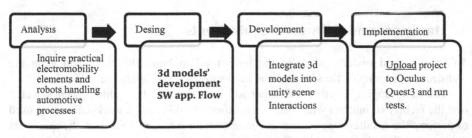

**Fig. 1.** Project stages.

The process proposed for development of the special case of application is shown at Fig. 2.

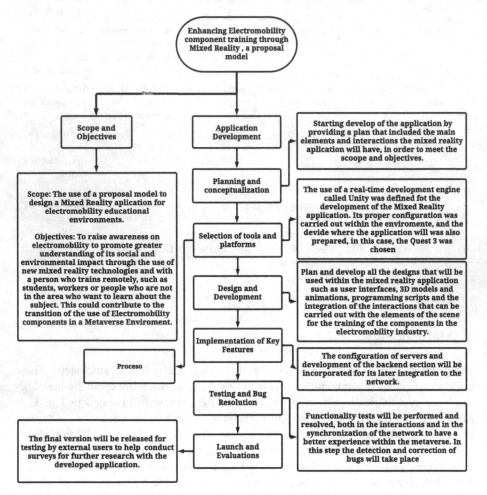

**Fig. 2.** Representation of the proposed model

# 4   Hardware and Software Requirements

To have a good understanding of the tools used to build the MX application the architecture diagram of the software and hardware elements is shown at Fig. 3.

The Unity engine together with other software, described at Table 2, were selected due the facility to interact with different headsets, in this case a workstation was used to perform the resultant application and then transfer into a MX headset, the minimum requirements are shown at Table 3.

**Table 2.** Software used to develop the MX application

| Tool | Description | Use |
| --- | --- | --- |
| Unity | Real-time development engine | Development of mixed reality application, integrating 3D models alongside scripts and audio files, handling Photon packages for network configuration |
| Visual Studio | Integrated Development Environment (IDE) | Application logic and programming of interactions for elements within the mixed reality scene |
| Photon Unity Networking (PUN) | Framework for developing multiplayer games in Unity | Development of multiplayer functionalities within the mixed reality application |
| Blender | Tool for creating 3D models | Development of 3D models and textures |
| Audacity | Audio recording and editing software | Development of audio files |

**Table 3.** Hardware

| Tool | Description | Use |
| --- | --- | --- |
| Oculus Quest 3 | Virtual reality headsets | Testing and experiencing the mixed reality environment |
| Workstation | Workstation,Procesador: Intel(R) Core(TM) i5-10300H CPU @ 2.50 GHz 2.50 GHz RAM 8 GB, NVIDIA GeForce GTX 1650 Ti,Operative System 64 bits, processor x64 | Application development |

A first approach to validate the user interface was made applying a pilot test, using the first version of the application, a group of 9 technical students of automotive program and 9 of mechatronic engineering program were selected. The area where the test took place was a normal laboratory of virtual reality class at engineering school. In order to evaluate the user satisfaction and interface intuitiveness of the early beta version of our application, a structured survey was conducted. The survey aimed to gather feedback on various aspects of the application, including the clarity of instructor instructions, the intuitiveness of project controls, the comfort of the testing environment, and the overall fluidity of process performance.

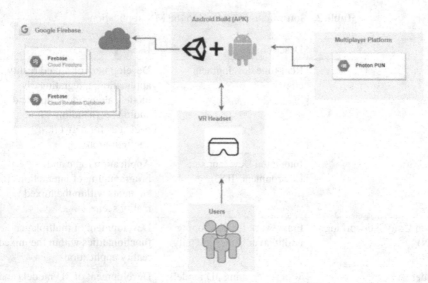

**Fig. 3.** Application architecture showing the MX framework

The results of the survey are summarized, Fig. 4, the key findings highlighted through the use of descriptive statistics and visual representations in the form of charts and graphs. This result shows that there is an acceptance of the environment conducted and the instructions given are understandable for trainers.

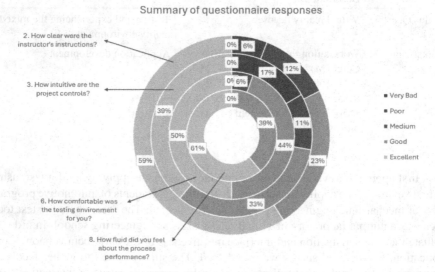

**Fig. 4.** Summary of pilot test

The application aims to use this proposed model to development a mixed reality simulator for electromobility in educational environments [10], the first step in the development of the application is the planning and conceptualization, here arise all the ideas of how the application will look like at the end of its development and what interactions it will have with the user [10], the tool selected to develop the application was Unity, which is a real-time development engine, then we develop the elements that will support the interaction activities to start the development process, gathering all the components, once we have the application with the main interactions where they explain the main elements within the electromobility industry, we implement the configuration of the servers and the configuration of the application to become multiplayer and create a metaverse within this educational environment, see Fig. 6. Before launching the application, a test process take place to find bugs and resolve them to subsequently have a metaverse within this educational environment (Fig. 5).

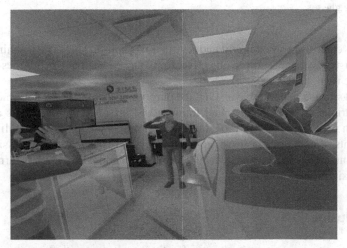

**Fig. 5.** Beta phase of the interaction within the metaverse in a Mixed Reality environment in the remote training of the elements of an electric car

Within Fig. 6, it can observe the first tests within the mixed reality training application, we can see that the environment is in the real world and that within it virtual elements appear with which there are interactions for the training of people within of this metaverse, an electric car can be seen representing that within the application the elements that will be taught to the operators will be integrated as well as later activities will be added and also more resources that feedback the learning of each of the elements of this branch.

This kind of tools can be implemented in production lines and due to the increase in electromobility companies, it is also required to hire and increase the head count on these facilities. Meanwhile teaching large groups of new personnel, an option can be the use of mixed reality to reduce the learning curve in every new entry. Making a person understand with precise examples, such as, the interaction with a real time CAD model in a real environment to learn step-by-step how to interact or assemble a new product

**Fig. 6.** Demonstration of the real-world environment and what it looks like through the Quest 3 mixed reality glasses.

working together from a real world and a virtual workplace, [11], The teaching process used must agree with the learning objective, for which educational techniques using mix reality were used, [12].

The last step includes double testing, the purpose is to obtain feedback when seeking to cover various aspects of personnel training and instils a more cautious attitude to protect both personnel and equipment/clothing and thus reduce the possibility of risks and incidents, thus helps the instructors to cover a greater variety of possibilities of training as interaction on the part of the user, greater functionality which in turn increases the complexity of the simulator.

## 5   Conclusion

Mixed reality environments can give us effective results and with this proposed model we can achieve a great learning into the electromobility components, this application can be improved with training features for new entry personnel. By the time we start with the initial phase of this project, we notice different tasks to implement, in order to achieve a complete design of an effective environment, this will lead us to separate this road into more phases between development, an improved conceptualization, testing and issue resolution and finally a complete launch and evaluation. The activities that can be carried out include the beginning of a structure for digital twin projects that facilitate training in the production of products in the field of electromobility, [13]. In addition, after the first pilot test, an approach to support the digital twins design environments, [14], was detected for future works.

The next step for this work, the results of a practical on site test will be presented to demonstrate the level of effectiveness of the learning session, that the operators show and fulfill one of the targets to improve the training process of Electric Vehicle and its Components, based on area trends. [15].

**Acknowledgments.** This study was supported by the lab of virtual reality at FIME-UANL, best regard to Chritopher Diaz mechatronic student for his collaboration.

**Disclosure of Interests.** The authors have no competing interests to declare that are relevant to the content of this article.

# References

1. Kucera, E., Haffner, O., Leskovský, R.: Interactive and virtual/mixed reality applications for mechatronics education developed in unity engine. In: 2018 Cybernetics & Informatics (K&I), pp. 1–5 (2018). https://doi.org/10.1109/CYBERI.2018.8337533
2. Almeida, L.G.G., Vasconcelos, N.V.d., Winkler, I., Catapan, M.F.: Innovating industrial training with immersive metaverses: a method for developing cross-platform virtual reality environments. Appl. Sci. **13**, 8915 (2023). https://doi.org/10.3390/app13158915
3. Un-Noor, F., Padmanaban, S., Mihet-Popa, L., Mollah, M.N., Hossain, E.: A comprehensive study of key electric vehicle (ev) components, technologies, challenges, impacts, and future direction of development. Energies **10**(8), 1217 (2017). https://doi.org/10.3390/en10081217
4. Çöltekin, A., et al.: Extended reality in spatial sciences: a review of research challenges and future directions. ISPRS Int. J. Geo Inf. **9**, 439 (2020). https://doi.org/10.3390/ijgi9070439
5. Nassif, J., Tekli, J., Kamradt, M.: Synthetic Data: Revolutionizing the Industrial Metaverse. Springer Nature (2024). https://doi.org/10.1007/978-3-031-47560-3
6. Mystakidis, S.: Metaverse. Encyclopedia **2**, 486–497 (2022). https://doi.org/10.3390/encyclopedia2010031
7. Nassif, J., Tekli, J., Kamradt, M.: How Visual Data Is Revolutionizing the Industry World. In: Synthetic Data: Revolutionizing the Industrial Metaverse, pp. 75–88. Springer Nature Switzerland (2024). https://doi.org/10.1007/978-3-031-47560-3_4
8. Husain, I.: Electric and hybrid vehicles: design fundamentals. CRC Press (2021)
9. Josan, P.K., de Leon, P., Srivastava, P.: Enhancing the human-machine interface using visr-an interactive 3d visualization/desensitization training tool in a variable gravity model. In: 66th International Astronautical Congress, Jerusalem, Israel, IAC-15-B3.9-YPVF.2. International Astronautical Federation (2015)
10. Kaluza, A., Juraschek, M., Büth, L., Cerdas, F., Herrmann, C.: Implementing mixed reality in automotive life cycle engineering: a visual analytics based approach. Procedia CIRP **80**, 717–722 (2019)
11. Šímová, T., Zychová, K., Fejfarová, M.: Metaverse in the virtual workplace: who and what is driving the remote working research? a bibliometric study. Vision. J. Bus. Perspective (2023). https://doi.org/10.1177/09722629231168690
12. Suryodiningrat, D., Ramadhan, A., Prabowo, H., Santoso, H., Hirashima, T.: Mixed reality systems in education: a systematic literature review. J. Comput. Educ. (2023). https://doi.org/10.1007/s40692-023-00281-z
13. Chinoracký, R., Stalmašeková, N., Corejova, T.: Trends in the field of electromobility—from the perspective of market characteristics and value-added services. Literat. Rev. Energ. **15**(17), 6144 (2022). https://doi.org/10.3390/en15176144
14. Ali, W.A., Fanti, M.P., Roccotelli, M., Ranieri, L.: A review of digital twin technology for electric and autonomous vehicles. Appl. Sci. **13**(10), 5871 (2023). https://doi.org/10.3390/app13105871
15. Rohini, M., Asha, S.: A review of electric vehicle components. In: Kolhe, M.L., Jaju, S.B., Diagavane, P.M. (eds.) Smart Technologies for Energy, Environment and Sustainable Development, vol. 1, pp. 131–145. Springer Nature Singapore, Singapore (2022). https://doi.org/10.1007/978-981-16-6875-3_45

# Training Attention Skills in Individuals with Neurodevelopmental Disorders Using Virtual Reality and Eye-Tracking Technology

Alberto Patti[1]([✉])[iD], Francesco Vona[1][iD], Anna Barberio[1][iD],
Marco Domenico Buttiglione[1][iD], Ivan Crusco[1][iD], Marco Mores[2][iD],
and Franca Garzotto[1][iD]

[1] Department of Electronics, Information, and Bioengineering, Politecnico di Milano, Milan, Italy
{alberto.patti,francesco.vona,franca.garzotto}@polimi.it,
{anna.barberio,marcodomenico.buttiglione,ivan.crusco}@mail.polimi.it
[2] Fraternità e Amicizia Soc. Coop. Soc. Onlus, Milan, Italy
marco.mores@fraternitaeamicizia.it
https://i3lab.polimi.it/, https://www.fraternitaeamicizia.it/

**Abstract.** Neurodevelopmental disorders (NDD), encompassing conditions like Intellectual Disability, Attention Deficit Hyperactivity Disorder, and Autism Spectrum Disorder, present challenges across various cognitive capacities. Attention deficits are often common in individuals with NDD due to the sensory system dysfunction that characterizes these disorders. Consequently, limited attention capability can affect the overall quality of life and the ability to transfer knowledge from one circumstance to another. The literature has increasingly recognized the potential benefits of virtual reality (VR) in supporting NDD learning and rehabilitation due to its interactive and engaging nature, which is critical for consistent practice. In previous studies, we explored the usage of a VR application called Wildcard to enhance attention skills in persons with NDD. The application has been redesigned in this study, exploiting eye-tracking technology to enable novel and more fine-grade interactions. A four-week experiment with 38 NDD participants was conducted to evaluate its usability and effectiveness in improving Visual Attention Skills. Results show the usability and effectiveness of Wildcard in enhancing attention skills, advocating for continued exploration of VR and eye-tracking technology's potential in NDD interventions.

**Keywords:** Virtual Reality · Visual Attention Skills · Neurodevelopmental Disorders

## 1 Introduction

Neurodevelopmental disorders (NDD) are a group of conditions that typically manifest early in development, often before a child enters grade school. These disorders are characterized by developmental deficits that impair personal, social, academic, or occupational functioning. Neurodevelopmental disorders include autism spectrum disorders (ASD), intellectual disabilities (ID), communication disorders, and attention-deficit/hyperactivity disorders (ADHD). These disorders, typically identified in early childhood, have common areas of involvement (comorbidity) and can significantly impact a child's development and learning ability. They vary in severity and may persist into adulthood, requiring ongoing support and intervention[2].

Attention deficits are often common in individuals with NDD due to the sensory system dysfunction that characterizes these disorders [23]. Consequently, limited attention capability affects learning, social interactions, daily functioning, emotional regulation, safety, cognitive abilities, overall quality of life, and the ability to transfer knowledge from one circumstance to another. Strengthening attention skills can improve relationships, enhance independence, safer behavior, and a higher sense of well-being. This is why attention skills are often targeted in therapeutic interventions to support individuals in achieving their treatment goals.

Virtual Reality (VR) is achieving promising results in improving various aspects of neurodevelopmental disorders, including cognitive, motor, and social skills [16,19,22] thanks to the possibility of creating a safe learning space where the user can train without unexpected events of the real environments while offering more engaging activities compared to traditional therapeutic ones.

Virtual reality has also proven effective in the case of attention skills [11,12], and in previous research, the potential of virtual reality to improve the attention skills of individuals with neurodevelopmental disorders was already been explored by designing Wildcard, an application for Google Cardboard[10]. With the arrival of more affordable virtual reality headsets and considering the various limitations of Wildcard related to the interaction paradigm (gaze-based, without controllers) and the graphic quality, it has been decided to upgrade Wildcard by moving from Google Cardboard to the Pico Neo3 Pro Eye, a standalone headset equipped with an eye-tracker and better performance and to run an exploratory study with the new version. The objectives of the study were twofold:

1. explore the usability of the new version of Wildcard with persons with NDD. Since the new version of Wildcard has a different interaction paradigm, it was necessary to verify that it was usable.
2. explore the effectiveness of the new version of Wildcard in training attention skills. Since the primary goal of Wildcard is to improve attention skills, it was necessary to verify that the new interaction paradigm would lead to improvements in attention skills.

## 2   Related Work

In the last decades, the literature has increasingly recognized the potential benefits of immersive technologies such as virtual reality in supporting the learning process and rehabilitation in individuals with NDD [7,20] thanks to the possibility of creating a safe learning environment where the user can train without

370    A. Patti et al.

unexpected events of real environments. However, it is not easy to find applications that use virtual reality exclusively for attention skill enhancement; instead, these applications usually bring together multiple benefits that can improve the quality of life of people with NDD.

An example is the work of [12] that shows how training joint attention skills can also benefit social and communication skills. This study is significant as joint attention, the ability to coordinate attention with another individual towards a common point of interest is challenging for many persons with ASD. The VR system simulates a classroom environment where children interact with avatars (virtual characters) that provide cues (like gaze direction, head-turning, and finger-pointing) directing attention to various objects. The children's task is to identify these objects based on the avatars' cues correctly [12]. Another example of how attention skills are trained with other abilities is the study of [5]. It emphasizes recognizing affective states (like engagement, enjoyment, frustration, and boredom) through physiological signals during driving in VR [5]. Attention skills are addressed indirectly through this framework. The VR environment requires participants to navigate and respond to various driving scenarios, implicitly engaging their attention skills. Although the primary focus isn't on attention skills per se, their treatment and enhancement are integral to the driving task and the study's broader goals [5].

In [11], the authors utilize a VR classroom to create an immersive, controlled environment where children's responses to various stimuli can be observed and measured. It looks at gaze patterns as an indicator of attention skills, analyzing where and how long children focus their gaze during different classroom scenarios. This is crucial as gaze patterns in children with NDDs can significantly differ from typically developing children, impacting their learning and social interactions [11]. Additionally, the study explores interoception – the awareness of internal body states – which is another key aspect of how children with NDDs process sensory information and react to their environment [11]. Another study involving a classroom scenario is the one by [21] that presents an ADHD assessment using a virtual reality system. The core of the system is a simulated classroom environment designed to evaluate attention skills in individuals. The system's design integrates various elements to mimic real-life classroom distractions, allowing for a more accurate assessment of attention-related issues in ADHD. The methodology involves tracking behavioral responses and attention patterns in the VR setting, such as response time, accuracy, and focus consistency [21].

The integration of virtual reality with eye-tracking technology is giving good results and allows researchers and therapists to assess the condition of the user [4,13,17,18], providing training tools to individuals with NDD [14,15] for better practicing memory and attention skills. A system that exploits eye tracking is also presented in [1], which is used for enhancing joint attention skills in children with Autism Spectrum Disorder (ASD). The system aims at fostering gaze sharing and gaze following, two critical components of joint attention [1]. It encourages children to share their gaze by looking at an avatar's eye region and following the avatar's gaze to various objects in the virtual environment.

This is significant because gaze sharing and following are essential for effective social communication but are often challenging for children with ASD [1]. The system utilizes eye-tracking technology to monitor and analyze the child's gaze behavior, which is critical for assessing improvements in joint attention skills [1].

# 3   Wildcard

In its first version, Wildcard was an immersive virtual reality mobile application running on smartphones and usable on Google Cardboard [9]. Wildcard aims to improve people's attention skills with NDD through different gamified and customizable experiences. The activities contained in Wildcard were the output of an extensive collaboration with six caregivers, a game-pedagogy professor, and two computer scientists. For this reason, Wildcard tasks and graphics have been explicitly designed to promote attention. For example, i) requiring the child to point to an assigned visual element placed among multiple irrelevant ones, and ii) stabilizing their attention on an object and progressively changing direction to move it. Caregivers suggested creating experiences that evoked the visual content of storybooks used in regular interventions. Familiar content was used to reduce the potential distress caused by unpredictable content. The stories have simple plots, a clear distinction between the main character and the subsidiary elements, and appropriate graphics (e.g., simple shapes, clear lines, and colors) (Fig. 1).

## 3.1   Wildcard Activities

**Fig. 1.** Example of a 360° environment for the *Story* activity

The Wildcard experience encompasses three distinct activities: Research, Story, and Exploration. While the core design of these activities has been retained from the previous version, they have been improved to align with the new device's capabilities.

*Research.* In Research, users are tasked with locating and focusing on objects placed in the 360° environment, following the sequence of a story. The application guides users by highlighting the next target with an arrow to facilitate this task (Fig. 2b). Once the correct object is identified, users employ a combination of gaze, controller pointing, and button press to interact, resulting in the disappearance of the targeted element and progression to the subsequent narrative element.

*Story.* The Story activity involves steering the experience's protagonist through the immersive environment, directing his actions while maintaining focus on him through gaze and controller pointing. The user's gaze initiates the constant movement of the protagonist, ensuring a measured pace that aligns with the narrative. This design choice reduces the need for users to accurately predict the protagonist's movements, promoting a more immersive and user-friendly experience (Fig. 2a).

(a) Story activity with la Pimpa

(b) Object to find in Research activity

**Fig. 2.** Examples from the Story and Research activities

*Exploration.* In Exploration, users navigate a maze filled with story-related images on the walls. A model of a child is included as a companion to aid users in identifying the next picture of the story. Users can traverse the maze at a controlled, continuous pace using gaze and controller pointing to the correct picture, providing a well-integrated combination of exploration and narrative engagement (Fig. 3).

### 3.2    Interaction in Wildcard

Previous user interaction within Wildcard was based on head orientation and focus. By changing head direction, users update their view of the virtual environment and have the illusion of moving in different directions. Since smartphone sensors (accelerometer and gyroscope) track only movement and orientation of the user's head, the center of the smartphone screen was taken as a reference for the user's head (assumption: eye-gaze and head-gaze match). The center of the device was marked with a yellow dot (viewfinder). Users could control the viewfinder and interact with the system by moving their head. Although this system was usable by people with NDD the approximation that "head-gaze

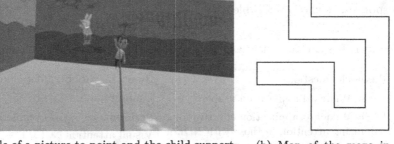

(a) Example of a picture to point and the child support in the Exploration Activity

(b) Map of the maze in the Exploration activity

**Fig. 3.** Examples from the Exploration activity

coincides with eye-gaze" was too strong for an application that is used to train attentional skills. This is why, in its second iteration, Wildcard was designed for the Pico Neo3 Pro Eye, a VR HMD equipped with motion controllers and eye-tracking technology. This technological upgrade expanded the application's functionalities and introduced a more refined and immersive user experience. The integration of eye-tracking technology has proven critical, allowing for more detailed interactions within the virtual environment by precisely identifying the user's focal points. This can enhance the user's concentration on specific objectives, a crucial aspect of the proposed activities in Wildcard. To interact with the system, the user will not only have to look at the object they want to interact with but also point at it with the raycast of the controller. This additional action was added also to improve hand-eye coordination in these individuals which can equally contribute to improving attentional skills.

## 4  Empirical Evaluation

### 4.1  Research Questions and Variables

The main goals of our study were the evaluation of Wildcard usability and efficacy in enhancing user focus and attention, considering the introduction of different interaction methods in the new version. The research questions guiding this investigation are delineated as follows:

- Is the Wildcard application usable?
- Is the Wildcard application effective in improving the attention skills of individuals with NDD?

By addressing these questions, the study aims to provide insights into the application's usability and to discern the efficacy of immersive experiences and eye-tracking technology in contributing to improve attentional skills among users with NDD.

From the research questions, three research variables with corresponding measurement tools were derived to obtain practical quantitative measures and responses, as shown in Table 1.

**Table 1.** Research questions and associated research variables and measurement tools

| Research Question | Research Variable | Measurement tool |
|---|---|---|
| Is the Wildcard application usable? | Usability | SUS |
| Is the Wildcard application effective for enhancing attention in those with NDD? | Performance | Completion Time |
| | Visual attention | TMT |

## 4.2   Participants

A total of 38 adult users (age $\mu$: 30.89, $\sigma$: 8.13) were recruited for the study from a care center with a gender distribution of 32% females and 68% males. All participants have been diagnosed with a disorder falling within the spectrum of neurodevelopmental disorders, with their primary language proficiency being Italian. Additionally, to be eligible for the study, individuals had to be older than 16, exhibit cooperative behavior, demonstrate adequate verbal and vocal production capabilities, and concurrently demonstrate poor attentional stability. These criteria were established to ensure that participants possessed a baseline level of cognitive and communicative abilities while still representing the challenges associated with attentional deficits characteristic of NDD.

Conversely, exclusion criteria were implemented to maintain the integrity of the study sample. Individuals who exhibited oppositional behavior towards technology, aggression, hypersensitivity to visual and auditory stimuli, or poor hand-eye coordination were intentionally omitted from participation. These exclusion criteria were designed to mitigate factors that could impact the study's objectives, ensuring a more homogenous participant group and enhancing the reliability of the findings.

## 4.3   Procedure

The study unfolded over four weeks, structured within a three-step training protocol encompassing a pre-test, four weekly training sessions, and a concluding post-test. The sequential steps of the study were organized to assess the impact of the Wildcard application on individuals with NDD.

The beginning of the study involved a comprehensive pre-test phase where participants underwent an initial evaluation session under the supervision of caregivers. This session aimed to measure the baseline level of visual attention, employing the Trail Making Test (TMT) [6]. The TMT is a neuropsychological test focusing on visual attention and task-switching, requiring participants to connect 25 consecutive targets as rapidly as possible. It comprises two parts: connecting numbers 1 to 25 and alternating between letters and numbers (1-A-2-B...).

Following the pre-test, participants engaged in a structured training involving four sessions conducted at a frequency of one session per week. Researchers were present as observers, providing assistance and technical support during these sessions. Participants, seated on swivel chairs, were equipped with the Pico Neo3 Pro Eye device after the streaming of the user's view was enabled. This facilitated a real-time understanding of the participant's virtual environment, enabling caregivers and researchers to intervene if necessary. Each session commenced with a calibration phase, utilizing the standard app provided by Pico to fine-tune the eye tracker according to the user's eyes. Subsequently, participants engaged in the Wildcard activities, following the sequence of *Research*, *Story*, and *Exploration*. An essential aspect of the study design involved providing different stories for the activities in each session to prevent monotony and repetition, thereby enhancing participant engagement.

At the end of the first session, participants were invited to respond to the SUS questionnaire to gather valuable data and feedback concerning the system's usability and other relevant information. The four consecutive sessions were concluded by a post-test, mirroring the TMT conducted during the pre-test to gather more information about possible improvements.

## 4.4  Data Gathering Methods

The study employed multiple methods to assess the impact and efficacy of the Wildcard application. The data-gathering methods are delineated as follows:

- **Usability:** the System Usability Scale (SUS) [8] was utilized to gather data concerning the usability of the system. This standardized questionnaire comprises ten Likert-scale questions designed to quantitatively measure the users' perceptions and satisfaction levels regarding the Wildcard application's usability. The final scores were computed using the formula:

$$(\sum_{n=1}^{5}(Score_{2n-1} - 1) + \sum_{n=1}^{5}(5 - Score_{2n})) * 2.5$$

- **Performance:** the time required for participants to complete each activity during the training sessions was recorded to gather insights into the participants' engagement and proficiency with the Wildcard application.
- **Visual attention:** the Trail Making Test was a fundamental tool for evaluating the level of visual attention. By comparing the pre-test and post-test scores, it is possible to quantify any improvements resulting from the Wildcard training sessions.

# 5   Results and Discussion

## 5.1   Usability

Of the 38 users involved in the study, only 37 answers have been considered for the evaluation of the usability of Wildcard through the SUS questionnaire. This exclusion was necessary because one participant's responses were considered nonsensical since he consistently provided the lowest score for all questions, irrespective of their nature, making the evaluation unreliable and inconsistent.

Despite this isolated instance, the overall analysis of the collected usability data shows a positive picture regarding the Wildcard application's usability for individuals with NDD. The average SUS score, calculated from the valid responses, is an encouraging 80.26 (Fig. 4). According to the interpretative guidelines by Bangor et al. [3], this score falls within the "Good" interval. This denotes that, on average, participants perceived the Wildcard application as user-friendly and navigable, indicating a positive usability experience within the group of individuals with NDD.

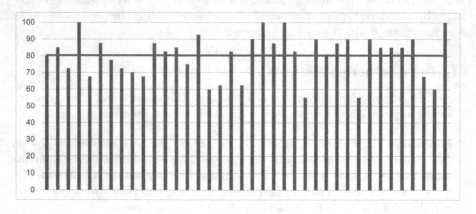

**Fig. 4.** SUS: user and average scores

## 5.2   Performance

Figure 5 illustrates the trend in the overall time required to complete each task across the sessions, showing a consistent decrease in completion times after each session. This observed pattern signifies a tangible improvement in task completion efficiency as participants engaged with the Wildcard application over successive sessions.

Notably, the *Research* activity slightly differed from this trend. However, this difference can be attributed to a deliberate increase in the number of elements within the environment after each session. As the complexity of the task increased with additional elements, the marginal decrease in completion times for this specific activity aligns with the logical expectation that more elements demand a proportionally longer time to complete the task.

Additionally, it is important to notice that, despite the overall positive trends in task completion, organizational challenges and technical issues with the eye tracker resulted in a decline in participant participation across successive sessions. While most of the 38 users successfully completed the first session, logistical constraints and unanticipated problems with the eye tracker hindered continued participation for some individuals in subsequent sittings.

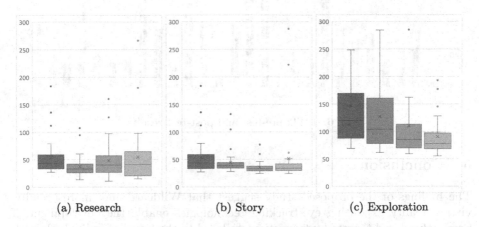

(a) Research          (b) Story          (c) Exploration

**Fig. 5.** Time required to execute the activities (in seconds)

## 5.3   Visual Attention

A selective approach was employed in analyzing the study data, considering participants who consistently engaged with the Wildcard application. Specifically, only those who completed a minimum of three out of the four Wildcard test sessions were included, resulting in an evaluation group of 27 participants. This decision aimed to ensure that the analysis encompassed individuals with substantial and consistent experience with the application, enhancing the reliability and value of the findings.

The analysis revealed a positive trend (Fig. 6), with most participants demonstrating improvement in the time required to complete the TMT. Out of the 27 participants, only six did not exhibit a reduction in completion time. This consistent improvement was also evident in the average completion time, which decreased from 183.22 s to 161.04 s.

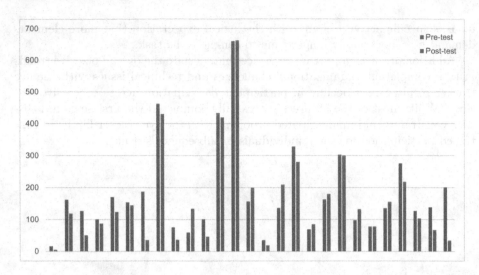

**Fig. 6.** TMT: pre-test and post-test results

## 6 Conclusion

The findings of the proposed study suggest that Wildcard and, more broadly, virtual reality exploiting eye-tracking technologies enable the development of personalized and targeted interventions tailored to the needs of individuals with neurodevelopmental disorders. The positive results observed in visual attention improvement highlight these technologies' potential to address attentional challenges associated with NDD, creating opportunities for more effective and customized therapeutic interventions.

These preliminary results do not prove that Wildcard is a therapeutic tool. However, this study serves as a stepping stone, encouraging further exploration and refinement of these innovative approaches to contribute to the well-being and cognitive development of individuals facing challenges in attentional stability.

### 6.1 Limitations

Despite the promising outcomes of the study highlighting the potential of Wildcard in enhancing visual attention among individuals with NDD, several limitations must be acknowledged.

Firstly, the heterogeneity within the NDD spectrum poses a challenge in understanding the effectiveness of Wildcard on a specific group of disorders. Therefore, it is necessary to involve more individuals with the same diagnosis to offer more specific results.

Secondly, the study encountered challenges related to organizational and technological issues, impacting the completion of sessions within the four weeks. Despite efforts to reschedule sessions, logistical constraints occasionally led to skipped meetings, potentially affecting the overall reliability of the findings.

A notable concern also arose from difficulties in assisting participants when interactions occurred through the eye tracker embedded in the HMD. While caregivers could address issues related to the controller by guiding users, assisting with the eye tracker proved more challenging. Even with screen casting to display the user's perspective, direct assistance remained impossible, leading to certain activities taking longer than expected.

## 6.2   Future Works

While acknowledging the limitations, the study's positive outcomes show that it is possible to improve attentional abilities in individuals with NDD by leveraging VR and eye-tracking technology. To further improve the validity of the study and the usage of these technologies, some considerations for future research can be considered.

Given the difficulties in providing direct assistance during eye-tracking interactions, possible technology support could be explored. Developing more user-friendly interfaces, providing a visible indicator of the user's focus (possibly visible only by the caregiver through the screen casting) or incorporating real-time assistance features could enhance the overall experience for individuals with NDD.

Moreover, further studies will be carried out with stricter inclusion criteria in order to recruit a more homogeneous sample. This approach would contribute to a deeper understanding of whether Wildcard can improve attention skills on specific kinds of NDD.

**Acknowledgments.** This work is partially funded by TIM S.p.A. through its UniversiTIM granting program.

**Disclosure of Interests.** The authors have no competing interests to declare that are relevant to the content of this article.

# References

1. Amat, A.Z., Zhao, H., Swanson, A., Weitlauf, A.S., Warren, Z., Sarkar, N.: Design of an interactive virtual reality system, invirs, for joint attention practice in autistic children. IEEE Trans. Neural Syst. Rehabil. Eng. **29**, 1866–1876 (2021). https://doi.org/10.1109/TNSRE.2021.3108351
2. American Psychiatric Association, D., Association, A.P., et al.: Diagnostic and statistical manual of mental disorders: DSM-5, vol. 5. American Psychiatric Association, Washington, DC (2013)
3. Bangor, A., Kortum, P., Miller, J.: Determining what individual sus scores mean: adding an adjective rating scale. J. Usability Studies **4**(3), 114-123 (may 2009)
4. de Belen, R.A., Pincham, H., Hodge, A., Silove, N., Sowmya, A., Bednarz, T., Eapen, V.: Eye-tracking correlates of response to joint attention in preschool children with autism spectrum disorder. BMC Psychiatry **23**(1) (Mar 2023). https://doi.org/10.1186/s12888-023-04585-3, https://doi.org/10.1186/s12888-023-04585-3

5. Bian, D., Wade, J., Swanson, A., Warren, Z., Sarkar, N.: Physiology-based affect recognition during driving in virtual environment for autism intervention. In: PhyCS 2015 - 2nd International Conference on Physiological Computing Systems, Proceedings, pp. 137–145 (2015)

6. Bowie, C.R., Harvey, P.D.: Administration and interpretation of the trail making test. Nat. Protoc. **1**(5), 2277–2281 (2006). http://dx.doi.org/10.1038/nprot.2006.390

7. Bozgeyikli, L., Raij, A., Katkoori, S., Alqasemi, R.: A survey on virtual reality for individuals with autism spectrum disorder: design considerations. IEEE Trans. Learn. Technol. **11**(2), 133–151 (2018). https://doi.org/10.1109/TLT.2017.2739747

8. Brooke, J.: SUS: a quick and dirty usability scale. Usabil. Eval. Ind. **189** (1995)

9. Garzotto, F., Gelsomini, M., Clasadonte, F., Montesano, D., Occhiuto, D.: Wearable immersive storytelling for disabled children. In: Proceedings of the International Working Conference on Advanced Visual Interfaces. ACM (2016). https://doi.org/10.1145/2909132.2909256

10. Garzotto, F., Gelsomini, M., Occhiuto, D., Matarazzo, V., Messina, N.: Wearable immersive virtual reality for children with disability: a case study. In: Proceedings of the 2017 Conference on Interaction Design and Children. IDC '17, pp. 478–483. Association for Computing Machinery, New York, NY, USA (2017). https://doi.org/10.1145/3078072.3084312

11. Ide-Okochi, A., Matsunaga, N., Sato, H.: A preliminary study of assessing gaze, interoception and school performance among children with neurodevelopmental disorders: the feasibility of VR classroom. Children **9**(2) (2022). https://doi.org/10.3390/children9020250, https://www.mdpi.com/2227-9067/9/2/250

12. Jyoti, V., Gupta, S., Lahiri, U.: Virtual reality based avatar-mediated joint attention task for children with autism: implication on performance and physiology. In: 2019 10th International Conference on Computing, Communication and Networking Technologies (ICCCNT), pp. 1–7 (2019). https://doi.org/10.1109/ICCCNT45670.2019.8944467

13. Lee, D.Y., et al.: Use of eye tracking to improve the identification of attention-deficit/hyperactivity disorder in children. Sci. Rep. **13**(1) (2023). https://doi.org/10.1038/s41598-023-41654-9

14. Lee, T., Yeung, M., Sze, S., Chan, A.: Computerized eye-tracking training improves the saccadic eye movements of children with attention-deficit/hyperactivity disorder. Brain Sci. **10**(12), 1016 (2020). https://doi.org/10.3390/brainsci10121016

15. McParland, A., Gallagher, S., Keenan, M.: Investigating gaze behaviour of children diagnosed with autism spectrum disorders in a classroom setting. J. Autism Dev. Disord. **51**(12), 4663–4678 (2021). https://doi.org/10.1007/s10803-021-04906-z

16. Nordahl-Hansen, A., et al.: An overview of virtual reality interventions for two neurodevelopmental disorders: intellectual disabilities and autism. In: Schmorrow, D.D., Fidopiastis, C.M. (eds.) HCII 2020. LNCS (LNAI), vol. 12197, pp. 257–267. Springer, Cham (2020). https://doi.org/10.1007/978-3-030-50439-7_17

17. Selaskowski, B., et al.: Gaze-based attention refocusing training in virtual reality for adult attention-deficit/hyperactivity disorder. BMC Psychiatry **23**(1) (2023). https://doi.org/10.1186/s12888-023-04551-z

18. Stokes, J.D., Rizzo, A., Geng, J.J., Schweitzer, J.B.: Measuring attentional distraction in children with ADHD using virtual reality technology with eye-tracking. Front. Virtual Real. **3** (2022). https://doi.org/10.3389/frvir.2022.855895

19. Tan, B.L., et al.: The use of virtual reality and augmented reality in psychosocial rehabilitation for adults with neurodevelopmental disorders: a systematic review.

Front. Psychiatry **13** (2022). https://doi.org/10.3389/fpsyt.2022.1055204, https://www.frontiersin.org/journals/psychiatry/articles/10.3389/fpsyt.2022.1055204

20. Tan, B.L., et al.: The use of virtual reality and augmented reality in psychosocial rehabilitation for adults with neurodevelopmental disorders: a systematic review. Front. Psychiatry **13** (2022). https://doi.org/10.3389/fpsyt.2022.1055204

21. Tan, Y., et al.: Virtual classroom: an ADHD assessment and diagnosis system based on virtual reality. In: 2019 IEEE International Conference on Industrial Cyber Physical Systems (ICPS), pp. 203–208 (2019). https://doi.org/10.1109/ICPHYS.2019.8780300

22. Vona, F., Silleresi, S., Beccaluva, E., Garzotto, F.: Social MatchUP: collaborative games in wearable virtual reality for persons with neurodevelopmental disorders. In: Ma, M., Fletcher, B., Göbel, S., Baalsrud Hauge, J., Marsh, T. (eds.) JCSG 2020. LNCS, vol. 12434, pp. 49–65. Springer, Cham (2020). https://doi.org/10.1007/978-3-030-61814-8_4

23. Zomeren, A.H., Brouwer, W.H.: Clinical Neuropsychology of Attention. Oxford University Press, USA (1994)

# EasyCaption: Investigating the Impact of Prolonged Exposure to Captioning on VR HMD on General Population

Sunday D. Ubur[1], Naome A. Etori[2], Shiva Ghasemi[1], Kenneth King[1], Denis Gračanin[1(✉)], and Maria Gini[2]

[1] Virginia Tech, Blacksburg, VA 24060, USA
{uburs,shivagh,kking935,gracanin}@vt.edu
[2] University of Minnesota, Minneapolis, MN 55455, USA
{etori001,gini}@umn.edu

**Abstract.** Recent research explores the potential of captioning within virtual environments. However, the effects of prolonged exposure to captioning in these environments have received scant attention. This study delves into the impacts of extended exposure to captions in a virtual reality (VR) setting, utilizing Head-Mounted Displays (HMDs). Its objective is to augment communication accessibility for individuals who are Deaf or Hard of Hearing (DHH), as well as the broader populace, by evaluating aspects such as user experience, cognitive load, and comprehension. To achieve this, the study adopts a mixed-methods framework, integrating quantitative data gathered via user surveys with qualitative insights obtained from semi-structured interviews. The findings suggest that prolonged eye gaze negatively impacts engagement levels, with participants without avatars exhibiting higher attention and engagement. Additionally, participants with avatars tend to experience slightly higher stress levels. The study concludes by recommending further exploration of robust personalization features and conducting user experience studies to refine captioning environments for improved readability and user satisfaction. This research contributes to the understanding of accessibility and VR technology for both Deaf and Hard of Hearing (DHH) and non DHH populations, offering valuable insights for designers, developers, and educators working towards creating more inclusive VR experiences.

**Keywords:** Virtual Reality · User Experience · Captions · Eye Tracking · Cognitive Load

## 1 Introduction

Virtual, augmented, and mixed reality (VR/AR/MR) together known as extended reality (XR) have become increasingly popular in recent years, offering new opportunities for education, entertainment, and communication. The potential of captioning within virtual environments (VEs) has been extensively

M. Antona and C. Stephanidis (Eds.): HCII 2024, LNCS 14697, pp. 382–403, 2024.
https://doi.org/10.1007/978-3-031-60881-0_24

explored in research, particularly in the context of enhancing communication accessibility for DHH individuals [11].

While some research has explored the impact of extended exposure to captions in virtual reality (VR) settings [32], there remains a notable gap in our understanding of how this prolonged exposure affects the user experience, cognitive burden, and comprehension. Further investigation is warranted, as highlighted by recent work emphasizing the need for additional research in this area [36].

Our primary objectives are to assess users' tolerance for prolonged gaze while absorbing information from real-time captions and to determine whether active user participation in the caption environment can yield positive or negative effects on sustained gaze, an aspect that remains understudied [5]. Additionally, we have established secondary objectives that involve evaluating the suitability of using Automatic Speech Recognition (ASR) captions as a means of communication in classroom settings. To address these objectives, our study seeks answers to the following research questions:

**RQ1:** What is the relationship between prolonged exposure to captioning on VR HMD and cognitive load for individuals with DHH and general population?

**RQ2:** How does the continuous visual processing of captions impact cognitive resources and mental effort during VR interactions?

**RQ3:** Can user interaction within the caption environment such as active engagement enhance user experience and minimize prolonged gaze?

**RQ4:** What is the mean optimal gazing distance between the eye and HMD caption display to maintain user experience?

This study contributes significantly to the field, augmenting the current understanding of accessibility within VR technology, especially for DHH individuals. It extends existing knowledge, shedding light on the potential benefits and challenges inherent in VR technology. The critical insights gained from this research hold substantial value for designers, developers, and educators striving to create more inclusive VR experiences for DHH individuals. Moreover, with a primary goal of enhancing communication accessibility, the study seeks to improve the overall quality of life for the DHH community and the wider population reliant on captions for communication. Leveraging augmented reality technology, the research underscores the significance of effective communication tools in VR environments. The findings are poised to influence the development of more accessible and user-friendly VR systems, contributing to the broader discourse on integrating technology and accessibility.

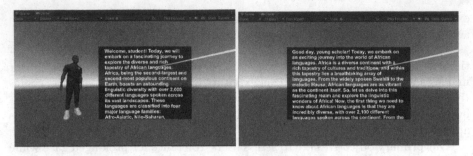

**Fig. 1. Left:** User reading caption on VR via ChatGPT Avatar. **Right:** User reading long text captions on VR.

## 2    Related Work

### 2.1    Impact of ASR Captioning on User's Focus

The integration of automatic speech recognition (ASR) captioning in VR has drawn a lot of attention for its potential to improve accessibility, especially for the DHH population [12]. However, research suggests prolonged exposure to ASR captions may impact user focus during VR interactions. According to [18], ASR captioning can be distracting even if it provides real-time information, especially for people not used to VR interfaces. Subtitles can compromise the quality of users' VR experiences on the display since they distract users' attention from their intended duties or environment [25]. ASR captioning can be essential for DHH population in helping them focus while engaging in VR encounters [22]. ASR captioning helps close communication gaps and encourages more active participation in the VR environment by providing contextual information and fostering conversation [24]. The influence of ASR captioning on user focus depends on personal preferences, past VR experience, and the particular AR application used.

Hence, it is crucial to acknowledge the variety within the DHH population [35]. It is necessary to consider elements like cognitive load to examine the effect on user focus [16]. Some research has shown that users increase cognitive load due to ASR captions since they must concurrently digest the textual content and the VR environment [3]. Cognitive load can impact users' ability to concentrate on their intended activities and gain knowledge from the VR experience [17]. ASR captions can improve accessibility for some users, but they may also reduce immersion and presence in VR experiences. The captions divide attention between reading text and perceiving the augmented environment [13]. This split attention effect seems to be more pronounced for users who are new to VR technology. As people gain more experience with VR over time, the distracting effect of captions may lessen [18].

## 2.2   Existing Approaches to Display ASR on VR HMDs

Various methods for presenting ASR captions in VR HMDs have been explored, with factors such as visibility, immersion, and usability requiring consideration. A common technique places text directly in the user's field of view to provide real-time subtitles blended into the VR environment [26,27]. These captions can be static or dynamically track speakers and objects. Although visibility is excellent, this could still be a design issue hence ensure text does not block important visual components or cause legibility issues under different lighting conditions citewu2020phrase2vec.

Another approach uses spatial audio cues to render captions, matching the auditory location of captions to their visual sources [4]. This can be used to render captions as audio explanations that emanate from the same location as the corresponding visual source in the VR environment. Linking the auditory captions to specific objects or people creates an aural connection that matches the visual information. In theory, spatially matching the audio and visual elements in this way can heighten the user's sense of presence and immersion in the VR experience [19].

However, the effectiveness of the spatial audio approach depends on the user's aural skills and the intricacy of the VR environment. Additionally, the complexity of the VR environment itself plays a role. Spatial audio captioning may work well for simple VR scenes but could become confusing or congested when multiple audio sources are present in complex environments [19]. A thorough review is essential to establish the best strategy for DHH patients and the general population [2].

When utilizing text-based techniques for VR ASR captions, factors such as legibility and readability should be thoroughly evaluated [42]. Design considerations including font size, color contrast, and text arrangement must account for user needs across diverse VR applications [9]. Additionally, adapting these text-based strategies to real-world environments, and lighting conditions warrants examination to ensure consistent performance [29]. For spatial audio ASR captioning methods, usability evaluations should assess the accuracy and clarity of auditory cues [30]. Users' ability to comprehend dispersed geographic captions and their impacts on VR experience immersion requires evaluation. Furthermore, audio congestion issues must be addressed, especially in complex VR scenes [37].

## 2.3   Current Design Principles

The primary design guideline is ensuring caption legibility through appropriate text font, size, and contrasting backdrops suited to the VR environment [10,23]. Careful evaluation of text placement within the user's field of view is crucial to avoid visual obstruction while maintaining readability and unobtrusiveness. Allowing user customization of caption positioning is optimal [38]. Additionally, designers must consider caption or backdrop color contrast to accommodate different visual acuity levels, especially for DHH users who rely on visual cues [1, 15]. An extensive VR HMD interface customization of text characteristics and positioning should be enabled to meet diverse user needs [7,8]. As dynamic VR landscapes change, captions should adapt seamlessly within the user's view while remaining anchored to relevant objects or speakers [41]. Reliable ASR performance across varied real-world settings from well-lit interiors to challenging exteriors requires rigorous evaluation [35].

### 2.4   Comprehensive Test Suite for VR Applications with ASR Captioning

In the context of VR applications, the effective assessment of ASR captioning's performance and influence calls for an elaborate test suite. This rigorously designed suite serves as a structured platform to scrutinize the intricate components of VR applications that are synergized with ASR captioning. Its design and purpose are twofold, catering to the specific needs of DHH individuals while also ensuring functionality and relevance for the wider audience. Integral to this suite are the Standardized Accessibility Tests. As explained by [28], these tests are critical in measuring the degree to which ASR captioning bolsters accessibility, with a particular emphasis on fostering the inclusivity of VR applications for DHH individuals. Additionally, a thorough cognitive burden assessment is essential. This involves evaluating the cognitive demands ASR captioning places on users. To this end, the suite should embed metrics that quantify the mental exertion required by users to both grasp the captions generated by ASR and navigate the VR interface [21,39]. Furthermore, the suite enriches its evaluative depth by incorporating Engagement Metrics [7]. It is essential to ascertain if the ASR captioning serves as a catalyst for, or a deterrent to, user immersion and engagement with VR content. In terms of quality assurance [6], it underscores the test suite to embed standardized protocols. These protocols should rigorously evaluate the precision of captions, their synchronicity in real-time, and their fluid integration within the VR environment. Recognizing the diverse user base of VR applications, the suite also integrates diverse User evaluations. Tailored with precision, these evaluations acknowledge and anticipate the unique challenges posed to both the DHH individuals and the broader user demographic. There is a need for tailor-made evaluations within the suite, which can aptly discern the nuanced ramifications of ASR captioning across diverse user segments [33].

## 3   Experiment

In this study, we employed a mixed-methods approach, combining quantitative data collection through user surveys with qualitative insights gathered through semi-structured interviews. The participant pool consisted of individuals from the general population who engaged in Virtual Reality (VR) Head-Mounted Display (HMD) experiences featuring real-time captions.

Quantitative data were gathered by measuring participants' subjective experiences, encompassing perceived usefulness, ease of use, and overall satisfaction. Standardized scales were utilized for a consistent and comparable evaluation of these metrics. Additionally, to delve into the cognitive aspects of the VR HMD experience, an Electroencephalogram (EEG) test was administered to assess cognitive load.

Qualitative data were collected through semi-structured interviews, providing participants with the opportunity to articulate detailed insights into their experiences with prolonged exposure to captions in VR HMD. Thematic analysis was employed to identify recurring themes and patterns related to comprehension, engagement, and the broader impact of VR HMD captions on the daily lives of Deaf and Hard of Hearing (DHH) individuals, as well as the general population relying on captions.

This comprehensive approach allowed for a holistic understanding of the effects of VR HMD captions, combining both quantitative metrics and qualitative narratives to enrich our insights into user experiences.

## 3.1 Participants

All 22 participants were Virginia Tech students, with a total of 22 respondents.

In terms of knowledge about the history of African Languages, participants provided self-reported ratings on a scale of 0 to 5, with an average score of 2.06. This suggests a limited level of familiarity or knowledge among the participants regarding the history of African Languages. Additionally, all 22 participants indicated using captions in the past, either as DHH individuals or as general users who may use captions to complement audio information. The overwhelming majority, 95.45%, affirmed the use of captions, underscoring the relevance of this aspect in their communication experiences. Furthermore, all participants reported English as their medium of communication, highlighting linguistic homogeneity within the sample.

## 3.2 Apparatus

For data collection, we utilized Emotiv Epoc+ [31] to conduct Electroencephalographic (EEG) testing, providing insights into eye tracking and cognition by measuring key performance metrics (Fig. 2). Simultaneously, surveys were administered using Question Pro [34]. The Meta Quest Pro headset [40] facilitated interaction within the virtual environment for reading captions and engaging with the Avatar.

Our meticulously crafted Avatar, developed with ReadyPlayerMe [14] and seamlessly integrated into Unity software, added a personalized touch to the virtual experience. To analyze the collected data, t-tests and Analysis of Variance (ANOVA) were conducted to explore differences and relationships between crucial variables: attention, engagement, and stress. These analyses are pivotal in comprehending the impact of prolonged gaze and cognitive load on user experiences.

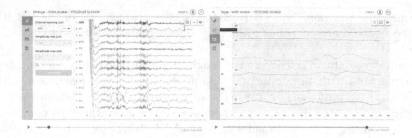

**Fig. 2. Left:** EEG Processing Participant Activity. **Right:** Participant's Performance Metric Data.

### 3.3 Tasks

Based on research questions, we employed two prototypes for distinct tasks. Task 1 involves the utilization of ASR captions displayed in a VR HMD (right side). In contrast, Task 2 involves the use of captions alongside a ChatGPT-based avatar on the left side (Fig. 1) to facilitate interactive experiences. All methods were carried out by relevant guidelines and regulations as approved by the Institutional Review Board at Virginia Tech, IRB-23-820. Participants were required to wear VR HMDs before undertaking any assigned tasks. Task 1 entails reading a concise historical overview of African languages presented through VR HMD captions, while Task 2 requires participants to engage with an avatar and pose questions about African languages. To minimize potential bias, participants for both tasks were chosen at random, and both methods did not require hearing speech. Our measurements focused on assessing participants' level of attention, excitement, engagement, interest, stress, and horizontal eye direction while reading captions to determine the effects of cognitive load and eye gaze.

### 3.4 Implementation

We implemented two prototypes to carry out two tasks: ASR captions in VR HMD, and captions using ChatGPT based Avatar to facilitate active interaction between the participant and the captions environment. Participants for this study used a VR HMD for both tasks after they were shown how to wear the hardware correctly, and how to adjust it to fit their optimal gazing level. To minimize bias in task completion, the study was conducted randomly in which some participants began with Task 1, and others began with Task 2.

In the first activity (Task 1), participants were attended to individually, listening to a brief history of languages in Africa via the VR HMD caption. In the second activity (Task 2), participants had an opportunity to ask further questions on the history of languages in Africa via ChatGPT captions on VR HMD in the form of interaction with an avatar. The purpose of Task 2 is to determine the impact of active engagement on prolonged gaze [20]. In both instances, par-

ticipants have been measured on duration they were able to concentrate gazing
on captions, and the optimal distance between their eyes to the caption display.

## 4 Results

**Table 1.** EEG with no avatar.

| Attention | Engagement | Excitement | Interest | Relaxation | Stress |
|---|---|---|---|---|---|
| 41 | 91 | 40 | 39 | 34 | 19 |
| 39 | 74 | 47 | 77 | 34 | 65 |
| 38 | 82 | 11 | 45 | 24 | 22 |
| 44 | 95 | 42 | 50 | 41 | 43 |
| 43 | 68 | 10 | 48 | 48 | 35 |
| 48 | 75 | 5 | 43 | 47 | 30 |
| 41 | 81 | 32 | 56 | 50 | 53 |
| 38 | 81 | 38 | 43 | 69 | 27 |
| 55 | 77 | 18 | 46 | 57 | 35 |
| 66 | 65 | 27 | 43 | 70 | 47 |
| 57 | 71 | 25 | 38 | 28 | 37 |
| 48 | 95 | 37 | 60 | 69 | 47 |
| 45 | 70 | 15 | 48 | 36 | 37 |
| 52 | 42 | 46 | 56 | 70 | 39 |
| 54 | 77 | 35 | 50 | 45 | 40 |
| 42 | 73 | 48 | 43 | 35 | 36 |
| 43 | 80 | 28 | 65 | 57 | 47 |
| 31 | 69 | 19 | 39 | 24 | 34 |
| 41 | 74 | 24 | 49 | 29 | 39 |
| 46 | 69 | 31 | 56 | 36 | 45 |
| 39 | 69 | 19 | 49 | 29 | 39 |
| 43 | 73 | 23 | 53 | 33 | 42 |

The data shown in Tables 1 and 2 were extracted from the Emotiv Pro after
experiments were performed with over 20 participants. The data generated by
the system was continuous, so we extracted 5 representative sample readings of
which we further calculated average values for each column, then we compared
each row to these average values and identify the row with values closest to
the averages. The representative values are what we extracted to work with
in Tables 1 and 2. In this analysis we settled with only 17 participants EEG
recorded data as the rest of the data had wrong and missing values due to poor
signal that was less than 70 microvolts (mV). To ensure EEG data reliability, we
used Performance Metrics data and signal 75–100 mV (Figs. 5 and 6).

**Table 2.** EEG with avatar.

| Attention | Engagement | Excitement | Interest | Relaxation | Stress |
|---|---|---|---|---|---|
| 33 | 76 | 54 | 45 | 45 | 34 |
| 35 | 95 | 41 | 45 | 34 | 63 |
| 35 | 82 | 13 | 46 | 26 | 38 |
| 38 | 95 | 68 | 43 | 53 | 41 |
| 39 | 71 | 23 | 46 | 31 | 38 |
| 35 | 60 | 9 | 43 | 26 | 34 |
| 59 | 62 | 15 | 42 | 24 | 40 |
| 29 | 74 | 33 | 60 | 66 | 53 |
| 38 | 67 | 19 | 45 | 43 | 32 |
| 31 | 79 | 5 | 38 | 70 | 28 |
| 35 | 60 | 21 | 51 | 52 | 43 |
| 35 | 95 | 14 | 51 | 66 | 35 |
| 43 | 68 | 19 | 51 | 63 | 39 |
| 40 | 72 | 16 | 41 | 56 | 29 |
| 47 | 81 | 9 | 49 | 50 | 36 |
| 39 | 76 | 26 | 46 | 42 | 36 |
| 32 | 95 | 21 | 45 | 51 | 28 |
| 30 | 70 | 20 | 40 | 26 | 36 |
| 40 | 73 | 25 | 50 | 30 | 41 |
| 45 | 70 | 30 | 55 | 33 | 45 |
| 38 | 68 | 18 | 47 | 25 | 38 |
| 42 | 74 | 22 | 52 | 32 | 42 |

## 4.1 Interpretation

*Attention:* In terms of attention, Table 1 shows values ranging from 38 to 66, averaging around 47. In contrast, Table 2 presents a range from 29 to 59 with an average of around 39. The interpretation here is that participants in Table 1, who read only captions, had higher attention levels compared to those in Table 2, who read captions while interacting with an avatar.

*Engagement:* For engagement, Table 1's values vary from 65 to 95, with an average of around 79. Table 2, on the other hand, ranges from 60 to 95, averaging about 74. This suggests that participants in Table 1 tended to be more engaged than those in Table 2.

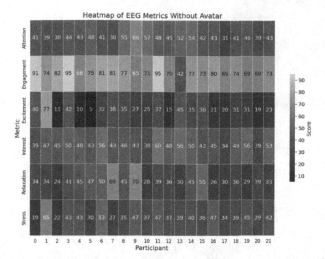

**Fig. 3.** Heatmap of EEG Metrics without Avatar: High engagement scores prevail (above 70), indicating sustained participant immersion. Attention varies widely, reflecting personal differences in interacting with the VR environment. Excitement and interest show fluctuation, excitement levels are generally lower and show significant fluctuations between participants. While relaxation scores vary, with some participants showing high levels of relaxation in the 50 s and 60 s. Overall, stress remains low with no scores above 50 underscoring a comfortable and non-stressful VR experience (from Table 1).

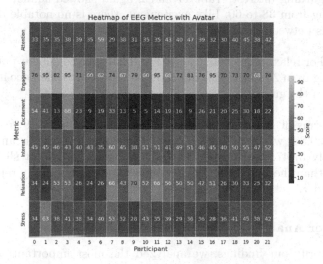

**Fig. 4.** Heatmap of EEG Metrics with Avatar: The heatmap reveals diverse EEG metric responses to an avatar, with high engagement scores dominating (above 70), reflecting a robust interaction. Varied attention levels hint at individual focus disparities. Excitement and interest are lower yet varied, suggesting mixed arousal and curiosity towards the avatar. Moderate relaxation scores imply calmness for some, while generally low-stress levels indicate minimal stress impact from the avatar interaction (from Table 2).

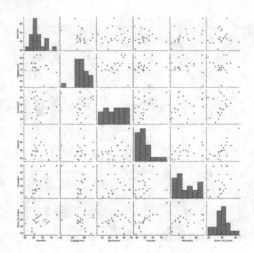

**Fig. 5.** Pair plot of EEG data from a study with no avatar.

*Excitement:* In the case of excitement, both Tables 1 and 2 exhibited similar patterns, with values ranging from 5 to 68. There appears to be no significant difference in excitement levels between the two groups.

*Interest:* Regarding interest, Tables 1 and 2 again showed similar trends, with values ranging from 38 to 60. Like excitement, there is no notable difference in interest levels between the groups.

*Relaxation:* For relaxation levels, Tables 1 and 2 displayed similar patterns, with values ranging from 24 to 70. This indicates no significant difference in relaxation levels between the groups.

*Stress:* In terms of stress, Table 1 had values ranging from 19 to 65, averaging around 39.88, whereas Table 2 ranged from 28 to 63 with an average of approximately 37.47. Participants in Table 2 tended to exhibit slightly higher stress levels than those in Table 1. This difference is also visually represented in Figs. 3, 4, and 7.

### 4.2  Further Analysis Using t-Test and ANOVA

To further verify our findings, we analyzed the most important performance metrics relating to our study, Attention, Engagement, and Stress.

The t-test and ANOVA results in Figs. 8, 9 and Tables 5 and 6 provide insights into the differences between participating in the two tasks for each metric (Attention, Engagement, and Stress). Let's interpret each result:

*Attention:* **T-Statistic (3.4958):** indicates the number of standard deviations by which the mean of the Attention metric for the two groups differs. A positive

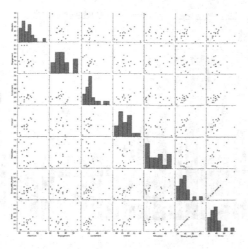

**Fig. 6.** Pair plot of EEG data from a study with avatar ChatGPT.

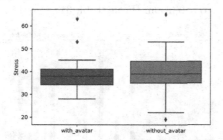

**Fig. 7.** Pair plot of stress with and without avatar.

value suggests that the mean of results from participants who read only captions is higher than those who read captions while interacting with Avatar. **P-Value (0.0014):** is the probability of observing such extreme results (or more extreme) if there is no true difference between the groups. A low p-value (typically below 0.05) suggests that you can reject the null hypothesis, indicating a significant difference in Attention between the groups.

For the ANOVA test, we have an F-statistic: of 12.2208 and a p-value: of 0.0014 Since the p-value of 0.0014 is less than the commonly used significance level of 0.05, therefore, there is evidence to reject the null hypothesis. This suggests that there are statistically significant differences in the means of the two tasks for the "Attention" metric.

*Engagement:* **T-Statistic (−0.1530):** suggests that the mean of the Engagement metric for the first group may be lower than the mean for the second group. However, the magnitude of the t-statistic is small. **P-Value (0.8793):** suggests no significant difference in Engagement between the groups. We fail to reject the null hypothesis.

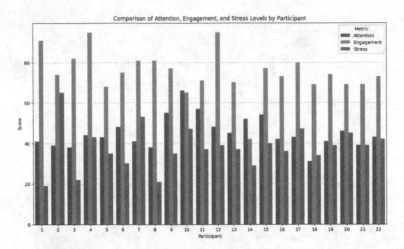

**Fig. 8.** EEG Data with no Avatar: Comparison of Attention, Engagement, and Stress Levels by Participant derived from EEG measurements, indicating variable engagement and stress levels relative to attention. (From Table 3)

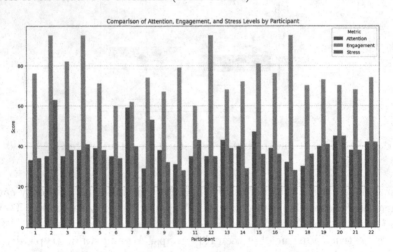

**Fig. 9.** EEG Data with Avatar: Comparison of Attention, Engagement, and Stress Levels by Participant derived from EEG measurements, indicating variable engagement and stress levels relative to attention (From Table 4).

**Table 3.** EEG Data with No Avatar

| Participant | Attention | Engagement | Stress |
|---|---|---|---|
| 1 | 41 | 91 | 19 |
| 2 | 39 | 74 | 65 |
| 3 | 38 | 82 | 22 |
| 4 | 44 | 95 | 43 |
| 5 | 43 | 68 | 35 |
| 6 | 48 | 75 | 30 |
| 7 | 41 | 81 | 53 |
| 8 | 38 | 81 | 27 |
| 9 | 55 | 77 | 35 |
| 10 | 66 | 65 | 47 |
| 11 | 57 | 71 | 37 |
| 12 | 48 | 95 | 47 |
| 13 | 45 | 70 | 37 |
| 14 | 52 | 42 | 39 |
| 15 | 54 | 77 | 40 |
| 16 | 42 | 73 | 36 |
| 17 | 43 | 80 | 47 |
| 18 | 31 | 69 | 34 |
| 19 | 41 | 74 | 39 |
| 20 | 46 | 69 | 45 |
| 21 | 39 | 69 | 39 |
| 22 | 43 | 73 | 42 |

Similarly, from the ANOVA test, F-statistic: 0.0234, p-value: 0.8793 which means the p-value of 0.8793 is greater than the significance level of 0.05. In this case, there is not enough evidence to reject the null hypothesis. This suggests that there are no statistically significant differences in the means of the two tasks for the "Engagement" metric.

*Stress:* **T-Statistic (0.2027):** The positive value suggests that the mean of the Stress metric for the first group may be higher than the mean for the second group. Again, the magnitude of the t-statistic is small. **P-Value (0.8406):** Similar to Engagement, the high p-value for Stress indicates that there is no significant difference between the groups in terms of Stress.

Also, the ANOVA test for Stress gives an F-statistic: of 0.0411, p-value: 0.8406, and similar to Engagement, the p-value of 0.8406 is greater than 0.05. There is insufficient evidence to reject the null hypothesis for the Stress metric, indicating that there are no statistically significant differences in the means of the two tasks.

**Table 4.** EEG Data with Avatar

| Participant | Attention | Engagement | Stress |
|---|---|---|---|
| 1 | 33 | 76 | 34 |
| 2 | 35 | 95 | 63 |
| 3 | 35 | 82 | 38 |
| 4 | 38 | 95 | 41 |
| 5 | 39 | 71 | 38 |
| 6 | 35 | 60 | 34 |
| 7 | 59 | 62 | 40 |
| 8 | 29 | 74 | 53 |
| 9 | 38 | 67 | 32 |
| 10 | 31 | 79 | 28 |
| 11 | 35 | 60 | 43 |
| 12 | 35 | 95 | 35 |
| 13 | 43 | 68 | 39 |
| 14 | 40 | 72 | 29 |
| 15 | 47 | 81 | 36 |
| 16 | 39 | 76 | 36 |
| 17 | 32 | 95 | 28 |
| 18 | 30 | 70 | 36 |
| 19 | 40 | 73 | 41 |
| 20 | 45 | 70 | 45 |
| 21 | 38 | 68 | 38 |
| 22 | 42 | 74 | 42 |

**Table 5.** T-Test Results

| | T-statistic | p-value |
|---|---|---|
| Attention | 3.4958 | 0.0014 |
| Engagement | −0.1530 | 0.8793 |
| Stress | 0.2027 | 0.8406 |

*Summary:* For "Attention," there are significant differences among the two tasks. For "Engagement" and "Stress," there is no evidence of significant differences among the two tasks. These results are based on the specified significance level (often set at 0.05).

*Facial Expression Eye Gaze:* The horizontal eye direction remains consistently centered around zero with occasional minor variations, indicating a stable gaze Fig. 10. Blinking and winking (FE.BlinkWink) are largely absent or minimal. The

**Table 6.** ANOVA Results

| Metric | F-statistic | p-value |
| --- | --- | --- |
| Attention | 12.2208 | 0.0014 |
| Engagement | 0.0234 | 0.8793 |
| Stress | 0.0411 | 0.8406 |

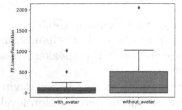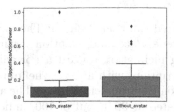

**Fig. 10. Left:** Eye gaze: Lower Face Action. **Right:** Upper Face Action.

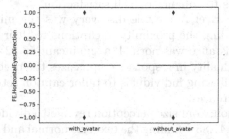

**Fig. 11.** Pair plot of Stress with and without Avatar.

upper and lower face actions seem to be more pronounced on captions without avatar (Fig. 10).

Similarly, the horizontal eye direction displays greater variability, including occasional negative values, suggesting shifts in gaze direction. While FE.BlinkWink remains generally minimal, there are instances of higher values. This is also observed in the upper and lower face actions which is more pronounced on captions without avatars.

Meanwhile, the most important parameter for analyzing eye gaze is the Horizontal Eyes Direction as it is a pertinent indicator of eye gaze. Given the absence of a dedicated column expressly labeled "eye gaze" or a comparable metric, the decision was made to prioritize the column that appeared most directly associated with the direction of the eyes. However, as shown in Fig. 11, there is no noticeable difference between the two studies regarding horizontal eye gaze. The mean values for Horizontal Eyes Direction exhibit no discernible difference between the two datasets. Consequently, concerning this particular column, it seems that the presence or absence of an avatar does not exert a significant influence on prolonged eye gaze, as shown in Fig. 11 .

# 5   Discussions

After Task 1 which required participants to read captions, they completed a survey assessing user preferences in captioning and transcription services, and several interesting patterns and insights emerged. The survey focused on aspects such as preferred caption position, speaker's pace, caption environment, feelings about the eyes, font size perception, and the overall preference for using captions in a classroom setting.

1. Preferred Caption Position: The majority of participants (56.52).
2. Speaker's Pace and Caption Transcription Speed: Participants showed a strong inclination toward a normal pace for both the speaker and caption transcription, with an overwhelming 81.82.
3. Caption Environment Rating: The average rating of the caption environment, calculated at 32.04 out of 100, indicates a moderate satisfaction level among participants. This suggests that while there might be aspects of the captioning environment that users appreciate, there is room for improvement or additional features to enhance overall satisfaction.
4. Feeling about the Eye: A notable discovery was the mixed feelings among participants regarding the proximity of captions to their eyes. While 43.48% felt the caption distance was normal, a significant 56.52% found it too close to the eyes. This duality in responses emphasizes the need for a customizable user experience, allowing individuals to tailor caption settings based on their comfort and preferences.
5. Font Size Perception: Font size perception revealed a divided sentiment among participants, with 47.83% finding the text size normal and an equal percentage split between those who found it too large or too small. This underscores the importance of offering adjustable font settings to cater to diverse user preferences.
6. Preference for Using Captions in a Classroom: Participants expressed a moderate preference for using captions as a mode of listening to lectures in a classroom, with an average score of 37.48 out of 100. This suggests that while captions are viewed favorably, there may be factors influencing the preference, such as the quality of transcription or additional features. The participants' survey responses provide additional insights into their subjective experiences during the tasks. Let's compare these findings with the EEG data:

Similarly, upon participants's completion of Task 2, which involved reading captions and interacting with ChatGPT Avatar, they were asked to complete a second survey. Below are the findings after completing the Task survey:

1. Gaze or Concentration Length: Participants reported similar average scores for the length of gaze or concentration in both tasks (Task 1: 29.71, Task 2: 29.26). No significant differences were observed between the tasks based on the average scores.
2. Adjusting Viewing Distance: In Task 1, a higher percentage (52.17%) felt the need to refocus or look away compared to Task 2 (47.83%). This aligns with the EEG data, where the "Attention" metric was higher in Task 1.

3. Comfortable Viewing Distance: In Task 1, more participants (56.52%) felt the distance between their eyes and the caption display was comfortable compared to Task 2 (43.48%). This corresponds with the subjective reports about the comfort of viewing distance in Task 1.

4. Influence of Avatar on Concentration: Participants were divided on whether the ChatGPT-based avatar in Task 2 influenced their concentration. This aligns with the EEG data, where there were no significant differences in "Engagement" and "Stress" between the tasks.

**Effect of Avatar on Focus Duration:** Among those who felt the avatar influenced concentration, most reported that it had no noticeable effect on focus duration (59.09%). This suggests that the avatar, while noticed, did not significantly impact attention, as supported by the EEG data.

5. Comfort with Avatar Interaction: Participants, on average, rated their comfort with viewing distance when interacting with the avatar in Task 2 as 35.39 (on a scale of 1 to 5). This aligns with the subjective reports on the comfort of viewing distance in Task 2.

6. Concentration and Comfort: Participants felt they were able to concentrate better on the captions in Task 2 (56.52%), and both tasks were perceived as similarly natural or comfortable in terms of the viewing experience.

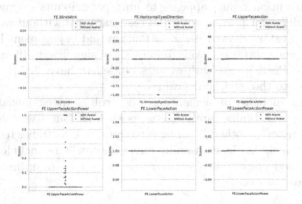

**Fig. 12.** Comparison of Eye Gaze Metrics With and Without Avatar Interaction: The swarm plots illustrate a clear distribution of eye gaze metrics across participants under two different conditions. In the presence of an avatar, the FE.UpperFaceActionPower metric shows a wider range of responses, suggesting a greater variation in participants' upper facial muscle activation. In contrast, the FE.HorizontalEyesDirection metric indicates a similar response pattern in both conditions, implying consistent horizontal eye movements regardless of avatar interaction. Notably, FE.BlinkWink and FE.LowerFaceActionPower metrics exhibit minimal variation, reflecting a lack of influence from the avatar's presence on these specific facial expressions.

The findings from eye gaze data shown in Fig. 12, and in addition to user survey results imply that the presence of an avatar may contribute to more consistent and less variable eye movements, influencing users' gaze direction. Moreover, the nature of the content, specifically the inclusion or exclusion of an avatar, appears to impact users' engagement and focus during caption reading. Notably, the minimal occurrence of blinking and winking in both conditions suggests a relatively stable and focused user state across the experimental settings.

*Challenges and Recommendations:* Challenges reported during Task 1 included headset discomfort, the need to move the head, and text size issues. Challenges reported during Task 2 included distraction by the avatar, the need to move the head, and issues with scrolling and paragraph breaks. Recommendations for Task 2 included reconsidering the avatar, indicating it was perceived as distracting.

## 6   Conclusion

The subjective survey responses provide qualitative insights that align with the quantitative EEG data. Participants' experiences, comfort, and preferences varied, emphasizing the importance of considering subjective and objective measures in evaluating user experiences. The challenges and recommendations offer valuable input for refining the tasks in future iterations. Prolonged eye gaze (as indicated by attention levels) appears to hurt participants' engagement levels, as shown in Table 1 for participants who read captions without avatars. Participants without avatars showed higher attention and engagement levels. Excitement, interest, and relaxation levels did not show significant differences between the two groups. Participants with avatars tended to have slightly higher stress levels compared to those without avatars.

Future work includes implementing more robust personalization features, allowing users to customize caption settings such as font size, color, and background transparency. Another direction is to conduct UX studies to identify areas for UI enhancements in the captioning environment. This includes refining the layout, design, and placement of captions on the screen to optimize readability and minimize distraction.

## References

1. Agulló, B., Matamala, A.: Subtitling for the deaf and hard-of-hearing in immersive environments: results from a focus group. J. Special. Transl. **32**, 217–235 (2019)
2. Aljedaani, W., Krasniqi, R., Aljedaani, S., Mkaouer, M.W., Ludi, S., Al-Raddah, K.: If online learning works for you, what about deaf students? Emerging challenges of online learning for deaf and hearing-impaired students during COVID-19: a literature review. Univ. Access Inf. Soc. **22**(3), 1027–1046 (2023)
3. Amal, A.I.: Deaf and hard of hearing students' perceptions of the flipped classroom strategy in an undergraduate education course. Eur. J. Educ. Res. **8**(1), 325–336 (2019)

4. Bastas, G., et al.: Towards a DHH accessible theater: real-time synchronization of subtitles and sign language videos with ASR and NLP solutions. In: Proceedings of the 15th International Conference on PErvasive Technologies Related to Assistive Environments, pp. 653–661 (2022)
5. Bektaş, K., et al.: Gear: gaze-enabled augmented reality for human activity recognition. In: Proceedings of the 2023 Symposium on Eye Tracking Research and Applications. ETRA '23. ACM, New York (2023). https://doi.org/10.1145/3588015.3588402
6. Buxton, J.: Design for accessible collaborative engagement: making online synchronous collaborative learning more accessible for students with sensory impairments. Ph.D. thesis, The Open University (2023)
7. Creed, C., Al-Kalbani, M., Theil, A., Sarcar, S., Williams, I.: Inclusive augmented and virtual reality: a research agenda. Int. J. Hum.–Comput. Interact. 1–20 (2023)
8. Cui, M., Zheng, C., Shi, W., Wang, Z.: Research of the typography design for digital reading on mobile devices. Ergon. Design **77**, 110–121 (2023)
9. Fan, M., Li, Y.: The application of computer graphics processing in visual communication design. J. Intell. Fuzzy Syst. **39**(4), 5183–5191 (2020)
10. Gabbard, J.L., Smith, M., Merenda, C., Burnett, G., Large, D.R.: A perceptual color-matching method for examining color blending in augmented reality head-up display graphics. IEEE Trans. Visual Comput. Graphics **28**(8), 2834–2851 (2020)
11. Glasser, A., Riley, E.M., Weeks, K., Kushalnagar, R.: Mixed reality speaker identification as an accessibility tool for deaf and hard of hearing users. In: Proceedings of the 25th ACM Symposium on Virtual Reality Software and Technology (2019). https://doi.org/10.1145/3359996.3364720
12. Jain, D.: Sound sensing and feedback techniques for deaf and hard of hearing people. Ph.D. thesis, University of Washington (2022)
13. Jain, D., et al.: Head-mounted display visualizations to support sound awareness for the deaf and hard of hearing. In: Proceedings of the 33rd Annual ACM Conference on Human Factors in Computing Systems, pp. 241–250 (2015)
14. Karaarslan, E., Altundas, S.: Cross-platform and personalized avatars in the metaverse: ready player me case. Available at SSRN 4249064 (2022)
15. Kodera, T.: Accessibility-friendly approach for responsive web design—perspectives for user experience and user interface. Bachelor's thesis, Metropolia University of Applied Sciences, 1 May 2023
16. Kopp, T., Riekert, M., Utz, S.: When cognitive fit outweighs cognitive load: redundant data labels in charts increase accuracy and speed of information extraction. Comput. Hum. Behav. **86**, 367–376 (2018)
17. Lai, C.F., Zhong, H.X., Chiu, P.S.: Investigating the impact of a flipped programming course using the DT-CDIO approach. Comput. Educ. **173**, 104287 (2021)
18. Li, J.: Augmented reality visual-captions: enhancing captioning experience for real-time conversations. In: Streitz, N.A., Konomi, S. (eds.) HCII 2023. LNCS, vol. 14037, pp. 380–396. Springer, Cham (2023). https://doi.org/10.1007/978-3-031-34609-5_28
19. Li, Z., Connell, S., Dannels, W., Peiris, R.: SoundVizVR: sound indicators for accessible sounds in virtual reality for deaf or hard-of-hearing users. In: Conference on Computers and Accessibility (ASSETS'22) (2022)
20. Liao, C.C.: Using occluded text as a cue attracting visual attention and preference in packaging and advertising. SAGE Open **13**(1), 21582440231154480 (2023)
21. Liu, X.B., et al.: Visual captions: augmenting verbal communication with on-the-fly visuals. In: Proceedings of the 2023 CHI Conference on Human Factors in Computing Systems, pp. 1–20 (2023)

22. Mathew, R., Dannels, W.A., Parker, A.J.: An augmented reality based approach for optimization of language access services in healthcare for deaf patients. In: Antona, M., Stephanidis, C. (eds.) HCII 2023. LNCS, vol. 14021, pp. 29–52. Springer, Cham (2023). https://doi.org/10.1007/978-3-031-35897-5_3

23. McCarron, L.: Creating accessible videos: captions and transcripts. Commun. Assoc. Inf. Syst. **48**(1), 19 (2021)

24. McDonnell, E.J., Liu, P., Goodman, S.M., Kushalnagar, R., Froehlich, J.E., Findlater, L.: Social, environmental, and technical: factors at play in the current use and future design of small-group captioning. Proc. ACM Hum.-Comput. Interact. **5**(CSCW2), 1–25 (2021)

25. Meng, L.M., Duan, S., Zhao, Y., Lü, K., Chen, S.: The impact of online celebrity in livestreaming e-commerce on purchase intention from the perspective of emotional contagion. J. Retail. Consum. Serv. **63**, 102733 (2021)

26. Moraru, O.A.: Real-time subtitle for the hearing impaired in augmented reality. Ph.D. thesis, Wien (2018)

27. Nuorivaara, T.: Finnish voice command in head mounted display devices. Master's thesis, Aalto University, Espoo, Finland, 25 July 2016

28. Olwal, A., et al.: Wearable subtitles: augmenting spoken communication with lightweight eyewear for all-day captioning. In: Proceedings of the 33rd Annual ACM Symposium on User Interface Software and Technology, pp. 1108–1120 (2020)

29. Osaba, E., et al.: A tutorial on the design, experimentation and application of metaheuristic algorithms to real-world optimization problems. Swarm Evol. Comput. **64**, 100888 (2021)

30. Raina, A.S., Mohanty, R.R., Bhuvanesh, A., Swaminathan, M., Krishnamurthy, V.R., et al.: Pointing tasks using spatial audio on smartphones for people with vision impairments. J. Comput. Information Sci. Eng. **23**(6) (2023)

31. Ramele, R., Villar, A.J., Santos, J.M.: Report: Epoc emotiv EEG basics. arXiv preprint arXiv:2206.09051 (2022)

32. Resibisma, B., Ramdhani, N.: Virtual reality heights exposure and its impact on college student's physiological response and emotional condition. Gadjah Mada J. Prof. Psychol. (Gamajpp) **6**(2), 140–150 (2020). https://doi.org/10.22146/gamajpp.54872

33. Rusli, M.S., Ibrahim, Z.: Augmented reality (AR) for deaf and hard of hearing (DHH) for animation. e-Academia J. **11**(2) (2022)

34. Schuck, L.: Question pro survey creation software. Research and Dessert 11-2012, Western Michigna University (2012)

35. Seita, M., Lee, S., Andrew, S., Shinohara, K., Huenerfauth, M.: Remotely co-designing features for communication applications using automatic captioning with deaf and hearing pairs. In: Proceedings of the 2022 CHI Conference on Human Factors in Computing Systems, pp. 1–13 (2022)

36. Shimizu, Y., Ohnishi, A., Terada, T., Tsukamoto, M.: Gaze-adaptive subtitles considering the balance among vertical/horizontal and depth of eye movement. In: 2021 IEEE International Symposium on Mixed and Augmented Reality Adjunct (ISMAR-Adjunct), pp. 127–132. IEEE (2021)

37. Son, S., Choi, J., Lee, S., Song, J.Y., Shin, I.: It is okay to be distracted: how real-time transcriptions facilitate online meeting with distraction. In: Proceedings of the 2023 CHI Conference on Human Factors in Computing Systems, pp. 1–19 (2023)

38. Tang, X.T., Yao, J., Hu, H.F.: Visual search experiment on text characteristics of vital signs monitor interface. Displays **62**, 101944 (2020)

39. Teófilo, M.R.d.S., et al.: Enabling deaf or hard of hearing accessibility in live theaters through virtual reality. Ph.D. thesis, Universidade Federal do Amazonas (2019)
40. Wei, S., Bloemers, D., Rovira, A.: A preliminary study of the eye tracker in the meta quest pro. In: Proceedings of the 2023 ACM International Conference on Interactive Media Experiences, pp. 216–221 (2023)
41. Weir, K., Loizides, F., Nahar, V., Aggoun, A., Pollard, A.: I see therefore I read: improving the reading capabilities of individuals with visual disabilities through immersive virtual reality. Univ. Access Inf. Soc. **22**(2), 387–413 (2023)
42. Yulianto, Y.: An analysis on readability of English reading texts with automated computer tool. J-SHMIC: J. Engl. Acad. **6**(1), 81–91 (2019)

# Shared Boundary Interfaces: Can One Fit All? A Controlled Study on Virtual Reality vs Touch-Screen Interfaces on Persons with Neurodevelopmental Disorders

Francesco Vona[1]($\boxtimes$) (ID), Eleonora Beccaluva[1] (ID), Marco Mores[2] (ID),
and Franca Garzotto[1] (ID)

[1] Department of Electronics, Information and Bioengineering, Politecnico di Milano,
Milan, Italy
{francesco.vona,eleonora.beccaluva,franca.garzotto}@polimi.it
[2] Fraternità e Amicizia Soc. Coop. Soc. Onlus, Milan, Italy
marco.mores@fraternitaeamicizia.it
https://i3lab.polimi.it/, https://www.fraternitaeamicizia.it/

**Abstract.** Technology presents a significant educational opportunity, particularly in enhancing emotional engagement and expanding learning and educational prospects for individuals with Neurodevelopmental Disorders (NDD). Virtual reality emerges as a promising tool for addressing such disorders, complemented by numerous touchscreen applications that have shown efficacy in fostering education and learning abilities. VR and touchscreen technologies represent diverse interface modalities. This study primarily investigates which interface, VR or touchscreen, more effectively facilitates food education for individuals with NDD. We compared learning outcomes via pre- and post-exposure questionnaires. To this end, we developed GEA, a dual-interface, user-friendly web application for Food Education, adaptable for either immersive use in a head-mounted display (HMD) or non-immersive use on a tablet. A controlled study was conducted to determine which interface better promotes learning. Over three sessions, the experimental group engaged with all GEA games in VR (condition A), while the control group interacted with the same games on a tablet (condition B). Results indicated a significant increase in post-questionnaire scores across subjects, averaging a 46% improvement. This enhancement was notably consistent between groups, with VR and Tablet groups showing 42% and 41% improvements, respectively.

**Keywords:** Touchscreen · Virtual Reality · Neurodevelopmental Disorders

## 1 Introduction

Neurodevelopmental disorders (NDD) are a group of conditions that typically manifest during childhood [1]. Common diagnoses within this category include

ASD -Autism Spectrum Disorder, ADHD -Attention Deficit and Hyperactivity Disorder, and ID - Intellectual Disability [1]. Children with these conditions often require support in developing cognitive skills such as attention and language, social abilities like interacting with others, and personal and household independence skills. Concerning the prevalence of these disorders, precise data is elusive, yet there is a consensus on its increasing occurrence. The World Health Organization (WHO) reports that ASD affects one in every 160 children [27]. In numerous neurodevelopmental disorders, the significance of food management and, consequently, food education cannot be overstated, acting as a pivotal component in the overall treatment and quality of life improvement for affected individuals [17]. The prevalence of obesity among individuals with Neurodevelopmental Disorders (NDD) is notably higher compared to the general population. This increased prevalence is attributed to a combination of factors including genetic predispositions, medication side effects, reduced physical activity, and dietary challenges. In this context, diverse eating disorders have been noted. Sisson and Van Hasselt [25] detailed four general types of feed behaviors typical of NDD:

- Challenges in eating independently
- Disruptive eating behaviors
- Inconsistent eating volume (over or under-eating)
- Food pickiness

These classifications, however, do not cover all scenarios. Matson and Bamburg [16] discovered a significant prevalence (9–25%) of Pica—a condition marked by eating non-food items, heightening poisoning risks-in those with cognitive impairments that can lead to disruptive and impulsive behavior known as Picacisim. Among the various NDD syndromes that are significantly affected by diet or picacism, there is a particular syndrome where this aspect is most pronounced and crucial: the Prader-Willi Syndrom (PWS). Prader-Willi Syndrome is a genetic disorder identified by anomalies in the hypothalamic-pituitary axis, leading to initial symptoms of hypotonia and poor weight gain, followed by hyperphagia and potential pathological obesity. This condition affects around 1 in 25,000 newborns. The disorder was initially thought to undergo two main nutritional phases [3]. However, subsequent research by Cassidy and Miller indicates a more intricate progression, involving seven phases and sub-phases [4]. The critical phase of hyperphagia, beginning at approximately 4 years, is characterized by an increased focus on food and persistent food-seeking, driven by hypothalamic dysfunction. This can lead to dangerous behaviors, such as eating inedible objects and food theft, potentially resulting in severe obesity and other health complications. Therefore, controlling or regulating these eating behaviors is essential for patient well-being.

Moreover, NDD subjects may exhibit selective eating habits based on food characteristics, which can lead to malnutrition or obesity, sometimes necessitating intensive care such as tube feeding. Children with certain NDDs often exhibit also restricted eating patterns and preferences for high-calorie, low-nutrient foods, contributing to obesity risk [15]. Literature confirms that especially children with Down syndrome are very often morbidly or severely obese [19].

Medications used to treat NDD symptoms can increase appetite and decrease metabolism, further exacerbating the risk of obesity. This prominence is also rooted in the multifaceted impact that nutrition has on cognitive, emotional, and physical development. For instance, certain NDDs are often accompanied by sensory sensitivities and gastrointestinal issues, making dietary choices and habits particularly challenging [24].

Optimal food management in these contexts can mitigate symptoms, improve gut health, and enhance the effectiveness of other therapeutic interventions [10]. Additionally, specific nutrients or dietary patterns may influence neurological development and function, suggesting that tailored nutritional strategies can be integral to managing NDDs [20].

However, implementing these strategies requires comprehensive food education, tailored not only to the needs of the individuals with NDD but also to their caregivers and educators [6]. This education encompasses understanding the nutritional requirements, developing skills to handle dietary restrictions or sensory aversions, and recognizing the links between diet, behavior, and symptom management [11]. Therefore, in the landscape of NDDs, an informed and personalized approach to food management, underpinned by robust food education, is essential in fostering optimal development and enhancing the overall well-being of those affected.

In the sphere of education, technology plays a pivotal role, offering unique opportunities for what is termed as "stealth learning." This approach, as detailed in Sharp's research [23], leverages technology to enhance emotional engagement and expand learning opportunities, making it particularly effective for those with mental disabilities to develop a range of skills. Gaming, due to its inherent appeal, is frequently used in this context. Recent experiences, such as those documented by Mazzone [18], affirm the success of using games in educational settings, especially for individuals with neurodevelopmental disorders who are often attracted to technological devices.

Virtual reality (VR) emerges as a promising tool in this domain. Strickland's work [26] emphasizes VR's benefits, including controlled input stimuli and personalized learning environments. Recent interest in VR's application in NDD, as explored by researchers like Yufang [5] and Garzotto [8], underscores its adaptability to the specific learning needs of this demographic.

Our research aims to discern the most effective interface, VR or tablet, for imparting food education to individuals with NDD. We developed GEA, a web application with dual-interface functionality suitable for immersive experiences through a head-mounted display (HMD) or non-immersive experience on a tablet. The effectiveness of these interfaces is evaluated by comparing pre- and post-exposure questionnaire results.

## 2    Related Work

In the specialized area of food education, diverse interactive games for touchscreen devices have been introduced. A notable example is the Food Pyramid game by Colorado State University [22], designed to educate children about the five primary food groups and apply this knowledge to meal and snack planning, thus boosting self-efficacy. The game's structure includes various challenges centered around the food pyramid, with findings indicating that challenge-based games are more impactful than storyline-based ones.

On the Healthy Eating website[1], a collection of educational computer games related to food education is available. One of these games, titled "My Plate Match Game," is designed to instruct users in categorizing various types of food for a well-balanced diet, emphasizing the recommended daily quantities. The primary drawback of this game lies in its absence of proper feedback, as it continues without error tracking until all objectives are correctly achieved. Furthermore, the website also offers another game specifically centered around promoting a healthy breakfast, titled "Power Up Your Breakfast." This game shares similarities with the previously mentioned one, where users begin by responding to questions regarding the significance of a nutritious breakfast. Additionally, there is "My Very Own Pizza," a game that enables users to create a customized pizza without a specific end goal, allowing users to add any ingredients they desire. While exploring the realm of food education games on the internet, we observed their prevalence, with another example being the Nourish Interactive website[2], which hosts a vast array of food-themed games.

Virtual reality technology has undergone significant development over the past half-century, starting from the creation of the Sensorama device in 1962, designed to provide an immersive film-watching experience, to the current devices that, although advanced, have not yet achieved complete sensory immersion [2]. Numerous applications of virtual reality technology have emerged over the years, prompting various experiments to assess their effectiveness and efficiency with persons with NDD. Some examples are the studies include those conducted by Lin [13], Lotan [14], and Yalon-Chamovitz [28].

In Lin's study, 21 students with various disabilities engaged with an application comprising six games designed to enhance their understanding of geometry. The results were promising, as the repeated use of the application led to improved learning outcomes, reflected in increased success rates [13]. In Lotan's research, a group of 44 adults, divided into two groups and affected by different intellectual and developmental disabilities (IDD), explored a virtual reality application aimed at supporting their physical fitness. However, the findings did not yield statistically significant results [14]. In the final example, 32 participants divided into two groups, all affected by various intellectual disabilities and severe cerebral palsy, interacted with a virtual reality application simulating leisure experiences and subsequently provided feedback through a questionnaire to assess their level of success and enjoyment [28].

In the context of food education, VR applications have the potential to revolutionize how individuals acquire knowledge about nutrition, cooking techniques, and food-related concepts. Following, we provide a selection of innovative

---

[1] https://www.healthyeating.org/Healthy-Kids/Kids-Games-Activities.

[2] http://www.nourishinteractive.com/kids/healthy-games.

VR-based food education games and experiences designed to engage learners while imparting essential culinary and nutritional insights.

One notable VR application is the "Cooking Simulator VR," which offers users a dynamic and interactive virtual kitchen environment. This simulation equips participants with the skills required to prepare a variety of dishes, including chopping ingredients, adhering to recipes, and monitoring the cooking process [9]. Real-time feedback enhances the learning process, making it an immersive platform for acquiring practical culinary expertise. The "Farm to Table VR" experience immerses users in the entire food production cycle. This includes farming and harvesting practices, animal husbandry, and an exploration of sustainable agricultural methods. Users gain insights into diverse cuisines and recipes while simultaneously learning about responsible and eco-friendly food production practices [21].

In the realm of nutrition education, the "Virtual Nutrition Adventure" VR application takes participants on a journey through the intricacies of the human digestive system. Users receive instruction on the significance of essential nutrients the process of food digestion, and are presented with opportunities to make informed dietary choices. Promoting food safety awareness, the "Food Safety VR" application immerses users in a virtual kitchen environment. Participants engage in interactive exercises to identify potential food safety hazards and acquire knowledge about proper food handling, storage, and hygiene practices [7].

In the "Virtual Food Science Lab," participants engage in experiments to understand food chemistry and explore the fundamental principles behind various cooking techniques, bridging the gap between scientific knowledge and culinary practice. The "Culinary Challenge VR" game challenges users to test and enhance their culinary skills in a competitive setting. Participants are required to prepare dishes under time constraints and follow specific instructions, fostering skill development, multitasking abilities, and culinary creativity [12].

"Food World VR" offers an immersive journey around the world, enabling users to explore diverse cuisines, cultures, and food traditions. Through virtual visits to restaurants, markets, and street food stalls, participants gain insights into global food diversity, ingredient profiles, and cooking styles. The "Healthy Eating Quest VR" game encourages users to adopt healthy dietary choices through a virtual world filled with food-related challenges and puzzles. By navigating this immersive environment, participants gain an understanding of the importance of a balanced diet and the impact of food choices on overall health [9].

The integration of immersive VR technology into food education has paved the way for engaging and informative learning experiences. However, based on our knowledge, very little has been done to develop a specific app for food education for individuals with NDD.

# 3   GEA

GEA (acronym for "Gioco di Educazione Alimentare" - Food Education Game) is an immersive virtual reality mobile application running on smartphones and tablets and usable in virtual reality on Google Cardboard that aims to teach food education to individuals with NDD. GEA was the result of a codesign process carried out with therapists and specialists. The idea of food education activity arose because several studies have indicated that NDD patients frequently experience feeding difficulties [17]. The activities contained in GEA, therefore seek to teach people with NDD very simple concepts concerning nutrition, such as i) at what time of day a certain food can be eaten, ii) which foods are healthier and which are not, iii) the allergens contained in a food.

## 3.1   GEA Activities

**Learn with the Pyramid.** The objective of this game is to educate how to complete the food pyramid by selecting the appropriate foods for each level. A pyramid with five tiers displays in the virtual environment, with a pointer showing which level the user is currently finishing and a table containing three food possibilities. The pyramid consists of five levels, and the importance of foods for each level is based on the Mediterranean diet, so we used well-known foods (not only Italian but also belonging to other countries). At the lowest level (the largest), there are foods that have to be consumed daily, such as fruits, vegetables, and water. On the second level, there are carbohydrates and cereals, on the third level, there are meat and fish, on the penultimate level, dairy products such as cheese and yogurt, and on the final level (the smallest), foods that have to be consumed as little as possible, such as sweets and alcohol. In order to provide a response, the user must select one of the foods on the table. If the answer is incorrect, a red circle appears, and the active level of the pyramid turns red; if the answer is accurate, the mascot appears with a joyful expression, and the level turns green.

**Healthy or Not?** This game is intended to teach users to determine if a food is healthy or not. When the game begins, two dishes appear on the table of the virtual room, along with a bin and a visual explanation of how the game is played; the user must select the "junk food" and move it by maintaining their gaze on it until it is thrown into the bin. There are three repeats of this game, each with a new set of options, and after each response, similar feedback is displayed. This initially appeared to be a bad idea due to the thought of "throwing" away food, but it has been adopted and interpreted as a representation of the close correlation between junk foods and the trash can, so that the user may understand that these meals are highly unhealthy.

**Let's Eat!** This game aims to educate players on which is the best meal to eat a particular food. It was designed specifically for people who have trouble recognizing when they may and cannot consume certain foods. In this task, the virtual environment displays four images representing the four primary meals (breakfast, lunch, afternoon snack, and supper) as well as a dish; the objective is to select the correct meal/s during which the dish can be consumed. The selection can be done by staring at one of the meal options present on the wall. Similar to the second game, there are three repeats, and feedback is provided after each answer. This game is based on the Mediterranean diet, thus there are specified items for each meal.

**Find the Allergens.** This activity aims to teach users about food allergens. The game environment is the same as the others; on the wall, there is a predefined number of allergens icons (4 for the first level of difficulty, 6 for the second, and 10 for the third) and food on the table. The allergens included in the task are celery, clams, eggs, fish, dairy products, peanuts, shellfish, soy, nuts, and gluten. The task difficulty is based on the allergen itself and not on the type of food since some allergens are very common, like gluten, whereas others are very hard to detect, like celery. For this reason, in the Easy level, there are foods containing egg, fish, dairy products, and gluten, in the Medium one also soy and nuts. Finally, in the Difficult level also the remaining allergens.

The user must select all the allergens contained in the food. A countdown indicating the number of remaining allergens is also shown on the wall. Once the user has selected the correct number of allergens contained in the food, a confirm button appears. Then, the user receives the feedback back, showing also correct answers and wrong ones.

### 3.2   VR vs Touchscreen Version

The two major differences there are between the versions of *GEA* are related to user interaction and the design of the environment. Concerning user interaction in the case of VR, it is based on gaze orientation and focus. By changing gaze direction, users update their view of the virtual environment and have the illusion of moving in different directions. Since, smartphone sensors (accelerometer and gyroscope) track only movement and orientation of the user's head, the center of the smartphone screen is taken as a reference for the user's head. In case of the Tablet or Touchscreen interface, the user interaction is based on the Tap Gestures. The view of the environment is fixed, and the user can only interact with the food in the scene in order to give their answer. Figure 1 shows the difference between the two versions.

## 4   Study

The study aimed to assess the potential of GEA through empirical research. Specifically, the objective was to compare the effectiveness of two different interfaces: Tablet (utilizing a touchscreen) and Virtual Reality. The study collected data on two key variables:

**Fig. 1.** Comparison of each activity between the two versions of GEA

- The time interval it took patients to complete each mini-game at different levels of difficulty.
- The number of errors made during the gameplay.

To evaluate the effectiveness of these interfaces, a pre-test and a post-test were conducted to measure the learning delta related to food education.

### 4.1 Participants

An initial group of 45 participants with NDD was initially enrolled for the pre-test. The purpose of the pre-test was to determine which participants to include based on their existing knowledge of food education. The pre-test had a maximum score of 21 points. Participants with scores exceeding 17 were excluded from the study. Consequently, 20 participants remained eligible and took part in the research. Subsequently, these participants were randomly allocated to one of two conditions, namely Condition 1 (VR) or Condition 2 (Tablet). Participant information is detailed in the table below 1.

Table 1. Selected patients information

| ID | Age | Gender | Diagnosis | Condition |
|---|---|---|---|---|
| FEA49 | 18 | M | Prader-Willi | 2 |
| FEA18 | 26 | M | Cognitive delay and epilepsy | 2 |
| FEA55 | 32 | M | Down syndrome | 2 |
| FEA41 | 26 | M | Autistic | 2 |
| FEA30 | 18 | M | Cognitive delay, epilepsy and encephalopathy | 2 |
| FEA23 | 29 | F | Autism and cognitive delay | 2 |
| FEA51 | 32 | F | Cognitive delay and epilepsy | 2 |
| FEA19 | 29 | F | Medium-high cognitive delay | 2 |
| FEA62 | 33 | M | High mental insufficiency | 1 |
| FEA63 | 19 | M | Medium-high cognitive delay | 1 |
| FEA52 | 27 | M | Cognitive delay | 1 |
| FEA17 | 26 | M | Autism | 1 |
| FEA44 | 27 | F | Low cognitive delay | 1 |
| FEA11 | 37 | F | High mental insufficiency, psychosis | 1 |
| FEA10 | 20 | F | Down syndrome | 1 |
| FEA20 | 34 | F | Encephalopathy | 1 |
| P4 | 51 | M | High cognitive delay | 2 |
| P3 | 60 | M | Medium cognitive delay | 1 |
| P6 | 59 | M | Medium cognitive | 1 |
| P5 | 68 | F | High cognitive delay | 2 |

## 4.2  Procedure

The evaluation took place at two therapeutic centers in Milan, and the experimental study spanned three weeks. During each week of the study, participants had the opportunity to engage with all three tasks of GEA. The difficulty level of the games was systematically increased throughout the study. Before the commencement of the study, all participants responded to a 21-item questionnaire designed to assess their awareness regarding food and food education. The questionnaire was divided into three sections, each comprising seven questions, to cover the content of the three games offered by the application evenly. The questionnaire items are in the table below (Table 2). In the first week of the study, all games were set to the "Easy" difficulty level. The games were adjusted to a "Medium" difficulty level during the second week. In the third week, the games were more challenging at the "Difficult" level. An additional fourth week was introduced to accommodate users who were absent during one of the previous sessions or had started the evaluation one week later than the initial group. The specific version of the tasks varied depending on the condition assigned to each participant. Following the three weeks of training, a post-test was conducted to assess the participants' knowledge of food education after their engagement with the GEA application using the same questionnaire with slightly different questions to avoid a learning effect. The post-test used the same test format as the pre-test and was administered to all 20 participants. The GEA sessions occurred in a designated room at the daycare centres. We specifically selected quiet rooms to minimize ambient noise during recording. The furniture was minimal to reduce distractions. During the session, subjects sat in front of the researcher and wore the VR headset or played with the tablet. Participants could interrupt the experience whenever they wanted and/or request a break from the experimenter. The sessions lasted approximately 20 min.

**Table 2.** Questions in Pre-test and Post-test

| Task | Question |
|------|----------|
| Learn with Pyramid | Do you know what is the food pyramid? a) Yes b) No |
| | On the pyramid you put: a) Foods b) Seasons |
| | Pyramid's base represents foods that must be eaten.. a) Everyday b) Sometimes |
| | What foods should be on the top of the pyramid? a) Sweet b) Vegetables |
| | Pyramid's top represents foods that must be eaten... a) More b) Less |
| | What is better to eat more often? a) Meat b) Fried foods |
| | How many steps does the pyramid have? a) 5 b) 7 |
| Healty or Not | What is more healthy between fried fish and boiled one? a) Fried b) Boiled |
| | Is it a good habit to eat every lunch at the fast-food? a) Yes b) No |
| | Select the healthy food among the ones below: a) Apple b) Sweets |
| | It is good to eat some fruit every day. a) True b) False |
| | Fried chips are healthy. a) True b) False |
| | What is less healthy between plain fish and fried one? a) Plain b) Fried |
| | What is better between water and chocolate? a) Water b) Chocolate |
| Let's Eat | Can you eat pizza at breakfast? a) Yes b) No |
| | Vegetables soup is often eaten at... a) Breakfast b) Dinner |
| | Can foods be divided into groups based on daytime? a) Yes b) No |
| | At lunch you eat: a) Pasta b) Milk with grains |
| | At dinner you would eat: a) Meat and vegetables b) Snack and fruit juice |
| | Is milk good at breakfast? a) Yes b) No |
| | Is meat good for a snack? a) Yes b) No |

## 5    Results and Discussion

Table 3 presents the pre-test and post-test outcomes for each participant. An additional column has been included to compute the delta score, representing the difference between the scores from the two sessions. It is noteworthy that, in every instance, there was an improvement or no decrease in scores between the pre-test and post-test. The delta score ranged from a minimum of 2 to a maximum of 9.

The data collected underwent analysis using SPSS (Statistical Package for Social Science). In the initial step, an assessment was conducted to ascertain

**Table 3.** Pre-test and Post-test results

| ID | Pre-test Results | Post-test Results | Delta Score |
|---|---|---|---|
| FEA49 | 17/21[1] | 19/21 | 2 |
| FEA18 | 15/21 | 19/21 | 4 |
| FEA55 | 11/21 | 16/21 | 5 |
| FEA41 | 14/21 | 19/21 | 5 |
| FEA30 | 16/21 | 20/21 | 4 |
| FEA23 | 11/21 | 17/21 | 6 |
| FEA51 | 8/21 | 17/21 | 9 |
| FEA19 | 13/21 | 19/21 | 6 |
| FEA62 | 15/21 | 18/21 | 3 |
| FEA63 | 13/21 | 18/21 | 5 |
| FEA52 | 13/21 | 20/21 | 7 |
| FEA17 | 12/21 | 20/21 | 8 |
| FEA44 | 16/21 | 20/21 | 4 |
| FEA11 | 15/21 | 21/21 | 6 |
| FEA10 | 16/21 | 21/21 | 5 |
| FEA20 | 10/21 | 19/21 | 9 |
| P4 | 15/21 | 20/21 | 5 |
| P3 | 15/21 | 19/21 | 4 |
| P6 | 15/21 | 20/21 | 5 |
| P5 | 16/21 | 20/21 | 4 |

the normality of the distribution. This involved the computation of values for skewness and kurtosis. The skewness index serves to determine the symmetry

**Table 4.** Average, asymmetry and kurtosis

|  | Pre-test | Post-test |
|---|---|---|
| Population | 20 | 20 |
| Average | 13,80 | 19,10 |
| Standard deviation | 2,375 | 1,334 |
| Asymmetry | −0,940 | −0,793 |
| Asymmetry's standard error | 0,512 | 0,512 |
| Kurtosis | 0,286 | 0,223 |
| Kurtosis' standard error | 0,992 | 0,992 |
| Minimum | 8 | 16 |
| Maximum | 17 | 21 |

of data distribution in relation to a particular value, characterized as follows: a positive value indicates right skewness, where data points tend to cluster toward the lower end with an extended tail toward higher values, causing the distribution graph to stretch rightward. A negative value indicates left skewness, where the opposite situation prevails, causing the distribution graph to stretch leftward. The kurtosis index, on the other hand, indicates the degree of deviation from a normal distribution, thereby signifying the relative weight of values located at the distribution's tails compared to those in its central region. Table 4 provides evidence that the distribution adheres to normality based on the aforementioned values. This confirms the suitability for conducting inferential analysis despite the relatively small sample size. Regarding the results obtained in the pre-test and post-test, the average score increased from 13.80 to 19.10, the minimum score doubled (from 8 to 16), and the maximum attainable score (21) was also reached in the post-test.

In general, all participants exhibited a notable increase in their post- questionnaire scores, demonstrating an average improvement of 46%. This improvement was consistently observed in both groups, with the VR group showing a 42% increase and the Tablet group showing a 41% increase. Specifically, the results within the VR condition indicated a statistically significant difference ($t = -9.333$; $df = 9$; $p < .01$) between the pre-test score ($M = 14$) and the post-test score ($M = 19.6$). Similarly, in the Tablet condition, there was a statistically significant difference ($t = -8.660$; $df = 9$; $p < .01$) between the pre-test score ($M = 13.6$) and the post-test score ($M = 18.6$). An unpaired t-test was conducted to explore whether there was a significant difference between the VR and Tablet conditions in improving participants' performance. The results showed no significant difference ($t = 0.81$; $df = 18$; $p = 0.93$) between the two conditions. Our study did not yield evidence to support the superiority of one interface over the other in enhancing knowledge. These results affirm the effectiveness of GEA as a valuable learning tool for individuals with NDD. Both the VR and Tablet interfaces demonstrated suitability for our target population.

## 6 Conclusions

The target user group of GEA primarily consists of individuals with neurodevelopmental disorders. These individuals often require more extensive support, even in nutrition education, given their daily cognitive challenges. GEA proved to be an effective learning tool, with tested patients exhibiting an increase in their scores on general knowledge about food after engaging with the game, demonstrating a positive outcome. Generally, there was no significant difference in terms of improvement between the two versions of the game. However, our data indicated that virtual reality performed particularly well with individuals experiencing high cognitive delay and autism disorders, suggesting its potential benefits in these specific cases. The results of our study do not provide significant evidence in favor of a VR interface over a tablet interface. This finding is particularly interesting in a context where there has been a rush towards new and highly advanced technologies as the sole means of improving learning capabilities, especially in recent times and in the field of education. However, our study demonstrates that this assertion is not necessarily true. In our study, the improvement achieved was comparable between the two interfaces, without the more advanced VR interface proving superior to the more traditional and commonly adopted tablet interface. It's crucial to recognize that not all advanced technologies necessarily represent an advancement in every context. In education, particularly, choosing the most suitable tool should take precedence over pursuing the latest and most cutting-edge solution. The effectiveness of an educational tool depends on its alignment with the learning objectives and the needs of the students. Therefore, educators should carefully evaluate whether a technological innovation enhances the learning experience and outcomes before adopting it. This is particularly relevant in the NDD arena.

## 6.1   Limitation and Future Work

In our evaluation, we encountered certain limitations, including the relatively small number of participants. A larger sample size could have generated more robust results, potentially revealing differences in performance between the two technology interfaces. Another constraint was the limited time available for experimentation. We could only assess GEA over a three-week period, and a more extended period of use might have led to even greater learning outcomes. As part of our future work, we have several ideas to expand and enhance the application. First, conduct a more extensive and long-term evaluation of the application to gain a deeper understanding of its potential for improving learning outcomes including an evaluation of the fourth game, "Find the allergen!" which has not been tested yet. Second, develop additional games related to food and nutrition, such as helping users understand and balance their intake of carbohydrates, sugars, proteins, and fats, or suggesting suitable seasonal food choices.

## References

1. American Psychiatric Association, DSMTF and American Psychiatric Association et al.: Diagnostic and statistical manual of mental disorders: DSM-5, vol. 5. American psychiatric association Washington, DC (2013)
2. Biocca, F., Levy, M.R.: Communication in the Age of Virtual Reality. Routledge, Abingdon (2013)
3. Cassidy, S.B., Driscoll, D.J.: Prader-Willi syndrome. Eur. J. Hum. Genet. 17(1), 3 (2009)
4. Cassidy, S.B., Schwartz, S., Miller, J.L., Driscoll, D.J.: Prader-Willi syndrome. Genet. Med. 14(1), 10 (2012)
5. Cheng, Y., Huang, C.L., Yang, C.S.: Using a 3d immersive virtual environment system to enhance social understanding and social skills for children with autism spectrum disorders. Focus Autism Other Dev. Disabil. 30(4), 222–236 (2015)

6.  Curtin, C., Anderson, S.E., Must, A., Bandini, L.: The prevalence of obesity in children with autism: a secondary data analysis using nationally representative data from the national survey of children's health. BMC Pediatr. **10**(1), 1–5 (2010)
7.  Davis, A.: Virtual reality simulation: an innovative teaching tool for dietetics experiential education. Open Nutr. J. **9**(1) (2015)
8.  Gelsomini, M., Garzotto, F., Montesano, D., Occhiuto, D.: Wildcard: a wearable virtual reality storytelling tool for children with intellectual developmental disability. In: 2016 IEEE 38th Annual International Conference of the Engineering in Medicine and Biology Society (EMBC), pp. 5188–5191. IEEE (2016)
9.  Gorman, D., Hoermann, S., Lindeman, R.W., Shahri, B.: Using virtual reality to enhance food technology education. Int. J. Technol. Des. Educ. **32**(3), 1659–1677 (2022)
10. Hyman, S.L., et al.: Nutrient intake from food in children with autism. Pediatrics **130**(Supplement_2), S145–S153 (2012)
11. Johnson, C.R., Handen, B.L., Mayer-Costa, M., Sacco, K.: Eating habits and dietary status in young children with autism. J. Dev. Phys. Disabil. **20**, 437–448 (2008)
12. Karkar, A., Salahuddin, T., Almaadeed, N., Aljaam, J.M., Halabi, O.: A virtual reality nutrition awareness learning system for children. In: 2018 IEEE Conference on e-Learning, e-Management and e-Services (IC3e), pp. 97–102. IEEE (2018)
13. Lin, C.Y., et al.: Augmented reality in educational activities for children with disabilities. Displays **42**, 51–54 (2016)
14. Lotan, M., Yalon-Chamovitz, S., Weiss, P.L.T.: Virtual reality as means to improve physical fitness of individuals at a severe level of intellectual and developmental disability. Res. Dev. Disabil. **31**(4), 869–874 (2010)
15. Marí-Bauset, S., Zazpe, I., Mari-Sanchis, A., Llopis-González, A., Morales-Suárez-Varela, M.: Food selectivity in autism spectrum disorders: a systematic review. J. Child Neurol. **29**(11), 1554–1561 (2014)
16. Matson, J.L., Bamburg, J.W.: A descriptive study of pica behavior in persons with mental retardation. J. Dev. Phys. Disabil. **11**(4), 353–361 (1999)
17. Matson, J.L., Kuhn, D.E.: Identifying feeding problems in mentally retarded persons: development and reliability of the screening tool of feeding problems (step). Res. Dev. Disabil. **22**(2), 165–172 (2001). https://doi.org/10.1016/S0891-4222(01)00065-8. http://www.sciencedirect.com/science/article/pii/S0891422201000658
18. Mazzone, E., Iivari, N., Tikkanen, R., Read, J.C., Beale, R.: Considering context, content, management, and engagement in design activities with children. In: Proceedings of the 9th International Conference on Interaction Design and Children, pp. 108–117. ACM (2010)
19. O'Shea, M., O'Shea, C., Gibson, L., Leo, J., Carty, C.: The prevalence of obesity in children and young people with down syndrome. J. Appl. Res. Intellect. Disabil. **31**(6), 1225–1229 (2018)
20. Rucklidge, J.J., Kaplan, B.J.: Nutrition and mental health. Clin. Psychol. Sci. **4**(6), 1082–1084 (2016)
21. Ruppert, B.: New directions in the use of virtual reality for food shopping: marketing and education perspectives (2011)
22. Serrano, E.L., Anderson, J.E.: The evaluation of food pyramid games, a bilingual computer nutrition education program for Latino youth. J. Fam. Consum. Sci. Educ. **22**(1), 1–16 (2004)
23. Sharp, L.A.: Stealth learning: unexpected learning opportunities through games. J. Instr. Res. **1**, 42–48 (2012)

24. Sharp, W.G., et al.: Feeding problems and nutrient intake in children with autism spectrum disorders: a meta-analysis and comprehensive review of the literature. J. Autism Dev. Disord. **43**, 2159–2173 (2013)

25. Sisson, L.A., Van Hasselt, V.B.: Feeding disorders. In: Luiselli, J.K. (ed.) Behavioral Medicine and Developmental Disabilities, pp. 45–73. Springer, New York (1989). https://doi.org/10.1007/978-1-4613-8844-9_3

26. Strickland, D.: A virtual reality application with autistic children. Presence Teleoperators Virtual Environ. **5**(3), 319–329 (1996)

27. Wing, L.: The definition and prevalence of autism: a review. Eur. Child Adolesc. Psychiatry **2**, 61–74 (1993)

28. Yalon-Chamovitz, S., Weiss, P.L.T.: Virtual reality as a leisure activity for young adults with physical and intellectual disabilities. Res. Dev. Disabil. **29**(3), 273–287 (2008)

# Correction to: A Study on the Design of an Emotional Interaction Device for Children with Autism Spectrum Disorder Based on Focused Attention Mindfulness

Yujia Jia, Jiaqi Wang, and Yujun Zhou

**Correction to:**
**Chapter 12 in: M. Antona and C. Stephanidis (Eds.):** *Universal Access in Human-Computer Interaction*, **LNCS 14697,**
**https://doi.org/10.1007/978-3-031-60881-0_12**

In the original version of this chapter, the affiliation and email-ID for the first author, Yujia Jia, were wrong. This has been corrected.

---

The updated version of this chapter can be found at
https://doi.org/10.1007/978-3-031-60881-0_12

# Author Index

## A

Aldossary, Dalal III-429
Alfredsson Ågren, Kristin II-213
Aljasem, Dalal III-363
Alsos, Ole Andreas II-267
Al-Wabil, Areej III-429
André, Luis I-106
Antunes, Carlos III-203
Arias-Flores, Hugo III-382
Atarashi, Yui I-88
Azab, Mohammad III-234

## B

Bächler, Liane III-3
Baker, Pamela III-222
Barberio, Anna II-368
Barthwal, Parth III-159
Baumann, Lukas II-19
Beccaluva, Eleonora II-404
Behravan, Majid II-301
Bekkvik Szentirmai, Attila II-267, II-282
Bellman, Scott III-112
Berget, Gerd I-337
Bernardino, Elidéa L. A. III-290
Bernasconi, Tobias III-3
Bhole, Palavi V. I-3
Biancur, Cooper I-19
Bonyani, Mahdi I-197
Branig, Meinhardt III-32
Buck, Andrew III-112
Bursy, Miriam II-171
Burzagli, Laura I-213, I-224
Busch, Matthias I-35
Buttiglione, Marco Domenico II-368

## C

Cabrita, Cristiano I-234
Calle-Jimenez, Tania III-382
Cardoso, Pedro III-16
Carvalho, Isabel F. de III-290
Carvalho, Jailson I-234

Ceccacci, Silvia I-326
Cerutti, Paolo III-246
Chadwick, Darren D. II-213
Chan, Angela III-58
Chaparro, Barbara S. I-162
Chen, Yueh-Peng III-334
Chien, Wei-Chi II-198
Chinnici, Marta I-300
Crusco, Ivan II-368
Cunha, António III-203

## D

D'Angelo, Ilaria I-326
Del Bianco, Noemi I-326
Deuss, Chantal III-144
Diaz, Christopher II-358
Dirks, Susanne II-19, II-171
Dreslin, Brandon D. I-162

## E

Emiliani, Pier Luigi I-213, I-224
Engel, Christin III-32, III-393
Ersoy, Baha Mert II-321
Esparza, Francisco J. II-358
Etori, Naome A. II-382
Etzold, Emma F. II-100

## F

Federspiel, Esther III-94
Feichtinger, Marcel III-3
Ferreira, João I-106
Fitzpatrick, Donal III-174
Freberg, Giske Naper II-3

## G

Garzotto, Franca II-368, II-404
Generosi, Andrea I-250
Ghasemi, Shiva II-301, II-382, III-234
Giaconi, Catia I-326
Giesteira, Bruno III-16

M. Antona and C. Stephanidis (Eds.): HCII 2024, LNCS 14697, pp. 419–422, 2024.
https://doi.org/10.1007/978-3-031-60881-0

Gini, Maria   II-382
Goldshtein, Maria   I-271
Gollasch, David   III-32
Gračanin, Denis   II-301, II-382, III-234
Guedes, Leandro S.   II-151
Guerreiro, J.   II-51
Gupta, Richa   III-159
Gustavsson, Catharina   II-213
Guyser, Sacha   III-275

**H**

Hafeez, Shireen   III-47
Hansen, Marit Fredrikke   I-122
Heimgärtner, Rüdiger   I-75
Heitplatz, Vanessa N.   II-171, II-213
Higashi, Ariaki   III-305
Hirata, Kazuhiko   III-305
Hordemann, Glen   III-58
Howell, Joshua   III-58
Howes, Andrew   III-363
Hsu, Chien-Lung   III-334
Husnes, Sandra Helen   I-122

**I**

Ibs, Robin   I-35
Illenberger, Andreas   III-275
Inal, Yavuz   II-267
Inverno, Armando   I-234
Iovane, Gerardo   I-300
Iversen, Kasper   III-246

**J**

Jaccheri, Letizia   I-122, I-143, II-66
Jenda, Overtoun   III-112
Jenson, Ronda   III-112
Jeong, Kyuman   I-291
Jia, Yujia   II-186
Johansson, Stefan   II-213
Jordan, JBern   III-185
Jung, Woosoon   I-291

**K**

Kakaraparthi, Vishnu   III-259
Kamin, Anna-Maria   III-125
Karaca, Murat   II-321
Kärpänen, Terhi   II-32
Kaya, Cem   II-321

Keates, Simeon   III-222
Keebler, Joseph R.   I-162
Keller, Thomas   III-275
Kimogol, Stephen Simei   III-78
King, Kenneth   II-382
Kinoshita, Fumiya   I-51
Krüger, Daniel   I-63
Kundaliya, Kripa K.   I-3
Kurita, Yuichi   III-305
Kurokawa, Masaomi   III-305
Kvilhaug Magnussen, Knut Ole   III-246

**L**

Lai, Michael T.   II-129
Landi, Riccardo Emanuele   I-300
Landoni, Monica   II-151
Liao, Tsai-Ling   II-198
Lien, Yu-Ling   II-129
Lilleby, Anton   I-337
Lin, Ling-Yi   II-198
Lo, Hsin-Yu   III-334
Loch, Frieder   III-94
Loitsch, Claudia   II-100

**M**

Maar, Aliaa   III-429
Marcolino, Milena Soriano   III-290
Marghitu, Daniela   III-112
Marstein, Steffen   I-337
Marte, Crystal   III-185
Martinez, Christopher   I-19
Maskut, Nele   II-171
Massey-Garrett, Tamara   III-112
Mastrogiuseppe, Marilina   II-151
Mathew, Roshan   II-334
Matos, T.   II-51
McCullough, Brittany   III-112
McDaniel, Troy   III-259
Mengoni, Maura   I-250
Mertens, Claudia   III-125
Milallos, Rezylle   III-413
Minghim, Rosane   III-174
Moises de Souza, Ana Carolina   II-66
Montanari, Roberto   I-250
Monteiro, Jânio   I-234
Mores, Marco   II-368, II-404
Musule, Ahmed   II-358

**N**

Naldini, Simone  I-224
Nebe, Karsten  I-75
Neira-Tovar, Leticia  II-358
Nishikawa, Yoshiki  I-88
Normand, Claude L.  II-213
Nussbaumer, Daniela  III-144

**O**

Ocumpaugh, Jaclyn  I-271
Oh, Tae  III-413
Oh, Yoosoo  I-291
Oliveira, Hélder P.  III-317
Oliveira, Miguel  I-234

**P**

Park, KyoungOck  I-291
Pathak, Shourya  III-159
Patti, Alberto  II-368
Peçaibes, Viviane  III-16
Peiris, Roshan L.  I-3, II-334, III-413
Pelka, Bastian  I-63
Pereira, Tania  III-317
Petri, Alexis  III-112
Pettis, Carl  III-112
Pitt, Ian  III-174
Potter, Andrew  I-271
Prates, Raquel Oliveira  III-290

**Q**

Quaresma, Isabel  III-16
Quayyum, Farzana  II-3
Quek, Francis  III-58

**R**

Rodrigues, João M. F.  III-203
Roscoe, Rod D.  I-271
Ryu, Jeong Tak  I-291

**S**

Sanchez-Gordon, Sandra  III-382
Sand, Erik  II-231
Sanderson, Norun Christine  III-78
Sandnes, Frode Eika  II-80
Santos, Salvador  I-106
Schaper, Franziska  III-125
Scherer, Christian  III-275

Schmalfuß-Schwarz, Jan  III-32, III-393
Schulz, Ann Christin  I-63
Sekiguchi, Shogo  I-88
Shannon, David  III-112
Sharma, Deep  III-159
Shashwat, Saumik  III-159
Shizuki, Buntarou  I-88
Shoaib, Muhammad  III-174
Siegert, Ingo  I-35
Silva, Francisco  III-317
Soares, Julia Manuela G.  III-290
Sohaib, Muhammad  I-311
Soleymani, Maryam  I-197
Sousa, Joana  I-106
Sousa, Joana Vale  III-317
Span, Stefania  II-151
Striegl, Julian  II-100
Szlavi, Anna  I-122

**T**

Takahashi, Kiriko  III-112
Takaoka, Alicia Julia Wilson  I-143
Takeda, Yuma  III-305
Tang, Hsien-Hui  II-112, II-129
Teiga, Inês  III-317
Tigwell, Garreth W.  I-3, II-334
Torkildsby, Anne Britt  II-267
Torrado, Juan C.  III-246
Traiger, Jeff  III-112
Tsai, Shin-Yu  II-112
Tsai, Tsai-Hsuan  III-334
Tseng, Kevin C.  III-345

**U**

Ubur, Sunday D.  II-301, II-382
Uchôa Conte, Tayana  I-122
Uricchio, Tiberio  I-326

**V**

Valencia-Aragón, Kevin  III-382
Van Ommen, Carmen A.  I-162
Vanderheiden, Gregg  III-185
Verne, Guri  I-337
Vila-Maior, Guilherme  III-16
Villafan, Josè Yuri  I-250
Vona, Francesco  II-368, II-404

**W**

Wang, Chao   I-197
Wang, Jiaqi   II-186
Wang, Tzu-Yang   I-179
Wang, Yi-Han   III-345
Wang, Yunqi   II-250
Weber, Gerhard   II-100, III-32
Wilkens, Leevke   II-171
Wu, Qiu-Ze   II-129
Wu, Shih-Lin   III-334

**Y**

Yuizono, Takaya   I-179

**Z**

Zanardi, Irene   II-151
Zhang, Han   II-250
Zhou, Lingchuan   II-250
Zhou, Yujun   II-186
Zubairi, Amaan   III-429
Zuo, Zhaoxin   I-179

he United States
ylor Publisher Services